# *Experience* HISTORY

## INTERPRETING AMERICA'S PAST

# Experience
# HISTORY

## INTERPRETING AMERICA'S PAST

### EIGHTH EDITION

**James West Davidson**

ꝏꝏꝏ

**Brian DeLay**

UNIVERSITY OF CALIFORNIA, BERKELEY

ꝏꝏꝏ

**Christine Leigh Heyrman**

UNIVERSITY OF DELAWARE

ꝏꝏꝏ

**Mark H. Lytle**

BARD COLLEGE

ꝏꝏꝏ

**Michael B. Stoff**

UNIVERSITY OF TEXAS, AUSTIN

**HST201
United States History to 1820
Volume 1
Central Oregon Community College**

Mc
Graw
Hill
Education

3 4 5 6 7 8 9 0  FRD FRD  19 18 17 16 15

ISBN-13: 978-1-259-18475-8
ISBN-10: 1-259-18475-7

*Learning Solutions Consultant: Michelle Payne*
*Associate Project Manager: Janie Larsen*
*Cover Photo Credits: SNA0087 © Royalty-Free/CORBIS*

# Brief Contents

# Contents

## Chapter 1

# THE FIRST CIVILIZATIONS OF NORTH AMERICA  2

ⲟⲟⲟⲟⲟ AN AMERICAN STORY ⲟⲟⲟⲟⲟ

*The Power of a Hidden Past*  3

## After the Fact

**Tracking the First Americans    22**

## Chapter 2

# OLD WORLDS, NEW WORLDS 1400–1600  26

ⲟⲟⲟⲟⲟ AN AMERICAN STORY ⲟⲟⲟⲟⲟ

*Fishing Nets and Far Horizons*  27

## Chapter 6

# IMPERIAL TRIUMPH, IMPERIAL CRISIS 1754–1776  130

∞∞∞ AN AMERICAN STORY ∞∞∞

*George Washington and the Half King*  131

## Chapter 7

# THE AMERICAN PEOPLE AND THE AMERICAN REVOLUTION 1775–1783  156

∞∞∞ AN AMERICAN STORY ∞∞∞

*"Will He Fight?"*  157

## Chapter 8
# CRISIS AND CONSTITUTION
# 1776–1789   180

# After the Fact
## White and Black Southerners Worshiping Together   204

## Chapter 9
# THE EARLY REPUBLIC
# 1789–1824   208

# After the Fact
## Sally Hemings and Thomas Jefferson 240

# LIST OF Maps and Charts

# From the Authors

## How do you make history?

There are two very different answers to the question, depending on whether you're living it or writing it. Yet both actions are more closely connected than appears at first glance. The American past is filled with people who have made history in ways they could not have anticipated when they were younger.

- Jean L'Archevêque, a 12-year-old French servant setting sail across the Atlantic in 1684 (see Chapter 5), could not have predicted that centuries later he would be remembered for his role as a decoy in an assassination plot, for the striking tattoos that were engraved on his face, and for his violent death along the Platte River, half a world away from his place of birth.

- Biology student Rachel Carson (Chapter 30) would have been astonished in 1928 to hear that 30 years later she would challenge the largest chemical companies in the United States, whose pesticides were damaging the environment.

- When a young Filipino soldier named Valentine Untalan (Chapter 26) was captured by the Japanese during World War II, the last thing on his mind, as he was herded into what was later called the Bataan death march, was whether one day his story might be told. He simply wanted to stay alive.

All these people made history—became a part of history—in large ways and small—as you yourself may someday, in a manner that is yet unknowable. However, there is another way to "make" history, and that is by thinking and writing about the past, as historians do.

## THE EXPERIENCE OF "MAKING HISTORY"

The operative word is *make*. History is not the past; it is a reconstruction assembled from the past's raw materials. It is not a set of agreed-upon facts. Events happened and are relayed to us through a wide variety of surviving records, but—because we were not there—it is always through the gauze of someone's interpretation.

By nature textbook programs strive to be comprehensive, smooth, and seamless. They project an aura of omniscience; the narrative speaks with a single authoritative voice. But history does not consist of one voice; it has multiple voices, like our diverse nation. It must take into account the dialogues, disagreements, and diverse actors that all have been a part of American history.

Of course, it is impossible to convey even a fraction of the debates that go into the "making" of history. However, in *Experience History,* we suggest a bit of the substance and flavor of the process by examining some of the debates and disagreements around a particular historical question. We place the reader in the role of historical detective. You are asked to examine historical evidence—whether a cartoon, an artifact, or two conflicting documents—and see what can be made of it. In short, you will learn what it means to make—to construct—history.

# Experiencing the Stories of History

As historians, we use narrative as a way to give life to the past. The choice of narrative puts a great deal of emphasis on the individual and acknowledges that individuals can affect history in surprising ways. Personal decisions, sudden deaths, natural catastrophes, and chance all combine to make history unpredictable. And by telling these unpredictable stories we illustrate what historians refer to as "contingency"—the idea that history is not an inevitable series of events, but is changed and shaped by often-unanticipated events and actions of individuals.

Then, too, these stories fascinate us for the sheer wonder of watching individuals of all kinds grappling with how to shape the worlds around them.

- Take Wingina, chief of the Roanoke Indians, who in 1584 had to decide what to do about the savage, strangely behaved white men who had just landed on his shores;

- Or gaze in wonder at the quirky Henry Ford, who turned out identical Model T automobiles—because, as he put it, "Everybody wants to be somewhere he ain't"—and who also insisted that his factory workers wear identical expressions, which he referred to as "Fordization of the Face."

- Consider young Thurgood Marshall, crisscrossing the South in his own "little old beat-up '29 Ford," typing legal briefs in the backseat, trying to get black teachers to sue for equal pay, hoping to change African American lives for the better. Because (to quote Henry Ford) everybody wants to be somewhere he ain't.

Of course, narrative also allows us to comprehend broad trends—like the transportation revolution that proceeded from canals and steamboats to railroads and automobiles—but it does so without depriving us of history's irreducible details, like Wingina's dilemma or Marshall's dreams.

In *Experience History,* we hope we have combined a narrative whose stories engage you with a set of features that explore what historians do and how history is created. How you reflect upon the past, engage with it, and reconstruct it, will in no small measure determine your understanding and enjoyment of history, as well as your success in it.

# Improve Your Course

***Connect® History*** is a highly interactive learning environment designed to help students connect to the resources they will need to achieve success. Map activities, primary source exercises, image analysis, key term quizzes, and review questions provide a wealth of assignments to ensure that students are comprehending the reading and will succeed in the course. *ConnectPlus® History* offers all of the above with the addition of an integrated, interactive e-book. Optimized for the web, the e-book immerses students in a flexible, interactive environment.

***ConnectPlus® History*** offers all of the above with the addition of an integrated, interactive e-book. Optimized for the web, the e-book immerses students in a flexible, interactive environment.

**LearnSmart**, McGraw-Hill's adaptive learning system, helps assess student knowledge of course content and maps out a personalized study plan for success. Accessible within *Connect History*, LearnSmart uses a series of adaptive questions to pinpoint the concepts students understand—and those they don't. The result is an online tool that helps students learn faster and study more efficiently and enables instructors to customize classroom lectures and activities to meet their students' needs.

**SMARTBOOK**™

Fueled by LearnSmart—the most widely used and intelligent adaptive learning resource—SmartBook is the first and only adaptive reading experience available today.

Distinguishing what a student knows from what they don't, and honing in on concepts they are most likely to forget, SmartBook personalizes content for each student in a continuously adapting reading experience. Reading is no longer a passive and linear experience, but an engaging and dynamic one where students are more likely to master and retain important concepts, coming to class better prepared. Valuable reports provide instructors insight as to how students are progressing through textbook content, and are useful for shaping in-class time or assessment. As a result of the adaptive reading experience found in SmartBook, students are more likely to retain knowledge, stay in class and get better grades. This revolutionary technology is available only from McGraw-Hill Education and for hundreds of course areas as part of the LearnSmart Advantage series.

 **create**™

Design your ideal course materials with McGraw-Hill's **Create—www.mcgrawhillcreate.com!** Rearrange or omit chapters, combine material from other sources, and/or upload your syllabus or any other content you have written to make the perfect resources for your students. Search thousands of leading McGraw-Hill textbooks to find the best content for your students, then arrange it to fit your teaching style. You can even personalize your book's appearance by selecting the cover and adding your name, school, and course information. When you order a Create book, you receive a complimentary review copy. Get a printed copy in three to five business days or an electronic copy (eComp) via e-mail in about an hour. Register today at **www.mcgrawhillcreate. com** and craft your course resources to match the way you teach.

 **Course**Smart
Learn Smart. Choose Smart.

**CourseSmart** offers thousands of the most commonly adopted textbooks across hundreds of courses from a wide variety of higher education publishers. It is the only place for faculty to review and compare the full text of a textbook online, providing immediate access without the environmental impact of requesting a printed exam copy. At CourseSmart, students can save up to 50 percent off the cost of a printed book, reduce their impact on the environment, and gain access to powerful web tools for learning, including full text search, notes and highlighting, and e-mail tools for sharing notes among classmates. Learn more at **www.coursesmart.com**.

 **Campus**

**McGraw-Hill Campus** is the first-of-its-kind institutional service providing faculty with true single sign-on access to all of McGraw-Hill's course content, digital tools, and other high-quality learning resources from any learning management system (LMS). This innovative offering allows for secure and deep integration and seamless access to any of our course solutions such as McGraw-Hill *Connect,* McGraw-Hill Create, McGraw-Hill LearnSmart, or Tegrity. McGraw-Hill Campus includes access to our entire content library, including e-books, assessment tools, presentation slides, and multimedia content, among other resources, providing faculty open and unlimited access to prepare for class, create tests/quizzes, develop lecture material, integrate interactive content, and much more.

## Online Learning Center for *Experience History*

The **Online Learning Center (OLC)** at **www.mhhe.com/eh8** contains a wealth of instructor resources, including an Instructor's Manual, Test Bank, and PowerPoint presentations for each chapter. All maps and most images from the print text are included.

A **Computerized Test Bank**, McGraw-Hill's EZ Test, allows you to quickly create a customized test using the publisher's supplied test banks or your own questions. You decide the number, type, and order of test questions with a few simple clicks. EZ Test runs on your computer without a connection to the Internet.

# Primary Source Documents

The following primary source documents, carefully selected by the authors to coordinate with this program, are available on the Online Learning Center for *Experience History* at www.mhhe.com/eh8 and as assignable assessments on *Connect* at http://connect.mcgraw-hill.com. Documents include an explanatory headnote and are followed by discussion questions.

Choose from many of these documents—or hundreds of others—to customize your print text by visiting McGraw-Hill's Create at www.mcgrawhillcreate.com.

# Acknowledgments

We are grateful to the many advisors and reviewers who generously offered comments and suggestions at various stages in our development of this manuscript. Our thanks go to:

Thomas Altherr,
*Metropolitan State College of Denver*

Melissa Anyiwo,
*Curry College*

Darren Bardell,
*Ohlone College*

Daniel Barr,
*Robert Morris University*

Melissa Biegert,
*Temple College*

Lisa Blank,
*Tarrant County Community College*

Margaret Brown,
*Brevard College*

Owen Chariton,
*Metropolitan State College of Denver*

Ann Short Chirhart,
*Indiana State University*

George Fain,
*University South Carolina - Upstate*

Jessica Feveryear,
*Salt Lake Community College*

Melody Flowers,
*McLennan Community College*

Amy Forss,
*Metropolitan Community College*

Rick Gianni,
*Indiana University Northwest*

Shawn Gladden,
*Community College of Baltimore County*

Mark Goldman,
*Tallahassee Community College*

Wendy Gunderson,
*Collin College*

David Haney,
*Austin Community College*

Ken Hansen,
*Salt Lake Community College*

Carmen Harris,
*University of South Carolina - Upstate*

Ely Janis,
*Massachusetts College of Liberal Arts*

Russell Jones,
*Eastern Michigan University*

Richard Kitchen,
*New Mexico Military Institute*

John Leland,
*Salem International University*

Charles Levine,
*Mesa Community College*

Manuel Medrano,
*University of Texas, Brownsville*

Mark Mengerink,
*Lamar University*

Don Mohr,
*University of Alaska Anchorage*

Kimberly Nichols,
*Northeast Texas Community College*

Michelle Anne Novak,
*Houston Community College - Southeast*

Shannon O'Bryan,
*Greenville Technical College*

Richard Owens,
*West Liberty University*

David Porter,
*Northern Virginia Community College*

Gretchen Reilly,
*Temple College*

John Selby,
*Roanoke College*

Richard Straw,
*Radford University*

Michael Thetford,
*Lone Star College, Montgomery*

Mark Van Ells,
*Queensborough Community College*

Melissa Weinbrenner,
*Northeast Texas Community College*

Scott Williams,
*Weatherford College*

Chad Wooley,
*Tarrant County Community College*

**Digi-posium Attendees**

Wayne Ackerson,
*Technical College of Low Country*

Ceci Barba,
*El Paso Community College*

Gene Barnett,
*Calhoun Community College*

Eric Duchess,
*High Point University*

Caroline Emmons,
*Hampden-Sydney College*

John Frongillo,
*Florida Tech University*

Mindy Green Reynolds,
*Southern Union State Community College*

Phyllis Jestice,
*University of Southern Mississippi*

Lloyd Johnson,
*Campbell University*

Haile Larebo,
*Morehouse College*

Jason Ramshur,
*Pearl River Community College*

Mark Roehrs,
*Lincoln Land Community College*

Robert A. Saunders,
*Farmingdale State College*

Keith Sisson,
*University of Memphis*

Matt Zembo,
*Hudson Valley Community College*

One acknowledgment we can never make too often is to the work of our co-author, colleague, and friend, William E. Gienapp. Bill traveled with us on this journey from the book's earliest conception up until his untimely passing in 2003. His insight, erudition, and good humor made him a pleasure to work with, and his contribution to the book will endure no matter how many new revisions appear.

JAMES WEST DAVIDSON, BRIAN DELAY,
CHRISTINE LEIGH HEYRMAN,
MARK H. LYTLE, MICHAEL B. STOFF

# About the Authors

◇◇◇◇◇◇◇◇◇◇◇◇◇◇◇◇◇◇◇◇◇◇◇◇◇◇◇◇◇◇◇◇◇◇◇◇◇◇◇◇◇◇◇◇◇◇◇◇◇◇◇◇◇◇◇◇◇◇◇◇◇◇◇◇◇◇◇◇◇◇

## JAMES WEST DAVIDSON

RECEIVED HIS PHD FROM YALE UNIVERSITY. A historian who has pursued a full-time writing career, he is the author of numerous books, among them *After the Fact: The Art of Historical Detection* (with Mark H. Lytle), *The Logic of Millennial Thought: Eighteenth-Century New England*, and *Great Heart: The History of a Labrador Adventure* (with John Rugge). He is co-editor with Michael Stoff of the *Oxford New Narratives in American History*, in which his own most recent book appears: *'They Say': Ida B. Wells and the Reconstruction of Race*.

## BRIAN DELAY

RECEIVED HIS PHD FROM HARVARD University and is Associate Professor of History at the University of California, Berkeley. He is a frequent guest speaker at teacher workshops across the country and has won several prizes for his book *War of a Thousand Deserts: Indian Raids and the U.S.-Mexican War*. He is currently at work on the history of guns, business, and freedom in the Americas.

## CHRISTINE LEIGH HEYRMAN

IS THE ROBERT W. AND SHIRLEY P. Grimble Professor of American History at the University of Delaware. She received a PhD in American Studies from Yale University and is the author of *Commerce and Culture: The Maritime Communities of Colonial Massachusetts, 1690–1750*. Her book *Southern Cross: The Beginnings of the Bible Belt* was awarded the Bancroft Prize in 1998.

## MARK H. LYTLE

RECEIVED HIS PHD FROM YALE University and is Professor of History and Environmental Studies at Bard College. He served two years as Mary Ball Washington Professor of American History at University College, Dublin, in Ireland. His publications include *The Origins of the Iranian-American Alliance, 1941–1953*, *After the Fact: The Art of Historical Detection* (with James West Davidson), *America's Uncivil Wars: The Sixties Era from Elvis to the Fall of Richard Nixon*, and most recently, *The Gentle Subversive: Rachel Carson, Silent Spring, and the Rise of the Environmental Movement*. He is currently working on a book on the environmental impacts of consumerism in the post–World War II era.

## MICHAEL B. STOFF

IS ASSOCIATE PROFESSOR OF HISTORY and Director of the Plan II Honors Program at the University of Texas at Austin. The recipient of a PhD from Yale University, he has been honored many times for his teaching, most recently with the University of Texas System Regents' Outstanding Teaching Award. He is the author of *Oil, War, and American Security: The Search for a National Policy on Foreign Oil, 1941–1947*, co-editor (with Jonathan Fanton and R. Hall Williams) of *The Manhattan Project: A Documentary Introduction to the Atomic Age*, and series co-editor (with James West Davidson) of the *Oxford New Narratives in American History*. He is currently working on a narrative of the bombing of Nagasaki.

# *Experience* HISTORY

## INTERPRETING AMERICA'S PAST

From the air, this serpentine mound fashioned thousands of years ago still stands out in bold relief. Located in southern Ohio, it extends from the snake's coiled tail at the left of the photo to the open mouth at the top right, which is pointed in the direction of the summer solstice sunset. The snake's tail points toward the winter solstice sunrise.

# The First Civilizations of North America

∞∞∞ **AN AMERICAN STORY** ∞∞∞

## THE POWER OF A HIDDEN PAST

Stories told about the past have power over both the present and the future. Until recently, most students were taught that American history began several centuries ago—with the "discovery" of America by Columbus, or with the English colonization of Jamestown and Plymouth. History books ignored or trivialized the continent's precontact history. But the reminders of that hidden past are everywhere. Scattered across the United States are thousands of ancient archaeological sites and hundreds of examples of monumental architecture, still imposing even after centuries of erosion, looting, and destruction.

Man-made earthen mounds, some nearly 5,000 years old, exist throughout eastern North America in a bewildering variety of shapes and sizes. Many are easily mistaken for modest hills, but others evoke wonder. In present-day Louisiana an ancient town with earthworks took laborers an estimated 5 million work hours to construct. In Ohio a massive serpent effigy snakes for a quarter-mile across the countryside, its head aligned to the summer solstice. In Illinois a vast, earthen structure covers 16 acres at its base and once reached as high as a 10-story building.

Observers in the colonial and revolutionary eras looked on such sites as curiosities and marvels. George Washington, Thomas Jefferson, and other prominent Americans collected ancient artifacts, took a keen interest in the excavation of mounds, and speculated about the Indian civilizations that created them. Travelers explored these strange mounds, trying to imagine in their mind's eye the peoples who had built them. In 1795 the Reverend James Smith traced the boundaries of a mound wall that was strategically placed to protect a neck of land along a looping river bend in the Ohio valley. "The wall at present is so mouldered down that a man could easily ride over it. It is however about 10 feet, as near as I can judge, in perpendicular height. . . . In one place I observe a breach in the wall about 60 feet wide, where I suppose the gate formerly stood through which the people passed in and out of this stronghold." Smith was astonished by the size of the project. "Compared with this," he exclaimed, "what feeble and insignificant works are those of Fort Hamilton or Fort Washington! They are no more in comparison to it than a rail fence is to a brick wall."

But in the 1830s and 1840s, as Americans sought to drive Indians west of the Mississippi and then confine them on smaller and smaller reservations, many observers began thinking differently about the continent's ancient sites. Surely the simple and "savage" people just then being expelled from American life could not have constructed such inspiring monuments. Politicians, writers, and even some influential scientists instead attributed the mounds to peoples of Europe, Africa, or Asia—Hindus, perhaps, or Israelites, Egyptians, or Japanese. Many nineteenth-century Americans found special comfort in a tale about King Madoc from Wales who, supposedly shipwrecked in the Americas in the twelfth century, had left behind a small but ingenious population of Welsh pioneers who built the mysterious mounds before being overrun by Indians. Some observers even thought Indian skin boats resembled Welsh coracles, designs brought over by King Madoc. The Welsh hypothesis seemed to offer poetic justice, because it implied that nineteenth-century Indians were only receiving a fitting punishment for what their ancestors had done to the remarkable mound builders from Wales.

These fanciful tales were discredited in the late nineteenth and twentieth centuries. In recent decades archaeologists working across the Americas have discovered in more detail how native peoples built the hemisphere's ancient architecture. They have also helped to make clear the degree to which prejudice and politics have blinded European Americans to the complexity, wonder, and significance of America's history before 1492. Fifteen thousand years of human habitation in North America allowed a broad range of cultures to develop, based on agriculture as well as hunting and gathering. In North America a population in the millions spoke hundreds of languages. Cities evolved as well as towns and farms, exhibiting great diversity in their cultural, political, economic, and religious organization. ∞∞∞

| *The skilled craftspeople of the Hopewell tradition worked most often with copper but made exquisite objects from a variety of materials. This image of a human hand, discovered in a Hopewell mound, was cut from a single sheet of mica.*

# A Continent of Cultures

**IMMIGRANTS FROM ASIA**

RECENT BREAKTHROUGHS IN ARCHAEOLOGY AND genetics have demonstrated that the first inhabitants of the Americas arrived from Siberia at least 15,500 years ago BP.* (For more details, see the After the Fact essay "Tracking the First Americans," beginning on page 22). Gradually these **nomads** filtered southward, some likely following

---

*Before the Present, used most commonly by archaeologists when the time spans are in multiple thousands of years. This text will also use CE for Common Era, equivalent to the Christian Era or AD; BCE is Before the Common Era, equivalent to BC.

the Pacific coastline in small boats, others making their way down a narrow, glacier-free corridor along the eastern base of the Rocky Mountains and onto the northern Great Plains. There they found and hunted a stunning array of huge mammals, so-called megafauna. These animals included mammoths that were twice as heavy as elephants, giant bison, sloths that were taller than giraffes, several kinds of camels, and terrifying, 8-foot-long lions. Within a few thousand years the descendants of these Siberians, people whom Columbus would wishfully dub "Indians," had spread throughout the length and breadth of the Americas.

This first colonization of the Americas coincided with, and perhaps accelerated, profound changes in the natural world. The last Ice Age literally melted away as warmer global temperatures freed the great reservoirs of water once locked in glaciers. A rise in sea levels inundated the Bering Strait, submerging the land bridge, and creating new lakes and river systems. The emergence of new **ecosystems**—climates, waterways, and land environments in which humans interacted with other animals and plants—made for ever greater diversity. The first human inhabitants of the Americas had fed, clothed, warmed, and armed themselves in part by hunting megafauna, and some combination of overhunting and climate change resulted in the extinction of most of these giants by the end of the Ice Age. As glaciers receded and human populations increased, the first Americans had to adapt to changing conditions. They adjusted by hunting smaller animals with new, more specialized kinds of stone tools and by learning to exploit particular places more efficiently.

**DIVERSIFIED SOCIETIES** So it was that between 10,000 and 2,500 years ago distinctive regional cultures developed among the peoples of the Americas. Those who remained in the Great Plains turned to hunting the much smaller descendants of the now-extinct giant bison; those in the deserts of the Great Basin survived on small game, seeds, and edible plants; those in the Pacific Northwest relied mainly on fishing; and those east of the Mississippi, besides fishing and gathering, tracked deer and bear and trapped smaller game animals and birds. Over these same centuries, what seems to have been one original, common language evolved into regional dialects and eventually into a multitude of distinct languages. Linguistic diversity paralleled other sorts of divergences, in social organizations, kinship practices, politics, and religion. Technological and cultural unity gave way to striking regional diversity as the first Americans learned how to best exploit their particular environments. Glimpses of these profound changes may be found today in burials, stone tools, and some precious sites of long-term or repeated occupation.

## Civilizations of Ancient Mexico

**AGRICULTURAL REVOLUTION** To the south, pioneers in **Mesoamerica** began domesticating squash 10,000 years ago. Over the next several thousand years farmers added other crops including beans, tomatoes, and especially corn to an agricultural revolution that would transform life through much of the Americas. Because many crops could be dried and stored, agriculture allowed these first farmers to settle in one place.

By about 1500 BCE, farming villages began giving way to larger societies, to richer and more complex cultures. As the abundant food supply steadily expanded their populations, people began specializing in certain kinds of work. While most continued to labor on the land, others became craftworkers and merchants, architects and artists, warriors and priests. Their built environment reflected this social change as humble villages expanded into skillfully planned urban sites that were centers of trade, government, artistic display, and religious ceremony.

**OLMEC CITY-BUILDERS** The Olmecs, the first city-builders in the Americas, constructed large plazas and pyramidal buildings, and sculpted enormous heads chiseled from basalt. The Olmec cultural influence gradually spread throughout Mesoamerica, perhaps as a result of their trade with neighboring peoples. By about 100 BCE, the Olmecs' example had inspired the flowering of Teotihuacán from a small town in central Mexico into a metropolis of towering pyramids. The city had bustling marketplaces, palaces decorated with mural paintings that housed an elite of warriors and priests, schools for their children, and sprawling suburbs for commoners. At its height, around 650 CE, Teotihuacán spanned 15 square miles and had a population of nearly 200,000—making it the sixth largest city in the world.

**MAYAN CIVILIZATION** More impressive still were the achievements of the Mayas, who benefited from their contacts with both the Olmecs and Teotihuacán. In the lowland jungles of Mesoamerica they built cities filled with palaces, bridges, aqueducts, baths, astronomical observatories, and pyramids topped with temples. Their priests developed a written language, their mathematicians discovered the zero, and their astronomers devised a calendar more accurate than any then existing. In its glory, between the third and ninth century CE, the Mayan civilization boasted some 50 urban centers scattered throughout the Yucatán Peninsula, Belize, Guatemala, and Honduras.

## PLAY BALL

The band strikes up—trumpets blaring, drums pounding, flutes trilling. Dancers whirl and gymnasts cavort. Then the players parade into the stadium, and the crowd goes wild, cheering their favorites. So many magnificent athletes trained to win, looking all the more formidable in their heavily padded gear. Which team will carry the day? A great deal is at stake for both players and spectators— honor, wealth, perhaps even life itself. The outcome hangs on the arc of a ball.

The Super Bowl? The World Series? Good guesses, because those present-day athletic spectacles bear striking resemblances to the scene described above: the beginning of a ball game in pre-Columbian Mesoamerica. Those contests, with all their accompanying fanfare, consumed the attention of both elites and commoners for many centuries.

It was the Olmecs who got the ball rolling (and flying), around 1500 BCE. In the main plazas of their cities, they built ornate stone ball courts for teams to compete and celebrated star athletes with towering stone sculptures. Even as civilizations rose and fell in Mesoamerica, the passion for playing ball, following the games, and gambling on their outcome not only endured but even spread to the Hohokam in the American Southwest. Archaeological digs have revealed that nearly every city built by the Mayas, Toltecs, and Aztecs boasted its own ball court: the most impressive were larger than present-day football fields, painted in vivid colors, and decorated with intricately carved birds, jaguars, and skeletal heads. Renowned players inspired artists to paint murals or to fashion clay figurines depicting ballplayers in full athletic regalia—kneepads, gloves, and belts festooned with images of their gods or skeletal heads.

In most cultures the rules of the game dictated that players could use only their hips, buttocks, or knees to bounce the ball against the parallel walls of the court and the alley lying between. And after about 800 CE the game became even more challenging: teams earned the most points by shooting hoops—that is, by sending the ball through a stone ring set in the center of the side walls. No mean feat, since players could not use their hands or feet, and the impact of a flying ball—about six pounds of solid rubber—could inflict serious and even fatal injuries.

But it was the ritual significance of these competitions that made for greater danger. In the Southwest, ball games often figured as friendly rivalries, festive occasions intended to strengthen military or trading alliances among neighboring peoples. In Mesoamerica, however, the games typically celebrated military conquests: during postgame rituals, the captain of the losing team—a captive taken in war—was beheaded with an obsidian knife by the winning captain. That practice seems to have stemmed from the religious significance invested in the ball games, which both the winning players and spectators understood as a religious ceremony celebrating their main deity, the Sun, an orb greater than any other celestial body, and encouraging the soil's fertility with a sacrifice of human blood.

### *Thinking Critically*

*What similarities and dissimilarities do modern athletic festivals share with ancient ballplaying festivals in the following areas: equipment, social violence, aesthetic appearance, and religious significance?*

*Heavy padding protects the internal organs of this Aztec ballplayer from being injured by the heavy, dangerous rubber ball; the player's headdress is a vulture painted brilliant Mayan blue.*

But neither the earliest urban centers of the Olmecs nor the glittering city-state of Teotihuacán survived. Even the enduring kingdom of the Mayas had collapsed by 900 CE. Like the ancient civilizations of Greece and Rome, they thrived for centuries and then declined. Scholars still debate the reasons for their collapse. Military attack may have brought about their ruin, or perhaps their large populations exhausted local resources.

**AZTEC EMPIRE** Mayan grandeur was eventually rivaled in the Valley of Mexico. In the middle of the thirteenth century the Aztecs, a people who had originally lived on Mesoamerica's northern frontiers, swept south and settled in central Mexico. By the end of the fifteenth century they ruled over a vast empire from their capital at Tenochtitlán, an island metropolis of perhaps a quarter of a million people. At its center lay a large plaza bordered by sumptuous palaces and the Great Temple of the Sun. Beyond stood three broad causeways connecting the island to the mainland; many other tall temples were adorned with brightly painted carved images of the gods, zoological and botanical gardens, and well-stocked marketplaces. Through Tenochtitlán's canals flowed gold, silver, exotic feathers and

*Aztec merchants, or pochtecas, spoke many languages and traveled on foot great distances throughout Mesoamerica and parts of North America. Pictured at left is Yacatecuhtli, Lord Nose, the patron god of merchants. He carries a symbol of the crossroads, with bare footprints. The merchant on the right carries a cargo of quetzal birds.*

jewels, cocoa, and millions of pounds of maize—all trade goods and tribute from the several million other peoples in the region subjugated by the Aztecs.

Unsurpassed in power and wealth, in technological and artistic attainments, theirs was also a highly stratified society. The Aztec ruler, or Chief Speaker, shared governing power with the aristocrats who monopolized all positions of religious, military, and political leadership, while the commoners—merchants, farmers, and craftworkers—performed all manual labor. There were slaves as well, some captives taken in war, others from the ranks of commoners forced by poverty to sell themselves or their children.

## Farmers, Potters, and Builders of the Southwest

MOGOLLON AND HOHOKAM PEOPLES

Mesoamerican crops and farming techniques began making their way north to the American Southwest by 1000 BCE. At first the most successful farmers in the region were the Mogollon and the Hohokam peoples, two cultures that flourished in New Mexico and southern Arizona during the first millennium CE. Both tended to cluster their dwellings near streams, relying on either floodplain irrigation or a system of floodgates and canals to sustain their crops. The Mogollon came to be the master potters of the Southwest. The Hohokam pioneered vast and complex irrigation systems in arid southern Arizona that allowed them to support one of the largest populations in precontact North America.

THE ANCESTRAL PUEBLO

Their neighbors to the north in what is now known as the Four Corners Region of Arizona, Colorado, New Mexico, and Utah, commonly referred to by the term Anasazi, are today more properly known as the Ancestral Pueblo peoples. The Ancestral

Pueblo peoples adapted corn, beans, and squash to the relatively high altitude of the Colorado Plateau and soon parlayed their growing surplus and prosperity into societies of considerable complexity. Their most stunning achievements were villages of exquisitely executed masonry buildings—apartment-like structures up to four stories high and containing hundreds of rooms at such places as Mesa Verde (Colorado) and Canyon de Chelly (Arizona). Villages in Chaco Canyon (New Mexico), the largest center of Ancestral Puebloan settlement, were linked to the wider region by hundreds of miles of wide, straight roads.

Besides their impressive dwellings, the Ancestral Pueblo people filled their towns with religious shrines, astronomical observatories, and stations for sending signals to other villages. Their craftworkers fashioned delicate woven baskets, beautiful feather and hide sashes, decorated pottery, and turquoise jewelry that they traded throughout the region and beyond. For more than a thousand years, this civilization prospered, reaching a zenith between about 900 and 1100 CE. During those three centuries, the population grew to approximately 30,000 spread over 50,000 square miles, a total area larger than present-day California.

*The remains of Pueblo Bonito, one of the nine Great Houses built by Ancestral Puebloans in Chaco Canyon. By the end of the eleventh century, Pueblo Bonito stood four stories high at the rear and contained 800 rooms as well as many towers, terraces, a large central plaza, and several round "kivas" for religious and ceremonial purposes.*

# Chiefdoms of the Eastern Woodlands

East of the Mississippi, Indian societies prospered in valleys near great rivers (Mississippi, Ohio, Tennessee, and Cumberland), the shores of the Great Lakes, and the coast of the Atlantic. Everywhere the earliest inhabitants depended on a combination of fishing, gathering, and hunting—mainly deer but also bear, raccoon, and a variety of birds. Around 2000 BCE some groups in the temperate, fertile Southeast began growing the gourds and pumpkins first cultivated by Mesoamerican farmers, and later they also adopted the cultivation of maize. But unlike the ancient peoples of the Southwest, most Eastern Woodland peoples continued to subsist largely on animals, fish, and nuts, all of which were abundant enough to meet their needs and even to expand their numbers.

**ADENA AND HOPEWELL**
Indeed, many of the mysterious earthen mounds that would so fascinate Europeans were built by peoples who did not farm. About 1000 BCE, residents of a place now known as Poverty Point in northeastern Louisiana fashioned spectacular earthworks—six semicircular rings that rose 9 feet in height and covered more than half a mile in diameter. Although these structures might have been sites for studying the planets and stars, hundreds of other mounds—built about 2,000 years ago by the Adena and the Hopewell cultures of the Ohio and Mississippi valleys—served as the burial places of their leading men and women. Alongside the corpses mourners heaped their richest goods—headdresses of antlers, necklaces of copper, troves of shells and pearls—rare and precious items imported from as far north as Canada, as far west as Wyoming, and as far east as Florida. All these mounds attest powerfully not only to the skill and sheer numbers of their builders but also to the complexity of these ancient societies, their elaborate religious practices, and the wide scope of their trading networks.

**MISSISSIPPIAN CULTURE**
Even so, the most magnificent culture of the ancient Eastern Woodlands, the Mississippian, owed much of its prominence to farming. By the twelfth century CE these peoples had emerged as the premier city-builders of North America, and their towns radiated for hundreds of miles in every direction from the hub of their trading network at Cahokia, a port city of perhaps 30,000 located directly across from present-day St. Louis at the confluence of the Missouri and Mississippi Rivers. Cahokia's many broad plazas teemed with farmers hawking their corn, squash, and beans and with craftworkers and merchants displaying their wares. But what commanded every eye were the structures surrounding the plazas—more than 100 flat-topped pyramidal mounds crowned by religious temples and the palaces of rulers.

*An artist's reconstruction of the city of Cahokia, ca. 1100 CE, the hearth of Mississippian culture. Note how tiny the human figures are in comparison to the temples.*

## Life on the Great Plains

MIGRATORY
PEOPLES
Cahokia's size and power depended on consistent agricultural surpluses. Outside the Southwest and the river valleys of the East, agriculture played a smaller role in shaping North American societies. On the Great Plains, for example, some people did cultivate corn, beans, squash, and sunflowers, near reliable rivers and streams. But more typically plains communities relied on hunting and foraging, migrating to exploit seasonally variable resources. Plains hunters pursued game on foot; the horses that had once roamed the Americas became extinct after the last Ice Age. Sometimes large groups of people worked together to drive the buffaloes over cliffs or to trap them in corrals. The aridity of the plains made it a dynamic and unpredictable place to live. During times of reliable rainfall, bison populations boomed, hunters flocked to the region, and agricultural communities blossomed along major rivers. But sometimes centuries passed with lower-than-average precipitation, and families abandoned the plains for eastern valleys or the foothills of the Rocky Mountains.

## Survival in the Great Basin

Some peoples west of the Great Plains also kept to older ways of subsistence. Among them were the Numic-speaking peoples of the Great Basin, which includes present-day Nevada and Utah, eastern California, and western Wyoming and Colorado. Small family groups scoured their stark, arid landscape for the limited supplies of food it yielded, moving with each passing season to make the most of their environment. Men tracked elk and antelope and trapped smaller animals, birds, even toads, rattlesnakes, and insects. But the staples of their diet were edible seeds, nuts, and plants, which women gathered and stored in woven baskets to consume in times of scarcity. Several families occasionally hunted together or wintered in common quarters, but because the desert heat and soil defied farming, these bands usually numbered no more than about 50 people.

## The Plenty of the Pacific Northwest

The rugged stretch of coast from the southern banks of present-day British Columbia to northern California has always been an extraordinarily rich natural environment. Its mild climate and abundant rainfall yield forests lush with plants and game; its bays and rivers teem with salmon and halibut, its oceans with whales and porpoises, and its rocky beaches with seals, otters, abalone, mussels, and clams. Agriculture was unnecessary in such a bountiful place. From their villages on the banks of rivers, the shores of bays, and the beaches of low-lying offshore islands, the ancestors of the Nootkans, Makahs, Tlingits, Tshimshians, and Kwakiutls speared or netted salmon, trapped sea

mammals, gathered shellfish, and launched canoes. The largest of these craft, from which they harpooned whales, measured 45 feet bow to stern and nearly 6 feet wide.

SOCIAL AND
CEREMONIAL
DISTINCTIONS
By the fifteenth century these fecund lands supported a population of perhaps 130,000. They also permitted a culture with the leisure time needed to create works of art as well as an elaborate social and ceremonial life. The peoples of the Northwest built houses and canoes from red cedar; carved bowls and dishes from red alder; crafted paddles and harpoon shafts, bows, and clubs from Pacific yew; and wove baskets from bark and blankets from mountain goat wool. They evolved a society with sharp distinctions among nobles, commoners, and slaves, the latter being mainly women and children captured in raids on other villages. Those who were free devoted their lives to accumulating and then redistributing their wealth among other villagers in elaborate potlatch ceremonies in order to confirm or enhance their social prestige.

## The Frozen North

Most of present-day Canada and Alaska were equally inhospitable to agriculture. In the farthest northern reaches—a treeless belt of Arctic tundra—temperatures fell below

*This ornately carved and painted house post once supported the main beams of a dwelling belonging to a Kwakiutl whaler in the Pacific Northwest. Depicting a man of wealth and high rank, the figure has a whale painted on his chest and copper ornaments on his arms. Two smaller figures, in shadow by the whaler's knees, each support one end of a plank seat. These were his household slaves, most likely children captured in an attack on rival tribes.*

## EARLY PEOPLES OF NORTH AMERICA

**Bering land bridge**

**Extent of ice cap during most recent glaciation**

**Adena cultures**

**Hopewell cultures**

**Primary Mississippian cultures**

→ Possible migration routes of early Indians

◆ Adena/Hopewell site

■ Mississippian site

● Mayan site

● Olmec site

● Southwestern sites

ANCESTRAL PUEBLO
Mesa Verde
Canyon de Chelly
Chaco Canyon
HOHOKAM
MOGOLLON
Poverty Point

*Migration routes across the Bering Strait from Asia were taken by peoples whose descendants created the major civilizations of ancient America. The influence of Mesoamerica is most striking among the cultures of the Southwest and the Mississippians. Based on the information in After the Fact, "Tracking the First Americans" (pages 22–25), which migration route on this map is being more closely considered due to recent archaeological discoveries?*

freezing for most of the year. The Subarctic, although densely forested, had only about 100 frost-free days each year. As a result, the peoples of both regions survived by fishing and hunting. The Inuit, or Eskimos, of northern Alaska harvested whales from their umiaks, boats made by stretching walrus skin over a driftwood frame and that could bear more than a ton of weight. In the central Arctic, they tracked seals. The inhabitants of the Subarctic, both Algonquian-speaking peoples in the East and Athapaskan speakers of the West, moved from their summer fishing camps to berry patches in the fall to moose and caribou hunting grounds in the winter.

 **REVIEW**

How did native cultures differ from region to region, and what accounts for these differences?

# Innovations and Limitations

The first Americans therefore expressed, governed, and supported themselves in a broad variety of ways. And yet they shared certain core characteristics, including the desire and ability to reshape their world. Whether they lived in forests, coastal regions, jungles, or prairies, whether they inhabited high mountains or low deserts, native communities experimented constantly with the resources around them. Over the course of millennia, nearly all the hemisphere's peoples found ways to change the natural world in order to improve and enrich their lives.

## America's Agricultural Gifts

 **RISE OF AGRICULTURE** No innovation proved more crucial to human history than native manipulation of individual plants. Like all first farmers, agricultural pioneers in the Americas began experimenting accidentally. Modern-day species of corn, for example, probably derive from a Mesoamerican grass known as teosinte. It seems that ancient peoples gathered teosinte to collect its small grains. By selecting the grains that best suited them and bringing them back to their settlements, and by returning the grains to the soil through spillage or waste disposal, they unintentionally began the process of domestic cultivation. Soon these first farmers began deliberately saving seeds from the best plants and sowing them in gardens. In this way, over hundreds of generations, American farmers transformed the modest teosinte grass into a staple crop that would give rise to the hemisphere's mightiest civilizations.

 **WORLDWIDE SPREAD OF AMERICAN CROPS** Indeed, ever since contact with Europe, the great breakthroughs in Native American farming have sustained peoples around the world. In addition to corn, the first Americans gave humanity scores of varieties of squash, potatoes, beans, and other basic foods. Today, plants domesticated by indigenous Americans account for three-fifths of the world's crops, including many that have revolutionized the global diet. For good or ill, a handful of corn species occupies the center of the contemporary American diet. In addition to its traditional forms, corn is consumed in chips, breads, and breakfast cereals; corn syrup sweeteners are added to many of our processed foods and nearly all soft drinks; and corn is fed to almost all animals grown to be consumed, even farmed fish.

Other Native American crops have become integral to diets all over the world. Potatoes revolutionized northern European life in the centuries after contact, helping to avert famine and boost populations in several countries. Ireland's population tripled in the century after the introduction of potatoes. Beans and peanuts became prized for their protein content in Asia. And in Africa, corn, manioc, and other New World crops so improved diets and overall health that the resulting rise in population may have offset the population lost to the Atlantic slave trade.

## Landscapers

Plant domestication requires the smallest of changes, changes farmers slowly encourage at the genetic level. But native peoples in the precontact Americas transformed their world on grand scales as well. In the Andes, Peruvian engineers put people to work by the tens of thousands creating an astonishing patchwork of terraces, dikes, and canals designed to maximize agricultural productivity. Similar public-works projects transformed large parts of central Mexico and the Yucatán. Even today, after several centuries of disuse, overgrowth, and even deliberate destruction, human-shaped landscapes dating from the precontact period still cover thousands of square miles of the Americas.

 **CULTIVATED TREES OF THE AMAZON** Recently, scholars have begun to find evidence of incredible manipulation of landscapes and environments in the least likely of places. The vast Amazon rain forest has long been seen by Westerners as an imposing symbol of untouched nature. But it now seems

| Teosinte, a Mesoamerican grass. Selective harvesting by native peoples helped transform teosinte into maize (corn).

Theodore de Bry, Florida Indians Planting Maize. *Both men and women were portrayed as involved in agriculture. Except for the digging stick at the center rear, however, the farming implements drawn by the artist are European in origin.*

In both North and South America native peoples used techniques to shape their physical environment, from burning prairies and forests (to harvest/hunt animals) to creating irrigation systems (to control floodwaters for agriculture). This photograph from present-day Peru shows the exquisite terracing Incas employed to maximize agricultural yields amid hills, valleys, and mountains. Some researchers think these circular terraces were used for agronomic experiments.

that much of the Amazon was in fact made by people. Whereas farmers elsewhere in the world domesticated plants for their gardens and fields, farmers in the Amazon cultivated food-bearing trees for thousands of years, cutting down less useful species and replacing them with ones that better suited human needs. All told there are more than 70 different species of domesticated trees throughout the Amazon. At least one-eighth of the nonflooded rain forest was directly or indirectly created by humans. Likewise, native peoples laboriously improved the soil across as much

as a tenth of the Amazon, mixing it with charcoal and a variety of organic materials. These managed soils are more than 10 times as productive as untreated soils in the Amazon. Today, farmers in the region still eagerly search for the places where precontact peoples enriched the earth.

Native North Americans likewise transformed their local environments. Sometimes they moved forests. Ancestral Puebloans cut down and transported more than 200,000 trees to construct the floors and roofs of the monumental buildings in Chaco Canyon. Sometimes they moved rivers. By taming the waters of the Salt and Gila Rivers in present-day Arizona with the most extensive system of irrigation canals anywhere in precontact North America, the Hohokam were able to support large populations in a desert environment. And sometimes they moved the land itself. Twenty-two million cubic feet of earth were moved to construct just one building in the Mississippian city of Cahokia.

FIRE AS A TOOL   Indians also employed fire to systematically reshape landscapes across the continent. Throughout North America's great eastern and western forests, native peoples periodically set low fires to consume undergrowth and fallen trees. In this way the continent's first inhabitants managed forests and also animals. Burning enriched the soil and encouraged the growth of grasses and bushes prized by game animals such as deer, elk, beaver, rabbit, grouse, and turkey. The systematic use of fire to reshape forests helped hunters in multiple ways: it increased the overall food supply for grazing animals, it attracted those animal species hunters valued most, and, by clearing forests of ground debris, fire made it easier to track, kill, and transport game. Deliberate burns transformed forests in eastern North America to such an extent that bison migrated from their original ranges on the plains and thrived far to the east. Thus, when native hunters from New York to Georgia brought down a buffalo, they were harvesting a resource that they themselves had helped to cultivate.

## The Shape of a Problem

No matter how great their ingenuity, the first Americans were constrained by certain natural realities. One of the most important is so basic that it is easy to overlook. Unlike Eurasia, which stretches across the Northern Hemisphere along an east-west axis, the Americas fall along a north-south axis, stretching nearly pole to pole. Consequently, the Americas are broken up by tremendous geographic and climactic diversity, making communication and technology transfer far more difficult than it was in the Old World.

Consider the agricultural revolution in Eurasia. Once plants and animals were first domesticated in the Fertile Crescent around 10,000 years ago, they quickly began spreading east and west. Within 1,500 years these innovations had been adopted in Greece and India. A thousand years later the domesticated plants and animals of the Fertile Crescent had reached central Europe, and, from there, it took perhaps 200 years for them to be embraced in present-day Spain. Eurasia's east-west axis facilitated these transfers. Locations at roughly the same latitude share the same seasonal variation, have days of the same length, and often have similar habitats and rates of precipitation, making it relatively easy for plants and animals to move from one place to the next.

In contrast, the north-south orientation of the Americas erected natural barriers to plant and animal transfer. Mesoamerica and South America, for example, are about as far apart as the Balkans and Mesopotamia. It took roughly 2,000 years for plants and animals domesticated in Mesopotamia to reach the Balkans. But because Mesoamerica and South America are separated by tropical, equatorial lowlands, it took domesticated plants such as corn several thousand years to jump between the two regions. Sometimes the transfer never happened at all before European contact. South American potatoes would have thrived in central Mexico, but the tropics stopped their northward migration. Equatorial jungles also denied Mesoamerican societies the llama and the alpaca, domesticated more than 5,000 years ago in the Andes. One wonders what even greater heights the Olmec, Toltec, Mayan, and Aztec civilizations would have achieved if they had had access to these large creatures as draft animals and reliable sources of protein.

**TRANSFER OF TECHNOLOGY, AGRICULTURE, AND ANIMALS**

Dramatic variations in climate likewise delayed the transfer of agriculture from Mexico to regions north of the Rio Grande. Archaeologists have discovered evidence of 10,000-year-old domesticated squash in a cave in southern Mexico, an indication that agriculture began in the Americas nearly as early as anywhere else in the world. Yet squash and corn were not cultivated in the present-day American Southwest for another 7,000 years, and the region's peoples did not embrace a fully sedentary, agricultural lifestyle until the start of the Common Era. Major differences in the length of days, the growing season, average temperatures, and rainfall between the Southwest and central Mexico meant that farmers north of the Rio Grande had to experiment for scores of generations before they perfected crops suited to their particular environments. Corn took even longer to become a staple crop in eastern North America, which is why major urban centers did not arise there until approximately 1000 CE.

By erecting barriers to communication and the spread of technology, then, the predominantly north-south orientation of the Americas made it more difficult for the hemisphere's inhabitants to build on one another's successes. Had American innovations spread as quickly as innovations in Eurasia, the peoples of the Western Hemisphere would likely have been healthier, more numerous, and more powerful than they were when Europeans first encountered them in 1492.

## Animals and Illness

One other profound difference between the Eurasian world and the Americas concerned animals and disease. Most diseases affecting humans originated from domesticated animals, which came naturally into frequent and close contact with the humans who raised them. As people across Eurasia embraced agriculture and started living with one another and with domesticated animals in crowded villages, towns, and cities, they created ideal environments for the evolution and transmission of infectious disease. For example, measles, tuberculosis, and smallpox all seem to have derived from diseases afflicting cattle.

 **EURASIA'S DEADLY ADVANTAGE**

Eurasians therefore paid a heavy price for living closely with animals. Yet in the long run, the continent's terrible illnesses hardened its population. Victims who survived into adulthood enjoyed acquired immunity to the most common diseases: that is, if they had already encountered a particular illness as children, their immune systems would recognize and combat the disease more effectively in the event of reinfection. By the fifteenth century, then, Eurasian bodies had learned to live with a host of deadly communicable diseases.

But Native American bodies had not. With a few important exceptions, including tuberculosis, pneumonia, and possibly herpes and syphilis, human populations in the Western Hemisphere seem to have been relatively free from major communicable pathogens. Insofar as most major diseases emerge from domesticated animals, it is easy enough to see why. Indigenous Americans domesticated turkeys, dogs, Muscovy ducks, and guinea pigs but raised only one large mammal—the llama or alpaca (breeds of the same species).

## AN ANCIENT CALENDAR

**During summer solstice, the spiral is bisected by a single shaft of light.**

**Why might the Chacoans have used a spiral rather than another image to make this calendar?**

On a blazing hot summer day in 1977, Anna Sofaer climbed up to the top of Fajada Butte in Chaco Canyon, New Mexico, spotted three sandstone slabs resting carefully against a wall, and walked over to investigate. What she saw against the wall astounded her: a spiral glyph, bisected by a pure shaft of light. An artist and amateur archaeologist, Sofaer had keen interest in how indigenous American cultures harnessed light and shadow in their architecture. Knowing that it was nearly the summer solstice, she recognized instantly that she'd discovered an ancient Ancestral Puebloan calendar. Later research revealed that the device also marked the winter solstice, the summer and winter equinoxes, and the extremes of the moon's 18–19- year cycle (the major and minor standstills). These discoveries prompted still more research, and scholars now believe that there are structures throughout Chaco Canyon aligned to solar and lunar events.

*Thinking Critically*

What practical reasons might there have been to build these sorts of sun and moon calendars? Might there have been cultural, religious, or social purposes to track accurately the movements of the sun and moon?

This scarcity of domestic animals had more to do with available supply than with the interest or ability of their would-be breeders. The extinction of most species of megafauna soon after humans arrived in the Americas deprived the hemisphere of 80 percent of its large mammals. Those that remained, including modern-day bison, elk, deer, and moose, were more or less immune to domestication because of peculiarities in their dispositions, diets, rates of growth, mating habits, and social characteristics. In fact, of the world's 148 species of large mammals, only 14 were successfully domesticated before the twentieth century. Of those 14, only one—the ancestor to the llama/alpaca—remained in the Americas following the mass extinctions. Eurasia, in contrast, was home to 13—including the five most common and adaptable domestic mammals: sheep, goats, horses, cows, and pigs.

With virtually no large mammals to domesticate, Native Americans were spared the nightmarish effects of most of the world's major communicable diseases—until 1492. After that date, European colonizers discovered the grim advantage of their millennia-long dance with disease. Old World infections that most colonizers had experienced as children raged through indigenous communities, usually doing the greatest damage to adults

## Place and Timing of Pioneering Plant and Animal Domestications

| PLACE | PLANT | ANIMAL | APPROX. DATE |
|-------|-------|--------|--------------|
| Southwest Asia | Wheat, pea, olive | Sheep, goat | 8500 BCE |
| China | Rice, millet | Pig, silkworm | By 7500 BCE |
| New Guinea | Sugarcane, banana | None | ca. 7000 BCE? |
| Sahel | Sorghum, African rice | Guinea fowl | By 5000 BCE |
| Mesoamerica | Corn, beans, squash | Turkey | By 3500 BCE |
| Andes & Amazonia | Potato, manioc | Llama, guinea pig | By 3500 BCE |
| Tropical West Africa | African yams, oil palm | None | By 3000 BCE |
| Eastern North America | Sunflower, goosefoot | None | 2500 BCE |
| Ethiopia | Coffee, teff | None | ? |

*Source:* Jared M. Diamond, *Guns, Germs, and Steel: The Fates of Human Societies*, 1st ed. (New York: W.W. Norton, 1997).

whose robust immune systems reacted violently to the novel pathogens. Often native communities came under attack from multiple diseases at the same time. Combined with the wars that attended colonization and the malnutrition, dislocation, and despair that attend wars, disease would kill native peoples by the millions while European colonizers increased and spread over the land. Despite their ingenuity and genius at reshaping plants and environments to their advantage, native peoples in the Americas labored under crucial disadvantages compared to Europe—disadvantages that would contribute to disaster after contact.

 REVIEW

How did the native inhabitants of the Americas transform their environments, and what natural constraints put them at a disadvantage relative to Europeans?

# CRISIS AND TRANSFORMATION

**SUDDEN DECLINES**   WITH ITS COASTAL PLAINS, ARID deserts, broad forests, and vast grasslands, North America has always been a place of tremendous diversity and constant change. Indeed, many of the continent's most dramatic changes took place in the few centuries before European contact. Because of a complex and still poorly understood combination of ecological and social factors, the continent's most impressive civilizations collapsed as suddenly and mysteriously as had those of the Olmecs and the Mayas of Mesoamerica. In the Southwest, the Mogollon culture went into eclipse around the twelfth century, the Hohokam and the Ancestral Puebloans by about the fourteenth. In the Eastern Woodlands, the story

was strikingly similar. Most of the great Mississippian population centers, including the magnificent city of Cahokia, had faded by the fourteenth century.

## Enduring Peoples

**TRADING CITY OF PAQUIME**   The survivors of these crises struggled to construct new communities, societies, and political systems. In the Southwest, descendants of the Hohokam withdrew to small farming villages that relied on simpler modes of irrigation. Refugees embarked on a massive, coordinated exodus from the Four Corners region and established new, permanent villages in Arizona and New Mexico that the Spaniards would collectively call the Pueblos. The Mogollon have a more mysterious legacy, but some of their number may have helped establish the remarkable trading city of Paquime in present-day Chihuahua. Built around 1300, Paquime contained more than 2,000 rooms and had a sophisticated water and sewage system unlike any other in the Americas. The city included 18 large mounds, all shaped differently from one another, and three ball courts reminiscent of those found elsewhere in Mexico. Until its demise sometime in the fifteenth century Paquime was the center of a massive trading network, breeding macaws and turkeys for export and channeling prized feathers, turquoise, seashells, and worked copper throughout a huge region.

The dramatic transformations remaking the Southwest involved tremendous suffering. Southwesterners had to rebuild in unfamiliar and oftentimes less productive places. Although some of their new settlements endure even to this day, many failed. Skeletal analysis from an abandoned pueblo on the Rio Grande, for example, indicates that the average life expectancy was only 16.5 years. Moreover, drought and migrations increased conflict

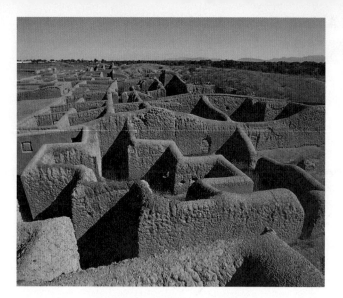

| The rooms of Paquime, divided by adobe mud walls, help archaeologists estimate population.

over scarce resources. The most successful new settlements were large, containing several hundred people, and constructed in doorless, defensible blocks, or else set on high mesas to ward off enemy attacks. These changes were only compounded by the arrival of Athapaskan-speaking peoples (known to the Spanish as Apaches and Navajos) in the century or two before contact with Europeans. These hunters and foragers from western Canada and Alaska moved in small bands, were sometimes friendly, sometimes hostile toward different Pueblos, and eventually became key figures in the postcontact Southwest.

**MUSKOGEAN PEOPLES** In the Eastern Woodlands, the great Mississippian chieftainships never again attained the glory of Cahokia, but key traditions endured in the Southeast. In the lower Mississippi valley, the Natchez maintained both the temple mound–building tradition and the rigid social distinctions of Mississippian civilization. Below the chief, or "Great Sun," of the Natchez stood a hereditary nobility of lesser "Suns," who demanded respect from the lowly "Stinkards," the common people. Other Muskogean-speakers rejected this rigid and hierarchical social model and gradually embraced a new, more flexible system of independent and relatively **egalitarian** villages that forged confederacies to better cope with outsiders. These groupings would eventually mature into three of the great southeastern Indian confederacies: Creek, Choctaw, and Chickasaw.

**IROQUOIANS** To the North lived speakers of Iroquoian languages, roughly divided into a southern faction including Cherokees and Tuscaroras, and a northern faction including the powerful Iroquois and Hurons. Like Muskogeans to the South, these Iroquoian communities mixed farming with a hunting/gathering economy and lived in semipermanent towns. The distinctive feature of Iroquois and Huron architecture was not the temple mound but rather the longhouse (some stretching up to 100 feet in length). Each sheltered as many as 10 families.

**ALGONQUINS** The Algonquins were the third major group of Eastern Woodlands people. They lived along the Atlantic seaboard and the Great Lakes in communities smaller than those of either the Muskogeans or the Iroquois. By the fifteenth century, the coastal communities from southern New England to Virginia had adopted agriculture to supplement their diets, but those in the colder northern climates with shorter growing seasons depended entirely on hunting, fishing, and gathering plants such as wild rice.

**CARIBBEAN CULTURES** Cultures of equal and even greater resources persisted and flourished during the fifteenth century in the Caribbean, particularly on the Greater Antilles—the islands of present-day Cuba, Haiti and the Dominican Republic, Jamaica, and Puerto Rico. Although the earliest inhabitants of the ancient Caribbean, the Ciboneys, may have come from the Florida peninsula, it was the Tainos, later emigrants from northern South America, who expanded throughout the Greater Antilles and the Bahamas. Taino chiefs, known as caciques, along with a small number of noble families, ruled island tribes, controlling the production and distribution of food and tools and exacting tribute from the great mass of commoners, farmers, and fisherfolk. Attending to these elites were the poorest Taino peoples—servants who bedecked their masters and mistresses in brilliant diadems of feathers, fine woven textiles, and gold nose and ear pieces and then shouldered the litters on which the rulers sat and paraded their finery.

## North America on the Eve of Contact

By the end of the fifteenth century, North America's peoples numbered between 5 and 10 million—with perhaps another million living on the islands of the Caribbean—and they were spread among more than 350 societies speaking nearly as many distinct languages. (The total precontact population for all of the Americas is estimated at between 57 and 112 million.)

**DIVERSE LIFEWAYS** These millions lived in remarkably diverse ways. Some peoples relied entirely on farming; others on hunting, fishing, and gathering; still others on a combination of the two. Some, like the Natchez and the Iroquois, practiced matrilineal forms of kinship, in which women owned land, tools, and even children. Among others, such as the Algonquins, patrilineal kinship prevailed, and all property and prestige descended in the male line. Some societies, such as those of the Great Plains and the Great Basin in the West, the Inuit in the Arctic, and the Iroquois and Algonquins in the East, were roughly egalitarian, whereas others, like

# HOW MANY PEOPLE LIVED ON HISPANIOLA IN 1492?

*Estimates of the precontact population of the Americas are necessarily speculative. Historians disagree sharply over these estimates, partly because they have used different data and methods and partly because of the moral or political implications that many people associate with high or low figures. The greater the initial population, so the argument goes, the greater the crime of its destruction. The range of estimates is particularly striking for the island of Hispaniola (present-day Haiti and the Dominican Republic), site of Europe's first American colony and of the hemisphere's first demographic catastrophe. Historians Sherburne Cook and Woodrow Borah, relying especially on population estimates in the primary sources, have argued that several million people lived on the island in 1492. The historical demographer Massimo Livi-Bacci, using other methods to estimate the island's precontact population, doubts that it could have exceeded 400,000. These short excerpts cannot capture the complexity of the arguments, but they illustrate some of the differences.*

## DOCUMENT 1    Sherburne Cook and Woodrow Borah

It is now more than four centuries since [Bartolomé de] las Casas insisted that when Columbus first sighted Hispaniola, the island had 3 to 4 million native inhabitants and perhaps more. This estimate has been denied vigorously. Yet if we accept as substantially correct the count for tribute carried out by Bartolomé Columbus in 1496, and we have seen that there is good evidence for it, we have to concede the reliability of Las Casas. We have set forth previously the reasons for estimating that in 1496 the entire island was inhabited by 3,770,000 souls. There must have been more than this number in

1492, particularly if in 1496 somewhere near 40 percent of the natives were dying annually. Hence we cannot consider a number below 4 million. . . . The most probable number may be put at 7 to 8 million. This is the order of magnitude obtained if we assume that the Columbus' count was relatively accurate, and after we have made all reasonable adjustments for area coverage and the omission of certain population categories. . . . [This figure] would give an average population density for Hispaniola of approximately double the density we found for central Mexico just before the coming of the

Europeans. . . . The American Indians in general had available to them food plants of far greater yield per hectare than any cultivated at that time in the Old World except the yams of sub-Saharan Africa and the rice of southeast Asia. The Indians of Hispaniola, relative to the Indians of central Mexico, had cassava, which yields more per hectare than maize and has remarkable storage qualities; they had also the more favorable agricultural conditions of Hispaniola.

*Source:* Sherburne F. Cook and Woodrow Borah, *Essays in Population History,* 3 vols. (Berkeley and Los Angeles: University of California Press, 1971–1979), 1:405–408.

## DOCUMENT 2    Massimo Livi-Bacci

There are many reasons to believe that the contact population could not have exceeded a few hundred thousand people, and to reject recent higher estimates. . . . The crown and the colonists were eager for gold. The Columbuses' failed tribute levy was probably based on rough calculation of the households of the Vega Real and Cibao. On this basis, [historian Luis] Arranz has estimated a total population of 90,000 for 1494 and 60,000 for 1496 in that area, and three times as much (180,000 and 270,000) for the whole of the island. Forcing the indios to work in the mines was a far more efficient way to obtain gold, and gold production reached a peak of 1,000 kg per year in the first years of Ovando's rule. Under the conservative hypothesis that annual individual productivity was 100 g, and that one third of adult males worked in the mines (about 8 percent of the total population), 10,000 laborers would have been needed to produce 1,000 kg, drawn from a total population of 120,000. This figure during Ovando's rule would be consistent with a population twice as large, or more, at the time of contact ten years before, as stipulated by Arranz.

[Another] approach is demographic in nature. It is during [Governor Nicolás de] Ovando's times (1502–1508) that the decline of the native population must have accelerated its pace—the logical consequence of the wars of "pacification," the Spanish occupation of the whole island, the growing number of colonists, and the increased demand for construction, agriculture, and mining labor. At the end of Ovando's rule in 1508, the native population was said to be 60,000: how many could they have been 14 years earlier? A contact population of 400,000—reduced to 200,000 after the high mortality of 1494–1496 and suffering three other major epidemic outbreaks, each one wiping out one third of the total population—would have been reduced to the estimated 60,000 of 1508. Although this is not impossible, epidemics are not mentioned in the abundant available literature prior to the smallpox epidemic of 1518–1519. The repartimiento of 1514 shows an age structure and a children-to-women ratio consistent with rates of decline approaching 5 percent a year. This rate, if carried backward to 1492, would yield a population of about 80,000. More

elaborate models would tell an only slightly different story.

These independent methods restrict the plausible range into which the initial contact population could fall. A probability distribution of this elusive number places the most likely figure between 200,000 and 300,000, with levels below 100,000 and above 400,000 both unlikely.

*Source:* Massimo Livi-Bacci, "Return to Hispaniola: Reassessing a Demographic Catastrophe," *Hispanic American Historical Review* 83, no. 1 (February 2003), pp. 3–51; pp. 48–49.

### Thinking Critically

*What evidence do Cook and Borah use to produce their population estimate? What evidence does Livi-Bacci employ? Why do you think their approaches produced such dramatically different figures? Do you think that the moral implications of Hispaniola's demographic collapse are different if the original population was 400,000, as opposed to 8 million? Why or why not?*

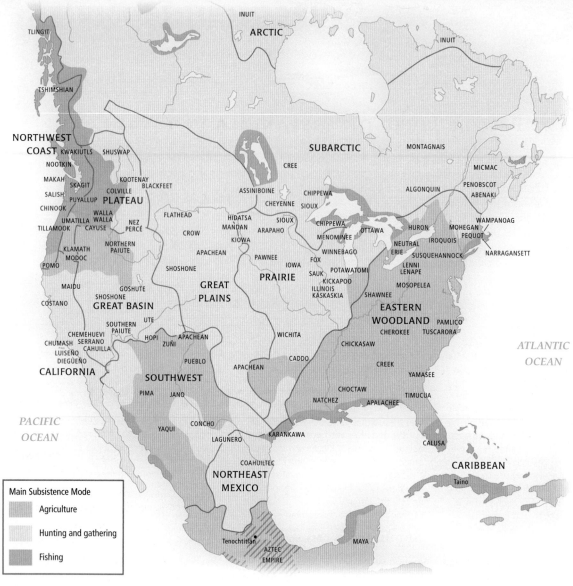

## INDIANS OF NORTH AMERICA, CA. 1500

*The map shows approximate locations of some Native groups.*

many in the Caribbean and the Pacific Northwest, were rigidly divided into nobles and commoners and servants or slaves. Some, such as the Natchez and the Tainos, were ruled by powerful chiefs; others, such as the Algonquins and the Pueblo peoples by councils of village elders or heads of family clans; still others in the Great Basin, the Great Plains, and the far North by the most skillful hunter or the most powerful shaman in their band. Those people who relied on hunting practiced religions that celebrated their kinship with animals and solicited their aid as guardian spirits, whereas predominantly agricultural peoples sought the assistance of their gods to make the rain fall and the crops ripen.

When Europeans first arrived in North America, the continent north of present-day Mexico boasted an ancient, rich, and dynamic history marked by cities, towns, and prosperous farms. At contact it was a land occupied by several million men, women, and children speaking hundreds of languages and characterized by tremendous political, cultural, economic, and religious diversity.

 REVIEW

What was life like in the Americas on the eve of European contact?

# CONCLUSION

## THE WORLD AT LARGE

Medieval Scandinavians sailed as far west as Greenland. Then in 1001 a party of men and women under Leif Ericsson established an encampment known as Vinland on the northern tip of Newfoundland. That European outpost in North America may have endured several seasons or even decades, but eventually it was extinguished or abandoned. In contrast, the contact between Eastern and Western Hemispheres that began in 1492 was permanent, and the effects rising out of it were far-reaching. Epidemic diseases and the traumas of colonization would kill millions of Native Americans; animals and vegetables from both hemispheres would transform lives across the globe. And the newcomers from Europe, Africa, and Asia embarked on a series of encounters that reshaped North and South America.

So it is important to grasp the extent of American cultures before 1492, because for most of our nation's short history we have not wanted to remember the Americas as a populous, diverse, and civilized hemisphere when Christopher Columbus first dropped anchor in the Bahamas. In 1830, for example, President Andrew Jackson tried to answer the many critics of his Indian- removal policies. Although "humanity has often wept over the fate of the aborigines of this country," Jackson said, the Indians' fate was as natural and inevitable "as the extinction of one generation to make room for another." Pointing to the mysterious mounds that had so captivated the founding fathers, he proclaimed, "we behold the memorials of a once powerful race, which was exterminated, or has disappeared, to make room for the existing savage tribes." Just as the architects of the mounds supposedly met their end at the hands of these "savage tribes," the president concluded, so, too, must Indians pass away before the descendants of Europe. "What good man would prefer a country covered with forests and ranged by a few thousand savages, to our extensive republic, studded with cities, towns, and prosperous farms . . . and filled with all the blessings of liberty, civilization, and religion!"

Jackson and many others of his era preferred a national history that contained only a few thousand ranging "savages" to one shaped by millions of indigenous hunters, farmers, builders, and inventors. Yet what seems clear from modern research is the rich diversity of American cultures on the eve of contact between the peoples of Eurasia, Africa, and the Americas. We are still struggling to find stories big enough to encompass not only Indians but all those who have forged this complex, tragic, and marvelous nation of nations. ∞∞∞

# CHAPTER SUMMARY

THOUSANDS OF YEARS AFTER SIBERIAN hunters migrated across the Bering Strait to Alaska, their descendants created civilizations that rivaled those of ancient Europe, Asia, and Africa.

- Around 1500 BCE Mesoamerica emerged as the hearth of civilization in the Western Hemisphere, a process started by the Olmecs and brought to its height by the Mayans. Their built cities are remarkable for their art, architecture, and trade.

- The adoption of agriculture gave peoples in the Southwest and the Eastern Woodlands the resource security necessary to develop sedentary cultures of increasing complexity.

- Inhabitants of the Great Plains, the Great Basin, the Arctic, and the Subarctic relied on fishing, hunting, and gathering.

- Peoples of the Pacific Northwest boasted large populations and prosperous economies as well as an elaborate social, ceremonial, and artistic life.

- The first Americans transformed their environments, pioneering crops and terraforming mountains and jungles.

- Nonetheless, the continent's north-south orientation inhibited the spread of agriculture and technology, and a lack of domesticatable animals compared to Europe would leave Native Americans with little protection against Old World diseases.

■ North America's most impressive early civilizations had collapsed by the end of the fifteenth century. In their wake a diverse array of cultures evolved.

- In the Southwest, Pueblo Indians were joined by Athapaskan-speakers eventually known as Apaches and Navajos.

- In much of eastern North America, stratified chiefdoms of the Mississippian era gave way to more egalitarian confederacies of independent villages.

# ADDITIONAL READING

THE MAGAZINE *ARCHAEOLOGY* OFFERS CLEAR explanations of the latest discoveries for nonscientific audiences. The best descriptions of ancient American civilizations are offered by Brian M. Fagan, *Kingdoms of Gold, Kingdoms of Jade: The Americas before Columbus* (1991); and, especially, Charles C. Mann, *1491: New Revelations of the Americas before Columbus* (2005). For North America specifically, see Alice Beck Kehoe, *America before the European Invasions* (2002). For the Southwest, see Stephen Plog, *Ancient Peoples of the Southwest* (2008, 2nd ed.). For the Eastern Woodlands, see George R. Milner, *The Moundbuilders: Ancient Peoples of Eastern North America* (2005). Roger G. Kennedy, *Hidden Cities: The Discovery and Loss of Ancient North American Civilization* (1994), gives a fascinating account of how white Americans responded to the ruins of ancient American cultures. For the consequences of axis alignment and of domesticated animals, see the captivating work by Jared Diamond, *Guns, Germs, and Steel: The Fates of Human Societies* (1998).

For the cultures of precontact Mexico, see Michael D. Coe and Rex Koontz, *Mexico: From the Olmecs to the Aztecs* (5th ed., 2002). For exhaustive surveys of all regional cultures in North America, see William C. Sturtevant, general editor, *Handbook of North American Indians,* 20 volumes projected (1978– ).

For a fuller list of readings, see the Bibliography at www.mhhe.com/eh8e.

# SIGNIFICANT EVENTS

ATLEAST

**15,500 BCE**
First humans arrive in the Americas

**CA. 10,000–7000 BCE**
Agriculture pioneered in the Western Hemisphere

**CA. 2500 BCE**
Agriculture practiced in the present-day Southeast

**CA. 1700–700 BCE**
Poverty Point flourishes in present-day Louisiana

**CA. 1500 BCE**
The Olmecs begin to build the first Mesoamerican cities

**CA. 500–100 BCE**
Adena culture reaches its height in North America

**CA. 100 BCE–400 CE**
Hopewell culture thrives in the Ohio and Mississippi valleys

**CA. 200–800 CE**
The Maya flourish on the Yucatán Peninsula

**CA. 200–900 CE**
Mogollon culture developing in present-day New Mexico

**CA. 800–1200 CE**
Mississippian civilization reaches its height

**CA. 900–1100 CE**
Ancestral Puebloan civilization reaches its height

**CA. 1300 CE**
Hohokam, Ancestral Pueblo, and Mississippian civilizations decline; Athapaskan peoples (Apache and Navajo) migrate to the Southwest from Canada

**CA. 1325–1500 CE**
Aztec Empire rises in Mesoamerica

| | NATURAL ENVIRONMENT | BUILT ENVIRONMENT | PRIMARY SUSTENANCE |
| --- | --- | --- | --- |
| Olmecs | Tropical lowlands of south central Mexico | First city-builders: large plazas, pyramidal structures, sculptured heads | Beans, squash, maize (corn) |
| Mayas | Lowland jungles of the Yucatán Peninsula | Cities contain palaces, bridges, aqueducts, baths, pyramids topped with temples | Beans, squash, maize |
| Aztecs | Valley of Mexico | Tenochtitlán—an island metropolis with canals, marketplaces, palaces, temples | Beans, squash, maize |
| Mogollon | Southern New Mexico | Exquisite pottery | |
| Hohokam | Southern Arizona | Canals, ball courts | Beans, squash, maize |
| Ancestral Pueblo | Colorado plateau | Masonry buildings | |
| Eastern Woodlands | Centered in valleys of great rivers, Great Lakes, and Atlantic coast | Mound building, sometimes figurative and monumental | Primarily animals, fish, and nuts; gourds and pumpkins in the southeast; and later maize |
| Great Plains | Semiarid long- and short-grass plains; rainfall varied and unpredictable | Hide shelters on poles | Primarily hunting and foraging, buffalo stampedes, but some maize, squash, beans, and sunflowers |
| Great Basin | Plateau between Rocky Mountains and the Sierras | Bands usually numbered less than 50; simple shelters | Elk, antelope trapped; also a wide variety of small game as available; seeds, nuts, and plants |
| Pacific Northwest | Coastal areas from British Columbia to northern California; abundant rainfall, mild climate | Large and long houses of cedar beams and hand-split boards; complex works of art | Lush forests provide plants and game; rivers and ocean, abundant fish and shellfish |
| Subarctic and Arctic Peoples | Open boreal forest and tundra stretch across Canada; usually fewer than 100 frost-free days a year | Skin tents and igloos in the arctic winters | Hunting and fishing (including whales, seals, muskrats); moose and caribou |

# Tracking the First Americans

What methods do historians use to discover the history of a past thousands of years before any humans knew how to write? Archaeological research is key; and by carefully unearthing layer after layer of soil, analyzing artifacts and their relation to these layers, scientists and historians have been able to discover a remarkable amount of information about the first immigrants to the Americas over 15,000 years ago.

But the deductions and inferences made about a past lacking historical documents are often contested. Like millions of other Americans who look to religious texts more than to evolutionary biology or archaeology for their deep history, many Indian people today reject what Western science has to say about their origins. Rather, they insist that their people are truly indigenous to America—that they didn't migrate here but *emerged* here from other planes of existence. A Navajo origin story, for example, explains how their ancestors came into this world, "the changeable world," after a harrowing journey through the Four Dark Worlds. For some these stories are profound metaphors; for others they describe actual events in ancient times. But adherents of either perspective often share an understandable skepticism about scientific "truth" that over the past two centuries has taken so little interest in their oral traditions, has gone through so many massive revisions, and has so often been used to justify native dispossession. After all, Andrew Jackson and other supporters of Indian removal insisted they had "science" on their side.

Archaeologists rarely question the basis of scientific knowledge, but they have continually argued with one another over the scant evidence discovered about early migrations. And progress often depends on accidental finds, such as the one made by an African American cowboy, George McJunkin. McJunkin, a former slave, was a talented rancher, not to mention a capable fiddler, amateur astronomer, and surveyor. Old fossils also fascinated him, and he happened upon one of the most important of the twentieth century.

## THE CLOVIS DISCOVERIES

ON HORSEBACK ONE DAY IN 1908 near Folsom, New Mexico, McJunkin spotted some very old bison bones eroding from a slope. Bringing some home, he soon realized that they were far too large—that they must have belonged to an extinct bison species. Professional archaeologists ignored McJunkin's discovery, and only in 1926 after his death did New Mexican locals manage to convince scholars from the University of Colorado to investigate the original site. In doing so, they uncovered an exquisitely crafted stone spear-point embedded in the bison's ribs.

Stone artifacts known as Clovis points have been found with skeletons of mammoths, mastodon, and bison.

The discovery rocked the scientific community, which had long declared confidently that Indians had first arrived in the Americas only about 4,000 BP. Eleven years later another shock followed when archaeologists digging near Clovis, New Mexico, found a different sort of projectile point near butchered mammoth bones. Finally, in 1949, scientists confirmed the great antiquity of both finds by using radiocarbon dating, a method for measuring decay rates of the radioactive isotope of carbon, which exists in organic matter such as bone and starts to break down immediately after an organism dies. Tests revealed that the Folsom site dated to 10,800 BP and that Clovis was nearly a thousand years older still. Soon archaeologists around the continent discovered other sites of comparable antiquity containing stone tools with the same Clovis characteristics. A new consensus emerged: Asian migrants first came to North America around 13,000 BP. These migrants brought with them a common stone-working technology, of the sort found at Clovis. The Clovis people fanned out across the Western Hemisphere and, within one or two millennia, their culture gave way to regionally specific cultural and stone-working traditions, like Folsom.

## EVIDENCE OF MIGRATION FROM SIBERIA TO NORTH AMERICA

BUT HOW DID ASIANS GET to North America? According to the long-standing consensus, they walked to Alaska—a region now separated from Siberia by 50 miles of ocean known as the Bering Strait. During the last Ice Age, with much of the world's water locked up in continent-straddling glaciers, ocean levels were far lower. Consequently, between around 25,000 BP and 15,000 BP, a now-submerged landmass called "Beringia" linked Alaska and Siberia. Following game onto and across Beringia, the first Americans gradually occupied this land and, over the course of many generations, some eventually moved east into what is now Alaska. For centuries massive glaciers blocked the way farther south. But geologists have argued that around 15,000 BP an ice-free corridor opened up along what is now the McKenzie River, east of the Canadian Rockies. Game animals and the people hunting them (with Clovis-point tools) eventually began to filter south, gradually emerging into the warmer and totally uninhabited lands of the present-day United States. This scenario enjoyed support for several decades, not only from geologists but also from some geneticists, who found that modern-day Native Americans diverged from Siberians perhaps 15,000 years ago.

Still, several provocative archaeological finds in Tennessee, Pennsylvania, Florida, and elsewhere suggested that humans had been living in the Americas longer—perhaps far longer. For example, a mastodon bone discovered in Washington State, some 800 years older than any Clovis site, had what seemed to be another bone embedded in it—perhaps from a projectile thrown by a human hunter. In the late 1970s researchers from Vanderbilt University discovered an ancient campsite dating to 14,600 BP at Monte Verde, Chile—a full millennium earlier than the oldest known Clovis tools. But the Monte Verde site was thousands of miles to the south and difficult to visit, dating techniques were open to multiple interpretations, and most archaeologists rejected these pre-Clovis claims. The standard story had endured for decades, and it would take incontrovertible evidence of earlier occupation to overthrow it.

## THE NEW CONSENSUS

FOR MOST ARCHAEOLOGISTS, THAT INCONTROVERTIBLE evidence has finally arrived. A 2008 study demonstrated that fossilized human feces excavated from a cave in Oregon were more than 14,000 years old. In 2011, archaeologist Michael R. Waters (himself once a staunch "Clovis-firster") led a team that confirmed the antiquity of the mastodon bone from Washington State. They found that the invasive bone chip was indeed from another animal and had almost certainly been fashioned into a weapon by an ancient hunter. Most significantly, in 2011 Waters published yet another analysis of a site he excavated on Buttermilk Creek, outside of Austin, Texas. It revealed a typical collection of Clovis tools. But digging deeper into a layer of clay sediments, Waters and his colleagues found dozens of stone tools made with a strikingly different technique. Lacking the organic material necessary for radiocarbon dating, the team instead employed a newer dating technology called optically-stimulated luminescence that can determine when stone was last exposed to the sun by measuring light energy trapped in minerals. The results were remarkable: the oldest tools at the site dated to 15,500 BP.

Most specialists now acknowledge that humans arrived in the present-day United States at least 15,000–16,000 years ago, and that the Clovis stone-working tradition emerged here, long after they arrived. The "shattering" of the Clovis barrier has reinvigorated the study of ancient America, but there now seem to be more questions than ever. Previously excavated sites are being reopened and tested anew in light of the revised theories. Some archaeologists insist that the earliest migrations took place as many as 20,000 or even 40,000 years ago. Though most scholars reject these very early dates, they now do so more tentatively, mindful of the way in which dogmatic loyalty to Clovis-first blinded the field to compelling evidence. And the controversy over dates has reopened the question of the routes Siberians first took into North America. Depending on the date of the first migration, immense glaciers may have made an overland route virtually impossible. For this reason archaeologists have become more interested in the possibility that the first arrivals came in small boats, gradually working their way down the Pacific coast.

Some of the most exciting developments in the study of ancient America are emerging from linguistics and genetics. Previous genetic research on the peopling of the Americas had compared present-day Native Americans and present-day Siberians by examining small regions of their respective genomes, usually Y chromosomes or mitochondrial DNA. These studies confirmed Siberia as the origin of the first migrants and suggested that all native peoples in the Americas descend from a single, ancestral migration. But today new technologies enable the sequencing of entire genomes, making research of this kind far more revealing and complete. In the summer of 2012, researchers unveiled a major new study demonstrating that there were in fact three totally separate migrations from Siberia to the Americas, an idea put forward long ago by linguist Stephen Greenberg but widely dismissed at the time. The first migration, at least 15,000 years ago, populated the entire hemisphere. The vast majority of today's Native Americans are descendants of this first founding group. Millennia later another migration brought the ancestors of the Eskimos and Aleutians who colonized the Arctic, and still another brought the Athapaskans of western Canada and the American Southwest (today's Apaches and Navajos).

It was the most ambitious study of Native American genetics ever undertaken, but the origins debate is hardly settled. Skeptics of the study note that a large majority of the hemisphere's native peoples perished in epidemics and wars in the centuries after contact, making any present-day genetic sample unrepresentative in critical respects. And many indigenous peoples remain deeply distrustful of the motivations behind such studies. They know all too well that stories told about the past have power over both the present and the future. The Genographic Project of the National Geographic Society recently asked all federally recognized tribes in the United States for genetic samples, in order to run an ambitious study on native origins. Out of 565 tribes, only 2 agreed.

Archaeologist Michael R. Waters excavated a site at Buttermilk Creek, near Austin, Texas, which revealed artifacts that are older and of a distinctly different style than the Clovis points found deposited above them, in a more recent layer. Such evidence suggests that migrants into North America arrived much earlier than most archaeologists believed.

With sails bellying in a gale, the Dutch ship in this painting has furled the rest of its canvas. Sailors from western Europe risked much as they crossed the Atlantic in search of fish, silver, gold, and other commodities of trade.

# Old Worlds, New Worlds

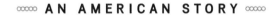

## 1400–1600

### *What's to Come*

⟨⟨⟨⟨⟨ **AN AMERICAN STORY** ⟩⟩⟩⟩⟩

## FISHING NETS AND FAR HORIZONS

All the world lay before them. Or so it seemed to mariners from England's seafaring coasts, pushing westward toward unknown lands in the far Atlantic.

The scent of the new land came first—not the sight of it, but the smells: the scent of fir trees wafted from beyond the horizon; or the sight of shorebirds wheeling about the masts. Straightaway the captain would call for a lead to be thrown overboard to sound the depths. At its end was a hollowed-out socket with a bit of tallow in it, so that some of the sea bottom would stick when the lead was hauled up. Even out of sight of land, a good sailing master could tell where he was by what came up—"oosy sand" or perhaps "soft worms" or "popplestones as big as beans."

Through much of the fifteenth century the search for cod had drawn West Country sailors north and west, toward Iceland. In the 1480s and 1490s a few English tried their luck farther west, looking for the mythical *Hy-Brasil*—Gaelic for "Isle of the Blessed"—somewhere west of Ireland. These western ventures returned with little to show for their daring until an Italian named Giovanni Caboto, called John Cabot by the English, obtained the blessing of King Henry VII to hunt for unknown lands. From the port of Bristol his lone ship sailed west in the spring of 1497. This time the return voyage brought news of a "new-found" island where the trees were tall enough to make fine masts and the codfish were plentiful. Cabot returned to England to inform His Majesty of his success, received 10 pounds as his reward, and with the proceeds dressed himself in dashing silks. Then he returned to Bristol to undertake a more ambitious search for a northwest passage to Asia. In 1498 his five ships disappeared over the horizon and were never heard from again.

By the 1550s Cabot's island, now known as Newfoundland, attracted 400 vessels annually, fishermen not only from England but also from France, Portugal, and Spain. The harbor of present-day St. John's, Newfoundland, served as the informal hub of the North Atlantic fishery. Sailors dropped anchor to take on supplies in the spring, trade with native peoples, or to prepare for the homeward voyage in autumn. There was a good deal of swapping tales, for these seafarers knew as much as anyone else—if not more—about the new world of wonders that was opening to Europeans. They were acquainted with names like Cristoforo Colombo, the Italian from Genoa whom Cabot might have known as a boy. They listened to Portuguese tales of sailing around the Horn of Africa in pursuit of spices and to stories of Indian empires to the south, rich in gold and silver that Spanish treasure ships were bringing home.

| *During the sixteenth century, West Country fisherfolk from England sailed from harbors such as Plymouth, shown here in a painting from the 1480s. Can you spot the primitive lighthouse?*

Indeed, Newfoundland was one of the few places in the world where so many ordinary folk of different nations could gather and talk, crammed aboard dank ships moored in St. John's harbor, huddled before blazing fires on its beaches, or crowded into smoky makeshift taverns. When the ships sailed home in autumn, the tales went with them, repeated in the tiniest coastal villages by those pleased to have cheated the sea and death one more time. Eager to fish, talk, trade, and take profits, West Country mariners were almost giddy at the prospect of Europe's expanding horizons.

Though most seafarers who fished the waters of Newfoundland remain unknown today, it is well to begin with these ordinary folk, for the European discovery of the Americas cannot be looked on simply as the voyages of a few bold explorers. Adventurers such as Columbus and Cabot were only the tip of a much larger expansion of European peoples and culture that began in the 1450s. That expansion arose out of a series of gradual but telling changes in the fabric of European society. Some of these changes were technological, arising out of advances in the arts of navigating and shipbuilding and the use of gunpowder. Some were economic, involving the development of trade networks like those linking Bristol with ports in Iceland and Spain. Some were **demographic,** bringing about a rise in Europe's population after a devastating century of plague. Other changes were religious, adding a dimension of belief to the political rivalries that fueled discoveries in the Americas. Yet others were political, making it possible for kingdoms to centralize and extend their influence across the ocean. Portugal, Spain, France, and England—all possessing coasts along the Atlantic—led the way in exploration, spurred on by Italian "admirals" such as Caboto and Colombo, Spanish *conquistadores*—"conquerors"—such as Hernán Cortés and Francisco Pizarro, and English sea dogs such as Humphrey Gilbert and Walter Raleigh. Ordinary folk rode these currents, too. The great and the small alike were propelled by forces that were remolding the face of Europe—and were beginning to remold the face of the world. ∞∞∞

# EURASIA AND AFRICA IN THE FIFTEENTH CENTURY

**CHINA'S GLORY** IN 1450, HOWEVER, THE WESTERN European kingdoms that would one day dominate much of the world still sat at the fringe of an international economy that revolved around China. By a variety of measures Ming China was the richest, most powerful, and most advanced society in the world. All Eurasia sought Chinese goods, especially spices, ceramics, and silks, and Chinese ships sped these goods to faraway ports. Seven times between 1405 and 1433, China's "treasure fleet"—300 ships manned by 28,000 sailors and commanded by Zheng He (pronounced "Jung Huh")—unfurled its red silk sails off the south China coast and traveled as far as the kingdoms of eastern Africa. The treasure fleet's largest craft were nine-masted junks measuring 400 feet long. They boasted multiple decks and luxury cabins with balconies. (By comparison, Columbus's largest ship in 1492 was a mere 85 feet long, and the crew aboard all three of his ships totaled just 90 men.) Chinese leaders soon grounded their trading fleet and put a stop to the long-distance voyages that might eventually have made Zheng He a forerunner to Columbus. But Chinese luxuries, most transported overland, continued to be Eurasia's most sought-after commodities.

**ISLAMIC KINGDOMS** The next mightiest powers in the Old World were not European kingdoms but rather huge Islamic empires, especially the Ottomans in the eastern Mediterranean. The Ottomans rose to prominence during the fourteenth and fifteenth centuries and expanded aggressively in every direction. Muslim rulers gained control of critical trade routes and centers of commerce between Asia and Europe. The Ottomans' greatest triumph came in 1453, when the sultan Mehmet II conquered Constantinople (now Istanbul), the ancient and supposedly impregnable Christian city that straddled Europe and Asia and was one of the world's premier trading hubs. Mehmet's stunning victory sounded alarms throughout Europe.

## Europe's Place in the World

Europe's rulers had good reason for alarm. Distant from Asia's profitable trade and threatened both economically and militarily by the Ottomans, most of the continent remained fractious and vulnerable. During the fourteenth and fifteenth centuries, 90 percent of Europe's people, widely dispersed in small villages, made their living from the land. But warfare, poor transportation, and low grain yields all created food shortages, and undernourishment produced a population prone to disease. Under these circumstances life was nasty, brutish, and usually short. One-quarter of all children died in the first year of life. People who reached the age of 40 counted themselves fortunate.

It was also a world of sharp inequalities, where nobles and aristocrats enjoyed several hundred times the income of peasants or craftworkers. It was a world with no strong, centralized political authority, where kings were weak and warrior lords held sway over small towns and tiny fiefdoms. It was a world of violence and sudden death, where homicide, robbery, and rape occurred with brutal frequency. It was a world where security and order of any kind seemed so fragile that many people clung to tradition, and more than a few used witchcraft in an attempt to master the chaotic and unpredictable world around them.

**THE BLACK DEATH** But Europe was changing, in part because of a great calamity. Between the late 1340s and the early 1350s, bubonic plague—known as the Black Death—swept away one-quarter of Europe's population. Some urban areas lost 70 percent of their people to the disease. The Black Death disrupted both agriculture and commerce, and provoked a spiritual crisis that resulted in violent, unsanctioned religious movements, scapegoating of marginal groups, even massacres of Jews. Although Europeans seem to have met recurrent outbreaks of the disease with less panic, the sickness continued to disrupt social and economic life nonetheless.

Yet the sudden drop in population relieved pressure on scarce resources. Survivors of the Black Death found that the relative scarcity of workers and consumers made for better wages, lower prices, and more land. These changes intersected in an overall expansion of trade. In earlier centuries Italian merchants had begun building wealth by encouraging commerce across Europe and by tapping into

As bubonic plague and other epidemic diseases wracked Europe, it brought the possibility of sudden death closer than ever. This skull pendant dating from the 1600s was designed as jewelry to hang from the wearer's breast. When opened, it revealed a skeleton in a coffin. In England, before the coming of the Black Death, funeral monuments usually portrayed deceased lords and ladies in their finest clothing. Afterward, the monuments increasingly featured death masks, contorted corpses, or skeletons with serpents slinking among their bones.

## A WITCH BOTTLE

Known as a "Bellarmine jar." Why? (Do a little web research!)

Pins and needles. Why might these have been deliberately bent?

*Exterior*

X-ray cross-section

Fingernail clippings: well manicured, suggesting someone of higher social standing.

Liquid: analysis shows it to be urine.

Historians often find clues about a culture from material artifacts discarded long ago. A Bellarmine jar was dug up in a cellar in England in 2004. Archaeologists recognized it as a "witch bottle," so called because some English folk used such items to defend against the perceived ill will of witches. "The whole rationale for these bottles was sympathetic magic—so you put something intimate to the bewitched person in the bottle and then you put in bent pins and other unpleasant objects which are going to poison and cause great pain to the witch," explained historian Owen Davies.

When shaken, this bottle splashed and rattled. An X ray showed the objects inside, whose contents were examined in a laboratory. Among other items, the bottle included hair, navel fluff, and a heart-shaped piece of leather with a nail through it. The liquid also contained traces of sulphur (popularly called brimstone in the seventeenth century). An estimated 40,000–60,000 witches were hanged and burned in early modern Europe, demonstrating that despite the Reformation's disdain for "Popish superstitions," supernaturalism and magic remained potent religious strains.

### Thinking Critically

*Why might brimstone have been added to the witch bottle? What social factors help explain why fifteenth-century Europeans saw witchcraft as a significant part of the way the world worked? Would illnesses such as the plague contribute to attitudes about witchcraft?*

---

trade from Africa, the Middle East, and, when able, from Asia. By the late fifteenth century, Europe's merchants and bankers had devised more efficient ways of transferring the money generated from manufacturing and trade and had established credit in order to support commerce across longer distances. Wealth flowed into the coffers of fifteenth-century traders, financiers, and landlords, creating a pool of capital that those investors could plow into new technologies, trading ventures, and, eventually, colonial enterprises.

**MONARCHS FORGE NATION-STATES**

The direction of Europe's political development also laid the groundwork for overseas colonization. After 1450 strong monarchs in Europe steadily enlarged the sphere of royal power at the expense of warrior lords. Henry VII, the founder of England's Tudor dynasty, Francis I of France, and Ferdinand and Isabella of Spain began the trend, forging modern nation-states by extending their political control over more territory, people, and resources. Such larger, more centrally organized states were able to marshal the resources necessary to support colonial outposts and to sustain the professional armies and navies capable of creating and protecting overseas empires. By the mid-fourteenth century western Europe had commercial networks, private fortunes, strong kingdoms, and ambitions that would lead to a transformative period of expansion.

## Africa and the Portuguese Wave

**IMPROVED NAVIGATION AND SAILING TECHNIQUES**

European expansion began with Africa. For centuries, African spices, ivory, and gold had entered the Eurasian market either westward, through ports on the Indian Ocean, or northward, through the Sahara Desert and into the Mediterranean Sea. Powerful African kingdoms controlled the routes through which these prized commodities moved, and prices ballooned by the time the goods reached cities in Europe. Islamic expansion in the fifteenth century made competition all the more intense. Merchants throughout the continent yearned to access West African markets directly, by ship. But navigational and shipbuilding technology was not yet up to the challenge of the Atlantic's prevailing currents, which sped ships south along Africa's coast but made the return voyage virtually impossible.

Portugal was the first to solve this problem and tap directly into West African markets, thanks in large part to the vision and tenacity of one man. Prince Henry "the Navigator," as he became known, was a passionate advocate for Portugal's maritime interests, an ardent Catholic, and a man who dreamed of turning back Islam's rising tide. He understood that direct commerce with West Africa would allow his kingdom to circumvent the costly trans-Sahara trade. To forward his vision, Henry funded exploratory voyages, established a maritime school, and challenged sailors and engineers to conquer the problem of the current. His advocacy helped the Portuguese develop the caravel, a lighter, more maneuverable ship that could sail better against contrary winds and in rough seas. More seaworthy than the lumbering galleys of the Middle Ages, caravels combined longer, narrower hulls—a shape built for speed—with triangular lateen sails, which allowed for more flexible steering. The caravel allowed the Portuguese to regularly do what few Europeans had ever done: sail down Africa's west coast and return home. Other advances, including a sturdier version of the Islamic world's astrolabe, enabled Portugal's vessels to calculate their position at sea with unprecedented accuracy.

The farther south the Portuguese extended their influence along the Atlantic rim of sub-Saharan Africa, the more likely they were to meet with peoples who had had no earlier encounters with Europeans and, indeed, had no knowledge of the existence of other continents. On catching their first sight of a Portuguese expedition in 1455, the inhabitants of one village on the Senegal River marveled at the strangers' clothing and their white skin. As an Italian member of that expedition recounted, some Africans "rubbed me with their spittle to discover whether my whiteness was dye or flesh."

**WEST AFRICAN STATES**

But the Portuguese were wrong to mistake such acts of innocence for economic or political naïveté. As they made their way south in stages, the newcomers found mature commercial networks and formidable African states, states eager to trade but intent on protecting their interests. Portugal could not simply take what it wanted from West Africa. With few exceptions, it proved impossible for European powers to colonize territory in West Africa before the nineteenth century because the region's people were too many and too organized. Furthermore, its disease environment was too dangerous. Malaria would kill between one-fourth and one-half of all Portuguese unwise and unlucky enough to try to stay. Hence the newcomers had to seek partners, to forge trading relationships with coastal elites. The Portuguese established forts and trading houses on the coast. They gave tribute or taxes to local powers in return for trading privileges and exchanged textiles, especially, but also raw and worked metal goods, currency (in the form of cowry shells), and beads for prized commodities such as gold, ivory, and malaguetta pepper. Portuguese traders also expressed interest in another commodity, one that would reshape the wider Atlantic world: slaves.

## Sugar and the Origins of the Atlantic Slave Trade

Unfree labor has existed in nearly all human societies. Although the norms, characteristics, and economic importance of slavery have varied widely over time and place, men, women, and children have been held as slaves from before recorded history to the present. (U.S. and international organizations estimate that today there are as many as 27 million people held in some form of labor bondage and that nearly 1 million unfree people are sold across international borders every year.)

By the Middle Ages, elites in Europe had largely abandoned the slave culture of the Roman Empire and relied instead on serfs or peasants for labor. Slaves became more important as status symbols than as workers, and most were young white women. Indeed, the word "slave" comes originally from "Slav"; Slavic girls and women from the Balkans and the coasts of the Black Sea were frequent targets of slave raids.

| Astrolabe

This African fortune-teller reads the palm of her white client in this seventeenth-century painting by a Franco-Flemish artist, Nicolas Regnier. In early modern Europe, class and religion were more important than color and ethnicity in defining social divisions. Slaves, servants, and free workers of all races often worked and socialized together.

**CHANGES IN EUROPEAN SLAVERY**

But European slavery began to change again following the Crusades. In 1099 Christian forces captured Jerusalem from the Seljuk Turks (forerunners to the Ottomans). In the Holy Land the crusaders discovered sugar plantations that the Turks had cultivated. At that time some sugar was being produced by Moors in North Africa and Iberia, yet it remained an expensive luxury item coveted by merchants and elites as a medicine and preservative. Crusaders recognized sugar's economic potential, but because it was so labor-intensive they found it a difficult commodity to produce. It required intense work during planting and close tending during the growing season. On maturity the crop had to be harvested and processed 24 hours a day to avoid being spoiled. In short, sugar demanded cheap, pliable labor. The newly arrived crusaders relied in part on slave labor to make their plantations turn a profit.

**SPREAD OF SUGAR**

Once Islamic forces under the famed leader Saladin reconquered Jerusalem in the twelfth century, European investors established new plantations on eastern Mediterranean islands. In addition to being labor intensive, though, sugar was a crop that quickly exhausted soils and forced planters to move operations regularly. Plantations spread to new islands, and by the early 1400s sugar was even being grown in Portugal. As production expanded, planters had to work harder than ever to obtain the necessary labor because of the Black Death and because Ottoman conquests restricted European access to the traditional slaving grounds of the eastern Mediterranean and the Balkans.

Thus by the fifteenth century the Portuguese were already producing sugar on slave-run plantations, but they were seeking new cropland and new sources of slaves. Once again Prince Henry's vision enhanced his kingdom's economic interests. While Portugal's merchants were establishing trading posts along the west coast of Africa, Iberian mariners were discovering or rediscovering islands in the eastern Atlantic: the Canaries, Madeira, and the Azores, islands with rich, volcanic soils ideally suited to sugarcane. By the late fifteenth century sugar plantations were booming on the Atlantic islands, staffed by West African slaves. By the middle of the sixteenth century people of African descent accounted for 10 percent of the population of Lisbon, Portugal's capital city.

**DIAS AND DA GAMA**

Portugal was growing great in wealth and in ambition. Convinced that they could reach coveted Asian markets by sea, bold mariners sailed their caravels farther and farther south. In 1488 Bartolomeu Dias rounded the Cape of Good Hope on the southern tip of Africa, sailing far enough up that continent's eastern coast to claim discovery of a sea route to India. Ten years later Vasco da Gama reached India itself, and Portugal's interests ultimately extended to Indochina and China.

Portuguese geographers had long felt certain that travel around Africa was the shortest route to the Orient, but an Italian sailor disagreed. Cristoforo Colombo was 25 years old when he shipwrecked on the Portuguese coast in 1476. The ambitious young man spent the next 10 years learning from the world's master mariners. He also threw himself into research, devouring Lisbon's books on geography and cartography. Columbus (the Latinized version of his name) became convinced that the fastest route from Portugal to China lay west, across the uncharted Atlantic Ocean. He appealed to Portugal's king to support an exploratory voyage, but royal geographers scoffed at the idea. They agreed that the world was round but insisted (correctly, as it turns out) that the globe was far larger than Columbus had calculated; hence the proposed westward route was too distant to be practical. Almost a decade of rejection had grayed Columbus's red hair, but—undaunted—he packed up in 1485 and took his audacious idea to Spain.

 **REVIEW**

Why did Europeans begin to develop commercial networks in the Atlantic, and how did the Portuguese operate in Africa?

# SPAIN IN THE AMERICAS

BUT COLUMBUS ARRIVED A FEW years too early. Spain's monarchs, Ferdinand and Isabella, were then engaged in a campaign to drive the Muslims out of their last stronghold on the Iberian Peninsula, the Moorish kingdom of Granada. At first the monarchs rejected Columbus's offer, leading him to make other (failed) overtures to the kings of England, France, and even Portugal again. Then in 1492 Ferdinand and Isabella took Granada and completed their reconquest of Spain, or *reconquista.* Flush with victory and ready to expand their horizons, the pair granted Columbus another audience. The mariner insisted that a westward route to Asia would allow Spain to compete with Portugal and generate sufficient revenue to continue the reconquest, even into the Holy Land itself. Ignoring the advice of their geographers, the monarchs agreed to his proposal.

COLUMBUS REACHES AMERICA

Columbus's first voyage across the Atlantic could only have confirmed his conviction that he was destiny's darling. His three ships, no bigger than fishing vessels that sailed to Newfoundland, plied their course over placid seas, south from Seville to the Canary Islands and then due west. On October 11, a little more than two months after leaving Spain, branches, leaves, and flowers floated by their hulls, signals that land lay near. Just after midnight, a sailor spied cliffs shining white in the moonlight. On the morning of October 12, the *Niña,* the *Pinta,* and the *Santa Maria* set anchor in a shallow sapphire bay, and their crews knelt on the white coral beach. Columbus christened the place San Salvador (Holy Savior).

## The Spanish Beachhead in the Caribbean

Like many men of destiny, Columbus mistook his true destination. At first he confused his actual location, the Bahamas, with an island off the coast of Japan. He coasted along Cuba and Hispaniola (today's Haiti and Dominican Republic), expecting

at any moment to catch sight of gold-roofed Japanese temples or fleets of Chinese junks. He encountered instead a gentle, generous people who knew nothing of the Great Khan but who welcomed the newcomers profusely. Columbus's journals note that these people wore little clothing (see Daily Lives, "'Barbaric' Dress—Indian and European," page 36), but they did wear jewelry—tiny pendants of gold suspended from the nose. He dubbed the Taino people "Indians"—inhabitants of the Indies.

Columbus would long insist that he had indeed reached the Indies, and it would take some years before other mariners and geographers understood clearly that these newfound islands and the landmasses beyond them lay between Europe and Asia. One of the earliest geographers to do so was the Florentine Amerigo Vespucci, who first described Columbus's Indies as *Mundus Novus,* a "New World." Rather than dub the new lands "Columbia," a German mapmaker called them "America" in Vespucci's honor. The German's maps proved wildly successful, and the name stuck.

 WEST AFRICA AND THE CARIBBEAN COMPARED

Whether Columbus had found Asian isles or a new world, Europeans seemed to agree that the simple societies he encountered were better suited to be ruled than partnered with. Unlike the kingdoms of West Africa, the Taino chiefdoms lacked the military power to resist European aggression. Moreover, although the newfound islands would eventually present their own threats to European health, they seemed a good deal more inviting than the deadly coast of West Africa. Hints of gold, a seemingly weak and docile population, and a relatively healthy climate all ensured that Columbus's second voyage would be one of colonization rather than commerce. During the 1490s and early 1500s Spanish colonizers imposed a terrifically brutal regime on the Tainos, slaughtering native leaders and forcing survivors to toil in mines and fields.

Only a few Spaniards spoke out against the exploitation. Among them was Bartolomé de Las Casas, a man who spent several years in the Caribbean, participating in conquests and profiting from native labor. Eventually, Las Casas had an epiphany, renounced his role in the conquest, and, as a Dominican friar, became a tireless foe of Spanish cruelties toward Indians. He railed against the "unjust, cruel, and tyrannical warfare" waged on Indians, war waged in order to disrupt native societies and force their people into "the hardest, harshest, and most heinous bondage to which men or beasts might ever be bound into." Las Casas's writings, translated throughout Europe and illustrated with gruesome drawings, helped give rise to the "Black Legend" of Spanish oppression in the Americas.

**PRINCIPAL ROUTES OF EUROPEAN EXPLORATION**

The warnings had some effect, but not for decades. Within a generation of Columbus's landfall, the Taino population had nearly collapsed from war, overwork, malnutrition, despair, and strange new Eurasian diseases. Ambitious Spaniards began scouring the Caribbean basin, discovering new lands and searching for new populations of Indians to subjugate or enslave in place of the vanishing Tainos. Soon the Bahamas were depopulated by Spanish slavers, and conquests had done to present-day Cuba, Jamaica, and Puerto Rico what they had done to Hispaniola.

## Conquest of the Aztecs

Would-be conquistadors turned their eyes to the mainland. Spanish sailors surveyed the Yucatán Peninsula and clashed with the formidable Maya. In 1519 an expedition led by the impetuous Hernán Cortés made contact with native peoples on Mexico's gulf coast. They spoke of an oppressive imperial people who occupied a fantastic city to the west. These were the Aztecs.

Aztecs had much in common with Spaniards. Both societies were predominantly rural, with most inhabitants living in small villages and engaging in agriculture. In both places, merchants and specialized craftworkers clustered in cities, organized themselves into guilds, and

clamored for protection from the government. Aztec noble and priestly classes, like those in Europe, took the lead in politics and religion, demanding tribute from the common people. Finally, both societies were robustly expansionist, bent on bringing new lands and peoples under their control.

Yet critical differences between these two peoples shaped the outcome of their meeting. The Aztecs lacked the knowledge of ocean navigation, metal tools and weaponry, and firearms. Equally important, the relatively young Aztec empire had not yet established total control over central Mexico. Formidable peoples remained outside Aztec domination, and conquered city-states within the empire bitterly resented Aztec rule. It was a weakness that Cortés exploited ably. Massing an army of disgruntled native warriors, Cortés and his men marched inland to the mighty Aztec capital Tenochtitlán, home to more people (roughly a quarter million) than any city then existing in Europe. When the emperor Moctezuma's ambassadors met Cortés on the road and attempted to appease him with gold ornaments and other gifts, an Indian witness noted that "the Spaniards . . . picked up the gold and fingered it like monkeys. . . . Their bodies swelled with greed." The newcomers were welcomed into the city as honored guests but soon siezed Moctezuma and took him captive. For months Cortés ruled the empire indirectly, but the Aztecs drove the Spanish out after Moctezuma's death.

Both the Aztecs and the Spanish tried to understand the new in terms of the familiar. Hence an Aztec artist portrayed Cortés as an Indian with strange clothes and stranger beard (left), whereas a European artist depicted Moctezuma in the style of a Greco-Roman warrior (right).

## "Barbaric" Dress—Indian and European

It was remarkable to sixteenth-century Europeans how many things seemed to be missing from Indian culture. Even more remarkable, the Indians themselves did not seem to notice. Michel de Montaigne, a French philosopher who had never been to America but liked to talk with explorers and read their accounts, managed to compile quite a list. According to Montaigne, Indians had "no kind of traffic [trade], no knowledge of letters, no intelligence of numbers, no name of magistrate, nor of politics, no use of service [servants], of riches, or of poverty, no contracts, no successions, no partitions, no occupation but idle, no apparel but natural. . . ." That last item—clothing—was crucial. European woodcuts, engravings, and paintings regularly showed native peoples either entirely nude or clad in skimpy loincloths or grass skirts.

Some Europeans interpreted the lack of clothing as evidence of "barbarism." André Thevet, a shocked French visitor to Brazil in 1557, voiced this point of view when he attributed nakedness to simple lust. If the Indians could weave hammocks, he sniffed, why not shirts? But other Europeans viewed unashamed nakedness as a badge of innocence. As remnants of a bygone "golden age," they believed, Indians needed clothing no more than government, laws, regular employment, or other corruptions of civilization.

In fact, Indians were no more "naked" than they were without trade, politics, employment, or religion. Although the simplest peoples of the Caribbean and Brazil wore little, the members of more advanced Indian cultures in South, Central, and North America clothed themselves with animal pelts sewn into mantles and robes, breechclouts, leggings, and moccasins. They wrought bird feathers into headdresses and ear decorations and fashioned reptile skins into belts and pouches. Even more formidably clad were the Inuits of the Far North, who dressed head to foot in sealskin suits with waterproofed seams.

If natives struck whites as underdressed, Europeans seemed, by the Indians' standards, grotesquely overdressed. Indeed, European fashion was ill suited to the environment between the Chesapeake and the Caribbean. Elizabethan gentlemen strutted in silk stockings attached with garters to padded, puffed knee breeches, topped by long-sleeved shirts and tight quilted jackets called "doublets." Men of lesser status wore coarse woolen hose, canvas breeches, shirts, and fitted vests known as "jerkins." Women wore gowns with long, full skirts, low-cut bodices, aprons, and hosiery held up by garters. Ladies went about in silk and wore hoods and mantles to ward off the sun, while women from humbler backgrounds dressed in flannels or canvas and covered their heads with linen caps or coifs.

Such fashions complicated life in the American environment, since heavy clothing and even shoes rotted rapidly from sweat and humidity. The pungent aroma of Europeans also compounded the discomfort of natives who came in contact with them—for the whites who swaddled themselves in woolens also disdained regular bathing. To them, Indian devotion to daily washing seemed just another uncivilized oddity.

It would have been natural for Indians to wonder why the barbaric newcomers did not adapt their dress to a new setting. The answer may be that for Europeans the psychological risk of shedding familiar apparel was simply too great. However inappropriate or even unhealthy, heavy, elaborate dress afforded the comfort of familiarity and distinguished "civilized" newcomer from "savage" native in America.

### Thinking Critically

*From the perspective of Europeans, how did Native American dress seem barbaric? From the point of view of Indian peoples, how did European dress seem barbaric?*

*Columbus meeting the Tainos on Hispaniola.*

In the midst of this victory the city encountered another foe—smallpox. Geographically isolated from Eurasia and its complex disease environment, the Aztecs and all other native peoples in the Americas lacked the acquired immunity that gave Europeans a degree of protection against Old World pathogens. The resulting **virgin soil epidemics**—so called because the victims had no prior exposure—took a nightmarish toll. Smallpox claimed millions in central Mexico between 1520 and 1521. This too presented Cortés with opportunities. Supported by a massive Indian force, he put Tenochtitlán to siege, killing tens of thousands before the ragged, starving survivors surrendered in August of 1521. The feared Aztec Empire lay in ruins. Conquistadors fanned out from central Mexico, overwhelming new populations and eventually learning of another mighty kingdom to the south. Again relying on political faction, disease, technological advantages, and luck, by 1532 Spaniards under Francisco Pizarro and his brothers had conquered the Inca Empire in South America, which in certain regards rivaled even the Aztecs.

 ## The Columbian Exchange

Virgin soil epidemics, which contributed to the devastation of the Indian populations, were only one aspect of a complex web of interactions between the flora and fauna of the Americas on the one hand and that of Eurasia and Africa on the other. Just as germs migrated along with humans, so did plants and animals. These transfers, begun in the decades after Columbus first landed in the Caribbean, are known by historians as the **Columbian exchange,** and they had far-reaching effects on either side of the Atlantic. Europeans brought a host of American crops home with them, as seen in Chapter 1 (page 11). They also most likely brought syphilis, an American disease that broke out across Europe in more virulent form than ever before. Europeans brought to the Americas the horses and large dogs that intimidated the Aztecs; they brought oranges, lemons, figs, and bananas from Africa and the Canary Islands. Escaped hogs multiplied so rapidly that they overran some Caribbean islands, as did European rats.

The Columbian exchange was not a short-lived event. In a host of different ways it continued to reshape the globe over the next half millennium as travel, exploration, and colonization brought cultures ever closer. Instead of smallpox, today H1N1 influenza or the West Nile virus threatens populations worldwide. But the exchanges of the sixteenth century were often more extreme, unpredictable, and far-reaching because of the previous isolation of the two hemispheres.

## The Crown Steps In

The proud conquistadors did not long enjoy their mastery in the Americas. Spain's monarchs, who had just tamed an aristocracy at home, were not about to allow a colonial nobility to arise across the Atlantic. The Crown bribed the conquistadors into retirement—or was saved the expense when men such as Francisco Pizarro were assassinated by their own followers. The task of governing Spain's new colonies passed from the conquerors to a small army of officials, soldiers, lawyers, and Catholic bishops, all appointed by the Crown, reporting to the Crown, and loyal to the Crown. Headquartered in urban centers such as Mexico City (formerly Tenochtitlán), an elaborate, centralized bureaucracy administered the Spanish Empire, regulating nearly every aspect of economic and social life.

Few Spaniards besides imperial officials settled in the Americas. By 1600 only about 5 percent of the colonial population was of Spanish descent, the other 95 percent being either Indian or African. Even by 1800 only 300,000 Spanish immigrants had come to Central and South America. Indians often remained on the lands that they had farmed under the Aztecs and the Incas, now paying Spanish overlords their taxes and producing livestock for export. More importantly, Indians paid for the new order through their labor, sometimes as slaves but more often through an evolving administrative system channeling native workers to public and private enterprises throughout New Spain. The Spanish also established sugar plantations in the West Indies; these were worked by black slaves who by 1520 were being imported from Africa in large numbers.

Spain's colonies returned even more spectacular profits to the mother country by the 1540s—the result of silver discoveries of epic proportions in both Mexico and Peru. Silver mining developed into a large-scale capitalist enterprise requiring substantial investment. European investors and Spanish immigrants who had profited from cattle raising and sugar planting poured their capital into equipment and supplies that would mine the silver deposits more efficiently: stamp mills, water-powered crushing equipment, pumps, and mercury. Whole villages of Indians were pressed into service in the mines, joining black slaves and free white workers employed there.

In the last decades of the sixteenth century the economies of Mexico and Peru revolved around the mines. By 1570 the town of Potosí, the site of a veritable mountain of silver, had become larger than any city in either Spain or its American empire, with a population of 120,000. Local farmers who supplied mining centers with food and Spanish merchants in Seville who exported European goods to Potosí profited handsomely. So, too, did the Spanish Crown, which claimed one-fifth of all extracted silver. During the sixteenth century some 16,000 tons of the precious metal were exported from Spanish America to Europe.

## The Search for North America's Indian Empires

Riches and glory radicalized Spanish expectations. Would-be conquistadors embarked on an urgent race to discover and topple the next Aztec or Inca Empire, a race to

# How Did Spaniards and Aztecs Remember First Contact?

*The first encounter between the Spaniards under Hernán Cortés and ambassadors of the emperor Moctezuma in 1519 represents a fateful turning point in history. While we have no full contemporary account of that meeting, two remarkable sources present Spanish and Mexican memories of the event written years later. The first selection below was written in the 1560s by one of Cortés's lieutenants, the conquistador Bernal Díaz. The second section comes from a work compiled in the 1540s by the missionary Bernardino de Sahagún, in which indigenous informants recalled Aztec culture, religion, society, and history up to and through the conquest.*

## DOCUMENT 1  Bernal Díaz

Seeing the big ship with the standards flying they knew that it was there that they must go to speak with the captain; so they went direct to the flagship and going on board asked who was the Tatuan [Tlatoan] which in their language means the chief. Doña Marina who understood the language well, pointed him out. Then the Indians paid many marks of respect to Cortés, according to their usage, and bade him welcome, and said that their lord, a servant of the great Montezuma, had sent them to ask what kind of men we were and of what we were in search. . . . [Cortés] told them that we came to see them and to trade with them and that our arrival in their country should cause them no uneasiness but be looked on by them as fortunate. . . .

[Several days later, one of Montezuma's emissaries] brought with him some clever painters such as they had in Mexico and ordered them to make pictures true to nature of the face and body of Cortés and all his captains, and of the soldiers, ships, sails, and horses, and of Doña Marina and Aguilar, even of the two greyhounds, and the cannon and cannon balls, and all of the army we had brought with us, and he carried the pictures to his master. Cortés ordered our gunners to load the lombards with a great charge of powder so that they should make a great noise when they were fired off. . . . [The emissary] went with all haste and narrated everything to his prince, and showed him the pictures which had been painted. . . .

*Source: Bernal Díaz, The True History of the Conquest of New Spain, excerpted in Stuart B. Schwartz, ed., Victors and Vanquished: Spanish and Nahua Views of the Conquest of Mexico (2000), pp. 85–91.*

## DOCUMENT 2  Fray Bernardino de Sahagún

When they had gotten up into [Cortes's] boat, each of them made the earth-eating gesture before the Captain. Then they addressed him, saying, "May the god attend: his agent Moteucçoma who is in charge in Mexico for him addresses him and says, 'The god is doubly welcome.' "

Then they dressed up the Captain. They put on him the turquoise serpent mask attached to the quetzal-feather head fan, to which were fixed, from which hung the greenstone serpent earplugs. And they put the sleeveless jacket on him, and around his neck they put the plaited green-stone neckband with the golden disk in the middle. On his lower back they tied the back mirror, and also they tied behind him the cloak called a *tzitzilli*. And on his legs they placed the green-stone bands with the golden bells. And they gave him, placing it on his arm, the shield with gold and shells crossing, on whose edge were spread quetzal feathers, with a quetzal banner. And they laid the obsidian sandals before him. . . .

Then the Captain ordered that they be tied up: they put irons on their feet and necks. When this had been done they shot off the cannon. And at this point the messengers truly fainted and swooned; one after another they swayed and fell, losing consciousness. . . . Then [Cortés] let them go.

[Upon returning to Tenochtitlán and reporting to Moteucçoma, he replied] "I will not hear it here. I will hear it at the Coacalco; let them go there." And he gave orders, saying, "Let some captives be covered in chalk [for sacrifice]."

Then the messengers went to the Coacalco, and so did Moteucçoma. There upon the captives died in their presence; they cut open their chests and sprinkled their blood on the messengers. (The reason they did it was that they had gone to very dangerous places and had seen, gazed on the countenances of, and spoken to the gods.) . . .

When this was done, they talked to Moteucçoma, telling him what they had beheld, and they showed him what [the Spaniards'] food was like.

And when he heard what the messengers reported, he was greatly afraid and taken aback, and he was amazed at their food. It especially made him faint when he heard how the guns went off at [the Spaniards'] command, sounding like thunder, causing people to actually swoon, blocking the ears. And when it went off, something like a ball came out from inside, and fire went showering and spitting out. And the smoke that came out had a very foul stench, striking one in the face. And if they shot at a hill, it seemed to crumble and come apart. . . . Their war gear was all iron. They clothed their bodies in iron, they put iron on their heads, their swords were iron, their bows were iron, and their shields were iron.

And the deer that carried them were as tall as the roof. And they wrapped their bodies all over; only their faces could be seen, very white. . . .

And their dogs were huge creatures, with their ears folded over and their jowls dragging. They had burning eyes, eyes like coals, yellow and fiery. . . .

When Moteucçoma heard it, he was greatly afraid; he seemed to faint away, he grew concerned and disturbed.

*Source: Fray Bernardino de Sahagún, The Florentine Codex, excerpted in Schwartz, ed., Victors and Vanquished, pp. 91–99.*

## *Thinking Critically*

*How did the Aztecs and the Spaniards communicate? Why does Díaz pay so little attention to the gifts the emissaries brought Cortés? Why might the painters be absent from the Nahua account? What principles of critical thinking should be kept in mind when reading such documents?*

Fabulous gold and silver discoveries in their New World empire led Spaniards to force Indians and Africans to labor in the mines under dangerous and brutal conditions. This late-sixteenth-century illustration portrays Africans mining for a Spaniard in Panama, but it seems almost pastoral, compared to the dangers of earthen collapses in the mining pits and tunnels or the risks of suffocation or black lung disease from the dust underground.

become the next Cortés or Pizarro. The prevailing mood was captured by the portrait of a Spanish soldier that adorns the frontispiece of his book about the West Indies. He stands with one hand on his sword and the other holding a pair of compasses on top of a globe. Beneath is inscribed the motto "By compasses and the sword / More and more and more and more."

**PONCE DE LEÓN** Some of the most ambitious adventurers felt certain that more lands and riches would be found in the North. Spanish slavers had been the first to skirt the North American mainland, going as far north as present-day South Carolina. These voyages likely inspired Juan Ponce de León, conquerer of Puerto Rico, to make the first official expedition to the mainland, which he named Florida to mark the day of his landfall, *Pascua Florida* (Easter). Everywhere he went he met armed resistance from Florida's native inhabitants, people who had come to know and despise Spaniards as slave raiders. Ponce de León

sailed back to Puerto Rico and then returned for some years to Spain, until Cortés's early exploits in Mexico rekindled his ambitions. Filled with visions of glory, he returned to Florida in 1521 only to be mortally wounded in a battle with Calusa Indians.

**PÁNFILO DE NARVÁEZ AND CABEZA DE VACA** Ponce de León died miserably, yet his countrymen still believed that wealthy Indian empires remained undiscovered in the North. In 1526 Spain established a settlement in present-day Georgia, but the endeavor soon collapsed. Two years later Pánfilo de Narváez, a red-bearded veteran from the conquest of Cuba, led a major expedition back to Florida. Ignoring advice from his second-in-command, Alvar Núñez Cabeza de Vaca, Narváez separated from his main force near Tampa Bay and led 300 men on a harrowing march in search of riches. For months the force plundered its way through Florida, while the men fell ill or fell victim to Indian archers, whose longbows could bury an arrow six inches into a tree. Disillusioned and desperate, 242 survivors lashed together makeshift rafts and tried to sail along the Gulf Coast to Mexico. Weeks later proud Narváez and most of his men had disappeared at sea, whereas Cabeza de Vaca and a handful of survivors washed up on islands off the Texas coast.

Local Indian groups then turned the tables and made slaves of the Spaniards. Cabeza de Vaca later recalled that his captors were appalled to learn that the starving castaways had eaten their dead. After years as prisoners, Cabeza de Vaca and three others, including a black slave named Esteban, escaped to make an extraordinary trek across Texas and northern Mexico. Somewhere in present-day Chihuahua they passed through what had been the trading hinterland of Paquime, and Cabeza de Vaca noted an enduring regional commerce in feathers and "green stones"—turquoise. Finally, in July 1536 a shocked party of Spanish slavers stumbled across the four rag-tag castaways and brought them to Mexico City.

**HERNÁN DE SOTO** The stories the four men told of their trek inspired two more massive expeditions to discover and conquer North America's elusive Indian empires. The first was led by Hernán de Soto, who had grown wealthy helping to conquer Peru. Confident that Florida held similar riches, de Soto scoured the Southeast's agricultural villages searching for gold and taking whatever he wanted: food, clothing, luxury goods, even young women whom he and his men "desired both as servants and for their foul uses. . . ." As they raped, stole, and killed their way through the Southeast, de Soto and his men unwittingly had the honor of being the first and last Europeans to glimpse several declining Mississippian chiefdoms, echoes of Cahokia's ancient majesty. Some native communities resisted, inflicting huge losses on de Soto's men. Others shrewdly feigned friendship and insisted that gold and glory could be found in this or that nearby village, thus ridding themselves of a great danger and directing it at enemies instead. De Soto's men ravaged Indian societies through parts of present-day Florida, Georgia, North and

South Carolina, Tennessee, Alabama, Mississippi, Arkansas, Louisiana, and Texas. The expedition never found the treasures it sought, but it did hasten the transformation of the southeastern chiefdoms into decentralized confederacies.

**VÁZQUEZ DE CORONADO**

Spanish ambition met a similar fate in the West. In 1539, 29-year-old Francisco Vázquez de Coronado led 300 Spaniards and 1,000 Mexican Indian warriors north into the present-day American Southwest. Emboldened by tales of cities more wondrous even than Tenochtitlán, Coronado's brash confidence began to fail him when instead he found only mud and straw pueblos inhabited by modest farmers. Determined to turn his hugely expensive expedition to advantage, Coronado sent men in all directions. Some went west, until they ran into the vastness of the Grand Canyon and had to turn back. Others traveled east, taking up temporary residence among the Pueblo peoples of the upper Rio Grande. The increasingly abusive visitors soon provoked battles with their hosts, forcing them to abandon 13 villages, which the Spaniards then destroyed. Desperate to redeem his reputation and investment, Coronado followed an Indian he dubbed the Turk out onto the Great Plains in search of a rumored kingdom called Quivira. Perhaps the Turk had in mind one of the easternmost Mississippian chiefdoms, but

As Hernán de Soto traveled through North America, he brought a herd of pigs much like this razorback hog. At times the herd numbered more than 700. The animals were an efficient way of providing protein to the expedition. More than 80 percent of a carcass could be consumed, compared with only 50 percent of a cow or sheep. Hogs could be herded on the march as well, foraging for food as they went. But some anthropologists and historians believe that the hogs were also carriers of disease that migrated to humans. The diseases may have sparked the deaths of thousands of Indians, who lacked the immunity built up by Europeans over centuries of exposure to Eurasian illnesses.

## SPANISH AMERICA, CA. 1600

*By 1600 Spain was extracting large amounts of gold and silver from Mexico and South America, as well as profits from sugar plantations in the Caribbean. Each year Spanish treasure ships ferried bullion from mines such as the one at Potosí to the Isthmus of Panama, where it was transported by land to the Caribbean coast, and from there to Spain. An expedition from Acapulco sailed annually to the Philippines as well, returning with Asian spices and other trade goods. For an English "sea dog" (read: pirate) looking to capture Spanish treasure, which geographic location would be the best place to pick off Spanish treasure ships?*

the frustrated conquistador became convinced he had been deceived. He had the Turk strangled somewhere in present-day Kansas and in 1542 returned to Mexico, where Crown authorities brought him to trial for inflicting "great cruelties" on Indians.

**SPAIN'S DOMINANCE IN THE AMERICAS** Conquistadors such as Coronado might be ruined by their unfulfilled ambitions, but Spain could afford its failed North American excursions. It had taken vast wealth from the Americas, conquered the hemisphere's mightiest peoples, and laid claim to most of the New World. Spaniards warily expected competition, and yet for most of the sixteenth century rival European powers took little interest in the Americas. England's fishermen continued to explore the North Sea, Labrador, and Newfoundland. Portugal discovered and laid claim to Brazil. France sent expeditions to explore North America's eastern shoreline (Giovanni da Verrazano, 1524) and the St. Lawrence River valley (Jacques Cartier, 1534, 1535, and 1541). These efforts proved important in the long run, but for most of the century Spain could treat the Americas as their own. They owed that luxury, in part, to religious upheaval in Europe. During the second decade of the sixteenth century—the same decade in which Cortés laid siege to Tenochtitlán—religious changes of enormous significance began spreading through Europe. That revolution in Christianity, known as the Protestant Reformation, occupied European attentions and eventually figured as a crucial force in shaping the history of the Americas.

REVIEW

How did the Spanish respond to the discovery of a "new world"?

# RELIGIOUS REFORM DIVIDES EUROPE

DURING THE MIDDLE AGES, THE Roman Catholic church defined what it meant to be a Christian in western Europe. Like other institutions of medieval society, the Catholic church was a hierarchy. At the top was the pope in Rome, and under him were the descending ranks of other church officials—cardinals, archbishops, bishops. At the bottom of the Catholic hierarchy were parish priests, each serving his own village, as well as monks and nuns living in monasteries and convents. But medieval popes were weak, and their power was felt little in the lives of most Europeans. Like political units of the era, religious institutions of the Middle Ages were local and decentralized.

**RISE OF THE PAPACY** Between about 1100 and 1500, however, as the monarchs of Europe grew more powerful so, too, did the popes. The Catholic church acquired land throughout Europe, and its swelling bureaucracy added to church income from tithing (taxes

contributed by church members) and from fees paid by those appointed to church offices. In the thirteenth century church officials also began to sell "indulgences." For ordinary believers who expected to spend time after death purging their sins in purgatory, the purchase of an indulgence promised to shorten that punishment by drawing on a "treasury of merit" amassed by the good works of Christ and the saints.

By the fifteenth century the Catholic church and the papacy had become enormously powerful but increasingly indifferent to popular religious concerns. Church officials meddled in secular politics. Popes and bishops flaunted their wealth, while poorly educated parish priests neglected their pastoral duties. At the same time, popular demands for religious assurance grew increasingly intense.

## The Teachings of Martin Luther

Into this climate of heightened spirituality stepped Martin Luther, who abandoned studying the law to enter a monastery. Like many of his contemporaries, Luther was consumed by fears over his eternal fate. He was convinced that he was damned, and he could not find any consolation in the Catholic church. Catholic doctrine taught that a person could be saved by faith in God and by his or her own good works—by leading a virtuous life, observing the sacraments (such as baptism, the Mass, and penance), making pilgrimages to holy places, and praying to Christ and the saints. Because Luther believed that human nature was innately evil, he despaired of being able to lead a life that "merited" salvation. If men and women are so bad, he reasoned, how could they ever win their way to heaven with good works?

**JUSTIFICATION BY FAITH ALONE** Luther finally broke through his despair with the Bible. It convinced him that God did not require fallen humankind to earn salvation. Salvation, he concluded, came by faith alone, the "free gift" of God to undeserving sinners. The ability to live a good life could not be the *cause* of salvation but its *consequence:* once men and women believed that they had saving faith, moral behavior was possible. Luther elaborated that idea, known as "justification by faith alone," between 1513 and 1517.

Luther was ordained a priest and then assigned to teach at a university in Wittenberg, Germany. He became increasingly critical, however, of the Catholic church as an institution. In 1517 he posted on the door of a local church 95 theses attacking the Catholic hierarchy for selling salvation in the form of indulgences.

The novelty of this attack was not Luther's open break with Catholic teaching. Challenges to the church had cropped up throughout the Middle Ages. What was new were the passion and force behind Luther's protest. Using the blunt, earthy Germanic tongue, he expressed the anxieties of many devout laypeople and their outrage at the church hierarchy's neglect. The "gross, ignorant asses and knaves at Rome," he warned, should keep their distance from Germany, or else "jump into the Rhine or the nearest river, and take . . . a cold bath."

The pope and his representatives in Germany at first tried to silence Martin Luther, then excommunicated him. But opposition only pushed Luther toward more radical positions. He asserted that the church and its officials were not infallible; only the Scriptures were without error. Every person, he said, should read and interpret the Bible for himself or herself. In an even more direct assault on church authority, he advanced an idea known as "the priesthood of all believers." Catholic doctrine held that salvation came only through the church and its clergy, a privileged group that possessed special access to God. Luther asserted that every person had the power claimed by priests.

Although Luther had not intended to start a schism within Catholicism, independent Lutheran churches were forming in Germany by the 1520s. And, during the 1530s, Luther's ideas spread throughout Europe, where they were eagerly taken up by other reformers.

| Martin Luther argued that salvation came by faith alone, a free gift of God to undeserving sinners.

## The Contribution of John Calvin

The most influential of Luther's successors was John Calvin, a French lawyer turned theologian. Calvin agreed with Luther that men and women could not merit their salvation. But, whereas Luther's God was a loving deity who extended his mercy to sinful humankind, Calvin conceived of God as awesome, all-knowing and all-powerful—the controlling force in human history that would ultimately triumph over Satan. To bring about that final victory, to usher in his heavenly kingdom, God had selected certain people as his agents, Calvin believed. These people—"the saints," or "the **elect**"—had been "predestined" by God for eternal salvation in heaven.

THE "ELECT" Calvin's emphasis on predestination led him to another distinctively Protestant notion—the doctrine of calling. How could a person learn whether he or she belonged to the elect who were saved? Calvin answered: strive to behave like a saint. God expected his elect to serve the good of society by unrelenting work in a "calling," or occupation, in the world. In place of the Catholic belief in the importance of good works, Calvin emphasized the goodness of work itself. Success in attaining discipline and self-control, in bringing order into one's own life and the entire society, revealed that a person might be among the elect.

Calvin fashioned a religion to change the world. Whereas Luther believed that Christians should accept the existing social order, Calvin called on Christians to become activists, reshaping society and government to conform with God's laws laid down in the Bible. He wanted all Europe to become like Geneva, the Swiss city that he had converted into a holy commonwealth in which the elect regulated the behavior and morals of everyone else. And unlike Luther, who wrote primarily for a German audience, Calvin addressed his most important book, *The Institutes of the Christian Religion* (1536), to Christians throughout Europe. Reformers from every country flocked to Geneva to learn more about Calvin's ideas.

## The Birth of Spanish Florida and French Huguenots

The Protestant Reformation shattered the unity of Christendom in western Europe. Spain, Portugal, Ireland, and Italy remained firmly Catholic. England, Scotland, the Netherlands, Switzerland, and France developed either dominant or substantial Calvinist constituencies. Much of Germany and Scandinavia opted for Lutheranism. As religious groups competed for political power and the loyalties of believers, brutal wars swept sixteenth-century Europe, and France experienced some of the worst violence. An influential group of Huguenots (Calvin's French followers) saw in North America a potential refuge from religious persecution. Under the leadership of Jean Ribault, 150 Huguenots from Normandy in 1562 established a simple village on Parris Island off present-day South Carolina. That experiment ended in desperation and cannibalism, but two years later Ribault led another, larger group to a site south of present-day Jacksonville, Florida. Here the Huguenots constructed a settlement they named Fort Caroline and nurtured a cordial relationship with the local Timucua Indians. It seemed a promising start.

HUGUENOTS AS A THREAT TO SPAIN
But Spanish authorities in the Caribbean took the Huguenots for a triple threat. First, French pirates had long sought to siphon silver from the Americas by waylaying Spanish galleons. Silver shipments rode the Gulf Stream past the Bahamas and up the southeastern coast of North America before turning east toward Spain. In only four years, from 1556 to 1560, French ships preying on this vulnerable route had helped cut Spain's colonial revenues in half. With good reason, Spanish administrators feared that Fort Caroline would entrench the threat of piracy. Second, Spain had to worry that France would

plant successful colonies and take a broader interest in the Americas, perhaps eventually making claims on all of North America. Finally, many Spanish Catholics saw Protestantism as a loathsome contagion, to be expunged from Europe and barred from the Americas.

These interlocking concerns prompted Spain to found a permanent colony in Florida. To do so the Crown turned to a focused and unforgiving man named Pedro Menéndez de Avilés. In 1565 Menéndez established a settlement on the coast called St. Augustine (still the United States' oldest continuously occupied, non-Indian settlement) and immediately marched north to destroy Fort Caroline. He and 500 soldiers slogged through the rain and marsh until they found the simple fort. In battle and through later executions, the attackers killed Ribault and about 500 of his Huguenots. Flush with victory, Menéndez established several more outposts on Florida's Atlantic and Gulf coasts, and in 1570 even encouraged a short-lived Jesuit mission just miles from where English colonists would establish Jamestown a generation later. As for the Huguenots, the calamity at Fort Caroline dashed hope that the New World would be their haven. Most had to resign themselves to intensifying persecution in France.

Protestants such as Luther and Calvin placed greater emphasis on the Word of Scripture than on church rituals controlled by priests and bishops. In this seventeenth-century portrait of John Calvin, sacred words from scripture literally help define him.

herself the defender of Protestantism. Elizabeth was no radical Calvinist, however. A vocal minority of her subjects were reformers of that stripe, calling for the English church to purge itself of bishops, elaborate ceremonies, and other Catholic "impurities." Because of the austerity and zeal of such Calvinist radicals, their opponents proclaimed them "**Puritans**."

**ELIZABETH'S FEARS** Radical Protestants might annoy Elizabeth as she pursued her careful, moderate policies, but radical Catholics frightened her. She had reason to worry that Spain might try to employ English Catholics to undermine her rule. More ominously, Elizabeth's advisors cautioned that Catholic Ireland to the west would be an ideal base from which Spain or France could launch an invasion of England. Beginning in 1565 the queen encouraged a number of her elite subjects to sponsor private ventures for subduing the native Irish and settling loyal English Protestants on their land. As events fell out, this Irish venture proved to be a prelude to England's bolder attempt to found colonies across the Atlantic.

## The English Reformation

While the Reformation wracked northern Europe, King Henry VIII of England labored at a goal more worldly than those of Luther and Calvin. He wanted a son, a male heir to continue the Tudor dynasty. When his wife, Catherine of Aragon, gave birth to a daughter, Mary, Henry petitioned the pope to have his marriage annulled in the hope that a new wife would give him a son. This move enraged the king of Spain, who also happened to be Catherine's nephew. He persuaded the pope to refuse Henry's request. Defiantly, England's king proceeded with the divorce nonetheless and quickly married Anne Boleyn. He then went further, making himself, not the pope, the head of the Church of England. Henry was an audacious but practical man, and he had little interest in promoting reformist doctrine. Apart from discarding the pope, the Church of England remained essentially Catholic in its teachings and rituals.

**ENGLISH PURITANS** England's Protestants gained ground during the six-year reign of Henry's son Edward VI but then found themselves persecuted when Edward's Catholic half-sister Mary became queen in 1553. Five years later the situation turned again, when Elizabeth I (Anne Boleyn's daughter) took the throne, proclaiming

✓ **REVIEW**
How did religious reform divide Europe in the sixteenth century?

# ENGLAND'S ENTRY INTO AMERICA

AMONG THE GENTLEMEN EAGER TO win fame and fortune were Humphrey Gilbert and Walter Raleigh, two adventurers with conquistador appetites for more and more. The pair were like most of the English who went to Ireland, ardent Protestants who viewed the native Catholic inhabitants as superstitious, pagan savages: "They blaspheme, they murder, commit whoredome," complained one Englishman, "hold no wedlocke, ravish, steal and commit all abomination without scruple." Thus the English found it easy enough to justify their conquest. They proclaimed it their duty to teach the Irish the discipline of hard work, the rule of law, and the truth of Protestant Christianity. And, while the Irish were learning these civilized, English ways, they would not be allowed to buy land or hold office or serve on juries or give testimony in courts or learn a trade or bear arms.

When the Irish rebelled at that program of "liberation," the English ruthlessly repressed them, slaughtering not only combatants but civilians as well. Most English in Ireland, like most Spaniards in America, believed that native peoples who resisted civilization and proper Christianity should be subdued at any cost. No scruples stopped Gilbert, in an insurgent country, from planting the path to his camp with the severed heads of Irish rebels.

**THE IRISH EXPERIENCE AS A MODEL**

The struggle to colonize and subdue Ireland would serve as a rough model for later English efforts at expansion. The approach was essentially military, like that of the conquistadors. It also set the ominous precedent that Englishmen could treat "savage" peoples with a level of brutal cruelty that would have been inappropriate in wars between "civilized" Europeans. But the campaigns in Ireland seemed to leave the queen's men with little more than lessons. "Neither reputation, or profytt is to be wonne" in Ireland, concluded Gilbert. He, Raleigh, and many other West Country gentry wanted to take their ambition and their Irish education to North America.

## The Ambitions of Gilbert, Raleigh, and Wingina

**GILBERT'S UTOPIAN DREAMS**

In 1578 Gilbert was the first to get his chance for glory when Elizabeth granted him a royal patent—the first English colonial **charter**—to explore, occupy, and govern any territory in America "not actually possessed of any Christian prince or people." The vague, wildly unrealistic charter matched Gilbert's vast ego. It ignored the Indian possession of North America and made him lord and proprietor of all the land lying between Florida and Labrador. In many ways his dreams looked backward. Gilbert hoped to set up a kind of medieval kingdom of his own, where loyal tenant farmers would work the lands of manors, paying rent to feudal lords. Yet his vision also looked forward to a utopian society.

Though Sir Walter Raleigh was a favorite of Queen Elizabeth, her successor, King James I, thought the West Country adventurer lively and dangerous enough to clap him in the Tower of London for fifteen years. When Raleigh defied James a second time, he lost his head.

He planned to encourage England's poor to emigrate by providing them free land and a government "to be chosen by consent of the people." Elizabeth had high hopes for her haughty champion, but a fierce storm got the better of his ship, and the Atlantic swallowed him before he could ever plant a settlement.

**WALTER RALEIGH**

Meanwhile, Gilbert's stepbrother Raleigh had been working more industriously to lay the groundwork for a British American empire. Raleigh enlisted the talents of Richard Hakluyt, a clergyman with a passion for spreading knowledge of overseas discoveries. At Raleigh's bidding, Hakluyt wrote an eloquent plea to Elizabeth for the English settlement of America, titled *A Discourse Concerning Westerne Planting*. The temperate and fertile lands of North America, Hakluyt argued, would prove ideal for growing tropical commodities and would be an excellent base from which to harry the Spanish, search for a northwest passage to the Orient, and extend the influence of Protestantism. He also stressed the advantages of colonies as potential markets for English goods and as havens for the poor and unemployed. Finally, Hakluyt predicted that because the "Spaniardes have executed most outragious and more then Turkishe crueltaies in all the west Indies," Indians would greet Englishmen as liberators.

**FIRST ROANOKE SETTLEMENT**

Raleigh's chance to test the prediction finally came in 1584, when Elizabeth granted him a patent nearly identical to Gilbert's. By the summer Raleigh had dispatched an exploratory voyage to the Outer Banks of present-day North Carolina. Expedition leaders reported making friendly contact with a people known as the Roanoke and ruled by a "weroance," or chief, named Wingina. The enthusiastic Hakluyt envisioned a colony that would become the Mexico of England, full of plantations producing sugar and silk and mountains yielding gold. Elizabeth knighted Raleigh and allowed him to name the new land "Virginia," after his virgin queen.

**WINGINA'S PLANS**

But Raleigh was not the only one with grand plans. Almost certainly Wingina had encountered or at least heard of Europeans before 1584. Like most coastal groups in the region, his people would have obtained prized European tools and commodities through indirect trade or by scouring wrecked ships. Preoccupied with the political geography of his own region and eager to fortify his own and his people's power, Wingina recognized that friendly relations with the English would give him privileged access to their trade and influence. Perhaps he believed he would act as patron to the newcomers. After all, they knew little of the region, spoke no Indian languages, and even lacked the basic skills necessary to survive in the area without native assistance. In short, Wingina seems to have welcomed the English and encouraged their return because he believed that they could be useful and that they could be controlled. It was a tragic if understandable miscalculation—one that Indian leaders would make again and again in colonial America.

Raleigh apparently aimed to establish on Roanoke a mining camp and a military garrison. In a stroke of genius, he included in the company of 108 men a scientist, Thomas Hariot, to study the country's natural resources and an artist, John White, to make drawings of the Virginia Indians. *A Briefe and True Reporte of the New Found Land of Virginia* (1588), written by Hariot and illustrated by White, served as one of the principal sources about North America and its Indian inhabitants for more than a century. Far less inspired was Raleigh's choice to lead the expedition—two veterans of the Irish campaigns, Sir Richard Grenville and Ralph Lane. Even his fellow conquistadors in Ireland considered Lane proud and greedy. As for Grenville, he was given to breaking wineglasses between his teeth and then swallowing the shards to show that he could stand the sight of blood, even his own.

The bullying ways of both men quickly alienated the natives of Roanoke. Wingina found the newcomers disrespectful, haughty, and cruel: when a local stole a cup, the English tried to teach everyone a lesson by torching his village and destroying its corn stores. As winter arrived and supplies ran low, the hungry colonists made greater and greater demands. The Roanokes' resentment fueled English anxiety that a revolt was brewing, and these anxieties led only to more brutality and more resentment. The following summer Wingina made a final attempt to regain control of the situation. He had agreed to parlay with Lane about improving relations. But the meeting was a ruse. Lane's men opened fire at the Indian envoys, killed Wingina, and hacked the head from his body. All that averted a massive counterattack was the arrival of England's preeminent privateer, Sir Francis Drake, fresh from freebooting up and down the Caribbean. The settlement's 102 survivors piled onto Drake's ships and put an ocean between themselves and the avenging Roanokes.

## A Second Roanoke—and Croatoan

Undaunted, Raleigh organized a second expedition to plant a colony farther north, in Chesapeake Bay. He now projected an agricultural community of manors, much like those in England. He recruited 119 men, women, and children, members of the English middle class, and granted each person an estate of 500 acres. He also appointed as governor the artist John White, who brought along a suit of armor for ceremonial occasions.

White deplored Lane's treachery toward Wingina and hated the brazen, senseless violence that had characterized the entire endeavor. The artist had spent his time on Roanoke closely observing native peoples, their material cultures, and their customs. His sensitive watercolors, especially those featuring women and children, indicate a genuine respect and affection. White felt strongly that under prudent, moral leaders an English colony could indeed coexist peacefully with American Indians.

Despite his best intentions, everything went wrong. In July of 1587 the expedition's pilot, Simon Ferdinando, insisted on leaving the colonists at Roanoke Island rather than along Chesapeake Bay. Understandably, the Roanokes took no pleasure in seeing the English return, and even before Ferdinando weighed anchor the settlers began skirmishing with Indians. Sensing that the situation on Roanoke could quickly become desperate, the colonists

*John White's sensitive watercolor* Indian Elder *or* Chief *may well be of Wingina. The portrayal includes the copper ornament worn hanging from his neck, indicating high social status and the presence of an active trade network, since copper is not found on the island. Just as Raleigh had to gauge his strategy in dealing with the Indians, Wingina had to decide how to treat the strange newcomers from across the Atlantic.*

prevailed on White to sail back with Ferdinando and bring reinforcements.

But White returned home in 1588 just as the massive Spanish navy, the Armada, was marshaling for an assault on England. Elizabeth enlisted every seaworthy ship and able-bodied sailor in her realm to stave off invasion. The Armada was defeated, but Raleigh left the Roanoke colonists to fend for themselves. When White finally returned to Roanoke Island in 1590, he found only an empty fort and a few cottages in a clearing. The sole clue to the colony's fate was carved on a post: CROATOAN. It was the name of a nearby island off Cape Hatteras.

Had the Roanoke colonists fled to Croatoan for safety? Had they moved to the mainland and joined Indian communities? Had they been killed by Wingina's people?

The fate of the "lost colony" remains a mystery, though later rumors suggest that the missing colonists merged with native societies in the interior. His dream of a tolerant, cooperative colony dashed, White sailed back to England, leaving behind the little cluster of cottages, which would soon be overgrown with vines, and his suit of armor, which was already "almost eaten through with rust."

 **REVIEW**

Why did Elizabeth agree to charter a colony in America, and how successful were the first attempts?

# CONCLUSION

## THE WORLD AT LARGE

All the world lay before them. Or so it had seemed to the young men from England's West Country who dreamed of gold and glory, conquest and colonization. True, they lived on the fringe of the civilized world in the fifteenth and sixteenth centuries. China remained the distant, exotic kingdom of power and wealth, supplying silks and spices and other luxurious goods. Islamic empires stood astride the land routes from Europe to the east. Nations on the western edge of Europe thus took to the seas. Portugal sent slave and gold traders to Africa, as well as merchants to trade with the civilizations of the Indies. Spanish conquerors such as Cortés toppled Indian empires and brought home mountains of silver. But England's West Country sea dogs—would-be conquistadors—met only with frustration. In 1600, more than a century after Columbus's first crossing, not a single English settlement existed in the Americas. The Atlantic had devoured Humphrey Gilbert before he could establish an outpost; Raleigh's Roanoke ventures lay in ruins.

What was left of the freebooting world of West Country adventurers? Raleigh, his ambition unquenchable, sailed to South America in quest of a rich city named El Dorado. In 1603, however, Elizabeth's death brought to the English throne her cousin James I, the founder of the Stuart dynasty. The new king arrested the old queen's favorite for treason and imprisoned him for 15 years in the Tower of London. Set free in 1618 at the age of 64, Raleigh returned to South America, his lust for El Dorado undiminished. Along the way he plundered some Spanish silver ships, defying King James's orders. It was a fatal mistake, because England had made peace with Spain. Raleigh lost his head.

James I did not want to harass the king of Spain; he wanted to imitate him. The Stuarts were even more determined than the Tudors had been to enlarge the sphere of royal power. There would be no room in America for a warrior nobility of conquistadors, no room for a feudal fiefdom ruled by the likes of Raleigh or Gilbert. Instead, there would be English colonies in America like the new outpost of Jamestown, planted on the Chesapeake Bay in Virginia in 1607. There would be profitable plantations and other bold enterprises, enriching English royalty and managed by loyal, efficient bureaucrats. Colonizing America would strengthen English monarchs, paving their path to greater power, just as the dominions of Mexico and Peru had enlarged the authority of the Spanish Crown. America would be the making of kings and queens.

Or would it? For some Europeans, weary of freebooting conquistadors and sea rovers, the order and security that Crown rule and centralized states promoted in western Europe would be enough. But others, men and women who were often desperate and sometimes idealistic, would cast their eyes west across the Atlantic and want more. ∞∞∞

# Chapter Summary

DURING THE LATE FIFTEENTH CENTURY, Europeans and Africans made their first contact with the Americas.

■ Western Europeans had lived on the fringes of an international economy drawn together by Chinese goods.

■ Technological advances, the rise of new trade networks and techniques, and increased political centralization made Europe's expansion overseas possible.

■ Led by Portugal, European expansion pushed south along the West African coast. Sugar plantations and a slave trade in Africans became critical to this expansive commerce.

■ Spain led in exploring and colonizing the Americas, consolidating a vast and profitable empire. Divisions within Indian empires and the devastating effects of European diseases made Spanish conquest possible.

■ The early conquistadors were replaced by a centralized royal bureaucracy. The discovery of vast silver deposits provided Spain with immense wealth, while leading to sharply increased mortality among the native population.

■ Conquistadors also explored much of the present-day southeastern and southwestern United States. The native peoples they encountered thwarted their efforts.

■ Martin Luther and later John Calvin spearheaded the Protestant Reformation, which spread to England, Scotland, the Netherlands, and the Huguenots in France.

■ England did not turn to exploration and colonization until the 1570s and 1580s. By that time, European rivalries were heightened by splits arising out of the Protestant Reformation.

■ England's merchants and gentry supported colonizing ventures, although early efforts, such as those at Roanoke, failed.

## ADDITIONAL READING

FOR ORDINARY FOLK IN THE era of exploration, see Kenneth R. Andrews, *Trade, Plunder, and Settlement* (1985). For Portugal's initial expansion, see Malyn Newitt, *A History of Portuguese Overseas Expansion, 1400–1668* (2004). John Thornton's *Africa and Africans in the Making of the Atlantic World, 1400–1680* (1998) explores West Africa's role in the international economy. For sugar and expansion, see Philip D. Curtin, *The Rise and Fall of the Plantation Complex* (2nd ed., 1998). The demographic catastrophe that followed contact is explored in Massimo Livi-Bacci, *Conquest: The Destruction of American Indios* (2008). For European expansion in global perspective, see Jared Diamond, *Guns, Germs, and Steel* (1998).

For Spain in the Caribbean, see David Abulafia, *The Discovery of Mankind* (2008). For Indians in central Mexico after Cortés, see James Lockhart, *The Nahuas after Conquest* (1992).

For a magisterial narrative of Spain's activities in North America, see David J. Weber, *The Spanish Frontier in North America* (1992). Coronado's sojourn is the subject of the exacting work by Richard Flint, *No Settlement, No Conquest* (2008). For the Southeast, see Daniel S. Murphree, *Constructing Floridians* (2006).

For a good introduction to the Reformation in England, see Christopher Haigh, *English Revolutions* (1993); Eamon Duffy's *The Voices of Morebath* (2001) asks how the Reformation transformed the lives of ordinary people. For early English attempts at colonization, in both Ireland and the Americas, consult the works of Nicholas Canny in the Bibliography, as well as Michael Leroy Oberg, *The Head in Edward Nugent's Hand* (2007).

For a fuller list of readings, see the Bibliography at www.mhhe.com/eh8e.

## SIGNIFICANT EVENTS

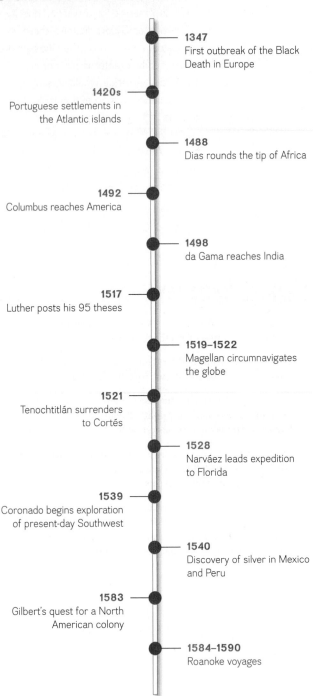

**1347**
First outbreak of the Black Death in Europe

**1420s**
Portuguese settlements in the Atlantic islands

**1488**
Dias rounds the tip of Africa

**1492**
Columbus reaches America

**1498**
da Gama reaches India

**1517**
Luther posts his 95 theses

**1519–1522**
Magellan circumnavigates the globe

**1521**
Tenochtitlán surrenders to Cortés

**1528**
Narváez leads expedition to Florida

**1539**
Coronado begins exploration of present-day Southwest

**1540**
Discovery of silver in Mexico and Peru

**1583**
Gilbert's quest for a North American colony

**1584–1590**
Roanoke voyages

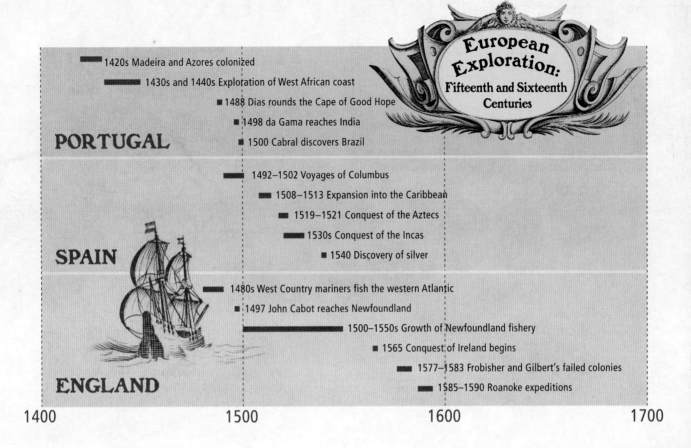

**European Exploration: Fifteenth and Sixteenth Centuries**

### PORTUGAL

- 1420s Madeira and Azores colonized
- 1430s and 1440s Exploration of West African coast
- 1488 Dias rounds the Cape of Good Hope
- 1498 da Gama reaches India
- 1500 Cabral discovers Brazil

### SPAIN

- 1492–1502 Voyages of Columbus
- 1508–1513 Expansion into the Caribbean
- 1519–1521 Conquest of the Aztecs
- 1530s Conquest of the Incas
- 1540 Discovery of silver

### ENGLAND

- 1480s West Country mariners fish the western Atlantic
- 1497 John Cabot reaches Newfoundland
- 1500–1550s Growth of Newfoundland fishery
- 1565 Conquest of Ireland begins
- 1577–1583 Frobisher and Gilbert's failed colonies
- 1585–1590 Roanoke expeditions

1400　　　1500　　　1600　　　1700

VIRGINIA

A.D. 1607

JAMES FORTE
AT
JAMES'TOWNE

the Discovery

the Susan Constant

the Godspeed

The River JAMES

In Jamestown's early years its military orientation was clear. The fort's heavy palisades and its strategic location upriver and some distance inland underscore the colonists' concern for defense—as does the imposing figure of Powhatan seated at the right.

## CHAPTER 3

# Colonization and Conflict in the South

## 1600–1750

⬭⬭⬭ **AN AMERICAN STORY** ⬭⬭⬭

## OUTLANDISH STRANGERS

In the year 1617, European time, on a bay Europeans called the Chesapeake, in a land they named Virginia, the mighty weroance Powhatan surveyed his domain with satisfaction. While in his prime, the tall, robust man had drawn some 30 villages along the Virginia coast into a powerful confederacy. As tribute for his protection and leadership, Powhatan collected food, furs, and skins. He forged alliances with communities too distant or too powerful for him to dominate. He married the daughters of prominent men, dozens in all, to solidify his network of patronage and power. His confederacy numbered perhaps 20,000 souls. Some coastal villages had fiercely resisted Powhatan's efforts to incorporate them; some peoples to the west still threatened the security of his confederacy.

John Hull

After 1607 Powhatan was forced to take into account yet another group. The English, as this new people called themselves, came by sea, crammed into three ships. They were 100 men and 4 boys, all clad in heavy, outlandish clothing, many dressed in gaudy colors. The ships followed a river deep into Powhatan's territory and built a fort on a swampy, mosquito-infested site that they called Jamestown.

Powhatan knew of these strangers from across the waters, who had larger boats and louder, more deadly weapons. But the Indians quickly learned how to use guns, and they vastly outnumbered the English, a clumsy and unprepared people who seemed unlikely to live long and prosper in Powhatan's land. Even amid the bounty of the Chesapeake they failed to feed themselves. With bows and arrows, spears and nets, Indian men brought in an abundance of meat and fish. Fields tended by Indian women yielded generous crops of corn, beans, squash, and melon, and edible nuts and fruits grew wild. Still, for several years the English starved. Powhatan could understand why the English refused to grow food. Cultivating crops was women's work—like building houses; or making clothing, pottery, and baskets; or caring for children. And the English settlement included no women until two arrived in the fall of 1608. Yet even after more women came, the English still starved, and they expected—no, they demanded—that Powhatan's people feed them.

When the English attempted to crown Powhatan as a subject king, he may have sent King James I this cloak as a reciprocal present. Made from four tanned deerskins, the mantle is decorated with many small marine shells sewn into designs. In addition to human and animal figures, the cloak has 34 roundlets that may represent the Indian districts under Powhatan's control.

Worse, these hapless folk put on such airs. They boasted about the power of their god—they had only one—and denounced the Indians' "devil-worship" of "false gods." They crowed endlessly about the power of their king, James I, who expected Powhatan to become his vassal. The English had even planned a "coronation" to crown Powhatan as a "subject king." He was unimpressed. "If your king has sent me presents," he responded, "I also am a king, and this is my land. . . . Your father is to come to me, not I to him." In the end the English did come to Powhatan, only to find what "a fowle trouble there was to make him kneele to receave his crowne. . . . [He] indured so many perswasions, examples and instructions as tired them all. At last by leaning hard on his shoulders, he a little stooped, and . . . put the Crowne on his head."

Inconceivable to Powhatan—that he should bow before this King James, the ruler of so small and savage a people! When the Indians made war, they killed the male warriors of rival communities but adopted their women and children. But when Powhatan's people defended their land from these invaders, the English retaliated by murdering Indian women and children. Worse, the English could not even keep order among themselves. Too many of them wanted to lead, and they squabbled constantly among themselves.

Only one man, a brash fellow called Captain John Smith, had briefly brought order to the English settlement. Powhatan granted him a grudging respect, though Smith bragged endlessly of his earlier exploits across the ocean, where he had fought as a soldier of fortune. He told fanciful tales of his irresistible appeal to beautiful women who had rescued him from harrowing perils. A rough man, he bullied the Indians for food and would have enslaved them if it had been in his power. Even so, Smith took a genuine interest in Indian ways. But the fellow returned to England in 1609 after being injured when some English gunpowder blew up by mistake. Thereafter the newcomers returned to squabbling and starving.

The temptation to wipe out the helpless, troublesome, arrogant tribe of English—or simply to let them starve to death—was almost overwhelming. But Powhatan had allowed the English to survive. Like Wingina before him, he decided that even these barbaric people had their uses. English labor, English trading goods, and, most important, English guns would help subdue his Indian rivals, within and beyond his confederacy. In 1614 Powhatan cemented his claim on the English and their weapons with the marriage between his favorite child, Pocahontas, and an ambitious Englishman, John Rolfe.

By 1617 events had vindicated Powhatan's strategy of tolerating the English. His chiefdom flourished, ready to be passed on to his brother. Powhatan's people still outnumbered the English, who seldom starved outright now but continued to fight among themselves and sicken and die.

Only one thing had changed in the Chesapeake by 1617: the English were clearing woodland along the rivers and planting tobacco.

That was the doing of Powhatan's son-in-law, Rolfe, a man as strange as the rest of the newcomers. Rolfe had been obsessed with finding a crop that could be grown in Virginia and then sold for gain across the sea. When he succeeded by growing tobacco, other English followed his lead. Odder still, not women but men tended the tobacco fields. Here was more evidence of English inferiority. Men wasted long hours laboring when they might supply their needs with far less effort.

In 1617 Powhatan, ruler of the Pamunkeys, surveyed his domain, and sometime in that year, he looked no longer. He had lived long enough to see the tobacco fields lining the riverbanks, straddling the charred stumps of felled trees. But perhaps he went to his grave believing that he had done what Wingina had failed to do: bend the English to his purposes. He died before those stinking tobacco weeds spread over the length of his land and sent his hard-won dominion up in smoke.

Wingina and Powhatan were not the only native leaders that dreamed of turning Europeans to their advantage. Across North America, the fleeting if destructive encounters of the sixteenth century gave way to sustained colonialism in the seventeenth. As Europeans began to settle the edges of North America in earnest, Indian peoples struggled not only to survive and adapt to new realities but also, when possible, to profit from the rapid changes swirling around them.

Those often dramatic changes reflected upheavals under way all across the globe. The tobacco John Rolfe had begun to cultivate was only one of several plantation **monocultures** that Europeans began to establish in their far-flung colonies. Sugar, already flourishing in the Atlantic islands off the coast of West Africa, was gaining a foothold in the islands of the Caribbean. Rice, long a staple in Asia and grown also in Africa, made its way into South Carolina toward the end of the seventeenth century. Because these crops were grown most efficiently on plantations and required intensive labor, African slavery spread during these years, fueled by an expanding international slave trade. Whites, blacks, and Indians were all, in different ways, caught up in the wrenching transformations. ∞∞∞∞

No stranger to self-promotion, Captain John Smith included this portrait of himself and verses celebrating his ennobling exploits at the beginning of his Description of New England (1616).

# SPAIN'S NORTH AMERICAN COLONIES

AND JUST AS SPAIN HAD been the first European power to explore North America's interior, so, too, it led the way in establishing lasting colonies north of Mexico. But while France and especially England would eventually colonize territory ideally suited to European-style agriculture, territory capable of sustaining large colonial populations, Spain confined its North American ventures to the ecologically challenging regions of the upper Rio Grande and coastal Florida. Because economic opportunities and quality farmland existed in abundance elsewhere in Spanish America, relatively few Spaniards chose to eke out an existence in distant and difficult northern outposts. Nonetheless, Spain's colonial endeavors would have tremendous implications for North America's native peoples and for the geopolitics of the continent as a whole.

## The Founding of a "New" Mexico

By the 1590s Coronado's dismal expedition a half century earlier had been all but forgotten. Again, rumors were circulating in Mexico about great riches in the North. New Spain's viceroy began casting about for a champion of means to establish a "new" Mexico, one perhaps as magnificent and profitable as its namesake. He chose Juan de Oñate, son of one of New Spain's richest miners and husband to Isabel de Tolosa Cortés Moctezuma, granddaughter of Hernán Cortés and great-granddaughter of Moctezuma. Oñate needed wealthy connections. Colonizing New Mexico would eventually cost him and his backers more than half a million pesos. But the would-be conquistador expected to recoup the investment with ease. Ignorant of North America's geography and overestimating New Mexico's riches, Oñate even requested and received permission to sail ships up the Pacific to Pueblo country, so that twice a year he could resupply his would-be colony and export its expected treasures.

CAUTIOUS RELATIONS

The magnitude of his mistaken assumptions began coming into focus in 1598, when he led 500 colonists, soldiers, and slaves to the Upper Rio Grande and, like Coronado before him, found modest villages, no ocean, and no evidence of significant mineral wealth. But, whatever the disappointments, Oñate had come with women and children, with livestock and tools, with artisans and tradesmen, with seeds and books and Bibles. He had come to stay. Eager to avoid the violence of earlier encounters, and perhaps hopeful of a mutually beneficial relationship, Tewa-speaking Pueblos evacuated a village for the newcomers to use. Many native leaders pledged Oñate their allegiance, Pueblo artisans labored on irrigation systems and other public works for the Spaniards, and Indian women (traditionally the builders in Pueblo society) constructed the region's first Catholic church.

THE ACOMA SIEGE

The colonizers mistook this cautious courtesy for subservience. Oñate's oldest nephew, Juan de Zaldívar, was bolder and cruder than most. At Acoma Pueblo, known today as "Sky City"

| Like many other Pueblo peoples, the founders of Acoma built their village atop a sandstone mesa to gain protection from enemies. As punishment for resisting his troops, Juan de Oñate ordered that every surviving Acoma male have one foot cut off. Four hundred years later, when this statue of Oñate was erected, vandals attacked the statue with a saw. "We took the liberty of removing Oñate's right foot on behalf of our brothers and sisters of Acoma Pueblo," they announced. Monuments to and celebrations of the "distant past" often provoke passionate disagreements in the present. What other monuments or commemorations have provoked disagreements?

because of its position high atop a majestic mesa, he brazenly seized several sacred turkeys to kill and eat, answering Indian protests with insults. Outraged, Acoma's men fell upon Zaldívar, killing him and several of his companions. Oñate responded by putting Zaldívar's younger brother Vicente in command of a punitive expedition. Fueled by grief and rage, Vicente de Zaldívar and his men laid siege to the Pueblo, killed perhaps 800 of its people, and made slaves of several hundred more. Following up on these punishments, Oñate decreed that all adult male survivors were to have one foot chopped off, so that they might spend their lives as limping advertisements for Spanish power. Scholars now doubt that this sentence was actually carried out, but even today, many Pueblos still consider Oñate's harsh edict as emblematic of Spanish cruelty. Whether or not Oñate executed his cruel judgment, the savagery of the Acoma siege and the brutal repression of other acts of defiance educated all of the region's native communities about the risks of resistance.

 **IMPOVERISHED NEW MEXICO** But it was easier to instill terror than grow rich. Desperate to salvage their enterprise and turn their investments to account, Oñate and key followers toiled on long, fruitless expeditions in search of gold, silver, and cities, and a place to dock those biannual ships. Some more practical entrepreneurs decided to exploit the resources they could see. The younger Zaldívar, headstrong conquerer of Acoma, spent time with Apache hunters and decided it would be more efficient to domesticate bison than search for them on the plains. He and his men labored for three days to build a sprawling cottonwood corral, only to discover that bison were "stubborn animals, brave beyond praise," dangerous to catch, and virtually impossible to hold. With varying degrees of enthusiasm, most Spaniards had to turn to more mundane and less hazardous pursuits, to farming and husbandry, in order to support themselves and their families. Others despaired of even securing a living in arid New Mexico, let alone getting rich. The Spanish Crown had promised to make minor nobles of those who stayed at least five years, but many spurned even this incentive and fled back into New Spain.

They were not the only ones losing confidence. In 1606 royal authorities removed Oñate from his position, brought him up on charges of mismanagement, and, as they had with Coronado, accused him of abusing Indians. Ruined, the would-be conquerer spent the rest of his days struggling to rebuild his fortune and clear his name. Meanwhile, a new viceroy decided that the colonization of "worthless" New Mexico had been an expensive mistake and began planning for its evacuation. The colony would have been abandoned but for the Franciscan religious order. Arguing that it would be a crime and a sin to forsake the many thousands of Indians they claimed to have baptized since 1598, the Franciscans convinced a skeptical King Philip III to continue supporting his outpost on the Upper Rio Grande.

## The Growth of Spanish Florida

**FRANCISCANS RENEW SPAIN'S EFFORTS** Franciscans would become key actors in Spanish North America. Members of a medieval religious order founded by St. Francis of Assisi, Franciscan monks foreswore property, remained **celibate,** and survived by begging for alms or accepting donations from wealthy patrons. Like their peers and occasional rivals the Jesuits, Franciscans wore only sandals, simple robes, and a rope belt and took it as their charge to live with and minister to the poor. Contact with the Americas reinvigorated their mission. Franciscans accompanied Columbus on his second voyage, and they began ministering to the Indians of central Mexico soon after Tenochtitlán fell. By the 1570s Spanish authorities started secularizing central Mexico's missions, transforming them into self-supporting parishes, and the friars looked to the frontiers for new fields of conversion. Jesuits established several missions in present-day Arizona, and Franciscans went on to become powerful figures in colonial New Mexico.

**FLORIDA'S STRATEGIC IMPORTANCE** The Crown needed them, nowhere more so than in Florida. Seventeenth-century New Mexico was a Catholic obligation for Spain's monarchs, but a small worry compared with the strategic importance of Florida. As long as pirates or rival colonies on the Atlantic seaboard threatened Spanish shipping, the king had to control Florida. Pedro Menéndez de Avilés did much to secure the peninsula in the 1560s when he destroyed France's Fort Caroline and established several Spanish posts on the coast (Chapter 2). By the 1580s, however, the energetic Menéndez was dead and nearly all his coastal establishments destroyed by Indians or privateers. Only St. Augustine endured, with a population of perhaps 500 in 1600. Spanish Florida needed something more than a beachhead along the coast if it was to survive.

**FRANCISCAN FLORIDA** The king turned to the Franciscans, as part of a two-stage policy to consolidate his influence over Florida's interior. First, royal administrators enticed or menaced the peninsula's many native peoples into alliances. In return for trade privileges and regular diplomatic presents, native leaders promised to trade with no other European power, support the Spanish in war, and tax their people on behalf of the Spaniards. Second, allied Indian communities were made to accept Franciscan missions and a few resident soldiers, a policy that would be critical to molding and monitoring native villages. Franciscans set about their work with characteristic determination. By 1675, 40 missions were ministering to as many as 26,000 baptized Indians. That same year, the bishop of Cuba toured Florida and spoke enthusiastically of converts who embraced "with devotion the mysteries of our holy faith."

Spain's plan for Florida seemed to be working, barely. St. Augustine had grown to a settlement of 1,500 by the time of the bishop's tour. Still, Florida's mission system and network of Indian alliances convinced Spanish authorities that they could maintain their grip on this crucial peninsula.

Artist Jacques Le Moyne recorded this scene of Florida Indians holding council in the 1560s. Observers from Jean Ribaut's French expedition can be seen in the foreground.

## Popé and the Pueblo Revolt

As the seventeenth century progressed, Spain's colony in New Mexico also seemed to stabilize. Although more than a few desperate colonists fled south, enough remained to establish a separate Spanish town, El Villa Real de Santa Fe, in 1610. Santa Fe (the second-oldest European town in the United States after St. Augustine) became the hub of Spanish life in New Mexico. The demands of agriculture and stock raising forced many families to settle elsewhere on the Rio Grande, on well-watered lands near Pueblo villages. Economic and political life revolved around a dozen prominent families. By 1675 New Mexico had a colonial population of perhaps 2,500. It was a diverse community, including Spaniards, Africans, Mexican Indians, mestizos (persons of mixed Spanish-Indian heritage), and mulattoes (of Spanish-African heritage).

INDIAN CAPTIVES This population of 2,500 also included large numbers of Indian captives. Occasionally captives came to Spanish households through war, as after the siege of Acoma. In addition, Spaniards purchased enslaved women and children from other Indians and regularly launched slave raids against so-called enemy Indians such as Utes, Apaches, and Navajos. By 1680 half of all New Mexican households included at least one Indian captive, someone who, depending on age, gender, and the master's disposition, could be treated affectionately as a low-status family member or terrorized and abused as disposable human property.

The colonists also extracted labor from Pueblo Indians. Officially Pueblo households had to surrender three bushels of corn and one processed hide or large cotton blanket each year. Pueblos were also sometimes made to labor on public works, and elite Spaniards often exploited their privileges by insisting on more tribute and labor than legally allowed. Still, the populous Pueblos would have been able to satisfy Spanish demands with little difficulty but for other changes in their world. First and most importantly, colonialism meant epidemics. Smallpox arrived in the early 1620s. In less than a generation the Pueblo population plumeted by 70 percent, to about 30,000. Whereas New Mexico had approximately 100 native villages at contact, by 1680 only 30 remained inhabited. Infestations of locusts, severe droughts, and crop failures compounded the crisis. By 1667 a distraught Franciscan reported widespread famine, with native men, women, and children "lying dead along the roads, in the ravines, and in their hovels." Mounted Utes, Apaches, and Navajos, embittered by New Mexican slaving and barred from their customary trade in the pueblos, launched punishing raids against the most vulnerable Pueblo villages.

PUEBLO SUFFERING In their deepening misery Pueblos turned to religion—their own. Since 1598 the Franciscans had worked tirelessly to supress the dances, idols, and ceremonies that long mediated Pueblo relationships with the divine. By the 1670s Pueblo elders could argue convincingly that the calamities of the past decades could be reversed only by a rejection of Christianity and a return to the old faith. Such revivalist sentiments threw the friars into a panic. Franciscans and civil authorities scrambled to extinguish the movement, arresting key Pueblo leaders, executing two and whipping 43 others in front of large crowds.

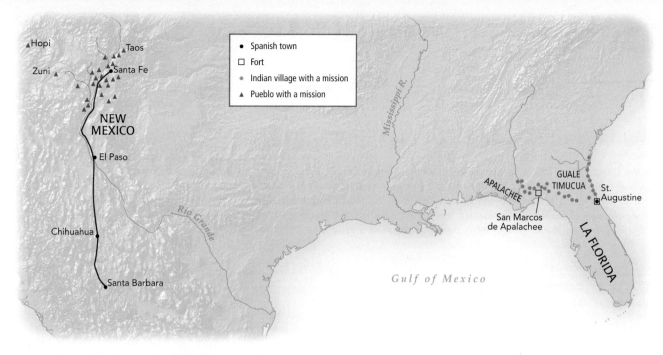

## SPANISH MISSIONS IN NORTH AMERICA, CA. 1675

*From St. Augustine, Spanish missionaries spread north into Guale Indian villages in present-day Georgia and westward among the Indians of Timucua, Apalachee, and Apalachicola. In New Mexico, missions radiated outward from the Rio Grande, as distant as Hopi Pueblos in the west.*

One of the 43, a prominent Tewa man known to history as Popé, nursed his wounds in Taos and laid the groundwork for a general uprising against the Spaniards. Appealing to headmen throughout the Pueblo world, Popé called for a war to purify the land. Many individuals and some entire villages refused to participate. But on August 10, 1680, Indians from across New Mexico rose up and began killing Spaniards. Astonished survivors fled to Santa Fe, followed by Popé and his army, who put the town to siege. Weeks later the desperate Spanish governor, wounded by an arrow in the face and a gunshot to the chest, gathered the remainder of the colonial population and fled south out of New Mexico. The most successful pan-Indian uprising in North American history, the Pueblo Revolt sent shock waves throughout Spanish America, and left the Catholic devout agonizing over what they might have done to provoke God's wrath.

 REVIEW

Where and why did Spain establish colonies in North America, and how did native peoples resist colonization?

# ENGLISH SOCIETY ON THE CHESAPEAKE

BY 1700, THEN, SPAIN VIEWED its situation in the Americas from a very different perspective than it had 100 years earlier. The Pueblo Revolt had checked its power at the northern reach of its American possessions. Equally disturbing was the progress of Spain's European rivals in the Americas during the seventeenth century. During the sixteenth, both France and England had envied the wealth Spain reaped from its American conquests. But neither nation did much to check Spain's power, beyond preying on Spanish ships and fishing for cod. During the seventeenth century, this would change.

MERCANTILISM    In fact, by 1600 other European kingdoms were beginning to view overseas colonies as essential to a nation's power and prosperity. They did so in part because of an economic model known as **mercantilism,** which guided Europe's commercial expansion for 200 years. (The theory was so named by the eighteenth-century economist Adam Smith.) Mercantilists called for the state to regulate and protect industry and commerce. Their primary objective was to enrich the nation by fostering a favorable balance of trade. Once the value of exports exceeded the cost of imports, they theorized, gold and silver would flow into home ports.

If a nation could make do without any imports from other countries, so much the better. It was here that the idea of colonies entered the mercantilist scheme. Colonial producers would supply raw materials that the mother country could not produce, while colonial consumers swelled demand for the finished goods and financial services that the mother country could provide. Convinced that colonies would enhance national self-sufficiency, mercantilists urged states to sponsor overseas settlements.

Mercantilist notions appealed to Europe's monarchs. A thriving trade meant that more taxes and customs

# DUELING DOCUMENTS

## WHAT CAUSED THE PUEBLO REVOLT?

*In the chaotic days following the outbreak of the Pueblo Revolt, shocked Spanish authorities detained several Indians and interrogated them about the rebels' motives. The first informant, Pedro García, was a Spanish-speaking Indian who had been raised in a Spaniard's household. Don Pedro Nanboa, the second informant, was captured by the Spanish and gave his testimony through an interpreter. The final declaration comes from Juan, detained and interrogated more than a year after the rebellion.*

### DOCUMENT 1  Pedro García

The deponent said that he was in the service of Captain Joseph Nieto, because he was born and has been brought up in his house. . . . While weeding part of a corn field on his master's estancia, which is something like a league from the pueblo of Galisteo, [he] saw coming to the place where he was an Indian named Bartolomé, the cantor mayor of the Pueblo of Galisteo. He came up weeping and said to him, "What are you doing here? The Indians want to kill the custodian, the fathers, and the Spaniards, and have said that the Indian who shall kill a Spaniard will get an Indian woman for a wife, and he who kills four will get four women, and he who kills ten or more will have a like number of women; and they have said that they are going to kill all the servants of the Spaniards and those who know how to speak Castilian, and they have also ordered that rosaries be taken away from everyone and burned. Hurry! Go! Perhaps you will be lucky enough to reach the place where the Spaniards are and will escape with your wife and an orphan girl that you have." Asked why they were plotting such treason and rebellion, he said that the said cantor told him that they were tired of the work they had to do for the Spaniards and the religious, because they did not allow them to plant or do other things for their own needs; and that, being weary, they had rebelled.

*Source:* "Declaration of Pedro García, an Indian of the Tagno nation, a native of Las Salinas, August 25, 1680," in Charles Wilson Hackett, ed., and Charmion Clair Shelby, trans., *Revolt of the Pueblo Indians of New Mexico and Otermín's Attempted Reconquest, 1680–1682* (Albuquerque: University of New Mexico Press, 1943), 1:23–26.

### DOCUMENT 2  Don Pedro Nanboa

Having been asked his name and of what place he is a native, his condition, and age, he said that his name is Don Pedro Nanboa, that he is a native of the pueblo of Alameda, a widower, and somewhat more than 80 years of age. Asked for what reason the Indians of this Kingdom have rebelled, forsaking their obedience to his Majesty and failing in their obligation as Christians, he said that for a long time, because the Spaniards punished sorcerers and idolaters, the nations of the Teguas, Taos, Pecuríes, Pecos, and Jemez had been plotting to rebel and kill the Spaniards and religious, and that they have been planning constantly to carry it out, down to the present occasion. . . . He declared that the resentment which all the Indians have in their hearts has been so strong, from the time this kingdom was discovered, because the religious and the Spaniards took away their idols and forbade their sorceries and idolatries; that they have inherited successively from their old men the things pertaining to their ancient customs; and that he has heard this resentment spoken of since he was of an age to understand. What he has said is the truth and what he knows, under the oath taken, and he ratifies it.

*Source:* "Declaration of one of the rebellious Christian Indians who was captured on the road, September 6, 1680," in Hackett, ed., *Revolt of the Pueblo Indians*, 1:60–62.

### DOCUMENT 3  Juan, of the Tegua Nation

Asked for what reasons and causes all the Indians of the Kingdom in general rebelled . . . he said that what he knows concerning this question is that not all of them joined the said rebellion willingly; that the chief mover of it is an Indian who is a native of the Pueblo of San Juan, named El Popé, and that from fear of this Indian all of them joined in the plot that he made. Thus he replied. Asked why they held the said Popé in such fear and obeyed him, and whether he was the chief man of the pueblo, or a good Christian, or a sorcerer, he said that the common report that circulated and still is current among all the natives is that the said Indian Popé talks with the devil, and for this reason all held him in terror, obeying his commands although they were contrary to the señores governors, the prelate and the religious, and the Spaniards, he giving them to understand that the word which he spoke was better than that of all the rest; and he states that it was a matter of common knowledge that the Indian Popé, talking with the devil, killed in his own house a son-in-law of his named Nicolás Bua, the governor of the pueblo of San Juan. On being asked why he killed him, he said that it was so that he might not warn the Spaniards of the rebellion, as he intended to do.

*Source:* "Declaration of the Indian, Juan, December 18, 1681," in Hackett, ed., *Revolt of the Pueblo Indians*, 2:232–238, 233–234.

### Thinking Critically

*Why does Pedro García say the Indians rebelled? Don Pedro Nanboa? Juan, the Tegua Indian? Can modern historians take these documents at face value? Why or why not? How might the circumstances of each informant have shaped his testimony?*

duties would fill royal coffers, increasing royal power. That logic led England's King James I to approve a private venture to colonize the Chesapeake Bay, a sprawling inlet of the Atlantic Ocean fed by over 100 rivers and streams.

## The Virginia Company

In 1606 the king granted a charter to a number of English merchants, gentlemen, and aristocrats, incorporating them as the Virginia Company of London. The members of the new **joint stock company** sold stock in their venture to English investors, as well as awarding a share to those willing to settle in Virginia at their own expense. With the proceeds from the sale of stock, the company planned to send to Virginia hundreds of poor and unemployed people as well as scores of skilled craftworkers. These laborers were to serve the company for seven years in return for their passage, pooling their efforts to produce any commodities that would return a profit to stockholders. If gold and silver could not be found, perhaps North America would yield other valuable commodities—furs, pitch, tar, or lumber. In the spring of 1607—nearly a decade after Oñate had launched Spain's colonies in New Mexico—the first expedition dispatched by the Virginia Company founded Jamestown.

 **JAMESTOWN'S PROBLEMS** Making the first of many mistakes, Jamestown's 104 men and boys pitched their fort on an inland peninsula in order to prevent a surprise attack from the Spanish. Unfortunately, the marshy, thickly wooded site served as an ideal breeding ground for malaria. The settlers, as well as those who followed them, were weakened by bouts of the disease and beset by dysentery, typhoid, and yellow fever. They died by the scores. During the summers, Indians familiar with the region's environment scattered beyond the estuary waters of the Chesapeake to find food. The English newcomers, by contrast, remained close to their fort, where the brackish waters became even more salty in the hot summer months. Salt poisoning in the wells left many colonists listless and apathetic.

Even before sickness took its toll, many of Jamestown's colonists had little taste for labor. The gentlemen of the expedition expected to lead rather than to work, and most of the other early settlers were gentlemen's servants and craftworkers who knew nothing about growing crops. As did the colonists on Roanoke, Jamestown's settlers resorted to bullying native people for food. Many colonists suffered from malnutrition, which heightened their susceptibility to disease. Only 60 of Jamestown's 500 inhabitants lived through the winter of 1609–1610, known as the "starving time." Some desperate colonists unearthed and ate corpses; one settler even butchered his wife. De facto martial law failed to turn the situation around, and skirmishes with the Indians became more brutal and frequent as rows of tobacco plants steadily invaded tribal lands.

## Reform and a Boom in Tobacco

**KEY REFORMS** Determined to salvage their investment, Virginia Company managers in 1618 set in place sweeping reforms. To attract more capital and colonists, the company established a "headright" system for granting land to individuals. Those already settled in the colony received 100 acres apiece. New settlers each received 50 acres, and anyone who paid the passage of other immigrants to Virginia—either family members or servants—received 50 acres per "head." The company also abolished martial law, allowing the planters to elect a representative assembly. Along with a governor and an advisory council appointed by the company, the House of Burgesses had the authority to make laws for the colony. It met for the first time in 1619, beginning what would become a strong tradition of representative government in the English colonies.

The new measures met with immediate success. The free and unfree laborers who poured into Virginia during the 1620s made up the first wave of an English migration to the Chesapeake that numbered between 130,000 and 150,000 over the seventeenth century. Drawn from the ranks of ordinary English working people, the immigrants were largely men, outnumbering women by six to one. Most were young, ranging in age from 15 to 24. Because of their youth, most lacked skills or wealth. Some of those who came to the Chesapeake as free immigrants prospered as Virginia's tobacco economy took off. When in the 1620s demand soared and prices peaked in European markets, colonists with an eye for profit planted every inch of their farms in tobacco and reaped windfalls.

**INDENTURED SERVANTS** Indentured servants accounted for three-quarters of all immigrants to Virginia. For most of them, the crossing was simply the last of many moves made in the hope of finding work. Although England's population had been rising since the middle of the fifteenth century, the demand for farm laborers was falling because many landowners were converting croplands into pastures for sheep. The search for work pushed young men and women out of their villages, sending them through the countryside and then into the cities. Down and out in London, Bristol, or Liverpool, some decided to make their next move across the Atlantic and signed **indentures.** Pamphlets promoting immigration promised abundant land and quick riches once servants had finished their terms of four to seven years.

Even the most skeptical immigrants were shocked at what they found. The death rate in Virginia during the 1620s was higher than that of England during times of epidemic disease. The life expectancy for Chesapeake men who reached the age of 20 was a mere 48 years; for women it was lower still. Servants fared worst of all, because malnutrition, overwork, and abuse made them vulnerable to disease. As masters scrambled to make quick profits, they extracted the maximum amount of work before death carried off their laborers. An estimated 40 percent of servants did not survive to the end of their indentured terms.

**WAR WITH THE CONFEDERACY** The expanding cultivation of tobacco also claimed many lives by putting unbearable pressure on Indian land. After Powhatan's death in 1617 leadership of the confederacy passed to Opechancanough, who watched, year after year, as the tobacco mania grew. In March 1622 he coordinated a sweeping attack on white settlements that killed about a quarter of Virginia's colonial population. English retaliation over the next decade cut down an entire generation of young Indian men, drove the remaining Powhatans to the west, and won the colonists hundreds of thousands more acres for tobacco.

News of the ongoing Indian war jolted English investors into determining the true state of their Virginia venture. It came to light that, despite the tobacco boom, the Virginia Company was plunging toward bankruptcy. Nor was that the worst news. Stockholders discovered that more than 3,000 immigrants had succumbed to the brutal conditions of Chesapeake life. An investigation by James I revealed the grisly truth, causing the king to dissolve the Virginia Company and take control of the colony himself in 1624. Henceforth Virginia would be governed as a royal colony.

**DECLINE IN MORTALITY RATES** As the tobacco boom broke in the 1630s and 1640s, Virginians began producing more corn and cattle. Nutrition and overall health improved as a result. More and more poor colonists began surviving their indenture and establishing modest farms of their own. For women who survived servitude, prospects were even better. With wives at a premium, single women stood a good chance of improving their status by marriage. Even so, high mortality rates still fractured families: one out of every four children born in the Chesapeake did not survive to maturity, and among those children who reached their 18th birthday, one-third had lost both parents to death.

By 1650 Virginia could boast about 15,000 colonists, although much of that increase resulted from servants and free immigrants arriving in the colony every year. But Virginians looking to expand into more northerly bays of the Chesapeake found their way blocked by a newer English colony.

## The Founding of Maryland and the Renewal of Indian Wars

Unlike Virginia, established by a private corporation and later converted into a royal colony, Maryland was founded in 1632 by a single aristocratic family, the Calverts. They held absolute authority to dispose of 10 million acres of land, administer justice, and establish a civil government. All these powers they exercised, granting estates, or "manors," to their friends and dividing other holdings into smaller farms for ordinary immigrants. From all these "tenants"—that is, every

settler in the colony—the family collected "quitrents" every year, fees for use of the land. The Calverts appointed a governor and a council to oversee their own interests while allowing the largest landowners to dispense local justice in manorial courts and make laws for the entire colony in a representative assembly.

Virginians liked nothing about Maryland. To begin with, the Calvert family was Catholic and had extended complete religious freedom to all Christians, making Maryland a haven for Catholics. Worse still, the Marylanders were a source of economic competition. Two thousand inhabitants had settled on Calvert holdings by 1640, virtually all of them planting tobacco on land coveted by the Virginians.

| Tobacco plant

Another obstacle to Virginia's expansion was the remnant of the Powhatan confederacy. Hounded for corn and supplies (most colonial fields grew tobacco rather than food), and constantly pressured by the expanding plantation economy, Virginia's native peoples became desperate and angry enough to risk yet another war. Aged Opechancanough led a new generation of Indians into battle in 1644 against the encroaching Virginia planters. Though his warriors killed several hundred English and brought the frontier to a standstill, Opechancanough was eventually captured and summarily shot through the head. The Powhatan confederacy died with him. Virginia's Indians would never again be in a position to resist the colony militarily. Over the next decades and centuries, many Indians fled the region altogether. But whole communities remained, quietly determined to continue their lives and traditions in their homeland.

## Changes in English Policy in the Chesapeake

Throughout the 1630s and 1640s colonial affairs drew little concern from royal officials. England itself had become engulfed first by a political crisis and then by a civil war.

**THE ENGLISH CIVIL WAR** Outraged at the contempt that King Charles I had shown toward Parliament, disaffected **elites** and radical Puritans overthrew the king and executed him in 1649. When the "republic" of Oliver Cromwell turned out to be something closer to a military dictatorship, most English were happy to see their throne restored in 1660 to Charles II, the son of the beheaded king. The new monarch was determined to ensure that not only his subjects at home but also his American colonies abroad contributed to England's prosperity. His colonial policy was reflected in a series of regulations known as the Navigation Acts.

**NAVIGATION ACTS** The first, passed by Parliament in 1660, gave England and English colonial merchants a monopoly on the shipping and marketing of all colonial goods. It also ordered that the colonies could export certain "enumerated commodities" only to England

## COLONIES OF THE CHESAPEAKE

*Settlements in Virginia and Maryland spread out along the many bays of the Chesapeake, where tobacco could easily be loaded from plantation wharves. The "fall line" on rivers, dividing Tidewater and Piedmont regions, determined the extent of commercial agriculture, since ships could not pick up exports beyond that point.*

or other British ports. These goods included sugar, tobacco, cotton, ginger, indigo (a blue dye), and eventually rice. In 1663 Parliament added another regulation, giving British merchants a virtual monopoly on the sale of European manufactured goods to Americans by requiring that most imports going to the colonies pass through England. In 1673 a third Navigation Act placed duties on the coastal trade of the American colonies and provided for customs officials to collect tariffs and enforce commercial regulations.

These acts were mercantilistic, insofar as they were designed to ensure that England—and no foreign nations or their merchants—would profit from colonial production and

trade. Chesapeake planters chafed under the Navigation Acts. They were used to conducting their affairs as they pleased—and they were often pleased to trade with the Dutch. What was worse, the new restrictions came at the same time as a downturn in tobacco prices. In the effort to consolidate its empire, England had unintentionally worsened the economic and social difficulties of Chesapeake society.

 REVIEW

How did the Chesapeake colonies support the aims of British mercantilism?

# CHESAPEAKE SOCIETY IN CRISIS

BY THE 1660S OVERPRODUCTION WAS depressing tobacco prices, and wealthy planters reacted by putting even more prime coastal land into production. Newly freed servants had either to become tenants or try to establish farms to the west in Indian country. Meanwhile, export duties on tobacco paid under the Navigation Acts helped plunge many small planters into crushing debt, and some were forced back into servitude. By 1676 one-quarter of Virginia's free white men remained landless and frustrated.

**DIMINISHING OPPORTUNITIES** Diminishing opportunities in the 1660s and 1670s provided the tinder for unrest in Virginia. As the discontent of the poor mounted, so did the worries of big planters. The assembly of the colony lengthened terms of servitude, hoping to limit the number of servants entering the free population. It curbed the political rights of landless men, hoping to stifle opposition by depriving them of the vote. But these measures only set off a spate of mutinies among servants and protests over rising taxes among small planters.

## Bacon's Rebellion and Coode's Rebellion

**NATHANIEL BACON** Those tensions came to a head in 1676. The rebellion was renewed fighting between desperate Indians and the expanding colonial population. Virginia's royal governor, William Berkeley, favored building forts to guard against Indians, but frontier farmers opposed his plan as an expensive and ineffective way to defend their scattered plantations. As they clamored for an expedition to punish the Indians, Nathaniel Bacon stepped forward to lead it.

Wealthy and well connected, Bacon had arrived recently from England, expecting to receive every favor from the governor—including permission to trade with the Indians from his frontier plantation. But Berkeley and a few select friends already held a monopoly on the Indian trade. When they declined to include Bacon, he took up the cause of his poorer frontier neighbors against their common enemy, the governor. Other recent, well-to-do immigrants who resented being excluded from Berkeley's circle of power and patronage also joined Bacon.

| This ceramic pipe from the 1670s was probably used by an indentured servant or tenant farmer living near Jamestown. Its design, featuring an animal carved around the pipe bowl, combined features typical of pipes made by English colonists, Indians, and African Americans. Virginia during this period experienced unstable relations between the expanding English population, the declining Indian population (due to wars and enslavement), and the growing number of enslaved Africans taking a larger role in the colony.

In the summer of 1676 Bacon marched into Jamestown with a body of armed men and bullied the assembly into approving his expedition to kill Indians. While Bacon carried out that grisly business, slaughtering friendly as well as hostile Indians, Berkeley rallied his supporters and declared Bacon a rebel. Bacon retaliated by turning his forces against those led by the governor. Both sides sought allies by offering freedom to servants and slaves willing to join their ranks. Many were willing: for months the followers of Bacon and Berkeley plundered one another's plantations. In September 1676 Bacon reduced Jamestown to a mound of ashes. It was only his death from dysentery a month later that snuffed out the rebellion.

Political upheaval also shook Maryland, where colonists had long resented the sway of the Calvert family. As proprietors, the Calverts and their favorites monopolized political offices, just as Berkeley's circle had in Virginia. Well-to-do planters wanted a share of the Calverts' power. Smaller farmers, like those in Virginia, wanted a less expensive and more representative government. Compounding the tensions were religious differences: the Calverts and their friends were Catholic, but other colonists, including Maryland's most successful planters, were Protestant.

The unrest among Maryland's discontented planters peaked in July 1689. A former member of the assembly, John Coode, gathered an army, captured the proprietary governor, and then took grievances to authorities in England. There Coode received a sympathetic hearing. The Calverts' charter was revoked and not restored until 1715, by which time the family had become Protestant.

**GROWING STABILITY** After 1690 rich planters in both Chesapeake colonies fought among themselves less and cooperated more. In Virginia older leaders and newer arrivals divided the spoils of political office. In Maryland Protestants and Catholics shared power and privilege. Those arrangements ensured that no future Bacon or Coode would mobilize restless gentlemen against the government. By acting together in legislative assemblies, the planter elite managed to curb the power of royal and proprietary governors for decades.

But the greater unity among the Chesapeake's leading families did little to ease that region's most fundamental problem—the sharp inequality of white society. The gulf between rich and poor planters, which had been etched ever more deeply by the troubled tobacco economy, persisted long after the rebellions of Bacon and Coode. All that saved white society in the Chesapeake from renewed crisis and conflict was the growth of black slavery.

## From Servitude to Slavery

Like the tobacco plants that spread across Powhatan's land, a labor system based on African slavery was an on-the-ground innovation. Both early promoters and planters preferred paying for English servants to importing alien African slaves. Black slaves, because they served for life, were more expensive than white workers, who served only for several years. Because neither white nor black immigrants lived long, cheaper servant labor was the logical choice. The black population of the Chesapeake remained small for most of the seventeenth century, constituting just 5 percent of all inhabitants in 1675.

THE LIVES OF SERVANTS AND SLAVES

Africans had arrived in Virginia by 1619, most likely via the Dutch, who dominated the slave trade until the middle of the eighteenth century. The lives of those newcomers resembled the lot of white servants, with whom they shared harsh work routines and living conditions. White and black bound laborers socialized with one another and formed sexual liaisons. They conspired to steal from their masters and ran away together; if caught, they endured similar punishments. There was more common ground: many of the first black settlers did not arrive directly from Africa but came from the Caribbean, where some had learned English and had adopted Christian beliefs. And not all were slaves: some were indentured servants. A handful were free.

A number of changes after 1680 caused planters to invest more heavily in slaves than in servants. First, as death rates in the Chesapeake began to drop, slaves became a more profitable investment. Although they were more expensive to buy than servants, planters could now expect to get many years of work from their bondspeople. Equally important, masters would have title to the children that slaves were now living long enough to have. At the same time, the influx of white servants was falling off just as the pool of available black labor was expanding. When the Royal African Company lost its monopoly on the English slave trade in 1698, other merchants entered the market. The number of Africans sold by British dealers swelled to 20,000 annually.

## Africa and the Atlantic Slave Trade

From 1492 to 1820, enslaved African migrants outnumbered European migrants to the New World by nearly five to one. Put differently, before the twentieth century, African workers did most of the heavy lifting in the economies of the Americas.

DIMENSIONS OF THE SLAVE TRADE

For a century after Columbus's arrival, the traffic in slaves to the Americas had numbered a few thousand annually. But as sugar cultivation steadily prospered after 1600, slave imports rose to 19,000 a year during the seventeenth century and mushroomed to 60,000 a year in the eighteenth century. All told, as many as 21 million people were captured in West Africa between 1700 and 1850: some 9 million among them entered the Americas as slaves, but millions died before or during the Atlantic crossing, and as many as 7 million remained slaves in Africa. Although slavery became indispensible to its economy, British North America played a relatively small role in the Atlantic slave trade.

Nine-tenths of all Africans brought to the New World landed in Brazil or the Caribbean islands.

TRANSFORMATION OF WEST AFRICAN SOCIETY

The rapid growth of the trade transformed not only the Americas but also Africa. Slavery became more widespread within African society, and slave trading more central to its domestic and international commerce. Most important, the African merchants and political leaders most deeply invested in the slave trade used their profits for political advantage—to build new chiefdoms and states such as Dahomey, Asante, and the Lunda Empire. Their ambitions and the greed of European slave dealers drew an increasingly large number of Africans, particularly people living in the interior, into slavery's web. By the late seventeenth century, Africans being sold into slavery were no longer only those who had put themselves at risk by committing crimes, running into debt, or voicing unpopular political and religious views. The larger number were instead captives taken by soldiers or kidnappers in raids launched specifically to acquire prisoners for the slave trade, or else desperate refugees captured while fleeing war, famine, and disease. During the decades after 1680, captives coming directly from Africa made up more than 80 percent of all new slaves entering the Chesapeake and the rest of mainland North America. Many were shipped from the coast of Africa that Portuguese explorers had first probed, between the Senegal and Niger Rivers. Most of the rest came from Angola, farther south.

Seized by other Africans, captives were yoked together at the neck and marched hundreds of miles through the interior to coastal forts or other outposts along the Atlantic. There, they were penned in hundreds of prisons, in lots of anywhere from 20 or 30 to more than 1,000. They might be forced to wait for slaving vessels in French *captiveries* below the fine houses of traders on the island of Gorée, or herded into "outfactories" on the Banana Islands upstream on the Sierra Leone River, or perhaps marched into the dank underground slaveholds at the English fort at Cape Coast. Farther south, captives were held in marshy, fever-ridden lowlands along the Bight of Benin, waiting for a slaver to drop anchor. One African, Ottobah Cugoano, recalled finally being taken aboard ship:

> There was nothing to be heard but the rattling of chains, smacking of whips, and the groans and cries of our fellowmen. Some would not stir from the ground, when they were lashed and beat in the most horrible manner. . . . And when we found ourselves at last taken away, death was more preferable than life, and a plan was concerted amongst us that we might burn and blow up the ship and to perish altogether in the flames.

THE MIDDLE PASSAGE

Worse than the imprisonment was the voyage itself: the so-called Middle Passage, a nightmarish journey across the Atlantic that could take anywhere between three weeks and three months, depending on currents, weather, and where ships

## AFRICAN TRANSATLANTIC SLAVE TRADE, 1450–1760

Toward the end of the seventeenth century, Chesapeake and Carolina planters began importing increasing numbers of slaves. In Africa the center of that trade lay along a mountainous region known as the Gold Coast, where more than a hundred European trading posts and forts funneled the trade. Unlike most of the rest of West Africa's shoreline, the Gold Coast had very little dense rain forest. Despite the heavy trade, only about 4 percent of the total transatlantic slave trade went to North America.

Katharina, sketched by Albrecht Dürer in 1521, was a servant of a Portuguese diplomat living in Antwerp. She was probably one of the increasing number of Africans being brought to Europe owing to the growing slave trade along the West African coast.

Slaves captured in the African interior were marched out in slave "coffles," a forced march in which captives were linked either by chains or by wooden yoke restraints linking two slaves together as they walked.

Africans found themselves in a variety of conditions in the Americas. Most toiled on plantations. Some, however, like these "watermen" along the James River in Virginia (lower right), claimed more independence. Still others ran away to Maroon communities in the interior. This armed Maroon (a runaway slave; lower left) is from Dutch Guiana, where conditions on the plantations were particularly harsh.

Slaves were often bought and sold on the decks of the ship they traveled on, as in this painting from the 1770s (top). Note that the ship has put up a barricade (left side of the illustration) to keep slaves separate from the rest of the ship while the selling is proceeding.

ENGLAND

3%

EUROPE

ATLANTIC OCEAN

NORTH AMERICA

BRITISH COLONIES

ARAB

BERBER

ARAB

SAHARA DESERT

ASIA

4%

WEST INDIES

French 17%

KAARTA

ARAB

British 24%

SEGU

KANEM-BORNU

Spanish 13%

HAUSA

CENTRAL AMERICA

The Middle Passage

DAHOMEY

ASHANTE

BENIN

AFRICA

Dutch 7%

OYO

GUIANAS

62%

Equator

TEKE

Portuguese 32%

NSUNDI

KONGO

SWAHILI CITY-STATES

BRAZIL

MBUNDU

36%

SOUTH AMERICA

ANGOLA

MADAGASCAR

2%

MOZAMBIQUE

Main slave sources 1450 to 1760

SUSU   Ethnic groups

## PENDANT MASK FROM BENIN

These images of mudfish alternate with those of Portuguese merchants. What might the mudfish be meant to symbolize? (Use a few key terms to find answers on the web.)

These pieces of inlaid iron represent medicine-filled incisions that were said to have given Idia metaphysical powers.

Object is hollow at the back; may have been used as a receptacle for medicines, as well as a pendant.

This exquisite sixteenth-century ivory mask, now in New York's Metropolitan Museum of Art, graced the neck of Benin's king during ceremonial occasions. Its subtlety and precision suggest that it was produced by Benin's famed guild of royal ivory carvers, specifically for royalty. The object communicates a tremendous amount of visual information. The face itself is a portrait of Idia, mother of Benin's great early-sixteenth-century leader Esigie.

A powerful political figure in her own right, Idia helped secure the throne for her son and remained an influential adviser throughout his reign. On her head and around her neck are miniature faces of Portuguese merchants who brought great wealth to Benin and enriched and empowered its leaders through the slave trade.

*Source:* Metropolitan Museum of Art, www.metmuseum.org/toah/ho/08/sfg/ho_1978.412.323.htm.

*Thinking Critically*

*Why pair the mudfish and the Portuguese? Do you think that the artist conceived of the Portuguese merchants as equals? Would you expect Benin's artistic sophistication to shape how the Portuguese regarded the kingdom?*

disembarked and landed. Often several hundred black men, women, and children were packed below-decks, squeezed onto platforms built in tiers spaced so close that sitting upright was impossible. It was difficult to know whether the days or the nights were more hellish. Slaves were taken out and forced to exercise for their health for a few hours each day; the rest of the day, the sun beat down and the heat below the decks was "so excessive," one voyager recalled, that the doctors who went below to examine slaves "would faint away, and the candles would not burn." At night, the slaves "were often heard making a howling melancholy kind of noise, something expressive of extreme anguish," noted a doctor aboard another ship. When he made inquiries, he discovered it was because the slaves, in sleeping, had dreamed "they were back in their own country again, amongst their families and friends" and "when they woke up to find themselves in reality on a slave ship they began to bay and shriek." Historians estimate that for every 85 enslaved Africans that set foot in the Americas, 15 died during the middle passage.

"SEASONING" After the numb, exhausted survivors reached American ports, they faced more challenges to staying alive. The first year in the colonies was the most deadly for new, "unseasoned" slaves. The sickle-cell genetic trait gave them a greater immunity to malaria than Europeans, but Africans were highly susceptible to respiratory infections. One-quarter of all Africans died during their first year in the Chesapeake, and among Carolina and Caribbean slaves, mortality rates were far higher. In addition to the new disease environment, Africans had to adapt to lives without freedom in a wholly unfamiliar country and culture.

Exchanging a labor system based on servitude for one based on slavery transformed the character of Chesapeake society. Most obviously, the number of Afro-Virginians rose sharply. By 1740, 40 percent of all Virginians were black, and most of those were African-born. Unlike many African men and women who had arrived earlier from the Caribbean, these new inhabitants had little familiarity with English language and culture. This larger, more distinctively African community was also locked into a slave system that was becoming ever more rigid and demeaning. By the late decades of the seventeenth century, new laws made it more difficult for masters to free slaves. Other legislation systematically separated the races by prohibiting free black settlers from having white servants and outlawing interracial marriages and sexual relationships. The legal code encouraged white contempt for black Virginians in a variety of other ways. While masters were prohibited from whipping their white servants on the bare back, slaves had no such protection. And "any Negro that shall presume to strike any white" was to receive 30 lashes for that rash act.

GROWING RACISM The new laws both reflected and encouraged **racism** among white colonists of all classes. Deepening racial hatred, in turn, made it unlikely that poor white planters, tenants, and servants would ever join with poor black slaves to challenge the privilege of great planters. Instead of identifying with the plight of the slaves, the Chesapeake's poorer white residents considered black Virginians their natural inferiors. They could pride themselves on sharing with wealthy white gentlemen the same skin color and on being their equals in the eyes of the law.

OPPORTUNITIES FOR WHITE SETTLERS The leaders of the Chesapeake colonies cultivated unity among white inhabitants by improving economic prospects for freed servants and lesser planters. The Virginia assembly made provisions for freed servants to get a better start as independent farmers. It lowered taxes, allowing small planters to keep more of their earnings. New laws also gave most white male Virginians a vote in elections, allowing them an outlet to express their grievances. Economic trends toward the end of the seventeenth century contributed to the greater prosperity of small planters, because tobacco prices rose slightly and then stabilized. As a result of Bacon's savage campaign against the Virginia Indians, new land on the frontier became available. Even the domestic lives of ordinary people became more secure as mortality rates declined and the numbers of men and women in the white population evened out. As a result, virtually all men were now able to marry, and families were fragmented less often by the premature deaths of spouses and parents.

After 1700 the Chesapeake evolved into a more stable society. Gone were the bands of wild, landless, young bachelors one step ahead of the law, the small body of struggling lesser planters one step ahead of ruin, and the great mass of exploited servants one step away from rebellion. Virginia and Maryland became colonies of farming families, most of them small planters who owned between 50 and 200 acres. These families held no slaves, or at most two or three. And they accepted, usually without question, the social and political leadership of their acknowledged "superiors," great planters who styled themselves the "gentry."

George Booth, the son of a wealthy planter family in Gloucester County, Virginia, was being raised for mastery. The young man's self-assured stance, the bow and arrows, the dog at his feet clutching the kill, the classical busts of women flanking his figure, and his family estate in the distance all suggest the gentry's concern for controlling the natural and social worlds.

The gentry's fortunes rested in part on the cultivation of tobacco on thousands of acres by hundreds of slaves. But the leading planters made even more money by marketing the tobacco of their humbler neighbors, selling them manufactured goods, supplying them with medical and legal services, lending money, and hiring out slaves. Unlike the rough-hewn barons of the early tobacco boom, the gentry did not owe their wealth to wringing work from poor whites. Instead, they amassed great estates by wringing work from black slaves while converting their white "inferiors" into modestly prosperous small planters and paying clients. But the gentry wanted more than money: they wanted the respect of lesser whites. And they received it. On court days, gentlemen served as justices of the peace, bedecked in wigs and robes and seated on raised benches. On Sundays, worshipers filed into the Anglican chapel in order of social rank, with gentlemen heading the procession. When the local militia trained, it did so at the head of gentlemen officers. The courthouse, the church, and the training field all served as theaters in which the new Chesapeake gentry dramatized their superiority and lesser men deferred.

### ✔ REVIEW

Why did slavery replace servitude as the dominant labor system in Virginia and Maryland?

# FROM THE CARIBBEAN TO THE CAROLINAS

**TRANSFORMATION OF THE CARIBBEAN**

DURING THE SAME DECADE THAT the English invaded Powhatan's land, they began to colonize the Caribbean, whose islands extended north and west, like beads on a string, from the Lesser Antilles toward the more substantial lands of Puerto Rico, Hispaniola, Jamaica, and Cuba (map, page 72). At their long journey's end English sailors found what seemed a paradise: shores rimmed with white sand beaches that rose sharply to coral terraces, then to broad plateaus or mountain peaks shrouded in rain forests. The earliest arrivals came intending not to colonize but to steal from the Spanish. Even after 1604, when some English settled on the islands, few intended to stay.

Yet the English did establish permanent plantation colonies in the West Indies. Beyond that, their Caribbean settlements became the jumping-off points for a new colony on the North American mainland—South Carolina. Because of the strong West Indian influence, South Carolina developed a social order in some ways distinct from that of the Chesapeake colonies. In other ways, however, the development paralleled Virginia and Maryland's path. In both regions, extreme violence, high mortality,

and uncertainty gave way to relative stability only over the course of many decades.

## Paradise Lost

The English had traded and battled with the Spanish in the Caribbean since the 1560s. From those island bases English buccaneers conducted an illegal trade with Spanish settlements, sacked the coastal towns, and plundered silver ships bound for Seville. Weakened by decades of warfare, Spain could not hold the West Indies. The Dutch drove a wedge into Caribbean trade routes, and the French and the English began to colonize the islands.

In the 40 years after 1604, some 30,000 immigrants from the British Isles planted crude frontier outposts on St. Kitts, Barbados, Nevis, Montserrat, and Antigua. The settlers—some free, many others indentured servants, and almost all young men—devoted themselves to working as little as possible, drinking as much as possible, and returning to England as soon as possible. They cultivated for export a poor quality of tobacco, which returned just enough profit to maintain straggling settlements of small farms.

 **CARIBBEAN SUGAR**

Then, nearly overnight, sugar cultivation transformed the Caribbean. In the 1640s Barbados planters learned from the Dutch how to process sugarcane. The Dutch also supplied African slaves to work the cane fields and marketed the sugar for high prices in the Netherlands. Sugar plantations and slave labor rapidly spread to other English and French islands as Europeans developed an insatiable sweet tooth for the once scarce commodity. Caribbean sugar made more money for England than the total volume of commodities exported by all the mainland American colonies.

Even though its great planters became the richest people in English America, they could not have confused the West Indies with paradise. Throughout the seventeenth century, disease took a fearful toll, and island populations grew only because of immigration. In the scramble for land, small farmers were pushed onto tiny plots that barely allowed them to survive.

**SLAVERY IN THE CARIBBEAN**

The desperation of bound laborers posed another threat. After the Caribbean's conversion to cultivating sugar, African slaves gradually replaced indentured servants in the cane fields. By the beginning of the eighteenth century resident Africans outnumbered English by four to one. Fear of servant mutinies and slave rebellions frayed the nerves of island masters. They tried to contain the danger by imposing harsh slave codes and inflicting brutal punishments on all laborers. But planters lived under a constant state of siege. One visitor to Barbados observed that whites fortified their homes with parapets from which they could pour scalding water on attacking servants and slaves. During the first century of settlement, seven major slave uprisings shook the English islands.

## A Taste for Sugar

It is said that shortly before his death in 735 CE, the Venerable Bede, an English abbot, bequeathed a precious treasure to his brother monks. It consisted of a cache of spices, including a little stock of sugar. What separated Bede's world, in which sugar was a costly luxury, from twenty-first-century Americans' world of ever-present sweetness was the discovery of America and the establishment of plantation economies in the Caribbean and Brazil.

Until the fourteenth century, Europe's merchants imported only small quantities of sugar at great expense from North Africa as well as from distant Persia and India, countries that had produced sugar since 500 CE.

Throughout the Middle Ages and the early modern era, only the royal and the rich of Europe could indulge their desire for sugar, and even those classes partook sparingly. Europeans classified sugar as a spice, like the equally scarce and exotic pepper, nutmeg, ginger, and saffron. Nobility valued sugar as a medicine for sore throats, stomach disorders, and infertility. The cooks of castle kitchens seasoned food and sauces with a pinch of sugar or sprinkled it on meat, fish, fowl, and fruit to preserve freshness—or to conceal rot. Only on great occasions did the confectioners of noble families splurge, fashioning for courtly feasts great baked sugar sculptures of knights and kings, horses and apes, called "subtleties."

For the ordinary folk of Europe, life was not as sweet. Their diets consisted of bread, peas, beans, and, in good years, a little milk, butter, and cheese. The occasional pig slaughtered, rabbit trapped, or fish caught supplied stray protein for the poor.

That pattern of consumption changed as Europeans turned to African slave labor to grow sugar for them. The early sugar plantations of Madeira and the Canary Islands (Chapter 2) were a foretaste of veritable sugar factories created in the Caribbean colonies of England and France.

By the sixteenth and seventeenth centuries, Europe's merchant classes could imitate elite patterns of eating by pouring sugar into pastries and puddings. And by the middle of the eighteenth century, an increasingly large supply from the Caribbean was making sugar essential to the poorest Europeans. Among England's laboring classes, another colonial import—Indian tea, laced heavily with sugar—began to accompany an otherwise cold supper of bread. Cheaper, warmer, and more stimulating than milk or beer (its prime competitors), sugared tea won the loyalty of England's mass market and ranked as the nonalcoholic beverage of national choice. By the nineteenth century English working families were also combining sugar and starch by pouring treacle (molasses) over porridge and spreading jams or marmalades on their bread.

Europe and America affected each other in many ways, but diet figured among the more fundamental conditions of life altered by colonization. More than coffee, chocolate, rum, or tobacco—indeed, more than any of the other "drug foods" produced by the colonies except tea—sugar provided a major addition to the diet of the English and other Europeans.

Even though sugar became a mass-marketed basic foodstuff, its association with power persisted. But it was no longer the consumption of sugar that bestowed status. Instead, after 1700 it was the production of sugar that conferred power. Planters who grew it, merchants who shipped and sold it, industrialists who refined it, and politicians who taxed it discovered in sugar sources of profit and distinction less perishable than sweetness on the tongue.

### *Thinking Critically*

*How did the growth of sugar cultivation in the Americas change European diets for different social classes?*

*Once harvested, sugarcane in the West Indies was crushed, as in this sugar mill. The juice was collected and channeled to the sugar works, where it was concentrated through boiling and evaporation. This neat diagrammatic picture belies the harsh conditions of labor and the high mortality that slaves experienced: sweetness came at a steep price.*

As more people, both white and black, squeezed onto the islands, some settlers looked for a way out. With all the land in use, the Caribbean no longer offered opportunity to freed servants or even planters' sons. It was then that the West Indies started to shape the history of the American South.

## The Founding of the Carolinas

The colonization of the Carolinas began with the schemes of Virginia's royal governor, William Berkeley, and Sir John Colleton, a supporter of Charles I who had been exiled to the Caribbean at the end of England's civil war. Colleton saw that the Caribbean had a surplus of white settlers, and Berkeley knew that Virginians needed room to expand as well. Together the two men set their sights on the area south of Virginia. Along with a number of other aristocrats, they convinced Charles II to make them joint proprietors in 1663 of a place they called the Carolinas, in honor of the king.

**NORTH CAROLINA** A few hardy souls from Virginia had already squatted around Albemarle Sound in the northern part of the Carolina grant. The proprietors provided them with a governor and a representative assembly. About 40 years later, in 1701, they set off North Carolina as a separate colony. The desolate region quickly proved a disappointment. Lacking good harbors and navigable rivers, the colony had no convenient way of marketing its produce. North Carolina

remained a poor colony, its sparse population engaged in general farming and the production of masts, pitch, tar, and turpentine.

**SOUTH CAROLINA** The southern portion of the Carolina grant held far more promise, especially in the eyes of one of its proprietors, Sir Anthony Ashley Cooper, Earl of Shaftesbury. In 1669 he sponsored an expedition of a few hundred English and Barbadian immigrants, who planted the first permanent settlement in South Carolina. By 1680 the colonists had established the center of economic, social, and political life at the confluence of the Ashley and Cooper Rivers, naming the site Charles Town (later Charleston) after the king. Like others before him, Cooper hoped to create an ideal society in America. His utopia was a place where a few landed aristocrats and gentlemen would rule with the consent of many smaller property holders. With his personal secretary, the renowned philosopher John Locke, Cooper drew up an intricate scheme of government, the Fundamental Constitutions. The design provided Carolina with a proprietary governor and a hereditary nobility who, as a Council of Lords, would recommend all laws to a Parliament elected by lesser landowners.

The Fundamental Constitutions met the same fate as other lordly dreams for America. Instead of peacefully observing its provisions, most of the Carolinians, emigrants from Barbados, plunged into the economic and political wrangling that had plagued Maryland's first government. They challenged proprietary rule, protested or

With large majorities of their populations enslaved, the sugar-producing islands of the Caribbean were anxious, fearful places of brutal labor and gruesome discipline. But they were also sites of rich social life and cultural development, as this slave dance on the island of St. Vincent suggests.

ignored laws and regulations imposed on them, and rejected the proprietors' relatively benevolent vision of Indian relations. Instead of forging genuine alliances with regional Indians, Carolina's colonists fomented a series of Indian slave wars that would nearly destroy the colony altogether.

## Carolina, Florida, and the Southeastern Slave Wars

Taking wealthy Barbados as the model, the colonists intended from the start to grow Carolina's economy around cash crops tended by African slaves. But before they could afford to establish such a regime, the newcomers needed to raise capital through trade with Indians. Colonists gave textiles, metal goods, guns, and alcohol in exchange for hundreds of thousands of deerskins, which they then exported.

GROWTH OF THE INDIAN SLAVE TRADE

But the trade soon came to revolve around a commodity dearer still. As did most peoples throughout history, southeastern Indians sometimes made slaves of their enemies. Carolina's traders vastly expanded this existing slave culture by turning captives into prized commodities. Convinced that local Indians were physically weaker than Africans and more likely to rebel or flee, colonial traders bought slaves from Indian allies and then exported them to other mainland colonies or to the Caribbean. They found eager native partners in this business. Contact with Europe had unleashed phenomenal changes in interior North America; epidemics ruined one people and gave advantage to another, new commercial opportunities sparked fierce wars over hunting and trading territories, and many thousands of Indian families became displaced and had to rebuild their lives somewhere new. The chaos, conflict, and movement gave enterprising Indians ample opportunity to enslave weak neighbors and stock Carolina's slave pens.

RAIDS INTO SPANISH FLORIDA

To ensure a steady supply of slaves and maximize profits, Carolinian merchants courted a variety of Indian allies during the late seventeenth and early eighteenth centuries and encouraged them to raid mission Indians in Spanish Florida. By 1700 Florida's Indian peoples were in sharp decline, and Charles Town's slave traders turned to the large and powerful Creek, Choctaw, Chickasaw, and Cherokee confederacies of the interior, encouraging them to raid one another. Before long the slave wars had a momentum all their own, extending as far west as the Mississippi River. Even native peoples who deplored the violence and despised the English felt compelled to participate, lest they, too, become victims. One small Indian community elected an elder representative to travel to Charles Town and discover what his people needed to do to stay safe. The town's traders seized the man and

sold him into slavery. The trade had become central to Carolina's growing economy, and colonists high and low sought to profit from it. In 1702 Governor James Moore, one of the colony's chief slave traders, launched an audacious raid against Spanish St. Augustine and Florida's missions, returning with hundreds of Indian captives. His campaign inspired still more raids, and over the next few years Creeks, Yamasees, and Englishmen laid waste to 29 Spanish missions, shattering thousands of lives and destroying Spain's precarious system of Indian alliances in Florida. By 1706 Spanish authority was once again confined to St. Augustine and its immediate vicinity, and within another 10 years most of Florida had been depopulated of Indians.

It seemed a double victory from Charles Town's perspective. The English had bested a European rival for the Crown and had reaped enormous profits besides. The fragmentary evidence suggests that Carolinians had purchased or captured between 30,000 and 50,000 Indian slaves before 1715. Indeed, before that date South Carolina was a net exporter of slaves: it exported more slaves than it imported from Africa or the Caribbean. But in 1715 Carolina's merchants finally paid a price for the wars that they had cynically fomented for over 40 years.

YAMASEE WAR

With Florida virtually exhausted of slaves, the Yamasees grew nervous. Convinced that Carolina would soon turn on them as it had on other onetime allies, the Yamasees struck first. They attacked traders, posts, and plantations on the outskirts of Charles Town, killing hundreds of colonists and dragging scores more to Florida to sell as slaves in St. Augustine. Panicked authorities turned to other Indian peoples in the region but found most had either joined the Yamasee or were too hostile and suspicious to help. Though it lasted only a few months, the Yamasee War finally put an end to the destructive regional slave trade. Animal skins again dominated regional commerce. The powerful southern confederacies grew wary of aligning too closely with any single European power and henceforth sought to play colonies and empires off each other. It was a strategy that would bring them relative peace and prosperity for generations.

## White, Red, and Black: The Search for Order

As for South Carolina, the Yamasee War set it back 20 years. In its aftermath, colonists invested more and more of their resources in African slaves and in the cultivation of rice, a crop that eventually made South Carolina's planters the richest social group in mainland North America. Unfortunately, South Carolina's swampy coast, so perfectly suited to growing rice, was less suited for human habitation. Weakened by chronic malaria, settlers died in epic numbers from yellow fever, smallpox, and respiratory infections. The white population grew slowly, through

## THE CAROLINAS AND THE CARIBBEAN

*The map underscores the geographic link between West Indian and Carolina settlements. Emigrants from Barbados dominated politics in early South Carolina, while Carolinians provided foodstuffs, grain, and cattle to the West Indies. As South Carolinians began growing rice, Caribbean slave ships found it an easy sail north and west to unload their cargoes in Charles Town. The fall line is marked here and on the map of the Chesapeake region on page 61. What is the fall line? Why is it significant?*

Mulberry Plantation in South Carolina was first carved from coastal swamps in 1714. This painting, done half a century later, shows the Great House visible in the distance, flanked by slave quarters. African slaves skilled in rice cultivation oversaw the arduous task of properly planting and irrigating the crop.

immigration rather than natural increase, and numbered only 10,000 by 1730.

Early South Carolinians had little in common but the harsh conditions of frontier existence. Most colonists lived on isolated plantations; early deaths fragmented families and neighborhoods. Immigration after 1700 further intensified the colony's ethnic and religious diversity, adding Swiss and German Lutherans, Scots-Irish Presbyterians, Welsh Baptists, and Spanish Jews. The colony's only courts were in Charles Town; churches and clergy of any denomination were scarce. On those rare occasions when early Carolinians came together, they gathered at Charles Town to escape the pestilential air of their plantations, to sue one another for debt and haggle over prices, or to fight over religious differences and proprietary politics.

Finally, in 1729, the Crown formally established royal government; by 1730 economic recovery had done much to ease the strife. Even more important in bringing greater political stability, the white colonists of South Carolina came to realize that they must unite if they were to counter the Spanish in Florida and the French and their Indian allies on the Gulf Coast.

**SLAVERY IN SOUTH CAROLINA** The growing black population gave white Carolinians another reason to maintain a united front. During the first decades of settlement, frontier conditions and the scarcity of labor had forced masters to allow enslaved Africans greater freedom within bondage. White and black laborers shared chores on small farms. On stock-raising plantations, called "cowpens," black cowboys ranged freely over the countryside. African contributions to the defense of the colony also reinforced racial interdependence and muted white domination. Whenever threats arose— during the Yamasee War, for example—black Carolinians were enlisted in the militia.

White Carolinians depended on black labor even more after turning to rice as their cash crop. In fact, planters began to import slaves in larger numbers partly because of West African skill in rice cultivation. But whites harbored deepening fears of the black workers whose labor built planter fortunes. As early as 1708 black men and women had become a majority in the colony, and by 1730 they outnumbered white settlers by two to one. As their colony recovered and began to prosper, white Carolinians put into effect strict slave codes like those in the Caribbean that converted their colony into an armed camp and snuffed out the marginal freedoms that African settlers once enjoyed.

## The Founding of Georgia

After 1730 white South Carolinians could take comfort not only in newfound prosperity and new political harmony but also in the founding of a new colony on their southern border. South Carolinians liked Georgia a great deal more than the Virginians had liked Maryland, because the colony formed a buffer between British North America and Spanish Florida in much the same way that Yamasees and Shawnees had, before the war.

**JAMES OGLETHORPE** Enhancing the military security of South Carolina was only one reason for the founding of Georgia. More important to General James Oglethorpe and other idealistic English gentlemen was the aim of aiding the "worthy poor" by providing them with land, employment, and a new start. They envisioned a colony of hardworking small farmers who would produce silk and wine, sparing England the need to import those commodities. That dream seemed within reach when George II made Oglethorpe and his friends the trustees of the new colony in 1732, granting them a charter for

The Yuchi were neighbors of one of Georgia's early settlements; one of the newly emigrated German colonists painted this watercolor of a Yuchi celebration. Judging from the guns hanging at the back of the shelter, these Indians were already trading with white colonists in the area.

21 years. At the end of that time Georgia would revert to royal control.

The trustees did not, as legend has it, empty England's debtors' prisons to populate Georgia. They freed few debtors but recruited from every country in Europe paupers who seemed willing to work hard—and who professed Protestantism. Trustees paid the paupers' passage and provided each with 50 acres of land, tools, and a year's worth of supplies. Settlers who could pay their own way were encouraged to come by being granted larger tracts of land. Much to the trustees' dismay, that generous offer was taken up not only by many hoped-for Protestants but also by several hundred Ashkenazim (German Jews) and Sephardim (Spanish and Portuguese Jews), who established a thriving community in early Savannah.

The trustees were determined to ensure that Georgia became a small farmers' utopia. Rather than selling land, the trustees gave it away, but none of the colony's settlers could own more than 500 acres. The trustees also outlawed slavery and hard liquor in order to cultivate habits of industry and sustain equality among whites. This design for a virtuous and egalitarian utopia was greeted with little enthusiasm by Georgians. They pressed for a free market in land and argued that the colony could never prosper until the trustees revoked their ban on slavery. Because the trustees had provided for no elective assembly, settlers could express their discontent only by moving to South Carolina—which many did during the early decades.

As mounting opposition threatened to depopulate the colony, the trustees caved in. They revoked their restrictions on land, slavery, and liquor a few years before the king assumed control of the colony in 1752. Under royal control, Georgia continued to develop an ethnically and religiously diverse society, akin to that of South Carolina. Similarly, its economy was based on rice cultivation and the Indian trade.

 REVIEW

How was the colonization of Carolina both distinct from and parallel to that of the Chesapeake?

# CONCLUSION

## THE WORLD AT LARGE

Empire . . . utopia . . . independence. . . . For more than a century after the founding of Oñate's colony on the upper Rio Grande in 1598, those dreams inspired residents of New Mexico, Florida, the Chesapeake, the English Caribbean, the Carolinas, and Georgia.

Although South Carolina and the English West Indies were more opulent and unstable societies than Virginia and Maryland, the colonies stretching from the Chesapeake to the Caribbean had much in common. So did the South American sugar and coffee plantations of the Guianas and the sugar plantations of Brazil. As Europeans put down colonies throughout the Americas, Indian farmers and hunters were enslaved or expelled. Planters depended on a single staple crop, which brought wealth and political power to those commanding the most land and the most labor. And the biggest planters relied for their success on the very people whom they most feared—enslaved African Americans. That fear was reflected in the development of repressive slave codes and the spread of racism throughout all classes of white society.

The dream of an expanding empire faltered for the Spanish, who discovered few riches in the Southwest and eventually found rebellion. The dream of empire failed, too, when James I and Charles I of England found their power checked by Parliament. And the dream foundered fatally for Indians, unable to resist Old World diseases and land-hungry colonists.

English lords dreamed of establishing feudal utopias in America. But proprietors in Maryland and the Carolinas were hounded by frontier planters and farmers looking for their own economic and political power. Georgia's trustees failed to erect their utopia for the poor. And Indian resistance dimmed the utopian dreams of Spanish Catholic missionaries in the American Southwest.

The dream of independence proved most deceptive, especially for English colonists. Almost half of white servant emigrants to the Chesapeake died from disease or were worn down by tobacco barons. And real independence eluded even English planters. The poorer ones depended on richer settlers for land and leadership, while even the richest needed English and Scottish merchants to supply credit and market their crops.

And everywhere in the American Southeast and Southwest, the dreams of Europeans depended on the labor of the least free members of colonial America. That stubborn reality would haunt Americans of all colors who continued to chase after freedom and independence. ∞∞∞∞

## CHAPTER SUMMARY

DURING THE SEVENTEENTH CENTURY, SPAIN and England moved to colonize critical regions of southern North America.

■ Native peoples everywhere in the American South resisted colonization, despite losses from warfare, disease, and enslavement.

■ Spanish colonies in New Mexico and Florida grew slowly and faced a variety of threats. By the late seventeenth century, Spanish New Mexico had been lost to the Pueblo Revolt and Florida's delicate mission system was under siege from English Carolina and its Indian allies.

■ Thriving monocultures were established in all of England's southern colonies—tobacco in the Chesapeake, rice in the Carolinas, and sugar in the Caribbean.

■ Despite a period of intense enslavement of native peoples, African slavery emerged as the dominant labor system throughout these regions.

■ Instability and conflict characterized both Spanish and English colonies in the South for most of the first century of their existence.

# Additional Reading

David J. Weber's *Spanish Frontier in North America* (1992) remains indispensible. For New Mexico, see also John L. Kessell's *Spain in the Southwest* (2002) and James F. Brook's pathbreaking *Captives and Cousins* (2002). For Spain in the Southeast, see Paul E. Hoffman's *Florida's Frontiers* (2002) and Daniel S. Murphree's *Constructing Floridians* (2006).

For enduring treatments of early Virginia, see Edmund S. Morgan, *American Slavery, American Freedom* (1975), and Kathleen Brown, *Good Wives, Nasty Wenches, and Anxious Patriarchs* (1996). James D. Rice's *Tales from a Revolution* (2012) explores the multiple perspectives of Indians to Bacon's Rebellion.

For Indians in the colonial Southeast, see Gregory A. Waselkov, Peter Wood, and Tom Hatley, eds., *Powhatan's Mantle* (2006). For native Virginia, see also Hellen C. Rountree, *Pocahontas, Powhatan, Opechancanough* (2005).

In recent years there has been a surge in scholarship on African slavery in the New World. For a magisterial overview, see David Brion Davis, *Inhuman Bondage* (2006). For British North America, see Ira Berlin, *Many Thousands Gone* (1998), and Philip D. Morgan, *Slave Counterpoint* (1998). The classic account of the British Caribbean remains Richard Dunn's *Sugar and Slaves* (2000 [1972]). Vincent Brown's *Reaper's Garden* (2008) examines the brutalities of the Jamaican slave system. Stephanie Smallwood's *Saltwater Slavery* (2007) provides a haunting portrait of the Middle Passage.

The best overview of South Carolina's development remains Robert Weir, *Colonial South Carolina* (1982). The complexities of Carolina's slave wars are explored in Alan Gallay, *The Indian Slave Trade* (2002). For the topic more broadly, see Christina Snyder, *Slavery in Indian Country* (2010).

For a fuller list of readings, see the Bibliography at www.mhhe.com/eh8e.

# Significant Events

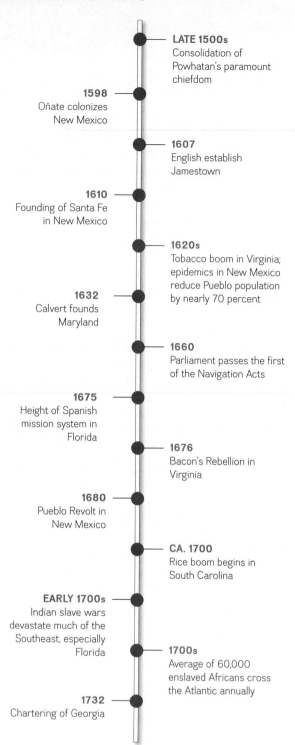

**LATE 1500s**
Consolidation of Powhatan's paramount chiefdom

**1598**
Oñate colonizes New Mexico

**1607**
English establish Jamestown

**1610**
Founding of Santa Fe in New Mexico

**1620s**
Tobacco boom in Virginia; epidemics in New Mexico reduce Pueblo population by nearly 70 percent

**1632**
Calvert founds Maryland

**1660**
Parliament passes the first of the Navigation Acts

**1675**
Height of Spanish mission system in Florida

**1676**
Bacon's Rebellion in Virginia

**1680**
Pueblo Revolt in New Mexico

**CA. 1700**
Rice boom begins in South Carolina

**EARLY 1700s**
Indian slave wars devastate much of the Southeast, especially Florida

**1700s**
Average of 60,000 enslaved Africans cross the Atlantic annually

**1732**
Chartering of Georgia

| COLONY | FOUNDING/ SETTLEMENT | CHARACTER AND DEVELOPMENT | APPROXIMATE COLONIAL POPULATION |
|---|---|---|---|
| New Mexico | Oñate expedition 1598; Santa Fe 1610 | Arid; few Spanish colonists; agriculture, stock raising, trade with Indians | 2,500, including Indian slaves, in 1675 |
| Florida | St. Augustine 1565 | Spain uses as a buffer against English settlements to the north | 40 Franciscan missions to c. 26,000 baptized Indians by 1675. 1,500 Spaniards in Florida by 1700. |
| Virginia | Jamestown 1607 | Tobacco boom 1620s; population of young, single, indentured servants; Bacon's Rebellion 1676; slavery replaces servitude as the prevailing labor system, 1680s | 72,000, including 56,000 white, 16,000 black, in 1700 |
| Maryland | Founded by the Calverts as proprietors, 1632 | Religious freedom for Christians; tobacco economy; Coode's Rebellion 1689 | 30,000, including 27,000 white, 3,000 black, in 1700 |
| West Indies (British) | English settlements after 1604: islands of Barbados, Antigua, St. Kitts, Nevis, and Montserrat | Tobacco gives way to sugar boom, 1640s; African slaves become majority population on sugar islands | 65,000, including 15,000 white, 50,000 black, in 1700 |
| Carolinas | Charles Town established by colonists from England and Barbados, 1669 | Trade in hides and Indian slaves; increased stability as rice cultivation established; made royal colony in 1729; North Carolina becomes separate colony in 1701 | South Carolina: 6,000—3,500 white, 2,500 black; North Carolina: 10,700—10,300 white, 400 black, in 1700 |
| Georgia | Chartered in 1732 | Refuge for debtors; slavery not allowed until shortly before it becomes a royal colony in 1752 | 5,000, including 4,000 white, 1,000 black, in 1752 |

By 1664, when this map of New Amsterdam was engraved, the town had grown considerably from its origins as a fort and fur-trading outpost. (Compare the engraving from 1626, on page 95.) Behind the houses in the foreground, a palisade fence still stands as a wall protecting against Indian attacks. A gallows stands in the foreground and a windmill in the distance. The English renamed the city New York when they pushed out the Dutch, in this year.

## CHAPTER 4

# Colonization and Conflict in the North

## 1600-1700

### *What's to Come*

∞∞ **AN AMERICAN STORY** ∞∞

## BEARS ON FLOATING ISLANDS

They came to her one night while she slept. Into her dreams drifted a small island, and on the island were tall trees and living creatures, one of them wearing the fur of a white rabbit. When she told of her vision, no one took her seriously, not even the wise men among her people, shamans and conjurers whose business it was to interpret dreams. No one, that is, until two days later, when the island appeared to all, floating toward shore. On the island, as she had seen, were tall trees, and on their branches—bears. Or creatures that looked so much like bears that the men grabbed their weapons and raced to the beach, eager for the good hunt sent by the gods. They were disappointed. The island was not an island at all but a strange wooden ship planted with the trunks of trees. And the bears were not bears at all but a strange sort of men whose bodies were covered with hair. Strangest among them, as she had somehow known, was a man dressed all in white. He commanded great respect among the bearlike men as their "shaman," or priest.

In that way, foretold by the dreams of a young woman, the Micmac Indians in 1869 recounted their people's first encounter with Europeans more than two centuries earlier. Uncannily, the traditions of other northern tribes record similar dreams predicting the European arrival: "large canoes with great white wings like those of a giant bird," filled with pale bearded men bearing "long black tubes."

Perhaps the dreamers gave shape in their sleep to stories heard from other peoples who had actually seen white strangers and ships. Or perhaps, long before they ever encountered the newcomers, these Indians imagined them, just as Europeans fantasized about a new world.

| Micmacs

However Micmacs and other northern Indians first imagined and idealized Europeans, they quickly came to see them as fully human. Traders might bring seemingly wondrous goods, goods that could transform the way labor, commerce, politics, and war functioned in native communities. And yet the traders themselves hardly seemed magical. They could be by turns generous and miserly, brave and frightful, confident and confused, kind and cruel. Moreover, it soon became clear that these newcomers hailed from different nations, spoke different languages, and often seemed to have different goals. English colonists, it seemed, were every day more numerous and wanted nothing so much as land. The French, in contrast, were relatively few and seemed to care for nothing so much as trade—unless it was their Christian God they brought with them from across the waters. Strange to say, the Europeans argued over their deity as they did over so many other things. The English, the French, and the Dutch were all rivals, and the Micmacs and others who encountered these new peoples studied them closely and began to make alliances.

As northern Indians became more and more aware of Europeans and their ways, they came also to realize that whatever their attitudes and intentions, the newcomers provoked dramatic changes everywhere they went. Thousands of English migrants coming into the land founded villages and towns that multiplied throughout the seventeenth century. They not only took up land but also brought animals and plants that changed the way Indians lived. The Dutch, Europe's most powerful commercial nation, established no more than a handful of trading settlements up and down the Hudson River, but they encouraged the Iroquois confederacy to push into rival Indian territories in a quest for furs to trade. Even the French, who styled themselves loyal allies to many Indian peoples and claimed to want little more than beaver pelts, brought with them profound, sometimes cataclysmic changes—changes that would upend the world that natives knew when Frenchmen were but bears on floating islands. ∞∞∞

# FRANCE IN NORTH AMERICA

**CARTIER AND CHAMPLAIN**

THE FIRST OFFICIAL EXPEDITION TO the land the French would call Canada took place in 1535, when Jacques Cartier sailed through the Gulf of St. Lawrence. But not until 1605 did the French plant a permanent colony, at Port Royal in Acadia (Nova Scotia). Three years later, Samuel de Champlain established Quebec farther up the St. Lawrence valley, where he could pursue the fur trade with less competition from rival Europeans. Champlain soon aligned himself with local Montagnais, Algonquins, and, especially, the mighty Hurons—a confederacy of farmers 20,000 strong whose towns near the Georgian Bay straddled a vast trading network.

# The Origins of New France

**FRENCH-INDIAN ALLIANCES** These allied peoples had reason to embrace Champlain. Like Europeans elsewhere in North America, the Frenchman came with wondrous goods, such as textiles, glass, copper, and ironware. In the early years of contact such things would have been treated as exotic commodities rather than utilitarian items. Copper kettles, for instance, might be cut into strips for jewelry. But before long, metal tools, especially, began transforming native life. Metal knives made it far easier to butcher animals; trees could be felled and buildings built far more easily with iron than stone axes; cooking became more efficient with brass kettles that could be placed directly on the fire; flint strike-a-lights eliminated the cumbersome need for transporting hot coals in bounded shells; beads, cloth, needles, and thread made possible a new level of creative and visual expression; and, because metal arrowheads traveled farther and truer than stone, they would make hunters and warriors more deadly than they had ever been.

Champlain found a warm welcome for all these reasons. But native peoples in North America seldom viewed exchange as a simple market transaction. All exchanges were bound up in complex social relations, and the Montagnais, Algonquins, and Hurons wanted assurance that Champlain would be a good friend as well as a good merchant. To satisfy his hosts, he agreed to accompany them on a campaign against their mutual enemies the Mohawks, one of the five confederated tribes of the Iroquois. The Frenchman proved his friendship, and his worth, in the spring of 1609 when he and his Indian companions confronted 200 Mohawk warriors in what is now upstate New York. According to Champlain, he strode to the front as the battle was about to begin, raised his musket, and shot dead two Mohawk chiefs. Few if any of the assembled warriors had ever seen a gun fired in combat. Champlain's allies let out a joyous cry, so loud "one could not have heard it thunder," attacked the astonished Mohawks, and drove the survivors from the field. It was not the last time that European newcomers would alter the balance of power in North America.

**THE FUR TRADE** Satisfied with their new ally, the Montagnais, Algonquins, and Hurons became eager trading partners over the next generation. In return for European goods, they provided tens of thousands of otter, raccoon, and especially beaver pelts. These furs went to make fashionable European hats, whereas mink and marten were sent to adorn the robes of high-ranking European officials and churchmen. Some in France derided the colonial endeavor, dismissing New France as a *comptoir,* a storehouse for the skins of dead animals. And yet Champlain wanted more. He struggled to encourage more immigration to Canada, to convince those who came to settle permanently, and, above all, to bind his native allies closer and closer to the colonial project. To that end, Champlain encouraged certain French men and boys to live with Indian families, to learn their language and become conversant in their customs.

**JESUIT MISSIONS** Along with these *coureurs de bois,* or "runners in the woods," French authorities engaged Jesuits, members of the Society of Jesus, to establish missions among the region's Indians. Just as devout but often more culturally flexible than Franciscan missionaries, Jesuit friars came to New France in the 1610s determined to master Indian languages and make inroads into native culture. They were also fired with the passions of the **Counter-Reformation** in Europe, a movement by devout Catholics to correct those abuses that had prompted the Protestant Reformation. Initially, Jesuit missionaries were tolerated more than listened to. But by the 1630s Champlain began pressing the Indians, insisting that trading partners accept resident Jesuits. More importantly, Christianized Indians got better prices for furs than did their unconverted counterparts. Such policies helped the French pursue what they saw as interlocked economic, strategic, and religious objectives. French pressure also caused friction in native communities, among the Huron in particular. Should they accept European customs and religion? Converts remained relatively few into the 1640s, and the debate over Huron cultural identity provoked internal quarrels that eventually left the confederacy fragmented and vulnerable to enemies.

## New Netherland, the Iroquois, and the Beaver Wars

 **THE DUTCH STRENGTH IN TRADE** If Canada was merely a *comptoir,* it was a profitable one. Potential revenues from the fur trade drew the attention of rival European powers, including the Dutch. By the beginning of the seventeenth century the Calvinist Dutch had finally freed their homeland from Spanish domination. Having won independence, they were equally determined to compete with Spanish merchants and to contain the spread of Spanish Catholicism. Along the Amazon River and the African coast, forts and trading posts of the Dutch West India Company protected and promoted Dutch commerce while harrying Spanish competitors.

Furthermore, by the early seventeenth century the Netherlands had the greatest manufacturing capacity in the world and had become the key economic power in Europe. Intent especially on trade, the Dutch had little desire to plant permanent colonies abroad because they enjoyed prosperity and religious freedom at home. But they did

| French women as well as men in religious orders dedicated their lives to missionary work in Canada. Marguerite Bourgeoys founded a religious community dedicated to the education of young girls.

This undated French engraving depicts something often overlooked or trivialized by European observers: native women's work. Two Iroquois women grind corn into meal while a swaddled infant rests in a backboard.

want to tap directly into the wealth flowing out of North America and therefore explored and laid claim to a number of sites around the Connecticut, Delaware, and Hudson Rivers (the last named for the Englishman Henry Hudson, who first explored it for the Dutch in 1609). Most of New Netherland's few settlers would cluster in the village of New Amsterdam on Manhattan Island at the mouth of the Hudson.

**COLLAPSE OF THE BEAVER POPULATION**

More important for the geopolitics of the continent, the Dutch West India Company also established a trading outpost 150 miles upriver known as Fort Orange (present-day Albany). Initially the traders at Fort Orange hoped to obtain cheap furs by fostering competition among rival Indian customers. But by 1630 the powerful Mohawks had displaced their competitors and come to dominate the fort's commerce. Ever since their encounter with Champlain's musket, the Mohawks and the other four members of the **Iroquois League** (the Oneidas, Onondagas, Cayugas, and Senecas) had suffered from their lack of direct access to European goods. With Mohawk ascendancy around Fort Orange, the Iroquois finally had reliable access to the tools and weapons necessary to go on the offensive against their northern enemies. They felt compelled to do so because the beaver population, always fragile, had collapsed within their own territory. To maintain their trading

position, they began preying on Huron convoys on their way to Quebec and then selling the plundered pelts to the Dutch.

**SMALLPOX EPIDEMIC**

Just as this old rivalry revived, and soon after the aging Champlain died of a stroke, two things happened to help plunge the region into catastrophe. First, waves of disease afflicted the settlements in the Northeast in the 1630s and took a nightmarish toll on nearly all the region's native peoples, especially agricultural communities in their densely populated towns. Between 1634 and 1640 smallpox killed more than 10,000 Hurons, reducing their total population by half and precipitating a spate of conversions to Christianity that divided the community all the more. The Iroquois likewise suffered greatly, but, unlike the Hurons, they reacted by waging war in an effort to obtain captives that could formally replace dead kin. The second transformative event was a dramatic expansion in the regional arms trade. Initally reluctant to deal in guns, by the late 1630s the Dutch at Fort Orange relaxed their policy in order to obtain more furs. Before long the Iroquois had many times more muskets than the Hurons, whom the French had traditionally refused to arm so long as they remained unconverted.

Reeling from disease and internal division, the Hurons saw their world collapsing. In 1648 well-armed Iroquois warriors destroyed three Huron towns. The attacks continued into the next year. At one town under siege the Jesuit Paul Ragueneau saw desperate Hurons seek baptism and Christian consolation. "Never was their faith more alive, nor their love for their good fathers and pastors more keenly felt." The Hurons made the wrenching decision to burn their remaining towns and abandon their lands for good. As many as 2,000 became Iroquois, as either war captives or humble refugees. Others merged with neighboring peoples, while thousands more fled in desperation and starved to death or died of exposure in the harsh winter of 1649–1650.

The Hurons, who became infected with smallpox in the 1630s, would have experienced fevers, aches, and vomiting before the telltale spots emerged on their skin. Agonizing pustules would have soon covered them from head to toe, as in the picture here, and sometimes the pustules merged into oozing sheets that caused large sections of the victims' skin to peel away from their bodies. This horrible disease claimed millions of lives in the Americas after 1492.

## A French Map

Information on Pawnee Indians on Great Plains suggests the scope of French exploration—or at least French interests—by the late seventeenth century.

Mapmaker included population estimates for some native groups.

"There are a number of unknown savages and villages whose names are unknown," says the mapmaker. Why don't we see similar notations elsewhere?

*Carte de Louisiane, by Jean Baptiste Louis Franquelin (1684)*

Maps are and always have been far more than simple representations of physical or political space. Maps should also be seen as arguments. Consider the choices made by the cartographer who made the map above. Through the inclusion of certain physical, demographic, and geo-political details, and through the exclusion of other information, this mapmaker sought to shape perceptions about North America. Choices about where to put boundaries, the relative size and boldness of the words used to identify different regions, the names applied to natural landmarks, and whether to even mention a given place or group all had political implications. The decisions Franquelin made along these lines would surely have been contested by mapmakers from rival empires and would likely have seemed bizarre and mostly useless to the continent's native peoples, who had their own methods for representing space through images.

### Thinking Critically

Locate New Spain, New France, and Louisiana. Which English colonies does the map indicate? Could maps be used as tools in interimperial rivalries? Would Spain have agreed with France about the boundaries around Texas? Would England have agreed with France about the boundaries of New England or Virginia? What might native peoples have thought about any of these claims?

So began the Beaver Wars, a series of conflicts at least as profoundly transformative for the colonial north as the Indian slave wars were for the south. Seeking new hunting grounds and new captives to replenish their diminishing population, Iroquois raiders attacked peoples near and far. After the Hurons, they struck and scattered the nearby Petuns, Eries, and Neutrals—peoples who, like the Hurons, were all Iroquoian speakers and could thus be integrated into Iroquois communities with relative ease. Iroquois warriors next moved against non-Iroquoian groups, including Delawares and Shawnees in the Ohio valley, and even extended their raids south to the Carolinas. To the north they attacked Algonquins in the Canadian Shield, and Abenakis and others in New England.

## The Lure of the Mississippi

The Beaver Wars continued in fits and starts for the rest of the seventeenth century, bringing dozens of Indian nations to grief and provoking a massive refugee crisis as families fled their traditional territories and tried to rebuild their lives in peace. The wars also very nearly led to the ruin of New France. About 300 Frenchmen were killed or captured in the wars, cutting the colony's meager population in half by 1666. The survivors saw Champlain's carefully managed trading system thrown into disarray. French authorities scrambled to find reliable new partners in the fur trade and henceforth were less reluctant to trade guns to Indian allies. More broadly, the scope of the conflict and the far-flung movement of refugees compelled the French to take a more expansive view of the continent and their place in it.

By the 1660s, French traders, priests, and officers were making inroads among diverse refugee villages in the Western Great Lakes, a region the French referred to as the **pays d'en haut.** These peoples sought trade, assistance against the Iroquois, and mediation of their own disputes. While the French set about building alliances in the *pays d'en haut,* they became aware of and began exploring the greatest watercourse in North America.

LA SALLE DESCENDS THE MISSISSIPPI

The Mississippi River travels nearly 2,500 miles from its source in present-day Minnesota to the Gulf of Mexico, carrying water from several other major rivers and dominating a drainage area larger than the Indian subcontinent in Asia. As the French began exploring the river in earnest in the 1670s, it dawned on them that the Mississippi valley could be the strategic key to success in North America. French officials set out courting Indian peoples along the river and its tributaries, employing their hard-won insights into native diplomatic culture along the way. The region's peoples—the Illinois, Shawnees, Quapaws, and others—expressed keen interest in French trade, as well as fear and hatred of their common Iroquois enemies. When René Robert Cavelier, Sieur de La Salle, became the first European to descend the river to the Gulf in 1682, he encountered the Natchez, Chickasaws, and others who had not seen Europeans since de Soto and his maniacal march

nearly a century and a half before. Other Frenchmen went further, erecting trading posts and simple missions, and even making contact and tentative alliances with Osages, Arkansas, Ottos, Pawnees, and others west of the great river.

By the early eighteenth century New France had helped broker an uneasy peace between the Iroquois and Indian nations to the west, extended its influence over a vast area, and fortified its colonial core along the St. Lawrence. In 1700 the colony had scores of simple missions and three modest towns—Quebec, Montreal, and Trois-Rivières—containing a population of approximately 15,000. Most immigrants to New France eventually returned to Europe, and shortsighted French monarchs insisted that Canada be a Catholic colony, off limits to France's most obvious emigrants, the Protestant Huguenots. But even with its small colonial population, New France emerged as a powerful player in North America, given its strategic and economic alliances with native peoples. The French had reason to hope that their native allies could help contain the Spanish to the west and limit English expansion from the east.

 REVIEW

What caused the Beaver Wars?

# THE FOUNDING OF NEW ENGLAND

AT FIRST THE ENGLISH REGARDED the northern part of North America as a place in which only the mad French could see possibility. English fisherfolk who strayed from Newfoundland to the coast of Acadia and New England carried home descriptions of the long, lonely coast, rockbound and rugged. Long winters of numbing cold melted into short summers of steamy heat. There were no minerals to mine, no crops suitable for export, no large native population available for enslaving. The Chesapeake, with its temperate climate and long growing season, seemed a much likelier spot.

But by 1620 worsening conditions at home had instilled in some English men and women the mixture of desperation and idealism needed to settle an uninviting, unknown world. Religious differences among English Protestants became a matter of sharper controversy during the seventeenth century. Along with the religious crisis came mounting political tensions and continuing problems of unemployment and recession. Times were bad—so bad that the anticipation of worse times to come swept English men and women to the shores of New England.

## The Puritan Movement

The colonization of New England started with a king who chose his enemies unwisely. James I, shortly after succeeding Elizabeth I in 1603, vowed to purge England of all radical Protestant reformers. The radicals James had in mind were the Puritans, most of whom were either Presbyterians or Congregationalists. Although both groups of Puritan reformers embraced Calvin's ideas, they differed on the best form of church organization. Individual **Presbyterian** churches (or congregations) were guided by higher governing bodies of ministers and laypersons. Those in the **Congregationalist** churches, in contrast, believed that each congregation should conduct its own affairs independently, answering to no other authority.

Like all Christians, Protestant and Catholic, the Puritans believed that God was all-knowing and all-powerful. And, like all Calvinists, the Puritans emphasized that idea of divine sovereignty known as **predestination.** At the center of their thinking was the belief that God had ordained the outcome of history, including the eternal fate of every human being. The Puritans found comfort in their belief in predestination because it provided their lives with meaning and purpose. They felt assured that a sovereign God was directing the fate of individuals, nations, and all of creation. The Puritans strove to play their parts in that divine drama of history and to discover in their performances some signs of personal salvation.

The divine plan, as the Puritans understood it, called for reforming both church and society along the lines laid down by John Calvin. It seemed to the Puritans that England's government hampered rather than promoted religious purity and social order. It tolerated drunkenness, theatergoing, gambling, extravagance, public swearing, and Sabbath-breaking. It permitted popular recreations rooted in pagan custom and superstition—sports such as bear baiting and maypole dancing and festivals such as the celebration of Christmas and saints' days.

**PURITAN CALLS FOR REFORM** — Even worse, the state had not done enough to purify the English church of the "corruptions" of Roman Catholicism. The Church of England counted as its members everyone in the nation, saint and sinner alike. To the Puritans, belonging to a church was no birthright. They wished to limit membership and the privileges of baptism and communion to godly men and women. The Puritans also deplored the hierarchy of bishops

and archbishops in the Church of England, as well as its elaborate ceremonies in which priests wore ornate vestments. Too many Anglican clergy were "dumb dogges" in Puritan eyes, too poorly educated to instruct churchgoers in the truths of Scripture or to deliver a decent sermon. In reformer John Foxe's vision of good and evil (below), Anglican priests on the right side of the drawing are shown in vestments and headdresses worshiping Satan before an altar. Anglican worshipers (bottom right) superstitiously count rosary beads and follow a priestly procession like so many dumb sheep. In contrast, Puritan worshipers (bottom left) conspicuously hold their Bibles and attend only to the word of God.

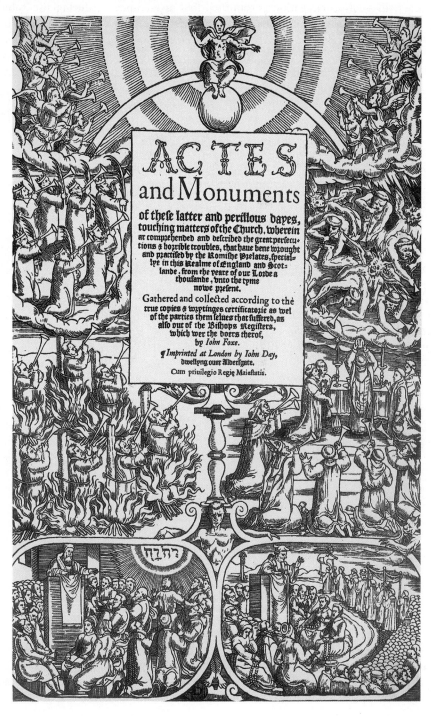

| John Foxe's Actes and Monuments *(1563), a book revered by the Puritan founders of New England,* arrayed the forces of righteousness (left side of page) *against a host of devils, priests, and their sheeplike followers within the Church of England at right. Under the Catholic Queen Mary, Protestants were regarded as heretics and some were burned at the stake* (middle left).

Because English monarchs had refused to take stronger measures to reform church and society, the Puritans became their outspoken critics. Elizabeth I had tolerated this opposition, but James I would not endure it and intended to rid England of these radicals. With some of the Puritans, known as the Separatists, he seemed to succeed.

## The Pilgrim Settlement at Plymouth Colony

The Separatists were devout Congregationalists who concluded that the Church of England was too corrupt to be reformed. They abandoned Anglican worship and met secretly in small congregations. From their first appearance in England during the 1570s, the Separatists suffered persecution from the government—fines, imprisonment, and, in a few cases, execution. Always a tiny minority within the Puritan movement, the Separatists were people from humble backgrounds: craftworkers and farmers without influence to challenge the state. By 1608 some had become so discouraged that they migrated to Holland, where the Dutch government permitted complete freedom of religion. But when their children began to adopt Dutch customs and other religions, some Separatists decided to move again, this time to Virginia.

**EARLY DIFFICULTIES** It can only be imagined what fate would have befallen the unworldly Separatists had they actually settled in the Chesapeake during the tobacco boom. But a series of mistakes—including an error in charting the course of their ship, the

## EARLY NEW ENGLAND

*Despite some variety among emigrants, New England's English settlements remained relatively homogeneous and stable. Over the years, groups of settlers "hived off" from the settlements around Massachusetts Bay, beginning new towns along the Connecticut River, southern and western Connecticut, Long Island, and East Jersey.*

*Mayflower*—brought the little band far to the North, to a region Captain John Smith had earlier dubbed "New England." In November 1620 some 88 Separatist "Pilgrims" set anchor at a place they called Plymouth on the coast of present-day southeastern Massachusetts. They were sick with scurvy, weak from malnutrition, and shaken by a shipboard mutiny, and neither the site nor the season invited settlement. As one of their leaders, William Bradford, later remembered:

> For summer being done, all things stand upon them with a weather beaten face, and the whole country, full of woods and thickets represented a savage hue. If they looked behind them, there was the mighty ocean which they had passed and was now as a main bar and gulf to separate them from all the civil parts of the world.

For some, the shock was too great. Dorothy Bradford, William's wife, is said to have fallen overboard from the *Mayflower* as it lay anchored off Plymouth. It is more likely that she jumped to her death.

Few Pilgrims could have foreseen founding the first permanent European settlement in New England, and many did not live long enough to enjoy the distinction. They had arrived too late to plant crops and had failed to bring an adequate supply of food. By the spring of 1621 half the immigrants had died. English merchants who had financed the *Mayflower* voyage failed to send supplies to the struggling settlement. Plymouth might have become another doomed colony had the Pilgrims not received better treatment from native inhabitants than they did from their English backers.

EFFECT OF EPIDEMIC DISEASE

Though they understood it only dimly, the Pilgrims were, in one historian's memorable phrase, the "beneficiaries of catastrophe." Only four years before their arrival, coastal New England had been devastated by a massive epidemic, possibly the plague. Losses varied locally, but overall the native coastal population may have been reduced by as much as 90 percent. Abandoned villages lay in ruins up and down the coast, including the village of Patuxet, where the Pilgrims established Plymouth. Years later visitors would still marvel at heaps of unburied human remains dating from the epidemic.

The Wampanoags dominated the lands around Plymouth. Still reeling from loss in 1620 and eager to obtain trade goods and assistance against native enemies, Massasoit, their chief, agreed to help the starving colonists. Initially, the peoples communicated through a remarkable Wampanoag named Squanto, who had been kidnapped by English sailors before the epidemic. Taken to Europe, Squanto learned English and eventually returned to America in time to play a crucial intermediary role between Massasoit and the newcomers. The Pilgrims accepted Wampanoag hospitality and instruction and invited native leaders to a feast in honor of their first successful harvest in 1621 (the genesis of the "First Thanksgiving" story).

THE MAYFLOWER COMPACT

The Pilgrims set up a government for their colony, the framework of which was the Mayflower Compact, drawn up on board ship before landing. That agreement provided for a governor and several assistants to advise him, all to be elected annually by Plymouth's adult males. In the eyes of English law the Plymouth settlers had no clear basis for their land claims or their government, because they had neither a royal charter nor approval from the Crown. But English authorities, distracted by problems closer to home, left the tiny colony of farmers alone.

# THE PURITAN SETTLEMENT AT MASSACHUSETTS BAY

AMONG THE CROWN'S DISTRACTIONS WERE two groups of Puritans more numerous and influential than the Pilgrims. They included both the Presbyterians and the majority of Congregationalists who, unlike the Pilgrim Separatists, still considered the Church of England capable of being reformed. But the 1620s brought these Puritans only fresh discouragements. In 1625 Charles I inherited his father's throne and all his enemies. When Parliament attempted to limit the king's power, Charles simply dissolved it, in 1629, and proceeded to rule without it. When Puritans pressed for reform, the king began to move against them.

This persecution swelled a second wave of Puritan migration that also drew from the ranks of Congregationalists. Unlike the humble Separatists, these emigrants included merchants, landed gentlemen, and lawyers who organized the Massachusetts Bay Company in 1629. Those able Puritan leaders aimed to build a better society in America, an example to the rest of the world. Unlike the Separatists, they had a strong sense of mission and destiny. They were not abandoning the English church, they insisted, but merely regrouping across the Atlantic for another assault on corruption.

Despite the company's Puritan leanings, it somehow obtained a royal charter confirming its title to most of present-day Massachusetts and New Hampshire. Advance parties in 1629 established the town of Salem on the coast well north of Plymouth. In 1630 the company's first governor, a tough-minded and visionary lawyer named John Winthrop, sailed from England with a dozen other company stockholders and a fleet of men and women to establish the town of Boston. The newcomers intended to build a godly "city on a hill" that would serve as an example to the world.

ESTABLISHING THE COLONY'S GOVERNMENT

Once established in the Bay Colony, Winthrop and the other stockholders transformed the charter for their trading company into the framework of government for a colony. The company's governor became the colony's chief executive, and the company's other officers became the governor's assistants. The charter provided for annual elections

Sudbury, Mass.
17th century

Commonly held land

Privately held lots

• Residences

0     1/4 Mile

0     1/4 Kilometer

*Everyday life in New England centered in small towns such as Sudbury, west of Boston. Families lived in houses clustered around the meetinghouse, in contrast to the decentralized plantations of the South. The privately held farm lots were mixed together as well, so that neighbors worked and lived in close contact with one another.* **How does the pattern of settlement in Sudbury differ from the pattern of settlement in the Chesapeake region?**

of the governor and his assistants by company stockholders, known as the freemen. But to create a broad base of support for the new government, Winthrop and his assistants expanded the freemanship in 1631 to include every adult male church member.

The governor, his assistants, and the freemen together made up the General Court of the colony, which passed all laws, levied taxes, established courts, and made war and peace. In 1634 the whole body of the freemen stopped meeting, and instead each town elected representatives or deputies to the General Court. Ten years later, the deputies formed themselves into the lower house of the Bay Colony legislature, and the assistants formed the upper house. By refashioning a company charter into a civil constitution, Massachusetts Bay Puritans were well on the way to shaping society, church, and state to their liking.

Contrary to expectations, New England proved more hospitable to the English than did the Chesapeake. The character of the migration itself gave New England settlers an advantage, for most arrived in family groups—not as young, single, indentured servants of the sort whose discontents unsettled Virginia society. The heads of New England's first households were typically freemen—farmers, artisans, and merchants. Most were skilled and literate. Since husbands usually migrated with their wives and children, the ratio of men to women within the population was fairly evenly balanced.

**THE "GREAT MIGRATION"** Most of the immigrants, some 21,000, came in a cluster between 1630 and 1642. Thereafter new arrivals tapered off because of the outbreak of the English Civil War. This relatively rapid colonization fostered solidarity because immigrants shared a common past of persecution and a strong desire to create an ordered society modeled on Scripture.

 **REVIEW**

Who settled the earliest New England colonies?

# STABILITY AND ORDER IN EARLY NEW ENGLAND

**LONG-LIVED NEW ENGLANDERS** PURITAN EMIGRANTS AND THEIR descendants thrived in New England's bracing but healthy climate. The first generation of colonists lived to an average age of 70, nearly twice as long as Virginians and 10 years longer than men and women living in England. With 90 percent of all children reaching adulthood, the typical family consisted of seven or eight children who came to maturity. Because of low death rates and high birthrates, the number of New Englanders doubled about every 27 years—while the populations of Europe and the Chesapeake barely reproduced

*Susan Gill, an English maidservant from the 1670s.*

themselves. By 1700 New England and the Chesapeake would both have populations of approximately 100,000. But, whereas the southern population grew because of continuing immigration and the importation of slaves, New England's expanded primarily through natural increase.

As immigrants arrived in the Bay Colony after 1630, they carved out an arc of villages around Massachusetts Bay. Within a decade settlers pressed into Connecticut, Rhode Island, and New Hampshire. Connecticut and Rhode Island received separate charters from Charles II in the 1660s, guaranteeing their residents the rights to land and government. New Hampshire, to which Massachusetts laid claim in the 1640s, did not become a separate colony until 1679. The handful of hardy souls settled along the coast of present-day Maine had also accepted the Massachusetts Bay Colony's authority.

| The Old Ship Meetinghouse, built in Hingham, Massachusetts in 1681, expresses the importance of hierarchy among New England Puritans. Wealthy families enjoyed the enclosed wooden pews on the ground floor, whereas poorer folk sat on benches in the second-floor gallery. The raised pulpit (front) bespeaks the congregation's respect for the authority and learning of the clergy. The American flag, of course, is a modern addition.

**PATTERNS OF SETTLEMENT**

Early New Englanders established most of their settlements with an eye to stability and order. Unlike the Virginians, who scattered across the Chesapeake to isolated plantations, most New Englanders established tightly knit communities like those they had left behind in England. Each family received a lot for a house along with about 150 acres of land in nearby fields. Farmers left many of their acres uncultivated as a legacy for future generations, for most had only the labor of their own families to work their land. While the Chesapeake abounded with servants, tenant farmers, and slaves, almost every adult male in rural New England owned property. With little hope of prospering through commercial agriculture, New England farmers also had no incentive to import large numbers of servants and slaves or to create large plantations.

Strong family institutions contributed to New England's order and stability. Although the early deaths of parents regularly splintered Chesapeake families, two adult generations were often on hand to encourage order within New England households. Husbands and fathers exacted submission from wives and strict obedience from children. Land gave New England's long-lived fathers great authority over even their grown children; sons and daughters relied on paternal legacies of farms in order to marry and establish their own families.

**CHURCH MEMBERSHIP**

Whereas churches were few and far between in seventeenth-century Virginia, they constituted the center of community life in colonial New England. Individual congregations ran their own affairs and regulated their own membership. Those wishing to join had to convince ministers and church members that they had experienced a genuine spiritual rebirth or "conversion." Most New Englanders sought and won membership. As majority institutions supported by public taxes, churches had the reach and the resources to oversee public morality, often censuring or expelling wayward neighbors. Still, ministers enjoyed less public power in New England than in the old country. New England's ministers did not serve as officers in the civil government, and the Congregational churches owned no property. In contrast, Catholic and Anglican church officials wielded real temporal power in European states, and the churches held extensive tracts of land.

Finally, New Englanders governed themselves more democratically than did their counterparts in England.

**HIERARCHY OF LEADERSHIP**

Communities throughout the region held regular town meetings of all resident white men. The town fathers generally set the meeting's agenda and offered advice, but the unanimous consent of townsmen determined all decisions. Colony governments in early New England also evolved into representative and responsive institutions. Typically the central government of each colony, such as the General Court of Massachusetts Bay, consisted of a governor and a bicameral legislature, including an upper house, or council, and a lower house, or assembly. All officials were elected annually by the freemen—white adult men entitled to vote in colony elections. Voting qualifications varied, but the number of men enfranchised made up a much broader segment of society than that in seventeenth-century England.

## Communities in Conflict

Although most New Englanders called themselves Puritans and Congregationalists, the very fervency of their convictions often led them to disagree about how best to carry out the teachings of the Bible and the ideas of John Calvin. During the first decades of colonization, such disagreements led to the founding of breakaway colonies. In 1636 Thomas Hooker, the minister of Cambridge, Massachusetts, led part of his congregation to Connecticut, where they established the first English settlement. Somewhat more liberal than other Bay Puritans, Hooker favored more lenient standards

# DAILY LIVES

## A WORLD OF WONDERS AND WITCHCRAFT

In 1684 the Reverend Increase Mather, a learned Boston minister, proudly issued a plump book titled *Remarkable Providence*. The work was packed with fantastic occurrences that had taken place during the first 50 years of New England's settlement. Those occurrences dealt with "wonders"—interventions of the supernatural in the normal order of things. Ministers throughout New England contributed marvels of all sorts: a "Conjuring Book" from Salem, which filled readers with "a strange kind of Horror" and caused their hair to stand on end; a house in Newbury inhabited by evil spirits and a "monstrous birth"; a phantom ship sighted sailing into New Haven harbor that suddenly disappeared.

Mather's book of wonders became one of many available to New England readers—a numerous group, for literacy was almost universal. Accounts of marvelous events poured from presses in England, the Continent, and the colonies. The authors drew their reports of visions and voices, untimely deaths and natural disasters from ancient and early Christian authors, medieval chronicles, the Bible, and local lore collected by contemporaries.

Most seventeenth-century New Englanders preferred to read religious books: the Bible, psalmbooks, sermons. Even so, authors such as Increase Mather recognized that a wider audience might be reached by volumes blending godly messages with sensational topics. Ministers recounted wonders to make the religious argument that the world was shot through with mystery and miracle and that men and women were at the mercy of God's will and the devil's wiles. At the same time, these books titillated readers with accounts of witches, apparitions, and freaks of nature. Published narratives of New Englanders taken captive by the Indians and the confessions of convicted murderers combined the same mixture of religion and sensationalism.

Knowing what early New Englanders liked to read offers a glimpse not only of their entertainments but of their inner world as well. Especially significant was their enduring fascination with wonders, which were believed to be true both by learned folks and by humble farmers and

their wives. The popularity of wonder lore is powerful proof that all New Englanders inhabited an enchanted universe. Their world brimmed with invisible forces and supernatural beings that could interrupt the order of nature.

That widely shared belief made witchcraft a crime punishable by death and allowed for the unfolding of the notorious witchcraft trials in Salem Village. There, in the early months of 1692, a group of adolescent girls used the white of a raw egg suspended in a glass of water as a kind of crude crystal ball to divine what sorts of men their future husbands might be. Somehow, the seance went sour, and the frightened adolescents began behaving in ways that other villagers took to be signs of bewitchment. Crying out in pain and terror, the afflicted girls claimed to see taunting specters of witches, whom they recognized as fellow villagers. In the hysteria that ensued, hundreds of accusations of witchcraft led to the trial and execution

*Witchcraft trials and executions took place throughout Europe in the sixteenth and seventeenth centuries, occurring far more frequently and claiming many more victims than in colonial America. But, as this engraving of an English hanging of witches indicates, women composed a majority of those charged and executed on both sides of the Atlantic.*

of 20 innocent women and men. Only when Increase Mather and 14 other Massachusetts ministers publicly warned against the trials' excesses did the killings stop.

Many historians have tried to explain the deeper causes behind the Salem episode. Some point to the Puritan mistrust of independent women, others to the bitter rivalries among Salem Village families. Still others have noted ties between accused witches and heretical groups such as the Quakers, or deep communal traumas stemming from conflicts with Indians and the French. Whatever the source of Salem's particular troubles, the witchcraft charges there and elsewhere in seventeenth-century New England were rooted in the widespread belief in a world of wonders, at once terrible and fascinating. Witchcraft trials and executions took place throughout Europe in the sixteenth and seventeenth centuries, occurring far more frequently and claiming many more victims than in colonial America. But, as this engraving (left) of an English hanging of witches indicates, women composed a majority of those charged and executed on both sides of the Atlantic.

The one arena in which women could attain something approaching equal standing with men was the churches. Puritan women could not become ministers, but after the 1660s they made up the majority of church members. In some churches membership enabled them to vote for ministerial candidates and to voice opinions about admitting and disciplining members. Puritan doctrine itself rejected the medieval Catholic suspicion of women as "a necessary evil," seeing them instead as "a necessary good." Even so, the Puritan ideal of the virtuous woman was a chaste, submissive "helpmeet," a wife and mother who served God by serving men.

### Thinking Critically

*What might account for the disproportionate number of women charged with witchcraft?*

for church membership. He also opposed the Bay's policy of limiting voting in colony elections to church members. In contrast, New Haven (a separate colony until it became part of Connecticut in 1662) was begun in 1638 by strict Congregationalists who found Massachusetts too liberal.

**ROGER WILLIAMS** While Connecticut and New Haven emerged from voluntary migration, enforced exile filled Rhode Island with men and women whose radical ideas unsettled the rest of Massachusetts. Roger Williams, Rhode Island's founder, had come to New England in 1631, serving as a respected minister of Salem. But soon Williams announced that he was a Separatist, like the Pilgrims of Plymouth. He encouraged the Bay Colony to break all ties to the corrupt Church of England. He also urged a more complete **separation of church and state** than most New Englanders were prepared to accept, and later in his career he endorsed full religious toleration. Finally, Williams denounced the Bay's charter—the legal document that justified Massachusetts's existence—on the grounds that the king had no right to grant land that he had not purchased from the Indians. When Williams boldly suggested that Massachusetts actually inform the king of his mistake, angry authorities prepared to deport him. Instead, Williams fled the colony in the dead of winter to live with the Indians. In 1636 he became the founder and first citizen of Providence, later to be part of Rhode Island.

**ANNE HUTCHINSON** Another charismatic heretic from Massachusetts arrived soon after. Anne Hutchinson, a skilled midwife and the spouse of a wealthy merchant, came to Boston in 1634. Enthusiasm for her minister, John Cotton, started her on a course of explaining his sermons to gatherings of her neighbors—and then to elaborating ideas of her own. The fact that a woman would do such things made the authorities uneasy; but they became alarmed when they learned that Hutchinson embraced controversial positions on doctrine. Soon a majority of the Bay's ministers accused the troublesomely popular Hutchinson of holding heretical views. She in turn denounced her detractors, and the controversy escalated. In 1638 the Bay Colony government expelled Hutchinson and her followers for sedition. She settled briefly in Rhode Island before moving on to Long Island, where she died in an Indian attack.

## Goodwives and Witches

If Anne Hutchinson had been a man, her ideas would still have been deemed heretical. However, if she had been a man, she might have found other ways to express her intelligence and magnetism. But life in colonial New England offered women, especially married women, little scope for their talents.

Most adult women were hardworking farm wives who cared for large households of children. Between marriage and middle age, most New England wives were pregnant except when breast-feeding. When they were not nursing or minding children, mothers were producing and preparing much of what was consumed and worn by their families. They planted vegetable gardens and pruned fruit trees, salted beef and pork and pressed cider, milked cows and churned butter, kept bees and tended poultry, cooked and baked, washed and ironed, spun, wove, and sewed. While husbands and sons engaged in farmwork that changed with the seasons, took trips to taverns and mills, and went off to hunt or fish, housebound wives and daughters were locked into a humdrum routine with little time for themselves.

**WITCHCRAFT** Communities sometimes responded to assertive women with accusations of witchcraft. Like most early modern Europeans, New Englanders believed in wizards and witches, men and women who

The artist who sketched this Quaker meeting called attention to one of that sect's most controversial practices by placing a woman at the center of his composition. Women were allowed to speak in Quaker worship services and to preach and proselytize at public gatherings of non-Quakers. The Puritans roundly condemned this liberty as contrary to the teachings of St. Paul.

## ACCUSATIONS AND DEFENSES IN THE SALEM WITCHCRAFT TRIALS

*The Salem witchcraft trials of 1692 set neighbor against neighbor and resulted in the execution of 20 women and men. One of the accused was tavern owner John Proctor, on whom Arthur Miller loosely based the main protagonist in his famous play* The Crucible. *The documents below include testimony of three witnesses against Proctor and his own remarkable response.*

### DOCUMENT 1  The Accusations

**Sarah Bibber**

The Deposition of Sarah Bibber agged about 36 years who testifieth and saith that on the 3 june 1692. Jno: proctor. sen'r came to me and did most greviously torment me by pinching pricking and almost presing me to death urging me to drink: drink as Red as blood which I refusing he did tortor me with variety of tortors and immediatly he vanished away also on the same day I saw Jno: proctor most greviously tortor Susannah Shelden by claping his hands on hir throat and almost choaking hir. also severall times sence Jno: proctor sen'r has most greviously tortored me a grat many times with a variety of tortors

Sara vibber ownid this har testimony to be the truth on har oath before the Juriars of Inqwest this: 30. of June 1692.
      Jurat in Curia
      (Reverse) Sarah Bibber

**Ann Putnam**

The Deposistion of Ann putnam Jun'r who testifieth and saith I have often seen the Apperishtion of Jno procktor senr. amongst the wicthes but he did not doe me much hurt tell a little before his examination which was on the 11th of April 1692 and then he sett upon me most greviously and did tortor me most dreadfully also in the time of his examination he afflected

me very much: and severall times sence the Apperishtion of John procktor senr, has most greviously tortored me by pinching and allmost choaking me urging me vehemently to writ in his book also on the day of his examination I saw the Apperishtion of Jno: proctor senr goe and afflect and most greviously tortor the bodys of Mistris pope mary walcott Mircy lewes. Abigail williams and Jno: Indian. and he and his wife and Sarah Cloys keept Elizabeth Hubburd speachless all the time of their examination

*(mark) Ann Putnam*

---

were said to acquire supernatural powers by signing a compact with Satan. A total of 344 New Englanders were charged with witchcraft during the first colonial century, with the Salem Village episode of 1692 producing the largest outpouring of accusations and 20 executions. More than three-quarters of all accused witches were women, usually middle-aged and older, and most of those accused were regarded as unduly independent. Before they were charged with witchcraft, many had been suspected of heretical religious beliefs, others of sexual impropriety. Still others had inherited or stood to inherit property.

## The People in the Way

SIMILARITIES BETWEEN PURITANS AND INDIANS

Whatever their political battles, doctrinal disputes, and inequalities, New Englanders were all participants in a colonial project that depended on taking land from other people. Perhaps 100,000 Algonquin men and women lived in the area reaching from the Kennebec River in Maine to Cape Cod at contact. Like the Puritans, they relied on fishing in spring and summer, hunting year-round,

and cultivating and harvesting corn and other crops in spring and fall. And, to an even greater degree than among the colonists, Indian political authority was local. Within each village, a single leader known as the "sachem" or "sagamore" directed economic life, administered justice, and negotiated with other tribes and English settlers. As with New England's town fathers, a sachem's power was contingent on keeping the trust and consent of his people.

Thus the newcomers had more in common with their hosts than they cared to admit. But English expansion in the region had to come at someone's expense, and colonists obtained Indian lands in one of three ways. Sometimes they purchased it. Sales varied—they might be free and fair, fraudulent, subtly coerced, or forced through intimidation and violence. Second, colonists eagerly expanded into lands emptied by epidemics. The English often saw God's hand in such events. Following a terrible smallpox epidemic in 1633–1634, for example, one observer exclaimed that "without this remarkable and terrible stroke of God upon the natives, [we] would with much more difficulty have found room, and at far greater charge have obtained and purchased land."

Ann Putman owned what is above written upon oath before and unto the Grand inquest on the 30'th Day of June 1692

(Reverse) Ann puttnam ag't John procter

**Mary Warren**

The deposition of mary warrin aged 20 y'rs ho testifieth I have seen the apparition of

John procter sen'r among the wiches and he hath often tortored me by penching me and biting me and Choakeing me and pressing me one my Stomack tell the blood came out of my mouth and all so I saw him tortor Mes poap and marcey lues and John Indian a pon the day of his examination and he hath allso temted me to right in his book

and to eat bread which he brought to me which I Refuseing to doe: Jno proctor did most greviously tortor me with variety of torturs all most Redy to kill me.

Mary Warren owned the above written upon her oath before & unto the Grand inquest on the 30'th Day of June 1692

DOCUMENT 2  **The Defense**

SALEM-PRISON, July 23, 1692. *Mr. Mather, Mr. Allen, Mr. Moody, Mr. Willard, and Mr. Bailey.*
*Reverend Gentlemen.*

The innocency of our Case with the Enmity of our Accusers and our Judges, and Jury, whom nothing but our Innocent Blood will serve their turn, having Condemned us already before our Tryals, being so much incensed and engaged against us by the Devil, makes us bold to Beg and Implore your Favourable Assistance of this our Humble Petition to his Excellency, That if it be possible our Innocent Blood may be spared, which undoubtedly otherwise will be shed, if the Lord doth not mercifully step in. The Magistrates, Ministers, Jewries, and all the People in general, being so much inraged and incensed against us by the Delusion of the Devil, which we can term no other, by reason we know in our own Consciences, we are all Innocent Persons. Here are five Persons who have lately confessed themselves to be Witches, and do accuse some of us, of being along with them at a Sacrament, since we

were committed into close Prison, which we know to be Lies. Two of the 5 are (Carriers Sons) Youngmen, who would not confess any thing till they tyed them Neck and Heels till the Blood was ready to come out of their Noses, and 'tis credibly believed and reported this was the occasion of making them confess that they never did, by reason they said one had been a Witch a Month, and another five Weeks, and that their Mother had made them so, who has been confined here this nine Weeks. My son William Procter, when he was examin'd, because he would not confess that he was Guilty, when he was Innocent, they tyed him Neck and Heels till the Blood gushed out at his Nose, and would have kept him so 24 Hours, if one more Merciful than the rest, had not taken pity on him, and caused him to be unbound. These actions are very like the Popish Cruelties. They have already undone us in our Estates, and that will not serve their turns, without our Innocent Bloods. If it cannot be granted that we can have our Trials at Boston, we humbly beg that you would endeavour to

have these Magistrates changed, and others in their rooms, begging also and beseeching you would be pleased to be here, if not all, some of you at our Trials, hoping thereby you may be the means of saving the sheeding our Innocent Bloods, desiring your Prayers to the Lord in our behalf, we rest your Poor Afflicted Servants,

*JOHN PROCTER, etc.*

*Source:* http://etext.virginia.edu/etcbin/salembrowse?id=684 (Click through to "next page" to see all the relevant documents.)

> ### Thinking Critically
>
> What patterns do you see in the accusations? What does the language in all four pieces tell you about how members of this community conceived of Satan? How does Proctor try to defend himself? What do you think he was trying to accomplish by comparing the interrogations his son and others faced to "Popish Cruelties"?

---

Third and finally, colonists commonly encouraged and participated in regional wars to obtain native lands. This proved easy enough to do, because, like Europeans, the Indians of New England quarreled frequently with neighboring nations. The antagonism among the English, Spanish, Dutch, and French was matched by the hostilities among the Abenakis, Pawtuckets, Massachusetts, Narragansetts, and Wampanoags of the north Atlantic coast. Epidemics often intensified existing rivalries. Affecting some villages and nations more than others, outbreaks of Old World disease opened up new opportunities for stronger neighbors to press the advantage. New England settlers, like those in the Chesapeake, studied Indian feuds to better exploit them.

The English began by aligning with Massasoit and his Wampanoags against other coastal peoples in New England. In 1637 colonial forces joined the Narragansetts in a campaign against the formidable Pequots, who controlled coveted territory in present-day Connecticut. The colonists shocked even their Indian allies when they set fire to the main Pequot village, killing hundreds of men, women, and children. Plymouth's William Bradford recalled that "it was

a fearful sight to see them thus frying in the fire, and the streams of blood quenching the same, and horrible was the stink and scent thereof; but the victory seemed a sweet sacrifice, and they gave the praise thereof to God, who had wrought so wonderfully for them." Several years later the colonists turned against their former allies, joining forces with the Mohegans to intimidate the Narragansetts into ceding much of their territory. Only a few colonists objected to those ruthless policies, among them Roger Williams. "God Land," he warned one Connecticut leader, "will be (as it now is) as great a God with us English as God Gold was with the Spainards."

 **REVIEW**

What were the sources of stability and conflict in early New England?

## Metacom's War

Throughout these wars, the colonists more or less nurtured their original alliance with Massasoit and his Wampanoags. As long as regional enemies bore the brunt of English expansion, Massasoit and his people could live in relative safety. Indeed, certain colonists tried to bring the two societies closer together. While the impulse to convert was not nearly as strong in New England as in New Spain or New France, a few Englishmen worked tirelessly to bring the word of their God to Indians.

MISSIONS TO THE INDIANS

Most famously, Puritan minister John Eliot began preaching in Algonquian in the 1640s. Over the next two decades he oversaw a project to publish the scriptures in Algonquian using the Latin alphabet. He also trained scores of native ministers (many of whom became literate) and established seven villages or "praying towns" exclusively for Christian Indians. Eliot was not alone. According to its charter of 1650, for example, Harvard College defined its mission as "the education of English & Indian youth of this Country in knowledge and godliness." In 1655 Harvard established an Indian college and dormitory on campus specifically to instruct Wampanoag youth in the English language and in Protestantism. None of these efforts embodied respect for Indian culture or religion. But some in New England, at least, wanted to assimilate Indians rather than drive them away.

And yet the colony always grasped for more land. By the time Massasoit died and was succeeded by his son in the 1660s, the partnership had become a relationship of subordination and suspicion. Colonial authorities reacted to rumors of pending native rebellion with humiliating interrogations and increasingly severe rules and restrictions. The colonists' cows and pigs invaded and destroyed Indian fields, provoking innumerable conflicts as white pressures on Indian lands increased. When Indians tried to adapt by raising their own cows and pigs, colonial authorities barred them from using common pasture or selling meat in Boston. At the same time, as many as half the dwindling Wampanoags had followed Eliot into the praying towns, threatening tribal unity in a time of mounting crisis.

By 1675 these and other pressures convinced Massasoit's son, Metacom, whom the English called King Philip, that his nation could be preserved only by chancing war. Complaining that the English were plotting to kill him and other sachems and replace them with Christian Indians more willing to sell land, Metacom rallied most of southern New England's native peoples and laid waste to Plymouth Colony. Metacom's forces destroyed more than two dozen colonial towns. By the spring of 1676 they were closing in on the coast, raiding settlements within 20 miles of Boston.

But the momentum could not be sustained. Faced with shortages of food and ammunition, Metacom called for assistance from the Abenakis of Maine and the Mahicans of

*Though no images of Metacom survive from his time, in later years artists frequently portrayed him. This image is based on an engraving by Paul Revere.*

New York. Both refused his plea, and the English even recruited the powerful Mohawks to their cause. In the summer of 1676 Metacom met his death in battle; colonial forces dismembered his body and brought his severed head to Boston and his hands to Plymouth as trophies. The Indian offensive collapsed but not before threatening New England's very existence. In proportion to population, "King Philip's War" inflicted twice the casualties on New England that the United States as a whole would suffer in the American Civil War. And Metacom's desperate gamble exhausted native military power in southern New England, virtually destroyed the Wampanoags as a coherent people, and consigned the region's surviving Indians, Christian or not, to quiet and often desperate lives on the margins of colonial life.

# THE MID-ATLANTIC COLONIES

THE INHABITANTS OF THE MID-ATLANTIC colonies—New York, New Jersey, Pennsylvania, and Delaware—enjoyed more secure lives than most southern colonials. But they lacked the common bonds that lent stability to early New England. Instead, throughout the mid-Atlantic region a variety of ethnic and religious groups vied for wealth from farming and the fur trade and contended bitterly against governments that commanded little popular support.

## English Rule in New York

By the 1660s the Dutch experiment on the mid-Atlantic coast was faltering. While Fort Orange continued to secure furs for the Dutch West India company, the colonial population remained small and fractious. The company made matters worse by appointing corrupt, dictatorial governors who ruled without an elective assembly. It also provided little protection for outlying Dutch settlements; when it did attack neighboring Indian nations, it did so savagely, triggering terrible retaliations. By the time the company went bankrupt in 1654, it had virtually abandoned its American colony.

Taking advantage of the disarray in New Netherland, Charles II ignored Dutch claims in North America and granted his brother, James, the Duke of York, a proprietary charter there. The charter granted James all of New Netherland to Delaware Bay as well as Maine, Martha's Vineyard, and Nantucket Island. In 1664 James sent an

New Amsterdam (later New York City) in about 1626. Despite having this outpost in New Netherland, the Dutch had far more interest in vying with the Portuguese for control of commerce with the Far East than in competing with the English for the fur trade in North America.

invading fleet, whose mere arrival caused the Dutch to surrender.

**ETHNIC AND RELIGIOUS DIVERSITY**

New York's dizzying diversity would make it difficult to govern. The Duke inherited 9,000 or so colonists: Dutch, Belgians, French, English, Portuguese, Swedes, Finns, and Africans—some enslaved, others free. The colony's ethnic diversity ensured a variety of religions. Although the Dutch Reformed church predominated, other early New Netherlanders included Lutherans, Quakers, and Catholics. There were Jews as well, refugees from Portuguese Brazil, who were required by law to live in a ghetto in New Amsterdam. The Dutch resented English rule, and only after a generation of intermarriage and acculturation did that resentment fade. James also failed to win friends among New Englanders who had come to Long Island seeking autonomy and cheap land during the 1640s. He grudgingly gave in to their demand for an elective assembly in 1683 but rejected its first act, the Charter of Liberties, which would have guaranteed basic political rights. The chronic political strife discouraged prospective settlers. By 1698 the colony numbered only 18,000 inhabitants, and New York City, the former New Amsterdam, was an overgrown village of a few thousand.

## The Founding of New Jersey

Confusion attended New Jersey's beginnings. The lands lying west of the Hudson and east of the Delaware River had been part of the Duke of York's proprietary grant. But in 1664 he gave about 5 million of these acres to Lord Berkeley and Sir George Carteret, two of his favorites who were already involved in the proprietary colonies of the Carolinas. New Jersey's new owners guaranteed settlers land, religious freedom, and a representative assembly in exchange for a small quitrent, an annual fee for the use of the land. The proprietors' terms promptly drew Puritan settlers from New Haven, Connecticut. At the same time, unaware that James had already given New Jersey to Berkeley and Carteret, New York's Governor Richard Nicolls granted Long Island Puritans land there.

More complications ensued when Berkeley and Carteret decided to divide New Jersey into east and west and sell both halves to **Quaker** investors—a prospect that outraged New Jersey's Puritans. Although some English Quakers migrated to West Jersey, the investors quickly decided that two Jerseys were less desirable than one Pennsylvania and resold both East and West Jersey to speculators. In the end the Jerseys became a patchwork of religious and ethnic groups. Settlers who shared a common religion or national origin formed communities and established small family farms. When the Crown finally reunited East and West as a single royal colony in 1702, New Jersey was overshadowed by settlements not only to the north but now, also, to the south and west.

## Quaker Odysseys

Religious and political idealism similar to that of the Puritans inspired the colonization of Pennsylvania, making it an oddity among the mid-Atlantic colonies. The oddity began with an improbable founder, William Penn. Young Penn devoted his early years to disappointing his distinguished father, Sir William Penn, an admiral in the Royal Navy.

Several years after being expelled from college, young Penn finally chose a career that may have made the admiral yearn for mere disappointment: he undertook a lifelong commitment to put into practice Quaker teachings. By the 1670s he had emerged as an acknowledged leader of the Society of Friends, as the Quakers formally called themselves.

**QUAKER BELIEFS** The Quakers behaved in ways and believed in ideas that most people regarded as odd. They dressed in a deliberately plain and severe manner. They withheld from their social superiors the customary marks of respect, such as bowing, kneeling, and removing their hats. They refused to swear oaths or to make war. They allowed women public roles of religious leadership. That pattern of behavior reflected their egalitarian ideals, the belief that all men and women shared equally in the "Light Within." Some 40,000 English merchants, artisans, and farmers embraced Quakerism by 1660, and many suffered fines, imprisonment, and corporal punishment.

**PENNSYLVANIA ESTABLISHED** Since the English upper class has always prized eccentricity among its members, it is not surprising that Penn, despite his Quakerism, remained a favorite of Charles II. More surprising is that the king's favor took the extravagant form of presenting Penn in 1681 with all the land between New Jersey and Maryland. Perhaps the king was repaying Penn for the large sum that his father had lent the Stuarts. Or perhaps the king was hoping to export England's Quakers to an American colony governed by his trusted personal friend.

Penn envisioned that his proprietary colony would provide a refuge for Quakers while producing quitrents for himself. To publicize his colony, he distributed pamphlets praising its attractions throughout the British Isles and Europe. The response was overwhelming: by 1700 its population stood at 21,000. The only early migration of equal magnitude was the Puritan colonization of New England.

## Patterns of Growth

Perhaps half of Pennsylvania's settlers arrived as indentured servants; the families of free farmers and artisans made up the rest. The majority were Quakers from Britain, Holland, and Germany, but the colonists also included Catholics, Lutherans, Baptists, Anglicans, and Presbyterians. In 1682, when Penn purchased and annexed the Three Lower Counties (later the colony of Delaware), his colony included the 1,000 or so Dutch, Swedes, and Finns living there.

Quakers from other colonies—West Jersey, Maryland, and New England—also flocked to the new homeland. Those experienced settlers brought skills and connections that contributed to Pennsylvania's rapid economic growth. Farmers sowed their rich lands into a sea of wheat, which merchants exported to the Caribbean. The center of the colony's trade was Philadelphia, a superb natural harbor situated at the confluence of the Delaware and Schuylkill Rivers.

In contrast to New England's landscape of villages, the Pennsylvania countryside beyond Philadelphia was dotted with dispersed farmsteads. Commercial agriculture required larger farms, which kept settlers at greater distances from one another. As a result, the county rather than the town became the basic unit of local government in Pennsylvania.

**QUAKERS AND INDIANS** Another reason that farmers did not need to cluster their homes within a central village was that they were at peace with the coastal Indians, the Lenni Lenapes (also called Delawares by the English). Thanks to two Quaker beliefs—their commitment to pacifism and their conviction that the Indians rightfully owned their land—peace prevailed between native inhabitants and newcomers. Before Penn sold any land to colonists, he purchased it from the Indians. He also prohibited the sale of alcohol to the tribe, strictly regulated the fur trade, and learned the language of the Lenni Lenapes. "Not a language spoken in Europe," he remarked, "hath words of more sweetness in Accent and Emphasis than theirs."

"Our Wildernesse flourishes as a Garden," Penn declared late in 1683, and in fact, his colony lived up to its promises. New arrivals readily acquired good land on liberal terms, while Penn's Frame of Government instituted a representative assembly and guaranteed all inhabitants the basic English civil liberties and complete freedom of worship.

## Quakers and Politics

Even so, Penn's colony suffered constant political strife. Rich investors whom he had rewarded with large tracts of land and trade monopolies dominated the council, which held the sole power to initiate legislation. That power and Penn's own claims as proprietor set the stage for controversy. Members of the representative assembly battled for the right to initiate legislation. Farmers opposed Penn's efforts to collect quitrents. The Three Lower Counties agitated for separation, their inhabitants feeling no loyalty to Penn or Quakerism.

**PENN'S COMPROMISES** Penn finally bought peace at the price of approving a complete revision of his original Frame of Government. In 1701 the Charter of Privileges, Pennsylvania's new constitution, stripped the council of its legislative power, leaving it only the role of advising the governor. The charter also limited Penn's privileges as proprietor to the ownership of ungranted land and the power to veto legislation. Thereafter an elective unicameral assembly, the only single-house legislature in the colonies, dominated Pennsylvania's government.

As Pennsylvania prospered, Philadelphia became the commercial and cultural center of England's North American empire. Gradually the interior of Pennsylvania filled with immigrants—mainly Germans and Scots-Irish—who harbored no "odd" ideas about Indian rights, and the Lenni Lenapes and other native peoples were bullied into moving farther west. As for William Penn, he returned to England and spent time in a debtors' prison after being defrauded by his unscrupulous colonial agents. He died in 1718, an ocean away from his American utopia.

## REVIEW
In what ways were the mid-Atlantic colonies more diverse than the other colonies of the period?

# ADJUSTMENT TO EMPIRE

WHATEVER HIS PERSONAL DISAPPOINTMENTS, PENN'S colony had enjoyed spectacular growth—as indeed had British North America more generally. And yet by the 1680s England's king had reason to complain. Although North America now abounded in places named in honor of English monarchs, the colonies themselves lacked any strong ties to the English state. Until Parliament passed the first Navigation Acts in 1660, England had not even set in place a coherent policy for regulating colonial trade. And the acts had not produced the desired sense of patriotism in the colonies. While Chesapeake planters grumbled over the customs duties levied on tobacco, New Englanders, the worst of the lot, ignored the Navigation Acts altogether and traded openly with the Dutch. Royally appointed proprietors increasingly met defiance in New York, New Jersey, the Carolinas, and Pennsylvania. If England were to prosper from colonies as Spain's monarchs had, the Crown needed to take matters in hand.

## The Dominion of New England

And the Crown did so in 1686. At the urging of the new King James II (formerly the Duke of York), the Lords of Trade consolidated the colonies of Connecticut, Plymouth, Massachusetts Bay, Rhode Island, and New Hampshire into a single entity to be ruled by a royal governor and a royally appointed council. By 1688 James had added New York and New Jersey to that domain, now called the Dominion of New England. Showing the typical Stuart distaste for representative government, James also abolished all northern colonial assemblies. The king's aim to centralize authority over such a large territory made the Dominion not only a

| The tidy, productive farmsteads of the Pennsylvania countryside were the basis of that colony's prosperity during the eighteenth century. Their produce fueled the growth of Philadelphia and sustained the expansion of sugar plantations on England's Caribbean islands.

royal dream but also a radical experiment in English colonial administration.

The experiment proved to be short-lived. In England James II had revealed himself to be yet another Stuart who tried to dispense with Parliament and who had embraced Catholicism besides. Parliament dispensed with the king just as it had with Charles I during the English Civil War of the 1640s. In a quick, bloodless coup d'état known as the Glorious Revolution, Parliament forced James into exile in 1688. In his place it elevated to the throne his daughter, Mary, and her Dutch husband, William of Orange. Mary was a distinctly better sort of Stuart—a staunch Protestant—and she agreed to rule with Parliament.

**THE GLORIOUS REVOLUTION** William and Mary officially dismembered the Dominion of New England and reinstated representative assemblies everywhere in the northern colonies. Connecticut and Rhode Island were restored their old charters, but Massachusetts received a new charter in 1691. Under its terms Massachusetts, Plymouth, and present-day Maine were combined into a single royal colony headed by a governor appointed by the Crown rather than elected by the people. The charter also imposed religious toleration and made property ownership rather than church membership the basis of voting rights.

England, in an effort to regulate colonial trade, required all ships bound from America to pass through British ports and pay customs duties. Places such as Plymouth, Liverpool, and Bristol (shown here) thrived as a result. Contrast this large, bustling commercial center with the modest size of Plymouth 200 years earlier (illustration, page 28).

## Royal Authority in America in 1700

**CLOSER REGULATION OF TRADE** William and Mary were more politic than James II but no less interested in revenue. In 1696 Parliament enlarged the number of customs officials stationed in each colony to enforce the Navigation Acts. To help prosecute smugglers, Parliament established colonial vice-admiralty courts, tribunals without juries presided over by royally appointed justices. To keep current on all colonial matters, the king appointed a new Board of Trade to replace the old Lords of Trade. The new enforcement procedures generally succeeded in discouraging smuggling and channeling colonial trade through England.

These changes were enough for England and its monarchs for half a century thereafter. English kings and queens gave up any dreams of imposing the kind of centralized administration of colonial life represented by the Dominion of New England. Clearly, royal control had increased over the previous half century. By 1700 royal governments had been established in Virginia, New York, Massachusetts, and New Hampshire. New Jersey, the Carolinas, and Georgia would shortly be added to the list. Royal rule meant that the monarch appointed governors and (everywhere except Massachusetts) also appointed their councils. Royally appointed councils could veto any law passed by a colony's representative assembly, royally appointed governors could veto any law passed by both houses, and the Crown could veto any law passed by both houses and approved by the governor.

**THE LIMITS OF ROYAL POWER** Nonetheless, the sway of royal power remained more apparent than real after 1700. The Glorious Revolution asserted once and for all that Parliament's authority—rule by the legislative branch of government—would be supreme in the governing of England. In the colonies members of representative assemblies grew more skilled at dealing with royal governors and more protective of their rights. They guarded most jealously their strongest lever of power—the right of the lower houses to levy taxes.

The political reality of the assemblies' power reflected a social reality as well. No longer mere outposts along the Atlantic, the colonies of 1700 were becoming more firmly rooted societies. Their laws and traditions were based not only on what they had brought from England but also on the conditions of life in America. That social reality had already blocked Stuart ambitions to shape the future of North America, just as it had thwarted the designs of lordly proprietors and the dreams of religious reformers.

 REVIEW

How did William and Mary try to increase colonial revenues?

# CONCLUSION

## THE WORLD AT LARGE

The dream of empire would revive among England's rulers in the middle of the eighteenth century—in part because the rulers of France had never abandoned their own imperial visions. France had long been Europe's largest kingdom in terms of land and overall population. By the 1660s, bureaucratic, financial, and political reforms had left the French with the mightiest military as well. Determined to have more territory, France's ambitious king, Louis XIV, unleashed this titanic war machine against his neighbors on four different occasions between 1667 and 1714.

Even after 1714, France, England and, to a lesser extent, Spain waged a kind of cold war for a quarter of a century, jockeying for position and influence. Western European monarchs had come to realize that confrontations in North America's vast and distant interior could influence the outcome of their feuds closer to home. In this global chess game, the British had the advantage of numbers: nearly 400,000 subjects in the colonies in 1720, compared with only about 25,000 French spread along a thin line of fishing stations and fur-trading posts, and a meager 5,000 or so Spaniards in New Mexico, Texas, and Florida combined. But by a considerable margin, native peoples still represented the majority population in North America. Moreover, they still controlled more than 90 percent of its territory. If events in North America could affect the balance of power in Europe, then French and Spanish administrators could still believe and hope that their Indian alliances might yet help them prevail against each other, especially against Britain's booming colonies. ∞∞∞

## CHAPTER SUMMARY

WHILE THE FRENCH COLONIZED CANADA, the Protestant Reformation in England spurred the colonization of New England and Pennsylvania.

■ During the seventeenth century, the French slowly established a fur trade, agricultural communities, and religious institutions in Canada while building Indian alliances throughout the Mississippi drainage.

■ Competition over the fur trade in New France and New Netherland contributed to a devastating series of wars between Iroquois, Hurons, and dozens of other Indian groups.

■ Over the same period, English Puritans planted more populous settlements between Maine and Long Island.

■ The migration of family groups and a rough equality of wealth lent stability to early New England society, reinforced by the settlers' shared commitment to Puritanism and a strong tradition of self-government.

■ The mid-Atlantic colonies also enjoyed a rapid growth of people and wealth, but political wrangling as well as ethnic and religious diversity made for a higher level of social conflict.

■ Whereas New Englanders attempted to subdue native peoples, colonists in the mid-Atlantic enjoyed more harmonious relations with the region's original inhabitants.

■ The efforts of the later Stuart kings to centralize England's empire ended with the Glorious Revolution in 1688, which greatly reduced tensions between the colonies and the parent country.

# ADDITIONAL READING

FOR INTRODUCTIONS TO FRENCH AND Indian encounters, see Olive Patricia Dickason, *Canada's First Nations* (1992), and Bruce G. Trigger, *Natives and Newcomers* (1995). Colin G. Calloway's *One Vast Winter Count* (2003) masterfully synthesizes the history of natives and Europeans in early North America west of the Appalachians, and Daniel K. Richter does the same for eastern North America in *Facing East from Indian Country* (2001). For a history of Dutch America, see Jaap Jacobs, *New Netherland* (2005). Jenny Hale Pulsipher's *Subjects unto the Same King* (2005) illuminates the complex tale of Indian-English relations in the Northeast by focusing on notions of authority. To understand the appeal of Puritanism, the best book to read is Charles Cohen, *God's Caress* (1986). To learn more about how English influences shaped the evolution of Puritanism in New England, read Stephen Foster's masterly study, *The Long Argument* (1991). And to learn more about the diversity of religious and super-natural views in New England, consult Philip Gura, *A Glimpse of Sion's Glory* (1984), and David Hall, *Worlds of Wonder, Days of Judgment* (1989).

For the everyday lives of northern colonists in New England and New York, rely on Virginia Dejohn Anderson's *New England's Generation* (1991) and Joyce Goodfriend's *Before the Melting Pot* (1991). The best assessment of British imperial policy in the late seventeenth century is Richard R. Johnson, *Adjustment to Empire* (1981). For the complex interplay among English colonialism, environmental change, and Indian power in the Northeast, see William Cronon's classic *Changes in the Land* (1983). The event and memory of "King Philip's War" is the subject of Jill Lepore's *The Name of War* (1998).

For a fuller list of readings, see the Bibliography at www.mhhe.com/eh8e.

# SIGNIFICANT EVENTS

**LATE 1500s**
Formation of the Iroquois League

**1535**
Cartier makes first voyage to the Gulf of St. Lawrence

**1608**
Champlain founds Quebec

**1616–1618**
Epidemic devastates native peoples of the coastal Northeast

**1620**
Puritans settle at abandoned village of Patuxet and rename it Plymouth

**1624**
Dutch found New Netherland

**1630**
Winthrop fleet arrives in Massachusetts Bay; Boston established

**1637**
Pequot War

**1664**
New Netherland becomes English New York; founding of New Jersey

**1675–1676**
Metacom's War

**1681**
Founding of Pennsylvania

**1682**
La Salle becomes first European to descend the Mississippi to its mouth

**1688**
Glorious Revolution; William and Mary become monarchs of England

**1692**
Witchcraft trials in Salem

| COLONY | FOUNDING/ SETTLEMENT | CHARACTER AND DEVELOPMENT | APPROXIMATE POPULATION (1700) |
|---|---|---|---|
| **New France** | 1605 Port Royal (Acadia); 1608 Quebec | Fur-traders and Jesuit missionaries; small number of farmers in 1660s; French into western Great Lakes in 1670s; Mississippi valley in 1680s | 15,000 |
| **Massachusetts** (including Maine) | Plymouth 1620; Massachusetts Bay 1629 | Separatist and Puritan settlements; most colonists arrive in family groups; village-centered agricultural settlements | 56,000 |
| **Connecticut** | Thomas Hooker leads congregation to Connecticut 1636 | New Haven, a separate, stricter settlement, joins Connecticut in 1662 | 26,000 |
| **Rhode Island** | Roger Williams 1636 | Williams champions separation of church and state, respect for Indian land claims | 6,000 |
| **New Hampshire** | Portsmouth 1631 | Allied with Massachusetts for several decades; becomes royal colony 1680 | 5,000 |
| **New Netherland/ New York** | Dutch settle 1624; England takes possession 1664 | Dutch at Fort Orange (later Albany) ally with Iroquois to vie for furs; Dutch arms trade helps fuel Beaver Wars | 9,000 by 1664 under Dutch; 18,000 in 1700 |
| **New Jersey** | Duke of York grants lands out of New York holdings 1664 | Patchwork of ethnic groups; small family farms; becomes royal colony 1702 | 14,000 |
| **Pennsylvania/Delaware** (separates in 1703) | Penn receives lands in 1681 from Charles II; Philadelphia principal town | Penn recruits colonists from across Britain and Europe; dispersed farms the norm rather than village settlements; Penn pledges to deal fairly with Indians | 20,000 |

In this detail from a remarkable painting, Don Pedro de Villasur lies dead, hands extended in the air as he is being dragged by the legs outside his blue tent. Just below, the Spanish (wearing hats) form a circle to fend off the attack of Pawnee warriors. Jean L'Archevêque stands bareheaded on the right side of the circle, wearing blue clothing. The shadow across his face likely represents his tattoos.

## CHAPTER 5

# The Mosaic of Eighteenth-Century America

1689–1768

## What's to Come

∞∞∞ **AN AMERICAN STORY** ∞∞∞

## THE TALE OF A TATTOOED TRAVELER

August 13, 1720: morning sunlight breaks over the confluence of the Platte and Loup Rivers in what today is Nebraska. Jean L'Archevêque rises stiffly from where he slept and looks about camp. A few dozen Spanish soldiers huddle in the early light, donning their long, leather vests and their wide-brimmed hats. At another end of the encampment the Pueblo Indian men who have accompanied the expedition speak softly to one another, making less noise than the soldiers, though double their number. A friar in his habit passes among

*17 feet long by 4½ feet high, this painting on bison or elk hide was likely made by a mission-trained Indian, after Villasur's debacle.*

the tents. Don Pedro de Villasur, lieutenant governor of New Mexico and leader of the party, threads his arms through a bright, red officer's coat and orders the soldiers to bring in their horses.

Most of these men had known L'Archevêque for years—had come to appreciate his sly humor and grown accustomed to his thick French accent. But on this morning, as they set about the king's business some 600 miles from their homes and families, there must have been something unnerving about the dark, swirling tattoos that covered the Frenchman's face. They had been put there years earlier by Indians who had captured L'Archevêque in the aftermath of a Texas expedition that had ended in calamity. One had only to look at those tattoos to be reminded that things sometimes go badly for both kings and their servants.

Born in 1672 in Bayonne, France, L'Archevêque was only a boy when he boarded ship to the French Caribbean, fleeing his family's financial troubles. Then in 1684 he joined an expedition led by the French explorer René Robert Cavelier, Sieur de La Salle. Three years earlier La Salle had been the first to navigate the immense Mississippi River from the Great Lakes to the Gulf of Mexico. He was famous and respected. Now he was set to plant a permanent settlement near the Mississippi's mouth, as a strategic foothold for France. Yet try as he might, La Salle could not find the mouth of the Mississippi when he approached this time from the Gulf of Mexico. Instead, he landed on the coast of present-day Texas and threw up some ramshackle buildings. As months stretched into years, the expedition lost its ships, while the nearly 300 colonists sickened, starved, and died. The survivors blamed their leader and hatched a plan to be rid of him. Young L'Archevêque played a part, distracting the great explorer while an accomplice blew his head apart with a musket shot.

As the colony spiraled into ruin, L'Archevêque and a few desperate companions eventually found themselves unhappy guests among Caddo Indians in east Texas. These were the people who tattooed the young man's face, carefully inserting a dye made from walnuts into countless tiny cuts. Spanish explorers, determined to root out La Salle's French colony, stumbled across L'Archevêque in 1690, ransomed him from the Caddos, and imprisoned him—first in Mexico City and then for two and a half years in Spain. Finally he was freed and returned to Mexico City.

Meanwhile, news of La Salle's stillborn colony convinced Spanish officials to take more energetic measures to secure their claims on the North American West. A permanent French settlement could be used all too easily as a base to threaten New Spain and its famous silver mines. Crucially, Spain had to reconquer New Mexico, from which it had been driven out by Popé's Pueblo Revolt of 1680 (Chapter 3). When Spanish colonists returned in earnest in 1692, they met only fragmented resistance from the Pueblo villages.

It was in reconquered New Mexico that Jean L'Archevêque found his first real home since boyhood. Sent north perhaps because of his facility with not only French but also Indian languages, L'Archevêque quickly became a fixture in Santa Fe, prospering, marrying well, and gaining the trust of his neighbors. The Spanish had not long returned to New Mexico before they began hearing complaints from the plains Apaches about Pawnee raiders armed with French guns and mocking the Spanish, calling them "women." In 1720, with Spain and France at war in Europe, New Mexico's governor ordered his lieutenant Villasur to take L'Archevêque and a group of Indian and Spanish fighters to confront the French—hence the long trek to the Platte River, where the men awoke at daybreak on August 13 to do the king's business.

But things sometimes go badly for kings and their servants. Moments after ordering his men to bring in their horses, Villasur heard wild screams and saw dozens of painted Pawnee warriors rush the camp. The lieutenant governor was one of the first to die, killed with mouth agape just outside his tent; L'Archevêque fell soon after, his death demonstrating how unsettled the North American continent had become in the eighteenth century. The young Frenchman from Bayonne had been shipwrecked, recruited to murder, and tattooed in Texas, imprisoned in Mexico and Spain, married and made respectable on the upper Rio Grande, and finally shot dead and buried alongside Spanish and Indian companions somewhere in Nebraska. It was a remarkable and turbulent odyssey. ∞∞∞

# CRISIS AND TRANSFORMATION IN NORTHERN NEW SPAIN

JEAN L'ARCHEVÊQUE'S LIFE TESTIFIES IN a very personal way to the unpredictable changes unleashed by contact between European and American civilizations. As Europeans established colonies and began competing with one another across the far reaches of the continent, individuals throughout North America, especially native peoples, found life changing at astonishing speed. Europeans, with their animals, plants, technologies, diseases, and designs, drove the existing dynamism in the Americas to a fever pitch of transformation. But Europeans could not predict and did not control the process. Despite their grand ambitions, colonial newcomers often found their

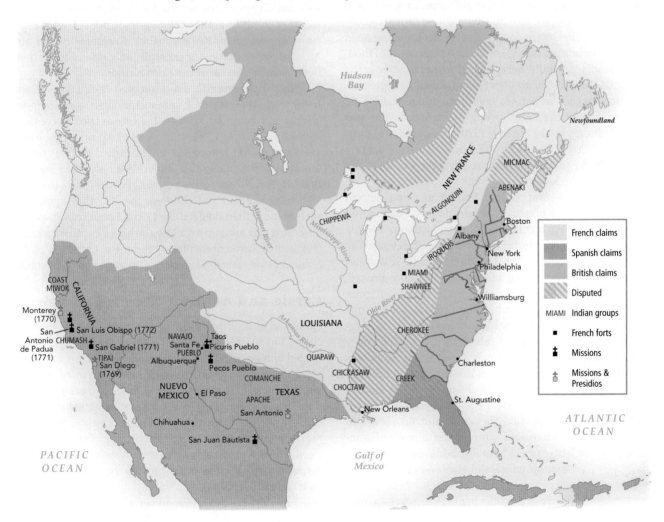

## EUROPEAN TERRITORIAL CLAIMS IN THE EIGHTEENTH CENTURY

*The French, English, and Indian nations all jockeyed for power and position across North America during the eighteenth century. The French expanded their fur trade through the interior, while the English at midcentury began to press the barrier of the Appalachians. But native peoples still controlled the vast majority of the continent and often held the balance of power in interimperial struggles. What geographic advantages did the French enjoy? And the English?*

own plans upended and their lives reordered by the same forces reworking native life.

## Defensive Expansion into Texas

As European rivals laid claim to more and more of North America, nervous Spanish officials stared at their maps. Around the region that had been the Aztec Empire, Spain controlled enormous cities, booming towns, and agricultural villages—a region still populated by millions despite waves of epidemic disease. Though drier and home to far fewer people, the lands hundreds of miles north of Mexico City were of special concern because of their remarkable silver mines. To protect these lands from French designs, Spain had to start paying more attention to the blank spaces still farther north on their maps—spaces entirely controlled by Indians.

**TEXAS AS A BUFFER AGAINST THE FRENCH** Nowhere did the French seem more menacing than in Texas, one of the most important blank spots on Spanish maps. La Salle's catastrophic adventure could have turned out differently: before his grisly death, the Frenchman pledged to invade northern New Spain with an army of thousands of Indians, who, he believed, had "a deadly hatred of the Spaniards." Fearful that another French expedition might actually acquire such an army, in 1690 Spain began establishing missions among the native peoples of Texas. The project started haltingly, but by the early 1720s the Spanish had fortified their claim on Texas with 10 Franciscan missions, 4 presidios (military garrisons), and the beginnings of a civilian settlement on the San Antonio River.

Still, missions disappointed Franciscans and natives alike. Missionaries hoped to create orderly, regimented communities where Indians could be shielded from outside influence and taught to be industrious and devout. The friars did baptize natives by the thousands in Texas. But Indians insisted on coming and going when they pleased. Many nonsedentary peoples sought the food and sanctuary missions offered, only to leave periodically to rendezvous with kin, hunt, and harvest wild plant foods. Their comings and goings confounded the missionaries. Matters were even worse for Franciscans in east Texas, where sedentary Caddos barely tolerated the missions. Farmers themselves, and relatively secure in their fixed villages of beehive-shaped homes, Caddos had no need for the missionaries' crops or protection. Just as important, they could and did trade with Frenchmen from Louisiana, who offered more manufactured goods at better prices than Spaniards did.

**INDIANS AND MISSIONS** However successful they were at retaining autonomy, Indians throughout Texas paid a steep price for any benefits they wrung from missions. Those compelled inside by hunger and insecurity often endured harsh discipline and corporal punishment for disobeying orders. Even worse, missions proved ideal vectors for epidemic disease. In the 1730s alone, smallpox killed more than 1,000 mission Indians near San Antonio. Other illnesses became commonplace as nomadic peoples

Comanche power derived in part from French guns, which they often obtained from Wichita Indians like these painted by Lino Sanchez y Tapia.

with sanitary practices suitable for life on the move crowded together in filthy, cramped buildings. Children were especially vulnerable to the new regime. In eighteenth-century Mission San Antonio, for example, only one in three newborns survived to his or her third birthday.

While friars and Indians negotiated their complex and tragic relationship, Spanish administrators struggled to foster civilian communities in Texas. The Crown tried to convince Spanish subjects to move to the infant colony and even sent agents to recruit among the impoverished families on the Canary Islands. These efforts met with only token success. In 1731 Texas's nonnative population barely amounted to 500 men, women, and children; by 1760 that figure had slightly more than doubled. In 1778 a Franciscan inspector described San Antonio as "a town so miserable that it resembles a most wretched village." The town consisted of "59 houses of stone and mud, and 79 of wood, but all poorly built."

## Crisis and Rebirth in New Mexico

Spain had pushed into the blank space on the map that was Texas, but after generations into the project it still controlled only an archipelago of missions, presidios, and a few towns—surrounded on all sides by unconquered Indians, whose power in the region was, if anything, expanding. At first Apaches posed the greatest threat to Spain's ambitions in Texas. Their raids thinned Spanish herds, prevented ranching and farming communities from expanding outward, and threatened missions with destruction. Spaniards responded with slave raids on Apache camps, and the violence escalated.

**COMANCHE NEWCOMERS** By the 1730s, however, a new force emerged to eclipse even Apaches. They called themselves Numunuu "the People." Their enemies came to call them Comanches. Emerging from the foothills of the Rockies in the late sixteenth century, Comanches integrated European horses into their lives, moved permanently onto the plains, and quickly became some of the most formidable equestrian warriors in history. They allied with Indians who could provide them French guns and ammunition from Louisiana and embarked on a program of territorial expansion. By the mid-eighteenth century Comanches drove most Apaches from the plains and took over their rich bison-hunting territories in what is today southern Colorado, eastern New Mexico, and west Texas. Without bison, Apaches turned more and more to stealing Spanish animals to survive. Spaniards from Santa Fe to San Antonio soon found themselves at war with Apaches and Comanches both; New Mexico often came into conflict with Navajos and Utes as well. Much of northern New Spain became a theater of desolation; abandoned villages up and down the Rio Grande testified to the limits of Spanish power.

Spaniards accused the "barbarians" of animalistic savagery, but all sides inflicted horrors on their enemies. Outside the little besieged town of Tucson, for example, Lieutenant Colonel Pedro de Allende boasted that he had decapitated a fallen Apache in front of the dead man's comrades and "charged the Apache line single-handed, with the head stuck on his lance." Away from the din of battle, a prominent Spaniard noted that his people accuse the Indians of cruelty but added, "I do not know what opinion they would have of us."

**A Brokered Peace**

By the 1780s nearly everyone had had enough of war. A farsighted Comanche leader named Ecueracapa helped broker peace with Spanish authorities in 1786, after which the new allies cooperated to entice or threaten Utes, Navajos, and Apaches into peace as well. Northern New Spain entered a period of relative calm, expansion, and economic growth. Changes were most dramatic in New Mexico, where Spanish subjects opened up new farms and ranches, enlarged their flocks and herds, and devoted new energy to local manufacturing. As New Mexico's non-Indian population grew (20,000 by the close of the eighteenth century), new roads funded by the Crown helped ease the province's isolation. Finally, peace meant that *nuevo mexicanos* could accumulate wealth by trading more with their Indian neighbors and with merchants in Chihuahua, Durango, and Mexico City. Trade and supply caravans began setting out from Santa Fe for Chihuahua once or even twice a year.

**Distinctive New Mexican Culture**

Some of the New Mexicans who profited most from the newfound opportunities began to patronize artists and skilled craftsmen.

By the late eighteenth century a distinctive New Mexican culture started to emerge, one marked by new traditions in such crafts as woodworking and weaving, as well as in religious art and practice. A master craftsman known only as the Laguna Santero helped define this movement by training local apprentices in his workshop and making pieces for wealthy patrons. The Laguna Santero, his apprentices, and others he inspired began making exquisite portraits of saints on pine boards (*retablos*), hide paintings, elaborate altar screens for churches, and wooden statues of saints (*bultos*)—all art forms still associated with New Mexican folk culture today.

## Spanish California

Spanish California was the empire's last major colonial project in North America. Like the colonies in Texas and Florida, settlement was sparked by a fear of foreign competition, this time from Russians moving south from Alaska. Though Spaniards first explored the California coast in 1542, not until 1768 did the Crown authorize permanent colonization. A joint expedition of military men and Franciscans led by the pragmatic Gaspar de Portolá and the iron-willed Fray (Friar) Junípero Serra, braved shipwrecks, scurvy, and earthquakes to establish ramshackle **presidios** (military garrisons) and missions at San Diego and Monterey.

This retablo, *or alterpiece,* of San Jose (Saint Joseph) is typical of the work produced by the Laguna Santero and his workshop.

# The Founders of Spanish California

Historians often turn to census data for insights into people's lives that are difficult to come by in other records. Often scholars analyze masses of historic census data with the help of computers. But these censuses from early colonial California survey households in what were then the tiny villages of Los Angeles and San José, making it relatively easy for us to look for patterns. For example, these documents reveal the striking heterogeneity of the "Spanish" colonization of California. Preoccupied with blood and birthright, officials throughout Spanish America routinely labeled people according to their supposed heritage. Mestizo/a referred to children of a Spaniard and an Indian; mulato/a to a child of a Spaniard and an African; coyote to a child of a mestizo/a and an Indian; chino/a to a child of a Spaniard and a salta-atras (a person with African features born of white parents); and pardo/a (child of an African and Indian). The second census, from San José, includes occupation and birthplace information for the head of house.

## Census of Los Angeles, 1781

| NAME | AGE |
| --- | --- |
| (1) Lara, Josef de; español | 50 |
| Maria Antonio Campos, india sabina | 23 |
| Josef Julian | 4 |
| Juana de Jesus | 6 |
| Maria Faustina | 2 |
| (2) Navarro, Josef Antonio; mestizo | 42 |
| Maria Rufina Dorotea; mulata | 47 |
| Josef Maria | 10 |
| Josef Clemente | 9 |
| Maria Josefa | 4 |
| (3) Rosas, Basillio; indio | 67 |
| Maria Manuela Calixtra; mulata | 43 |
| Jose Maximo | 15 |
| Carlos | 12 |
| Antonio Rosalino | 7 |
| Josef Marcelino | 4 |
| Juan Esteban | 2 |
| Maria Josefa | 8 |
| (4) Mesa, Antonio; negro | 38 |
| Ana Gertrudis Lopez; mulata | 27 |
| Antonio Maria | 8 |
| Maria Paula | 10 |
| (5) Villavicencio, Antonio; español | 30 |
| Maria de los Santos Seferina; india | 26 |
| Maria Antonio Josefa | 8 |

| NAME | AGE |
| --- | --- |
| (6) Vanegas, Josef; indio | 28 |
| Maria Maxima Aguilar; India | 20 |
| Cosme Damien | 1 |
| (7) Rosas, Alejandro; indio | 19 |
| Juana Rodriguez; coyote india | 20 |
| (8) Rodriguez, Pablo; indio | 25 |
| Maria Rosalia Noriega; india | 26 |
| Maria Antonia | 1 |
| (9) Camero, Manuel; mulatto | 30 |
| Maria Tomasa; mulata | 24 |
| (10) Quintero, Luis; negro | 55 |
| Maria Petra Rubio; Mulata | 40 |
| Josef Clemente | 3 |
| Maria Gertrudis | 16 |
| Maria Concepcion | 9 |
| Tomasa | 7 |
| Rafaela | 6 |
| (11) Moreno, Jose; mulato | 22 |
| Maria Guadalupe Gertrudis | 19 |
| (12) Rodriguez, Antonio Miranda; chino | 50 |
| Juana Maria | 11 |

Source: David Weber, *Foreigners in Their Native Land: Historical Roots of the Mexican Americans*, 30th Anniversary ed. (Albuquerque: University of New Mexico Press, 2003), 33–35.

## Census of San José, 1790

| NAME | AGE |
| --- | --- |
| (1) Romero, Antonio, farmworker, pardo, from Guadalajara | 40 |
| Petra Aceves; parda | 28 |
| [Antonio] | 14 |

| NAME | AGE |
| --- | --- |
| (2) Archuleta, Ignacio; farmworker, Spaniard, from Horcasitas [Sonora] | 36 |
| Gertrudis Pacheco; Spaniard | 36 |
| [Petra] | 9 |

| NAME | AGE | | NAME | AGE |
|------|-----|---|------|-----|
| [Miguel] | 11 | (10) | Lugo, Serafino; farmworker, español, from Villa Sinaloa | 50 |
| [Gregorio] | 8 | | Gertrudis Pacheco, española | 50 |
| [Florentino] | 6 | | [Juan] | 19 |
| [Juan José] | 5 | | [Nicolas] | 13 |
| | | | [Rafael] | 11 |
| (3) Alvírez, Claudio; farmworker, coyote, from Tetuache [Sonora] | 48 | (11) | Castro, Joaquín; farmworker, español, from Villa Sinaloa | 50 |
| Ana María Gonzales; india | 30 | | Martina Botiller, española | 50 |
| [José] | 8 | | [Francisco María] | 18 |
| [Brígida] | 5 | | [Carlos] | 15 |
| [Juan] | 2 | | [unnamed orphan] | ? |
| [Jacoba] | baby | | [unnamed orphan] | ? |
| (4) Gonzales, Manuel; farmworker, indio, from San Bartolomé [Chihuahua] | 70 | (12) | Alegre, Antonio; farmworker, español, from Genoa [Italy] | 50 |
| Gertrudis Aceves; parda | 20 | | Catarina; India | 28 |
| [Francisco] | 18 | | [Vicenta Anastacia] | 6 |
| [Romualdo] | 13 | | | |
| (5) Rosales, Bernardo; farmworker, mulato, from Terrenate [Sonora] | ? | (13) | Bojórquez, Pedro; cowboy, español, from Villa Sinaloa | 36 |
| Mónica; india, from Mission San Antonio | 28 | | Angela Trejo; española | 43 |
| [Josefa] | 14 | | [Hermenegildo Ignacio] | 12 |
| [Cornelio] | 12 | | [Bartolomé Francisco] | 10 |
| [Petra] | 10 | | [Juan José] | 6 |
| [María Antonia] | 7 | | | |
| (6) Amézquita, Manuel; farmworker, mulato, from Terrenate [Sonora] | ? | (14) | Aceves, Antonio; farmworker, mulato, from San Bartolomé [Chihuahua] | 50 |
| Graciana Arroyo, mulata | 26 | | Feliciana Cortés, mestiza | 50 |
| [Gabriel] | 14 | | [José Antonio] | 18 |
| [Serafín] | 10 | | [José Maria] | 11 |
| [Ventura] | 6 | | | |
| [Augustina] | 4 | (15) | Sáez, Nazario; cowboy, español, from San Bartolomé [Chihuahua] | 48 |
| [Salvador] | 2 | | Micaela Sotelo, españa | 40 |
| (7) Vásquez, Tiburcio; farmworker, mestizo, from Ahualulco [Jalisco] | 35 | | [Juana] | 16 |
| María Bojórquez, española | 30 | | [Juan María] | 12 |
| [Francisco] | 12 | | [María Benita] | 10 |
| [Felipe] | 10 | | [María Felipa] | 8 |
| [Resurección] | 8 | (16) | Cagüelas, Pedro; cowboy, indio, from San Luis Obispo | 20 |
| [Hermenegildo] | 6 | | Secundina, India | 18 |
| [Rosalía] | 4 | | | |
| [Faustino] | 2 | (17) | Osuna, Miguel; tailor, español, from Real de San Francisco [Sonora], single | 52 |
| [Féliz] | 1 | | | |
| (8) Avila, Francisco; farmworker, español, from El Fuerte [Sinaloa], widower | 46 | (18) | Nervo, Pedro Ruiz; español, from San Blas [Nayarit], single | 21 |
| Francisco Xavier | 16 | | | |
| (9) Mesa, Valerio; farmworker, español, from San Juan Bautista [Sonora] | 60 | | | |
| Leonor Borboa, española | 50 | | | |
| [Juan] | 19 | | | |
| [Nicolas] | 13 | | | |
| [Rafael] | 11 | | | |

*Source:* William M. Mason, *The Census of 1790: A Demographic History of Colonial California,* Ballena Press anthropological papers no. 45 (Menlo Park, Calif.: Ballena Press, 1998), 98–100.

*Thinking Critically*

Other than individual ethnic heritage, what sorts of information or patterns can you find in these censuses? Can you spot any familial connections? What can these documents tell us about family size, marriage age, naming customs, or prevailing norms regarding interethnic unions? What sorts of cautions do historians need to keep in mind when working with documents such as these?

Officials found it difficult to recruit colonists for California and even turned to orphanages and prisons in New Spain, with little success. Moreover, it seemed nearly impossible to get colonists to California alive. The sea route along the Pacific coast proved costly and often deadly, and the backbreaking overland route from northwestern New Spain had to be abandoned after 1781, when an uprising of Yuma Indians shut down the crossing at the Colorado River. Still, the colony enjoyed steady if modest growth. By 1800 California had two more presidios (at San Francisco and Santa Barbara), three Spanish towns (San José, Los Angeles, and Branciforte, near present-day Santa Cruz), and a total of 18 Franciscan missions, ministering to 13,000 Indian converts.

**THE CHANGING CALIFORNIA ENVIRONMENT**

Like their colleagues in Texas and Florida, Franciscans tried to entice Indians into missions with promises of food, shelter, instruction, and protection. As time went on, missions became self-sufficient and more effective at both attracting Indians and policing those who came in. All the while, Indians saw the world changing around them. In Monterey, for example, imported pigs, sheep, mules, horses, and cows multiplied at astonishing speed. These animals radiated out from the mission and presidio, overgrazing and annihilating native plants. Soon weeds and plants that Spaniards had unwittingly brought with them began to spread throughout the region, outcompeting the disturbed native vegetation.

By 1800 the lands around Monterey had been thoroughly transformed. Pollen analysis of the vegetable matter in adobe from the early nineteenth century indicates that by the time the bricks were made, alien weeds had all but displaced native plants. With their lands transformed by overgrazing and invasive plant species, and their populations diminished by epidemics, native families around Monterey abandoned their villages and either fled to the interior or surrendered to the discipline and danger of mission life.

California's three colonial towns depended on missions for food and labor. Given the difficulties of immigrating to California, the colonial population grew mainly through natural increase. By 1800 California was home to only 1,800 Hispanic residents. Despite their relative poverty and isolation, these men, women, and children maintained distinctive traditions. An English visitor to Monterey savored local parties, bullfights, and hunts in the countryside. Most of all, he marveled at the "exhilarating" fandango, a dance that "requires no little elasticity of limbs as well as nimbleness of capers & gestures." The whirling men and women moved "with such wanton attitudes & motions, such leering looks, sparkling eyes and trembling limbs, as would decompose the gravity of a stoic."

Like most English-speaking visitors to California, this excitable traveler found Hispanic women both alluring and improper. Proper women knew their

| *Dame de Monterey*

place, and, while delightful to watch, fandango seemed a good deal too joyous and suggestive to be proper. Had the Englishman probed deeper, he would have learned of other, far more consequential differences between Spanish and English women than the former's love of bold and beautiful dance.

## Women and the Law in New Spain and British North America

Women in California and throughout the Spanish world had a host of important legal rights denied to women in English-speaking realms. For comparison's sake, consider a few critical moments in the lives of two imaginary women: Soledad Martínez, of Los Angeles, California; and Constance Snowling, of Albany, New York.

**SPANISH LEGAL ADVANTAGES FOR WOMEN**

When Soledad's parents passed away, Spanish law ensured that she would inherit their property on an equal footing with her brothers. English law, in contrast, allowed fathers to craft wills however they wished. Constance could theoretically receive nothing upon her parents' deaths. If, as was usually the case, Constance's father died without a will, by law his eldest son inherited all his land and any buildings on it. Constance and any other sisters or brothers would receive only a share of the remaining personal property (money, tools, furniture, clothing, and so on).

The legal advantages enjoyed by women in the Spanish Empire become even more apparent in marriage. Suppose that both Soledad and Constance were fortunate enough to come into their marriages with some personal property of their own and with modest dowries—sums of money meant to help the young couple get established. After her wedding, Soledad retained complete legal control over her personal property and could dispose of it however she wished (with or without her husband's blessing). Moreover, although her husband had the right to manage the dowry and invest it as he saw fit, it still belonged to Soledad. Once death or divorce ended the marriage, he was legally obliged to return its full value to her or her family. Finally, as a married woman Soledad retained the right to buy and sell land in her own name and could legally represent herself in court.

Wives in the English-speaking world had no such rights in the colonial era. Upon marriage, Constance surrendered her dowry and even her personal property to her new husband, who could dispose of all of it however he wished. As a married woman, Constance had virtually no control over property of any kind, could not write a will, and could initiate no legal actions without her husband's consent.

Finally, if our two imaginary colonial women had outlived their husbands, they would have experienced widowhood very differently. In addition to the full value of her dowry, Soledad was legally entitled to at least one-half of all property she and her deceased husband had accumulated in marriage. Upon Soledad's death, this property would pass to her own children or to her other family members. Constance had no claim on her dowry following her husband's death. She would have entered widowhood with her personal "paraphernalia" (clothes, jewelry, and similar items), any land she had been fortunate enough to inherit during marriage, and control over a third of her dead husband's property. Crucially, however, Constance could use this property only to support herself in life. Upon her death, it would pass into the hands of her husband's family.

Not all Spanish and English women would have felt these legal differences as keenly as Soledad and Constance. Poor women who inherited little, came into marriages with paltry dowries, and lived hand to mouth as adults endured poverty whether they lived under English or Spanish law. But for those who did have some property or wealth, it mattered a great deal whether they lived in New Spain or British North America.

**WOMEN'S LEGAL RIGHTS IN NEW FRANCE** France's legal traditions descended from the same Roman sources as Spain's, so women in New France enjoyed legal protections similar to women in Florida, Texas, New Mexico, and California. And France and Spain's colonies in North America had other, less happy things in common. Like northern New Spain, New France generally cost the Crown more money than it brought in. Like their Spanish counterparts, French administrators found it all but impossible to convince or compel large numbers of their fellow subjects to move to the colonies. As in Florida, Texas, New Mexico, and California, the colonial population of New France struck many well-heeled observers as degraded, insolent, lazy, and ignorant. And, as with all Spanish colonies north of the Rio Grande, New France remained dependent on Indians generations after its founding.

 REVIEW

Why did Spain establish colonies in Texas and California, and what role did missions play in establishing the Spanish presence?

# EIGHTEENTH-CENTURY NEW FRANCE

LIKE THE SPRAWLING VASTNESS OF Spain's territorial claims in North America, France's imperial reach was nothing if not ambitious. French colonial maps laid claim to the heart of the continent, a massive imperial wedge stretching from Newfoundland southwest to the Mississippi delta, then northwest across the Great Plains and into the cold north woods, and east again through Upper Canada to the North Atlantic. Of course it was one thing to draw an empire on a map, another to make the empire a reality.

## Colonial Compromises

Despite their grand claims, most eighteenth-century French Americans continued to live along the St. Lawrence River. Most dwelt in farming communities up and down the river valley between the small cities of Montreal and Quebec, capital of New France. Jesuit missions also lined the river, ministering to native converts. The Crown had given the valley a boost with an energetic colonization program in the 1660s and 1670s, but thereafter the French population grew almost totally through natural increase. Fortunately for France, the colonists excelled at natural increase—nurturing large, thriving families and basically doubling their own population every generation.

**GROWTH ALONG THE ST. LAWRENCE RIVER** Those determined enough to endure darkness, isolation, and numbing cold in winter, then heat, humidity, and swarming mosquitoes in summer, found life in Canada considerably easier than life in France. Colonists were healthier and lived longer, were much more likely to own their own land, and enjoyed significantly more autonomy over their lives than rural peasants across the Atlantic. By 1760 the valley was home to around 75,000 French colonists, soldiers, and priests. Many Canadian households also included Indian slaves: women and children, mostly, who had been captured by other Indians in places as faraway as the Arkansas valley and sold into trade networks that eventually brought them to New France. Though modest by Anglo-American standards, by the mid-eighteenth century the colonial project along the St. Lawrence River had nonetheless put an unmistakable French stamp upon the land.

**FRENCH AND INDIANS IN THE PAYS D'EN HAUT** To the west and north in the country known as the *pays d'en haut* ("upper country"), France's eighteenth-century venture took on a very different look. Around the Great Lakes, north around Lakes Manitoba and Winnipeg, and south along the Mississippi River basin, forts and missions rather than farms or towns anchored French ambition. More exactly, the goodwill of Indian peoples provided the anchor. Though as quick as other Europeans to use violence to get what they wanted, the French in North America recognized that they were too few to secure their interests through force alone. France gained an edge over its rivals in the interior by being useful to Indians, primarily the Algonquian-speaking nations who spread across eastern Canada and the upper Mississippi. French merchants brought coveted European presents and trade goods, while military men, administrators, and Jesuits often mediated in conflicts between native groups. Vastly outnumbered by Indians throughout most of the territory that it claimed in North America, France remained deeply dependent on native peoples.

Dependence meant compromise. Cultural differences between the French and their Indian allies often seemed vast and irreconcilable. The two peoples had radically divergent expectations about warfare, trade, marriage, child rearing, religion, food, beauty, and many other areas of life. Few cultural differences seemed as difficult to bridge as those concerning law. In 1706, for example, men associated with a prominent Ottawa leader known as Le Pesant killed a priest and a French soldier outside of Fort Detroit. Enraged French authorities demanded that Le Pesant be delivered to them so that he could be tried and, once found guilty, executed for murder. Ottawa leaders countered by offering to replace the dead Frenchmen with Indian slaves. "Raising" the dead this way was a common Ottawa remedy in cases of murder between allies, because it helped avoid a potentially disastrous cycle of blood revenge. Moreover, Le Pesant was a powerful man. His execution would have political consequences dangerous to the broader French alliance.

Neither side surrendered to the other. Instead, they crafted a novel solution that exemplified the pattern of creative, mutual compromises typical of what one scholar has called the "middle ground" characterizing French-Indian relations in the *pays d'en haut*. On a snowy morning, grim Ottawa leaders turned over Le Pesant to the French commander at Fort Detroit who then quickly condemned the man to death. But before the execution could be carried out, Le Pesant escaped to freedom. It is exceedingly difficult to believe that French authorities would have been careless enough to allow this most wanted of men to slip away. Moreover, Le Pesant was elderly and obese—hardly a nimble

escape artist. Clearly the French and their Ottawa allies came to an understanding. Le Pesant would be surrendered and, once condemned, quietly allowed to escape. This new compromise more or less satisfied both sides and became a model solution to later French-Indian murder cases.

Necessary and inevitable, such compromises nonetheless rankled authorities in Paris. In 1731 one such official bemoaned the fact that after more than a century, colonial administrators in New France had failed to make the "savages" obedient to the Crown. The colony's governor-general dashed off a terse reply: "If this has not been done, it is because we have found the task to be an impossible one. Kindly apprise me of any means you should conceive of for securing such obedience."

## France on the Gulf Coast

Forced into uncomfortable compromises in the north, authorities in Paris hoped to establish a colony on the Gulf Coast that could be more profitable and more French. When shipwreck

## Algonquin and French Views Regarding Trade and Justice

|  | ALGONQUIN VALUES | FRENCH VALUES |
|---|---|---|
| Trade | Trade embedded in personal relationships. Expectation that exchanges will be relatively uniform and consistent season to season. Negative changes in trade terms attributed to decay of personal relationship. | Trade structured mostly by markets, and only marginally by personal relationships. Trade terms will naturally change as market conditions change. Nothing inherently personal about fluctuations in prices or trade terms. |
| Justice | Upon a murder, most urgent question was "To what group did the killer belong?" Response to the murder would be determined and pursued by family of the victim. Families could (a) seek another death in revenge—especially if the killer belonged to an enemy people; (b) accept presents to "cover" the death; or (c) take an Indian slave in compensation and thereby "raise" the victim. | Upon a murder, most urgent question was "Who was the killer?" Response to the murder would be determined and pursued by state authorities. State authorities held that the only legitimate remedy for a murder was the apprehension, trial, and execution of the killer. |

on the Texas coast sealed La Salle's doom, it fell to Pierre Le Moyne d'Iberville to establish French Louisiana. A veteran sailor and soldier, d'Iberville spent much of the 1690s destroying British settlements in Newfoundland and the North Atlantic. Sent to the Gulf in 1698, he inaugurated the new colony of Louisiana with a post at Biloxi Bay. D'Iberville's successors established settlements at Mobile Bay and, in 1718, the town of New Orleans. Crown officers and entrepreneurs envisioned an agricultural bonanza, expecting Louisiana to have far more in common with the Caribbean's lucrative sugar islands than with the maddening *pays d'en haut*.

Nothing went according to plan. Here, too, Indians forced the French into painful concessions. While disease and aggression devastated the smaller Indian communities along the coast, more powerful peoples in the interior endured and protected their interests. Louisiana came into conflict with the mighty Chickasaws, and in 1729 the Natchez Indians rose up against French encroachment, killing or capturing some 500 colonists. Underfunded and usually neglected by the Crown, Louisiana's officials became notoriously corrupt and arbitrary. The colony was, according to one observer, a place "without religion, without justice, without discipline, without order, and without police."

**DIFFICULTIES IN FRENCH LOUISIANA** More to the point, the Gulf Coast was without many French colonists. The region quickly acquired a reputation among would-be French migrants as unattractive and unhealthy. When colonists were not fighting Indians, they contended with heat, humidity, hurricanes, droughts and crop failures, with never-ending battles to turn swamps and forests into farmland, and with the scourges of malaria and yellow fever. One despairing official lamented that "death and disease are disrupting and suspending all operations . . . the best workers are dead." By 1731, two-thirds of the French who had chanced the journey to Louisiana had died or fled. Still, like New Mexico, Canada, California, and Texas, colonial Louisiana persevered to become more populous and more prosperous. Nearly 4,000 French men, women, and children called the colony home by 1746. Their fortunes had in large part come to depend on another, even larger group of newcomers: French Louisiana's African slaves.

## Slavery and Colonial Society in French Louisiana

When the first colonists founded New Orleans in 1718, they immediately clamored for bound laborers. Their goal was to create prosperous plantations in the surrounding Mississippi delta. A year later the Company of the Indies, which managed France's slave trade, brought nearly 6,000 slaves, overwhelmingly men, directly from Africa to Louisiana. Unfortunately for white planters, Louisiana tobacco and, later, indigo proved inferior to the varieties exported from Britain's colonies. Instead of providing the formula for economic success, the sudden influx of Africans challenged French control. In 1729 some newly arrived slaves joined forces with the Natchez Indians in their rebellion. The alliance sent waves of panic through the colony, whose population by then had more slaves than free French. The French retaliated in a devastating counterattack, enlisting both the Choctaw Indians, rivals of the Natchez, and other enslaved blacks, who were promised freedom in return for their support.

The planters' costly victory persuaded French authorities to stop importing slaves into Louisiana. Thus the colony did not develop a plantation economy until the end of the eighteenth century, when the cotton boom transformed its culture. In the meantime, blacks continued to make up a majority of all Louisianans, and by the middle of the eighteenth century, nearly all were native-born. The vast majority were slaves, but their work routines—tending cattle, cutting timber, producing naval stores, manning boats—allowed them greater freedom of movement than most slaves enjoyed elsewhere in the American South. They were also encouraged to market the produce of their gardens, hunts, and handicrafts, which became the basis of a thriving trade with both white settlers and the dwindling numbers of coastal Native Americans. But the greatest prize—freedom—was awarded those black men who served in the French militia, defending the colony from the English and Indians as well as capturing slave runaways. The descendants of these black militiamen would become the core of Louisiana's free black community.

Male subjects throughout French America stood ready to perform militia duty, formally or informally. They had to. While the French struggled to sustain peaceful relations with key Indian allies, they turned to violent coercion when they thought it would work. Though not as devastating as the Beaver Wars (Chapter 3), conflicts with Indians proved to be common enough to require a ready defense.

 **IMPERIAL RIVALRIES** More fundamentally, France found itself in conflict with the English in the backcountry beyond the Appalachian Mountains. The rivalries had their beginnings in Europe

Louisiana's socially mixed society is evident from this market scene: the buyers and sellers include Indians as well as colonials of French, Spanish, and African descent.

and flared regularly throughout the late seventeenth century and into the eighteenth. In 1689 England joined the Netherlands and the League of Augsburg (several German-speaking states) in a war against France. While the main struggle raged in Europe, French and English colonials, joined by their Indian allies, skirmished in what was known as King William's War. Peace returned in 1697, but only until the Anglo-French struggle resumed with Queen Anne's War, from 1702 to 1713.

For a quarter of a century thereafter, the two nations waged a kind of cold war, competing for advantage. At stake was not so much control over people or even territory as control over trade. In North America, France and England vied for access to the sugar islands of the Caribbean, a monopoly on supplying manufactured goods to Spanish America, and dominance of the fur trade. The British had the advantage of numbers: nearly 400,000 subjects in the colonies in 1720, the year of L'Archevêque's death, compared with only about 25,000 French. But this is precisely where France's many compromises paid dividends. So long as the French maintained their network of alliances with powerful native peoples, British colonies had little chance of expanding west of the Appalachian Mountains.

 REVIEW

How did Louisiana differ from French Canada?

# FORCES OF DIVISION IN BRITISH NORTH AMERICA

BRITISH COLONIALS FROM MAINE TO the Carolinas distrusted the French and resented their empire of fish and furs. But the English were preoccupied with their own affairs and, by and large, uninterested in uniting against New France. Indeed a traveler during the first half of the eighteenth century would have been struck by how hopelessly divided and disunited England's mainland colonies were, split by ethnicity, race, region, wealth, and religion. The British colonies were a diverse and fragmented lot.

## Immigration and Natural Increase

One of the largest immigrant groups—250,000 black men, women, and children—had come to the colonies from Africa in chains. White arrivals included many English immigrants but also a quarter of a million Scots-Irish, the descendants of seventeenth-century Scots who had regretted settling in northern Ireland; perhaps 135,000 Germans; and a sprinkling of Swiss, Swedes, Highland Scots, and Spanish Jews. Most non-English white immigrants were fleeing lives torn by famine, warfare, and religious persecution. All the voyagers, English and non-English, risked the hazardous Atlantic crossing (Daily Lives, page 115). Many had paid for passage by signing indentures to work as servants in America. The immigrants and slaves who arrived in

the colonies between 1700 and 1775 swelled an American population that was already growing dramatically from natural increase. The birthrate in eighteenth-century America was triple what it is today. Most women bore between five and eight children, and most children survived to maturity.

 **NORTH AMERICA LEADS A GLOBAL RISE IN POPULATION**
This astonishing population explosion was quite possibly the fastest in the world at the time. Even so, the surge was merely one part of a more general global acceleration of population in the second half of the eighteenth century. China's population of 150 million in 1700 had doubled to more than 313 million by century's end. Europe's total rose from about 118 million to 187 million over the same period. The unprecedented global population explosion had several causes. Europe's climate, for one, had become warmer and drier, allowing for generally better harvests. Health and nutrition improved globally with the worldwide spread of Native American crops. Irish farmers discovered that a single acre planted with the American potato could support an entire family. The tomato added crucial vitamins to the Mediterranean diet, and in China the American sweet potato thrived in hilly regions where rice would not grow.

Dramatic population increase in the British colonies, fed by the importation of slaves, immigration, and natural increase, made it hard for colonials to share any common identity. Far from fostering political unity, almost every aspect of social development set Americans at odds with one another. And that process of division and disunity was reflected in the outpouring of new settlers into the backcountry.

## Moving into the Backcountry

To immigrants from Europe weary of war or worn by want, the seaboard's established communities must have seemed havens of order and stability. But by the beginning of the eighteenth century, Anglo-America's colonists had to look farther and farther west to obtain farmland. With older rural communities offering bleak prospects to either native-born or newly arrived families, both groups turned westward in search of new opportunities. The founding of frontier communities in New England was left mainly to the descendants of old Yankee families. Immigrants from Europe had more luck obtaining land south of New York. By the 1720s German and Scots-Irish immigrants as well as native-born colonists were pouring into western Pennsylvania. Some settled permanently, but others streamed southward into the backcountry of Virginia and the Carolinas, where they encountered native-born southerners pressing westward.

ISOLATION OF THE BACKCOUNTRY
Living in the West could be profoundly isolating. From many farmsteads it was a day's ride to the nearest courthouse, tavern, or church. Often lacking decent roads or navigable rivers, frontier families had no means of sending crops to market and aimed for self-sufficiency instead. Distance inhibited the formation of strong social bonds, as did the rapid turnover in western communities. Many families pulled up

# DAILY LIVES

## TRANSATLANTIC TRIALS

A mountain of water swelled from the Atlantic, towered over the *Jamaica Packet*, then toppled onto the small wooden passenger ship. The impact hurled Janet Schaw and her maid about their cabin like rag dolls. As seawater surged in, the ship pitched wildly, "one moment mounted to the clouds and whirled on the pointed wave," the next plunging into the heaving ocean. The ship's provisions—hogsheads of water, coops of chickens, and barrels of salted meat—snapped from their fastenings and careened across the deck before bouncing overboard.

For more than two days the *Jamaica Packet* hurtled in the gale's grip. Then its foremast splintered, and the ship flipped onto its side. Schaw found herself "swimming amongst joint-stools, chests, [and] tables" in her cabin and listening to the sound of "our sails fluttering into rags." It would have been the end of the *Jamaica Packet* if, at that moment, its masts had not washed overboard. With the weight of the masts gone, the ship righted itself.

Schaw, "a lady of quality," as she described herself, was traveling by the finest accommodations from Great Britain to America in the age of sail. For passengers who could not pay for a private cabin, the storm was worse. Twenty-two or more indentured servants from Scotland in that year of 1774 were bound aboard ship for the West Indies. Like thousands of others who came to America in the eighteenth century, they were consigned to steerage, the between-decks area or "upper hold."

Perhaps 4 to 5 feet high, that space was crowded with narrow wooden bunks arranged in tiers about 2 feet apart. It was impossible for most people to stand in steerage or to sit up in a bunk, where as many as four people huddled together at night. Sanitary facilities consisted of a few wooden buckets filled with seawater; candles and fish-oil lanterns supplied the only light. The sole source of air was the hatch opening onto the deck.

When the storm struck, the hatch was fastened tightly to keep the holds from filling with water. But as waves dashed over the decks, water streamed into steerage, forcing its occupants to stand, clutching their children to keep them from being crushed, drowned, or suffocated. For nine days they stood in water, without a fire or any food except raw potatoes and moldy biscuits. And they were without light or fresh air, except for one young man and his pregnant wife. During the storm the woman miscarried, and her "absolutely distracted" husband, Schaw reported, somehow forced open the hatch and carried her up to the deck, reviving the unconscious woman and saving her life.

Luckily, the *Jamaica Packet* escaped not only shipwreck but epidemic disease. Passengers on other transatlantic voyages were not so fortunate. Outbreaks of epidemic disease—smallpox, influenza, typhus, and diphtheria—were common. Although there are no reliable statistics for shipboard mortality during the eighteenth century, estimates range from 3 percent of all passengers to as

high as 10 to 15 percent, a rate nearly comparable to that for slave ships during the Middle Passage across the Atlantic.

For all who ventured abroad, transatlantic travel was tedious and dirty at best, hazardous and horrific at worst. With good reason, those who risked the crossing routinely made out wills and sought the prayers of loved ones. On the high seas, disease and misfortune took a heavy toll.

### *Thinking Critically*

*In what ways did the hazards of transatlantic travel shape the profile of people who willingly undertook these journeys?*

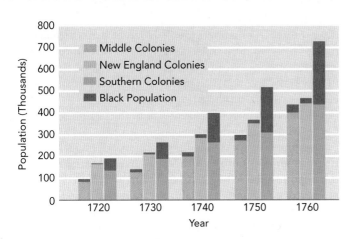

**ESTIMATED POPULATION BY REGION, 1720–1760**

stakes three or four times before settling permanently. Most backcountry inhabitants could not afford to invest in a slave or even a servant. Those conditions made the frontier, more than anywhere else in America, a society of equals. Most families crowded into one-room shacks walled with mud, turf, or crude logs. And everyone worked hard.

**FRONTIER WOMEN** Hard work dominated the lives of backcountry settlers. Besides doing the usual chores of farm women, western wives and daughters joined male family members in the fields. One traveler from the East expressed his astonishment at seeing German women in western Pennsylvania "at work abroad on the Farm mowing, Hoeing Loading Dung into a Cart." Perhaps even more difficult to endure than the hard labor was the loneliness of many women's lives. The reactions of women to being resettled on the frontier can be imagined from the promise that one Scottish husband offered his wife: "We would get all these trees cut down ... [so] that we would see from house to house."

## Social Conflict on the Frontier

Despite the discomforts of frontier life, cheap land lured many families to the West. Benjamin Franklin, Pennsylvania's most successful entrepreneur, inventor, and politician, had observed the hordes of Scots-Irish and German immigrants lingering in Philadelphia just long enough to scrape together the purchase price of a frontier farm. From Franklin's point of view, the backcountry performed a valuable service by siphoning off surplus people from congested eastern settlements. But he knew, too, that the opened frontier unleashed discord, especially between the Eastern Seaboard and the backcountry.

Ethnic differences heightened sectional tensions between East and West. People of English descent predominated along the Atlantic coast, whereas Germans, Scots-Irish, and other white minorities were concentrated in the interior. Many English colonials regarded these new immigrants as culturally inferior and politically subversive. Charles Woodmason, an Anglican missionary in the Carolina backcountry, lamented the arrival of "5 or 6,000 Ignorant, mean, worthless, beggarly Irish Presbyterians, the Scum of the Earth, the Refuse of Mankind," who "delighted in a low, lazy, sluttish, heathenish, hellish life."

German immigrants were generally credited with steadier work habits, as well as higher standards of sexual morality and personal hygiene. But like the clannish Scots-Irish, the Germans preferred to live, trade, and worship among themselves. By 1751 Franklin was warning that the Germans would retain their separate language and customs: the Pennsylvania English would be overrun by "the Palatine Boors."

| This log cabin, built in the North Carolina backcountry in 1782, would have been dark inside, given its lack of windows. The spaces between the logs in such cabins were usually chinked with thin stones or wedges of wood and then daubed with mortar.

Ethnic prejudices only aggravated clashes between wealthy landlords and backcountry tenants. In eastern New Jersey, landed proprietors insisted that squatters pay rent on land that had become increasingly valuable. When the squatters, many of them migrants from New England, refused to pay rents, the proprietors began evictions, touching off riots in the 1740s. Tenant unrest also raged in New York's Hudson River valley, where about 30 manors around New York City and Albany dominated the region. The estates encompassed some 2 million acres and were worked by several thousand tenants. Newcomers from New England, however, demanded to own land and preached their ideas to Dutch and German tenants. Armed insurrection exploded in 1757 and again, more violently, in 1766. Tenants refused to pay rents, formed mobs, and stormed the homes of landlords.

## Eighteenth-Century Seaports

While most Americans on the move flocked to the frontier, others swelled the populations of colonial cities. By present-day standards such cities were small, harboring from 8,000 to 22,000 citizens by 1750. The scale of seaports remained intimate, too: all of New York City was clustered at the southern tip of Manhattan island, and the length of Boston or Charleston could be walked in less than half an hour.

All major colonial cities were seaports, their waterfronts fringed with wharves and shipyards. A jumble of shops, taverns, and homes crowded their streets; the spires of churches studded their skylines. By the 1750s the grandest and most populous was Philadelphia, which boasted straight, neatly paved streets, flagstone sidewalks, and three-story brick buildings. Older cities such as Boston and New York had a medieval aspect: most of their dwellings and shops were wooden structures with tiny windows and low ceilings, rising no higher than two stories to steeply pitched roofs. The narrow cobblestone streets of Boston and New York City also challenged pedestrians, who competed for space with livestock being driven to the butcher, roaming herds of swine and packs of dogs, clattering carts, carriages, and horses.

**THE COMMERCIAL CLASSES** Commerce, the lifeblood of seaport economies, was managed by merchants who tapped the wealth of surrounding regions. Traders in New York City and Philadelphia shipped the Hudson and Delaware valleys' surplus of grain and livestock to the West Indies. Boston's merchants sent fish to the Caribbean and Catholic Europe, masts to England, and rum to West Africa. Charlestonians exported indigo to English dyemakers and rice to southern Europe. Other merchants specialized in the import trade, selling luxuries and manufactured goods produced in England—fine fabrics, ceramics, tea, and farming implements.

No large-scale domestic industry produced goods for a mass market: instead, craft shops filled orders for specific items placed by individual purchasers. Some **artisans** specialized in the maritime trades as shipbuilders, black-smiths, and sailmakers. Others, such as butchers, millers, and distillers, processed and packed raw materials for export. Still others served the basic needs of city dwellers—the men and, occasionally, women who baked bread, mended shoes, combed and powdered wigs, and tended shops and taverns.

On the lowest rung of a seaport's social hierarchy were free and bound workers. Free laborers were mainly young white men and women—journeyman artisans, sailors, fish-ermen, domestic workers, seamstresses, and prostitutes. The ranks of unfree workers in-cluded apprentices and indentured servants doing menial labor in shops and on the docks.

**INCREASE OF AFRICANS IN NORTHERN SEAPORTS**

Black men and women also made up a substantial part of the bound labor force of colo-nial seaports, but the character of slavery in northern seaports changed decisively during the mid-eighteenth century. When wars raging in Europe re-duced the supply of white indentured servants, colonial cities imported a larger number of Africans. In the two decades after 1730, one-third of all immigrants arriving in New York harbor were black; by 1760 blacks constituted more than three-quarters of all bound labor-ers in Philadelphia.

High death rates and a preference for importing African males inhibited the growth of slave families. Even so, city-dwelling African Americans forged an urban black culture exhibiting a new awareness of a common West African past. The influence of African traditions appeared most vividly in an an-nual event known as "Negro election day," celebrated in northern seaports. During the festival, similar to ones held in West Africa, some black men and women paraded in their masters' clothes or mounted on their horses. An election followed to choose black kings, governors, and judges who then held court and settled minor disputes among black and white members of the community. Negro election day did not challenge the established racial order with its temporary reversal of roles. But it did allow the black communities of seaports to honor their own leaders.

**WOMEN IN CITIES**

Working women found a num-ber of opportunities in port cities. Young single women from poor families worked in wealthier households as maids, cooks, laundresses, seamstresses, or nurses. The highest-paying occupations for women were midwifery and dressmaking, and both required long apprenticeships and

expert skills. The wives of artisans and traders sometimes assisted their husbands and, as widows, often continued to manage groceries, taverns, and print shops. But less than 10 percent of women in seaports worked outside their own homes. Most women spent their workday caring for households: seeing to the needs of husbands and children, tending to gardens and domestic animals, and engaged in spinning and weaving—activities crucial to the household economy.

## NON-ENGLISH SETTLEMENTS IN EIGHTEENTH-CENTURY BRITISH NORTH AMERICA

*Many non-English settlers spilled into the backcountry: the Scots-Irish and Germans followed the Great Wagon Road through the western parts of the middle colonies and southern colonies; the Dutch and other Germans moved up the Hudson River valley. In what ways did the concentration of non-English immigrants in the backcountry influence the development of that region?*

*In the mid-eighteenth century, Philadelphia became the largest city in the colonies and the second largest in all the British Empire. Its busy harbor served not only as a commercial hub but also as the disembarkation point for thousands of immigrants.*

PHILADELPHIA IN THE OLDEN TIME.

**URBAN DIVERSIONS AND HAZARDS**

All seaport dwellers—perhaps 1 out of every 20 Americans—enjoyed a more stimulating environment than other colonials did. Plays, balls, and concerts for the wealthiest; taverns, clubs, celebrations, and church services for everyone. Men of every class found diversion in drink and cockfighting. Crowds of men, women, and children swarmed to tavern exhibitions of trained dogs and horses or the spectacular waxworks of one John Dyer, featuring "a lively Representation of Margaret, Countess of Herrinburg, who had 365 Children at one Birth."

Then as now, cities were also places of economic insecurity. In seaports throughout British North America, poverty became increasingly apparent as the eighteenth century wore on. Although the major seaports established workhouses to employ the able-bodied poor, city governments continued to aid most of the dependent with small subsidies of money, food, and firewood. Furthermore, epidemics and catastrophic fires occurred with greater frequency and produced higher mortality rates in congested seaports than in the countryside.

## Social Tension in Seaports

The swelling of seaport populations, like the westward movement of whites, often churned up trouble. English, Scots-Irish, Germans, Swiss, Dutch, French, and Spanish jostled uneasily against one another in the close quarters of Philadelphia and New York City. To make matters worse, religious differences heightened ethnic divisions. Jewish funerals in New York City, for example, drew crowds of hostile and curious Protestants, who heckled mourners.

Class resentment also stirred unrest. Some merchant families flaunted their wealth, building imposing town mansions and dressing in the finest imported fashions. During hard times, symbols of merchant wealth such as expensive coaches and full warehouses became targets of

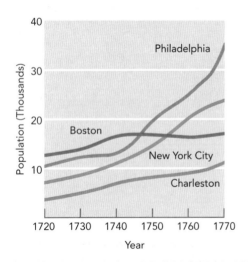

**ESTIMATED POPULATION OF COLONIAL CITIES, 1720–1770**

*Although Boston's population remained stable after 1740, it was surpassed owing to the sharp growth of New York City and, especially, Philadelphia.*

## A WOMAN'S CUPBOARD

Using a technique known as polarized light microscopy, researchers determined that the paint on the columns combined white lead with a shade of blue first synthesized in Berlin in 1704.

Eighteenth-century Americans spelled names, even their own, inconsistently. Beneath the first 'A' in 'Barnard' curators found a faint 'E' for 'Bernard.'

What sorts of possessions do you think Hannah might have kept in these drawers?

**O**bjects can help historians appreciate complex connections. For example, the owner of this exuberantly designed cupboard lived in western Massachusetts in the late seventeenth and early eighteenth centuries, a time of chronic warfare between the English and the French and their Indian allies. Hannah's husband John had been captured in a well-known Indian raid on Deerfield, Massachusetts, in 1704. Perhaps the cupboard can be seen as a defiant assertion of normality in a violent and insecure world. The imagery on the cupboard echoes patterns found on European manufactures from the time, illustrating transatlantic cultural connections even as the piece itself represents a distinct local craft tradition. Finally, the cupboard and the textiles it probably contained open a window into the sorts of property Anglo-American women retained in marriage and passed down to their descendants. According to historian Laurel Thatcher Ulrich, the cupboard's history "teaches us that material objects were not only markers of wealth but devices for building relationships and lineages over time, and it helps us to understand the cultural framework within which ordinary women became creators as well as custodians of household goods."

*Source:* Henry Ford Museum, www.thehenryford.org/exhibits/pic/1997/hannah.asp.

### *Thinking Critically*

*Why did the owner have her name emblazoned on the cupboard? Might it have something to do with restrictive English laws about what women could own in marriage? Do you think women in New Spain or New France would have done the same? What might objects such as these tell us about how women viewed property and identity in British North America?*

---

mob vandalism. Crowds also gathered to intimidate and punish other groups who provoked popular hostility—politicians, prostitutes, and "press gangs." Impressment, attempts to force colonials to serve in the British navy, triggered some of the most violent urban riots.

 **REVIEW**

What kinds of divisions led to social tensions and conflicts in British North America?

# SLAVE SOCIETIES IN THE EIGHTEENTH-CENTURY SOUTH

INEQUALITIES AND DIVISIONS BETWEEN SLAVE and free in the South dwarfed those between seaport dwellers. By 1775 one out of every five Americans was of African ancestry, and more than 90 percent of all black Americans lived in the South, most along the seaboard. Here, on tobacco and rice plantations, slaves fashioned a distinctive African

American society and culture. But they were able to build stable families and communities only late in the eighteenth century and against enormous odds.

THE CHESAPEAKE AND THE LOWER SOUTH

The character of a slave's life depended to a great extent on whether he or she lived in the Chesapeake or the Lower South. Slaves in the low country of South Carolina and Georgia lived on large plantations with as many as 50 other black workers, about half African-born. They had infrequent contact with whites. "They are as 'twere, a Nation within a Nation," observed Francis LeJau, an Anglican priest in the low country. And their work was arduous, because rice required constant cultivation. Black laborers tended young plants and hoed fields in the sweltering summer heat of the mosquito-infested lowlands. During the winter and early spring, they built dams and canals to regulate the flow of water into the rice fields. But the use of the **"task system"** rather than gang labor widened the window of freedom within slavery. When a slave had completed his assigned task for the day, one planter explained, "his master feels no right to call upon him."

Most Africans and African Americans in the Chesapeake lived on plantations with fewer than 20 fellow slaves. Less densely concentrated than in the low country, Chesapeake slaves also had more contact with whites. Unlike Carolina's absentee owners, who left white overseers and black drivers to run their plantations, Chesapeake masters actively managed their estates and subjected their slaves to closer scrutiny.

## The Slave Family and Community

The four decades following 1700 marked the heaviest years of slave importation into the Chesapeake and Carolina regions. Those Africans had survived the trauma of captivity, the Middle Passage, and sale at slave auctions only to be thrust into a bewildering new world: a sea of unfamiliar faces, a clamor of different languages, a host of demands and threats from men and women who called themselves masters.

AFRICAN SLAVES VS. AMERICAN-BORN SLAVES

The newcomers also had to adjust to their fellow slaves. The "new Negroes" hailed from a number of diverse West African peoples, each with a separate language or dialect and distinctive cultures and kinship systems. Often, they had little in common with one another and even less in common with the American-born black minority. Native-born African Americans enjoyed better health, command of English, and experience in dealing with whites. They were also more likely to enjoy a family life, because their advantages probably made the men the preferred partners of black women, who were outnumbered two to one by black

## DISTRIBUTION OF THE AMERICAN POPULATION, 1775

*The African American population expanded dramatically during the eighteenth century, especially in the southern colonies. The high volume of slave imports accounts for most of the growth in the first half of the century, but natural increase was responsible for the rising black population during later decades.*

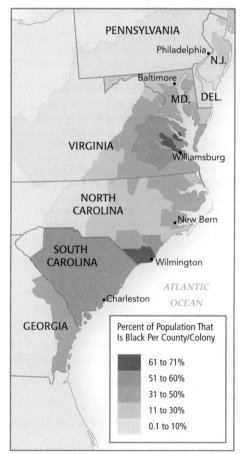

men. And, since immigrant women waited two or three years before marrying, some immigrant men died before they could find a wife. Competition for wives often bred conflict and division.

After the middle of the eighteenth century a number of changes fostered the growth of black families and the vitality of slave communities. At the same time that slave importations began to taper off, the rate of natural reproduction among blacks started to climb. Gender ratios became more equal. These changes, along with the rise of larger plantations throughout the South, made it easier for black men and women to find partners and start families. Elaborate kinship networks gradually developed, often extending over several plantations in a single neighborhood. And, as the immigrant generations were replaced by native-born offspring, earlier sources of tension and division within the slave community disappeared.

Even so, black families remained vulnerable. If a planter fell on hard times, members of black families might be sold off to different buyers to meet his debts. When an owner died, black spouses, parents, and children might be divided among surviving heirs. Even under the best circumstances, fathers might be hired out to other planters for long periods or sent to work in distant quarters. The migration of slaveholders from the coast to the interior also disrupted black efforts to fashion domestic and communal bonds. Between 1755 and 1782, masters on the move resettled fully one-third of all adult African Americans living in Tidewater, Virginia. Most slaves forced to journey west were men and women in their teens and early 20s, who had to begin again the long process of establishing families and neighborhood networks far from kin and friends.

Black families struggling with terrible uncertainties were sustained by the distinctive African American culture evolving in the slave community. The high percentage of native Africans among the eighteenth-century American black population made it easier for slaves to retain the ways of their lost homeland. Christianity won few converts, in part because white masters feared that baptizing slaves might make them more rebellious but also because African Americans preferred their traditional religions. African influence appeared as well in the slaves' agricultural skills and practices, folktales, music, and dances.

## Slave Resistance in Eighteenth-Century British North America

British North America had no shortage of African Americans who both resisted captivity and developed strategies for survival. Collective attempts at escape were most common among recently arrived Africans. Groups of slaves, often made up of newcomers from the same region, fled inland and formed **"Maroon" communities** of runaways. These efforts were rarely successful, because the Maroon settlements were too large to go undetected for long.

More-acculturated blacks turned to subtler subversions, employing what one scholar has called "weapons of the weak." Domestics and field hands alike faked illness, feigned stupidity and laziness, broke tools, pilfered from storehouses, hid in the woods for weeks at a time, or simply took off to visit other plantations. Other slaves, usually escaping bondage as solitary individuals, found a new life as craftworkers, dock laborers, or sailors in the relative anonymity of colonial seaports.

The Old Plantation *affords a rare glimpse of life in the slave quarters. At this festive gathering, both men and women dance to the music of a molo (a stringed instrument similar to a banjo) and drums. The gudugudu drum is an instrument common throughout West Africa and similar to the drum depicted* (far right) *in the painting.*

Sometimes slaves rebelled openly. Whites in communities with large numbers of blacks lived in gnawing dread of arson, poisoning, and insurrection. Four slave conspiracies were reported in Virginia during the first half of the eighteenth century. In South Carolina more than two decades of abortive uprisings and insurrection scares culminated in the Stono Rebellion of 1739, the largest slave revolt of the colonial period. Nearly 100 Africans, led by a slave named Jemmy, seized arms from a store in the coastal district of Stono and killed several white neighbors before they were caught and killed by the colonial militia. But throughout the eighteenth century, slave rebellions occurred far less frequently on the mainland of North America than in the Caribbean or Brazil. Whites outnumbered blacks in all of Britain's mainland colonies except South Carolina, and only there did rebels have a haven for a quick escape—Spanish Florida. Faced with those odds, most slaves reasoned that the risks of rebellion outweighed the prospects for success—and most sought opportunities for greater personal freedom within the slave system itself.

 REVIEW

How did African American culture evolve in the slave community, and what form did resistance to captivity take?

# ENLIGHTENMENT AND AWAKENING IN AMERICA

WHERE COLONISTS LIVED, HOW WELL they lived, whether they were male or female, native-born or immigrant, slave or free—all these variables fostered distinctive worldviews, differing attitudes and assumptions about the individual's relationship to nature, society, and God. The diversity of colonials' inner lives became even more pronounced during the eighteenth century because of the **Enlightenment,** an intellectual movement that started in Europe during the seventeenth century.

## The Enlightenment in America

The leading figures of the Enlightenment, the *philosophes,* stressed the power of human reason to promote progress by revealing the laws that governed both nature and society. Like many devotees of the Enlightenment, Benjamin Franklin of Philadelphia was most impressed by its emphasis on useful knowledge and experimentation. He pondered air currents and then invented a stove that heated houses more efficiently. He toyed with electricity and then invented lightning rods to protect buildings in thunderstorms. Other amateur colonial scientists constructed simple telescopes, classified animal species native to North America, and sought to explain epidemics in terms of natural causes.

American colleges helped promote Enlightenment thinking. Although institutions such as Harvard (founded 1636) and Yale (1701) initially focused on training ministers, by the eighteenth century their graduates included lawyers, merchants, doctors, and scientists. Most offered courses in mathematics and the natural sciences that taught students algebra and such advanced theories as Copernican astronomy and Newtonian physics.

By the middle of the eighteenth century, Enlightenment ideals had given rise to "rational Christianity," which commanded a small but influential following among Anglicans or liberal **Congregationalists** in the colonies. Their God was not the Calvinists' awesome deity but a benevolent creator who offered salvation not to a small, predestined elite, but to everyone. They believed that God's greatest gift to humankind was reason, which enabled all human beings to follow the moral teachings of Jesus. They muted the Calvinist emphasis on human sinfulness and the need for a soul-shattering conversion. An even smaller number of Americans steeped in the Enlightenment embraced deism, which rejected the divinity of Jesus and looked to nature rather than the Bible for proof of God's existence. In the magnificent design of creation, deists detected a Supreme Architect who had wrought the world and then withdrew to let events unfold through natural law.

Enlightenment philosophy and rational Christianity did little to change the lives of most colonials. French and Spanish authorities suppressed Enlightenment literature in their colonies. Likewise, innovations in Protestant doctrine were meaningless in New Spain and New France, where Catholicism was the only European religion tolerated. Eighteenth-century British North Americans suffered from fewer restrictions, and more than half of all white men (and a smaller percentage of white women) could read. But few colonial readers had the interest or the background necessary to tackle the learned writings of Enlightenment *philosophes.* The great majority still looked for ultimate truth in biblical revelation rather than human reason and explained the workings of the world in terms of divine providence rather than natural law.

Widespread attachment to traditional Christian beliefs was strengthened by the hundreds of new churches built during the first half of the eighteenth century. Church attendance ran highest in the northern colonies, where some 80 percent of the population turned out for public worship on the Sabbath. In the South, because of the greater distances involved and the shortage of clergy, about half of all colonials regularly attended Sunday services.

Despite the prevalence of traditional religious beliefs, many ministers grew alarmed over the dangerous influence of rational Christianity. They also worried that the lack of churches might tempt many frontier families to abandon Christianity altogether. Exaggerated as these fears may have been, they gave rise to a major religious revival that swept the colonies during the middle decades of the eighteenth century.

A sharp critic of the evangelical revivals that swept both sides of the Atlantic, the English artist William Hogarth satirized preaching in the style of George Whitefield. In this detail from an engraving of 1762 titled "Credulity, Superstition, and Fanaticism," the minister wears a clown's jacket under his gown and plays upon the superstitious beliefs of his congregation by dangling a witch from one hand, a devil from the other. The page before him reads, "I speak as a fool"; the ribbon to his right shows a scale of "vociferation" that runs from a "Natural Tone" of speaking all the way up to "Bull Roar." Hogarth did not think critical thinking was incompatible with biblical teachings, for below the engraving he included a bit of scripture: "Believe not every Spirit, but try the Spirits whether they are of God: because many false Prophets are gone out into the World."

## The First Great Awakening

The **Great Awakening,** as the revival came to be called, first appeared in the 1730s among Presbyterians and Congregationalists in the middle colonies and New England. Many ministers in these churches preached an "evangelical" message, emphasizing the need for individuals to experience "a new birth" through religious conversion. Among them was Jonathan Edwards, the pastor of a Congregational church in Northampton, Massachusetts. Edwards's Calvinist preaching combined moving descriptions of God's grace with terrifying portrayals of eternal damnation. "The God that holds you over the pit of hell, much as one holds a spider or some loathsome insect over the fire, abhors you and is dreadfully provoked," he declaimed to one congregation. "There is no other reason to be given, why you have not dropped into hell since you arise in the morning, but that God's hand has held you up."

These local revivals of the 1730s were mere tremors compared to the earthquake of religious enthusiasm that shook the colonies with the arrival in the fall of 1739 of George Whitefield. This handsome (though cross-eyed) "boy preacher" from England electrified crowds from Georgia to New Hampshire during his two-year tour of the colonies. He and his many imitators among colonial ministers turned the church into a theater, enlivening sermons with dramatic gestures, flowing tears, and gruesome depictions of hell. The drama of such performances appealed to people of all classes, ethnic groups, and races. By the time Whitefield sailed back to England in 1741, thousands of awakened souls were joining older churches or forming new ones.

## The Aftermath of the Great Awakening

Whitefield also left behind a raging storm of controversy. Many "awakened" church members now openly criticized their ministers as cold, unconverted, and uninspiring. To supply the missing fire, some laymen—"and even Women and Common Negroes"—took to "exhorting" any audience willing to listen. The most popular ministers became **itinerants,** traveling as Whitefield did from one town to another.

RELIGIOUS DIVISIONS

Although Americans had been fighting over religion well before the Great Awakening, the new revivals left colonials even more divided along religious lines. The largest single group of churchgoers in the northern colonies remained within the Congregational and Presbyterian denominations. But both of these groups split into factions over the revivals. Quakers and Anglicans shunned them. In contrast, the most radical converts joined forces with the warmest champions of the Awakening, the Baptists.

While northern churches splintered and bickered, the fires of revivalism spread to the South and its back-country. From the mid-1740s until the 1770s scores of new Presbyterian and Baptist churches formed, sparking controversy. Ardent Presbyterians disrupted Anglican worship by loosing packs of dogs in local chapels. County officials, prodded by resentful Anglican parsons, harassed, fined, and imprisoned Baptist ministers.

And so a diverse lot of Americans found themselves continually at odds with one another: arguing over religion and the Enlightenment, conflicted over racial and ethnic tensions, and divided between coastal and backcountry cultures. Benjamin Franklin, a man who made it his business to know, surely understood the depth of those divisions. Even he had brooded over the boatloads of non-English newcomers. He had lived in two booming seaports and felt the explosive force of the frontier. He personified the Enlightenment—and yet looked on in admiration at a George Whitefield sermon on the steps of the Philadelphia courthouse.

Franklin recognized these divisions. Yet oddly enough, even though he knew how little held colonials together, he still harbored hopes for their political unity. After all, most were English. That much they had in common.

 REVIEW

Describe the different outlooks of Enlightenment and evangelical Christians.

# ANGLO-AMERICAN WORLDS OF THE EIGHTEENTH CENTURY

MOST COLONISTS IN BRITISH NORTH America prided themselves on being English. Colonial towns bore English names; colonial governments drew on English precedents; colonial diets, dress, architecture, furniture, and literature all followed English models. And yet there were important differences. Some differences made colonials feel inferior, ashamed of their simplicity when compared with London's sophistication. But they also came to appreciate the greater equality of their society and the more representative character of their governments. If it was good to be English, it was better still to be English in America.

## English Economic and Social Development

The differences between England and America began with their economies. Large financial institutions such as the Bank of England and influential corporations such as the East India Company were driving England's commercial development. A growing number of textile factories and mines were deepening its industrial development. Although most English men and women worked at agriculture, it, too, had become a business. Gentry rented their estates to tenants, the rural middle class. In turn, these tenants hired men and women from the swollen ranks of England's landless to perform the farm labor. In contrast, most colonial farmers owned their land, and most family farms were a few hundred acres. The scale of commerce and manufacturing was equally modest, limited by the preference of colonials to farm instead.

England's more developed economy fostered the growth of cities, especially London, a teeming colossus of 675,000 in 1750. In contrast, 90 percent of all eighteenth-century colonials lived in towns of fewer than 2,000.

## The Consumer Revolution

But in another respect, England's more advanced economy drew the colonies and the parent country together. Americans were so eager to acquire British-made commodities that their per capita consumption of imported manufactures rose 120 percent between 1750 and 1773. People of all classes demanded and indulged in small luxuries such as a tin of tea, a pair of gloves, and a bar of Irish soap. In both England and its colonies, the spare and simple material life of earlier centuries was giving way to a new order in which even people of ordinary means owned a wider variety of things.

## Inequality in England and America

Then there were people of no means. In England they were legion. London seethed with filth, crime, and desperate poverty. The poor and the unemployed as well as pickpockets and prostitutes crowded into its gin-soaked slums, taverns, and brothels. The contrast between the luxuries enjoyed by a wealthy few Londoners and the misery of the many disquieted colonial observers. Ebenezer Hazard, an American Quaker visiting London, knew for certain he was in "a Sink of Sin."

**CLASS DISTINCTIONS** New wealth and the inherited privileges of England's landed aristocracy made for deepening class divisions. Two percent of England's population owned 70 percent of its land. By right of birth, English aristocrats claimed membership in the House of Lords; by custom, certain powerful gentry families dominated the other branch of Parliament, the House of Commons.

The colonies had their own prominent families, but no titled ruling class holding political privilege by hereditary right. And even the wealthiest colonial families lived far more humbly than their English counterparts. Probably the finest mansion in eighteenth-century America, William Byrd's plantation at Westover, Virginia, was scarcely a tenth the size of the Marquis of Rockingham's country house, a sprawling edifice longer than two football fields.

If England's upper classes lived more splendidly, its lower classes were larger and worse off than those in the colonies. Less than a third of England's inhabitants belonged to the "middling sort" of traders, professionals, artisans, and tenant farmers. More than two-thirds struggled for survival at the bottom of society. In contrast, the colonial middle class counted for nearly three-quarters of the white population. With land cheap, labor scarce, and wages for both urban and rural workers 100 percent higher in America than in England, it was much easier for colonials to accumulate savings and farms of their own.

Colonials were both fascinated and repelled by English society. Benjamin Rush, a Philadelphia physician, felt in the House of Lords as if he "walked on sacred ground." He begged his guide for permission to sit on the throne therein and then sat "for a considerable time." Other colonials gushed over the grandeur of aristocratic estates and imported suits of livery for their servants, tea services for their wives, and wallpaper for their drawing rooms.

But colonials recognized that England's ruling classes purchased their luxury and leisure at the cost of the rest of the nation. In his autobiography, Benjamin Franklin painted a devastating portrait of the degraded lives of his fellow workers in a London print shop, who drowned their disappointments by drinking throughout the workday, even more excessively on the Sabbath, and then faithfully observing the holiday of "St. Monday" to nurse their hangovers. Like Franklin, many colonials regarded the idle among England's rich and poor alike as ominous signs of a degenerate nation.

## Politics in England and America

**ENGLAND'S BALANCED CONSTITUTION** Colonials were also of two minds about England's government. While they praised the English constitution as the basis of all liberties, they were alarmed by the actual workings of English politics. In theory, England's

**"balanced constitution"** gave every order of society a voice in government. Whereas the Crown represented the monarchy and the House of Lords the aristocracy, the House of Commons represented the democracy, the people of England.

In fact, webs of patronage and outright bribery compromised the whole system. The monarch and his ministers had the power to appoint legions of bureaucrats to administer the growing state and empire. By the middle of the eighteenth century, almost half of all members of Parliament held such Crown offices or government contracts. Many had won their seats in corrupt elections, where the small electorate (perhaps a quarter of all adult males) were bought off with money or liquor.

**COLONIAL GOVERNMENTS**

Americans liked to think that their colonial governments mirrored the ideal English constitution. Most colonies had a royal governor who represented the monarch in America and a bicameral (two-house) legislature made up of a lower house (the assembly) and an upper house (or council). The democratically elected assemblies, like the House of Commons, stood for popular interests, whereas the councils, some of which were elected and others appointed, more roughly approximated the House of Lords.

But these formal similarities masked real differences between English and colonial governments. On the face of it, royal governors had much more power than the English Crown. Unlike kings and queens, royal governors could veto laws passed by assemblies; they could dissolve those bodies at will; they could create courts and dismiss judges. However, governors who asserted their full powers quickly met opposition from their assemblies, who objected that such overwhelming authority endangered popular liberty. In any showdown with their assemblies, most royal governors had to give way, because they lacked the government offices and contracts that bought loyalty. The colonial legislatures possessed additional leverage, since all of them retained the sole authority to levy taxes.

At the same time, widespread ownership of land meant that more than half of the colonies' white adult male population could vote. The larger electorate made it more difficult to buy votes. The colonial electorate was also more watchful. Representatives had to reside in the districts that they served, and a few even received binding instructions from their constituents about how to vote.

Most Americans were as pleased with their inexpensive and representative colonial governments as they were

Coffeehouses such as this establishment in London were favorite gathering places for eighteenth-century Americans visiting Britain. Here merchants and mariners, ministers and students, lobbyists and tourists warmed themselves, read newspapers, and exchanged gossip about commerce, politics, and social life.

John Stuart, the third Earl of Bute (1713–1792), in the ceremonial robes of the House of Lords. The lavish style epitomizes the opulence of Britain's ruling class in the eighteenth century.

things. Those few Britons who thought about America at all believed that colonials resembled the "savage" Indians more than the "civilized" English. As a London acquaintance remarked to the Boston merchant Thomas Hancock, it was a pity Mrs. Hancock had to remain in Boston when he could "take her to England and make her happy with Christians."

The same indifference contributed to England's haphazard administration of its colonies. Aside from passing an occasional law to regulate trade, restrict manufacturing, or direct monetary policy, Parliament made no effort to assert its authority in America. Its members assumed that Parliament's sovereignty extended over the entire empire, and nothing had occurred to make them think otherwise.

**BENEFITS OF BENIGN NEGLECT** For the colonies, this chaotic and inefficient system of colonial administration left them a great deal of freedom. Even England's regulation of trade rested lightly on the shoulders of most Americans. Southern planters were obliged to send their rice, indigo, and tobacco to Britain only, but they enjoyed favorable credit terms and knowledgeable marketing from English merchants. Colonials were prohibited from finishing iron products and exporting hats and textiles, but they had scant interest in developing domestic industries. Americans were required to import all manufactured goods through England, but by doing so, they acquired high-quality goods at low prices. At little sacrifice, most Americans obeyed imperial regulations. Only sugar, molasses, and tea were routinely smuggled.

Following this policy of **benign neglect,** the British Empire muddled on to the satisfaction of most people on both sides of the Atlantic. Economic growth and political **autonomy** allowed most Americans to like being English, despite their misgivings about their parent nation. The beauty of it was that Americans could be English in America, enjoying greater economic opportunity and political equality. If imperial arrangements had remained as they were in 1754, the empire might have muddled on indefinitely.

horrified by the conduct of politics in England. John Dickinson, a young Pennsylvanian training as a lawyer in London, was scandalized by a parliamentary election he witnessed in 1754. The king and his ministers had spent over 100,000 pounds sterling to buy support for their candidates, he wrote his father, and "if a man cannot be brought to vote as he is desired, he is made dead drunk and kept in that state, never heard of by his family and friends, till all is over and he can do no harm."

This tea caddy, owned by a Massachusetts colonial, was a new consumer luxury, as was the tea it held.

## The Imperial System before 1760

Few Britons gave the colonists as much thought as the colonists gave them. It would be hard to overstate just how insignificant North America was in the English scheme of

✓ **REVIEW**

What were the similarities, differences, and connections between England and America?

*Commercial ties to Spain and Portugal, Africa, and the Caribbean sustained the growth of both seaports and commercial farming regions on the British North American mainland and enabled colonials to purchase an increasing volume of finished goods from England. The proceeds from exports in foodstuffs and lumber to the West Indies and trade in fish to Spain and Portugal enabled northern merchants and farmers to buy hardware and clothing from the mother country. Southern planters financed their consumption of English imports and their investment in African slaves with the profits from the sale of tobacco, rice, and indigo abroad.*

# CONCLUSION

## THE WORLD AT LARGE

By the 1750s North America was changing, both within the British world and in relation to the international order. For decades, Europe's imperial wars found their way to America almost as an afterthought. Colonial officials, traders, land speculators, and would-be pioneers regularly seized on news of the latest European conflict as an excuse to attack their Spanish or French or British counterparts in the North American borderlands. The interests of kings and queens had to be served, of course. And yet it was easier to exploit war for local or personal purposes out on the far margins of Europe's empires. Eastern North America's native peoples likewise sought advantage in these interimperial flare-ups. But for them the stakes were higher. When chiefs joined in a fight for profit or revenge, or to please one or another colonial ally, they also put their own people at risk.

However the various players positioned themselves, they often found that the outcome of their struggles could be determined by men they would never see: well-heeled diplomats sipping drinks around mahogany tables in European capitals. Victories, defeats, territories won or lost—all this could be and often was undone in Paris, Madrid, or London, where negotiators casually agreed to ignore territorial gains and losses in the colonies and return everything as it was before the fighting broke out. The message was clear: great imperial struggles began in Europe and ended in Europe. America followed.

Though few recognized it in 1754, this older model was about to be swept away. That year marked the beginning of yet another imperial war, one begun not in Europe but in the American borderlands. Rather than following events, this time Indians proved decisive to the war's origins, course, and outcome. And rather than the conflict ending with a return to the status quo, this time war would produce changes greater than anyone could have anticipated. In waging the war and managing its aftermath, London would pursue policies that made it difficult—and ultimately impossible—for its American subjects to remain within the empire. ∞∞∞

# Chapter Summary

During the eighteenth century, Spain, France, and Great Britain competed for power and influence in North America. Native peoples, too, played off these shifting alliances. British North Americans grew increasingly diverse, which made the prospect of any future colonial political union appear remote.

- Spain established mission systems in Texas and California, largely to preempt the expansion of European rivals.

- Low immigration compelled New France to seek sustainable alliances with Indian peoples throughout the Far North and the Mississippi drainage. French Louisiana grew very slowly and failed to develop into a booming plantation colony.

- Differences became more pronounced among whites because of the immigration of larger numbers of non-English settlers, the spread of settlement to the backcountry, and the growth of major seaports.

- The South became more embattled, too, as a result of the massive importation of slaves directly from Africa.

- Religious conflict among colonials was intensified by Enlightenment ideas and the first Great Awakening.

- Still, a majority of white colonials took pride in their common English ancestry.

# Additional Reading

For a richly textured history of early Texas, see Juliana Barr, *Peace Came in the Form of a Woman* (2007). H. Ross Frank's *From Settler to Citizen* (2000) recovers the economic and social changes that came to New Mexico with peace in the late eighteenth century. Steven Hackel's *Children of Coyote, Missionaries of St. Francis* (2005) has set a new standard for scholarship on colonial California. For France in America, see *The People of New France* by Allan Greer (2000). Alan Taylor's *American Colonies* (2001) takes a sweeping, continental perspective. For women's rights in comparison, see Deborah A. Rosen, "Women and Property across Colonial America, *William and Mary Quarterly* 60: 2(2003), 355–382.

On ethnic and racial diversity, see Bernard Bailyn, *Voyagers to the West* (1986), and Peter Silver, *Our Savage Neighbors* (2007). Philip Morgan's *Slave Counterpoint* (1998) offers an overview of African American cultures in the early South. For mounting tensions in American seaports, consult Jill Lepore, *New York Burning* (2005), and Gary Nash, *The Urban Crucible* (1979).

Nancy Shoemaker, *A Strange Likeness* (2004), and James M. Merrell, *Into the American Woods* (1999), are two compelling accounts of how Indians and white Americans came to perceive one another as different peoples. For the expansion of colonial settlement into the backcountry, begin with Eric Hinderaker and Peter C. Mancall, *At the Edge of Empire* (2003). On religion in eighteenth-century society, see Patricia Bonomi, *Under the Cope of Heaven* (1986), and George Marsden, *Jonathan Edwards* (2003).

For a fuller list of readings, see the Bibliography at www.mhhe.com/eh8e.

# Significant Events

**1689–1697**
King William's War (War of the League of Augsburg)

**1690**
Spain begins establishing missions in Texas

**1698**
d'Iberville inaugurates French colony of Louisiana

**1702–1713**
Queen Anne's War (War of the Spanish Succession)

**1729**
Natchez revolt against the French

**1730s**
Comanches begin conquest of the southern plains with the help of European horses and guns; rise in importation of black slaves in northern colonies

**1739**
George Whitefield's first preaching tour in America; Stono Rebellion in South Carolina

**1766**
Tenant Rebellion in New York

**1768**
Spanish begin to colonize California

# [Eighteenth-Century North America: A Mosaic]

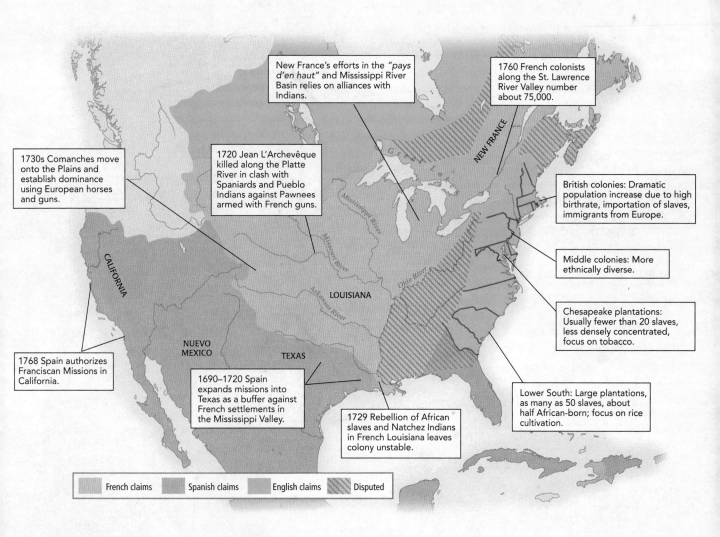

New France's efforts in the *"pays d'en haut"* and Mississippi River Basin relies on alliances with Indians.

1760 French colonists along the St. Lawrence River Valley number about 75,000.

1730s Comanches move onto the Plains and establish dominance using European horses and guns.

1720 Jean L'Archevêque killed along the Platte River in clash with Spaniards and Pueblo Indians against Pawnees armed with French guns.

British colonies: Dramatic population increase due to high birthrate, importation of slaves, immigrants from Europe.

Middle colonies: More ethnically diverse.

Chesapeake plantations: Usually fewer than 20 slaves, less densely concentrated, focus on tobacco.

1768 Spain authorizes Franciscan Missions in California.

1690–1720 Spain expands missions into Texas as a buffer against French settlements in the Mississippi Valley.

1729 Rebellion of African slaves and Natchez Indians in French Louisiana leaves colony unstable.

Lower South: Large plantations, as many as 50 slaves, about half African-born; focus on rice cultivation.

NEW FRANCE

CALIFORNIA

Mississippi River

Missouri River

Ohio River

Arkansas River

LOUISIANA

NUEVO MEXICO

TEXAS

| French claims | Spanish claims | English claims | Disputed |

George Washington was only 22 when he led 200 militiamen and a party of Indians to confront French forces in the Ohio Country in the spring of 1754. He came upon a French detachment at what is now called Jumonville Glen, shown in this 2007 photograph. By the time the encounter had ended, Washington's smart Virginia militia uniform was badly worn and most of his troops, he noted, were "almost naked, and scarcely a man has either Shoes, Stockings, or Hat."

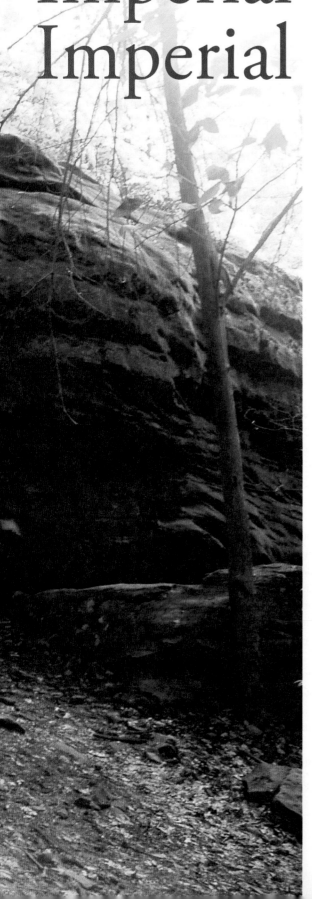

## CHAPTER 6

# Imperial Triumph, Imperial Crisis

1754–1776

## What's to Come

∞∞∞ AN AMERICAN STORY ∞∞∞

## GEORGE WASHINGTON AND THE HALF KING

Everyone seemed to want something from the Ohio Country. And when so many rivals—assertive, anxious, and aggressive—assembled in one location, it was a situation made for disaster. Young George Washington, deep in the forests of the Ohio Country, learned this lesson in the spring of 1754.

The region north of the Ohio River had been a no-man's-land for decades following the Beaver Wars (Chapter 4). Though the mighty Iroquois had no interest in occupying the territory, they claimed sovereignty over it into the 1750s by right of conquest. By then, however, Delawares, Shawnees, Mingos, and other native peoples had established villages in the territory. If they looked to the Iroquois it was for advice, not orders. Who, then, could claim dominion over the Ohio Country?

European rivalries compounded these uncertainties. By the 1750s both Britain and France saw the lands as vital to their strategic interests. Pennsylvania traders had wandered the territory for years, their reports drawing the interest of land speculators. The Ohio Country boasted forests of white oak, plentiful game, and grassy meadows, ideally suited for farming. Chunks of black coal thrust from the ground, hinting at mineral riches. Wealthy Virginians and Pennsylvanians envisioned colonies in the Ohio Country—schemes London happily encouraged in hopes of weakening New France. In 1745 the Virginia House of Burgesses granted 300,000 acres of land to a newly formed enterprise called the Ohio Company. For their part, the French in Quebec relied on the Ohio lands as a buffer between their own relatively small settlements and the populous British settlements to the east. Anxious, the French built new forts and shored up their Indian alliances.

The British countered. In 1754 Virginia's governor (a major investor in the Ohio Company) ordered 200 militiamen under 22-year-old Lieutenant Colonel George Washington (another investor) to assert British interests in the Ohio Country. Washington's militia marched west with the help of several Indians under the "Half King" Tanaghrisson, the Iroquois representative for the Ohio Country. Tanaghrisson had grown up near the important forks of the Ohio River (present-day Pittsburgh)

Indians and Europeans negotiate in the Ohio Country, an area coveted by the English, French, Delawares, Shawnees, and Mingos.

and advised the British to build a "strong house" at this key position. He had even laid down the fort's first log in a ceremony. Washington, who was intelligent, able, and disciplined but inexperienced and badly out of his depth, soon discovered how little control he had over the circumstances—or even over his own expedition.

To begin with, the French had beaten the Virginians to the forks of the Ohio, where they erected Fort Duquesne. On hearing of the approaching British militia, the French commander there dispatched 35 men under an ensign named Jumonville to advise Washington to withdraw. The Virginians learned of the approaching party and marched to intercept it, following Tanaghrisson's lead, "in a heavy rain and a night as dark as pitch," as Washington recalled. At dawn, just as the French were crawling out from under their bark lean-tos to make breakfast, the British and their Indian companions opened fire. Badly wounded along with nearly half of his men, the ensign cried out to stop shooting, that he had come only to talk. Once Washington had gotten control of his force, Jumonville handed him a letter from the French commander. But it was in French, which Washington did not read. He turned to fetch his translator. Just then Tanaghrisson stepped in front of the wounded Jumonville. The grave Iroquois representative was older and far more experienced than Washington, and he had his own agenda. Unhappy with the emboldened French posture in the region and convinced that Iroquois interests would be best served if the French and British were at each other's throats, he did something neither Washington nor his French counterpart could have possibly expected. "You're not dead yet, my father," he told Jumonville; and then sank a hatchet into the officer's head, ripped his skull apart, and pulled out his brains. Washington staggered back dumbstruck as Tanaghrisson's Indians set about killing the other wounded soldiers.

This was not how it was supposed to happen. Washington hastily retreated some way, threw up a makeshift structure, aptly named "Fort Necessity," and waited for reinforcements from Virginia. About a month later a formidable French force (led by Jumonville's grieving brother) laid siege and quickly compelled Washington's surrender. The Virginians returned home in defeat, bearing the news that the Shawnees, Delawares, and Mingos had either sided with the French or refused to fight at all. "The chief part" of his men, Washington wrote in dismay, "are almost naked, and scarcely a man has either Shoes, Stockings or Hat." It was an ignominious beginning to a long, exhausting war that would eventually spread across the entire globe. ∞∞∞

# The Seven Years' War

The Seven Years' War, which actually lasted nine years, pitted Britain and its ally, Prussia, against France, in league with Austria and Spain. The conflict raged from 1754 until 1763 and deserves to be called the first global war. Because the contending powers had colonial possessions and economic interests around the world, the fight spanned the continent of Europe, the coast of West Africa, India, the Philippines, the Caribbean, and North America. The spark that started this worldwide conflagration came from the Ohio Country.

Britain and France had come to blows in the backcountry before. And Indian peoples had long sought to profit from their interimperial rivalry and turn it to their own ends. But for the first time, bloodshed in the forests of North America would lead Europe into war, rather than the other way around. And Washington's misadventure at Fort Necessity set the pattern for the early years of the conflict more broadly, years marked by British missteps and British defeats.

## Years of Defeat

Washington's surrender only stiffened Britain's resolve to assert its claims to the Ohio Country: hence its decision to send two divisions under General Braddock to wrest the region from France. France responded by sending the equivalent of eight divisions to Canada. There was therefore great anticipation surrounding Braddock's campaign. Unfortunately for the English, General Braddock had all but sealed his doom before even marching into the backcountry. Ignoring American advisers who insisted that Indian alliances would be key to victory, Braddock alienated native leaders and refused to acknowledge their claims to land. "The English should inhabit and inherit the land . . . no savage should inherit the land," he insisted. In 1755 Braddock's divisions pushed into the Ohio Country with fewer than 10 Indians along. After five weeks of agonizing progress through dense woods and over rough terrain, the troops were ambushed by French and Indian sharpshooters firing into the British column from the cover of trees. As his men fell around him, Braddock calmly rode back and forth on horseback and ordered the troops to remain or get back in formation and return fire as they had been trained. But none had been trained for this kind of fighting, and gathering together only made them easier to shoot. The smoke and gunfire, the screams of dying men and horses, and—perhaps most memorably—the haunting cries of the attacking Indians gradually overcame British discipline. Three hours into the battle Braddock still sat atop his horse, as brave as he was unimaginative, yelling at his men to fight as if they were on a European battlefield. Finally, the general lurched up in his saddle and collapsed, a musket ball buried deep in his back. The British troops still able to walk or run fled the scene.

The monumental defeat sent shock waves throughout the empire, emboldened the French, and convinced many wavering Indian peoples that the French were the people to back. Raiding parties began striking backcountry settlements from New York to Virginia, and terrified refugees fled east.

**ALBANY PLAN OF UNION** — Britain's war went from bad to worse in North America. British colonists generally saw the French and their Indian allies as a common threat but found cooperation among colonies elusive. At the start of the war, representatives from throughout the colonies came to the so-called Albany Congress, designed in part to repair the "Covenant Chain," the long-standing alliance between Britain and the Iroquois that had been badly damaged by British missteps and French victories in the Ohio Country. More broadly, Benjamin Franklin presented the other colonial delegates with a plan for colonial cooperation, in which a federal council made up of representatives from each colony would assume responsibility for a united colonial defense. The Albany delegates were alarmed enough by the wavering Iroquois and the threatening French to accept the idea. But when they brought the proposal home to their respective legislatures, not a single one approved the Albany Plan of Union. "Everyone cries, a union is necessary," Franklin complained, "but when they come to the manner and form of the union, their weak noodles are perfectly distracted."

London did little to encourage collective self-sacrifice. When England and France formally declared war in May 1756, John Campbell, the Earl of Loudoun, took command of the North American theater. American soldiers and colonial assemblies alike despised Lord Loudoun. They balked at his efforts to take command over colonial troops and dragged their heels at his high-handed demands for men and supplies. Meanwhile, the French appointed an effective new commanding general of their forces in Canada, Louis Joseph, the marquis de Montcalm. Montcalm drove southward, capturing key British forts and threatening the security of both New York and New England.

 **THE WAR WIDENS** — France decided to press its advantage in Europe as well. In addition to threatening England itself, French ships began attacking British holdings throughout the Mediterranean. Meanwhile, the complex system of alliances that was supposed to keep continental Europe at peace began to fail. In August of 1756 Prussia, an English ally, invaded Austria, a French ally. France went to Austria's aid and Prussia suddenly found itself on the defensive, begging London for salvation. The war seemed to be spreading in all directions, and none of the changes seemed to bode well for the British Empire.

## A Shift in Policy

**WILLIAM PITT TURNS THE TIDE** — British fortunes rebounded only when the veteran English politician William Pitt came out of retirement to direct the war.

## THE SEVEN YEARS' WAR

*After Washington's surrender and Braddock's defeat in the Pennsylvania backcountry, the British and French waged their final contest for supremacy in North America in northern New York and Canada. But the rivalry for empire between France and Britain was worldwide, with naval superiority providing the needed edge to Britain. The British navy isolated French forces in India, winning a victory at Pondicherry, while English offensives captured the French sugar islands in the Caribbean and French trading posts along the West African coast. When Spain entered the war on the side of France, British fleets captured both Havana and the strategic port of Manila in the Philippines.* **Which victory sealed the British triumph over New France? Why was the win geographically important?**

Pitt was an odd character. Subject to bouts of depression and loathed for his opportunism and egotism, he was nonetheless buoyed by a strong sense of destiny—his own and that of England. He believed Great Britain must seize the world's trade, because trade meant wealth and wealth meant power. France seemed to him the greatest obstacle to this British destiny—and Pitt returned to the political fray charged with energy. "I know that I can save this country," he declared with typical confidence, "and that no one else can."

Pitt's strategy was bold. He would leave the fighting in Europe to the Prussians but support them with massive infusions of cash with which they could buy supplies and

recruit men. France was strongest in Europe, he reasoned, so Britain ought to focus its military energies elsewhere. Better to attack France around the world—in the Caribbean, in West Africa, and in the Indian Ocean. Most especially, Pitt would attack them in North America. He audaciously pledged to drive France out of the continent altogether. To do so he would have to convince the colonists who had been alienated by Braddock's arrogance and Loudoun's harsh policies that they would be treated as equals. Pitt recalled Loudoun, put limits on the powers enjoyed by his successor, pledged to respect the officers in colonial militias, and, crucially, promised that London—not the colonies—would bear the financial burden of the war.

| John Campbell

| William Pitt

**INDIANS AND THE WAR EFFORT** Last but certainly not least, the new government acknowledged the centrality of Indians to the war effort. The officers Pitt sent to execute the new approach listened to colonial Indian agents and go-betweens, authorized new, high-level conferences, and approved the distribution of presents to key leaders. These conciliatory gestures and more accommodating policies were well timed, because by then, the Indian peoples of the Ohio Country and the *pays d'en haut* had increasingly come to question the French alliance.

Though French authorities often took Indians more seriously than their English counterparts, they, too, struggled to reconcile cultural difference. In the aftermath of joint victories, for example, French officers sometimes felt obliged by European military protocol to deny their Indian allies customary war spoils—captives, plunder, and scalps. Disgruntled native warriors generally took them anyway and often refused to fight for France again. More critical than even such cultural differences, the economic toll of the war damaged French-Indian alliances. By 1757 Britain's unsurpassed navy had instituted a formidable blockade on the St. Lawrence that cut off supplies to Canada. Without arms, ammunition, and metal goods, French authorities found it more and more difficult to maintain their Indian alliances. More and more withdrew from the conflict or sided with Britain.

## Years of Victory

The reforms galvanized the colonies. Most British North Americans were proud to be part of the empire and welcomed the chance to help fight for it so long as they would be treated as equals. With Pitt's reforms in place, the tide of the war finally began to turn. In July of 1758 the British gained control of the St. Lawrence River when the French fortress at Louisbourg fell before the combined force of the Royal Navy and British and colonial troops. In August a force of New Englanders strangled France's frontier defenses by capturing Fort Frontenac, thereby isolating French forts lining the Great Lakes and the Ohio valley. More and more Indians, seeing the French routed from the interior, switched their allegiance to the English.

**WOLFE AND MONTCALM BATTLE FOR QUEBEC** The British succeeded even more brilliantly in 1759. In Canada, Brigadier General James Wolfe gambled on a daring stratagem and won Quebec from Montcalm. Under the cover of darkness, naval squadrons landed Wolfe's men beneath the city's steep bluffs, where they scaled the heights to a plateau known as the Plains of Abraham. Montcalm might have won by holding out behind the walls of his fortress and awaiting reinforcements. Instead, he matched Wolfe's recklessness and offered battle. Five days later both Wolfe and Montcalm lay dead, along with 1,400 French soldiers and 600 British and American troops. Quebec had fallen to the British. A year later the French surrender of Montreal ended the imperial war in North America, although it continued elsewhere around the world for another two years.

 **TREATY OF PARIS** The Treaty of Paris, signed in February 1763, ended the French presence on the continent of North America. The terms confirmed British title to all French territory east of the Mississippi. Spain had foolishly entered the war on France's side in 1762 and quickly lost Havana to British warships. The treaty restored Cuba to Spain, but at a high price: the Spanish relinquished Florida to Britain. With France driven from the continent, something had to be done with the vast and ill-defined territory of Louisiana, west of the Mississippi. Spain did not want the trouble and expense of administering this sprawling region, but it did not want Britain to have it. Somewhat reluctantly, then, Spain accepted nominal dominion over all land west of the great river, as well as the port of New Orleans, in the separate Treaty of San Ildefonso. In addition to its North America spoils, Britain won several Caribbean islands in the war, as well as Senegal in West Africa.

After generations of inconclusive imperial wars, British North Americans found the victory almost impossibly grand. Towns up and down the Atlantic coast glowed bright with celebratory bonfires and rang with the sounds of clanking tankards and jolly song. How good it was to be British!

## Postwar Expectations

Grand expectations came hot on the heels of joyful celebration. The end of the war, Americans felt sure, meant the end of high taxes. The terms of the peace, they were confident, meant that the fertile lands of the Ohio valley would be thrown open to English settlement. The prosperity of the war years alone made for a mood of optimism. British military spending and William Pitt's subsidies had made money for farmers, merchants, artisans, and anyone else who had anything to do with supplying the army or navy. Colonials also took pride in their contributions of troops and money to the winning of the war. In view of that support, Americans expected to be given more consideration within the British Empire. Now, as one anonymous pamphleteer put it, Americans would "not be thought presumptuous, if they consider[ed] themselves upon an equal footing" with English in the parent country.

ENGLISH RESENTMENTS

But most imperial officials in America thought that if Americans took pride in being English, they had done a poor job of showing it. British statesmen grumbled that colonial assemblies had been tightfisted when it came to supplying the army. British commanders charged that colonial troops had been lily-livered when it came to fighting the French. Such accusations were unjust, but they stuck in the minds of many Britons at home. The nation had accumulated a huge debt that would saddle it with high taxes for years to come. To make matters worse, some Britons suspected that, with the French removed from North America, the colonies would move toward independence. As early as 1755 Josiah Tucker, a respected English economist, had warned that "to drive the French out of all North America would be the most fatal step we could take."

Americans in 1763 were not, in truth, revolutionaries in the making. They were loyal British subjects in the flush of postwar patriotism. Americans in 1763, deeply divided,

| The British navy bombarded Quebec, reducing many of the city's buildings to smoldering ruins. The devastation presaged the end of France's empire in North America.

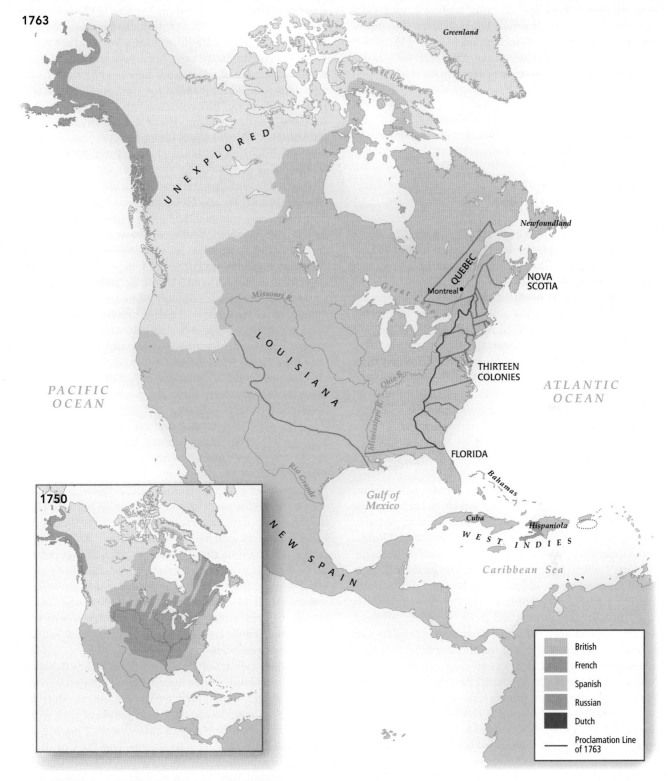

1763

Greenland

UNEXPLORED

Newfoundland

QUEBEC

Montreal

NOVA SCOTIA

Missouri R.

Great Lakes

L O U I S I A N A

Ohio R.

THIRTEEN COLONIES

PACIFIC OCEAN

ATLANTIC OCEAN

Mississippi R.

FLORIDA

Rio Grande

Gulf of Mexico

Bahamas

1750

N E W  S P A I N

Cuba

Hispaniola

W E S T   I N D I E S

Caribbean Sea

| | British |
|---|---|
| | French |
| | Spanish |
| | Russian |
| | Dutch |
| | Proclamation Line of 1763 |

## EUROPEAN CLAIMS IN NORTH AMERICA, 1750 AND 1763

*The British victory in the Seven Years' War secured Great Britain's title to a large portion of present-day United States and Canada. Colonials hoped to settle the newly won territory, but politicians in London intended to restrict westward movement with the Proclamation of 1763.*

were not even "Americans." But most postwar English colonials did expect to enjoy a more equal status in the empire. And most Britons had no inclination to accord them that equality. The differing expectations of the colonies' place in the empire poised the postwar generation for crisis.

 **REVIEW**

What started the Seven Years' War, and how did Britain emerge victorious?

# THE IMPERIAL CRISIS

IT WAS COMMON SENSE. Great Britain had waged a costly war to secure its empire in America; now it needed to consolidate those gains. The empire's North American territory needed to be protected, its administration tightened, and its colonies made as profitable as possible to the parent nation. In other words, the empire needed to be centralized. That conclusion dictated Britain's decision to leave a standing army of several thousand troops in America after the Seven Years' War. And, of course, armies needed to be paid for; that would mean taxes. That the colonists, who benefited most from the great victory, ought to pull out their purses for king and country—well, Britain's political leaders thought that, too, was common sense.

## Pontiac's Rebellion

British authorities justified the army's continued presence in part by pointing to the various foreign peoples that the Crown now had to administer. The army must be prepared to police French colonists in Canada, Spaniards in Florida, and, especially, dozens of native peoples west of the Appalachians. General Jeffery Amherst, the top British officer in North America, believed Indian troubles could be avoided if military and civil authorities simply projected strength. Now that French power had been expelled, Amherst thought, Britain need not purchase Indian friendship with presents, and subsidize trade, and sponsor tiresome diplomatic ceremonies. All this was to cease. Knowledgeable colonists saw too much of Edward Braddock in all of this. When they insisted that presents, favorable trade, and diplomacy were the indispensable elements of Indian relations, Amherst would have none of it. "When men of what race soever behave ill," the general insisted, "they must be punished but not bribed." Indians had to learn that the English now were masters of the land.

NEOLIN    Britain's new attitude of triumph provoked great anxiety within Indian communities that had troubles enough to contend with. Many had lost men in the war, crops had been destroyed or had failed, and whole villages and towns had been put to the torch. British traders, now untroubled by French competition, bartered eagerly but charged far more for their goods than previously. Finally, the end of the war brought a surge of speculators and colonists eager to claim land beyond the mountains. These interlocked crises prompted calls for a return to tradition—for a revival that would empower resistance movements across tribal lines. Such was the message of a Delaware holy man named Neolin, who told followers he spoke for God, or the Master of Life. The Master of Life commanded his Indian children to "drive [the British] out, make war on them. I do not love them at all; they know me not, and are my enemies. Send them back to the lands I have created for them and let them stay there."

Pontiac, a charismatic and tactically gifted Ottawa chief, embraced Neolin's message of renaissance and rebellion. In the summer of 1763 he organized attacks against British forts. Shawnees, Mingos, Potawatomis, Wyandots, and other Indian peoples in the Ohio Country, or the *pays d'en haut,* working with Pontiac or independently, captured every British fort west of Detroit by early July. Colonial settlements in the backcountry came under attack from Pennsylvania to Virginia, leaving hundreds of colonists dead and hundreds more fleeing east. Enraged and determined to assert British rule, Amherst organized troops to march west and attack Indian forces and native villages. He also authorized the commander at Fort Pitt to give Indians blankets from the forts' infirmary, where several men had been stricken with smallpox.

THE PAXTON BOYS    Hatreds mounted on all sides. In western Pennsylvania, where Indian raids had taken an especially grim toll, a number of Scots-Irishmen calling themselves the "Paxton Boys" set out to purge the colony of Indians altogether. In December of 1763 they burst into a small village of Christian Indians, killed the six people they found there, and burned it to the ground. Fourteen others who had been absent fled to the town of Lancaster. Learning that Lancaster's officials had put the survivors into protective custody, the Paxton Boys organized a mob, forced their way into the safe house, and massacred all 14 men, women, and children with broadswords. Colonists and natives alike were increasingly willing to simplify difference and see all "Indians" or all "whites" as despicable enemies.

When officials in London learned of Pontiac's Rebellion and all the violence it occasioned, they attributed it to bad leadership and immediately replaced Amherst. More important, the Crown issued the Proclamation of 1763, which transformed colonial policy in critical ways. Presents and respectful diplomacy were to resume, and the Crown put two Indian superintendents in place (one in South Carolina and one in New York) to help oversee good relations. Most critical, colonial settlement west of the Appalachians was to cease immediately. The so-called proclamation line designated all western territories as Indian territory and strictly off limits to colonization. (Quebec and Florida were the exceptions, divided into eastern and western halves, for colonials and Indians.) Restricting westward movement might ease Indian fears, the British hoped, and so stave off future conflicts.

## THE APPALACHIAN FRONTIER, 1750–1775

*Made bold by the presence of British forts and soldiers, land-hungry colonials spilled into the West through the Cumberland Gap, a notch in the chain of mountains stretching the length of the North American interior. Only Indians and some white hunters knew of the Cumberland Gap before it was scouted in 1750 by Dr. Thomas Walker and a party of Virginians on behalf of a company of land speculators. In 1763 Indians led by Pontiac seized eight British forts before troops under Colonel Henry Bouquet stopped the offensive at Bushy Run, Pennsylvania. In 1775 Daniel Boone took the first large party of pioneers through the Cumberland Gap and established a fort at Boonesborough in present-day Kentucky.*

 **THE PROCLAMATION VS. THE ENVIRONMENT ON THE GROUND**

In drawing their proclamation line, British officials in London adopted what they thought would be a commonsense boundary rooted in the environment on the ground. The Appalachian Mountains, after all, provided a natural barrier, and the line forbidding settlement could be defined in reference to physical features: "any lands beyond the heads or sources of any of the rivers which fall into the Atlantic Ocean from the west or northwest." Yet the real environment was more ambiguous and diverse. Rivers (and their valleys) often acted as pathways into the interior, beckoning Indians and white settlers alike to breach mountain "barriers." In some areas, Indians remained powerful to the east of the Appalachians (the Creeks and Cherokees to the south, the Iroquois to the north). In other areas west of the mountains, the chaos of the Seven Years' War had left lands largely unoccupied, into which white settlers had entered. Although the proclamation line did not ignore the environment on the ground, actual conditions were infinitely more complicated, and the British Indian commissioners almost immediately began redrawing the line in an effort to keep up with the realities.

Amherst's recall and the conciliatory measures helped defuse the conflict, and the violence had more or less subsided by the fall of 1764. Insofar as it helped push Britain to change its Indian policy, Pontiac's Rebellion helped the Indians who launched it. But the war's animosities endured. And however sensible and just the proclamation line might have seemed from the perspective of the Ohio Country or London, few British colonists would see it as anything but betrayal by their own government. Many of them wondered why they had fought and sacrificed in the war against France, if all the territory they helped win was to be set aside for Indians.

## George Grenville's New Measures

If Pontiac's Rebellion and the Proclamation of 1763 had been the only postwar disappointments colonists faced, that would have been trouble enough. But George Grenville, the first lord of the treasury, had yet to confront the dismal financial consequences of the Seven Years' War.

Britain's national debt had doubled in the decade after 1754. Adding to that burden was the drain of supporting troops in the colonies. As matters stood, heavy taxes were already triggering protests among hard-pressed Britons. Americans, in contrast, paid comparatively low taxes to their colonial governments and little in trade duties to the empire. Indeed, Grenville discovered that the colonial customs service paid out four times more in salaries to its collectors than it gathered in duties and was thereby operating at a net loss. Rampant bribery and tax evasion allowed merchants to avoid existing duties on foreign molasses, for example, which New England merchants imported in order to make rum.

**SUGAR ACT** George Grenville reasoned that if Americans could pay out a little under the table to protect an illegal trade, they would willingly pay a little more to go legitimate. Parliament agreed. In April 1764 it passed the Revenue Act, commonly called the Sugar Act. This **tariff** actually lowered the duty on foreign molasses from six to three pence a gallon. This time, however, the tax would be scrupulously collected, ships would be tightly monitored for compliance, and violators would be tried in admiralty courts, far harsher than typical colonial courts.

**CURRENCY AND QUARTERING ACTS** Grenville made other, similar proposals, all approved by Parliament. There was the Currency Act of 1764, which prohibited the colonies from making their paper money legal tender. That prevented Americans from paying their debts to British traders in currency that had fallen to less than its face value. There was the Quartering Act of 1765, which obliged any colony in which troops were stationed to provide them with suitable accommodations. That contributed to the cost of keeping British forces in America. Finally, in March of 1765, Parliament passed the Stamp Act.

**STAMP ACT** The Stamp Act placed **taxes** on legal documents, customs papers, newspapers, almanacs, college diplomas, playing cards, and dice. After November 1, 1765, all these items had to bear a stamp signifying that their possessor had paid the tax. Violators of the Stamp Act, like those disobeying the Sugar Act, were to be tried without juries in admiralty courts. The English had been paying a similar tax for nearly a century, so it seemed to Grenville and Parliament that colonials could have no objections.

Every packet boat from London that brought news of Parliament's passing another of Grenville's measures dampened postwar optimism. For all the differences between the colonies and England, Americans still held much in common with the English. Those shared ideas included firm beliefs about why the British constitution, British customs, and British history all served to protect liberty and the rights of the empire's freeborn citizens. For that reason the new measures, which seemed like common sense to Grenville and Parliament, did not make sense to Americans.

Visual imagery brought home the urgency of resistance to Americans who could not read political pamphlets or radical newspapers. This detail from an engraving by Paul Revere includes a liberty tree, from which is hung an effigy of the Boston stamp distributor, and a beast busily destroying the Magna Carta while trampling American colonials. The date on the tree, August 14, 1765, marked the first Stamp Act riot in Boston.

# The Beginning of Colonial Resistance

**LOCKE ON PROPERTY AND LIBERTY**

Like other Britons, colonials in America accepted a maxim laid down by the English philosopher John Locke: property guaranteed liberty. Property, in this view, was not merely real estate, or wealth, or material possessions. It was the source of strength for every individual, providing the freedom to think and act independently. Protecting the individual's right to own property was the main responsibility of government, because if personal property was not sacred, then neither was personal liberty.

It followed from this close connection between property, power, and liberty that no people should be taxed without consenting—either personally or through elected representatives. The power to tax was the power to destroy by depriving a person of property. Yet both the Sugar Act and the Stamp Act were taxes passed by members of Parliament, none of whom had been elected by colonials.

Like the English, colonials also prized the right of trial by jury as one of their basic constitutional liberties. Yet both the Sugar Act and the Stamp Act would prosecute offenders in the admiralty courts, not in local courts, thus depriving colonials of the freedom claimed by all other English men and women.

The concern for protecting individual liberties was only one of the convictions shaping the colonies' response to Britain's new policies. Equally important was their deep suspicion of power itself, a preoccupation that colonials shared with a minority of radical English thinkers. These radicals were known by a variety of names: the Country Party, the Commonwealthmen, and the **Opposition.** They drew their inspiration from the ancient tradition of classical **republicanism,** which held that representative government safeguarded liberty more reliably than either monarchy or oligarchy did. Underlying that judgment was the belief that human beings were driven by passion and insatiable ambition. One person (a monarch), or even a few people (an oligarchy), could not be entrusted with governing, because they would inevitably become corrupted by power and turn into despots. Even in representative governments, the people were obliged to watch those in power at all times. The price of liberty was eternal vigilance.

The Opposition believed that the people of England were not watching their rulers closely enough. During the first half of the eighteenth century, they argued, the entire executive branch of England's government—monarchs and their ministers—had been corrupted by their appetite for power. Proof of their ambition was the executive bureaucracy of civil officials and standing armies that steadily grew larger, interfered more with citizens' lives, and drained increasing amounts of money from taxpayers. Even more alarming, in the Opposition's view, was the executive branch's bribery of members of Parliament was corrupting the representative branch of England's government. They warned that a sinister conspiracy originating in the executive branch of government threatened English liberty.

Opposition thinkers commanded little attention in England, where they were dismissed as a discontented radical fringe. But they were revered by political leaders in the American colonies. The Opposition's view of politics confirmed colonial anxieties about England, doubts that ran deeper after 1763. Parliament's attempt to tax the colonies and the quartering of a standing army on the frontier confirmed all too well the Opposition's description of how powerful rulers turned themselves into tyrants and reduced the people whom they ruled to slaves. In sum, Grenville's new measures led some colonials to suspect that ambitious men ruling England might be conspiring against American liberties.

**IMPACT OF POSTWAR RECESSION**

Britain's attempt to raise revenue after 1763 was a disaster of timing, not just psychologically but also economically. By then, the colonies were in the throes of a recession. The boom produced in America by government spending during the war had collapsed once subsidies were withdrawn. Colonial merchants were left with stocks full of imported goods gathering dust on their shelves. Farmers lost the brisk and profitable market of the army.

Colonial response to the Sugar Act reflected the painful postwar readjustments. New England merchants led the opposition, objecting to the Sugar Act principally on economic grounds. But with the passage of the Stamp Act, the terms of the imperial debate widened. The Stamp Act hit all colonials, not just New England merchants. It took money from the pockets of anyone who made a will, filed a deed, traded out of a colonial port, bought a newspaper, consulted an almanac, graduated from college, took a chance at dice, or played cards. More important, the Stamp Act served notice that Parliament claimed the authority to tax the colonies directly and for the sole purpose of raising revenue.

## Riots and Resolves

That unprecedented assertion provoked an unprecedented development: the first display of colonial unity. During the spring and summer of 1765 American assemblies passed resolves denying that Parliament could tax the colonies. The right to tax Americans belonged to colonial assemblies alone, they argued, by the law of nature and by the liberties guaranteed in colonial charters and in the British constitution.

**PATRICK HENRY'S RESOLVES**

Virginia's assembly, the House of Burgesses, took the lead in protesting the Stamp Act, prodded by Patrick Henry. Just 29 years old in 1765, Henry had tried his hand at planting in western Virginia before recognizing his real talent—demagoguery. Blessed with the eloquence of an evangelical preacher, the dashing charm of a southern gentleman, and a mind uncluttered by much learning, Henry parlayed his popularity as a smooth-talking lawyer into a place among the Burgesses. He took his seat just 10 days before introducing the Virginia Resolves against the Stamp Act.

The Burgesses passed Henry's resolutions upholding their exclusive right to tax Virginians. They stopped short of adopting those resolves that called for outright resistance. When news of Virginia's stand spread to the rest of the colonies, other assemblies followed suit, affirming that the sole right to tax Americans resided in their elected representatives. But some colonial newspapers deliberately printed a different story—that the Burgesses had approved all of Henry's resolves, including one that sanctioned disobedience to any parliamentary tax. That prompted a few assemblies to endorse resistance. In October 1765, delegates from nine colonies convened in New York, where they prepared a joint statement of the American position and petitioned the king and Parliament to repeal both the Sugar Act and the Stamp Act.

| This idealized likeness of Patrick Henry, by the American artist Thomas Sully, conveys the subject's intensity. Henry's eloquence and passion as an orator made a vivid impression on his contemporaries.

Meanwhile, colonial leaders turned to the press to arouse popular opposition to the Stamp Act. Disposed by the writings of the English Opposition to think of politics in conspiratorial terms, they warned that Grenville and the king's other ministers schemed to deprive the colonies of their liberties by unlawfully taxing their property. The Stamp Act was only the first step in a sinister plan to enslave Americans.

Whether or not fears of a dark conspiracy haunted most colonials in 1765, many resisted the Stamp Act. The merchants of Boston, New York, and Philadelphia agreed to stop importing English goods in order to pressure British traders to lobby for repeal. In every colony, organizations emerged to ensure that the Stamp Act, if not repealed, would never be enforced.

SONS OF LIBERTY The new resistance groups, which styled themselves the "Sons of Liberty," consisted of traders, lawyers, and prosperous artisans. With great success, they organized the lower classes of seaports in opposition to the Stamp Act. The sailors, dockworkers, poor artisans, apprentices, and servants who poured into the streets resembled mobs that had been organized from time to time earlier in the century. Previous riots against houses of prostitution, merchants who hoarded goods, or supporters of smallpox inoculation had not been spontaneous, uncontrolled outbursts. Crowds chose their targets and their tactics carefully and then carried out the communal will with little violence.

In every colonial city, the mobs of 1765 burnt the stamp distributors in effigy, insulted them on the streets, demolished their offices, and attacked their homes. One hot night in August 1765 a mob went further than the Sons of Liberty

had planned. They all but leveled the stately mansion of Thomas Hutchinson, the unpopular lieutenant governor of Massachusetts and the brother-in-law of the colony's stamp distributor. The destruction stunned Bostonians, especially the Sons of Liberty, who resisted Britain in the name of protecting private property. Thereafter they took care to keep crowds under tighter control. By the first of November, the day that the Stamp Act took effect, most of the stamp distributors had resigned.

## Repeal of the Stamp Act

Meanwhile, the repeal of the Stamp Act was already in the works back in England. The man who came—unintentionally—to America's relief was George III. The young king was a good man, industrious and devoted to the empire, but he was also immature and not particularly bright. Insecurity made him an irksome master, and he ran through ministers rapidly. By the end of 1765 George had replaced Grenville with a new first minister, the Marquis of Rockingham. Rockingham had opposed the Stamp Act from the outset, and he had no desire to enforce it. He received support from London merchants, who were beginning to feel the pinch of the American nonimportation campaign, and secured repeal of the Stamp Act in March 1766.

VIRTUAL VS. ACTUAL The Stamp Act controversy demonstrated to colonials how similar in political outlook they were to one another and how different they were from the British. Americans found that they shared the same assumptions about the meaning of representation. To counter colonial objections to the Stamp Act, Grenville and his supporters had claimed that Americans *were* represented in Parliament, even though they had elected none of its members. Americans were virtually represented, Grenville insisted, for each member of Parliament stood for the interests of the whole empire, not just those of the particular constituency that had elected him.

Colonials could see no virtue in the theory of **virtual representation.** After all, the circumstances and interests of colonials, living an ocean away, were significantly different from those of Britons. The newly recognized consensus among Americans was that colonials could be truly represented only by those whom they had elected. Their view, known as **actual representation,** emphasized that elected officials were directly accountable to their constituents.

Americans also had discovered that they agreed about the extent of Parliament's authority over the colonies: it did not include the right to tax. Colonials conceded Parliament's right to legislate and to regulate trade for the good of the whole empire. But taxation, in their view, was the free

## LORD CHATHAM AND AMERICA

Note Pitt's stance, typical of portraits of European aristocrats in the eighteenth century.

Why is the woman's dress slipping from her shoulder?

The British lion, celebrating Pitt's long service to the British Empire

What's this animal? What meaning is conveyed by the woman kneeling on it? Why is it juxtaposed to the book next to Pitt?

This 1766 porcelain attests to the great popularity of William Pitt, earl of Chatham, among Americans who resisted the Stamp Act. Almost alone among British politicians, Pitt had grasped and approved the colonists' objections to taxation. During Parliament's debate over the repeal of the Stamp Act, Grenville asked sarcastically: "Tell me when the colonies were emancipated?" Pitt shot back, "I desire to know when they were made slaves." The porcelain's representation of "America" as an enslaved African American woman kneeling before him, her face raised in gratitude, references Pitt's celebrated remark and echoes the colonists' association of taxation with slavery

### Thinking Critically

What is the significance of the feather headdress worn by the "America" figure? Why choose a black woman to represent "America"? What do those choices suggest about the ways in which colonials disaffected with Britain regarded themselves and their place within the British Empire? Why is Pitt represented extending his hand to the kneeling woman but not meeting her gaze?

gift of the people through their representatives—who were not sitting in Parliament.

**DECLARATORY ACT** Members of Parliament brushed aside colonial petitions and resolves, all but ignoring these constitutional arguments. To make its own authority clear, Parliament accompanied the repeal of the Stamp Act with a Declaratory Act, asserting that it had the power to make laws for the colonies "in all cases whatsoever." In fact, the Declaratory Act clarified nothing. Did Parliament understand the power of legislation to include the power of taxation?

## The Townshend Acts

In the summer of 1766 George III—again inadvertently—gave the colonies what should have been an advantage by changing ministers again. The king replaced Rockingham with William Pitt, who enjoyed great favor among colonials for his leadership during the Seven Years' War and for his opposition to the Stamp Act. If the man who believed that Americans were "the sons not the bastards of England" had been well enough to govern, matters between Great Britain and the colonies might have turned out differently. But almost immediately after Pitt took office, his health collapsed, and power passed into the hands of Charles Townshend, the chancellor of the exchequer, who wished only to raise more revenue. In 1767 he persuaded Parliament to tax the lead, paint, paper, glass, and tea that Americans imported from Britain.

In addition, Townshend was determined to curb the power of the upstart American assemblies. To set a bold example, he singled out for punishment the New York legislature, which was refusing to comply with provisions of the Quartering Act of 1765. The troops that were left on the western frontier after the Seven Years' War had been pulled back into colonial seaports in 1766. In part their movement was meant to economize on costs, but royal officials also hoped the troops' presence would help quiet agitation over the Stamp Act. When the largest contingent came to New York, that colony's assembly protested, claiming that the cost of quartering the troops constituted a form of indirect taxation. But Townshend held firm, and Parliament backed him, suspending the New York assembly in 1767 until it agreed to obey the Quartering Act.

Townshend also dipped into the revenue from his new tariffs in order to make royal officials less dependent on the assemblies. Governors and other officers such as customs collectors and judges had previously received their salaries from colonial legislatures. The assemblies lost that crucial leverage when Townshend used the revenues to pay those bureaucrats directly. Finally, in order to ensure more effective enforcement of all the duties on imports, Townshend created an American Board of Customs Commissioners, who appointed a small army of new customs collectors. He also established three new vice-admiralty courts in Boston, New York City, and Charleston to bring smugglers to justice.

## The Resistance Organizes

**JOHN DICKINSON AND SAMUEL ADAMS**

In Townshend's efforts to centralize the administration of the empire, Americans saw new evidence that they were not being treated like the English. A host of newspapers and pamphlets took up the cry against taxation. The most widely read publication, "A Letter from a Farmer in Pennsylvania," was the work of John Dickinson—who was, in fact, a Philadelphia lawyer. He urged Americans to protest the Townshend duties by consuming fewer imported English luxuries. The virtues of hard work, thrift, and home manufacturing, Dickinson argued, would bring about repeal.

As Dickinson's star rose over Philadelphia, the Townshend Acts also shaped the destiny of another man, farther north. By the 1760s Samuel Adams was a leader in the Massachusetts assembly. In some ways his rise had been unlikely. Adams's earlier ventures as a merchant ended in bankruptcy; his stint as a tax collector left all of Boston

in the red. But he proved a consummate political organizer and agitator. First his enemies and later his friends claimed that Adams had decided on independence for America as early as 1768. In that year he persuaded the assembly to send to other colonial legislatures a circular letter condemning the Townshend Acts and calling for a united American resistance.

As John Dickinson and Samuel Adams whipped up public outrage, the Sons of Liberty again organized the opposition in the streets. Customs officials, like the stamp distributors before them, became targets of popular hatred. But the customs collectors gave as good as they got. Using the flimsiest excuses, they seized American vessels for violating royal regulations. With cold insolence they shook down American merchants for what amounted to protection money. The racketeering in the customs service brought tensions in Boston to a flash point in June 1768 after officials seized and condemned the *Liberty,* a sloop belonging to one of the city's biggest merchants, John Hancock. Several thousand Bostonians vented their anger in a night of rioting, searching out and roughing up customs officials.

The new secretary of state for the colonies, Lord Hillsborough, responded to the *Liberty* riot by sending two regiments of troops to Boston. In the fall of 1768 the redcoats, like a conquering army, paraded into town under the cover of warships lying off the harbor. In the months that followed, citizens bristled when challenged on the streets by armed soldiers. Even more disturbing to Bostonians was the execution of British military justice on the Common, an open field on the outskirts of the city. British soldiers were whipped savagely for breaking military discipline, and desertion was punished by execution.

The *Liberty* riot and the arrival of British troops in Boston pushed colonial assemblies to coordinate their resistance more closely. Most legislatures endorsed the Massachusetts circular letter sent to them by Samuel Adams. They promptly adopted agreements not to import or to consume British goods. The reluctance among some merchants to revive nonimportation in 1767 gave way to greater enthusiasm by 1768, and by early 1769 such agreements were in effect throughout the colonies.

The Stamp Act crisis had also called forth intercolonial cooperation and tactics such as nonimportation. But the protests against the Townshend Acts raised the stakes by creating new institutions to carry forward the resistance. Subscribers to the nonimportation agreements established "committees of inspection" to enforce the ban on trade with Britain. The committees publicly denounced merchants who continued to import, vandalized their warehouses, forced them to stand under the gallows, and sometimes resorted to tar and feathers.

After 1768 the resistance also brought a broader range of colonials into the politics of protest. Artisans, who recognized that nonimportation would spur domestic manufacturing, began to organize as independent political groups. In many towns, women took an active part in opposing the Townshend duties. The "Daughters of Liberty" took to heart John Dickinson's advice: they wore homespun clothing instead of English finery, served coffee instead of tea, and boycotted shops selling British goods.

##  Liberty's Other Sons

The resistance after 1768 grew broader in another sense as well. Many of its supporters in the colonies felt a new sense of kinship with freedom fighters throughout Europe. Eagerly they read about the doings of men such as Charles Lucas, an Irish newspaper editor and member of the Irish Parliament, and John Wilkes, a London journalist and a leading politician of the Opposition. Both men charged the king's ministers with corrupting the political life of the British Isles. The doings of political rebels even in distant Poland and Turkey engaged colonial sympathies, too. But perhaps the international cause that proved dearest to American lovers of liberty was the fate of Corsica.

COLONIALS FOLLOW PAOLI'S STRUGGLE

For years, this tiny island off the coast of Italy had fought for its independence, first from the Italian state of Genoa and then from France, which bought the island in 1768. The leader of the Corsican rebellion, Pascal Paoli, led what one New York newspaper touted as a "glorious struggle." Many in the British Empire hoped that England would rally to defend Corsica's freedom, if only to keep France from seizing this strategic point in the Mediterranean. But British statesmen had no intention of going to war with France over mere Corsica, and when French troops routed his rebel army, Paoli fled to exile in England in 1769. Adding insult to injury, this "greatest man of earth," as he was lionized, began to hobnob with British nobles. He even accepted a pension of 1,000 pounds sterling a year from George III. The moral of the sad story, according to more than one colonial newspaper, was that British corruption pervaded not only the empire but all of Europe as well. Paoli had been "bought"—and if the Corsican sons of liberty could not survive, would their American counterparts manage to remain virtuous for very long?

## The Boston Massacre

Meanwhile, the situation in Boston deteriorated steadily. British troops found themselves regularly cursed by citizens and occasionally pelted with stones, dirt, and human excrement. The British regulars were particularly unpopular among Boston's laboring classes because they competed with them for jobs. Off-duty soldiers moonlighted as maritime laborers, and they sold their services at rates cheaper than the wages paid to locals. By 1769 brawls between British regulars and waterfront workers broke out frequently.

With some 4,000 redcoats enduring daily contact with some 15,000 Bostonians under the sway of Samuel Adams, what happened on the night of March 5, 1770, was nearly

John Wilkes, an English journalist and member of the Opposition.

inevitable. A crowd gathered around the customshouse for the sport of heckling the 10 soldiers who guarded it. The redcoats panicked and fended off insults and snowballs with live fire, hitting 11 rioters and killing 5. Adams and other propagandists seized on the incident. Labeling the bloodshed "the Boston Massacre," they publicized that "atrocity" throughout the colonies. The radical *Boston Gazette* framed its account in an eye-catching black-bordered edition headed with a drawing of five coffins.

While Townshend's policies spurred the resistance in America, the obvious finally dawned on Parliament. It recognized that Townshend's duties on imported English goods only discouraged sales to colonials and encouraged them to manufacture at home. The argument for repeal was overwhelming, and the way had been cleared by the unexpected death of Townshend. In 1770 his successor, Lord North, convinced Parliament to repeal all the Townshend duties except the one on tea, allowing that tax to stand as a source of revenue and as a symbol of Parliament's authority.

## Resistance Revived

Repeal of the Townshend duties took the wind from the sails of American resistance for more than two years. But the controversy between England and the colonies had not been resolved. Colonials still paid taxes on molasses and tea, taxes to which they had not consented. They were still

## STREET THEATER

On the first night of November 1765 the narrow, winding streets of New York glowed with unaccustomed light. The Stamp Act was to have taken effect on that date, but the colony's stampmaster had long since resigned his office. What had frightened him into resignation could be seen in the moving shadows of men, women, and children, hundreds of them. The flaring torches and flickering candles that they carried aloft through the city's crooked byways cast on storefronts and doorways dark images of a crowd protesting the "death of Liberty."

Bringing up the rear of the procession was a seaman, bearing atop his head an old chair in which was seated a paper effigy. It represented Cadwallader Colden, "the most hated man in the province" and, as New York's temporary governor, the local representative of British authority. The crowd marched to the center of town, shouting insults at Colden's figure and peppering it with pistol shots. When some of the marchers decided that their effigy should evoke the Roman Catholic pope, the chief symbol of tyrannical power to colonial Americans, they broke into Colden's stable and stole his fine coach for a proper papal throne. A second group joined the crowd, bearing its own piece of portable political theater—a gallows illuminated with two lanterns. Hanging from the gallows were effigies of Colden and the devil, the "grand Deceiver of Mankind." The entire assembly climaxed the evening by burning the effigies in a bonfire and then vandalizing the homes of several Stamp Act supporters.

Similar protests were staged in seaports all over the colonies. Some crowds held mock trials of unpopular British officials and then tarred and feathered, beat, hung, or burned their effigies. Other crowds enacted mock funerals, parading effigies in carts or coffins as church bells tolled. Certain symbols appeared repeatedly: devils and gallows, lanterns and the paraphernalia of papal authority. The "people-out-of-doors," as such crowds were called in the eighteenth century, were making their views known—and their collective power felt.

*A Pope's Day parade in mid-eighteenth-century Boston. Dressed as the devil's imps, boys accompany a cart bearing an effigy of the pope.*

The frequency and the political focus of street protests were new, the actions taken after 1765 drew on rituals and symbols surrounding traditional forms of protest, punishment, and celebration. For centuries before the Revolution, crowds on both sides of the Atlantic had meted out to prostitutes, adulterers, and henpecked husbands punishments known in England as "rough music." After being tarred and feathered, the targets of rough music were often ridden "skimmington": placed on the back of a donkey, pelted with mud and dung, and driven through the streets to the accompaniment of hooting laughter and beating drums.

An even more important inspiration for resistance rituals came from Pope's Day, an elaborate annual outdoor celebration of anti-Catholic sentiment that started in Boston early in the eighteenth century. Craftworkers and apprentices from both the North End and the South End of town fashioned a cart bearing a lantern, effigies of the pope and the devil, and signs reading "The devil take the pope." Local boys with blackened faces and jester's caps played the part of the "devil's imps," taunting the pope's effigy as laboring people from both ends of town paraded their carts through the streets. Each group tried to destroy the other's creation before the final bonfire at the end of the evening.

It was not so great a leap, then, to jump from mocking a pope to vilifying a king. Beginning in 1776, Americans celebrated public readings of the Declaration by parading, burning, and burying effigies of George III. Strangely enough, Americans had converted symbols and ceremonies designed to honor monarchy to represent the killing of a king.

### *Thinking Critically*

*What explains the hostility to Roman Catholicism expressed by so many American colonials? Why did they identify the pope with tyranny?*

subject to trial in admiralty courts, which operated without juries. They still lived with a standing army in their midst. Beneath the banked fires of protest smoldered the live embers of Americans' political inequality. Any shift in the wind could fan those embers into flames.

The wind did shift, quite literally, on Narragansett Bay in 1772, running aground the *Gaspee,* a British naval schooner in hot pursuit of Rhode Island smugglers. Residents of nearby Providence quickly celebrated the *Gaspee's* misfortune by burning it down to the waterline. Outraged British officials sent a special commission to look into the matter, intending once again to bypass the established colonial court system. The arrival of the Gaspee Commission reignited the imperial crisis, and in America, once again, resistance flared.

**COMMITTEES OF CORRESPONDENCE** It did so through an ingenious mechanism, the **committees of correspondence.** Established in all the colonies by their assemblies, the committees drew up statements of American rights and grievances, distributed those documents within and among the colonies, and solicited responses from towns and counties. The brainchild of Samuel Adams, the committee structure formed a new communications network, one that fostered an intercolonial agreement on resistance to British measures. The strategy succeeded, and not only among colonies. The committees spread the scope of the resistance from colonial seaports into rural areas, engaging farmers and other country folk in the opposition to Britain.

The committees had much to talk about when Parliament passed the Tea Act in 1773. The law was an effort to bail out the bankrupt East India Company by granting that corporation a monopoly on the tea trade to Americans. Because the company could use agents to sell its product directly, cutting out the middlemen, it could offer a lower price than that charged by colonial merchants. Thus, although the Tea Act would hurt American merchants, it promised to make tea cheaper for ordinary Americans. Still, many colonials saw the act as Parliament's attempt to trick them into accepting its authority to tax the colonies. They set out to deny that power once and for all.

In the early winter of 1773 popular leaders in Boston called for the tea cargoes to be returned immediately to England. On the evening of December 16, thousands of Bostonians, as well as farmers from the surrounding countryside, packed into the Old South Meetinghouse. Some members of the audience knew what Samuel Adams had on the evening's agenda, and they awaited their cue. It came when Adams told the meeting that they could do nothing more to save their country. War whoops rang through the meetinghouse, the crowd spilled onto the streets and out to the waterfront, and the Boston Tea Party commenced. From the throng emerged 50 men dressed as

| *Like a swarm of angry bees, British troops disembark on one of Boston's long wharves in 1768. American colonials who had cheered the triumphs of British soldiers only a few years earlier now complained bitterly at the presence of a standing army designed to intimidate them.*

# WHO WAS TO BLAME FOR THE BOSTON MASSACRE?

*Following the shootings in King Street, Captain Thomas Preston and six of his men stood trial for murder. Two radical patriot lawyers, Josiah Quincy Jr. and future President John Adams, served as defense council. Convinced that Boston must prove itself fair and faithful to the rule of law, both lawyers performed brilliantly. The jury acquitted Preston and four of the soldiers, and convicted two others of manslaughter. The depositions from the trial provide some of our best evidence for how soldiers and Bostonians viewed the standoff differently.*

## DOCUMENT 1  Deposition of Captain Thomas Preston, March 12, 1770

The mob still increased and were more outrageous, striking their clubs or bludgeons one against another, and calling out, come on you rascals, you bloody backs, you lobster scoundrels, fire if you dare, G-d damn you, fire and be damned, we know you dare not, and much more such language was used. At this time I was between the soldiers and the mob, parleying with, and endeavouring all in my power to persuade them to retire peaceably, but to no purpose. They advanced to the points of the bayonets, struck some of them and even the muzzles of the pieces, and seemed to be endeavouring to close with the soldiers. On which some well-behaved persons asked me if the guns were charged. I replied yes. They then asked me if I intended to order the men to fire. I answered no, by no means, observing to them that I was advanced before the muzzles of the men's pieces, and must fall a sacrifice if they fired; that the soldiers were upon the half cock and charged bayonets, and my giving the word fire under those circumstances would prove me to be no officer. While I was thus speaking, one of the soldiers having received a severe blow with a stick, stepped a little on one side and instantly fired, on which turning to and asking him why he fired without orders, I was struck with a club on my arm, which for some time deprived me of the use of it, which blow had it been placed on my head, most probably would have destroyed me. On this a general attack was made on the men by a great number of heavy clubs and snowballs being thrown at them, by which all our lives were in imminent danger, some persons at the same time from behind calling out, damn your bloods—why don't you fire.

Instantly three or four of the soldiers fired, one after another, and directly after three more in the same confusion and hurry. The mob then ran away, except three unhappy men who instantly expired, in which number was Mr. Gray at whose rope-walk the prior quarrels took place; one more is since dead, three others are dangerously, and four slightly wounded. The whole of this melancholy affair was transacted in almost 20 minutes. On my asking the soldiers why they fired without orders, they said they heard the word fire and supposed it came from me. This might be the case as many of the mob called out fire, fire, but I assured the men that I gave no such order; that my words were, don't fire, stop your firing. In short, it was scarcely possible for the soldiers to know who said fire, or don't fire, or stop your firing.

## DOCUMENT 2  Deposition of Robert Goddard

The Soldiers came up to the Centinel and the Officer told them to place themselves and they formed a half moon. The Captain told the Boys to go home least there should be murder done. They were throwing Snow balls. Did not go off but threw more Snow balls. The Capt. was behind the Soldiers. The Captain told them to fire. One Gun went off. A Sailor or Townsman struck the Captain. He thereupon said damn your bloods fire think I'll be treated in this manner. This Man that struck the Captain came from among the People who were 7 feet off and were round on one wing. I saw no person speak to him. I was so near I should have seen it. After the Capt. said Damn your bloods fire they all fired one after another about 7 or 8 in all, and then the officer bid Prime and load again. He stood behind all the time. Mr. Lee went up to the officer and called the officer by name Capt. Preston. I saw him coming down from the Guard behind the Party. I went to Gaol the next day being sworn for the Grand Jury to see the Captain. Then said pointing to him that's the person who gave the word to fire. He said if you swear that you will ruin me everlastingly. I was so near the officer when he gave the word fire that I could touch him. His face was towards me. He stood in the middle behind the Men. I looked him in the face. He then stood within the circle. When he told 'em to fire he turned about to me. I looked him in the face.

*Source:* http://law2.umkc.edu/faculty/projects/ftrials/bostonmassacre/prestontrialexcerpts.html.

### *Thinking Critically*

*Preston and Goddard come to different conclusions about the shootings but describe similar details (the snowballs, the man who struck Preston). Can details from these two accounts be reconciled? Do they simply have different perspectives on the same event, or do you think one of the depositions must be misleading? Given the tensions these accounts relate, do you think that a violent confrontation between soldiers and Bostonians was inevitable?*

Indians to disguise their identities. The party boarded three vessels docked off Griffin's Wharf, broke open casks containing 90,000 pounds of tea, and brewed a beverage worth 10,000 pounds sterling in Boston harbor.

## The Empire Strikes Back

**COERCIVE ACTS** The Boston Tea Party proved to British satisfaction that the colonies aimed at independence. Lord North's assessment was grim: "We are now to dispute whether we have, or have not, any authority in that country." To reassert its authority, Parliament passed the Coercive Acts, dubbed in the colonies the "Intolerable Acts." The first of these came in March 1774, two months after hearing of the Tea Party, when Parliament passed the Boston Port Bill, closing that harbor to all oceangoing traffic until such time as the king saw fit to reopen it. And George, Parliament announced, would not see fit until colonials paid the East India Company for its losses.

During the next three months, Parliament approved three other "intolerable" laws designed to punish Massachusetts. The Massachusetts Government Act handed over the colony's government to royal officials. Even convening town meetings would require royal permission. The Impartial Administration of Justice Act permitted any royal official accused of a crime in Massachusetts to be tried in England or in another colony. The Quartering Act allowed the housing of British troops in uninhabited private homes, outlying buildings, and barns—not only in Massachusetts but in all the other colonies as well.

| While the new political activism of some American women merely amused male leaders of the resistance, it inspired the scorn of some partisans of British authority. When the women of Edenton, North Carolina, renounced imported tea, this British cartoon mocked them. Can you find at least five details in the painting used by the artist to insult the Americans?

**FEAR OF CONSPIRACY** Many colonials saw the Coercive Acts as proof of a plot to enslave the colonies. In truth, the taxes and duties, laws and regulations of the past decade *were* part of a deliberate design—a plan to centralize the administration of the British Empire that seemed only common sense to British officials. But those efforts by the king's ministers and Parliament to run the colonies more efficiently and profitably were viewed by more and more Americans as a sinister conspiracy against their liberties.

For colonials, the study of history confirmed that interpretation, especially their reading of the histories written by the English Opposition. The Opposition's favorite historical subject was the downfall of republics, whether those of ancient Greece and Rome or more recent republican governments in Venice and Denmark. The lesson of their histories was always the same: power overwhelmed liberty, unless the people remained vigilant. The pattern, argued radicals, had been repeated in America over the previous dozen years: costly wars waged; oppressive taxes levied to pay for them; standing armies sent to overawe citizens; corrupt governors, customs collectors, and judges appointed to enrich themselves by enforcing the measures. Everything seemed to fit.

**QUEBEC ACT** Week after week in the spring of 1774, reports of legislative outrages came across the waters. Shortly after approving the Coercive Acts, Parliament passed the Quebec Act, which established a permanent government in what had been French Canada. Ominously, it included no representative assembly. Equally ominous to Protestant colonials, the Quebec Act officially recognized the Roman Catholic church and extended the bounds of the province to include all land between the Mississippi and Ohio Rivers. Suddenly New York, Pennsylvania, and Virginia found themselves bordering a British colony whose subjects had no voice in their own government.

With the passage of the Coercive Acts, many more colonials came to believe not only that ambitious men plotted to enslave the colonies but also that those conspirators included almost all British political leaders. At the time of the Stamp Act and again during the agitation against the Townshend Acts, most colonials had confined their suspicions to the king's ministers. By 1774 members of Parliament were also implicated in that conspiracy—and a few radicals were wondering aloud about George III.

**FIRST CONTINENTAL CONGRESS CALLED** As alarm deepened in the wake of the Coercive Acts, one colony after another called for an intercolonial congress—like the one that had met during the Stamp Act crisis—to determine the best way to defend their freedom. But many also remained unsettled about where the logic of their actions seemed to be taking them: toward a denial that they were any longer English.

 REVIEW

How did British colonial policy change after the Seven Years' War, and what was the colonial response?

# Toward the Revolution

By the beginning of September 1774, when 55 delegates to the First Continental Congress gathered in Philadelphia, the news from Massachusetts was grim. The colony verged on anarchy, it was reported, as its inhabitants resisted the enforcement of the Massachusetts Government Act.

In the midst of this atmosphere of crisis, the members of Congress also had to take one another's measure. Many of the delegates had not traveled outside their own colonies. (All but Georgia sent representatives.) Although the delegates encountered a great deal of diversity, they quickly discovered that they esteemed the same traits of character, attributes that they called "civic virtue." These traits included simplicity and—self-reliance, industry and thrift, and above all, an unselfish commitment to the public good. Most members of the Congress also shared a common mistrust of England, associating the mother country with vice, extravagance, and corruption.

Still, the delegates had some misgivings about those from other colonies. Massachusetts in particular brought with it a reputation—well deserved, considering that Samuel Adams was along—for radical action and a willingness to use force to accomplish its ends.

## The First Continental Congress

As the delegates settled down to business, their aim was to reach agreement on three key points: How were they to justify the rights they claimed as American colonials? What were the limits of Parliament's power? And what were the proper tactics for resisting the Coercive Acts? Congress quickly agreed on the first point. The delegates affirmed that the law of nature, the colonial charters, and the British constitution provided the foundations of American liberties. This position was what most colonials had argued since 1765. On the two other issues, Congress charted a middle course between the demands of radicals and the reservations of conservatives.

Since the time of the Stamp Act, most colonials had insisted that Parliament had no authority to tax the colonies. But later events had demonstrated that Parliament could undermine colonial liberties by legislation as well as by taxation. The suspension of the New York legislature, the Gaspee Commission, and the Coercive Acts all fell into this category. Given those experiences, the delegates adopted a Declaration of Rights and Grievances on October 14, 1774, asserting the right of the colonies to tax and legislate for themselves. The Declaration of Rights thus limited Parliament's power over Americans more strictly than colonials had a decade earlier.

**JOSEPH GALLOWAY'S PLAN**

By denying Parliament's power to make laws for the colonies, the Continental Congress blocked efforts of the most conservative delegates to reach an accommodation with England. Their leading advocate, Joseph Galloway of Pennsylvania, proposed a plan of union with Britain similar to the one set forth by the Albany Congress in 1754. Under it, a grand council of the colonies would handle all common concerns, with any laws it passed subject to review and veto by Parliament. For its part, Parliament would have to submit for the grand council's approval any acts it passed affecting America. A majority of delegates judged that Galloway's proposal left Parliament too much leeway in legislating for colonials, and they rejected his plan.

Although the Congress denied Parliament the right to impose taxes or to make laws, delegates stopped short of declaring that it had no authority at all in the colonies. They approved Parliament's regulation of trade, but only because of the interdependent economy of the empire. And although some radical pamphleteers were attacking the king for plotting against American liberties, Congress acknowledged the continuing allegiance of the colonies to George III. In other words, the delegates called for a return to the situation that had existed in the empire before 1763, with Parliament regulating trade and the colonies exercising all powers of taxation and legislation.

**THE ASSOCIATION**

On the question of resistance, the Congress satisfied the desires of its most radical delegates by drawing up the Continental Association, an agreement to cease all trade with Britain until the Coercive Acts were repealed. They agreed that their fellow citizens would immediately stop drinking East India Company tea and that by December 1, 1774, merchants would no longer import goods of any sort from Britain. A ban on the export of American produce to Britain and the West Indies would go into effect a year later, during September 1775—the lag being a concession to southern rice and tobacco planters, who wanted to market crops already planted.

**REVERE AND THE SUFFOLK RESOLVES**

The Association provided for the total cessation of trade, but Samuel Adams and other radicals wanted bolder action. They received help from Paul Revere, a Boston silversmith who had long provided newspapers with many lurid engravings showing British abuses. On September 16, Revere galloped into Philadelphia bearing a copy of resolves drawn up by Bostonians and other residents of Suffolk County. The Suffolk Resolves, as they were called, branded the Coercive Acts as unconstitutional and called for civil disobedience to protest them. Congress endorsed the resolves, as Adams had hoped. But it would not approve another part of the radicals' agenda—preparing for war by authorizing proposals to strengthen and arm colonial militias.

Thus the First Continental Congress steered a middle course. Although determined to bring about repeal of the Coercive Acts, it held firm in resisting any revolutionary

*Samuel Adams, a radical who master-minded colonial resistance tactics.*

course of action. If British officials had responded to its recommendations and restored the status quo of 1763, the war for independence might have been postponed—perhaps indefinitely. However, even though the Congress did not go to the extremes urged by the radicals, its decisions drew colonials farther down the road to independence.

## The Last Days of the British Empire in America

Most colonials applauded the achievements of the First Continental Congress. They expected that the Association would bring about a speedy repeal of the Coercive Acts. But fear that the colonies were moving toward a break with Britain led others to denounce the doings of the Congress. Conservatives were convinced that if independence were declared, chaos would ensue. Colonials, they argued, would quarrel over land claims and sectional tensions and religious differences, as they had so often in the recent past. Without Britain to referee such disputes, they feared, the result would be civil war, followed by anarchy.

THOMAS GAGE IN BOSTON

The man in America with the least liking for the Continental Congress sat in the hottest seat in the colonies, that of the governor of Massachusetts. General Thomas Gage now watched as royal authority crumbled in Massachusetts and the rebellion spread to other colonies. In June 1774 a desperate Gage dissolved the Massachusetts legislature, only to see it reform, on its own, into a Provincial Congress. That new body assumed the government of the colony in October and began arming the militia. Gage then started to fortify Boston and pleaded for more troops—only to find his fortifications damaged by saboteurs and his requests for reinforcements ignored by Britain.

COLLAPSE OF ROYAL AUTHORITY

Outside Boston, royal authority fared no better. Farmers in western Massachusetts forcibly closed the county courts, turning out royally appointed justices and establishing their own tribunals. Popularly elected committees of inspection charged with enforcing the Association took over towns everywhere in Massachusetts, not only restricting trade but also regulating every aspect of local life. The committees called on townspeople to display civic virtue by renouncing "effeminate" English luxuries such as tea and fine clothing and "corrupt" leisure activities such as dancing, gambling, and racing. The committees also assigned spies to report on any citizen unfriendly to the resistance. "Enemies of American liberty" risked being roundly condemned in public or beaten and pelted with mud and dung by hooting, raucous mobs.

Throughout the other colonies a similar process was under way. During the winter

A British grenadier

and early spring of 1775 provincial congresses, county conventions, and local committees of inspection were emerging as revolutionary governments, replacing royal authority at every level. As the spectacle unfolded before General Gage, he concluded that only force could subdue the colonies. It would take more than he had at his command, but reinforcements might be on the way. In February of 1775 Parliament had approved an address to the king declaring that the colonies were in rebellion.

## The Fighting Begins

As spring came to Boston, the city waited. A band of artisans, organized as spies and express riders by Paul Revere, watched General Gage and waited for him to act. On April 14 word from Lord North finally arrived: Gage was to seize the leaders of the Provincial Congress, an action that would behead the rebellion, North said. Gage knew better than to believe North—but he also knew that he had to do something.

LEXINGTON AND CONCORD

On the night of April 18 the sexton of Boston's Christ Church hung two lamps from its steeple. It was a signal that British troops had moved out of Boston and were marching toward the arms and ammunition stored by the Provincial Congress in Concord. As the lamps flashed the signal, Revere and a comrade, William Dawes, rode out to arouse the countryside.

When the news of a British march reached Lexington, its Minuteman militia of about 70 farmers, chilled and sleepy, mustered on the Green at the center of the small rural town. Lexington Green lay directly on the road to Concord. About four in the morning 700 British troops massed on the Green, and their commander, Major John Pitcairn, ordered the Lexington militia to disperse. The townsmen, outnumbered and overawed, began to obey. Then a shot rang out—whether the British or the Americans fired first is unknown—and then two volleys burst from the ranks of the redcoats. With a cheer the British set off for Concord, 5 miles distant, leaving eight Americans dead on Lexington Green.

By dawn, hundreds of Minutemen from nearby towns were surging into Concord. The British entered at about seven in the morning and moved, unopposed, toward their target, a house lying across the bridge that spanned the Concord River. While three companies of British soldiers searched for American guns and ammunition, three others, posted on the bridge itself, had the misfortune to find those American arms—borne by the rebels and being fired with deadly accuracy. By noon, the British were retreating to Boston.

The narrow road from Concord to Boston's outskirts became a corridor of carnage. Pursuing Americans fired on the column of fleeing redcoats from the cover of fences and forests. By the end of

April 19, the British had sustained 273 casualties; the Americans, 95. It was only the beginning. By evening of the next day, some 20,000 New England militia had converged on Boston for a long siege.

## Common Sense

The bloodshed at Lexington Green and Concord's North Bridge committed colonials to a course of rebellion—and independence. That was the conclusion drawn by Thomas Paine, who urged other Americans to join the rebels.

Paine himself was hardly an American at all. He was born in England, first apprenticed as a corsetmaker, appointed later a tax collector, and fated finally to become midwife to the age of republican revolutions. Paine came to Philadelphia late in 1774, set up as a journalist, and made the American cause his own. "Where liberty is, there is my country," he declared. In January 1776 he wrote a pamphlet to inform colonials of their identity as a distinct people and their destiny as a nation. *Common Sense* enjoyed tremendous popularity and wide circulation, selling 120,000 copies.

After Lexington and Concord, Paine wrote, as the imperial crisis passed "from argument to arms, a new era for

| *Thomas Paine, the author of* Common Sense

politics is struck—a new method of thinking has arisen." That new era of politics for Paine was the age of republicanism. He denounced monarchy as a foolish and dangerous form of government, one that violated the dictates of reason as well as the word of the Bible. By ridicule and remorseless argument, he severed the ties of colonial allegiance to the king. *Common Sense* scorned George III as "the Royal Brute of Britain," who had enslaved the chosen people of the new age—the Americans.

Nor did Paine stop there. He rejected the idea that colonials were or should want to be English. The colonies occupied a huge continent an ocean away from the tiny British Isles—clear proof that nature itself had fashioned America for independence. England lay locked in Europe, doomed to the corruption of an Old World. America had been discovered anew to become an "asylum of liberty."

### ✓ REVIEW

What had happened by the mid-1770s to transform nonimportation and political protest into organized rebellion?

| *The Irish artist John Dixon created this mezzotint,* The Oracle, *in 1774. In it, Father Time puts on a magiclantern show for an audience of women who represent Britain, Scotland, Ireland, and America. The image projected on the wall conjures up a brilliant future for the British Empire, in which protest and discord give way to freedom and unity— wishful thinking, since little more than a year later American rebels fired the first shots at Lexington. Note that America, who sits in the shadows apart from the three other women, is a tawny Indian princess, her face hidden, a weapon at her side. What does this representation suggest about the ways that Britons viewed Americans?*

# CONCLUSION

## THE WORLD AT LARGE

Many Americans had liked being English, but being English hadn't worked. Perhaps that is another way of saying that over the course of nearly two centuries, colonial society and politics had evolved in such a way that for Americans an English identity no longer fit.

The radicals in America viewed this change in identity in terms of age-old conspiracies that repeated themselves throughout history. First, the people of a republic were impoverished by costly wars—as the colonists could well appreciate after the Seven Years' War. Then the government burdened the people with taxes to pay for those wars—as in the case of the Sugar Act or the Stamp Act or the Townshend duties. Next, those in power stationed a standing army in the country, pretending to protect the people but actually lending military force to their rulers. The rhetoric of the Opposition about ministerial conspiracies gave such talk a fervid quality that, to some modern ears, may seem an exaggeration.

Take away the rhetoric, however, and the argument makes uncomfortable sense. The British administration began its "backwoods" war with France, intending to limit it to the interior of North America. But the war aims of William Pitt—the leader Americans counted as their friend—grew with every victory, and he urged war with Spain even as France was looking for peace. Britain had already taken its war in Europe farther afield, driving France out of India. When it declared war against Spain, British naval forces in India sailed farther east, in a surprise attack on Spain's colony in the Philippines. At the same time, another fleet raced toward Spanish Cuba. Peace came only once Britain and the major powers had bankrupted their treasuries. Conspiracy may not have been at the heart of the plan. But wars must be paid for. And the prevailing assumptions in a monarchy about who should pay led to the effort to regulate and bring order to Britain's "ungrateful" colonies.

In America, colonists were ungrateful precisely because they had established political institutions that made the rights of "freeborn Britons" more available to ordinary citizens than they were in the nation that had created those liberties. Perhaps, in other words, most Americans had succeeded *too* well at becoming English, regarding themselves as political equals entitled to basic constitutional freedoms. In the space of less than a generation, the logic of events made clear that despite all that the English and Americans shared, in the distribution of political power they were fundamentally at odds. And the call to arms at Lexington and Concord made retreat impossible.

On that point Paine was clear. It was the destiny of Americans to be republicans, not monarchists. It was the destiny of Americans to be independent, not subject to British dominion. It was the destiny of Americans to be American, not English. That, according to Thomas Paine, was common sense. ∞∞∞

# CHAPTER SUMMARY

BRITAIN'S STUNNING VICTORY IN THE Seven Years' War prompted it to embrace policies designed to administer new territories and boost revenue. These policies provoked a backlash in the colonies that would ultimately lead to the Revolutionary War.

- French and Indian forces inflicted major defeats on the British during the mid-1750s, in large part thanks to British policies that had alienated colonists and Indians alike.

- Starting in 1757, William Pitt's reforms galvanized the colonies, secured Indian allies, and salvaged the war. By 1760 the French had been defeated throughout the continent.

- Partly thanks to Pontiac's Rebellion, the British prohibited colonial settlement west of the Appalachians.

- The acts by Parliament in the early 1760s—the Proclamation of 1763, the Sugar Act, the Stamp Act, the Currency Act, and the Quartering Act—were all designed to generate revenue and bind the colonies to the empire.

- These new measures violated what Americans understood to be their constitutional and political liberties.

- Although Parliament repealed the Stamp Act in the face of colonial protests, it reasserted its authority to tax Americans by passing the Townshend Acts in 1767.

- With the passage of the Coercive Acts in 1774, many Americans concluded that all British actions in the past decade were part of a deliberate plot to enslave Americans by depriving them of property and liberty.

- The First Continental Congress denied Parliament any authority in the colonies except regulating trade; it also prohibited trade with Britain until the Coercive Acts were repealed.

- When in April 1775 British troops tried to seize arms at Concord, the first battle of the Revolution took place

# ADDITIONAL READING

FOR COMPREHENSIVE OVERVIEWS OF THE revolutionary era, consult Edward Countryman, *The American Revolution* (1985), and Robert Middlekauff, *The Glorious Cause* (rev. ed., 2007). Fred Anderson, *Crucible of War* (2000), offers a magisterial account of the Seven Years' War. *The Stamp Act Crisis* (1953) by Edmund S. Morgan and Helen M. Morgan remains the clearest and most vivid portrayal of the issues, events, and people involved in that defining moment of the imperial crisis. To understand that struggle as lived and recalled by a Boston artisan, read Alfred F. Young's engaging book, *The Shoemaker and the Tea Party* (1999). Two important interpretations of how the logic of resistance took shape among colonials in Massachusetts and Virginia are Robert Gross, *The Minutemen and Their World* (1976), and Timothy Breen, *Tobacco Culture* (1985). A more recent study by Breen, *The Marketplace Revolution* (2005), sheds new light on the role of a transatlantic consumer culture in fueling tensions within the British Empire.

Bernard Bailyn, *The Ideological Origins of the American Revolution* (1967), remains the classic study of the English Opposition's influence on the evolution of republican political thought in the American colonies. Many fine biographies chronicle the careers of eighteenth-century Americans who led—or opposed—the resistance to Britain and also shed light on the times in which they lived. Of particular interest are Jack Rakove, *Revolutionaries* (2010), Gordon Wood, *Revolutionary Characters,* and two biographies of Thomas Paine (both published in 2006) by Harvey Kaye and Craig Nelson.

For a fuller list of readings, see the Bibliography at www.mhhe.com/eh8e.

# SIGNIFICANT EVENTS

**1755**
Braddock defeated by French and Indians

**1756**
England and France declare war

**1759**
Decisive English victory at Quebec

**1763**
Treaty of Paris ends the Seven Years' War; Pontiac's Rebellion begins

**1764**
Sugar Act; Currency Act

**1765**
Stamp Act; Quartering Act

**1766**
Repeal of the Stamp Act; Declaratory Act

**1767**
Townshend duties; Parliament suspends New York assembly

**1770**
Boston Massacre; repeal of most Townshend duties

**1772**
Gaspee Commission

**1773**
Boston Tea Party

**1774**
Coercive Acts; First Continental Congress meets at Philadelphia

**1775**
Battles of Lexington and Concord

**1776**
Thomas Paine's *Common Sense* published

| DATE | ACT | DETAILS | REACTION |
|---|---|---|---|
| 1764 | Sugar Act | Decreased existing tax on molasses but increased policing and punishment for violation | Angry protests by New England merchants |
| 1764 | Currency Act | Prohibited colonies making paper bills legal tender | |
| 1765 | Quartering Act | Compelled colonies to house army troops | New York refuses to comply |
| 1765 | Stamp Act | Taxed legal documents, various paper products, and dice | Assemblies deny Parliament's right to tax colonies; nonimportation campaign; mobs intimidate stamp distributors |
| 1766 | Declaratory Act | Though Stamp Act repealed, Parliament insists on power to tax colonies | Patriot writing flourishes; crowds attack customs agents; nonimportation more sophisticated |
| 1767 | Townshend Acts | Taxed lead, paper, paint, glass, and tea | Riots; propaganda; Townshend duties repealed except for tea |
| 1770 | Boston Massacre | 5 men shot dead by British troops in Boston | Refusal to let the tea shipments land; destruction of tea in Boston Harbor and elsewhere |
| 1773 | Tea Act | Allowed East India Company to sell tea in colonies at discount, but tea would still be taxed | First Continental Congress meets in Philadelphia |
| 1774 | Coercive Acts | Closed Boston's port; placed Massachusetts government under royal control | |

BOSTON

CHARLES

On June 17, 1775, thousands of colonials flocked to the rooftops and upper windows of their Boston homes to witness the British attack on Breed's Hill across the water on nearby Charlestown peninsula. As the British artillery sent shells into the peninsula, houses there caught fire and burst into flames. Then the redcoats, unloaded from their ships, launched their assault on the hill.

## CHAPTER 7

# The American People and the American Revolution

1775–1783

## What's to Come

∞∞∞ **AN AMERICAN STORY** ∞∞∞

## "WILL HE FIGHT?"

From a high place somewhere in the city—Beacon Hill, perhaps, or Copse Hill—General Thomas Gage looked down on Boston. Through a spyglass his gaze traveled over the church belfries and steeples, the roofs of brick and white frame houses. Finally he fixed his sights on a figure far in the distance across the Charles River. The man was perched atop a crude fortification on Breed's Hill, an elevation lying just below Bunker Hill on the Charlestown peninsula. Gage took the measure of his enemy: an older man, past middle age, a sword swinging beneath his homespun coat, a broad-brimmed hat shading his eyes. As he passed the spyglass to his ally, an American loyalist, Gage asked Abijah Willard if he knew the man on the fort. Willard peered across the Charles and identified his own brother-in-law, Colonel William Prescott. A veteran of the Seven Years' War, Prescott was now a leader in the rebel army laying siege to Boston.

"Will he fight?" Gage wondered aloud.

"I cannot answer for his men," Willard replied, "but Prescott will fight you to the gates of hell."

Fight they did on June 17, 1775, both William Prescott and his men. The evening before, three regiments had followed the colonel from Cambridge to Breed's Hill—soldiers drawn from the thousands of militia who had swarmed to surround British-occupied Boston after the bloodshed at Lexington and Concord. All through the night, they dug deep trenches and built up high earthen walls atop the hill. At the first light of day, a British warship spotted the new rebel outpost and opened fire. By noon barges were ferrying British troops under Major General William Howe across the half mile of river that separated Boston from Charlestown. The 1,600 raw rebel troops tensed at the sight of scarlet-coated soldiers streaming ashore, glittering bayonets grasped at the ready. The rebels were farmers and artisans, not professional soldiers, and they were frightened out of their wits.

But Prescott and his men held their ground. The British charged Breed's Hill twice, and Howe watched in horror as streams of fire felled his troops. Finally, during the third British frontal assault, the rebels ran out of ammunition and were forced to withdraw. Redcoats poured into the rebel fort, bayoneting its handful of remaining defenders. By nightfall the British had taken Breed's Hill and the rest of the Charlestown peninsula. They had bought a dark triumph at the cost of 228 dead and 800 wounded.

| *Will they fight? This Pennsylvania regimental flag gives one reason why some did.*

The cost came high in loyalties as well. The fighting on Breed's Hill fed the hatred of Britain that had been building since April. Throughout America, preparations for war intensified: militia in every colony mustered; communities stockpiled arms and ammunition. Around Charlestown civilians fled the countryside, abandoning homes and shops set afire by the British shelling of Breed's Hill. "The roads filled with frightened women and children, some in carts with their tattered furniture, others on foot fleeing into the woods," recalled Hannah Winthrop, one of their number.

The bloody, indecisive fight on the Charlestown peninsula known as the Battle of Bunker Hill actually took place on Breed's Hill. And the exchange between Thomas Gage and Abijah Willard that is said to have preceded the battle may not have taken place. But the story has persisted in the folklore of the American Revolution. Whether it really happened or not, the conversation between Gage and Willard raised the question that both sides wanted answered. Were Americans willing to fight for independence from British rule? It was one thing, after all, to oppose the British ministry's policy of taxation. It was another to support a rebellion for which the ultimate price of failure was hanging for treason. And it was another matter entirely for men to wait nervously atop a hill as the seasoned troops of their own "mother country" marched toward them with the intent to kill.

Indeed, the question "Will they fight?" was revolutionary shorthand for a host of other questions concerning how ordinary Americans would react to the tug of loyalties between long-established colonial governments and a long-revered parent nation and monarch. For slaves, the question revolved around their allegiance to masters who spoke of liberty or to their masters' enemies who promised liberation. For those who led the rebels, it was a question of strengthening the resolve of the undecided, coordinating resistance, instilling discipline—translating the *will* to fight into the *ability* to do so. And for those who believed the rebellion was a madness whipped up by artful politicians, it was a question of whether to remain silent or risk speaking out, whether to take up arms for the king or flee. All these questions were raised, of necessity, by the act of revolution. But the barrel of a rifle shortened them to a single, pointed question: Will you fight? ∞∞∞

# THE DECISION FOR INDEPENDENCE

THE DELEGATES TO THE SECOND Continental Congress gathered at Philadelphia on May 10, 1775, just one month after the battles at Lexington and Concord. They had to determine whether independence or reconciliation offered the best way to protect the liberties of their colonies.

For a brash, ambitious lawyer from Braintree, Massachusetts, British abuses dictated only one course. "The Cancer [of official corruption] is too deeply rooted," wrote John Adams, "and too far spread to be cured by anything short of cutting it out entire." Yet, during the spring and summer of 1775, even strong advocates of independence did not openly seek a separation from Britain. If the radicals' objective of independence was ever to be achieved, greater agreement among Americans had to be attained. Moderates and conservatives harbored deep misgivings about independence: they had to be brought along slowly.

## The Second Continental Congress

To bring them along, Congress adopted the "Olive Branch Petition" in July 1775. Drawn up by Pennsylvania's John Dickinson, the document affirmed American loyalty to George III and asked the king to disavow the policies of his principal ministers. At the same time, Congress issued a declaration denying that the colonies aimed at independence. Yet, less than a month earlier, Congress had authorized the creation of a rebel military force, the **Continental Army,** and had issued paper money to pay for the troops.

**AGGRESSIVE BRITISH RESPONSE** A Congress that sued for peace while preparing for war was a puzzle that British politicians—least of all, Lord George Germain—did not even try to understand. A tough-minded statesman now charged with overseeing colonial affairs, Germain was determined to subdue the rebellion by force. George III proved just as stubborn: he refused to receive the Olive Branch Petition. By the end of that year, Parliament had shut down all trade with the colonies and had ordered the Royal Navy to seize colonial merchant ships on the high seas. In November 1775 Virginia's royal governor, Lord Dunmore, offered freedom to any slaves who would join the British. During January of the next year, he ordered the shelling of Norfolk, Virginia, reducing that town to smoldering rubble.

British belligerence withered the cause of reconciliation within Congress and the colonies. Support for independence gained more momentum from the overwhelming reception of Paine's *Common Sense* in January 1776. Radicals in Congress realized that the future was theirs and were ready to act. In April 1776 the delegates opened American trade to every nation in the world except Great Britain; a month later Congress advised the colonies to establish new state governments. And on June 7 Virginia's Richard Henry Lee offered the motion "that these United Colonies are, and of right ought to be, free and independent States . . . and that all political connection between them and the State of Great Britain is, and ought to be, totally dissolved."

## The Declaration

Congress postponed a final vote on Lee's motion until July. Some opposition still lingered among delegates from the middle colonies, and a committee appointed to write a declaration of independence needed time to complete its work. That committee included some of the leading delegates in Congress: John Adams, Benjamin Franklin, Connecticut's Roger Sherman, and New York's Robert Livingston. But the man who did most of the drafting was a young planter and lawyer from western Virginia.

**THOMAS JEFFERSON** Thomas Jefferson was just 33 years old in the summer of 1776 when he withdrew to his lodgings on the outskirts of Philadelphia, pulled a portable writing desk onto his lap, and wrote the statement that would explain American independence to a "candid world." In the document's brief opening section, Jefferson set forth a general justification of revolution that invoked the "self-evident truths" of human equality and "unalienable rights" to "life, liberty, and the pursuit of happiness." These natural rights had been "endowed" to all persons "by their Creator," the Declaration pointed out; thus there was no need to appeal to the narrower claim of the "rights of Englishmen."

**BLAMING GEORGE III** While the first part of the Declaration served notice that Americans no longer considered themselves English, its second and longer section denied England any authority in the colonies. In its

| *Rough draft of the Declaration of Independence*

detailed history of American grievances against the British Empire, the Declaration referred only once to Parliament. Instead, it blamed George III for a "long train of abuses and usurpations" designed to achieve "absolute despotism." Unlike *Common Sense*, the Declaration denounced only the reigning king of England; it did not attack the institution of monarchy itself. But like *Common Sense*, the Declaration affirmed that government originated in the consent of the governed and upheld the right of the people to overthrow oppressive rule.

Later generations have debated what Jefferson meant by the "pursuit of happiness" and whether he had either women or black Americans in mind when he wrote the famous phrase "all men are created equal." His own contemporaries in Congress did not pause to consider those questions and surely would have found themselves divided if they had. No matter. By firmly grounding the Declaration on the natural rights due all people, Jefferson placed equality at the center of the new nation's identity, setting the framework for a debate that would continue over the next two centuries. Congress adopted the Declaration of Independence on July 4, 1776.

 **THE BRITISH PERSPECTIVE** The colonies thus followed the course set by common sense into the storms of independence. To those Britons who took a wide view of their empire, it made no sense whatsoever, and their perplexity is understandable. Since the end of the Seven Years' War, Britain had added to its overseas dominion a vast and diverse number of subjects formerly under French rule—Native Americans, French Catholic Canadians, peoples of African descent in the Caribbean. And then there was India, part Hindu, part Muslim, most of it ruled by the East India Company. What

better, more efficient way to regulate this sprawling empire than to bring all of its parts under the rule of a sovereign Parliament? What other way could the empire endure and prosper—and fend off future challenges from Catholic, monarchical France? Of course, it was impossible to grant colonials the same rights as Britons: it would require an empire firmly based on hierarchy to hold chaos at bay. Most colonial elites assented to the logic of that position—East India Company officials, Bengal nabobs, Canadian traders and landlords. Only the leading men in Britain's original 13 colonies would not go along.

## American Loyalists

But the sentiment for independence was not universal. Americans who would not back the rebellion, supporters of the king and Parliament, numbered perhaps one-fifth of the population in 1775. While they proclaimed themselves **loyalists,** their rebel opponents dubbed them "tories"—"a thing whose head is in England, whose body is in America, and whose neck ought to be stretched." That division made the Revolution a conflict pitting Americans against one another as well as the British. In truth, the war for independence was the first American civil war.

| *This detail from a painting, commemorating the signing of the Declaration of Independence, shows Benjamin Franklin (seated center) weighing the consequences of the decisions he and his colleagues are about to undertake. John Hancock, the president of the Congress, is reported to have remarked, "We must be unanimous; there must be no pulling different ways; we must all hang together." Franklin is said to have rejoined, "Yes, we must indeed all hang together, or most assuredly, we shall all hang separately."*

# ABIGAIL AND JOHN ADAMS SPAR ON WOMEN'S RIGHTS AND THE AMERICAN REVOLUTION

*While she managed the family farm in Braintree, Massachusetts, he served as a delegate to the Continental Congress at Philadelphia, running the war and framing a new national government. She had concerns about the war and advice about the future government:*

## DOCUMENT 1   Abigail Adams to John Adams, March 31, 1776

I wish you would ever write me a Letter half as long as I write you; and tell me if you may where your Fleet are gone? What sort of Defence Virginia can make against our common Enemy . . . ? Whether it is so situated as to make an able Defence? Are not the Gentery Lords and the common people vassals . . . ?

I have sometimes been ready to think that the passion for Liberty cannot be Eaquelly Strong in the Breasts of those who have been accustomed to deprive their fellow Creatures of theirs. . . .

I long to hear that you have declared an independency—and by the way in the new Code of Laws which I suppose it will be necessary for you to make I desire you would Remember the Ladies, and be more generous and favourable to them than your ancestors. Do not put such unlimited power into the hands of the Husbands. Remember all Men would be tyrants if they could. If perticuliar care and attention is not paid to the Ladies we are determined to foment a Rebelion, and will not hold ourselves bound by any Laws in which we have no voice, or Representation.

That our Sex are Naturally Tyrannical is a Truth so thoroughly established as to admit of no dispute, but such of you as wish to be happy willingly give up the harsh title of Master for the more tender and endearing one of Friend. Why then, not put it out of the power of the vicious and the Lawless to use us with cruelty and indignity with impunity. Men of Sense in all Ages abhor those customs which treat us only as the vassals of your Sex. Regard us then as Beings placed by providence under your protection and in imitation of the Supreem Being make use of the power only for our happiness.

## DOCUMENT 2   John Adams to Abigail Adams, April 14, 1776

You justly complain of my short Letters, but the critical State of Things and the Multiplicity of Avocations must plead my Excuse. . . . You ask what Sort of Defence Virginia can make. I believe they will make an able Defence. Their Militia and minute Men have been some time employed in training them selves. . . . Their neighbouring Sister or rather Daughter Colony of North Carolina, which is a warlike Colony, and has several Battallions at the Continental Expence, as well as a pretty good Militia, are ready to assist them. . . . The Gentry are very rich, and the common People very poor.

This Inequality of Property, gives an Aristocratical Turn to all their Proceedings, and occasions a strong Aversion in their Patricians, to Common Sense. But the Spirit of these Barons, is coming down, and it must submit. . . .

As to your extraordinary Code of Laws, I cannot but laugh. We have been told that our Struggle has loosened the bands of Government every where. That Children and Apprentices were disobedient—that schools and Colledges were grown turbulent—that Indians slighted their Guardians and Negroes grew insolent to their Masters. But your Letter was the first Intimation that another

Tribe more numerous and powerfull than the rest were grown discontented. —This is rather too coarse a Complement but you are so saucy I wont blot it out.

Depend upon it, We know better than to repeal our Masculine systems. Altho they are in full Force, you know they are little more than Theory. We dare not exert our Power in its full Latitude. We are obliged to go fair, and softly, and in Practice you know We are the subjects. We have only the Name of Masters, and rather than give up this, which would completely subject Us to the Despotism of the Peticoat, I hope General Washington, and all our brave Heroes would fight.

## DOCUMENT 3   Abigail Adams to John Adams, May 7, 1776

I can not say that I think you very generous to the Ladies, for whilst you are proclaiming peace and good will to Men, Emancipating all Nations, you insist on retaining an absolute power over Wives, But you must remember that Arbitrary power is like most other things which are very hard, very liable to be broken—and notwithstanding all your wise Laws and Maxims we have it in our power not only to free ourselves but to

subdue our Masters, and without violence throw both your natural and legal authority at our feet

> Charm by accepting, by submitting sway
> Yet have our Humour most when we obey.

*Source:* Adams Family Papers, Massachusetts Historical Society.

### Thinking Critically

*What rights for women did Abigail Adams advocate? What rights receive no mention in her March 31st letter? What did John Adams mean by "another tribe"? How did he respond to his wife's advice? Both Adamses were keenly aware of class and racial inequalities. How did that awareness shape their respective views of gender inequality?*

Predictably, the king and Parliament commanded the strongest support in colonies that had been wracked by internal strife earlier in the eighteenth century. In New York, New Jersey, Pennsylvania, and the Carolinas, not only did memories of old struggles sharpen worries of future upheaval, but old enemies often took different sides in the Revolution. The Carolina backcountry emerged as a stronghold of loyalist sentiment because of influential local men who cast their lot with Britain. To win support against Carolina's rebels, whose ranks included most wealthy coastal planters, western loyalist leaders played on ordinary settlers' resentments of privileged easterners. Grievances dating back to the 1760s also influenced the revolutionary allegiances of former land rioters of New York and New Jersey. If their old landlord opponents opted for the rebel cause, the tenants took up loyalism.

Other influences also fostered allegiance to Britain. Government officials who owed their jobs to the empire, major city merchants who depended on British trade, and Anglicans living outside the South retained strong ties to the parent country. Loyalists were also disproportionately represented among recent emigrants from the British Isles. The inhabitants of Georgia, the newest colony, inclined toward the king, as did the Highland Scots, many of whom had arrived in the colonies as soldiers during the Seven Years' War or had worked for a short time in the southern backcountry as tobacco merchants and Indian traders.

Although a substantial minority, loyalists never became numerous enough anywhere to pose a serious menace to the Revolution. A more formidable threat was posed by the British army. And the greatest threat of all was posed by those very Americans who claimed that they wanted independence. For the question remained: Would they fight?

 REVIEW

What were the arguments for and against independence, and how did the advocates for independence prevail?

# THE FIGHTING IN THE NORTH

IN THE SUMMER OF 1775 Americans who wished to remain neutral probably outnumbered either loyalists or rebels. From the standpoint of mere survival, staying neutral made more sense than fighting for independence. Even the most ardent advocates of American rights had reason to harbor doubts, given the odds against the rebel colonists defeating the armed forces of the British Empire.

GEORGE
WASHINGTON,
GENERAL

Perhaps no friend of American liberty saw more clearly how slim the chances of a rebel victory were than George Washington. But Washington's principles, and his sense of honor, prevailed. June of 1775 found him, then 43 years old, attending the deliberations of the Second Continental Congress and dressed—a bit conspicuously—in his officer's uniform. The other delegates listened closely to his opinions on military matters, because Washington was the most celebrated American veteran of the Seven Years' War who remained young enough to lead a campaign. Better still, as a southerner he could bring his region into what thus far had remained mostly New England's fight. Congress readily appointed him commander-in-chief of a newly created Continental Army.

## The Two Armies at Bay

Thus did Washington find himself, only a month later, looking to bring some order to the rebel forces massing around Boston. He knew he faced a formidable foe.

Highly trained, ably led, and efficiently equipped, the king's troops were seasoned professionals. Rigorous drills and often severe discipline welded rank-and-file soldiers, men drawn mostly from the bottom of British society, into a savage fighting machine. At the height of the campaign in America, reinforcements brought the number of British troops to 50,000, strengthened by some 30,000 **Hessian** mercenaries from Germany and the support of half the ships in the British navy, the largest in the world.

"REGULARS" VS.
THE MILITIA

Washington was more modest about the army under his command, and he had much to be modest about. At first Congress recruited his fighting force of 16,600 rebel "regulars," the Continental Army, from the ranks of local New England militia bands. Although enlistments swelled briefly during the patriotic enthusiasm of 1775, for the rest of the war Washington's Continentals suffered chronic shortages of men and supplies. Even strong supporters of the Revolution hesitated to join the regular army, with its low pay and strict discipline and the constant threat of disease and danger. Most men preferred to fight instead as members of local **militia** units, the "irregular" troops who turned out to support the regular army whenever British forces came close to their neighborhoods.

The general reluctance to join the Continental Army created a host of difficulties for its commander and for Congress. Washington wanted and needed an army whose size and military capability could be counted on in long campaigns. He could not create an effective fighting force out of militias that mustered occasionally or men who enlisted for short stints in the Continental Army. In contrast, most republican leaders feared standing armies and idealized "citizen-soldiers"—men of civic virtue who volunteered whenever needed—as the backbone of the common defense. "Oh, that I was a soldier," chubby John Adams fantasized in 1775. "Everyone must and will and shall be a soldier."

But everyone did not become a soldier, and the dwindling number of volunteers gradually overcame republican fears of standing armies. In September 1776 Congress set terms in the Continental Army at a minimum of three years or for the duration of the war and assigned each state to

*Although most New Englanders rallied behind the rebel cause, support for the Revolution was not as widespread in the middle colonies and southern colonies.*

Hudson
Bay

NEWFOUNDLAND

Anticosti I.

St. Pierre and
Miquelon (Fr.)

NOVA SCOTIA

• Halifax

LOWER
CANADA

ME.
(MASS.)

UPPER
CANADA

N.H.
• Boston

MASS.

NEW YORK
CONN.

L. Superior

L. Michigan

L. Huron

L. Ontario

L. Erie

PENNSYLVANIA

N.J.

MD.   DEL.

ATLANTIC
OCEAN

VIRGINIA

Bermuda

N.C.

SPANISH
LOUISIANA

S.C.

• Charleston

GEORGIA

| | |
|---|---|
| | Strongly loyalist |
| | Loyalist or neutral Indians |
| | Strongly neutralist |
| | Strong support for rebels |
| | Other British territory |

FLORIDA

BAHAMAS

Gulf of
Mexico

SPANISH CUBA

raise a certain number of troops. They offered every man who enlisted in the army a cash bounty and a yearly clothing issue; enlistees for the duration were offered 100 acres of land as well. Still the problem of recruitment persisted. Less than a year later, Congress recommended that the states adopt a draft, but Congress had no authority to compel the states to meet their troop quotas.

Even in the summer of 1775, before enlistments fell off, Washington was worried. As his inexperienced Continentals laid siege to British-occupied Boston, most officers provided no real leadership, and the men under their command shirked their duties. They slipped away from camp at night; they left sentry duty before being relieved; they took potshots at the British; they tolerated filthy conditions in their camps.

**WOMEN OF
THE ARMY**
While Washington strove to impose discipline on his Continentals, he also attempted, without success, to rid himself of "the Women of the Army." When American men went off to fight,

## RADICAL CHIC AND REVOLUTIONARY WOMEN

Women and men of revolutionary America sought to invest themselves with virtue as they escaped British "corruption." The most zealous partisans of colonial rights took that "investiture" to a literal extreme: they made and wore particular clothing as an emblem of political commitment. In the 1760s "homespun," any coarse cloth made in America, became a badge of opposition to British colonial policy.

Clothes sewn from domestic textiles identified the men and women who wore them as friends of liberty, freed from the vanity of British fashion and the humiliating dependence on British imports. As early as 1766 the radical press called for increased domestic industry to offset American reliance on English cloth. It aimed its pleas particularly at the women who managed colonial households.

By 1769 radical propaganda had produced a new ritual of American resistance, the patriotic spinning competition. Wives and daughters from some of the wealthiest and most prominent families, women who had earlier vied to outdo one another in acquiring the latest English finery, were the featured players in this new form of political theater. Its setting was usually the home of a local minister, where, early in the morning, "respectable" young ladies, all dressed in homespun, assembled with their spinning wheels. They spent the day spinning furiously, stopping only to sustain themselves with "American produce . . . which was more agreeable to them than any foreign Dainties and Delicacies" and to drink herbal tea. At

*A wheel for spinning flax, made around 1775.*

the end of the day the minister accepted their homespun and delivered an edifying sermon to all present. That was a large group, often including from 20 to 100 "respectable" female spinners as well as hundreds of other townsfolk who had come to watch the competition or to provide food and entertainment.

Women reveled in the new attention and value that the male resistance movement and the radical press now attached to a common and humdrum domestic task. By the beginning of 1769 New England newspapers were highlighting spinning bees and their female participants, sometimes termed the "Daughters of Liberty." Wives and daughters from families of every rank were made to feel that they could play an important role in the resistance by imitating the elite women showcased in public spinning spectacles.

Spinning bees and "dressing down" in homespun thus contributed to the solidarity of the resistance by narrowing the visible distance between rich and poor Americans. In accounts of spinning competitions, the radical press emphasized that even the daughters of the elite sacrificed for the cause of resistance by embracing domestic economy and simplicity.

American women took pride in the new political importance that radical propaganda attributed to domestic pursuits. Writing to her English cousin, Charity Clarke of New York City cast herself as one of America's "fighting army of amazones . . . armed with spinning wheels."

*Thinking Critically*

*What are some other historical examples of people using dress or other visible emblems to express their political opinions?*

their wives usually stayed at home. To women then fell the sole responsibility for running farms and businesses, raising children, and keeping households together. They helped to supply the troops by sewing clothing, making blankets, and saving rags and lead weights for bandages and bullets. Other women on the home front organized relief for the widows and orphans of soldiers and protests against merchants who hoarded scarce commodities.

But the wives of poor men who joined the army were often left with no means to support their families. Thousands of such women—1 for every 15 soldiers—drifted after the troops. In return for half-rations, they cooked and washed for the soldiers; and after battles, they nursed the wounded, buried the dead, and scavenged the field for clothing and

equipment. An even larger number of women accompanied the redcoats: their presence was the only thing that Washington did not admire about the British army and could barely tolerate in his own. But the services that they performed were indispensable, and women followed the troops throughout the war.

## Laying Strategies

At the same time that he tried to discipline the Continentals, Washington designed a defensive strategy to compensate for their weakness. To avoid exposing raw rebel troops on "open ground against their Superiors in number and Discipline," he planned to fight the British from strong fortifications. With that aim in mind, in March 1776, Washington barricaded his army on Dorchester Heights, an elevation commanding Boston harbor from the south. That maneuver, which allowed American artillery to fire on enemy warships, confirmed a decision already made by the British to evacuate their entire army from Boston and sail for Halifax, Nova Scotia.

THE BRITISH CHOOSE CONVENTIONAL WAR

Britain had hoped to reclaim its colonies with a strategy of strangling the resistance in Massachusetts. But by the spring of 1776 it saw clearly that more was required than a show of force against New England. Instead, Britain's leaders chose to wage a conventional war in America, capturing major cities and crushing the Continental forces in a decisive battle. Military victory, the British believed, would enable them to restore political control and reestablish imperial authority.

The first target was New York City. General William Howe and Lord George Germain, the British officials now charged with overseeing the war, chose that seaport for its central location and—they hoped—its large loyalist population. Howe's army intended to move from New York City up the Hudson River, meeting with British troops under General Sir Guy Carleton coming south from Canada. Either the British drive would lure Washington into a major engagement, crushing the Continentals, or, if unopposed, the British offensive would cut America in two, smothering resistance to the south by isolating New England.

HOWE BROTHERS

The strategy was sounder than the men placed in charge of executing it. Concern for preserving troops addicted General Howe to caution, when daring more would have carried the day. Howe's brother, Admiral Lord Richard Howe, the head of naval operations in America, also stopped short of pressing the British advantage, owing to his personal desire for reconciliation. The reluctance of the Howe brothers to fight became the formula for British frustration in the two years that followed.

THE CAMPAIGNS IN NEW YORK AND NEW JERSEY

By mid-August, 32,000 British troops, including 8,000 Hessians, the largest expeditionary force of the eighteenth century, faced Washington's army of 23,000, which had marched down from Boston to take up positions on Long Island. At dawn on August 22 the Howe brothers launched their offense, easily pushing the rebel army back across the East River to Manhattan. After lingering on Long Island for a month, the Howes again lurched into action, ferrying their forces to Kip's Bay, just a few miles south of Harlem. When the British landed, the handful of rebel defenders at Kip's Bay fled—straight into the towering wrath of Washington, who happened on the scene during the rout. For once the general lost his habitual self-restraint, flogged both officers and men with his riding crop, and came close to being captured himself. But the Howes remained reluctant to hit hard, letting Washington's army escape from Manhattan to Westchester County.

At the Battle of Princeton, British troops bayoneted the rebel general Hugh Mercer, an assault later memorialized in this painting by George Washington Parke Custis, the adopted step-grandson of George Washington. This rendering focuses attention not only on Mercer's courage but also on the savagery of the redcoats, both of which helped the rebels gain civilian support.

BRITISH CAPTURE NEW YORK CITY

Throughout the fall of 1776 General Howe's forces followed as Washington's fled southward across New Jersey. On December 7, with the British nipping at their heels, the rebels crossed the Delaware River into Pennsylvania. There Howe stopped, pulling back most of his army to winter in New York City and leaving the Hessians to hold the British line of advance along the New Jersey side of the Delaware River.

REBEL VICTORIES AT TRENTON AND PRINCETON

Although the retreat had shriveled rebel strength to only 3,000 men, Washington decided that the campaign of 1776 was not over. On a snowy Christmas night, the Continentals floated back across the Delaware, picked their way over roads iced with sleet, and finally slid into Hessian-held Trenton at eight in the morning. One thousand German soldiers, still recovering from their spirited Christmas celebration and caught completely by surprise, quickly surrendered. Washington's luck held when, on January 3, 1777, the Continentals defeated British troops on the outskirts of Princeton, New Jersey.

During the winter of 1776–1777 the British lost more than battles: they alienated the very civilians whose loyalties they had hoped to maintain. In New York City the presence of the main body of the British army brought shortages of food and housing and caused constant friction between soldiers and city dwellers. In the New Jersey countryside still held by the Hessians, the situation was more desperate. Forced to live off the land, the Germans aroused resentment among local

## THE FIGHTING IN THE NORTH, 1775–1777

*After the British withdrew from Boston in 1775, they launched an attack on New York City the following year. Washington was forced to retreat northward, then across the Hudson and south into New Jersey and Pennsylvania, before surprising the British at Trenton and Princeton. Burgoyne's surrender at Saratoga in 1777 marked a turning point in the war. If General Howe had moved forces toward Albany, could he and General Burgoyne have split rebel New England from the rest of the former colonies? How?*

farmers by seizing "hay, oats, Indian corn, cattle, and horses, which were never or but very seldom paid for," as one loyalist admitted. The Hessians ransacked and destroyed homes and churches; they kidnapped and raped young women.

Many repulsed neutrals and loyalists now took their allegiance elsewhere. Bands of militia on Long Island, along the Hudson River, and all over New Jersey rallied to support the Continentals.

## Capturing Philadelphia

BRANDYWINE AND
GERMANTOWN

In the summer of 1777 General Howe still hoped to entice the Continentals into a decisive engagement. But he had now decided

to goad the Americans into battle by capturing Philadelphia. Rather than risk a march through hostile New Jersey, he sailed his army to Maryland and began a march to Philadelphia, 50 miles away. Washington had hoped to stay on the strategic defensive, holding his smaller army together and harassing the enemy but avoiding full-scale battles. Howe's march on the new nation's capital made that impossible. Washington engaged Howe twice—in September at Brandywine Creek and in October in an early dawn attack at Germantown—but both times the rebels were beaten back. He had been unable to prevent the British occupation of Philadelphia.

But in Philadelphia, as in New York, British occupation created hostile feelings, as the flood of troops drove up the price of food, fuel, and housing. While inflation hit hardest at the poor, the wealthy resented British officers who became their uninvited house guests. Philadelphians complained of redcoats looting their shops, trampling their gardens, and harassing them on the streets. Elizabeth Drinker, the wife of a Quaker merchant, confided in her diary that "I often feel afraid to go to bed."

Even worse, the British march through Maryland and Pennsylvania had outraged civilians, who fled before the army and then returned to find their homes and barns bare, their crops and livestock gone. Everywhere Howe's men went in the mid-Atlantic, they left in their wake Americans with compelling reasons to support the rebels. Worst of all, just days after Howe marched his occupying army into Philadelphia in the fall of 1777, another British commander in North America was surrendering his entire army to rebel forces at Saratoga, New York.

## Disaster at Saratoga

The calamity that befell the British at Saratoga was the doing of a glory-mongering general, John "Gentleman Johnny" Burgoyne. After his superior officer, Sir Guy Carleton, bungled a drive into New York in 1776, Burgoyne won approval to command another attack from Canada. The following summer he set out from Quebec with a force of 9,500 redcoats, 2,000 women and children, and a baggage train that included the commander's silver dining service, his dress uniforms, and numerous cases of his favorite champagne. As Burgoyne's entourage lumbered southward, it was slowed by a winding road that was broken by boulders, felled trees, and ramshackle bridges. Meanwhile, a handful of Continentals and a horde of New England militia assembled several miles below Saratoga at Bemis Heights under the command of General Horatio Gates.

**BURGOYNE SURRENDERS AT SARATOGA** On September 19 Gates's rebel scouts, nested high in the trees, spied the glittering bayonets of Burgoyne's approaching force. Benedict Arnold, a brave young officer, led several thousand rebels into battle at a clearing at Freeman's Farm. At the end of the day British reinforcements finally pushed the rebels back from a battlefield piled high with the bodies of soldiers from both sides. Burgoyne tried to flee to Canada but got no farther than Saratoga, where he surrendered his army to Gates on October 17.

Saratoga changed everything. Burgoyne had not just been nipped in a skirmish; he had lost his entire army. The triumph was enough to convince Britain's old rival France that, with a little help, the Americans might well reap the fruits of victory.

 **REVIEW**

What challenges did the Continental Army face between 1775 and 1777?

# THE TURNING POINT

FRANCE HAD BEEN WAITING FOR revenge against Britain since its humiliating defeat in the Seven Years' War. And for some years a scheme for evening the score had been taking shape in the mind of the French foreign minister, Charles Gravier de Vergennes. He reckoned that France might turn discontented colonials into willing allies against Britain.

 ## The American Revolution Becomes a Global War

Vergennes approached the Americans cautiously. He wanted to make certain that the rift between Britain and its colonies would not be reconciled and that the rebels in America stood a fighting chance. Although France had been secretly supplying the Continental Army with guns and ammunition since the spring of 1776, Vergennes would go no further than covert assistance.

Congress approached its former French enemies with equal caution. Would France, the leading Catholic monarchy in Europe, make common cause with the republican rebels? A few years earlier American colonials had fought against the French in Canada. Only recently they had renounced a king. For centuries they had overwhelmingly adhered to Protestantism.

The string of defeats dealt the Continental Army during 1776 convinced Congress that they needed the French. In November Congress appointed a three-member commission to negotiate not only aid from France but also a formal alliance. Its senior member was Benjamin Franklin, who enchanted all of Paris when he arrived sporting a simple fur cap and a pair of spectacles (something no fashionable Frenchman wore in public). Hailed as a homespun sage,

The French public's infatuation with Benjamin Franklin knew no bounds. They particularly delighted in his rustic dress and styled him a representative of "frontier" America. He appears in this guise on a snuffbox along with two revered French philosophers, Voltaire and Rousseau.

Franklin played the role of American innocent to the hilt and watched as admiring Parisians stamped his face on everything from the top of snuffboxes to the bottom of porcelain chamber pots.

Still, Franklin understood that mere popularity could not produce the alliance sought by Congress. It was only news that Britain had surrendered an entire army at Saratoga that convinced Vergennes that the rebels could actually win. In February 1778 France signed a treaty of commerce and friendship and a treaty of alliance, which Congress approved in May. Under the terms of the treaties, both parties agreed to accept nothing short of independence for America. The alliance left the British no choice other than to declare war on France. Less than a year later Spain joined France, hoping to recover territory lost to England in earlier wars.

## Winding Down the War in the North

The Revolution widened into a global war after 1778. Preparing to fight France and Spain dictated a new British strategy in America. No longer could the British concentrate on crushing the Continental Army. Instead, they would disperse their forces to fend off challenges all over the world. In May Sir Henry Clinton replaced William Howe as commander-in-chief and received orders to withdraw from Philadelphia to New York City.

Only 18 miles outside Philadelphia, at Valley Forge, Washington and his Continentals were assessing their own situation. Some 11,000 rebel soldiers had passed a harrowing winter in that isolated spot, starving for want of food, freezing for lack of clothing, huddling in miserable huts, and hating the British who lay so close and yet so comfortably in Philadelphia. Both officers and rank-and-file cursed their fellow citizens, blaming their suffering on congressional disorganization and civilian indifference. Congress lacked both money to pay and maintain the army and an efficient system for dispensing provisions to the troops. Most farmers and merchants preferred to supply the British, who could pay handsomely, than to do business with a financially strapped Congress. What little did reach the army often was food too rancid to eat or clothing too rotten to wear. Perhaps 2,500 perished at Valley Forge, the victims of cold, hunger, and disease.

Why did civilians who supported the rebel cause allow the army to suffer? Probably because by the winter of 1777, the Continentals came mainly from social classes that received little consideration at any time. The respectable, propertied farmers and artisans who had laid siege to Boston in 1775 had stopped enlisting. Serving in their stead were single men in their teens and early 20s, some who joined the army out of desperation, others who were drafted, still others who were hired as substitutes for the more affluent. The landless sons of farmers, unemployed laborers, drifters, petty criminals, vagrants, indentured servants, slaves, even captured British and Hessian soldiers—all men with no other means and no other choice—were swept into the Continental Army. The social composition of

| A member of the Continental Congress (center) refuses to look at the sufferings of cold, poorly clad white soldiers and a wounded African American fallen to the ground. Why would the British have published such a cartoon in 1778? What messages are conveyed?

the rebel rank and file had come to resemble that of the British army. It is the great irony of the Revolution: a war to protect liberty and property was waged by those Americans who were poorest and least free.

The beginning of spring in 1778 brought a reprieve. Supplies arrived at Valley Forge, and so did a fellow calling himself Baron von Steuben, a penniless Prussian soldier of fortune. Although Washington's men had shown spirit and resilience ever since Trenton, they still lacked discipline and training. Those defects and more von Steuben began to remedy. Barking orders and spewing curses in German and French, the baron (and his translators) drilled the rebel regiments to march in formation and to handle their bayonets like proper Prussian soldiers. By the summer of 1778 morale had rebounded.

Spoiling for action after their long winter, Washington's army, now numbering nearly 13,500, harassed Clinton's army as it marched overland from Philadelphia to New York City. On June 28 at Monmouth Courthouse a long, confused battle ended in a draw. After both armies retired for the night, Clinton's forces slipped away to safety in New York City. Washington pursued, but he lacked the numbers to launch an all-out assault on New York City.

**ARMY UPRISINGS** During the two hard winters that followed, resentments mounted among the rank and file over spoiled food, inadequate clothing, and arrears in pay. The army retaliated with mutinies. Between 1779 and 1780, officers managed to quell uprisings in three New England regiments. But in January 1781 both the Pennsylvania and New Jersey lines in an outright **mutiny** marched on Philadelphia, where Congress had reconvened. Order returned only after Congress promised back pay and provisions and Washington put two ringleaders in front of a firing squad.

## War in the West

The battles between Washington's Continentals and the British made the war in the West seem, by comparison, a sideshow of attacks and counterattacks that settled little. American fighters such as George Rogers Clark, with great daring, captured outposts such as Kaskaskia and Vincennes, without materially affecting the outcome of the war. Yet the conflict sparked a tremendous upheaval in the West, both from the dislocations of war and from the disease that spread in war's wake.

**INDIANS CAUGHT IN A CROSSFIRE** The disruptions were so widespread because the "War for Independence" had also become a war involving the imperial powers of Britain, France, and Spain. The same jockeying for advantage went on in the West as had occurred in previous imperial wars. The United States as well as the European powers pressed Indian tribes to become allies and attacked them when they did not. Caught in the crossfire, some Indian nations were pushed to the brink of their

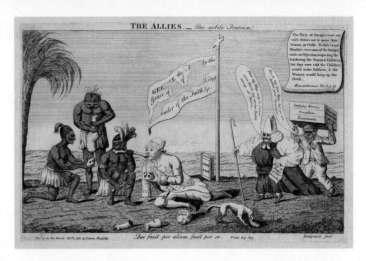

While both sides in the Revolution sought Indian allies, the American rebels spread sensationalized stories of British and Indian cruelties. This London cartoon shows the prime minister, Lord North, joining with Indians to feast on a child, an act of cannibalism that revolts even a dog. The archbishop of York promises to walk in God's ways, but is followed by his porter, who professes that "we are hellish good Christians" and carries boxes of scalping knives, tomahawks, and crucifixes. Such propaganda fueled Americans' hatred of Indians as they pushed westward.

own civil war, splitting into pro-American or pro-British factions. None suffered more than the mighty Iroquois. When days of impassioned speeches failed to secure a unified Iroquois policy regarding the Revolution, the six confederated tribes went their own ways. Most Tuscaroras and Oneidas remained neutral or joined the Americans, whereas Mohawk, Onondaga, Seneca, and Cayuga warriors aided the British by attacking frontier settlements. This pro-British faction rallied around the remarkable Mohawk leader Joseph Brant. Bilingual, literate, and formidable in war, Brant helped lead devastating raids across the frontiers of New York and Pennsylvania. In response Washington dispatched troops into Iroquois country, where they put the torch to 40 towns and destroyed fields and orchards everywhere they went. Many Iroquois perished the following winter—whichever side they had supported in the war—and the confederacy emerged from the Revolution with but a shadow of its former power.

Other native peoples switched allegiances more than once. Near St. Louis, a young Kaskaskia chief, Jean Baptiste de Coigne, allied first with the French, then joined the British and briefly threw in his lot with the Spanish, before finally joining the Virginians. Indians understood well that the pressures of war always threatened to deprive them of their homelands. "You are drawing so close to us that we can almost hear the noise of your axes felling our Trees," one Shawnee told the Americans. Another group of Indians concluded in 1784 that the Revolutionary War had been "the greatest blow that could have been dealt us, unless it had been our total destruction." Thousands fled the

## THE SMALLPOX PANDEMIC, 1775–1782

Smallpox spread across North America beginning late in 1775 as American forces launched an unsuccessful attack on the city of Quebec in Canada. The routes of transmission give only a rough idea of the disease's spread and impact, as it moved down the Eastern Seaboard and around the Gulf of Mexico, and then penetrated the interior, where the scattered surviving data make the pandemic's progress much harder to track. But the ravages of smallpox, combined with the disruptions sparked by the western raids of the Revolutionary War, placed severe stress on Indian peoples all across the continent. The disruption continued through the end of the eighteenth century.

Known transmission route
Probable transmission route

---

raids and counter-raids, while whole villages relocated. Hundreds made their way even beyond the Mississippi, to seek shelter in territory claimed by Spain. The aftershocks and dislocations continued for the next two decades; an entire generation of Native Americans grew up with war as a constant companion.

 **SMALLPOX PANDEMIC** — The political instability was vastly compounded by a smallpox epidemic that broke out first among American troops besieging Quebec in 1775. The disease soon spread to Continentals in New England, and Washington was obliged to inoculate them—secretly, for the vaccination left many soldiers temporarily weakened. From New England, the pox spread south along the coast, eventually reached New Orleans and next leapt to Mexico City by the autumn of 1779. From New Orleans it spread via fur traders up the Mississippi River and across the central plains, and from New Spain northward as well. By the time the pandemic burned out in 1782, it had felled over 130,000. By contrast, the Revolutionary War caused the deaths of some 8,000 soldiers while fighting in battle and another 13,000 from disease, including the mortality from smallpox.

## The Home Front in the North

Although in 1779 most northern civilians on the Eastern Seaboard enjoyed a respite from the war, the devastation lingered. Refugees on foot and in hastily packed carts filled the roads, fleeing the advancing armies. Those who remained to protect their homes and property might be caught in the crossfire of contending forces or cut off from supplies of food and firewood. Loyalists who remained in areas occupied by rebel troops faced harassment, imprisonment, or the confiscation of their property. Rebel sympathizers met similar fates in regions held by the British.

**WOMEN AND THE WAR** — The demands of war also disrupted family economies throughout the northern countryside. The seasons of intense fighting drew men off into military service just when their labor was most needed on family farms. Wives and daughters were left to assume the work of husbands and sons while coping with loneliness, anxiety, and grief. Two years after she fled before Burgoyne's advance into upstate New York, Ann Eliza Bleecker confessed to a friend, "Alas! the wilderness is within: I muse so long on the dead until I am unfit for the company of the living."

Despite these hardships, many women vigorously supported the revolutionary cause in a variety of ways. The Daughters of Liberty joined in harassing opponents to the rebel cause. One outspoken loyalist found himself surrounded by angry women who stripped off his shirt, covered him with molasses, and plastered him with flower petals. In more genteel fashion, groups of well-to-do women collected not only money but also medicines, food, and pewter to melt for bullets.

 **R E V I E W**

How did the Revolution become a global war, and what were conditions like for both soldiers and civilians?

# THE STRUGGLE IN THE SOUTH

DESPITE THEIR ARMED PRESENCE IN the North, the British had come to believe by the autumn of 1778 that their most vital aim was to regain their colonies in the mainland South. The Chesapeake and the Carolinas were more profitable to the empire and more strategically important, being so much closer to rich British sugar islands in the West Indies. Inspired by this new "southern strategy," Clinton dispatched forces to the Caribbean and Florida. In addition, the British laid plans for a new offensive drive into the Carolinas and Virginia.

BRITAIN'S SOUTHERN STRATEGY

English politicians and generals believed that the war could be won in the South. Loyalists were numerous, they believed, especially in the backcountry, where resentment of the patriot seaboard would encourage frontier folk to take up arms for the king at the first show of British force. And southern rebels—especially the vulnerable planters along the coast—could not afford to turn their guns away from their slaves. So, at least, the British theorized. All that was needed, they concluded, was that the British army establish a beachhead in the South and then, in league with loyalists, drive northward, up the coast.

## The Siege of Charleston

The southern strategy worked well for a short time in a small place. In November 1778 Clinton sent 3,500 troops to Savannah, Georgia. The resistance in the tiny colony quickly collapsed, and a large number of loyalists turned out to help the British. Encouraged, the army moved on to South Carolina.

During the last days of 1779 an expedition under Clinton himself set sail from New York City. Landing off the Georgia coast, his troops mucked through malarial swamps to the peninsula lying between the Ashley and Cooper Rivers. At the tip of that neck of land stood Charleston, and the British began to lay siege. By then, an unseasonably warm spring had set in, making the area a heaven for

mosquitoes and a hell for human beings. Sweltering and swatting, redcoats weighted down in their woolen uniforms inched their siege works toward the city. By early May Clinton's army had closed in, and British shelling was setting fire to houses within the city. On May 12 Charleston surrendered.

Clinton sailed back to New York at the end of June 1780, leaving behind 8,300 redcoats to carry the British offensive northward to Virginia. The man charged with leading that campaign was his ambitious and able subordinate, Charles, Lord Cornwallis.

## The Partisan Struggle in the South

Cornwallis's task in the Carolinas was complicated by the bitter animosity between rebels and loyalists there. Many Carolinians had taken sides years before Clinton's conquest of Charleston. In the summer and fall of 1775 the supporters of Congress and the new South Carolina revolutionary government mobbed, tortured, and imprisoned supporters of the king in the backcountry. These attacks only hardened loyalist resolve: roving bands seized ammunition, broke their leaders out of jail, and besieged rebel outposts. But within a matter of months, a combined force of rebel militias from the coast and the frontier managed to defeat loyalist forces in the backcountry.

REBELS AND LOYALISTS BATTLE FOR THE BACKCOUNTRY

With the fall of Charleston in 1780, the loyalist movement on the frontier returned to life. Out of loyalist vengefulness and rebel desperation issued the brutal civil war that seared the southern backcountry after 1780. Neighbors and even families fought and killed each other as members of roaming rebel and tory militias. The intensity of **partisan warfare** in the backcountry produced unprecedented destruction. Loyalist militia plundered plantations and assaulted local women; rebel militias whipped suspected British supporters and burned their farms; both sides committed brutal assassinations and tortured prisoners. All of society, observed one minister, "seems to be at an end. Every person keeps close on his own plantation. Robberies and murders are often committed on the public roads. . . . Poverty, want, and hardship appear in almost every countenance."

Cornwallis, when confronted with the chaos, erred fatally. He did nothing to stop his loyalist allies or his own troops from mistreating civilians. A Carolina loyalist admitted that "the lower sort of People, who were in many parts originally attached to the British Government, have suffered so severely . . . that Great Britain has now a hundred enemies, where it had one before." Although rebels and loyalists alike plundered and terrorized the backcountry, Cornwallis's forces bore more of the blame and suffered the consequences.

A growing number of civilians outraged by the behavior of the king's troops cast their lot with the rebels. That upsurge of popular support enabled Francis Marion, the

"Swamp Fox," and his band of white and black raiders to cut British lines of communication between Charleston and the interior. It swelled another rebel militia led by "the Gamecock," Thomas Sumter, who bloodied loyalist forces throughout the central part of South Carolina. It mobilized the "over-the-mountain men," a rebel militia in western Carolina who claimed victory at the Battle of Kings Mountain in October 1780. By the end of 1780 these successes had persuaded most civilians that only the rebels could restore order.

**BRITISH VICTORY AT CAMDEN**

If rebel fortunes prospered in the partisan struggle, they faltered in the conventional warfare being waged at the same time in the South. In August of 1780 the Continentals commanded by Horatio Gates lost a major engagement to the British force at Camden, South Carolina. In the fall of 1780 Congress replaced Gates with Washington's candidate for the southern command, Nathanael Greene, an energetic 38-year-old Rhode Islander and a veteran of the northern campaigns.

## Greene Takes Command

Greene bore out Washington's confidence by grasping the military situation in the South. He understood the needs of his 1,400 hungry, ragged, and demoralized troops and instructed von Steuben to lobby Virginia for food and clothing. He understood the importance of the rebel militias and sent Lieutenant Colonel Henry "Lighthorse Harry" Lee to assist Marion's raids. He understood the weariness of southern civilians and prevented his men from plundering the countryside.

Above all, Greene understood that his forces could never hold the field against the whole British army, a decision that led him to break the first rule of conventional warfare: he divided his army. In December 1780 he dispatched to western South Carolina a detachment of 600 men under the command of Brigadier General Daniel Morgan of Virginia.

*General Nathanael Greene*

**COWPENS**

Back at the British camp, Cornwallis worried that Morgan and his rebels, if left unchecked, might rally the entire backcountry against the British. However, Cornwallis reckoned that he could not commit his entire army to the pursuit of Morgan's men, because then Greene and his troops might retake Charleston. The only solution, unconventional to be sure, was that Cornwallis divide *his* army. That he did, sending Lieutenant Colonel Banastre Tarleton and 1,100 men west after Morgan. Cornwallis had played right into Greene's hands: the rebel troops

## THE FIGHTING IN THE SOUTH, 1780–1781

*In December 1780 Nathanael Greene made the crucial decision to split his army, sending Daniel Morgan west, where he defeated the pursuing Banastre Tarleton at Cowpens. Meanwhile, Greene regrouped and replenished at Cheraw, keeping Cornwallis off balance with a raid (dotted line) toward Charleston and the coast. Then, with Cornwallis in hot pursuit, Greene and Morgan rejoined at Salisbury, retreating into Virginia. Cornwallis was worn down in this vain pursuit and lost three-quarters of the troops he began with before finally abandoning the Carolina campaign.*

In 1845 painter William Ranney re-created a traditional retelling or account of the Battle of Cowpens recorded in John Marshall's biography of George Washington. According to Marshall, "a waiter, too small to wield a sword" saved the life of a relative of George Washington during the battle. Just as Lieutenant Colonel William Washington, leader of the patriot cavalry, was about to be cut down by a sword, the black man "saved him by wounding the officer with a ball from a pistol." Ranney depicts the unnamed man as a bugler astride a horse, as Morgan and Washington battle three British soldiers.

might be able to defeat a British army split into two pieces. For two weeks Morgan led Tarleton's troops on a breakneck chase across the Carolina countryside. In January 1781 at an open meadow called Cowpens, Morgan routed Tarleton's force.

Now Cornwallis took up the chase. Morgan and Greene joined forces and kept going north until the British army wore out. Cornwallis finally stopped at Hillsboro, North Carolina, but few local loyalists responded to his call for reinforcements. Greene decided to make a show of force near the tiny village of Guilford Courthouse. On a brisk March day the two sides joined battle, each sustaining severe casualties before Greene was forced to retreat. But the high cost of victory convinced Cornwallis that he could not put down the rebellion in the Carolinas. "I am quite tired of marching about the country in quest of adventures," he informed Clinton.

**VALUE OF THE MILITIA** Although Nathanael Greene's command provided the Continentals with effective leadership in the South, it was the resilience of rebel militia that thwarted the British offensive in the Carolinas. Many Continental Army officers complained about the militia's lack of discipline, its habit of melting away when homesickness set in or harvest approached, and its cowardice under fire in conventional engagements. But when set the task of ambushing supply trains, harrying bands of local loyalists, or raiding isolated British outposts, the militia came through. Many southern civilians refused to join the British or to provide the redcoats with food and information, because they knew that once the British army left their neighborhoods, the rebel militia would be back. The Continental Army in the South lost many conventional battles, but the militia kept the British from restoring political control over the backcountry.

## African Americans in the Age of Revolution

The British also lost in the Carolinas because they did not seek greater support from those southerners who would have fought for liberty *with* the British—African American slaves.

Black Americans, virtually all in bondage, made up one-third of the population between Delaware and Georgia. Since the beginning of the resistance to Britain, white southerners had worried that the watchwords of *liberty* and *equality* would spread to the slave quarters. Gripped by the fear of slave rebellion, southern revolutionaries began to take precautions. Marylanders disarmed black inhabitants and issued extra guns to the white militia. Charlestonians hanged and then burned the body of Thomas Jeremiah, a free black who was convicted of spreading the word to others that the British "were come to help the poor Negroes."

**WHITE FEARS OF REBELLION** Southern whites fully expected the British to turn slave rebelliousness to their strategic advantage. As early as 1775 Virginia's royal governor, Lord Dunmore, confirmed white fears by offering to free any slave who joined the British. When Clinton invaded the South in 1779 he renewed that offer. One North Carolina planter heard that loyalists were "promising every Negro that would murder his master and family he should have his Master's plantation" and that "the Negroes have got it amongst them and believe it to be true."

## RUNAWAYS

**What is implied by the tallying of children ["girls" and "boys"] with slave women?**

**What is the significance of the list specifying occupations for some of the slave men?**

**How does the number of female runaways compare with that of males? Children with adults?**

*"A List of Negroes That Went Off to Dunmore," dated April 14, 1776, Library of Virginia, Richmond.*

Americans in earlier centuries were inveterate listmakers, providing present-day historians with a rich trove of evidence. College students recorded the titles of books they read; ministers noted the Bible passages on which they preached; clerks kept count of church members; tax assessors enumerated household members and the rates owed and paid; probate court officers inventoried the possessions of the dead, often down to chipped crockery and broken tools. But the roster of slaves shown above is an extraordinary list, drawn up not on account of their master's death but because these 87 men, women, and children had fled their Virginia plantation, emboldened by Lord Dunmore's promise of freedom. It is impossible to know whether they ran away in small groups, stealing off over a period of several months between 1775 and 1776, or whether they ran away in larger companies within the space of a few days. But we do know that throughout Virginia, as on this plantation, women and children made up a significant percentage of the runaways.

### Thinking Critically

*For what purposes might the Virginia master have composed this list? Why are slave artisans so well represented among the men on this list? Why were slave women and their children willing to risk escape in such large numbers?*

But in Britain there was overwhelming opposition to organizing support among African Americans. British leaders dismissed Dunmore's ambitious scheme to raise a black army of 10,000 and another plan to create a sanctuary for black loyalists on the southeastern coast. Turning slaves against masters, they recognized, was not the way to conciliate southern whites.

Even so, southern fears of insurrection made the rebels reluctant to enlist black Americans as soldiers. At first, Congress barred African Americans from the Continental Army. But as the rebels became more desperate for manpower, policy changed. Northern states actively encouraged black enlistments, and in the Upper South, some states allowed free men of color to join the army or permitted slaves to substitute for their masters.

AFRICAN AMERICAN QUESTS FOR LIBERTY

Slaves themselves sought freedom from whichever side seemed most likely to grant it. Perhaps 10,000 slaves took up Dunmore's offer in 1775 and deserted their masters, and thousands more flocked to Clinton's forces after the fall of Charleston. For many runaways the hope of liberation proved an illusion. Although some served the British army as laborers, spies, and soldiers, many died of disease in army camps (upward of 27,000 by one estimate) or were sold back into slavery in the West Indies. About 5,000 black soldiers served in the revolutionary army in the hope of gaining freedom. In addition, the number of runaways to the North soared during the Revolution. In total, perhaps 100,000 men and women—nearly a fifth of the total slave population—attempted to escape bondage. Their odysseys to freedom took some to far-flung destinations: loyalist communities in Nova Scotia, a settlement established by the British in Sierra Leone on the West African coast, even the Botany Bay penal colony in Australia.

The slave revolts so dreaded by southern whites never materialized. Possibly the boldest slaves were drawn off into the armies; possibly greater white precautions discouraged schemes for black rebellions. In South Carolina, where the potential for revolt was greatest, most slaves chose to remain on plantations rather than risk a collective resistance and escape in the midst of the fierce partisan warfare.

✓ REVIEW

Why did the British fail to achieve their military and political goals in the South?

# THE WORLD TURNED UPSIDE DOWN

DESPITE HIS LOSSES IN THE Carolinas, Cornwallis still believed that he could score a decisive victory against the Continental Army. The theater he chose for that showdown was the Chesapeake. During the spring of 1781 he had marched his army to the Virginia coast and joined forces with the hero of Saratoga and newly turned loyalist, Benedict Arnold. Embarrassed by debt and disgusted by Congress's shabby treatment of the Continental Army, Arnold had started exchanging rebel secrets for British money in 1779 before defecting outright in the fall of 1780. By June of 1781 Arnold and Cornwallis were fortifying a site on the tip of the peninsula formed by the York and James Rivers, a place called Yorktown.

Meanwhile, Washington and his French ally, the comte de Rochambeau, met in Connecticut to plan a major attack. Rochambeau urged a coordinated land-sea assault on the Virginia coast. Washington insisted instead on a full-scale offensive against New York City. Just when the rebel commander was about to have his way, word arrived that a French fleet under the comte de Grasse was sailing for the Chesapeake to blockade Cornwallis by sea. Washington's Continentals headed south.

## Surrender at Yorktown

By the end of September, 7,800 Frenchmen, 5,700 Continentals, and 3,200 militia had sandwiched Yorktown between the devil of an allied army and the deep blue sea of French warships. "If you cannot relieve me very soon," Cornwallis wrote to Clinton, "you must expect to hear the worst." The British navy did arrive—but seven days after Cornwallis surrendered to the rebels on October 19, 1781. When Germain carried the news from Yorktown to the king's first minister, Lord North replied, "Oh, God, it is over." Then North resigned, Germain resigned, and even George III murmured something about abdicating.

It need not have ended at Yorktown, but timing made all the difference. At the end of 1781 and early in 1782, the British army received setbacks in the other theaters of the war: India, the West Indies, and Florida. The French and the Spanish were everywhere in Europe as well, gathering in the English Channel, planning a major offensive against Gibraltar. The cost of the fighting was already enormous. British leaders recognized that the rest of the empire was at stake and set about cutting their losses in America.

The Treaty of Paris, signed on September 3, 1783, was a diplomatic triumph for the American negotiators: Benjamin Franklin, John Adams, and John Jay. They dangled before Britain the possibility that a generous settlement might weaken American ties to France. The British jumped at the bait. They recognized the independence of the United States and agreed to ample boundaries for the new nation: the Mississippi River on the west, the 31st parallel on the south, and the present border of Canada on the north. American negotiators then persuaded a skeptical France to approve the treaty by arguing that, as allies, they were bound to present a united front to the British. Spain, the third member of the alliance, settled for retaining Florida and Minorca, an island in the Mediterranean.

| On September 30, 1780, a wagon bearing this two-faced effigy was drawn through the streets of Philadelphia. The effigy represents Benedict Arnold, who sits between a gallows and the devil. Note the similarities between this piece of street theater and the demonstrations mounted on Pope's Day several decades earlier, shown on page 146.

If the Treaty of Paris marked both the end of a war and the recognition of a new nation, the surrender at Yorktown captured the significance of a revolution. Those present at Yorktown on that clear autumn afternoon in 1781 watched as the British second in command to Cornwallis (who had sent word that he was "indisposed") surrendered his superior's sword. He offered the sword first, in a face-saving gesture, to the French commander, Rochambeau, who politely refused and pointed to Washington. But the American commander-in-chief, out of a mixture of military protocol, nationalistic pride, and perhaps even wit, pointed to *his* second in command, Benjamin Lincoln.

Some witnesses recalled that British musicians arrayed on the Yorktown green played "The World Turned Upside Down." Their recollections may have been faulty, but the story has persisted as part of the folklore of the American Revolution—and for good reasons. The world had, it seemed, turned upside down with the coming of American independence.

 REVIEW

How did the United States manage to prevail in the war and in the treaty negotiations?

# CONCLUSION

## THE WORLD AT LARGE

The colonial rebels shocked the British with their answer to the question "Would they fight?" The answer had been yes—but on their own terms. By 1777 most propertied Americans avoided fighting in the Continental Army. Yet whenever the war reached their homes, farms, and businesses, many Americans gave their allegiance to the new nation by turning out with rifles or supplying homespun clothing, food, or ammunition. They rallied around Washington in New Jersey, Gates in upstate New York, Greene in the Carolinas. Middle-class American men fought, some from idealism, others out of self-interest, but always on their own terms, as members of the militia. These citizen-soldiers turned the world upside down by defeating professional armies.

Of course, the militia did not bear the brunt of the fighting. That responsibility fell to the Continental Army, which by 1777 drew its strength from the poorest ranks of American society. Yet even the Continentals, for all their desperation, managed to fight on their own terms. Some asserted their rights by raising mutinies, until Congress redressed their grievances. All of them, as the Baron von Steuben observed, behaved differently than European soldiers did. Americans followed orders only if the logic of commands was explained to them. The Continentals, held in contempt by most Americans, turned the world upside down by sensing their power and asserting their measure of personal independence.

Americans of African descent dared as much and more in their quests for liberty. Whether they chose to escape slavery by fighting for the British or the Continentals or by striking out on their own as runaways, their defiance, too, turned the world upside down. Among the tens of thousands of slaves who would not be mastered was one Henry Washington, a native of Africa who became the slave of George Washington in 1763. But Henry Washington made his own declaration of independence in 1776, slipping behind British lines and serving as a corporal in a black unit. Thereafter, like thousands of former slaves, he sought to build a new life elsewhere in the Atlantic world, settling first in Nova Scotia and finally in Sierra Leone. By 1800 he headed a community of former slaves who were exiled to the outskirts of that colony for their determined efforts to win republican self-government from Sierra Leone's white British rulers. Like Thomas Paine, Henry Washington believed that freedom was his only country.

In all those ways, a revolutionary generation turned the world upside down. They were a diverse lot—descended from Indians, Europeans, and Africans, driven by desperation or idealism or greed—but joined, even if they did not recognize it, by their common struggle to break free from the rule of monarchs or masters. What now awaited them in the world of the new United States? ∞∞∞

## CHAPTER SUMMARY

THE AMERICAN REVOLUTION BROUGHT INDEPENDENCE to Britain's former colonies after an armed struggle that began in 1775 and concluded with the Treaty of Paris in 1783.

- When the Second Continental Congress first convened, many delegates still hoped for reconciliation—even as they created the Continental Army.

- The Second Continental Congress adopted the Declaration of Independence on July 4, 1776.

- British victories in the North throughout 1776 and 1777 secured both New York City and Philadelphia. But harsh tactics alienated much of the populace.

- The British suffered a disastrous defeat at the Battle of Saratoga in early 1778, which prompted France to openly ally with the American rebels soon thereafter.

- By 1780 Britain aimed to win the war by claiming the South, and captured both Savannah, Georgia, and Charleston, South Carolina.

- Although the war in the West contributed little to the outcome of the Revolution, the competition for Indian allies among the United States, Britain, France, and Spain sparked two decades of dislocation and conflict across the continent, a situation made worse by a smallpox pandemic.

- The Continental Army in the South, led by Nathanael Greene and aided by guerrilla fighters in the partisan struggle, foiled the British strategy, and Cornwallis surrendered at the Battle of Yorktown in 1781.

- Except during the first year of fighting, the rank and file of the Continental Army were drawn from the poorest Americans, whose needs for food, clothing, and shelter were neglected by the Continental Congress.

# ADDITIONAL READING

THE OUTSTANDING MILITARY HISTORIES OF the American Revolution are Don Higginbotham, The *War for American Independence* (1971), and Robert Middlekauff, *The Glorious Cause*, 1763 to 1789 (1982). For a compelling treatment of the lives of soldiers in the Continental Army, read Caroline Cox, *A Proper Sense of Honor* (2004), and to become better acquainted with their commander-in-chief, turn to *His Excellency: George Washington* (2004) by Joseph Ellis. Colin Calloway, *The American Revolution in Indian Country* (1995), probes the role of American Indians in that conflict, and Peter Silver explores the Revolution's spur to Indian-hating in *Our Savage Neighbors* (2008). Benjamin Franklin's efforts to secure an alliance with France are vividly told in Stacy Schiff, *A Great Improvisation* (2005), and the best introductions to the global context of the American Revolution are David Armitage, *The Declaration of Independence* (2007), and P. J. Marshall, *The Making and Unmaking of Empires* (2005).

Impressive interpretations of the war's impact on American society include Alfred Young, *Liberty Tree* (2006), Charles Royster, *A Revolutionary People at War* (1979), and John Shy, *A People Numerous and Armed* (1976). Sylvia Frey offers a thoughtful history of African Americans during this era in *Water from the Rock* (1991), and Cassandra Pybus, *Epic Journeys of Freedom* (2006), recounts the experiences of runaway slaves who seized on the wartime crisis to gain liberty. The role of women in revolutionary America receives excellent coverage in Carol Berkin, *Revolutionary Mothers* (2005), and in Mary Beth Norton's classic study, *Liberty's Daughters* (1980).

For a fuller list of readings, see the Bibliography at www.mhhe.com/eh8e.

## SIGNIFICANT EVENTS

**1775**
Second Continental Congress convenes at Philadelphia; Congress creates the Continental Army; Battle of Bunker Hill

**1776**
Publication of *Common Sense*; British troops evacuate Boston; Declaration of Independence; British occupy New York City, forcing Washington to retreat through New Jersey into Pennsylvania; Washington counterattacks at Battle of Trenton

**1777**
British summer drive to occupy Philadelphia; battles of Brandywine Creek, Germantown; Burgoyne surrenders at Saratoga; Continental Army encamps for winter at Valley Forge

**1778**
France allies with rebel Americans; France and Britain declare war; British shift focus to the South; Savannah falls

**1780**
British occupy Charleston; partisan warfare of Marion, Sumter; rebel victory at King's Mountain, South Carolina; Nathanael Greene takes southern command

**1781**
Engagements at Cowpens, Guilford Courthouse; Cornwallis surrenders at Yorktown

**1783**
Treaty of Paris

# British and American Forces in the Revolutionary War Compared

| | IN THEORY | ON THE GROUND |
|---|---|---|

**British**

| IN THEORY | ON THE GROUND |
|---|---|
| Advantage: superior army | Advantage: training paid off in winning many major battles and controlling cities |
| | Disadvantage: but formal training left British forces vulnerable to guerrilla attacks |
| Advantage: superior navy | Advantage neutralized by French navy at Cornwallis's surrender |
| | Disadvantage: entry of France into the war in 1778 obliged the British to divide their forces |
| | Disadvantage: British troops alienated rather than conciliated civilians |

**American**

| IN THEORY | ON THE GROUND |
|---|---|
| Disadvantage: badly trained, supplied, and equipped | Disadvantage: took years for the Continentals to gain training, discipline, and experience |
| Advantage: militias turned out to defend home territories | Disadvantage: militias tended to disappear when the immediate threat passed |
| Advantage: French alliance | Disadvantage: took Franklin's diplomacy nearly 3 years to secure alliance |
| Disadvantage: slaves running for freedom undermined rebel resolve | Disadvantage neutralized: except for Dunmore, British were reluctant to enlist African Americans |

South Carolina's low country supplies the background for this portrait of a wealthy Charleston couple, John Purves and his wife, Anne Pritchard Purves. John saw military service in both the state militia and the Continental Army; Anne, with her classically draped dress, evokes the goddess of Liberty. What do you make of the expressions on their faces?

## CHAPTER 8

# Crisis and Constitution

## 1776–1789

## *What's to Come*

∞∞∞ **AN AMERICAN STORY** ∞∞∞

## "*THESE* UNITED STATES"

"I am not a Virginian, but an American," Patrick Henry declared in the Virginia House of Burgesses. Most likely he was lying. Certainly no one listening took him seriously, for the newly independent colonists did not identify themselves as members of a nation. They would have said, as did Thomas Jefferson, "Virginia, Sir, is my country." Or as John Adams wrote to another native son, "Massachusetts is our country." Jefferson and Adams were men of wide political vision and experience: both were leaders in the Continental Congress and more inclined than most to think nationally. But like other members of the revolutionary generation, they identified deeply with their home states and even more deeply with their home counties and towns.

It followed that allegiance to the states, not the Union, determined the shape of the first republican political experiments. For a decade after independence, the revolutionaries were less committed to creating an American nation than to organizing 13 separate state republics. The Declaration of Independence referred explicitly not to *the* United States but to *these* United States. It envisioned not one republic so much as a federation of 13.

Only when peace was restored during the decade of the 1780s were Americans forced to face some unanswered questions raised by their revolution. The Declaration proclaimed that these "free and independent states" had "full power to levy war, conclude peace, contract alliances, establish commerce." Did that mean that New Jersey, as a free and independent state, could sign a trade agreement with France, excluding the other states? If the United States were to be more than a loose federation, how could it assert power on a national scale? Similarly, American borderlands to the west presented problems. If these territories were settled by Americans, would they eventually join the United States? Go their own ways as independent nations? Become new colonies of Spain or England?

Such problems were more than political; they were rooted in social realities. For a political union to succeed, the inhabitants of 13 separate states had to start thinking of themselves as Americans. When it came right down to it, what united a Vermont farmer working his rocky fields and a South Carolina gentleman presiding over a vast rice plantation? What bonds existed between a Kentuckian rafting the Ohio River and a Salem merchant sailing to China for porcelain?

And in a society in which all citizens were said to be "created equal," the inevitable social inequalities had to be confronted. How could women participate in the Revolution's bid for freedom if they were not free to vote or to hold property? How would free or enslaved African Americans live in a republic based on equality? As the British began leaving Yorktown, Charleston, and other ports, they transferred thousands of slaves who had been in their charge to New York City. Southern slaveholders followed, looking to reclaim their bondspeople. "The dreadful rumor" that slave masters were searching for their property "filled us all with inexpressible anguish and horror," reported Boston King, an escaped slave who had fought for the British; ". . . for some days we lost our appetite for food and sleep from our eyes." Repossessing such slaves could be perilous. One master was murdered by "about 12 or 15 of the Ward's blacks" when he came looking. How could black Americans feel a bond with white Americans when so often the only existing bonds had been forged with chains?

| The Revolution provided many humble folk a new sense of pride and potential. These men, who manufactured pewter mugs and teapots, gave their support to the new Constitution: a "Federal Plan most solid and secure."

To such questions there were no final answers in 1781. There was ferment, excitement, and experimentation as 13 states each sought to create their governments anew; as Americans—or rather, Virginians and New Yorkers and Georgians and citizens of other countries—began to imagine how the revolutionary virtue of equality might transform their societies. But as the decade progressed, the sense of crisis deepened. ∞∞∞

# REPUBLICAN EXPERIMENTS

AFTER INDEPENDENCE WAS DECLARED IN July 1776, many of America's best political minds turned to drawing up **constitutions** for their individual states. Thomas Jefferson deserted the Continental Congress, leaving the conduct of the war and national affairs to other men, for the more important business of creating Virginia's new government.

BELIEF IN THE NEED FOR SMALL REPUBLICS

In truth, the state constitutions were crucial republican experiments, the first efforts at establishing a government of and by the people. All the revolutionaries agreed that the people—not a king or a few privileged aristocrats—should rule. Yet they were equally certain that republican governments were best suited to small territories. They believed that the new United States was too sprawling and its people too diverse to be safely consolidated into a single national republic. They feared, too, that the government of a large republic would inevitably grow indifferent to popular concerns, being distant from many of its citizens. Without being under the watchful eye of the people, representatives would become less accountable to the electorate and turn tyrannical. A federation of small state republics, they reasoned, would stand a far better chance of enduring.

## The State Constitutions

The new state constitutions retained the basic form of their old colonial governments, all except Georgia and Pennsylvania providing for a governor and a bicameral legislature. But although most states did not alter the basic structure of their governments, they changed dramatically the balance of power among the different branches of government.

**CURBING EXECUTIVE POWER** From the republican perspective in 1776, the greatest problem of any government lay in curbing executive power. What had driven Americans into rebellion was the abuse of authority by the king and his appointed officials. To ensure that the executive could never again threaten popular liberty, the new states either accorded almost no power to their governors or abolished that office entirely. The governors had no authority to convene or dissolve the legislatures. They could not veto the legislatures' laws, grant land, or erect courts. Most important from the republican point of view, governors had few powers to appoint other state officials. All these limits were designed to deprive the executive of any patronage or other form of influence over the legislature. By reducing the governors' power, Americans hoped to preserve their states from the corruption that they deplored in British political life.

**STRENGTHENING LEGISLATIVE POWERS** What the state governors lost, the legislatures gained. Sam Adams, the Boston rebel leader, expressed the political consensus when he declared that "every legislature of every colony ought to be the sovereign and uncontrollable Power within its own limits of territory." To ensure that those powerful legislatures truly represented the will of the people, the new state constitutions called for annual elections and required candidates for the legislature to live in the districts they represented. Many states even asserted the right of voters to instruct the men elected to office about how to vote on specific issues. Although no state granted universal manhood suffrage, most reduced the amount of property required of qualified voters. Finally, state supreme courts were also either elected by the legislatures or appointed by elected governors.

By investing all power in popular assemblies, Americans abandoned the British system of mixed government. In one sense, that change was fairly democratic. A majority of voters within a state could do whatever they wanted, unchecked by governors or courts. On the other hand, the arrangement opened the door for legislatures to turn as tyrannical as governors. The revolutionaries brushed that prospect aside: republican theory assured them that the people possessed a generous share of civic virtue, the capacity for selfless pursuit of the general welfare.

**WRITTEN CONSTITUTIONS** In an equally momentous change, the revolutionaries insisted on written state constitutions. Whenever government appeared to exceed the limits of its authority, Americans wanted to have at hand the written contract between rulers and ruled. When eighteenth-century Britons used the word *constitution,* they meant the existing arrangement of government—not an actual document but a collection of parliamentary laws, customs, and precedents. But Americans believed that a constitution should be a written code that stood

Americans responded to independence with rituals of "killing the king," like the one enacted by this New York crowd in 1776 as it pulls down a statue of George III. Americans also expressed their mistrust of monarchs and their ministers by establishing new state governments with weak executive branches.

| First Seal of the United States

apart from and above government, a yardstick against which the people measured the performance of their rulers. After all, they reasoned, if Britain's constitution had been written down, available for all to consult, would American rights have been violated?

## From Congress to Confederation

While Americans lavished attention on their state constitutions, the national government nearly languished during the decade after 1776. With the coming of independence, the Second Continental Congress conducted the common business of the federated states. It created and maintained the Continental Army, issued currency, and negotiated with foreign powers.

But while Congress acted as a central government by common consent, it lacked any legal basis for its authority. To redress that need, in July 1776 Congress appointed a committee to draft a constitution for a national government. The urgent business of waging the war made for delay, but Congress approved the first national constitution in November 1777. It took four more years—until February 1781—for all the states to ratify these Articles of Confederation.

ARTICLES OF CONFEDERATION The Articles of Confederation provided for a government by a national legislature— essentially a continuation of the Second Continental Congress. That body had the authority to declare war and make peace, conduct diplomacy, regulate Indian affairs, appoint military and naval officers, and requisition men from the states. In affairs of finance it could coin money and issue paper currency. Extensive as these responsibilities were, Congress could not levy taxes or even regulate trade. The crucial power of the purse rested entirely with the states, as did the final power to make and execute laws. Even worse, the national government had no distinct executive branch. Congressional committees, constantly changing in their membership, not only had to make laws but had to administer and enforce them as well. With no executive to carry out the policies of finance, war, and foreign policy, the federal government's influence was extremely limited.

Those weaknesses appear more evident in hindsight. For Congress in 1777 it was no easy task to frame a new government in the midst of a war. And most American leaders of the 1770s had given little thought to federalism, the means by which political power could be divided among the states and the national government. In any case, to have given significant powers to the national government would have aroused only opposition among the states, each jealous of its independence. Creating a strong national government would also have antagonized many Americans, who after all had just rebelled against the distant, centralized authority of Britain's king and Parliament.

Guided by republican political theory and by their colonial experience, American revolutionaries created a loose confederation of 13 independent state republics under a nearly powerless national government. They succeeded so well that the United States almost failed to survive the first decade of its independence. The problem was that republican theory and lessons from the colonial past were not always useful guides to postwar realities. Only when events forced Americans to think nationally did they begin to consider the possibility of reinventing "these United States"—this time under the yoke of a truly federal republic.

 REVIEW

What political concerns shaped the first constitutions?

# THE TEMPTATIONS OF PEACE

THE SURRENDER OF CORNWALLIS AT Yorktown in 1781 marked the end of military crisis in America. But as the threat from Britain receded, so did the source of American unity. The many differences among Americans, most of which lay submerged during the struggle for independence, surfaced in full force. Those domestic divisions, combined with challenges to the new nation from Britain and Spain, created conflicts that neither the states nor the national government proved equal to handling.

## The Temptations of the West

The greatest opportunities and the greatest problems for postwar Americans awaited in the rapidly expanding West. With the boundary of the new United States now set at the Mississippi River, more settlers spilled across the Appalachians, planting farmsteads and raw frontier towns throughout Ohio, Kentucky, and Tennessee. By 1790 places that had been almost uninhabited by whites in 1760 held more than 2.25 million people, one-third of the nation's population.

After the Revolution, as before, western settlement fostered intense conflict. American claims that its territory stretched all the way to the Mississippi were by no means taken for granted by European and Indian powers. The West also confronted Americans with questions about their own national identity: Would the newly settled territories enter the nation as states on an equal footing with the original 13 states? Would they be ruled as dependent colonies? Could the federal government reconcile conflicting interests, cultures, and traditions over so great an area? The fate of the West, in other words, constituted a crucial test of whether "these" United States could grow and still remain united.

## Foreign Intrigues

Both the British from their base in Canada and the Spanish in Florida and Louisiana hoped to chisel away at American borders. Their considerable success in the 1780s exposed the weakness of Confederation diplomacy.

Before the ink was dry on the Treaty of Paris, Britain's ministers were secretly instructing Canadians to maintain their forts and trading posts inside the United States' northwestern frontier. They reckoned—correctly—that with the Continental Army disbanded, the Confederation could not force the British to withdraw.

The British also made mischief along the Confederation's northern borders, mainly with Vermont. For decades, Ethan Allen and his Green Mountain Boys had waged a war of nerves with neighboring New York, which claimed Vermont as part of its territory. After the Revolution the Vermonters petitioned Congress for statehood, demanding independence from both New York and New Hampshire. When Congress dragged its feet, the British tried to woo Vermont into their empire as a province of Canada. That flirtation with the British pressured Congress into granting Vermont statehood in 1791.

SPANISH DESIGNS ON THE SOUTHWEST — The loyalty of the southwestern frontier was even less certain. By 1790 more than 100,000 settlers had poured through the Cumberland Gap to reach Kentucky and Tennessee. Along with the farmers came speculators, who bought up large tracts of land from the Indians. But the commercial possibilities of the region depended entirely on access to the Mississippi and the port of New Orleans, since it was far too

Rivalries flared along the southwestern frontier of the United States as Spain vied to win the allegiance of Indians by supplying them with British trade goods. The Indians welcomed such goods (note the shovel, at left, the plow, center, and European clothing worn by some of the Indians). Here a white man, probably the American Indian agent Benjamin Hawkins, visits an Indian village during the 1790s.

## WESTERN LAND CLAIMS, 1782–1802

*The Confederation's settlement of conflicting western land claims was an achievement essential to the consolidation of political union. Some states asserted that their original charters extended their western borders to the Mississippi River. A few states, such as Virginia, claimed western borders on the Pacific Ocean. Which states claimed western lands that they eventually ceded to the Confederation?*

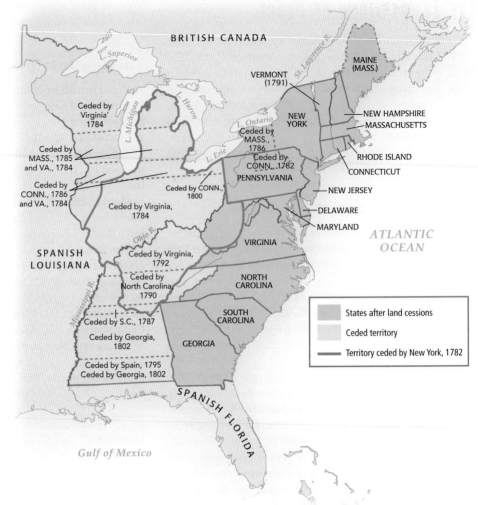

costly to ship southwestern produce over the rough trails east across the Appalachians. And the Mississippi route was still dominated by the Spanish, who controlled Louisiana as well as forts along western Mississippi shores as far north as St. Louis. The Spanish, seeing their opportunity, closed the Mississippi to American navigation in 1784. That action prompted serious talk among southwesterners about seceding from the United States and joining Spain's empire.

The Spanish also tried to strengthen their hold on North America by making common cause with the Indians. Of particular concern to both groups was protecting Spanish Florida from the encroachment of American settlers filtering south from Georgia—backwoods folk, Florida's governor complained, who were "nomadic like Arabs and . . . distinguished from savages only in their color, language, and the superiority of their depraved cunning and untrustworthiness." So Spanish colonial officials responded eagerly to the overtures of Alexander McGillivray, a young Indian leader whose mother was of French-Creek descent and whose father was a Scots trader. His efforts brought about a treaty of alliance between the Creeks and the Spanish in 1784, quickly followed by similar alliances with the Choctaws and the Chickasaws. What cemented such treaties were the trade

goods that the Spanish agreed to supply the tribes, for, as McGillivray explained, "Indians will attach themselves to and serve them best who supply their necessities." Securing European gunpowder and guns had become essential to southeastern Indians, because their entire economies now revolved around hunting and selling deerskins to white traders. So eager were the Spanish to "serve" the Indians in that matter that they even permitted British merchants, who could command a steady supply of manufactured goods, to monopolize the Indian trade. The largest dealers developed a trading network that reached all the way to the Mississippi by the 1790s. This flood of British merchandise sustained the alliance between the Spanish and the Indians, while British guns enabled the Creeks to defend their hunting territory from American invaders.

## Disputes among the States

**LANDED VS. LANDLESS STATES**

As if foreign intrigues were not divisive enough, the states continued to argue among themselves over western land claims. The old royal charters for some colonies had extended their boundaries all the way to the Mississippi and beyond. But the charters were often vague, granting both Massachusetts and Virginia, for example, undisputed possession of present-day Wisconsin. In contrast, other charters limited state boundaries to within a few hundred miles of the Atlantic coast. **Landed states** such as Virginia wanted to secure control over the large territory granted them by their charters. **Landless states** (which included Maryland, Delaware, Pennsylvania, Rhode Island, and New Jersey) called on Congress to restrict the boundaries of landed states and to convert western lands into a domain administered by the Confederation.

The landless states argued that the landed states enjoyed an unfair advantage from the money they could raise selling their western claims. That revenue would allow landed states to reduce taxes, and lower taxes would lure settlers from the landless states. Meanwhile, landless states would have to raise taxes to make up for the departed taxpayers, causing even more residents to leave. Speculators were also eager to see Congress control the western lands. Before the Revolution, many prominent citizens of landless Pennsylvania, Maryland, and New Jersey had purchased tracts in the West from Indians. These speculators now also lobbied for congressional ownership of all western lands—except those tracts that they had already purchased from the Indians.

The landless states lost the opening round in the contest over ownership of the West. The Articles of Confederation acknowledged the old charter claims of the landed states. Then Maryland, one of the smallest landless states, retaliated by refusing to ratify the Articles. Since every state had to approve the Articles before they were formally accepted, the fate of the United States hung in the balance. One by one the landed states relented, Virginia being the last. Only then did Maryland ratify the Articles, in February 1781.

## The More Democratic West

An even greater bone of contention concerned the sort of men westerners elected to political office. The state legislatures of the 1780s were both larger and more democratic in their membership than the old colonial assemblies. Before the Revolution no more than a fifth of the men serving in the assemblies were middle-class farmers or artisans. Government was almost exclusively the domain of the wealthiest merchants, lawyers, and planters. After the Revolution twice as many state legislators were men of moderate wealth. The shift was more marked in the North, where middle-class men predominated among representatives. But in every state, some men of modest means, humble background, and little formal education attained political power.

CHANGING COMPOSITION OF STATE LEGISLATURES

State legislatures became more democratic in their membership mainly because as backcountry districts grew, so too did the number of their representatives. Since western districts tended to be less developed economically and culturally, their leading men were less rich and cultivated than the Eastern Seaboard elite. But many of these eastern republican gentlemen, while endorsing government by popular consent, doubted whether ordinary people were fit to rule. The problem, they contended, was that the new western legislators concerned themselves only with the narrow interests of their constituents, not with the good of the whole state. As Ezra Stiles, the president of Yale College, observed, the new breed of politicians was those with "the all-prevailing popular talent of coaxing and flattering," who "whenever a bill is read in the legislature . . . instantly thinks how it will affect his constituents." And if state legislatures could not rise above narrow self-interest, how long would it be before a concern for the general welfare simply withered away?

This sketch of a new cleared farm idealizes many aspects of life on the late-eighteenth-century frontier. Although western farmers first sought to "improve" their acreage by felling trees, as the stumps dotting the landscape indicate, their dwellings were far less substantial than those depicted in the background above. And although Indians sometimes guided parties of white surveyors and settlers into the West, as shown in the foreground, Indians more often resisted white encroachment. For that reason, dogs, here perched placidly in a canoe, were trained to alert their white masters to the approach of Indians.

# The Northwest Territory

Such fears of "democratic excess" also influenced policy when Congress finally came to decide what to do with the **Northwest Territory.** Carved out of the land ceded by the states to the national government, the Northwest Territory comprised the present-day states of Ohio, Indiana, Illinois, Michigan, and Wisconsin. With so many white settlers moving into these lands, Congress was faced with a crucial test of its federal system. If an orderly way could not be devised to expand the confederation of states beyond the original 13 colonies, the new territories might well become independent countries or even colonies of Spain or Britain. Congress dealt with the issue of expansion by adopting three ordinances.

**JEFFERSON'S PLAN FOR THE NORTHWEST** The first ordinance, drafted by Thomas Jefferson in 1784, divided the Northwest Territory into 10 states, each to be admitted to the Union on equal terms as soon as its population equaled that in any of the existing states. In the meantime, Jefferson provided for democratic self-government of the territory by all free adult males. A second ordinance of 1785 set up an efficient mechanism for dividing and selling public lands. The Northwest Territory was surveyed into townships 6 miles square. Each township was then divided into 36 lots of 1 square mile, or 640 acres.

Congress waited in vain for buyers to flock to the land offices it established. The cost of even a single lot—$640—was too steep for most farmers. Disappointed by the shortage of buyers and desperate for money, Congress finally accepted a proposition submitted by a private company of land speculators who offered to buy some 6 million acres in present-day southeastern Ohio. That several members of Congress numbered among the company's stockholders no doubt added to enthusiasm for the deal.

**NORTHWEST ORDINANCE** The transaction concluded, Congress calmed the speculators' worries that incoming settlers might enjoy too much self-government by scrapping Jefferson's democratic design and substituting the Northwest Ordinance of 1787. That ordinance provided for a period in which Congress held sway in the territory through its appointees—a governor, a secretary, and three judges. When the population reached 5,000 free adult males, a legislature was to be established, although its laws required the governor's approval. A

## THE ORDINANCE OF 1785

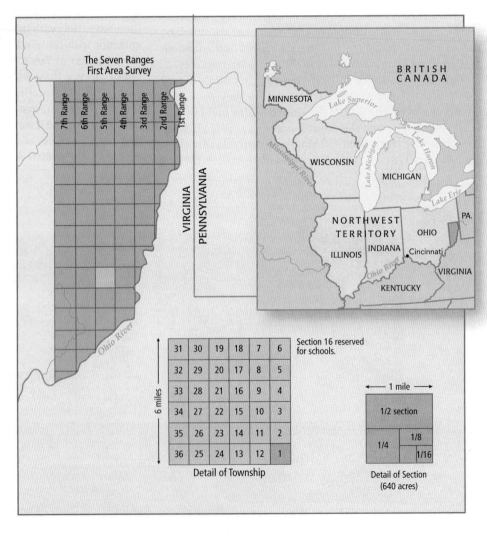

Surveyors entered the Northwest Territory in September of 1785, imposing on the land regular grids of 6 square miles to define new townships, as shown on this range map of a portion of Ohio. Farmers purchased blocks of land within townships, each 1 mile square, from the federal government or from land speculators. This pattern was followed in mapping and settling public lands all the way to the Pacific coast.

The Seven Ranges
First Area Survey

7th Range  6th Range  5th Range  4th Range  3rd Range  2rd Range  1st Range

VIRGINIA
PENNSYLVANIA

Ohio River

BRITISH CANADA

MINNESOTA
Lake Superior
WISCONSIN
Lake Michigan
MICHIGAN
Lake Huron
Lake Erie
Mississippi River
NORTHWEST TERRITORY
PA.
OHIO
ILLINOIS  INDIANA  Cincinnati
Ohio River
VIRGINIA
KENTUCKY

| 31 | 30 | 19 | 18 | 7 | 6 |
| 32 | 29 | 20 | 17 | 8 | 5 |
| 33 | 28 | 21 | 16 | 9 | 4 |
| 34 | 27 | 22 | 15 | 10 | 3 |
| 35 | 26 | 23 | 14 | 11 | 2 |
| 36 | 25 | 24 | 13 | 12 | 1 |

6 miles

Section 16 reserved for schools.

Detail of Township

← 1 mile →

1/2 section

1/4   1/8

1/16

Detail of Section
(640 acres)

representative could sit in Congress but had no vote. When the population reached 60,000, the inhabitants might apply for statehood, and the whole Northwest Territory was to be divided into not less than three or more than five states. The ordinance also guaranteed basic rights—freedom of religion and trial by jury—and provided for the support of public education. Equally significant, it also outlawed slavery throughout the territory.

With the Northwest Ordinance in place, Congress had succeeded in extending republican government to the West and incorporating the frontier into the new nation. The Republic now had an orderly way to expand its federation of states in a way that minimized the tensions between the genteel East and the democratic West that had plagued the colonies and the Confederation throughout much of the eighteenth century. Yet ironically, the new ordinance served to heighten tensions in a different way. By limiting the spread of slavery in the northern states, Congress deepened the critical social and economic differences between the North and the South, evident already in the 1780s.

**THE TERRITORIAL SYSTEM AND NATIVE AMERICANS**

The consequences of the new territorial system were also significant for hundreds of thousands of the continent's other inhabitants. In the short term, the ordinance ignored completely the rights of the Shawnee, Chippewa, and other Indian peoples who lived in the region. In the long term, the system "laid the blueprint," as one historian noted, for bringing new lands into the United States. The ordinance thus accelerated the pressures on Indian lands and aggravated the social and geographic dislocations already set in motion by disease and the western conflicts of the Revolutionary War.

Branding irons like these were sometimes used to burn a slaveholder's initials into the skin of his property to make running away more difficult.

## Slavery and Sectionalism

When white Americans declared their independence, they owned nearly half a million black Americans. African Americans of the revolutionary generation, most of them enslaved, constituted 20 percent of the total population of the colonies in 1775, and nearly 90 percent of them lived in the South. Yet few political leaders directly confronted the issue of whether slavery should be permitted to exist in a truly republican society.

**REPUBLICANISM AND SLAVERY**

When political discussion did stray toward the subject of slavery, southerners—especially ardent republicans—bristled defensively. Theirs was a difficult position, riddled with contradictions.

On the one hand, they had condemned parliamentary taxation as tantamount to political "slavery" and had rebelled, declaring that all men were "created equal." On the other hand, enslaved African Americans formed the basis of the South's plantation economy. To surrender slavery, southerners believed, would be to usher in economic ruin.

Some planters in the Upper South resolved the dilemma by freeing their slaves. Such decisions were made easier by changing economic conditions in the Chesapeake. As planters shifted from tobacco toward wheat, a crop demanding a good deal less labor, Virginia and Maryland liberalized their manumission statutes, laws providing for freeing slaves. Between 1776 and 1789, most southern states also joined the North in prohibiting the importation of slaves, and a few antislavery societies appeared in the Upper South. But no southern state legally abolished slavery. Masters defended their right to hold human property in the name of republicanism.

**REPUBLICANISM AND PROPERTY**

Eighteenth-century republicans regarded property as crucial, for it provided a man and his family with security, status, and wealth. More important, it provided a measure of independence: to be able to act freely, without fear or favor of others. People without property were dangerous, republicans believed, because the poor could never be politically independent. Southern defenders of slavery thus argued that free, propertyless black people would pose a political threat to the liberty of propertied white citizens. Subordinating the human rights of blacks to the property rights of whites, southern republicans reached the paradoxical conclusion that their freedom depended on keeping African Americans in bondage.

The North followed a different course. Because its economy depended far less on slave labor, black emancipation did not run counter to powerful economic interests. Antislavery societies, the first founded by the Quakers in 1775, spread throughout the northern states during the next quarter century. Over the same period the legislatures of most northern states provided for the immediate or gradual abolition of slavery. Freedom for most northern African Americans came slowly, but by 1830 there were fewer than 3,000 slaves out of a total northern black population of 125,000.

The Revolution, which had been fought for liberty and equality, did little to change the status of most black Americans. By 1800 more enslaved African Americans lived in the United States than had lived there in 1776. Slavery continued to grow in the Lower South as the rice culture of the Carolinas and Georgia expanded and as the new cotton culture spread westward.

In 1787 in Philadelphia, the year delegates to the Constitutional Convention met, Richard Allen and Absalom Jones founded Bethel African Methodist Episcopal Church. The first church was a former blacksmith's shop that the members hauled to a site they purchased on Sixth Street. By the time this illustration was created in 1829, a more spacious building had replaced the first church.

Still, a larger number of slaves than ever before became free during the war and in the following decades, whether through military service, successful escape, manumission, or gradual emancipation. All these developments fostered the growth of free black communities, especially in the Upper South and in northern cities. By 1810 free African Americans made up 10 percent of the total population of Maryland and Virginia.

GROWTH OF THE
FREE BLACK
COMMUNITY

The composition of the postwar free community changed as well. Before independence most free blacks had been either mulattoes—the offspring of interracial unions—or former slaves too sick or aged to have value as laborers. In contrast, a larger proportion of the free population of the 1780s were darker skinned, younger, and healthier. This group injected new vitality into black communal life, organizing independent schools, churches, and mutual benefit societies for the growing number of "free people of color." Richard Allen and Absalom Jones led the way in these efforts after being ejected from their pews in the midst of prayers one Sunday at St. George **Methodist** Episcopal Church in Philadelphia. Both men ended up founding independent black churches.

After the Revolution, slavery ceased to be a national institution. It became the **peculiar institution** of a single region, the American South. The isolation of slavery in one section set North and South on radically different courses of social development, sharpening economic and political divisions.

## Wartime Economic Disruption

With the outbreak of the Revolution, Americans had suffered an immediate economic loss. Formerly, Britain had supplied manufactured goods, markets for American exports, and credit that enabled commerce to flourish. No longer. Hardest hit were southern planters, who had to seek new customers for their tobacco, cotton, and rice as well as find new sources of capital to finance production. Northerners too faced difficulties, for their major seaports were occupied for a time by British troops, whose presence disrupted commercial activity.

PUBLIC AND
PRIVATE DEBT

Matters did not improve with the coming of peace. France and Britain flooded the new states with their manufactures, and postwar Americans, eager for luxuries, indulged in a most unrepublican spending spree. The flurry of buying left some American merchants and consumers as deeply in debt as their governments. When loans from private citizens and foreign creditors like France proved insufficient to finance the fighting, both Congress and the states printed paper money—a whopping total of $400 million. The paper currency was backed only by the government's promise to redeem the bills with money from future taxes, because legislatures balked at the unpopular alternative of levying taxes during the war. For the bills to be redeemed, the United States had to survive, so by the end of 1776, when Continental forces sustained a series of defeats, paper money started to depreciate dramatically. By 1781 it was virtually without value, and Americans coined the expression "not worth a Continental."

POSTWAR
INFLATION

The printing of paper money, combined with a wartime shortage of goods, triggered an inflationary spiral. As goods became scarcer and scarcer, they cost more and more worthless dollars. In this spiral, creditors were gouged by debtors, who paid them back with depreciated currency. At the same time, soaring prices for food and manufactured goods eroded the buying power of wage earners and small farmers. And the end of the war brought on demands for prompt repayment from the new nation's foreign creditors as well as from soldiers seeking back pay and pensions.

Congress could do nothing. With no power to regulate trade, it could neither dam the stream of imported goods rushing into the states nor stanch the flow of gold and silver to Europe to pay for these items. With no power to prohibit the states from issuing paper money, it could not halt depreciation. With no power to regulate wages or prices, it could not curb inflation. With no power to tax, it could not reduce the public debt. Efforts to grant Congress greater powers met with determined resistance from the states. They refused Congress any revenue of its own, fearing the first steps toward "arbitrary" government.

**POLITICAL DIVISIONS OVER ECONOMIC POLICY** Within states, too, economic problems aroused discord. Some major merchants and large commercial farmers had profited handsomely during the war by selling supplies to the American, British, and French armies at high prices. Eager to protect their windfall, they lobbied state legislatures for an end to inflationary monetary policies. They pushed for the passage of high taxes to pay wartime debts, a paper currency that was backed by gold and silver, and an active policy to encourage foreign trade.

Less affluent men fought back, pressing legislatures for programs that met their needs. Western farmers, often in debt, urged the states to print more paper money and to pass laws lowering taxes and postponing the foreclosure of mortgages. Artisans opposed merchants by calling for protection from low-priced foreign imports that competed with the goods they produced. They set themselves against farmers as well by demanding price regulation of the farm products they consumed. In the continuing struggle, the state legislatures became the battleground of competing economic factions, each bent on gaining its own particular advantage.

As the 1780s wore on, conflicts mounted. As long as the individual states remained sovereign, the Confederation was crippled—unable to conduct foreign affairs effectively, unable to set coherent economic policy, unable to deal with discontent in the West. Equally dismaying was the discovery that many Americans, instead of being selflessly concerned for the public good, selfishly pursued their private interests.

 **REVIEW**

What challenges did the West pose for the new republic?

# REPUBLICAN SOCIETY

THE WAR FOR INDEPENDENCE TRANSFORMED not only America's government and economy but also its society and culture. Inspired by the Declaration's ideal of equality, some Americans rejected the subordinate position assigned to them under the old colonial order. Westerners, newly wealthy entrepreneurs, urban artisans, and women all claimed greater freedom, power, and recognition. The authority of the traditional leaders of government, society, and the family came under a new scrutiny; the impulse to defer to social superiors became less automatic. The new assertiveness demonstrated how deeply egalitarian assumptions were taking root in American culture.

## The New Men of the Revolution

The Revolution gave rise to a new sense of social identity and a new set of ambitions among several groups of men who had once accepted a humbler status. The more democratic society of the frontier emboldened westerners to believe themselves the equals of easterners. One Kentuckian explained that the western migrants "must make a very different mass from one which is composed of men born and raised on the same spot. . . . They see none about them to whom or to whose families they have been accustomed to think themselves inferior."

The war also offered opportunities to aspiring entrepreneurs everywhere, and often they were not the same men who had prospered before the war. At a stroke, independence swept away the political prominence of loyalists, whose ranks included an especially high number of government officials, large landowners, and major merchants. And while loyalists found their properties confiscated by revolutionary governments, other Americans grew rich. Many northern merchants gained newfound wealth from privateering or military contracts. Commercial farmers in the mid-Atlantic states prospered from the high food prices caused by wartime scarcity and army demand.

**URBAN ARTISANS** The Revolution effected no dramatic redistribution of wealth. Indeed, the gap between rich and poor increased during the 1780s. But the republican ideal of equality emboldened city artisans to demand a more prominent role in politics. Calls for men of their own kind to represent them in government came as a rude shock to such gentlemen as South Carolina's William Henry Drayton, who balked at sharing power with men "who were never in a way to study" anything except "how to cut up a beast in the market to best advantage, to cobble an old shoe in the neatest manner, or to build a necessary house." The journeymen who worked for master craftsmen also exhibited a new sense of independence, forming new organizations to secure higher wages.

| Gilbert Stuart's The Skater *captures one American gentleman's characteristic sense of mastery over himself, nature, and society. But the Revolution gave other republican men a sense of power, too, including western backcountry farmers, aspiring entrepreneurs, and urban artisans such as the pewterers.*

But the greatest gains accrued to those men newly enriched by the war and by the opportunities of independence. Representative of this aspiring group was William Cooper, a Pennsylvania Quaker who did not support the Revolution but in its aftermath strove to transform himself from a wheelwright into a gentleman. He hoped to become a gentleman by transforming thousands of acres of hilly, heavily forested land around Otsego Lake in upstate New York into wheat-producing farms clustered around a market village called Cooperstown. Yankee emigrants fleeing the shrinking farms of long-settled New England made Cooper's vision a reality and made him the leading land developer of the 1790s. But the influx of white settlement radically altered the environment of what had once been part of Iroquoia. Farmers killed off panthers, bears, and wolves to protect their livestock. Grains farming leeched nutrients from the thin topsoil, forcing farmers to clear more trees, and as the forest barrier fell, weeds and insects invaded. By the beginning of the nineteenth century, the children of many small farmers were migrating even farther west, to western New York and northern Ohio.

Similar scenarios played out on frontiers throughout the new United States. And everywhere, too, men like William Cooper demanded and received social recognition and political influence. Even though some, like Cooper, never lost the crude manners that betrayed humble origins, they styled themselves as the "aristocracy of merit" enshrined by republican ideals.

## The New Women of the Revolution

Not long after the fighting with Britain had broken out, Margaret Livingston of New York wrote to her sister Catherine, "You know that our Sex are doomed to be obedient in every stage of life so that we shant be great gainers by this contest." By war's end, however, Eliza Wilkinson from rural South Carolina was complaining boldly to a woman friend: "The men say we have no business with political matters . . . it's not our sphere. . . . [But] I won't have it thought that because we are the weaker Sex (as to bodily strength my dear) we are Capable of nothing more, than minding the Dairy . . . surely we may have enough sense to give our Opinions."

What separated Margaret Livingston's resignation from Eliza Wilkinson's assertion of personal worth and independence was the Revolution. Eliza Wilkinson had managed her parents' plantation during the war and defended it from British marauders. Other women discovered similar reserves of skill and resourcefulness. When soldiers returned home, some were surprised to find their wives and daughters, who had been running family farms and businesses, less submissive and more self-confident.

**EXCLUSION OF
WOMEN FROM
POLITICS**

But American men had not fought a revolution for the equality of American women. In fact, male revolutionaries gave no thought whatsoever to the role of women in the new nation, assuming that those of the "weaker sex" were incapable of making informed and independent political deci-

sions. Most women of the revolutionary generation agreed that the proper female domain was the home, not the public arena of politics. Still, the currents of the Revolution occasionally left gaps that allowed women to display their keen political interests. When a loosely worded provision in the New Jersey state constitution gave the vote to "all free inhabitants" owning a specified amount of property, white widows and single women went to the polls. Only in 1807 did the state legislature close the loophole.

##  Mary Wollstonecraft's *Vindication*

In the wake of the Revolution there also appeared in England a book that would become a classic text of modern feminism, Mary Wollstonecraft's *A Vindication of the Rights of Women* (1792). Attracting a wide, if not widely approving, readership in America as well, it called not only for laws to guarantee women civil and political equality but also for educational reforms to ensure their social and economic equality.

**EDUCATION AS
A ROUTE TO
EQUALITY**

Like many young, single English women with more wit than fortune, Wollstonecraft started her working life as a governess and a school's headmistress. Then she turned to writing for her livelihood, producing book reviews, translations, a novel, and a treatise on women's education before dashing off *Vindication* in only six months. She charged that men deliberately conspired to keep women in "a state of perpetual childhood" by giving them inferior, frivolous educations. That encouraged young girls to fixate on fashion and flirtation and made them "only anxious to inspire love, when they ought to cherish a nobler ambition, and by their abilities and virtues exact respect." Girls, she proposed, should receive the same education as boys, including

A devoted mother with her daughter from the 1790s: but note the generation gap. While the mother holds fancy needlework in her lap, her daughter looks up from an opened book. Many women—especially younger women—in the decades around 1800 chose to include books in their portraits, indicating that literacy and education were becoming essential to their identity and self-esteem.

## A WOMAN'S COMPASS

A woman drinking spirits as her baby tumbles from her lap.

A woman crying, pointing to letters on a table. Was she jilted by a lover? Other possibilities?

A woman at hard labor in prison.

A woman being apprehended by the authorities. For prostitution? Drunkenness? Debt?

*Keep Within Compass, illustration, ca. 1785–1805, Winterthur Museum.*

Could there be any more eloquent testimony to the anxieties aroused by the newly confident (and sometimes outspoken) women of postrevolutionary America? Much like jokes, idealized images (for example, the smiling woman within the compass) can point historians toward areas of tension and conflict in the past. In this illustration, the four scenes displayed outside the compass send even clearer signals. Published sometime between 1785 and 1805 and titled *Keep Within Compass*, the illustration celebrates domesticity and wifely devotion while also warning women tempted to stray from that straight and narrow path. It promises a contented and prosperous life—lovely home, thriving garden, swishy silk dress, killer hat, and even a pet squirrel—to the woman "whose bosom no passion knows." But woe betide her erring sisters who strayed from the path of virtue, disgracing themselves as well as the men in their lives! Those twin themes proved equally popular in American novels published during the decades after the American Revolution.

### Thinking Critically

*Is the kind of virtue promoted by the illustration similar to or different from the republican understanding of virtue? What accounts for the concern about the virtue of women in the decades after the American Revolution? Why did the virtue of women loom so large, since they had few legal or political rights?*

| Contrast the portrait of Mary Wollstonecraft rendered just before her death in 1797 (left) with a strikingly masculinized rendering in a book published in the United States in 1809 (right), which placed her in the company of "actresses, adventurers, authoresses, fortunetellers, gipsies, dwarfs, swindlers, and vagrants."

training that would prepare them for careers in medicine, politics, and business. No woman should have to pin her hopes for financial security on making a good marriage, Wollstonecraft argued. On the contrary, well-educated and resourceful women capable of supporting themselves would make the best wives and mothers, assets to the family and the nation.

*Vindication* might have been written in gunpowder rather than ink, given the reaction it aroused on both sides of the Atlantic. At first, Wollstonecraft won more than a few defenders among both men and women. This favorable reception ended abruptly after her death in childbirth in 1797, when a memoir written by her husband revealed that she had lived out of wedlock with him—and before him, with another lover. Even so, some of her readers continued to admire her views. The Philadelphia Quaker Elizabeth Drinker confided to her diary that "In very many of her sentiments, [Wollstonecraft] . . . *speaks my mind.*"

## Republican Motherhood and Education

Wollstonecraft's ideas also lent support to the leading educational reformers in the revolutionary generation. Her sentiments echo in the writings of Judith Sargent Murray, a New Englander who urged the cultivation of women's minds to encourage self-respect and celebrated "excellency in our sex." Her fellow reformer, the Philadelphian Benjamin Rush, agreed that only educated and independent-minded women could raise the informed and self-reliant citizens that a republican government required.

The Revolution also prompted some states to reform their marriage laws, making divorce somewhat easier, although it remained extremely rare. But while women won greater freedom to divorce, courts became less concerned with enforcing a widow's traditional legal claim to one-third of her spouse's real estate. And married women still could not sue or be sued, make wills or contracts, or buy and sell property. Any wages that they earned went to their husbands; so did all personal property that wives brought into a marriage; so did the rents and profits of any real estate they owned. Despite the high ideals of **republican motherhood,** most women remained confined to the domestic sphere of the home and deprived of the most basic legal and political rights.

## The Attack on Aristocracy

Why wasn't the American Revolution more revolutionary? Independence secured the full political equality of white men who owned property, but women were still deprived of political rights, African Americans of human rights. Why did the revolutionaries stop short of extending equality to the most unequal groups in American society—and with so little sense that they were being inconsistent?

REPUBLICAN VIEW OF EQUALITY

In part, the lack of concern was rooted in republican ideas themselves. Republican ideology viewed property as the key to independence and power. Lacking property, women and black Americans were easily consigned to the custody of husbands and masters. Then, too, prejudice played its part: the perception of women and blacks as naturally inferior beings.

But revolutionary leaders also failed to press for greater equality because they conceived their crusade in terms of eliminating the evils of a European past dominated by kings and aristocrats. They believed that the great obstacle to equality was monarchy—kings and queens who bestowed hereditary honors and political office on favored individuals and granted legal privileges and monopolies to favored churches and businesses. These artificial inequalities posed the real threat to liberty, most republicans concluded. In other words, the men of the Revolution were intent on attaining equality by leveling off the top of society. It did not occur to most republicans that the cause of equality could also be served by raising up the bottom—by attacking the laws and prejudices that kept African Americans enslaved and women dependent.

**DISESTABLISHMENT OF STATE-SUPPORTED CHURCHES**

The most significant reform of the republican campaign against artificial privilege was the dismantling of state-supported churches. Most states had a religious establishment. In New York and the South, it was the Anglican church; in New England, the Congregational church. Since the 1740s, dissenters who did not worship at state churches had protested laws that taxed all citizens to support the clergy of established denominations. After the Revolution, dissenters argued that equality required ending such privileges. As more dissenters became voters, state legislators gradually abolished state support for Anglican and Congregational churches.

**SOCIETY OF CINCINNATI**

In the same anti-aristocratic spirit, reformers attacked the Society of Cincinnati, a group organized by former officers of the Continental Army in 1783. The society, which was merely a social club for veterans, was forced to disband for its policy of passing on its membership rights to eldest sons.

| A medal of the Society of the Cincinnati

In this way, critics charged, the Cincinnati was creating artificial distinctions and perpetuating a hereditary warrior nobility.

Today, many of the republican efforts at reform seem misdirected. While only a handful of revolutionaries worked for the education of women and the emancipation of slaves, enormous zeal went into fighting threats from a monarchical past that had never existed in America. Yet the threat from kings and aristocrats was real to the revolutionaries—and indeed remained real in many parts of Europe. Their determination to sweep away every shred of formal privilege ensured that these forms of inequality never took root in America. And if eighteenth-century Americans did not extend equality to women and racial minorities, it was a failure they shared with later revolutionary movements that promised more.

 **REVIEW**

How did the Revolution alter American society?

# FROM CONFEDERATION TO CONSTITUTION

WHILE AMERICANS IN MANY WALKS of life sought to realize the republican commitment to equality, Congress wrestled with the problem of preserving the nation itself. With the new republic slowly rending itself to pieces, some political leaders concluded that neither the Confederation nor the state legislatures were able to remedy the basic difficulties facing the nation. But how could the states be convinced to surrender their sovereign powers? The answer came in the wake of two events—one foreign, one domestic—that lent momentum to the cause of strengthening the central government.

## The Jay-Gardoqui Treaty

The international episode was a debate over a proposed treaty with Spain. In 1785 southwesterners still could not legally navigate the Mississippi and still were threatening to secede from the union and annex their territory to Spain's American empire. To shore up southwestern loyalties, Congress instructed its secretary of foreign affairs, John Jay, to negotiate an agreement with Spain preserving American rights to navigate the Mississippi River. But the Spanish emissary, Don Diego de Gardoqui, sweet-talked Jay into accepting a treaty by which the United States would give up all rights to the Mississippi for 25 years. In return, Spain agreed to grant trading privileges to American merchants.

Jay, a New Yorker, knew more than a few northern merchants who were eager to open new markets. But when the proposed treaty became public knowledge, southwesterners denounced it as nothing short of betrayal. The treaty

## THE SPIRITS OF INDEPENDENCE

If God had intended man to drink water, Ben Franklin remarked, he would not have made him with an elbow capable of raising a wineglass. Colonials from all across America agreed with Franklin on the virtues of drink. The ruddy glow of colonial cheeks (still visible in the portraits in museums) reflected not only good health but also substantial daily doses of alcohol. Colonials consumed about twice as much alcohol as Americans today, though in different forms. Beer was not popular, the only sort consumed being a weak, homemade "small beer" containing about 1 percent alcohol. Only the wealthy, like Franklin, could afford imported Madeira and port wines, but the produce of apple orchards allowed Americans northward from Virginia to drink their fill of hard cider. Far and away the most popular distilled liquor was rum, a potent 90 proof beverage (45 percent alcohol) that they sipped straight or mixed with water and sugar to make "toddies."

The liquor flowed freely at special occasions: ministerial ordinations in New England towns, court days in the South, house-raisings, corn-huskings, and quilting bees on the frontier, and weddings, elections, and militia musters everywhere in the colonies. But Americans did not confine their drinking to occasional celebrations. Some, like John Adams, started the day with a tankard of hard cider. Laborers in seaport docks and shipyards, fishermen and sailors at sea, and farmworkers in the countryside commonly received a daily allotment of liquor as part of their wages.

Women drank, too, although they sometimes explained their use of distilled liquor as serving some "medicinal" purpose. Slaves got around laws restricting their consumption of alcohol by stealing from masters or bartering with white peddlers.

Until the middle of the eighteenth century, most colonials (and Europeans) considered spirits an essential supplement to their diet. They did not condone public drunkenness, but they saw nothing amiss in the regular use of alcohol or even in occasional intoxication.

This easy acceptance of drinking prevailed for two reasons. First, until about the 1760s, frequent access to the strongest spirits, rum, lay beyond the means of most Americans. Second, the leaders of local communities were able to oversee most public drinking and to keep disorder to a minimum. But by the middle of the eighteenth century, some Americans developed misgivings about the drinking culture. Increased production and importation made rum so cheap that an ordinary laborer could earn enough in a day to stay "drunk as a lord" for the rest of the week. Taverns spread, making it impossible for community leaders to monitor the popular consumption of alcohol.

The new concern that the drinking of rum fostered crime and social disruption prompted the first steps toward temperance reform. By the 1770s Quakers such as Anthony Benezet were urging that alcohol, like slavery, was an "unrepublican vice," for both forms of bondage deprived their victims of liberty and the capacity for rationality and self-control. Some members of the medical profession, most notably Benjamin Rush, also joined early temperance ranks.

Although the advocates of more moderate consumption won some support, most Americans altered their drinking habits by consuming *more* hard liquor, as rum lost much of its ground to a new rival, whiskey. Whiskey was democratic and cheap, for it could be made in the lowliest backcountry farmhouse. It was patriotic, since it did not

*New England sea captains in Surinam drink rum the two-handed way—out of a silver bowl.*

depend on imports from the Caribbean. Gradually these "spirits of independence" supplanted rum not only in the frontier West but also in the urban East. Consumption of alcohol was on a steady rise that would finally result, half a century after the Revolution, in louder calls for temperance reform.

### Thinking Critically

*What factors besides the availability of inexpensive whiskey might account for the increased consumption of alcohol in the decades after the American Revolution?*

---

was never ratified, but the hostility stirred up during the debate revealed the strength of sectional feelings. Only a decade later, when the Senate ratified a treaty negotiated with Spain by Thomas Pinckney in 1796, did Americans gain full access to the Mississippi.

## Shays's Rebellion

On the heels of this humiliation by Spain came an internal conflict that challenged the notion that individual states could maintain order in their own territories. The trouble erupted in western Massachusetts, where many small farmers were close to ruin. By 1786 farm wages and prices had fallen sharply and farmers were selling little produce. Yet they still had to pay mortgages on their farms and other debts. In 1786 the lower house of the Massachusetts legislature obliged the farmers with a package of relief measures. But creditors in eastern Massachusetts, determined to safeguard their own investments, persuaded the upper house to defeat the measures.

In the summer of 1786 western farmers responded, demanding that the upper house of the legislature be abolished and that the relief measures go into effect. That autumn 2,000 farmers rose in armed rebellion, led by Captain Daniel Shays, a veteran of the Revolution. They closed the county courts to halt creditors from foreclosing on their farms and marched on the federal arsenal at Springfield. The state militia quelled the uprising by February 1787, but the insurrection left many in Massachusetts and the rest of the country thoroughly shaken.

RESPONSE TO AGRARIAN UNREST Alarmed conservatives saw Shays's Rebellion as the consequence of radical democracy. "The natural effects of pure democracy are already produced among us," lamented one republican gentleman; "it is a war against virtue, talents, and property carried on by the dregs and scum of mankind." He was wrong. The rebels with Daniel Shays were no impoverished rabble. They were reputable members of western communities who wanted their property protected and believed that government existed to provide that protection. The Massachusetts state legislature had been unable to safeguard the property of farmers from the inroads of recession or to protect the property of creditors from the armed debtors who closed the courts. It had failed, in other words, to fulfill the most basic aim of republican government.

What if such violent tactics spread? Other states with discontented debtors feared what the example of western Massachusetts might mean for the future of the Confederation itself. But by 1786 Shays's Rebellion supplied only the sharpest jolt to a movement for reform that was already under way. Even before the rebellion, a group of Virginians had proposed a meeting of the states to adopt a uniform system of commercial regulations. Once assembled at Annapolis in September 1786, the delegates from five states agreed to a more ambitious undertaking. They called for a second, broader meeting in Philadelphia, which Congress approved, for the "express purpose of revising the Articles of Confederation."

## Framing a Federal Constitution

SOCIAL PROFILE OF THE DELEGATES It was the wettest spring anyone could remember. The 55 men who traveled over muddy roads to Philadelphia in May 1787 arrived drenched and bespattered. Fortunately, most of the travelers were men in their 30s and 40s, young enough to survive a good soaking. Since most were gentlemen of some means—planters, merchants, and lawyers with powdered wigs and prosperous paunches—they could recover from the rigors of their journey in the best accommodations offered by America's largest city.

| James Madison, the scholar and statesman whose ideas and political skill shaped the Constitution.

The delegates came from all the states except Rhode Island. The rest of New England supplied shrewd backroom politicians—Roger Sherman and Oliver Ellsworth from Connecticut and Rufus King and Elbridge Gerry, Massachusetts men who had learned a trick or two from Sam Adams. The middle states marshaled much of the intellectual might: two Philadelphia lawyers, John Dickinson and James Wilson; one Philadelphia financier, Robert Morris; and the aristocratic Gouverneur Morris. From New York there was Alexander Hamilton, the mercurial and ambitious young protégé of Washington. South Carolina provided fiery orators Charles Pinckney and John Rutledge.

It was "an assembly of the demi-gods," gushed Thomas Jefferson, who, along with John Adams, was serving as a diplomat in Europe when the convention met. In fact, the only delegate who looked even remotely divine was the convention's presiding deity. Towering a full half foot taller than most of his colleagues, George Washington displayed his usual self-possession from a chair elevated on the speaker's platform in the Pennsylvania State House, where the delegates met. At first glance, the delegate of least commanding presence was Washington's fellow Virginian, James Madison. Short and slightly built, the 36-year-old Madison had no profession except hypochondria; he read a great deal and dressed in black. But he was an astute politician and a brilliant political thinker who, more than anyone else, shaped the framing of the federal Constitution.

The delegates from 12 different states had two things in common. They were all men of considerable political experience, and they all recognized the need for a stronger national union. So, when the Virginia delegation introduced Madison's outline for a new central government, the convention was ready to listen.

## The Virginia and New Jersey Plans

What Madison had in mind was a truly national republic, not a confederation of independent states. His "Virginia Plan" proposed a central government with three branches: legislative, executive, and judicial. Furthermore, the legislative branch, Congress, would possess the power to veto all state legislation. In place of the Confederation's single assembly, Madison substituted a bicameral legislature, with a lower house elected directly by the people and an upper house chosen by the lower, from nominations made by state legislatures. Representatives to both houses would be apportioned according to population—a change from practice under the Articles, in which each state had a single vote in Congress. Madison also revised the structure of government that had existed under the Articles by adding an executive, who would be elected by Congress, and an independent federal judiciary.

After two weeks of debate over the Virginia Plan, William Paterson, a lawyer from New Jersey, presented a less radical counterproposal. Although his "New Jersey Plan" increased Congress's power to tax and to regulate trade, it kept the national government as a unicameral assembly, with each state receiving one vote in Congress under the policy of equal representation. The delegates took just four days to reject Paterson's plan. Most endorsed Madison's design for a stronger central government.

Even so, the issue of apportioning representation continued to divide the delegates. While smaller states pressed for each state's having an equal vote in Congress, larger states backed Madison's provision for basing representation on population. Underlying the dispute over representation was an even deeper rivalry between southern and northern states. While northern and southern populations were nearly equal in the 1780s, and the South's population was growing more rapidly, the northern states were more numerous. Giving the states equal votes would put the South at a disadvantage. Southerners feared being outvoted in Congress by the northern states and felt that only proportional representation would protect the interests of their section.

That division turned into a deadlock as the wet spring burned off into a blazing summer. Delegates suffered the daily torture of staring at a large sun painted on the speaker's chair occupied by Washington. The stifling heat was made even worse because the windows remained shut to keep any news of the proceedings from drifting out into the Philadelphia streets.

## The Deadlock Broken

**COMPROMISE OVER REPRESENTATION**

Finally, as the heat wave broke, so did the political stalemate. On July 2nd a committee headed by Benjamin Franklin suggested a compromise. States would be equally represented in the upper house of Congress, each state legislature appointing two senators to six-year terms. That satisfied the smaller states. In the lower house of Congress, which alone could initiate money bills, representation was to be apportioned according to population. Every 30,000 inhabitants would elect one representative for a two-year term. A slave was to count as three-fifths of a free person in the calculation of population, and the slave trade was to continue until 1808. That satisfied the larger states and the South.

**ELECTORAL COLLEGE**

By the end of August the convention was prepared to approve the final draft of the Constitution. The delegates agreed that the executive, now called the president, would be chosen every four years. Direct election seemed out of the question—after all, how could citizens in South Carolina know anything about a presidential candidate who happened to live in distant Massachusetts, or vice versa? But if voters instead chose presidential electors, those eminent men would likely have been involved in national politics, have known the candidates personally, and be prepared to vote

wisely. Thus the Electoral College was established, with each state's total number of senators and representatives determining its share of electoral votes.

**SEPARATION OF POWERS**

An array of other powers ensured that the executive would remain independent and strong. He would have command over the armed forces, authority to conduct diplomatic relations, responsibility to nominate judges and officials in the executive branch, and the power to veto congressional legislation. Just as the executive branch was made independent, so too the federal judiciary was separated from the other two branches of government. Madison believed that this clear **separation of powers** was essential to a balanced republican government.

**AMENDING THE CONSTITUTION**

Madison's only real defeat came when the convention refused to give Congress veto power over state legislation. Still, the new bicameral national legislature enjoyed much broader authority than Congress had under the Confederation, including the power to tax and to regulate commerce. The Constitution also limited the powers of state legislatures, prohibiting them from levying duties on trade, coining money or issuing paper currency, and conducting foreign relations. The Constitution and the acts passed by Congress were declared the supreme law of the land, taking precedence over any legislation passed by the states. And changing the Constitution would not be easy. Amendments could be proposed only by a two-thirds vote of both houses of Congress or in a convention requested by two-thirds of the state legislatures. Ratification of amendments required approval by three-quarters of the states.

**A REPUBLIC OF THE PEOPLE, NOT A CONFEDERATION OF STATES**

On September 17, 1787, 39 of the 42 delegates remaining in Philadelphia signed the Constitution. It was fortunate that the signatories included so many lawyers, because the summer's proceedings had been of such dubious legality that many skilled attorneys would be needed to make them seem otherwise. Charged only to revise the Articles, the delegates had instead written a completely new frame of government. And to speed up ratification, the convention decided that the Constitution would go into effect after only nine states had approved it, overlooking the fact that even a revision of the Articles would have required the assent of all state legislatures. They further declared that the people themselves—not the state legislatures—would pass judgment on the Constitution in special ratifying conventions. To serve final notice that the new central government was a republic of the people and not merely another confederation of states, Gouverneur Morris of Pennsylvania hit on a happy turn of phrase to introduce the Constitution. "We the People," the document begins, "in Order to form a more perfect Union . . ."

## Ratification

**THE ANTI-FEDERALISTS**

With grave misgivings on the part of many, the states called for conventions to decide whether to ratify the new Constitution.

Those Americans with the gravest misgivings—the Anti-Federalists as they came to be called—voiced familiar republican fears. Older and less cosmopolitan than their **Federalist** opponents, the Anti-Federalists drew on their memories of the struggle with England to frame their criticisms of the Constitution. Expanding the power of the central government at the expense of the states, they warned, would lead to corrupt and arbitrary rule by new aristocrats. Extending a republic over a large territory, they cautioned, would separate national legislators from the interests and close oversight of their constituents.

**THE FEDERALIST PAPERS**   Madison responded to these objections in *The Federalist Papers,* a series of 85 essays written with Alexander Hamilton and John Jay during the winter of 1787–1788. He countered Anti-Federalist concerns over the centralization of power by pointing out that each separate branch of the national government would keep the others within the limits of their legal authority. That mechanism of **checks and balances** would prevent the executive from oppressing the people while preventing the people from oppressing themselves.

To answer Anti-Federalist objections to a national republic, Madison drew on the ideas of an English philosopher, David Hume. In his famous tenth essay in *The Federalist Papers,* Madison argued that in a great republic, "the Society becomes broken into a greater variety of interests, of pursuits, of passions, which check each other." The larger the territory, the more likely it was to contain multiple political interests and parties, so that no single faction could dominate. Instead, each would cancel out the others.

**BILL OF RIGHTS**   The one Anti-Federalist criticism Madison could not get around was the absence of a national bill of rights. Opponents insisted on an explicit statement of rights to secure the freedoms of individuals and minorities from being violated by the federal government. Madison finally promised to place a bill of rights before Congress immediately after the Constitution was ratified.

Throughout the early months of 1788, Anti-Federalists continued their opposition. But they lacked the articulate and influential leadership that rallied behind the Constitution and commanded greater access to the public press. In the end, too, Anti-Federalist fears of centralized power proved less compelling than Federalist prophecies of the chaos that would follow if the Constitution were not adopted.

**BILL OF RIGHTS RATIFIED**   By the end of July 1788 all but two states had voted in favor of ratification. The last holdout—Rhode Island, to no one's surprise—finally came aboard in May 1790, after Madison had carried through on his pledge to submit a bill of rights to the new Congress. Indeed, these 10 amendments—ratified by enough states to become part of the Constitution by the end of 1791—proved to be the Anti-Federalists' most impressive

*Ratification of the Constitution*

| State | Date | Vote For | Vote Against |
|---|---|---|---|
| Delaware | December 8, 1787 | 30 | 9 |
| Pennsylvania | December 12, 1787 | 46 | 23 |
| New Jersey | December 18, 1787 | 38 | 0 |
| Georgia | January 3, 1788 | 26 | 0 |
| Connecticut | January 9, 1788 | 128 | 40 |
| Massachusetts | February 6, 1788 | 187 | 168 |
| Maryland | April 26, 1788 | 63 | 11 |
| South Carolina | May 23, 1788 | 149 | 73 |
| New Hampshire | June 21, 1788 | 57 | 47 |
| Virginia | June 25, 1788 | 89 | 79 |
| New York | July 26, 1788 | 30 | 27 |
| North Carolina | November 21, 1788 | 194 | 77 |
| Rhode Island | May 29, 1790 | 34 | 32 |

## REPUBLICAN REMEDY?

*James Madison and "Brutus"—perhaps the Anti-Federalist judge Robert Yates—debated the proposed Constitution in the New York newspapers during 1787. One of the most contentious issues was whether a republic could effectively govern a territory as extensive as the United States.*

### DOCUMENT 1  James Madison

The two great points of difference between a democracy and a republic are: first, the delegation of the government in the latter, to a small number of citizens elected by the rest; secondly, the great number of citizens and greater sphere of country over which the latter may be extended.

The effect of the first difference is, on the one hand, to refine and enlarge the public views by passing them through the medium of a chosen body of citizens, whose wisdom may best discern the true interest of their country and whose patriotism and love of justice will be least likely to sacrifice it to temporary or partial considerations. Under such a regulation it may well happen that the public voice, pronounced by the representatives of the people, will be more consonant to the public good than if pronounced by the people themselves, convened for the purpose. On the other hand . . . men of factious tempers, of local prejudices, or of sinister designs, may, by intrigue, by corruption, or by other means, first obtain the suffrages, and then betray the interests of the people. The question resulting is, whether small or extensive republics are more favorable to the election of proper guardians of the public weal; and

it is clearly decided in favor of the latter by two obvious considerations.

In the first place . . . if the proportion of fit characters be not less in the large than in the small republic, the former will present a greater option, and consequently a greater probability of a fit choice.

In the next place, as each representative will be chosen by a greater number of citizens in the large than in the small republic, it will be more difficult for unworthy candidates to practice with success the vicious arts by which elections are too often carried. . . .

The other point of difference is the greater number of citizen and extent of territory which may be brought within the compass of republican than democratic government; and it is this circumstance principally which render factious combinations less to be dreaded in the former than in the latter. The smaller the society, the fewer probably will be the distinct parties and interests composing it; the fewer the distinct parties and interests, the more frequently will a majority be found of the same party; and the smaller the number of individuals compassing a majority . . . the more easily will they concert and execute their plans of oppression. Extend the sphere and you take in a

greater variety of parties and interests; you make it less probable that a majority of the whole will have a common motive to invade the rights of other citizens; or if such a common motive exists, it will be more difficult for all who feel it to discover their own strength and to act in unison with each other.

The influence of factious leaders may kindle a flame within their particular States but will be unable to spread a general conflagration through the other States. A religious sect may degenerate into a political faction in a part of the Confederacy; but the variety of sects dispersed over the entire face of it must secure the national councils against any danger from that source. A rage for paper money, for an abolition of debts, for an equal division of property, or for any other improper or wicked project, will be less apt to pervade the whole body of the Union than a particular member of it. . . .

In the extent and proper structure of the Union, therefore, we behold a republican remedy for diseases most incident to republican government.

*Source:* James Madison, Federalist No. 10, *The Federalist: A Collection of Essays, Written in Favour of the New Constitution* (New York, 1788).

### DOCUMENT 2  "Brutus"

A free republic cannot succeed over a country of such immense extent, containing such a number of inhabitants, and these increasing in such rapid progression as that of the whole United States. . . .

Now, in a large extended country, it is impossible to have a representation, possessing the sentiments and of integrity, to declare the minds of the people, without having it so numerous and unwieldly, as to be subject in great measure to the inconveniency of a democratic government. . . .

In a republic, the manners, sentiments, and interest of the people should be similar. If this be not the case . . . [it] will retard the operations of government, and prevent such conclusions as will promote the public good. . . . The productions of the different

parts of the union are very variant, and their interests, of consequence, diverse. Their manners and habits differ as much as their climates and production; and their sentiments are by no means coincident.

The confidence which people have in their rulers, in a free republic, arises from their knowing them, from their being responsible to them for their conduct, and from the power they have of displacing them when they misbehave: but in a republic of the extent of this continent, the people in general would be acquainted with few of their rulers. . . . The consequence will be, they will have no confidence in their legislature, suspect them of ambitious views, be jealous of every measure they adopt, and will not support the laws they pass . . . no way will be

left to render it otherwise, but by establishing an armed force to execute laws at the point of a bayonet.

*Source:* "Brutus," in the *New York Journal,* October 18, 1787.

### Thinking Critically

*How did Madison define the differences between a democracy and a republic? What did he regard as the chief advantage of a large republic? On what grounds did "Brutus" argue against large republics? Has our republican form of government been successful in avoiding the kinds of oppression and "improper projects" that Madison describes?*

legacy. The bill of rights set the most basic terms for defining personal liberty in the United States. Among the rights guaranteed were freedom of religion, the press, and speech, as well as the right to assemble and petition and the right to bear arms. The amendments also established clear procedural safeguards, including the right to a trial by jury and protection against illegal searches and seizures. They prohibited excessive bail, cruel and unusual punishment, and the quartering of troops in private homes.

 REVIEW

What short-term crises precipitated the Constitutional Convention, and what were the main points of debate at that meeting?

# CONCLUSION

# THE WORLD AT LARGE

Within the span of a single generation, Americans had declared their independence twice. In many ways the political freedom claimed from Britain in 1776 was less remarkable than the intellectual freedom from the Old World that Americans achieved by agreeing to the Constitution. The Constitution represented a triumph of the imagination—a challenge to many beliefs long cherished by western Europe's republican thinkers.

Revolutionary ideals had been deeply influenced by the conflicts of British politics, in particular the Opposition's warnings about the dangers of executive power. Those concerns at first committed the revolutionaries to making legislatures supreme. In the end, though, Americans ratified a constitution that provided for an independent executive and a balanced government. The Opposition's fears of distant, centralized power had at first prompted the revolutionaries to embrace state sovereignty. But in the Constitution Americans established a national government with authority independent of the states. Finally, the common sense among all of western Europe's republican theorists—that large national republics were an impossibility—was rejected by Americans, making the United States an impossibility that still endures.

What, then, became of the last tenet of the old republican creed—the belief that civic virtue would sustain popular liberty? The hard lessons of the war and the crises of the 1780s withered confidence in the capacity of Americans to sacrifice their private interests for the public welfare. The Constitution reflected the view that interest rather than virtue shaped the behavior of most people most of the time and that the clash of diverse interest groups would remain a constant of public life.

Yet Madison and many other Federalists did not believe that the competition between private interests would always foster the public welfare. That goal would be met instead by the new national government acting as "a disinterested and dispassionate umpire in disputes between different passions and interests in the State." A large republic, Federalists believed, with its millions of citizens, would yield more of that scarce resource—disinterested gentlemen dedicated to serving the public good. Such gentlemen, in Madison's words, "whose enlightened views and virtuous sentiments render them superior to local prejudices," would fill the small number of national offices.

Not all the old revolutionaries agreed. Anti-Federalists drawn from the ranks of ordinary Americans still believed that the national government should be composed of representations from every social class and occupational group, not dominated by "enlightened" gentlemen. "These lawyers and men of learning, and moneyed men, that talk so finely," complained one Anti-Federalist, would "get all the power and all of the money into their own hands, and then they will swallow up all us little folks."

That fear made Patrick Henry so ardent an Anti-Federalist that he refused to attend the Constitutional Convention in 1787, saying that he "smelt a rat." "I am not a Virginian, but an American," Henry had once declared. Most likely he was lying. Or perhaps Patrick Henry, a southerner and a slaveholder, could see himself as an "American" only so long as sovereignty remained firmly in the hands of the individual states. Henry's convictions, 70 years later, would rise again to haunt the Union. ∞∞∞

# Chapter Summary

Leading Americans gave more thought to federalism, the organization of a United States, as events in the 1780s revealed the weaknesses of the state and national governments.

- For a decade after independence, the revolutionaries were less committed to creating a single national republic than to organizing 13 separate state republics, each dominated by popularly elected legislatures.

- The Articles of Confederation's national legislature left the crucial power of the purse, as well as all final power to make and execute laws, entirely to the states.

- Many conflicts in the new republic were occasioned by westward expansion, which created both international difficulties with Britain and Spain and internal tensions over the democratization of state legislatures.

- After the Revolution, Americans struggled to define republican society; workers began to organize, some women claimed a right to greater political, legal, and educational opportunities, and religious dissenters called for disestablishment.

- The Revolution's egalitarian principles sparked a debate over slavery that increased the split between northern and southern states. Antislavery societies appeared in the North; some planters in the Upper South freed their slaves, but no southern state abolished slavery.

- In the mid-1780s the political crisis of the Confederation came to a head, prompted by the controversy over the Jay-Gardoqui Treaty and Shays's Rebellion.

- The Constitutional Convention of 1787 produced an entirely new frame of government that established a truly national republic and provided for a separation of powers among a judiciary, a bicameral legislature, and a strong executive.

- The Anti-Federalists, opponents of the Constitution, pushed for a bill of rights, which was incorporated into the Constitution by 1791.

# Additional Reading

The work of Gordon Wood is indispensable for understanding the transformation of American politics and culture during the 1780s and thereafter; see especially *The Creation of the American Republic* (1969) and *The Radicalism of the American Revolution* (1992). Other good accounts of the Confederation period and the framing of the Constitution include Forrest MacDonald, *E Pluribus Unum* (1965) and *Novus Ordo Seclorum* (1985), and Woody Holton's *Unruly Americans* (2007). To understand the arguments in favor of the Constitution, consult Garry Wills, *Explaining America* (1981), and to appreciate the contributions of its opponents, read Saul Cornell, *The Other Founders* (1999), and Cecilia Kenyon's *Men of Little Faith* (2003). The proceedings of the Constitutional Convention receive full coverage in Christopher Collier and James Lincoln Collier, *Decision in Philadelphia* (1987), and Clinton Rossiter, *1787: The Grand Convention* (1973).

To explore the meaning of republicanism for American women, see two fine studies by Linda Kerber, *Women of the Republic* (1980) and *No Constitutional Right to Be Ladies* (1998), as well as Rosemarie Zagarri's provocative *Revolutionary Backlash* (2007). For a vivid sense of how the 1780s transformed one Massachusetts county, read John Brooke, *The Heart of the Commonwealth* (1991), and for a fascinating tale of how the Revolution made one ordinary man's life extraordinary, enjoy Alan Taylor, *William Cooper's Town* (1995). For the effects of the Revolution on African Americans in the North, see Joan Pope Melish, *Disowning Slavery* (1998), and James Sidbury, *Becoming African in America* (2007).

For a fuller list of readings, see the Bibliography at www.mhhe.com/eh8e.

# Significant Events

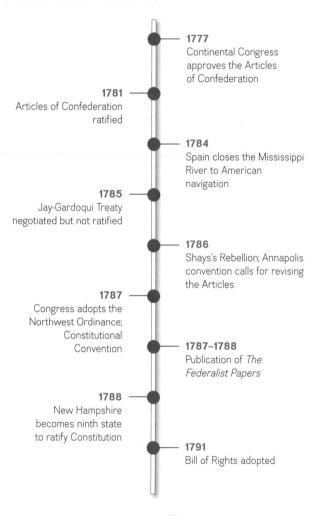

**1777**
Continental Congress approves the Articles of Confederation

**1781**
Articles of Confederation ratified

**1784**
Spain closes the Mississippi River to American navigation

**1785**
Jay-Gardoqui Treaty negotiated but not ratified

**1786**
Shays's Rebellion; Annapolis convention calls for revising the Articles

**1787**
Congress adopts the Northwest Ordinance; Constitutional Convention

**1787–1788**
Publication of *The Federalist Papers*

**1788**
New Hampshire becomes ninth state to ratify Constitution

**1791**
Bill of Rights adopted

# Crises of the 1780s—and Consequences

| INTERNATIONAL CRISES | EXPOSED |
|---|---|
| British efforts to annex Vermont to Canada | Weakness of confederation diplomacy; consequences of having no national army |
| Spanish efforts to ally with Indians in the Southeast and with white settlers in the Ohio valley | Weakness of confederation diplomacy and Indian policy; consequences of having no national army |
| ↓ | |
| Culminated in debate over the Jay-Gardoqui Treaty, 1785 | Simmering tensions between East and West, North and South; potential of sectional conflict to threaten national union |

| DOMESTIC CRISES | EXPOSED |
|---|---|
| Postwar inflationary spiral | Confederation Congress's lack of power to set national economic policy, tax, regulate trade |
| Debtor vs. creditor interests producing political divisions and deadlock in state legislatures | Inability of sovereign states to solve economic conflicts |
| ↓ | |
| Culminated in Shays's Rebellion (1786) | Potential for future agrarian violence; failure of state governments to protect property |

# White and Black Southerners Worshiping Together

Religious beliefs, gatherings, and rituals reflect some of the deepest human emotions. Often they also lay bare some of society's deepest divisions. For both these reasons and more, historians often study religious institutions and practices to understand how a society functions.

During the 50 years before 1800, **evangelicals** introduced southerners to new ways of being religious. Those attending their worship services were drawn into the earliest southern Baptist, Methodist, and Presbyterian churches by the First Great Awakening and other revivals that followed. Some of these early services were held in private homes, others in crudely constructed churches, and still others in open fields. As evangelical preachers stressed the importance of being "reborn" by faith in Jesus Christ, some southerners wept, confessed their sins, and encouraged one another with hopeful words and warm embraces. Those who came to such gatherings engaged in the most intimate kind of sharing and self-revelation.

What made the services even more extraordinary is that some participants were white and some black. These religious fellowships were truly biracial and remained so until after the Civil War. That remarkable fact has intrigued historians. In a society increasingly shaped by the institution of slavery, evangelical churches were one of the few southern institutions that brought blacks and whites together rather than keeping them apart. How did members behave toward one another daily? Were born-again converts from both races treated equally? How was authority within such churches distributed among black and white members?

The questions are tantalizing, but the answers by no means easy to come by. Some letters and diaries survive from the last half of the eighteenth century, among them the daily journals and correspondence of ministers. A few preachers even published autobiographies

Church book record: "Names of Black Members." Note the treatment of black names.

of their experiences. But even more valuable information can be gathered from what might seem at first a rather drab source. There are scores of church records dating from this period, most kept by Virginia Baptists. The members of each Baptist church elected a clerk, always a white male "brother," whose duty it was to record all the business transacted at their monthly meetings, often in a ledger-sized bound volume called the "church book." Church books provide an insight into relations between whites and blacks in part because their clerks are not consciously trying to write about race relations. They are simply recording the everyday business of churches, week in, week out.

## DECODING THE CHURCH BOOKS

SOMETIMES PRACTICAL CONCERNS DOMINATED THE meeting. Should the church building be repaired? Who among the brethren will be permitted to preach? (Many Baptist churches boasted several preachers besides the pastor.) On other occasions, members debated what, according to the Bible, was the holiest way to govern their churches. But at most meetings, members fixed their attention on admitting new converts to their fellowship and "disciplining" older members suspected of sexual misconduct or theft, slander or swearing, drinking or fighting. Church clerks duly noted all those accepted as new members, as well as the names of wayward brothers and sisters—and whether they were merely scolded for their faults or expelled.

Such records offer the most direct and vivid sense of African Americans' presence and participation in early evangelical churches. First, historians can start by doing a little counting. How many members are white and how many black? The records show that blacks made up a substantial minority—perhaps one-fifth to one-quarter—of the members in most churches. In a few, they constituted a majority. Many churches, too, authorized at least one African American brother to preach, sometimes permitting him that "liberty" only among other blacks but in other instances allowing him to address racially mixed gatherings. There were even a few predominantly white churches in early Virginia that black preachers served as pastors.

What about voting? In some churches, too, black men and, more rarely, black women were permitted to vote in meetings. In all, African American members could participate in deliberations and give testimony in discipline cases. Indeed, there are several instances of masters being disciplined after slave members complained of being abused. Black members, too, were sometimes charged with wrongdoing, but white men were far more likely than any other group of members to be hauled before the church for reported misdeeds. In short, evangelical churches like these Baptist fellowships were among the most racially egalitarian institutions in early southern society. They offered African Americans unusual opportunities to hold positions of authority, to voice their opinions, and to gain leverage over their masters.

## LIMITS OF RACIAL EQUALITY

YET THESE SAME CHURCH RECORDS also reveal the limits of racial equality among early evangelicals. Like all evidence mined by historians, the sources yield data that are sometimes complex and contradictory.

Records of those meetings at which members discussed the mundane matter of church repair reveal, for example, that the Baptists segregated seating at public worship. African Americans were consigned to the least choice spots at the back of the church or in "sheds" attached to the side. Moreover, when white members filled every available seat, black members were ordered outdoors to listen from underneath open windows. The attitude that such practices convey—that whites regarded African Americans as "second-class" members—is also suggested by the manner in which many clerks

*"Uncle Jack," shown in this 1849 engraving, preaches informally to a white congregation. He began his career as a minister in the 1790s and continued until 1832.*

recorded new church members. They always entered the full names of white converts; however, new African American members were usually listed last and often collectively as "several Negroes."

Church discussions about who might preach also show a growing concern on the part of white members to restrict the activities of black preachers. Increasingly after 1750, those allowed that "liberty" were given ever stricter instructions about whom they might preach to, at which times, and from what texts of the Bible. At meetings in which the rules of conducting church business were discussed, white members also began to express concern about whether African American members should be allowed to vote. Most churches revoked that right before the end of the eighteenth century. Tracing how churches dealt with black members accused of misbehavior suggests a similar anxiety among white members, which increased over time. Although African Americans continued to make up only a tiny minority of church members suspected of misbehavior, those convicted of wrongdoing were far more likely than white members to be expelled rather than to receive a milder punishment.

In other words, a closer inspection of church records suggests that white evangelicals drifted toward more racially restrictive policies over the latter half of the eighteenth century. Why? The numbers in the church books are suggestive. After the Revolution, increasing numbers of African Americans were entering Baptist (and other evangelical) churches.

As the percentage of black members rose, white evangelicals feared that the "freedoms" given to black worshipers might detract from the church's ability to win converts among slaveholders.

## SEEKING A SEPARATE WAY

CLEARLY, EVANGELICALS WERE WINNING CONVERTS among African Americans. Yet other evidence suggests that black members were left unsatisfied by their treatment in white churches. The diaries and letters of white evangelicals reveal that many black members of biracial churches had also begun conducting their own separate devotions. Even by the 1790s, African American Christians were meeting nightly in the slave quarters to pray, sing, and hear the sermons of black preachers. Such "shadow churches" served as the crucible of Afro-Christianity, a melding of evangelical Protestant and West African religious traditions. John Antrobus's painting *Plantation Burial* (in a detail shown above) reflects the situation that prevailed by the mid-nineteenth century. Although blacks attended white services in greater numbers, their most vital worship often took place elsewhere. White masters and preachers were like the shadowy couple Antrobus painted on the right: divorced from the Christian worship of their slaves.

Citizens staged Fourth of July parades as one way to define the identity of their young republic. This New York parade in 1812 was led by the Tammany Society, whose members rejected the aristocratic inclinations of the Federalist Party. The society was named to honor a Delaware Indian chief; its members often marched wearing Indian style garb, as seen here. But by 1812 the patriotic associations of Indian dress (recall the Boston Tea Party disguises) were less popular due to increased clashes with Indians on the frontier.

# The Early Republic

1789–1824

## What's to Come

∞∞∞ **AN AMERICAN STORY** ∞∞∞

## "I FELT MY BLOOD BOIL"

One spring evening in 1794 General John Neville rode home from Pittsburgh with his wife and granddaughter. As they went up a hill, his wife's saddle started to slip, so Neville dismounted. As he adjusted the strap, a rider galloped up and in a gruff voice asked, "Are you Neville the excise officer?"

"Yes," Neville replied, without turning around.

"Then I must give you a whipping!" cried the rider and leapt from his horse. He grabbed Neville by the hair and lunged at his throat. Breaking free, Neville finally managed to knock the man down, after which he fled. But Neville could not help but be shaken as he resumed his journey. The general was not accustomed to such treatment. As one of the wealthiest men in the area, he expected respect from those of lower social rank. And he had received it—until becoming embroiled in a controversy over the new "whiskey tax" on distilled spirits. In a frontier district like western Pennsylvania, farmers regularly distilled their grain into whiskey for barter and sale. Not surprisingly, the **excise tax,** passed by Congress in 1791, was notoriously unpopular. Still, Neville had accepted an appointment to be one of the tax's regional inspectors. For three years he had endured the occasional threat, but this roadside assault showed that popular hostility was rising.

As spring turned to summer the grain ripened, and so did the people's anger. In mid-July a federal marshal arrived to serve summonses to a number of farmer-distillers who had not paid taxes. One, William Miller, squinted at the paper and was amazed to find the government ordering him to appear in court—hundreds of miles away in Philadelphia—in little more than a month. Worse, the papers claimed he owed $250.

And there, next to this unknown federal marshal, stood John Neville.

"I thought $250 would ruin me," recalled Miller; "and I felt my blood boil at seeing General Neville along to pilot the sheriff to my very door." Within minutes 30 or 40 laborers had swarmed from a nearby field. Armed with muskets and pitchforks, they forced Neville and the marshal to beat a hasty retreat. Next morning, the local militia company marched to Neville's estate. A battle ensued, and the general, aided by his slaves, beat back the attackers. A larger group, numbering 500 to 700, returned the following day to find Neville fled and his home garrisoned by a group of soldiers from nearby Fort Pitt. The mob burned down most of the outbuildings and, after the soldiers surrendered, torched Neville's elegantly furnished home.

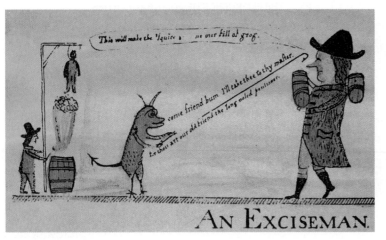

*A tax collector in league with the devil.*

That summer, marauding bands roamed the countryside, burning homes and attacking tax collectors. Western Pennsylvania experienced the greatest unrest, but farmers in the western districts of several other states also defied federal officials, thus launching a full-scale "Whiskey Rebellion" in the summer of 1794.

Alexander Hamilton, a principal architect of the strong federal government established by the Constitution, knew a challenge to authority when he saw one: "Shall there be a government, or no government?" So did an alarmed George Washington, now president and commander-in-chief of the new republic, who led an army of 13,000 men—larger than that he had commanded at Yorktown against the British—into the Pennsylvania countryside. That show of force cowed the Pennsylvania protesters, snuffing out the Whiskey Rebellion.

Federalists such as Washington and Hamilton—supporters of a powerful national government— had high hopes for their newly created republic. But the riots and rebellion deepened fears for its future. The nation's founders recognized all too well how risky it was to unite such a vast territory. Yankee merchants living along Boston wharves had economic interests and cultural traditions distinct from those of backcountry farmers who raised hogs, tended a few acres of corn, and distilled whiskey. Even among farmers there was a world of difference between a South Carolina planter who shipped tons of rice to European markets and a New Hampshire family whose stony fields yielded barely enough to survive. Could the new government established by the Constitution provide a framework strong enough to unite such a patchwork of peoples, cultures, and classes? These newly united states were a fragile creation, buffeted by changes beyond their borders and struggling to create a stable government at home. During the nation's first three decades, the republic's survival depended on balancing the interests of a socially and economically diverse population. ∞∞∞∞∞

# A Social and Political Portrait of the New Republic

When the constitution went into effect, the United States stretched from the Atlantic Ocean to the Mississippi River. Comprising some 840,000 square miles in 1789, it was approximately four times the size of France, five times the size of Spain, ten times the size of Great Britain. The first federal census, compiled in 1790, counted approximately 4 million people, divided about evenly between the northern and southern states. Only about 100,000 settlers lived beyond the Appalachians in the Tennessee and Kentucky territories, which were soon to become states.

Within the Republic's boundaries were two major groups that lacked effective political influence: African Americans and Indians. In 1790 black Americans numbered 750,000, almost one-fifth the total population. More than 90 percent lived in the southern states from Maryland to Georgia; most were slaves who worked on tobacco and rice plantations, but there were free blacks as well. The census did not count the number of Indians living east of the Mississippi. North of the Ohio, the powerful Miami Confederacy discouraged settlement, while to the south, five strong, well-organized tribes—the Creeks, Cherokees, Chickasaws, Choctaws, and Seminoles—dominated the region from the Appalachians to the Mississippi River.

**POPULATION GROWTH** That composition would change as the white population continued to double about every 22 years. Immigration contributed only a small part to this astonishing growth. On average, fewer than 10,000 Europeans arrived annually between 1790 and 1820. The primary cause was natural increase, since, on average, American white women gave birth to nearly eight children each. As a result, the United States had an unusually youthful population: in 1790 almost half of all white Americans were under 16 years old. The age at first marriage was about 25 for men, 24 for women—and three or four years younger in newly settled areas—which contributed to the high birthrate.

This youthful, growing population remained overwhelmingly rural. Only 24 towns and cities boasted 2,500 or more residents, and 19 out of 20 Americans lived outside them. In fact, more than 80 percent of American families in 1800 were engaged in agriculture. In such a rural environment the movement of people, goods, and information was slow. Few individuals used the expensive postal system, and most roads were still little more than dirt paths hacked through the forest. In 1790 the country had 92 newspapers, but they were published mostly in towns and cities along major avenues of transportation.

Life in isolated regions contrasted markedly with that in bustling urban centers like New York City and Philadelphia. But the most basic division in American society was not between the cities and the countryside, important as that was. What would divide Americans most broadly over the coming decades was the contrast between semisubsistence and commercial ways of life. Semisubsistence farmers lived on the produce of their own land and labor. Americans in the commercial economy were tied more closely to the larger markets of a far-flung world.

## Semisubsistence and Commercial Economies

Most rural white Americans in the interior of the northern states and the backcountry of the South lived off the produce of their own land. Wealth in those areas, although not distributed equally, was spread fairly broadly. And subsistence remained the goal of most white families. "The great effort was for every farmer to produce anything he required within his own family," one European visitor noted. In such an economy women played a key role. Wives and daughters had to be skilled in making articles such as candles, soap, clothing, and hats, since the cost of buying such items was steep.

With labor scarce and expensive, farmers also depended on their neighbors to help clear fields, build homes, and harvest crops. If a farm family produced a small surplus, it usually exchanged it locally rather than selling it for cash in a distant market. In this barter economy, money was seldom seen and was used primarily to pay taxes and purchase imported goods.

**INDIAN ECONOMIES** Indian economies were also based primarily on subsistence. In the division of labor women raised crops, while men fished or hunted—not only for meat but also for skins to make clothing. Because Indians followed game more seasonally than did white settlers, they moved their villages to several different locations over the course of a year. But both whites and Indians in a **semisubsistence economy** moved periodically to new fields after they had exhausted the old ones. Indians exhausted agricultural lands less quickly because they planted beans, corn, and squash in the same field, a technique that better conserved soil nutrients.

Despite the image of both the independent "noble savage" and the self-reliant yeoman farmer, virtually no one in the backcountry operated within a truly self-sufficient economy. Although farmers tried to grow most of the food their families ate, they normally bought salt, sugar, and coffee, and they often traded with their neighbors for food and other items. In addition, necessities such as iron, glass, lead, and gunpowder had to be purchased, and many farmers hired artisans to make shoes and weave cloth. Similarly, Indians were enmeshed in the wider world of European commerce, exchanging furs for iron tools or clothing and ornamental materials.

Outside the backcountry, Americans were tied much more closely to a **commercial economy.** Here, merchants, artisans, and even farmers did not subsist on what they produced but instead sold goods or services in a wider market and lived on their earnings. Cities and towns, of

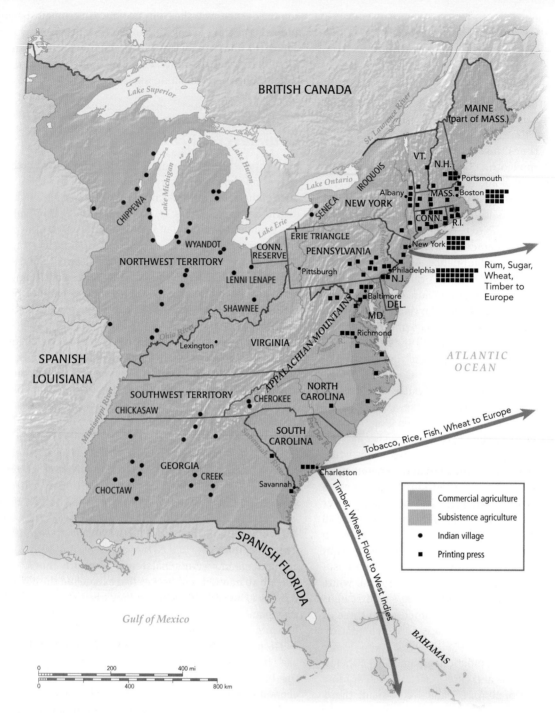

## SEMISUBSISTENCE AND COMMERCIAL AMERICA, 1790

*To prosper, a commercial economy demanded relatively cheap transportation to move goods. Thus in 1790 American commerce was confined largely to settled areas along the coast and to navigable rivers below the fall line. Because commerce depended on an efficient flow of information and goods, newspapers flourished in these areas. Did the split between commercial and semisubsistence ways of life reflect a division more between east and west or north and south? Why?*

course, played a key part in the commercial economy. But so did the agricultural regions near the seaboard and along navigable rivers.

For commerce to flourish, goods had to move from producers to market cheaply enough to reap profits. Water

offered the only cost-effective transportation over any distance; indeed, it cost as much to ship goods a mere 30 miles over primitive roads as to ship by boat 3,000 miles across the Atlantic to London. Cost-effective transportation was available to the planters of the Tidewater South, and city merchants used their access to the sea to establish trading ties to the West Indies and Europe. But urban artisans and workers were also linked to this market economy, as were many farm families in the Hudson valley, southeastern Pennsylvania, and southern New England.

In commercial economies wealth was less equally distributed. By 1790 the richest 10 percent of Americans living in cities and in the plantation districts of the Tidewater South owned about 50 percent of the wealth. In the backcountry the top 10 percent was likely to own 25 to 35 percent of the wealth.

## The Constitution and Commerce

In many ways the fight over ratification of the Constitution represented a struggle between the commercial and the subsistence-oriented elements of American society. Urban merchants and workers as well as commercial farmers and planters generally rallied behind the Constitution. They took a broader, more cosmopolitan view of the nation's future, and they had a more favorable view of government power than did subsistence farmers.

Americans who remained a part of the semisubsistence **barter economy** tended to oppose the Constitution. More provincial in outlook, they feared concentrated power, were suspicious of cities and commercial institutions, opposed aristocracy and special privilege, and in general just wanted to be left alone.

And so in 1789 the United States embarked on its new national course, with two rival visions of the direction that the fledgling Republic should take. Which vision would prevail—a question that was as much social as it was political—increasingly divided the generation of revolutionary leaders in the early republic.

## Washington Organizes the Government

Whatever the Republic was to become, Americans agreed that George Washington personified it. When the first Electoral College cast its votes, Washington was unanimously elected, the only president in history so honored. John Adams became vice president. Loyalty to the new Republic, with its untried form of government and diversity of peoples and interests, rested to a great degree on the trust and respect Americans gave Washington.

George Washington realized that as the first occupant of the executive office, everything he did was fraught with significance. "I walk on untrodden ground," he commented. "There is scarcely any part of my conduct which may not hereafter be drawn into precedent."

THE CABINET The Constitution made no mention of a cabinet. Yet the drafters of the Constitution, aware of the experience of the Continental Congress under the Articles of Confederation, clearly assumed that the president would have some system of advisers. Congress authorized the creation of four departments—War, Treasury, State, and Attorney General—whose heads were to be appointed with the consent of the Senate. Washington's most important choices were Alexander Hamilton as secretary of the treasury and Thomas Jefferson to head the State Department. Washington gradually excluded Adams from cabinet discussions, and any meaningful role for the vice president, whose duties were largely undefined by the Constitution, soon disappeared.

The Constitution created a federal Supreme Court but beyond that was silent about the court system. The Judiciary Act of 1789 set the size of the Supreme Court at 6 members; it also established 13 federal district courts and 3 circuit courts of appeal. Supreme Court justices spent much of their time serving on these circuit courts, a distasteful duty whose long hours "riding the circuit" caused one justice to grumble that Congress had made him a "traveling postboy." The Judiciary Act made it clear that federal courts had the right to review decisions of the state courts and specified cases over which the Supreme Court would have original jurisdiction. Washington appointed John Jay of New York, a staunch Federalist, as the first chief justice.

## Hamilton's Financial Program

HAMILTON'S TWO GOALS When Congress called on Alexander Hamilton to prepare a report on the nation's finances, the new secretary of the treasury undertook the assignment eagerly. A brilliant thinker and an ambitious politician, he did not intend to be a minor figure in the new administration. Convinced that human nature was fundamentally selfish, Hamilton was determined to link the interests of the wealthy with those of the new government. He also intended to use federal power to encourage manufacturing and commerce in order to make the United States economically strong and independent of Europe.

FUNDING AND ASSUMPTION Neither goal could be achieved until the federal government solved its two most pressing financial problems: revenue and credit. Without revenue it could not be effective. Without credit—the faith of merchants and other nations that the government would repay its debts—it would lack the ability to borrow. Hamilton proposed that all $52 million of the federal debt, much of it generated by the Revolutionary War, be paid in full (or funded). He also recommended that the federal government assume responsibility for the remaining $25 million in debts that individual states owed—a policy of "assumption." He intended with these twin policies to put the new federal government on a sound financial footing and enhance its power by increasing its need for revenue and making the wealthy look to the national government, not the states. Hamilton also proposed a series of excise taxes, including a controversial 25 percent levy on whiskey, to help meet government expenses.

**BANK OF THE UNITED STATES** After heated debate, Congress deadlocked over funding and assumption. Finally, at a dinner with Hamilton, Jefferson and James Madison of Virginia agreed to support his proposal if, after 10 years in Philadelphia, the permanent seat of government would be located in the South, on the Potomac River between Virginia and Maryland. Aided by this understanding, funding and assumption passed Congress. In 1791 Congress also approved a 20-year charter for the first Bank of the United States. The bank would hold government deposits and issue banknotes that would be received in payment of all debts owed the federal government. Congress proved less receptive to the rest of Hamilton's program, although a limited tariff to encourage manufacturing and several excise taxes, including the one on whiskey, won approval.

The passage of Hamilton's program caused a permanent rupture among supporters of the Constitution. Madison, who had collaborated closely with Hamilton in the 1780s, broke with his former ally over funding and assumption. Jefferson finally went over to the opposition when Hamilton announced plans for a national bank. Eventually the two warring factions organized themselves into political

Debt $75.6 Million

Foreign
Debt
$11.7

State Debt
$21.5

Domestic
Debt
$42.4

Excise
and Other
$1.2

Customs
$4.4

Revenue
$5.6 Million

Other
$1.0

Interest
on Debt
$4.6

Annual Expenditures
$5.6 Million

*Under Hamilton's financial system, more than 80 percent of federal revenues went to pay the interest on the national debt. Note that most of the revenue came from tariff duties (customs).*

parties: the Republicans, led by Jefferson and Madison, and the Federalists, led by Hamilton and Adams.* But the division emerged slowly over several years.

**FEARS OF A FINANCIAL ARISTOCRACY** Hamilton's program promoted the commercial sector at the expense of semisubsistence farmers. Thus it rekindled many of the concerns that had surfaced during the struggle over ratification of the Constitution. The ideology of the Revolution had stressed that republics inevitably contained groups who sought power in order to destroy popular liberties and overthrow the republic. To some Americans, Hamilton's program seemed a clear threat to establish a privileged and powerful financial aristocracy—perhaps even a monarchy.

**SYSTEMS OF CORRUPTION** Who, after all, would benefit from the funding proposal? During and after the Revolution, the value of notes issued by the Continental Congress dropped sharply. Speculators had bought up most

of these notes for a fraction of their face value from small farmers and workers. If the government finally paid back the debt, speculators would profit accordingly. Equally disturbing, members of Congress had been purchasing the notes before the adoption of Hamilton's program. Nearly half the members of the House of Representatives owned U.S. securities, a dangerous mimicking of Britain, where the Bank of England's loans to many members of Parliament gave it great political influence.

Fears were heightened because Americans had little experience with banks: only three existed in the country when the Bank of the United States was chartered. One member of Congress expressed a common attitude when he said that he would no more be caught entering a bank than a house of prostitution. Then, too, banks and commerce were a part of the urban environment that rural Americans so distrusted. Although Hamilton's opponents admitted that a certain amount of commerce was necessary, they believed that it should remain subordinate. Hamilton's program, in contrast, encouraged manufacturing and urbanization, developments that history suggested were incompatible with liberty and equality.

---

*The Republican Party of the 1790s, sometimes referred to as the Jeffersonian Republicans, is not to be confused with the modern-day Republican Party, which originated in the 1850s.

| *A study in contrasts, Jefferson and Hamilton increasingly came into conflict in Washington's administration. Despite his aristocratic upbringing, Jefferson (left) was awkward, loose-jointed, reserved, and ill at ease in public. Testifying before a congressional committee, he casually lounged in a chair and spoke in a rambling, nonstop manner. "Yet he scattered information wherever he went," conceded Senator William Maclay of Pennsylvania, "and some even brilliant sentiments sparkled from him." Hamilton (right), though short of stature, cut a dashing figure with his erect bearing, strutting manner, meticulous dress, and carefully powdered hair. Declared the wife of the British ambassador: "I have scarcely ever been more charmed with the vivacity and conversation of any man."*

**STRICT CONSTRUCTION OF THE CONSTITUTION**

After Congress approved the bank bill, Washington hesitated to sign it. When he consulted his cabinet, Jefferson stressed that the Constitution did not specifically authorize Congress to charter a bank. Both he and Madison upheld the idea of strict construction—that the Constitution should be interpreted narrowly and the federal government restricted to powers expressly delegated to it. Otherwise, the federal government would be the judge of its own powers, and there would be no safeguard against the abuse of power.

Hamilton countered that the Constitution contained implied as well as enumerated powers. He particularly emphasized the clause that permitted Congress to make all laws "necessary and proper" to carry out its duties. A bank would be useful in carrying out the enumerated powers of regulating commerce and maintaining the public credit; Congress thus had a right to decide whether to establish one. In the end Washington accepted Hamilton's arguments and signed the bill.

Economically Hamilton's program was a success. The government's credit was restored, and the national bank ended the inflation of the previous two decades and created a sound currency. In addition, Hamilton's theory of implied powers and broad construction gave the nation the flexibility necessary to respond to unanticipated crises.

 **REVIEW**

Analyze the relationship between economic interests and politics in the 1790s.

# THE EMERGENCE OF POLITICAL PARTIES

MEMBERS OF THE REVOLUTIONARY GENERATION fervently hoped that political parties would not take root in the United States. "If I could not go to heaven but with a party, I would not go at all," remarked Jefferson. Influenced by radical English republican thought, American critics condemned parties as narrow interest groups that placed selfishness and party loyalty above a concern for the public good. Despite Americans' distrust of such institutions, however, the United States became the first nation to establish truly popular parties.

**SOCIAL CONDITIONS ENCOURAGING POLITICAL PARTIES**

Social conditions encouraged the rise of parties. Because property ownership was widespread, the nation had a broad **suffrage.** During the American Revolution legislatures lowered property requirements in many states, increasing the number of voters still further. If party members hoped to hold office, they had to offer a program attractive to the broader voting public. When parties acted as representatives of economic and social interest groups, they became one means by which a large electorate could make its feelings known. In addition, the United States had the highest literacy rate in the world and the largest number of newspapers, further encouraging political interest and participation. Finally, the fact that well-known patriots of the Revolution headed both the Federalists and the Republicans helped defuse the charge that either party was hostile to the Revolution or the Constitution.

| The execution of King Louis XVI by guillotine left Americans divided over the French Revolution.

## Americans and the French Revolution

Although domestic issues first split the supporters of the Constitution, it was a crisis in Europe that pushed the nation toward political parties. Americans had hoped that their revolution would spark similar movements for liberty on the European continent, and in fact the American Revolution was only one of a series of revolutions in the late eighteenth century that shook the Western world, the most important of which began in France in 1789. There a rising population and the collapse of government finances sparked a challenge to royal authority that became a mass revolution. The French revolutionary ideals of "liberty, equality, and fraternity" eventually spilled across Europe.

**DIFFERING VIEWS OF THE FRENCH REVOLUTION**

Americans first hailed the Revolution. Many rejoiced to learn that the Bastille prison had been stormed and that a new National Assembly had abolished feudal privileges and adopted the Declaration of the Rights of Man. But by 1793, American enthusiasm for the Revolution had cooled after radical elements instituted a reign of terror, executing the king and queen and many of the nobility. The French Republic even outlawed Christianity and substituted the worship of Reason. Finally, in 1793 republican France and monarchical England went to war. Americans were deeply divided over whether the United States should continue its old alliance with France or support Great Britain.

Hamilton and his allies viewed the French Revolution as sheer anarchy. French radicals seemed to be destroying the very institutions that held civilization together: the church, social classes, property, law and order. The United States, Hamilton argued, should renounce the 1778 treaty of alliance with France and side with Britain. By contrast, Jefferson and his followers supported the treaty and

regarded France as a sister republic. They believed that despite deplorable excesses, its revolution was spreading the doctrine of liberty.

## Washington's Neutral Course

Washington, for his part, was convinced that in order to prosper, the United States must remain independent of European quarrels and wars. Thus he issued a proclamation of American neutrality and tempered Jefferson's efforts to support France.

**NEUTRAL RIGHTS**

Under international law, neutrals could trade with belligerents—nations at war—as long as the trade had existed before the outbreak of hostilities and did not involve war supplies. But both France and Great Britain refused to respect the rights of neutrals in the midst of their desperate struggle. They began intercepting American ships and confiscating cargoes. In addition, Britain, which badly needed manpower to maintain its powerful navy, impressed into service American sailors it suspected of being British subjects. Britain also continued to maintain the western forts it had promised to evacuate in 1783, and it closed the West Indies, a traditional source of trade, to American ships.

**JAY'S TREATY**

Recognizing that the United States was not strong enough to challenge Britain militarily, Washington sent John Jay to negotiate the differences between the two countries. Although Jay did persuade the British to withdraw their troops from the Northwest, he could gain no other concessions. Disappointed, Washington nonetheless submitted Jay's Treaty to the Senate. After a bitter debate, the Senate narrowly ratified it in June of 1795.

## The Federalists and the Republicans Organize

Thus events in Europe contributed directly to the rise of parties in the United States by stimulating fears over the course of American development. By the mid-1790s both sides were organizing on a national basis. Hamilton took the lead in coordinating the Federalist party, which grew out of the voting bloc in Congress that had enacted his economic program. Increasingly, Washington drew closer to Federalist advisers and policies and became the symbol of the party, although he clung to the vision of a nonpartisan administration.

REPUBLICANS IN OPPOSITION The guiding genius of the opposition movement was Hamilton's onetime colleague James Madison. Jefferson, who resigned as secretary of state at the end of 1793, became the symbolic head of the party, much as Washington reluctantly headed the Federalists. But it was Madison who orchestrated the Republican strategy and lined up their voting bloc in the House. The disputes over Jay's Treaty and over the whiskey tax in 1794 and 1795 gave the Republicans popular issues, and they began organizing on the state and local levels. Republican leaders had to be careful to distinguish between opposing the administration and opposing the Constitution. And they had to overcome the ingrained idea that an opposition party was seditious.

As more and more members of Congress allied themselves with one faction or the other, voting became increasingly partisan. By 1796 even minor matters were decided by partisan votes. Gradually, party organization filtered downward to local communities.

## The 1796 Election

As long as Washington remained head of the Federalists, they enjoyed a huge advantage. But in 1796 the weary president, stung by the abuse heaped on him by the opposition press, announced that he would not accept a third term. In doing so, he set a two-term precedent that future presidents followed until Franklin Roosevelt. In his Farewell Address, Washington warned against the dangers of parties and urged a return to the earlier nonpartisan system. That vision, however, had become obsolete: parties were an effective way of expressing the interests of different social and economic groups within the nation. When the Republicans chose Thomas Jefferson to oppose John

| John Adams

Adams, the possibility of a constitutional system without parties ended.

The framers of the Constitution did not anticipate that political parties would run competing candidates for both the presidency and the vice presidency. Thus they provided that, of the candidates running for president, the one with the most electoral votes would win and the one with the second highest number would become vice president. But Hamilton strongly disliked both Adams and Jefferson. Ever the intriguer, he tried to manipulate the electoral vote so that the Federalist vice presidential candidate, Thomas Pinckney of South Carolina, would be elected president. In the ensuing confusion, Adams won with 71 electoral votes, and his rival, Jefferson, gained the vice presidency with 68 votes.

## Federalist and Republican Ideologies

The fault line between Federalists and Republicans reflected basic divisions in American life. Geographically, the Federalists were strongest in New England, with its commercial ties to Great Britain and its powerful tradition of hierarchy and order. Moving farther south, the party became progressively weaker. Of the southernmost states, the Federalists enjoyed significant strength only in aristocratic South Carolina. The Republicans won solid support in semisubsistence areas such as the West, where farmers were only weakly involved with commerce. The middle states were closely contested, although the most cosmopolitan and commercially oriented elements remained the core of Federalist strength.

In other ways, each party looked both forward and backward: toward certain traditions of the past as well as toward newer social currents that would shape America in the nineteenth century.

FEDERALIST IDEAS Most Federalists viewed themselves as a kind of natural aristocracy making a last desperate stand against the excesses of democracy. They clung to the notion that the upper class should rule over its social and economic inferiors. In supporting the established social order, most Federalists opposed unbridled individualism. In their view, government should regulate individual behavior for the good of society and protect property from the violent and unruly.

Yet the Federalists were remarkably forward-looking in their economic ideas. They sensed that the United States would become a major economic and military power only by government encouragement of economic development.

REPUBLICAN IDEAS The Republicans, in contrast, looked backward to the traditional Revolutionary fear that government power threatened liberty. The Treasury, they warned, was corrupting Congress, the army would enslave the people, and interpreting the Constitution broadly would make the federal government all-powerful. Nor did Republican economic ideals anticipate future American development. For the followers of Madison and Jefferson, agriculture—not commerce or manufacturing—was the foundation of American liberty and virtue. Republicans also failed to appreciate the role of financial institutions in promoting economic growth, condemning speculators, bank directors, and holders of the public debt.

Yet the Jeffersonians were more farsighted in matters of equality and personal liberty. Their faith in the people put them in tune with the emerging egalitarian temper of society. They embraced the virtues of individualism, hoping to reduce government to the bare essentials. And they looked to the West—the land of small farms and a more equal society—as the means to preserve opportunity and American values.

## The Presidency of John Adams

As president, John Adams became the head of the Federalists, although in many ways he was out of step with his party. Unlike Hamilton, Adams felt no pressing need to aid the wealthy, nor was he fully committed to Hamilton's commercial-industrial vision. As a revolutionary leader who in the 1780s had served as American minister to England, Adams also opposed any alliance with Britain.

Increasingly, Adams and Hamilton clashed over policies and party leadership. Part of the problem stemmed from personalities. Adams was so thin-skinned that it was difficult for anyone to get along with him, and Hamilton's intrigues in the 1796 election had not improved relations between the two men. Although Hamilton had resigned from the Treasury Department in 1795, key members of Adams's cabinet regularly turned to the former secretary for advice. Indeed, they opposed Adams so often that the frustrated president sometimes dealt with them, according to Jefferson, "by dashing and trampling his wig on the floor."

**NAVAL WAR WITH FRANCE** Adams began his term trying to balance relations with both Great Britain and France. Because the terms of Jay's Treaty were so favorable to the British, the French in retaliation set their navy and privateers to raiding American shipping. To resolve the conflict, Adams dispatched three envoys to France in 1797, but the French foreign minister demanded a bribe before negotiations could even begin. The American representatives refused, and when news of these discussions became public, the situation became known as the XYZ Affair.

In the public's outrage over French bribery, Federalist leaders saw a chance to retain power by going to war. In 1798 Congress repudiated the French alliance of 1778 and enlarged the army and navy. Republicans suspected that the real purpose of the army was not to fight the French army—none existed in North America—but to crush the opposition party and establish a military despotism. All that remained was for Adams to whip up popular feeling and lead the nation into war.

But Adams feared he would become a scapegoat if his policies failed. Furthermore, he distrusted standing armies and preferred the navy as the nation's primary defense. So an unofficial naval war broke out between the United States and France as ships in each navy raided the fleets of the other, while Britain continued to impress American sailors and seize ships suspected of trading with France.

## Suppression at Home

**ALIEN AND SEDITION ACTS** Meanwhile, Federalist leaders attempted to suppress disloyalty at home. In the summer of 1798 Congress passed several measures known together as the Alien and Sedition Acts. The Alien Act authorized the president to arrest and deport aliens suspected of "treasonable" leanings. Although never used, the act directly threatened immigrants who had not yet become citizens, many of whom were prominent Jeffersonians. To limit the number of immigrant voters—again, most of them Republicans—Congress increased the period of residence required to become a **naturalized** citizen from 5 to 14 years. But the most controversial law was the Sedition Act, which established heavy fines and even imprisonment for writing, speaking, or publishing anything of "a false, scandalous and malicious" nature against the government or any officer of the government.

Because of the partisan way it was enforced, the Sedition Act quickly became a symbol of tyranny. Federalists convicted and imprisoned a number of prominent Republican editors, and several Republican papers ceased publication. In all, 25 people were arrested under the law and 10 convicted and imprisoned.

The crisis over the Sedition Act forced Republicans to develop a broader conception of freedom of the press. Previously, most Americans had agreed that newspapers should not be restrained before publication but that they could be punished afterward for sedition. Jefferson and others now argued that the American government was uniquely based on the free expression of public opinion, and thus criticism of the government was not a sign of criminal intent. Only overtly seditious acts, not opinions, should be subject to prosecution. The courts eventually endorsed this view, adopting a new, more absolute view of freedom of speech guaranteed by the First Amendment.

**VIRGINIA AND KENTUCKY RESOLUTIONS** The Republican-controlled legislatures of Virginia and Kentucky each responded to the crisis of 1798 by passing a set of resolutions. Madison secretly wrote those for Virginia, and Jefferson those for Kentucky. These resolutions proclaimed that the Constitution was a compact among sovereign states that delegated strictly limited powers to the federal government. When the government exceeded those limits and threatened the liberties of citizens, states had the right to interpose their authority. In the 1830s the two resolutions would serve as the precedent for state efforts to nullify federal laws.

But Jefferson and Madison were not ready to rend a union that had so recently been forged. The two men intended for the Virginia and Kentucky resolutions only to rally public opinion to the Republican cause. They opposed any effort to resist federal authority by force.

## The Election of 1800

With a naval war raging on the high seas and the Alien and Sedition Acts sparking debate at home, Adams shocked his party by negotiating a peace treaty with France. It was a courageous act, for Adams not only split his party in two but also ruined his own chances for reelection by driving Hamilton's pro-British wing of the party into open opposition. But the nation benefited, as peace returned.

With the Federalist Party split, Republican prospects in 1800 were bright. Again the party chose Jefferson to run against Adams, along with Aaron Burr for vice president. Sweeping to victory, the Republicans won the presidency, as well as control of both houses of Congress for the first time. Yet the election again demonstrated the fragility of the fledgling political system. Jefferson and Burr received an equal number of votes, but the Constitution did not distinguish between the votes for president and vice president. With the election tied, the decision lay with the House of Representatives, where each state was allotted one vote. Because Burr refused to step aside for Jefferson, the election remained deadlocked for almost a week, until the Federalists decided that Jefferson represented the lesser of two evils. They allowed his election on the 36th ballot. In 1804 the Twelfth Amendment corrected the problem, specifying that electors were to vote separately for president and vice president.

## John Marshall and Judicial Review

Having lost both the presidency and control of Congress in 1800, the Federalists took steps to shore up their power before Jefferson took office. They did so by expanding the size of the federal court system, the one branch of the federal government that they still controlled. The Judiciary Act of 1801 created 6 circuit courts and 16 new judgeships. Federalists justified these "midnight appointments" (executed by Adams in the last weeks of his term) on the grounds that the expanding nation required a larger judiciary.

*MARBURY V. MADISON* Among Adams's last-minute appointments was that of William Marbury as justice of the peace for the District of Columbia. When James Madison assumed the office of secretary of state under the new administration, he found a batch of undelivered commissions, including Marbury's. Wishing to appoint loyal Republicans to these posts, Jefferson instructed Madison not to hand over the commissions, whereupon Marbury sued. The case of *Marbury v. Madison* went directly to the Supreme Court in 1803.

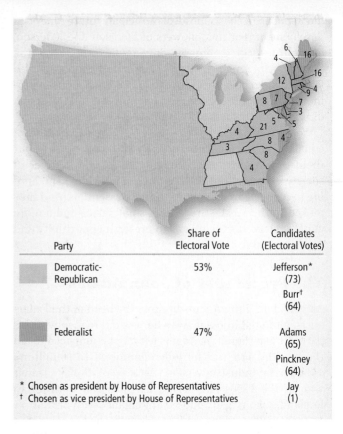

| John Marshall

| Party | Share of Electoral Vote | Candidates (Electoral Votes) |
|---|---|---|
| Democratic-Republican | 53% | Jefferson* (73) |
| | | Burr† (64) |
| Federalist | 47% | Adams (65) |
| | | Pinckney (64) |
| * Chosen as president by House of Representatives | | Jay (1) |
| † Chosen as vice president by House of Representatives | | |

## ELECTION OF 1800

Chief Justice John Marshall, a Federalist and one of Adams's late-term appointments, actually ruled in favor of Madison—but in a way that strengthened the power of the federal courts. Marshall affirmed the right of the Supreme Court to review statutes and interpret the meaning of the Constitution. "It is emphatically the province of and duty of the judicial department to say what the law is," he wrote in upholding the doctrine of **judicial review.** In Marshall's view, the Court "must of necessity expound and interpret" the Constitution and the laws when one statute conflicted with another or when a law violated the framework of the Constitution.

Marshall and his colleagues later asserted the power of the Court to review the constitutionality not only of federal but also of state laws. In fact, during his long tenure as chief justice (over 30 years), John Marshall extended judicial review to all acts of government.

*FEDERALIST ACHIEVEMENTS AND DISAPPOINTMENTS* As John Adams left office, he looked back with mixed feelings on the 12 years that the Federalist Party had held power. Under Washington's firm leadership and his own, his party had made the Constitution a workable instrument of government. The Federalists had proved that a republican form of government was compatible with stability and order. They had established economic policies that brought a return of prosperity. Washington had established the principle of American neutrality in foreign affairs, which became an accepted ideal by both parties for decades to come.

But most Federalists took no solace in such reflections, because the forces of history seemed to be running against them. In the election of 1800 they stood as the champions of order and hierarchy, of government by the wellborn, of a society in which social betters guided their respectful inferiors. They had waged one last desperate battle to save their disintegrating world—and had lost. Power had fallen into the hands of the ignorant rabble, led by that demagogue Thomas Jefferson.

This festive gathering of frontier Pennsylvanians depicted in a painting of 1813 illustrates the access among middle-class Americans to an expanding array of consumer goods. Gone were the sparsely furnished interiors of the colonial era; the owners of this dwelling have purchased a tall clock, a hutch filled with pewter and glassware, a quilting frame, framed pictures, a tea service, even a pet bird. What is the significance of the two African Americans in this scene?

## The Political Culture of the Early Republic

Such extreme views poisoned the political atmosphere of the early republic. Two distinct parties had emerged during the 1790s, but both longed to reestablish a one-party system. Neither Federalists nor Republicans could accept the novel idea that political parties might peacefully resolve differences among competing social, geographic, and economic interests. Instead, each party regarded its opponents as a dangerous faction of ambitious men striving to increase their wealth and power at the expense of republican liberty.

What resulted was a **political culture** marked by verbal and, at times, physical violence. Republicans accused Washington and Hamilton of being British agents and monarchists; Federalists denounced Jefferson as an atheist and his partisans as a pack of "blood-drinking cannibals." The leading Republican newspaper editor in Philadelphia plunged into a street brawl with his Federalist rival; two members of Congress slugged it out on the floor of the House of Representatives. Mobs threatened the leaders of both parties, and at the height of the crisis of 1798–1799, Adams smuggled guns into his home for protection.

The deepening divisions among national leaders also encouraged ordinary Americans to take an interest in politics. Beginning in the 1790s and for decades thereafter, activists in cities and villages everywhere in the new republic organized grand festivals to celebrate American patriotism and the glories of the Republicans or the Federalists. That grassroots movement democratized the conduct of politics by educating men and women, white and black, voters and nonvoters alike, about the issues of the day. In doing so, such activities encouraged strong partisan loyalties.

PARADES AND CELEBRATIONS Holidays such as the Fourth of July or Washington's Birthday became prime occasions for local party leaders to rally their fellow citizens. They hosted celebrations that began with parades in which marchers, hoisting banners to identify their particular trade, militia company, or social club, processed through the main street to a church, meeting hall, or public square. There the assembled throng of marchers and onlookers sang patriotic songs, recited prayers, and listened to the reading of the Declaration of Independence, all capped by a rousing sermon or political oration. Then the party started: in the North, taverns and hotels hosted community banquets; in the South, the crowds flocked to outdoor barbecues. Everywhere the feasts ended with many toasts to the glories of republican liberty and, of course, to the superiority of Federalists or Republicans.

These local celebrations not only made an impact on those who were able to attend the festivities but also reached a wider audience through newspaper accounts. During the 1790s and beyond, the number of local or regional newspapers in the new republic mushroomed, but their coverage was far from objective. Most editors were either staunch Federalists or ardent Republicans who could be counted on to publish glowing accounts of the festivities sponsored by their party and to instruct a much wider audience about party policies and values.

## African American Celebrations

African Americans, too, were drawn to political festivals, but only to discover that party organizers were determined to keep them away. In the years after 1800, bullies often drove black men and women from Fourth of July celebrations with taunts, threats, and assaults. James Forten, a leading citizen of Philadelphia's African American community, complained that because of the hostility of drunken whites, "black people, upon certain days of public jubilee, dare not to be seen" on the streets after noon.

The growing free black population of northern cities countered that opposition by organizing celebrations to express their own political convictions. They established annual holidays to celebrate the abolition of the slave trade in Britain and the United States as well as the successful slave revolt in the Caribbean led by Toussaint L'Ouverture, that resulted in the founding of Haiti in 1804. Those acts of defiance—the spectacle of blacks marching down the main streets with banners flying and bands of music playing, and of black audiences cheering orators who publicly condemned slavery—only inflamed racial hatred and opposition among many whites.

**CALLING FOR FULL CITIZENSHIP** But African Americans continued to press for full citizenship by persuading sympathetic white printers to publish poetry, slave narratives, and pamphlets composed by black authors. The strategy of those writings was to refute racist notions by drawing attention to the intelligence, virtue, and patriotism of black American women and men, both free and enslaved. Typical was the autobiography of Venture Smith, the first slave narrative published in the United States (1798), which followed his captivity as a young boy in West Africa through his lifelong struggle in New England to purchase his own freedom and that of his wife and children. Hardworking and thrifty, resourceful and determined to better himself and his family, Venture Smith's story invited white readers to conclude that he was as true a republican and a self-made man as Benjamin Franklin.

| The artist used watercolor and ink to draw this scene on silk cloth. Young women were no longer being educated merely in the polite arts of dancing, sewing, and embroidery. An increasing number were taking such academic subjects as algebra, history, and geography (note the young woman making measurements on the globe).

# Women's Education and Civic Participation

The new republic's political festivals and partisan newspapers aimed to woo the loyalty of white adult males who held enough property to vote. But they also sought the support of white women, some of whom joined in the crowds and even took part in the parades. In one New Jersey village the folks lining the parade route cheered as "16 young ladies uniformed in white with garlands in their hats" marched past, playing a patriotic anthem on their flutes. Federalists and Republicans alike encouraged women's involvement on those occasions, hoping that displays of approval from "the American Fair" would encourage husbands and male admirers to support their parties.

Many women seized on such opportunities for greater civic involvement. True, the law excluded most from taking direct part in voting and governing, but those prohibitions did not prevent women from taking an active interest in politics and voicing their opinions. When a female guest in a best-selling novel of the 1790s (the first by an American woman) "simpered" that their sex should not meddle with politics, her hostess shot back, "Why then should the love of our country be a masculine passion only? Why should government, which involves the peace and order of society, of which we are a part, be wholly excluded from our observation?"

**WOMEN'S ACADEMIES** What contributed to women's interest in the wider world was the formal education that increasing numbers of elite and middle-class girls received. By the 1790s the number of seminaries and academies for female students was skyrocketing, encouraged by a new ideal of republican motherhood (see Chapter 8). Although the curricula of those schools still included "ornamental" training in dancing, needlework, penmanship, and music, their offerings increasingly emphasized history, geography, geometry, algebra, chemistry, botany, and geology—even Greek and Latin. In the course of this solid academic training, students also spoke at school exhibitions and published school newspapers. Such activities encouraged young women to imagine themselves as independent citizens—not simply as republican mothers. And, after graduation, many women continued to cultivate their intellects in reading circles, literary societies, and mutual improvement associations. Those experiences habituated women to presenting their views before an audience in an articulate and self-possessed manner.

**RISING FEMALE LITERACY** Even young women unable to attend the new academies benefited from access to an increasing number of books and magazines, many of them aimed at a female audience. The new importance of reading to the identity of women appears in a striking number of portraits depicting young girls, middle-aged matrons, and elderly dowagers with books in hand. By 1850,

# CAN THIS MARRIAGE BE SAVED?

*Proponents of providing women with greater educational opportunities—here identified as "The Female Advocate"—often held ideals of marriage that differed dramatically from those embraced by more conservative Americans such as Samuel Jennings, a Methodist minister and the founder of a medical college in Baltimore.*

### DOCUMENT 1    "The Female Advocate" on the Virtues of an Educated Wife

How greatly doth a man of science [knowledge] misjudge in choosing a companion for life, if he selects one from the class of ignorant and untaught, that he may, by this mean, the more securely retain his favorite supremacy. Is it not a total blindness to the ideas of refined happiness, arising from a reciprocity of sentiments and the exchange of rational felicity, as well as an illiberal prejudice, thus to conduct? Shall a woman be kept ignorant, to render her more docile in the management of domestic concerns? How illy capable is such a person of being a companion for a man of refinement? How miserably capable of augmenting his social joys, or managing prudently the concerns of a family, or educating his children? Is it not of the utmost consequence, that the tender mind of the youth receive an early direction for future usefulness? And is it not equally true, that the first direction of a child

necessarily becomes the immediate and peculiar province of the woman? And may I not add, is not a woman of capacious and well stored mind, a better wife, a better widow, a better mother, and a better neighbor; and shall I add, a better friend in every respect. . . .

When women, no longer the humble dependent, or the obsequious slave, but the companion and friend, is party to an attachment founded on mutual esteem, then, and not till then, does man assume his intended rank in the scale of creation. . . .

Suppose one who has from her youth been indoctrinated and habituated to sentiments of female inferiority, one who has never been suffered to have an opinion of her own, but on the reverse, has been taught, and accustomed to rely, and implicitly believe, right or wrong, on her parents, guardians, or husband. What will be the

consequence of this, in a situation when deprived of the counsel of either or all of them, she is necessitated to act for herself, or be exposed to the fraudulence of an unfriendly world? Perhaps she is left a widow with a large property and a flock of small dependent children? But where have they to look for protection, or on whom to rely, but on their insufficient, helpless mother? How poorly capable is she to fill the vacancy, and act to her tender babes and orphans, in their bereaved situation, as is absolutely necessary, both father and mother? How incapable also is she of assisting in the settlement and adjustment of the estate; how liable to fraud, and how probable to be injured by unreal or exaggerated debts.

*Source: The Female Advocate, Written by a Lady (New Haven, Conn., 1801).*

### DOCUMENT 2    Samuel K. Jennings on the Virtues of a Submissive Wife

As it is your great wish and interest, to enjoy much of your husband's company and conversation, it will be important to acquaint yourself with his temper, his inclination, and his manner, that you may render your house, your person, and your disposition quite agreeable to him. . . .

Your choice in forming the connexion [marriage], was at best a passive one. Could you have acted the part of a courtier and made choice of a man whose disposition might have corresponded precisely with yours, there would have been less to do afterwards. But under present circumstances, it is your interest to adapt yourself to your husband, whatever may be his peculiarities. Again, nature has made man the stronger, the consent of mankind has given him superiority over his wife, his inclination is, to claim his natural and acquired rights. He

of course expects from you a degree of condescension, and he feels himself the more confident of the propriety of his claim, when he is formed, that St. Paul adds to his authority its support. "Wives submit to your own husbands, as unto the Lord, for the husband is the head of his wife."

In obedience then to this precept of the gospel, to the laws of custom and of nature, you ought to cultivate a cheerful and happy submission. . . .

Do not suppose, that my plan implies that the husband has nothing to do. So far from this he is bound "To love and cherish his wife, as his own flesh." But I repeat, this obligation seems, in a great degree, to rest on the condition of a loving and cheerful submission on the part of the wife. Here again perhaps you object and say, "Why not the husband, first shew a

little condescension as well as the wife?" I answer for these plain reasons. It is not his disposition; it is not the custom but with the henpecked; it is not his duty; it is not implied in the marriage contract; it is not required by law or the gospel.

*Source: Samuel K. Jennings, The Married Lady's Companion, or Poor Man's Friend (revised 2nd ed., New York, 1808).*

### *Thinking Critically*

*How did "The Female Advocate" advise men to choose their wives? How to behave as husbands? Why did she believe that her advice served the best interests of men? On what grounds did Samuel Jennings argue that women should submit to their husbands?*

for the first time in American history, there were as many literate women as there were men.

 **REVIEW**
What fostered the intense political loyalties of the 1790s?

# THE REPUBLICANS IN POWER

THE GROWING POLITICAL ENGAGEMENT OF ordinary white Americans played an important role in electing Thomas Jefferson to the presidency. He later referred to his election as "the Revolution of 1800," asserting that it "was as real a revolution in the principles of our government as that of 1776 was in its form." That claim exaggerates: Jefferson's presidency did little to enhance political rights or social opportunities of white women or African Americans. Even so, during the following two decades Republicans did set the United States on a more democratic course. And in their dealings with Britain and France, as well as with the Indian tribes of the West, Republican administrations defined, for better and worse, a fuller sense of American nationality.

## The New Capital City

Thomas Jefferson was the first president to be inaugurated in the new capital, Washington, D.C. In 1791 George Washington had commissioned Pierre Charles L'Enfant, a French architect and engineer who had served in the American Revolution, to draw up plans for the new seat of government. L'Enfant designed a city with broad avenues, statues and fountains, parks and plazas, and a central mall. Because the Federalists believed that government was the paramount power in a nation, they had intended that the city would be a new Rome—a cultural, intellectual, and commercial center of the Republic.

The new city fell far short of this grandiose dream. It was located in a swampy river bottom near the head of the Potomac, and the surrounding hills rendered the spot oppressively hot and muggy during the summer. The streets were filled with tree stumps and became seas of mud after a rain. Much of the District was wooded, and virtually all of it remained unoccupied. When the government moved to its new residence in 1800, the Senate chamber, where Jefferson took the oath of office, was the only part of the Capitol that had been completed.

This isolated and unimpressive capital reflected the new president's attitude toward government. Distrustful of centralized power of any kind, Jefferson deliberately set out to remake the national government into one of limited scope that touched few people's daily lives. The states rather than the federal government were "the most competent administrators for our domestic concerns," he asserted in his inaugural address. Ever the individualist, he recommended a government that left people "free to regulate their own pursuits of industry and improvement."

## Jefferson's Philosophy

Jefferson was a product of the Enlightenment, with its faith in the power of human reason to improve society and decipher the universe. He considered "the will of the majority" to be "the only sure guardian of the rights of man," which he defined as "life, liberty, and the pursuit of happiness." Although he conceded that the masses might err, he was confident they would soon return to correct principles. His faith in human virtue exceeded that of most of the founding generation, yet in good republican fashion, he feared those in power, even if they had been elected by the people. Government seemed to Jefferson a necessary evil at best.

**AGRARIAN VALUES** To Jefferson, agriculture was a morally superior way of life. "Those who labour in the earth are the chosen people of God, if ever he had a chosen people," he wrote in *Notes on the State of Virginia* (1787). Jefferson praised rural life for nourishing the honesty, independence, and virtue so essential in a republic.

Although Jefferson asserted that "the tree of liberty must be refreshed from time to time by the blood of patriots and tyrants," his reputation as a radical was undeserved. While he wanted to extend the suffrage to a greater number of Americans, he clung to the traditional republican idea that voters should own property and thus be economically independent. One of the largest slaveholders in the country, he increasingly muffled his once-bold condemnation of slavery, and in the last years of his life he reproached critics of the institution who sought to prevent it from expanding westward.

Slaveholding aristocrat and apostle of democracy, lofty theorist and pragmatic politician, Jefferson was a complex, at times contradictory, personality. But like most politicians, he was flexible in his approach to problems and tried to balance means and ends. And like most leaders, he quickly discovered that he confronted very different problems in power than he had in opposition.

## Jefferson's Economic Policies

The new president quickly proceeded to cut spending and to reduce the size of the government. He also abolished the internal taxes enacted by the Federalists, including the controversial excise on whiskey, and thus was able to get rid of all tax collectors and inspectors. Land sales and the tariff duties would supply the funds needed to run the scaled-down government.

The most serious spending cuts were made in the military branches. Jefferson slashed the army budget in half, decreasing the army to 3,000 men. In a national emergency, he reasoned, the militia could defend the country. Jefferson reduced the navy even more, halting work on powerful frigates authorized during the naval war with France.

**COMING TO ACCEPT HAMILTON'S POLICIES** By such steps, Jefferson made significant progress toward paying off Hamilton's national debt. Still, he did not entirely dismantle the Federalists' economic program. Funding and assumption could not be reversed—the nation's honor was pledged to paying these debts, and Jefferson understood the importance of maintaining the nation's credit. More surprising, Jefferson argued that the national bank should be left to run its course until 1811, when its charter would expire. In reality, he expanded the bank's operations and, in words reminiscent of Hamilton, advocated tying banks and members of the business class to the government by rewarding those who supported the Republican Party. In effect, practical politics had triumphed over agrarian economics.

## The Miami Confederacy Resists

For all his pragmatism, Jefferson still viewed the lands stretching from the Appalachians to the Pacific through the perspective of his agrarian ideals. America's vast spaces provided enough land to last for a thousand generations, he predicted in his inaugural address, enough to transform the United States into "an empire of liberty."

That optimistic vision contrasted sharply with the views of most Federalists, who feared the West as a threat to social order and stability. In the 1790s they had good reason to fear. British troops refused to leave their forts in the Northwest, and Indian nations still controlled most of the region. Recognizing that fact, the United States conceded that Indian nations had the right to negotiate as sovereign powers. North of the Ohio, leaders of the Miami Confederacy, composed of eight tribes, stoutly refused to sell their homelands without "the united voice of the confederacy."

**VICTORIES OF LITTLE TURTLE AND BLUE JACKET** In response the Washington administration sent 1,500 soldiers in 1790 under General Josiah Harmar to force the Indians to leave by burning their homes and fields. The Miami Confederacy, led by Blue Jacket and Little Turtle, roundly defeated the whites. Harmar was court-martialed, the nation embarrassed, and a second expedition organized the following year under General Arthur St. Clair. This force of over 2,000 was again routed by Little Turtle, whose warriors killed 600 and wounded another 300. The defeat was the worst in the history of Indian wars undertaken by the United States. (In contrast, Custer's defeat in 1876 counted 264 fatalities.)

**TREATY OF GREENVILLE** President Washington dispatched yet another army of 2,000 to the Ohio valley, commanded by "Mad Anthony" Wayne, an accomplished general. At the Battle of Fallen Timbers in August 1794, Wayne won a decisive victory, breaking the Indians' hold on the Northwest. In the Treaty of Greenville (1795), the tribes **ceded** the southern two-thirds of the area between Lake Erie and the Ohio River, opening it up to white families. Federalists were still not eager to see the land settled. Although they allowed the sale of federal land, they kept the price high, with a required purchase of at least 640 acres—more than four times the size of most American farms.

Once in power, Jefferson and the Republicans encouraged settlement by reducing the minimum tract that buyers could purchase (to 320 acres) and by offering land on credit. Sales boomed. By 1820 more than 2 million whites lived in a region they had first entered only 50 years earlier. From Jefferson's perspective, western expansion was a blessing economically, socially, and even politically, because most of the new westerners were Republican.

## Doubling the Size of the Nation

**LOUISIANA PURCHASE** With Spain's colonial empire weakening, Americans were confident that before long they would gain control of Florida and the rest of the Mississippi, either through purchase or by military occupation. Spain had already agreed, in Pinckney's Treaty (see page 196), to allow Americans to navigate the lower Mississippi River. But in 1802 Spain suddenly retracted this right. More alarming, word came that France was about to take control of Louisiana—the territory lying between the Mississippi River and the Rocky Mountains—after a secret agreement with Spain. Under the leadership of Napoleon Bonaparte, France had become the most powerful nation on the European continent, with the military might to protect its new colony and to block American expansion.

Jefferson dispatched James Monroe to Paris to join Robert Livingston, the American minister, in negotiating the purchase of New Orleans and West Florida from the French and thus securing control of the Mississippi. The timing was fortunate: with war looming again in Europe, Napoleon lost interest in Louisiana. He needed money, and in April 1803 he offered to sell not just New Orleans but all of Louisiana to the United States. This proposal flabbergasted Livingston and Monroe. Their instructions said nothing about acquiring all of Louisiana, and they had not been authorized to spend what the French demanded. But here was an opportunity to expand dramatically the boundaries of the United States. Pressed for an immediate answer, Livingston and Monroe took a deep breath and, after haggling over a few details, agreed to purchase Louisiana for approximately $15 million. In one fell swoop, the American negotiators had doubled the country's size by adding some 830,000 square miles.

While Jefferson was pleased at the prospect of acquiring so much territory, he found the legality of the act troubling. The Constitution, after all, did not authorize the acquisition of territory by treaty. In the end, the president sent the treaty to the Senate for ratification, noting privately, "The less we say about constitutional difficulties the better." Once again pragmatism triumphed over theory.

**LEWIS AND CLARK** Even before the Louisiana Purchase was completed, Congress secretly funded an expedition up the Missouri River to the Pacific. Leading that party were Meriwether Lewis, Jefferson's secretary, and William Clark, a younger brother of George Rogers Clark. Jefferson instructed them to make detailed

## EXPLORATION AND EXPANSION: THE LOUISIANA PURCHASE

*The vast, largely uncharted Louisiana Purchase lay well beyond the most densely populated areas of the United States. The Lewis and Clark expedition, along with Lieutenant Zebulon Pike's exploration of the upper Mississippi River and the Southwest, opened the way for westward expansion.* **What geographic factors helped to determine Lewis and Clark's route across North America?**

observations of the soil, climate, rivers, minerals, and plant and animal life. They were also to investigate the practicability of an overland route to the Pacific and engage in diplomacy with the Indians along the way. By pushing onward to the Pacific, Lewis and Clark would strengthen the American title to Oregon, which several nations claimed but none effectively occupied.

In the spring of 1804 Lewis and Clark left St. Louis and headed up the Missouri River with 48 men. They laboriously hauled their boats upstream to present-day North Dakota, where they spent the winter with the Mandan Indians. The next spring, they headed west again. Only with great difficulty did the expedition pass the rugged mountains ahead of the winter snows and then float down first the Snake and then the Columbia River to the Pacific.

**A LAND TRANSFORMED BY CHANGE** The western country Lewis and Clark traversed had been shaken by momentous changes over the previous quarter of a century. The trade routes across the plains and through the mountains circulated goods in greater quantities than ever before. Horses and guns in particular upset older Indian ways, making tribes more mobile and more dangerous. Lewis and Clark's expedition

spotted Spanish horse gear from Mexico in villages along the upper Missouri River, guns from French traders to the northeast, and British teapots along the Columbia River. In one example of these trading networks at work, members of Lewis and Clark's expedition sold war hatchets to Indians during their winter stay at Fort Mandan. The expedition ran into the same hatchets the following summer in distant Idaho, the trade goods having made their trip across the plains faster than the expedition.

Most disruptive to these western lands was smallpox, which had made its way along the same trade routes ever since the pandemic of the 1780s (see Chapter 7). The disease decimated Indian populations and forced many tribes to resettle. The Arikaras, who before 1780 had numbered perhaps 24,000, had dwindled to about 2,000 by the time Lewis and Clark passed through. Portions of tribes to the east had migrated westward, including the Delawares, Shawnees, Miamis, Chickasaws, and Cherokees. Captain Clark, who was present when the Treaty of Greenville was signed in 1795, discovered a Delaware chief he had seen there, along the Missouri, 500 miles west of his earlier home.

After a bleak winter in Oregon, the expedition returned home over the Rockies in 1806. It brought back thousands of plant and animal specimens and produced a remarkably accurate map of its journey. Lewis and Clark had crossed a continent disrupted by change. In the century to come the changes would only accelerate.

## Pressure on Indian Lands and Culture

East of the Mississippi, white settlers continued to flood into the backcountry. Jefferson endorsed the policy that Indian tribes either would have to assimilate into American culture by becoming farmers and abandoning their semi-nomadic hunting or would have to move west. Jefferson defended these alternatives as in the best interests of the Indians, because he believed that otherwise they faced extermination. But he also recognized that by becoming farmers they would need less land. He encouraged the policy of selling goods on credit in order to lure Indians into debt. "When these debts get beyond what the individuals can pay," the president observed, "they become willing to lop them off by a cession of lands."

Between 1800 and 1810, whites pressed Indians into ceding more than 100 million acres in the Ohio River valley. The loss of so much land devastated Indian cultures and transformed their environment by reducing hunting grounds and making game and food scarce. "Stop your people from killing our game," the Shawnees complained in 1802 to federal Indian agents. "They would be angry if we were to kill a cow or hog of theirs, the little game that remains is very dear to us." Tribes also became dependent on white trade to obtain blankets, guns, metal utensils, alcohol, and decorative beads. To pay for these goods with furs, Indians often overtrapped, which forced them to invade the lands of neighboring tribes, provoking wars.

The strain produced by white expansion led to alcoholism, growing violence among tribe members, family disintegration, and the collapse of the clan system designed to regulate relations among different villages. The question of how to deal with white culture became a matter of anguished debate. Although some Native Americans attempted to take up farming and accommodate to white ways, for most the course of assimilation proved unappealing and fraught with risk.

## White Frontier Society

Whites faced their own problems on the frontier. In the first wave of settlement came backwoods families who cleared a few acres of forest by girdling the trees, removing the brush, and planting corn between the dead trunks. Such settlers were mostly squatters without legal title to their land. As a region filled up, these pioneers usually sold their improvements and headed west again.

| The Prophet

Taking their place, typically, were young single men from the East, who married and started families. These pioneers, too, engaged in semisubsistence agriculture, save for the lucky few whose prime locations allowed them to transport their crops down the Ohio and Mississippi Rivers to New Orleans for shipment to distant markets. But many frontier families struggled, moving several times but never managing to rise from the ranks of squatters or tenant farmers to become independent landowners. Fledgling western communities lacked schools, churches, and courts, and inhabitants often lived miles distant from even their nearest neighbors.

## The Beginnings of the Second Great Awakening

This hardscrabble frontier proved the perfect tinder for sparking a series of dramatic religious revivals in the decades surrounding 1800. What lit the fire were missionary efforts by major Protestant churches—particularly the Baptists and the Methodists—who sent their ministers to travel the countryside on horseback and to preach wherever they could gather a crowd. Often those religious meetings took place outdoors and drew eager hearers from as far as 100 miles away, who camped for several days in makeshift tents to listen to sermons and to share in praying and singing hymns.

CANE RIDGE    Thus was born a new form of Protestant worship, the camp meeting, which drew national notice after a mammoth gathering at Cane Ridge, Kentucky, in August of 1801. At a time when the largest city in the state had only 2,000 people, more than 10,000 men, women, and children, white and black, flocked there to hear dozens of ministers preaching the gospel. Many in the crowd were overwhelmed by powerful religious feelings, some shrieking and shaking over guilt for their sins, others laughing and dancing from their high hopes of eternal salvation.

Some Protestant ministers denounced the "revival" at Cane Ridge and elsewhere as yet another instance of the ignorance and savagery of westerners. Other ministers were more optimistic: they saw frontier camp meetings as the first sign of a Protestant Christian renewal that would sweep the new republic. Their hopes set the stage for what would come to be called the Second Great Awakening, a wave of religious revivals that swept throughout the nation after 1800 (see Chapter 12).

## The Prophet, Tecumseh, and the Pan-Indian Movement

Native peoples also turned to religion to meet the challenges of the early national frontier. Indeed, in traditional Indian religions, they found the resource to revitalize their cultures by severing all ties with the white

## THE FRONTIER CAMP MEETING

The Cane Ridge revival, one of the earliest along the frontier, was a chaotic, disorganized affair. But as western clergy became more experienced with outdoor camp meetings, they standardized the format. About a week in advance, organizers chose a forest clearing, removed nearby underbrush, erected pulpits, and constructed benches. Usually the camp went up near an established church, which provided lodging for the ministers. Since a water supply was essential, camps were located near springs, creeks, or rivers. A good site needed dry ground, shade so worshipers could escape the blazing sun, and pasturage for the horses.

The tents of the worshipers formed a ring around the outdoor auditorium where services were held. At large meetings as many as 200 tents were set up in rows with streets in between to allow easy access. To help people find their lodgings, the streets were sometimes even named. This outer perimeter constituted the meeting's private space. Here, beneath tents of sailcloth or even shelters patched together from old blankets and sheets, individuals could withdraw from the larger group to find relative solitude, cook meals in front of campfires, and sleep on rude beds of straw or simply on the ground.

Worshipers filled bench after bench in the central public space at the periodic call of a bugle. Rising above the listeners stood the preachers' pulpit. Sometimes it was merely a 10-foot-square platform on stilts; other times it was more elaborate, with several levels and a roof. Services were held in the open, and neither rain nor thunderstorms would interrupt them. At night, the dancing light and shadows produced by the candles, torches, campfires, and fire altars heightened the feeling of awe.

The democracy of the frontier did not automatically break down customary social constraints. For reasons of authority as well as practicality, the ministers' pulpit rose above the congregation. And the audience itself was segregated: women on one side of the clearing, men on the other. In the South black worshipers were seated in an area behind the pulpit, where they set up their own camp and conducted separate services.

Since the purpose of camp meetings was to "revive" religion and stir listeners'

Tents ringed the central area of a camp meeting where benches faced the preachers' platform. What does this illustration of an 1837 camp meeting suggest about gender relations and religious experience?

hearts, several rows of planks were set aside directly in front of the pulpit as an "anxious bench," for those whose souls struggled in the agony of conversion. The design of the space thus focused the attention of both congregation and ministers on the "mourners," who were prayed over in hopes that they would receive a new birth in Christ.

But the social boundaries between public and private, male and female, and even black and white could be broken down. As excitement grew, several services might be held at once, some people praying, others singing, shouting, or listening to ministers who stood on wagons. And when formal services ended, men and women often continued in small groups, searching one another's souls by campfires late into the night. Indeed, the spontaneous excitement was great enough that meeting sponsors quickly learned that supervision was necessary to prevent unseemly activities. The nearby forest and the numerous tents at nightfall all

offered temptations for drinking, carousing, or lovemaking. Official patrols regularly investigated suspicious activities.

On the final day, white and black worshipers joined in a singing and marching festival before disbanding to their humdrum daily routines. Successful camp meetings depended on more than the talents of the clergy and the enthusiasm of participants. In their layout they were carefully planned and regulated communities in the forest, designed to reduce the distance between public and private space and thereby instill a sense of religion into all the activities that took place in the meeting as well as those that would be resumed in the regular world.

### Thinking Critically

Why does this portrayal of a camp meeting focus on the emotional responses of women?

## THE INDIAN RESPONSE TO WHITE ENCROACHMENT

*With land cessions and white western migration placing increased pressure on Indian cultures after 1790, news of the Prophet's revival fell on eager ears. It spread especially quickly northward along the shores of Lake Michigan and westward along Lake Superior and the interior of Wisconsin. Following the Battle of Tippecanoe, Tecumseh eclipsed the Prophet as the major leader of Indian resistance, but his trips south to forge political alliances met with less success.* **How far south did Tecumseh travel in his attempt to unite Indian resistance?**

world. During the 1790s a revival led by Handsome Lake took hold among the Iroquois, following the loss of most of the Iroquois lands and the collapse of their military power in western New York. Later, Lalawethika, also known as the Prophet, sparked a religious renewal among the Shawnees. The Prophet's early life was bleak: he was a poor hunter and as a child accidentally blinded himself in the right eye with an arrow; the ridicule of his fellow tribe members drove him to alcoholism. Suddenly, in April 1805 he lapsed into a trance so deep that he was given up for dead. When he revived he spoke of being reborn. From this vision and others he outlined a new creed for the Shawnees.

**INDEPENDENCE FROM WHITE SOCIETY**

Taking a new name—Tenskwatawa (Open Door)—the Prophet urged the Shawnees to renounce whiskey and white goods and return to their old ways of hunting with bows and arrows, eating customary foods such as corn and beans, and wearing traditional garb. The Shawnees could revitalize their culture, he insisted, by condemning intertribal violence, embracing monogamous marriage, and rejecting the idea of private instead of communal property. Except for guns, which could be used in self-defense, his followers were to discard all items made by whites. Intermarriage with white settlers was forbidden.

Setting up headquarters in 1808 at the newly built village of Prophetstown in Indiana, Tenskwatawa led a wider revival among the tribes of the Northwest. Just as thousands of white settlers traveled to Methodist or Baptist camp meetings in the woods, where preachers denounced the evils of liquor and called for a return to a purer way of life, so thousands of Indians from northern tribes traveled to the Prophet's village for inspiration. Many were concerned about the threatened loss of Indian lands.

**TECUMSEH'S POLITICAL STRATEGY** Whereas Tenskwatawa's strategy of revitalization was primarily religious, his older brother Tecumseh turned to political and military solutions. William Henry Harrison described Tecumseh as "one of those uncommon geniuses which spring up occasionally to produce revolutions and overturn the established order of things." Tall and athletic, an accomplished hunter and warrior, Tecumseh traveled throughout the Northwest, urging tribes to forget ancient rivalries and unite to protect their lands. Just as Indian nations in the past had adopted the strategy of uniting in a confederacy, Tecumseh's alliance brought together the Wyandot, Chippewa, Sauk and Fox, Winnebago, Potawatomi, and other tribes on an even larger scale.

**OBSTACLES TO A CONFEDERACY** But the campaign for pan-Indian unity ran into serious obstacles. Often, Tecumseh was asking tribes to unite with their traditional enemies in a common cause. When he headed south in 1811, he encountered greater resistance. Most southern tribes were more prosperous, were more acculturated, and felt less immediate pressure on their land from whites. His southern mission ended largely in failure.

To compound Tecumseh's problems, while he was away a force of Americans under Governor Harrison defeated the Prophet's forces at the Battle of Tippecanoe in November 1811 and destroyed Prophetstown. As a result, Tecumseh became convinced that the best way to contain white expansion was to play off the Americans against the British, who still held forts in the Great Lakes region. Indeed, by 1811, the United States and Great Britain were on the brink of war.

 **REVIEW**

How did Jefferson's presidency shape the settlement of the West?

# THE SECOND WAR FOR AMERICAN INDEPENDENCE

AS TECUMSEH WORKED TO ACHIEVE a pan-Indian alliance, Jefferson encountered his own difficulties in trying to achieve American political unity. The president hoped to woo all but the most extreme Federalists into the Republican camp. His reelection in 1804 showed how much progress he had made, as he defeated Federalist Charles Cotesworth Pinckney and carried 15 of 17 states. With the Republicans controlling three-quarters of the seats in Congress, one-party rule seemed at hand.

**WAR BETWEEN BRITAIN AND FRANCE** But events across the Atlantic complicated the efforts to unite Americans. Only two weeks after Napoleon agreed to sell Louisiana to the United States, war broke out between France and Great Britain. As in the 1790s the United States found itself caught between the world's two greatest powers. Jefferson insisted that the nation should remain neutral in a European war. But the policies he proposed to maintain neutrality sparked sharp divisions in American society and momentarily revived the two-party system.

 **THE BARBARY PIRATES** In the past, Jefferson had not shrunk from the use of force in dealing with foreign nations—most notably the Barbary States of North Africa—Algiers, Morocco, Tripoli, and Tunis. During the seventeenth and eighteenth centuries their corsairs plundered the cargo of enemy ships and enslaved the crews. European nations found it convenient to pay tributes to the Barbary States so that their ships could sail unmolested. But both Jefferson and John Adams disliked that idea. The "policy of Christendom" of paying tribute, complained Adams, "has made Cowards of all their Sailors before the Standard of Mahomet [Mohammed]."

By the time John Adams became president, he had subdued his outrage and agreed to tributes. But when Tripoli increased its demands in 1801, President Jefferson sent a squadron of American ships to force a settlement. In 1803 Tripoli captured the U.S.S. *Philadelphia*. Only the following year did Lieutenant Stephen Decatur repair the situation by sneaking into Tripoli's harbor and burning the vessel. The American blockade that followed forced Tripoli to give up its demands for tribute. Even so, the United States continued paying tribute to the other Barbary states until 1816.

## The Embargo

Jefferson was willing to fight the Barbary States, but he drew back from declaring war against Britain or France. Between 1803 and 1807, Britain seized more than 500 American ships; France more than 300. The British navy also impressed into service thousands of sailors, some of whom were deserters from England's fleet but others, native-born Americans. Despite such harassment, Jefferson pursued a program of "peaceable coercion" designed to protect neutral rights without war. His proposed **embargo** not only prohibited American ships from trading with foreign ports but also stopped the export of all American goods. The president was confident that American exports were so essential to the two belligerents that they would quickly agree to respect American neutral rights. In December 1807 Congress passed the Embargo Act.

Jefferson had seriously miscalculated. France did not depend on American trade and so managed well enough, while British ships quickly took over the carrying trade as American vessels lay idle. Under the embargo, both

*The young United States, like many European powers, found its trading vessels challenged by the Barbary states of Morocco, Algiers, Tunisia, and Tripoli. When the pasha of Tripoli declared war on the United States in 1801, Jefferson dispatched a force that blockaded Tripoli to bring the war to an end in 1805. Tribute paid to the other Barbary States continued until 1816, after a new naval force, led by Captain Stephen Decatur, forced the ruler of Algiers to end the practice.*

American imports and exports plunged. As the center of American shipping, New England port cities protested the loudest, and their merchants smuggled behind officials' backs.

## Madison and the Young Republicans

Following Washington's example, Jefferson did not seek a third term. A caucus of Republican members of Congress selected James Madison to run against Federalist Charles Cotesworth Pinckney. Madison triumphed easily, although in discontented New England, the Federalists picked up 24 seats in Congress.

**MADISON'S CHARACTER** Few men have assumed the presidency with more experience than James Madison, yet his tenure as president proved disappointing. Despite his intellectual brilliance, he lacked the force of leadership and the inner strength to impose his will on less capable men.

**WAR HAWKS** With a president reluctant to fight for what he wanted, leadership passed to Congress. The elections of 1810 swept in a new generation of Republicans, led by the magnetic 34-year-old Henry Clay of Kentucky, who gained the rare distinction of being elected Speaker of the House in his first term. These younger Republicans were more nationalistic than the generation

led by Jefferson and Madison. They sought an ambitious program of economic development and were aggressive expansionists, especially those from frontier districts. Their willingness to go to war earned them the name of War Hawks. Though they numbered fewer than 30 in Congress, they quickly became the driving force in the Republican Party.

## The Decision for War

**REPEAL OF THE EMBARGO** During Jefferson's final week in office in early 1809, Congress repealed the Embargo Act. The following year Congress authorized trade with France and England but decreed that if one of the two belligerents agreed to stop interfering with American shipping, trade with the other would be prohibited.

Given these circumstances, Napoleon outmaneuvered the British by announcing that he would put aside the French trade regulations. Madison took the French emperor at his word and reimposed a ban on trade with England. French raiders continued to seize American ships, but American anger focused on the British, who then seized many more ships and continued to impress American sailors. Finally, on June 16, 1812, the British ministry suspended the searches and seizures of American ships.

## THE WAR OF 1812

*After the American victory on Lake Erie and the defeat of the western Indians at the Battle of the Thames, the British adopted a three-pronged strategy to invade the United States, climaxing with an attempt on New Orleans. But they met their match in Andrew Jackson, whose troops marched to New Orleans after fighting a series of battles against the Creeks and forcing them to cede a massive tract of land.*

The concession came too late. Two days earlier, unaware of the change in policy, Congress granted Madison's request for a declaration of war against Britain. The vote was mostly along party lines, with every Federalist voting against war. By contrast, members of Congress from the South and the West clamored most strongly for war. Their constituents were consumed with a desire to seize additional territory in Canada or in Florida (owned by Britain's ally Spain). In addition, they accused the British of stirring up hostility among the Indian tribes.

Perhaps most important, the War Hawks were convinced that Britain had never truly accepted the verdict of the American Revolution. To them, American independence—

and with it republicanism—hung in the balance. For Americans hungering to be accepted in the community of nations, nothing rankled more than still being treated by the British as colonials.

With Britain preoccupied by Napoleon, the War Hawks expected an easy victory. In truth, the United States was totally unprepared for war. Crippled by Jefferson's cutbacks, the navy was unable to lift the British blockade of the American coast, which bottled up the country's merchant marine and most of its navy. As for the U.S. Army, it was small and poorly led. When Congress moved to increase its size to 75,000, even the most hawkish states failed to meet their quotas. Congress was also reluctant to levy taxes to finance the war.

A three-pronged American invasion of Canada from Detroit, Niagara, and Lake Champlain failed dismally in 1812. Americans fared better the following year, as both sides raced to build a navy on the strategically located Lake Erie. Led by Commander Oliver Hazard Perry, American forces won a decisive victory at Put-In Bay in 1813.

As the United States struggled to organize its forces, Tecumseh sensed that his long-awaited opportunity had come to drive Americans out of the western territories. "Here is a chance . . . such as will never occur again," he told a war council, "for us Indians of North America to form ourselves into one great combination." Allying with the British, Tecumseh traveled south in the fall to talk again with his Creek allies. To coordinate an Indian offensive for the following summer, he left a bundle of red sticks with eager Creek soldiers. They were to remove one stick each day from the bundle and attack when the sticks had run out.

**JACKSON DEFEATS THE CREEK INDIANS**

Some of the older Creeks were more acculturated and preferred an American alliance. But about 2,000 younger "Red Stick" Creeks launched a series of attacks, climaxed by the destruction of Fort Mims along the Alabama River in August 1813. Once again, the Indians' lack of unity was a serious handicap, as warriors from the Cherokee, Choctaw, and Chickasaw tribes, traditional Creek enemies, allied with the Americans. At the Battle of Horseshoe Bend in March 1814, General Andrew Jackson and his Tennessee militia soundly defeated the Red Stick Creeks. Jackson promptly dictated a peace treaty under which the Creeks ceded 22 million acres of land in the Mississippi Territory. They and the other southern tribes still retained significant landholdings, but Indian military power had been broken in the South, east of the Mississippi.

**DEATH OF TECUMSEH**

Farther north, in October 1813, American forces under General William Henry Harrison defeated the British and their Indian allies at the Battle of the Thames. In the midst of heavy fighting Tecumseh was killed. With him died any hope of a pan-Indian movement.

## The British Invasion

As long as the war against Napoleon continued, the British were unwilling to divert army units to North America. But in 1814 Napoleon was at last defeated. Free to concentrate on America, the British devised a coordinated strategy to invade the United States in the northern, central, and

After Andrew Jackson's victory at New Orleans, the Hartford Convention looked to many like a traitorous leap into the arms of the British king.

## REMEMBERING LAFAYETTE

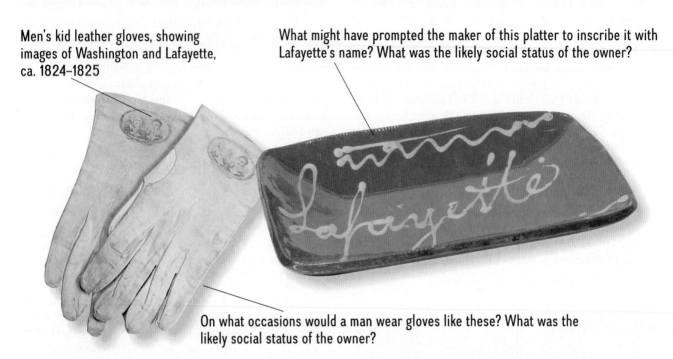

Men's kid leather gloves, showing images of Washington and Lafayette, ca. 1824–1825

What might have prompted the maker of this platter to inscribe it with Lafayette's name? What was the likely social status of the owner?

On what occasions would a man wear gloves like these? What was the likely social status of the owner?

Events that were commemorated even as they unfolded hold a special fascination for historians. Just as the celebration of Franklin's arrival in Paris tells us much about the French in the 1770s, the hoopla in the United States over the return of the Marquis de Lafayette reveals a great deal about early national Americans. A major general in the Continental Army, a comrade-in-arms of Washington, and a lifelong defender of liberal values and human rights, Lafayette made his second voyage from France to the United States in 1824 at the invitation of President James Monroe. A triumphal 13-month tour of all 24 states followed, the Marquis traveling by stagecoach and steamboat and drawing crowds that numbered in the tens of thousands. While only a lucky few Americans basked in the 67-year-old hero's presence at dinners and balls, nearly all could afford to purchase one of the souvenirs produced by artisans of both humble and fine crafts.

*Thinking Critically*

*Consider the challenges confronting President Monroe's administration. What might he have hoped to accomplish by inviting Lafayette to the United States? What do the two objects suggest about Lafayette's popularity as a public figure?*

---

southern parts of the country. The main army headed south from Montreal but was checked when Americans destroyed the British fleet on Lake Champlain.

Meanwhile, a smaller British force captured Washington and burned several public buildings, including the Capitol and the president's home. To cover the scars of this destruction, the executive mansion was painted with whitewash and became known as the White House. The burning of the capital was a humiliating event: President Madison and his wife, Dolley, were forced to flee. But the defeat had little military significance. The principal British objective was Baltimore, where for 25 hours their fleet bombarded

Fort McHenry in the city's harbor. When Francis Scott Key saw the American flag still flying above the fort at dawn, he hurriedly composed the verses of "The Star Spangled Banner," which was eventually adopted as the national anthem.

The third British target was New Orleans, where a formidable army of 7,500 British troops was opposed by a hastily assembled force commanded by Major General Andrew Jackson. The Americans included regular soldiers; frontiersmen from Kentucky and Tennessee; citizens of New Orleans, including several companies of free African Americans; Choctaw Indians; and a group of pirates. Jackson's outnumbered and ill-equipped forces won a stunning victory, which made the general an overnight hero.

**HARTFORD CONVENTION**

In December 1814, while Jackson was organizing the defense of New Orleans, New England Federalists met in Hartford to map strategy against the war. Angry as they were, the delegates still rejected calls for secession. Instead, they proposed a series of amendments to the Constitution that showed their displeasure with the government's economic policies and their resentment of the South's national political power.

**JACKSON'S VICTORY AT NEW ORLEANS**

To the convention's dismay, its representatives arrived in Washington to present their demands just as news of Andrew Jackson's victory was being trumpeted on the streets. The celebrations badly undercut the Hartford Convention, as did news from across the Atlantic that American negotiators in Ghent, Belgium, had signed a treaty ending the war. Hostilities had ceased, technically, on Christmas Eve 1814, two weeks before the Battle of New Orleans. Both sides were relieved to end the conflict, even though the Treaty of Ghent left unresolved the issues of impressment, neutral rights, or trade.

**COLLAPSE OF THE FEDERALIST PARTY**

The return of peace hard on the heels of Jackson's victory sparked a new confidence in many Americans. The new nationalism sounded the death knell of the Federalist Party, for even talk of secession at the Hartford Convention had tainted the party with disunion and treason. In the 1816 election Madison's secretary of state, James Monroe, resoundingly defeated Federalist Rufus King of New York. Four years later Monroe ran for reelection unopposed.

## Monroe's Presidency

The major domestic challenge that Monroe faced was the renewal of sectional rivalries in 1819, when the Missouri Territory applied for admission as a slave state. Before the controversy over Missouri erupted, slavery had not been a major issue in American politics. Congress had debated the institution when it prohibited the African slave trade in 1808, the earliest year this step could be taken under the Constitution. But lacking any specific federal legislation to stop it, slavery had crossed the Mississippi River into the Louisiana Purchase. Louisiana entered the Union in 1812 as a slave state, and in 1818 Missouri, which had about 10,000 slaves in its population, asked permission to come in, too.

In 1818 the Union contained 11 free and 11 slave states. As the federal government became stronger and more active, both the North and the South worried about maintaining their political power. The North's greater population gave it a majority in the House of Representatives, 105 to 81. The Senate, of course, was evenly balanced, because each state had two senators regardless of population. But Maine, which previously had been part of Massachusetts, requested admission as a free state. That would upset the balance unless Missouri came in as a slave state.

**MISSOURI COMPROMISE**

Representative James Tallmadge of New York disturbed this delicate state of affairs when in 1819 he introduced an amendment that would establish a program of gradual emancipation in Missouri. For the first time Congress directly debated the morality of slavery, often bitterly. The House approved the Tallmadge amendment, but the Senate refused to accept it, and the two houses deadlocked.

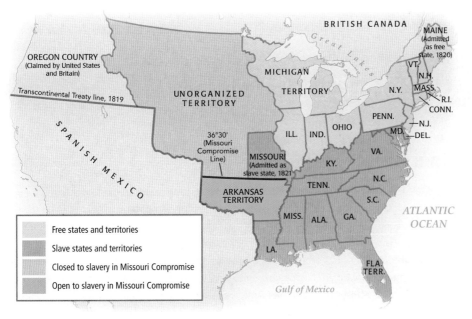

**THE MISSOURI COMPROMISE AND THE UNION'S BOUNDARIES IN 1820**

When Congress reconvened in 1820, Henry Clay of Kentucky promoted what came to be known as the Missouri Compromise. Under its terms Missouri was admitted as a slave state and Maine as a free state. In addition, slavery was forever prohibited in the remainder of the Louisiana Purchase north of 36°30′ (the southern boundary of Missouri). Clay's proposal, the first of several sectional compromises he would engineer in his long career, won congressional approval and Monroe signed the measure, ending the crisis. But southern fears for the security of slavery and northern fears about its spread remained.

Monroe's greatest achievements were diplomatic, accomplished largely by his talented secretary of state, John Quincy Adams, the son of President John Adams. An experienced diplomat, Adams thought of the Republic in continental terms and was intent on promoting expansion to the Pacific. Such a vision required dealing with Spain, which had never recognized the legality of the Louisiana Purchase. In addition, between 1810 and 1813 the United States had occupied and unilaterally annexed Spanish West Florida.

But Spain was preoccupied with events farther south in the Americas. In the first quarter of the nineteenth century, its colonies one after another revolted and established themselves as independent nations. These revolutions increased the pressure on the Spanish minister to America, Luis de Onís, to come to terms with the United States. So, too, did Andrew Jackson, who marched into East Florida and captured several Spanish forts in 1818. Jackson had exceeded his instructions, but Adams understood the additional pressure this aggression put on Onís and refused to disavow it.

**TRANSCONTINENTAL TREATY**

Fearful that the United States might next invade Texas or other Spanish territory, Spain agreed to the Transcontinental

Treaty in February 1819. Its terms set the boundary between American and Spanish territory all the way to the Pacific. Spain not only gave up its claims to the Pacific Northwest but also ceded Florida. To obtain the line to the Pacific, the United States abandoned its contention that Texas was part of the Louisiana Purchase.

More importantly, the United States also came to terms with Great Britain. Following the War of 1812, the British abandoned their connections with the western Indian tribes and no longer attempted to block American expansion to the Rocky Mountains. In a growing spirit of cooperation, the countries agreed in 1818 to the 49th parallel as the northern boundary of the Louisiana Purchase and also to joint control of the Oregon Territory for 10 years, subject to renewal.

In his annual message to Congress, on December 2, 1823, Monroe also announced that the United States would not interfere with already established European colonies in the Western Hemisphere. But any intervention in the new republics of Latin America, he warned, would be considered a hostile act: "The American continents . . . are henceforth not to be considered as subjects for future colonization by any European powers." The essence of this policy was the concept of two worlds, one old and one new, each refraining from interfering in the other's affairs. American public opinion hailed Monroe's statement and then promptly forgot it. Only years later would it be referred to as the Monroe Doctrine.

**MONROE DOCTRINE**

### REVIEW

What were the causes of the War of 1812?

# CONCLUSION

## THE WORLD AT LARGE

The three decades after 1789 demonstrated how profoundly events in the wider world could affect life within the United States, shaping its politics, its boundaries, its economy—its future.

The French Revolution contributed to splintering the once-united leaders of the American Revolution into two rival parties. The wars that followed, between France and England, deepened the divisions between Federalists and Republicans and prompted both parties to mobilize the political loyalties of ordinary white American men and women. Napoleon's ambitions to conquer Europe handed Jefferson the Louisiana Territory, while British efforts to reclaim its American empire tempted some New Englanders to secede from the Union and encouraged Tecumseh's hopes of mounting a pan-Indian resistance on the frontier. The Haitian Revolution in the Caribbean prompted free blacks in northern cities to protest racial inequalities and slavery within the United States.

But by the 1820s most white Americans paid less attention to events abroad than to expanding across the vast North American continent. Jefferson had dreamed of an "empire of liberty," delighting in expansion as the means to preserve a nation of small farmers. But younger, more nationalistic Republicans had a different vision of expansion. They spoke of internal improvements, protective tariffs to foster American industries, roads and canals to link farmers with towns, cities, and wider markets. These new Republicans were not aristocratic, like the Federalists of old. Still, their dream of a national, commercial republic resembled Franklin's and Hamilton's more than Jefferson's. They had seen how handsomely American merchants and commercial farmers profited when European wars swelled demand for American wheat and cotton. They looked to profit from speculation in land, the growth of commercial agriculture, and new methods of industrial manufacturing. If they represented the rising generation, what would be the fate of semisubsistence farm communities? The answer was not yet clear. ∞∞∞

# CHAPTER SUMMARY

BASIC SOCIAL DIVISIONS BETWEEN THE commercial and semisubsistence regions shaped the politics of the new United States. Between 1789 and the 1820s the first parties emerged and, along with them, a more popular and participatory political culture. Over the same decades, Indian confederacies mounted a sustained resistance to westward expansion, while events in Europe deepened divisions among Federalists and Republicans and threatened the very existence of the fledgling American republic.

■ The first party to organize in the 1790s was the Federalists, led by Alexander Hamilton and George Washington.

■ Divisions over Hamilton's policies as secretary of the treasury led to the formation of the Republicans, led by James Madison and Thomas Jefferson.

■ The commercially minded Federalists believed in order and hierarchy, supported loose construction of the Constitution, and wanted a powerful central government to promote economic growth.

■ The Republican Party, with its sympathy for agrarian ideals, endorsed strict construction of the Constitution, wanted a less active federal government, and harbored a strong fear of aristocracy.

■ The French Revolution, the XYZ Affair, the naval war, and the Alien and Sedition Acts also deepened the partisan division between Federalists and Republicans during the 1790s. The Federalists demonstrated that the new government could be a more active force in American society, but their controversial domestic and foreign policies, internal divisions, and open hostility to the masses led to their downfall.

■ Before becoming president, Jefferson advocated the principles of agrarianism, limited government, and strict construction of the Constitution. But once in power, he failed to dismantle Hamilton's economic program and promoted western expansion by acquiring Louisiana from France.

■ Chief Justice John Marshall proclaimed that the courts were to interpret the meaning of the Constitution (judicial review), a move that helped the judiciary emerge as an equal branch of government.

■ Lewis and Clark produced the first reliable information and maps of the Louisiana territory. The lands they passed through had been transformed over the previous 25 years by disease, dislocation, and the arrival of horses and guns.

■ The Shawnee prophet Tenskwatawa and his brother Tecumseh organized the most important Indian resistance to the expansion of the new republic, but the movement collapsed with the death of Tecumseh during the War of 1812.

■ France and Britain both interfered with neutral rights, and the United States went to war against Britain in 1812.

■ In the years after 1815 there was a surge in American nationalism, reinforced by Britain's recognition of American sovereignty and the Monroe Doctrine's prohibition of European intervention in the Western Hemisphere. But the Missouri crisis was an early indication of growing sectional rivalries.

## ADDITIONAL READING

TWO GOOD OVERVIEWS OF EARLY national politics are Stanley Elkins and Eric McKitrick's *The Age of Federalism* (1993) and James Roger Sharp's *American Politics in the Early Republic* (1993). For a fuller understanding of Federalist political thought, consult Linda Kerber, *Federalists in Dissent* (1970), and David Hackett Fischer, *The Revolution of American Conservatism* (1965); for the Republicans, read Lance Banning, *The Jeffersonian Persuasion* (1978), and Drew R. McCoy, *The Elusive Republic* (1980). Another approach to understanding the politics of this period is to read about the lives of leading political figures: among the best are Joseph Ellis's biographies of John Adams (*Passionate Sage,* 1993) and Thomas Jefferson (*American Sphinx,* rev. ed., 1998) and two biographies of Alexander Hamilton by Ron Chernow and Gerald Stourzh (all cited in the full bibliography). To become better acquainted with the popular political culture of the early republic, consult *Beyond the Founders* (2004), a superb collection of essays edited by Jeffrey Pasley, Andrew W. Robertson, and David Waldstreicher. For an engaging narrative about the political influence exerted by white women, see Catherine Allgor, *Parlor Politics* (2000), and for an outstanding analysis of women's education and their civic participation, read Mary Kelley, *Learning to Stand and Speak* (2006). Rich descriptions of the social and political interactions among whites, African Americans, and Indians in the new republic include Joshua-Rothman, *Notorious in the Neighborhood* (2003), and John Wood Sweet, *Bodies Politic* (2003). To gain a fuller understanding of the lives of both Indians and western frontier settlers, rely on Gregory Evans Dowd, *A Spirited Resistance* (1993); Roger Kennedy, *Mr. Jefferson's Lost Cause* (2003); John Mack Faragher, *Sugar Creek* (1986); Adam Rothman, *Slave Country* (2005); and R. David Edmunds, *The Shawnee Prophet* (1983) and *Tecumseh and the Quest for Indian Leadership* (1984).

For a fuller list of readings, see the Bibliography at www.mhhe.com/eh8e.

## SIGNIFICANT EVENTS

**1789**
Washington inaugurated president; French Revolution begins

**1793**
War breaks out between France and England; Washington proclaims American neutrality

**1794**
Battle of Fallen Timbers; Whiskey Rebellion

**1796**
First contested presidential election—Adams defeats Jefferson

**1798**
XYZ Affair; Alien and Sedition Acts passed; Virginia and Kentucky Resolutions

**1801**
House elects Jefferson; Cane Ridge religious revival

**1803**
*Marbury v. Madison;* Louisiana Purchase

**1804–1806**
Lewis and Clark expedition

**1807**
Embargo Act passed

**1809**
Tecumseh's confederacy organized

**1812**
War declared against Great Britain

**1814**
Washington burned; Hartford Convention; Treaty of Ghent signed

**1815**
Battle of New Orleans

**1820**
Missouri Compromise enacted

**1823**
Monroe Doctrine proclaimed

## FEDERALIST POSITIONS

Rejection of political parties

Encouragement of commerce, manufacturing, urbanization

Importance of funding the national debt

Condemnation of the French Revolution as anarchy; support for British ties

Importance of order, hierarchy, curbing democratic excess and unbridled individualism

## FEDERALIST ACHIEVEMENTS

Restored credit of national government

Ended postwar inflation and created sound currency

Instituted policy of neutrality (Washington)

Negotiated peace with France (Adams)

Established Supreme Court's right of judicial review (Marshall)

Proved republican government compatible with stability and order; peaceful transition to Republican power in 1800

### DUBIOUS ACHIEVEMENTS

Alien and Sedition Acts

Forcible efforts to push Indian nations from the Ohio valley

## REPUBLICAN POSITIONS

Rejection of political parties

Encouragement of agriculture as the basis of liberty and virtue

Suspicion of banks, speculators, public debt, taxation, government spending

Celebration of France as a fellow republic; suspicion of Britain as former foe

Support for the values of individualism, egalitarianism, limited government

## REPUBLICAN ACHIEVEMENTS

Endorsed a broad conception of freedom of the press in response to Alien and Sedition Acts

Made significant progress in paying off the national debt; expanded the national bank

Dispatched Louis and Clark expedition (Jefferson)

Negotiated the Louisiana Purchase (Jefferson)

Proclaimed the Monroe Doctrine

Proved republican government compatible with stability and order; peaceful transition to power in 1800

### DUBIOUS ACHIEVEMENTS

Virginia and Kentucky Resolutions

Forced cessions of Indians lands in the Ohio valley and the South

Embargo of 1807

Missouri Compromise

# After the Fact

*Historians Reconstruct the Past*

## Sally Hemings and Thomas Jefferson

So much goes into the weighing of historical evidence: not only the application of logic and reason, and the use of large theories and small inferences, but also the influence of emotion and a culture's prevailing myths. The distortions created by the latter pair come into play especially when topics like race and sex are involved—as can be seen by following the trail of a story first made public more than two centuries ago.

### SOME RUMORS—AND SOME FACTS

THE RUMORS BEGAN IN ALBEMARLE County, Virginia, more than 200 years ago; they came to the notice of a contemporary journalist by the name of James Callender. A writer for hire, Callender had once lent his pen to the Republicans but turned from friend into foe when the party failed to reward him with a political appointment. When his story splashed onto the pages of the *Recorder,* a Richmond newspaper, the trickle of rumor turned into a torrent of scandal. Callender alleged that Thomas Jefferson, during his years in Paris as the American minister, had contracted a liaison with one of his own slaves. The woman was the president's mistress even now, he insisted, in 1802. She was kept at Monticello, Jefferson's plantation, and Jefferson had fathered children with her. Her name was Sally Hemings.

Solid information about Sally Hemings is scarce. She was one of six children, we know, born to Betty Hemings and her white master, John Wayles, a Virginia planter whose white daughter, Martha Wayles Skelton, married Jefferson in 1772. We know that Betty Hemings was the child of an African woman and an English sailor, which means Betty's children with Wayles, Sally among them, were quadroons—light-skinned and one-quarter African. We know that Sally accompanied one of Jefferson's daughters to Paris as her maid in 1787 and that, on returning to Virginia a few years later, she performed domestic work at Monticello. We know that she had six children and that the four who survived to adulthood escaped from slavery into freedom: Jefferson assisted her two eldest children, Beverly and Harriet, in leaving Monticello in 1822, and her two youngest children, Madison and Eston, were freed by Jefferson's will in 1827. We know that shortly after Jefferson's death, his daughter, Martha Jefferson Randolph, freed Sally Hemings and that she lived with her two sons in Charlottesville until her death in 1835.

## DUELING ORAL TRADITIONS

This view of Monticello was painted shortly after Jefferson's death. It portrays his white descendants surrounded by a serene landscape.

WE KNOW, TOO, THAT JEFFERSON'S white descendants stoutly denied (and, to this day, some still deny) any familial connection with the descendants of Sally Hemings. Even though Callender's scandal quickly subsided, doing Jefferson no lasting political damage, Jefferson's white grandchildren were still explaining away the accusations half a century later. In the 1850s Jefferson's granddaughter, Ellen Coolidge Randolph, claimed that her brother, Thomas Jefferson Randolph, had told her that one of Jefferson's nephews, Samuel Carr, fathered Hemings's children. In the 1860s Henry Randall, an early biographer of Jefferson, recalled a conversation with Thomas Jefferson Randolph in the 1850s in which he attributed paternity to another nephew, Samuel's brother Peter Carr.

Until the end of the twentieth century most scholars resolved the discrepancy of this dual claim by suggesting that one of the Carr nephews had fathered Sally Hemings's children. And all of Jefferson's most eminent twentieth-century biographers—Douglass Adair, Dumas Malone, John Chester Miller, and Joseph J. Ellis—contended that a man of Jefferson's character and convictions could not have engaged in a liaison with a slave woman. After all, Jefferson was a Virginia gentleman and an American *philosophe* who believed that reason should rule over passion; he was also an eloquent apostle of equality and democracy and an outspoken critic of the tyrannical power of masters over slaves. And, despite his opposition to slavery, Jefferson argued in his *Notes on the State of Virginia* (1785) for the likelihood that peoples of African descent were inferior intellectually and artistically to those of European descent. Because of that conviction he warned of the dire consequences that would attend the mixing of the races.

The official version of events did not go unchallenged. Madison Hemings, a skilled carpenter, in 1873 told an Ohio newspaper reporter of an oral tradition, long repeated among his family, that his mother had been Thomas Jefferson's "concubine" and that Jefferson had fathered all her children. Even so, nearly a century passed before Madison Hemings's claims won wider attention. In 1968 the historian Winthrop Jordan noted that Sally Hemings's pregnancies coincided with Jefferson's stays at Monticello. In 1975 Fawn Brodie's best-selling "intimate history" of Jefferson portrayed his relationship with Sally Hemings as an enduring love affair; four years later, Barbara Chase-Rimboud set Brodie's findings to fiction.

## OVERTURNING CULTURAL ASSUMPTIONS

AN EVEN MORE POWERFUL CASE for Jefferson's paternity of all of Hemings's children was made in 1997 by Annette Gordon-Reed. She drew on her legal training to subject the handling of the evidence by Jefferson's biographers to a close and telling cross-examination. Although they had dismissed Madison Hemings's recollections as mere family lore and wishful thinking, Gordon-Reed argued that such oral testimony was, in fact, no more or less reliable than the oral testimony of Jefferson's white Randolph descendants.

One year later Gordon-Reed's arguments crested on a tidal wave of new revelations: a team of DNA research scientists headed by Eugene A. Foster discovered an exact match on the Y-chromosome markers between Thomas Jefferson's line and the descendants of Eston Hemings. (Eston was Sally's youngest child and the only one who left male-line descendants whose DNA could be tested.) Since the chance of such a match occurring randomly was less than 1 in 1,000, the DNA evidence made it highly probable that Thomas Jefferson fathered at least one of Sally Hemings's children. In addition, Foster's team found no DNA match between the Hemings line and the Carr family, thus discrediting the assertions of Jefferson's white descendants. Intrigued by these findings, historian Fraser D. Neiman undertook a sophisticated statistical analysis of Hemings's conceptions and Jefferson's returns to Monticello (where he spent about half his time), which established a 99 percent probability that he had fathered all of Hemings's children.

This new evidence has persuaded most historians that Thomas Jefferson conducted a monogamous liaison with Sally Hemings over 38 years and that their union produced at least one and most likely all six of her children. As a result, the debate among historians has moved on to explore questions left unresolved by the new scientific findings.

## UNRESOLVED QUESTIONS

ONE SUCH QUESTION BEARS ON how historians should assess the credibility of their sources. Specifically, how reliable are the oral traditions passed down through families? Both the DNA and the statistical evidence bear out Madison Hemings's recollections. Surely that outcome, as Annette Gordon-Reed has urged, should prompt future historians to scrutinize the oral testimonies of white masters such as the Jeffersons and the Randolphs as closely as they do the narratives of slaves and the oral traditions of their descendants. But does it follow that historians should regard the recollections of nonliterate peoples as possessing a superior claim to being accurate recoveries of the past? Gordon-Reed and a host of other historians warn against that conclusion, arguing that all oral testimony must be tested against the findings yielded by the documentary record and scientific research. Their caution is warranted by the fact that the DNA findings to date have failed to show a match between the Jefferson line and that of Thomas Woodson, another Monticello slave whose African

The names of Sally Hemings and her sons appear on this list of Thomas Jefferson's slaves.

American descendants have long cited their own family's oral tradition as evidence of a biological connection to Jefferson.

An equally intriguing question concerns the character of the relationship between Sally Hemings and Thomas Jefferson. Was it forced and exploitative or consensual and even affectionate? On the one hand, the long duration of their liaison suggests that it may have been based on a shared emotional intimacy. (If Jefferson fathered all of Hemings's children, their involvement began in Paris during the late 1780s and endured at least until the birth of Eston Hemings in 1808.) As Annette Gordon-Reed points out, even stronger support for this interpretation is that Sally Hemings and all her children were the only nuclear slave family at Monticello who finally attained their freedom. Furthermore, biographers have never doubted Jefferson's affection for his first wife, Martha Wayles Skelton, before she died in 1782. Is it not likely that Jefferson felt similarly toward Sally, who was in fact Martha's unacknowledged half-sister?

This bell once belonged to Martha Wayles Jefferson, the wife of Thomas Jefferson. According to Hemings family tradition, she gave the bell to Sally Hemings, who was her half-sister.

On the other hand, the sexual exploitation of black women was common among white masters in the Chesapeake, the Carolinas, and the Caribbean. Like them, Jefferson may have availed himself of the privileges of ownership to compel sexual favors over many years from a slave whom he fancied. Or perhaps Sally Hemings submitted to Jefferson's sexual demands because she hoped to win better treatment—and, in the end, freedom—for herself and her children. Many bondswomen (among them, possibly, Sally's mother, Betty Hemings, and her grandmother) used that strategy to protect their children from the ravages of slavery. What lends added support to either of those interpretations is the testimony of Madison Hemings, who recalled that although Jefferson was affectionate with his white Randolph grandchildren, he was "not in the habit of showing partiality or fatherly affection" to his children with Sally Hemings.

In the last analysis, the significance of Sally Hemings's relationship with Thomas Jefferson may reside in its power to reveal the complexity of southern plantation societies between the American Revolution and the Civil War. In that place and time the American South was not starkly divided into whites and blacks; instead, it was a culture in which the races had been mingling for generations, yielding many people of mixed ancestry, such as Sally Hemings. Israel Jefferson, who passed part of his life in slavery at Monticello, remembered her as being "mighty near white," with "long straight hair down her back." Because of their shared bonds of blood, such light-skinned slaves sometimes enjoyed greater privileges and freedoms from their masters, but they also had to negotiate more complicated relationships with them and with less favored members of the slave community.

VIRGINIAN LUXURIES.

This painting was discovered on the reverse side of a portrait of a Virginia gentleman. Experts believe that it dates from the early republic, and the artist, still unknown, evidently shared Jefferson's criticisms of slavery.

# Appendix

## The Declaration of Independence

*In Congress, July 4, 1776,*

### THE UNANIMOUS DECLARATION OF THE THIRTEEN UNITED STATES OF AMERICA

When, in the course of human events, it becomes necessary for one people to dissolve the political bands which have connected them with another, and to assume, among the powers of the earth, the separate and equal station to which the laws of nature and of nature's God entitle them, a decent respect to the opinions of mankind requires that they should declare the causes which impel them to the separation.

We hold these truths to be self-evident, that all men are created equal; that they are endowed by their Creator with certain unalienable rights; that among these, are life, liberty, and the pursuit of happiness. That, to secure these rights, governments are instituted among men, deriving their just powers from the consent of the governed; that, whenever any form of government becomes destructive of these ends, it is the right of the people to alter or to abolish it, and to institute a new government, laying its foundation on such principles, and organizing its powers in such form, as to them shall seem most likely to effect their safety and happiness. Prudence, indeed, will dictate that governments long established, should not be changed for light and transient causes; and, accordingly, all experience hath shown, that mankind are more disposed to suffer, while evils are sufferable, than to right themselves by abolishing the forms to which they are accustomed. But, when a long train of abuses and usurpations, pursuing invariably the same object, evinces a design to reduce them under absolute despotism, it is their right, it is their duty, to throw off such government and to provide new guards for their future security. Such has been the patient sufferance of these colonies, and such is now the necessity which constrains them to alter their former systems of government. The history of the present King of Great Britain is a history of repeated injuries and usurpations, all having, in direct object, the establishment of an absolute tyranny over these States. To prove this, let facts be submitted to a candid world:

He has refused his assent to laws the most wholesome and necessary for the public good.

He has forbidden his governors to pass laws of immediate and pressing importance, unless suspended in their operation till his assent should be obtained; and, when so suspended, he has utterly neglected to attend to them.

He has refused to pass other laws for the accommodation of large districts of people, unless those people would relinquish the right of representation in the legislature; a right inestimable to them, and formidable to tyrants only.

He has called together legislative bodies at places unusual, uncomfortable, and distant from the depository of their public records, for the sole purpose of fatiguing them into compliance with his measures.

He has dissolved representative houses repeatedly for opposing, with manly firmness, his invasions on the rights of the people.

He has refused, for a long time after such dissolutions, to cause others to be elected; whereby the legislative powers, incapable of annihilation, have returned to the people at large for their exercise; the state remaining, in the meantime, exposed to all the danger of invasion from without, and convulsions within.

He has endeavored to prevent the population of these States; for that purpose, obstructing the laws for naturalization of foreigners, refusing to pass others to encourage their migration hither, and raising the conditions of new appropriations of lands.

He has obstructed the administration of justice, by refusing his assent to laws for establishing judiciary powers.

He has made judges dependent on his will alone, for the tenure of their offices, and the amount and payment of their salaries.

He has erected a multitude of new offices, and sent hither swarms of officers to harass our people, and eat out their substance.

He has kept among us, in time of peace, standing armies, without the consent of our legislatures.

He has affected to render the military independent of, and superior to, the civil power.

He has combined, with others, to subject us to a jurisdiction foreign to our Constitution, and unacknowledged by our laws; giving his assent to their acts of pretended legislation:

For quartering large bodies of armed troops among us:

For protecting them by a mock trial, from punishment, for any murders which they should commit on the inhabitants of these States:

For cutting off our trade with all parts of the world:

For imposing taxes on us without our consent:

For depriving us, in many cases, of the benefit of trial by jury:

For transporting us beyond seas to be tried for pretended offences:

For abolishing the free system of English laws in a neighboring province, establishing therein an arbitrary government, and enlarging its boundaries, so as to render it at once an example and fit instrument for introducing the same absolute rule into these colonies:

For taking away our charters, abolishing our most valuable laws, and altering, fundamentally, the powers of our governments:

For suspending our own legislatures, and declaring themselves invested with power to legislate for us in all cases whatsoever.

He has abdicated government here, by declaring us out of his protection, and waging war against us.

He has plundered our seas, ravaged our coasts, burnt our towns, and destroyed the lives of our people.

He is, at this time, transporting large armies of foreign mercenaries to complete the works of death, desolation, and tyranny, already begun, with circumstances of cruelty and perfidy scarcely paralleled in the most barbarous ages, and totally unworthy the head of a civilized nation.

He has constrained our fellow citizens, taken captive on the high seas, to bear arms against their country, to become the executioners of their friends, and brethren, or to fall themselves by their hands.

He has excited domestic insurrections amongst us, and has endeavored to bring on the inhabitants of our frontiers, the merciless Indian savages, whose known rule of warfare is an undistinguished destruction of all ages, sexes, and conditions.

In every stage of these oppressions, we have petitioned for redress, in the most humble terms; our repeated petitions have been answered only by repeated injury. A prince, whose character is thus marked by every act which may define a tyrant, is unfit to be the ruler of a free people.

Nor have we been wanting in attention to our British brethren. We have warned them, from time to time, of attempts made by their legislature to extend an unwarrantable jurisdiction over us. We have reminded them of the circumstances of our emigration and settlement here. We have appealed to their native justice and magnanimity, and we have conjured them, by the ties of our common kindred, to disavow these usurpations, which would inevitably interrupt our connections and correspondence. They, too, have been deaf to the voice of justice and consanguinity. We must, therefore, acquiesce in the necessity which denounces our separation, and hold them as we hold the rest of mankind, enemies in war, in peace, friends.

We, therefore, the representatives of the United States of America, in general Congress assembled, appealing to the Supreme Judge of the world for the rectitude of our intentions, do, in the name, and by the authority of the good people of these colonies, solemnly publish and declare, that these united colonies are, and of right ought to be, free and independent states: that they are absolved from all allegiance to the British Crown, and that all political connection between them and the state of Great Britain is, and ought to be, totally dissolved; and that, as free and independent states, they have full power to levy war, conclude peace, contract alliances, establish commerce, and to do all other acts and things which independent states may of right do. And, for the support of this declaration, with a firm reliance on the protection of Divine Providence, we mutually pledge to each other our lives, our fortunes, and our sacred honor.

The foregoing Declaration was, by order of Congress, engrossed, and signed by the following members:

### JOHN HANCOCK

**NEW HAMPSHIRE**
Josiah Bartlett
William Whipple
Matthew Thornton

**MASSACHUSETTS BAY**
Samuel Adams
John Adams
Robert Treat Paine
Elbridge Gerry

**RHODE ISLAND**
Stephen Hopkins
William Ellery

**CONNECTICUT**
Roger Sherman
Samuel Huntington
William Williams
Oliver Wolcott

**NEW YORK**
William Floyd
Philip Livingston
Francis Lewis
Lewis Morris

**NEW JERSEY**
Richard Stockton
John Witherspoon
Francis Hopkinson
John Hart
Abraham Clark

**PENNSYLVANIA**
Robert Morris
Benjamin Rush
Benjamin Franklin
John Morton
George Clymer
James Smith
George Taylor
James Wilson
George Ross

**DELAWARE**
Caesar Rodney
George Read
Thomas M'Kean

**MARYLAND**
Samuel Chase
William Paca
Thomas Stone
Charles Carroll, of Carrollton

**VIRGINIA**
George Wythe
Richard Henry Lee
Thomas Jefferson
Benjamin Harrison
Thomas Nelson, Jr.
Francis Lightfoot Lee
Carter Braxton

**NORTH CAROLINA**
William Hooper
Joseph Hewes
John Penn

**SOUTH CAROLINA**
Edward Rutledge
Thomas Heyward, Jr.
Thomas Lynch, Jr.
Arthur Middleton

**GEORGIA**
Button Gwinnett
Lyman Hall
George Walton

*Resolved*, That copies of the Declaration be sent to the several assemblies, conventions, and committees, or councils of safety, and to the several commanding officers of the continental troops; that it be proclaimed in each of the United States, at the head of the army.

# The Constitution of the United States of America[1]

We the People of the United States, in Order to form a more perfect Union, establish Justice, insure domestic Tranquility, provide for the common defence, promote the general Welfare, and secure the Blessings of Liberty to ourselves and our Posterity, do ordain and establish this CONSTITUTION for the United States of America.

## ARTICLE I

**Section 1.** All legislative Powers herein granted shall be vested in a Congress of the United States, which shall consist of a Senate and House of Representatives.

**Section 2.** The House of Representatives shall be composed of Members chosen every second Year by the People of the several States, and the Electors in each State shall have the Qualifications requisite for Electors of the most numerous Branch of the State Legislature.

No Person shall be a Representative who shall not have attained to the Age of twenty-five Years, and been seven Years a Citizen of the United States, and who shall not, when elected, be an Inhabitant of that State in which he shall be chosen.

[Representatives and direct Taxes[2] shall be apportioned among the several States which may be included within this Union, according to their respective Numbers, which shall be determined by adding to the whole Number of free Persons, including those bound to Service for a Term of Years, and excluding Indians not taxed, three fifths of all other Persons.][3] The actual Enumeration shall be made within three Years after the first Meeting of the Congress of the United States, and within every subsequent Term of ten Years, in such Manner as they shall by Law direct. The Number of Representatives shall not exceed one for every thirty Thousand, but each State shall have at Least one Representative; and until such enumeration shall be made, the State of New Hampshire shall be entitled to chuse three, Massachusetts eight, Rhode-Island and Providence Plantations one, Connecticut five, New York six, New Jersey four, Pennsylvania eight, Delaware one, Maryland six, Virginia ten, North Carolina five, South Carolina five, and Georgia three.

When vacancies happen in the Representation from any State, the Executive Authority thereof shall issue Writs of Election to fill such Vacancies.

The House of Representatives shall chuse their Speaker and other Officers; and shall have the sole Power of Impeachment.

**Section 3.** The Senate of the United States shall be composed of two Senators from each State, chosen by the Legislature thereof, for six Years; and each Senator shall have one Vote.

Immediately after they shall be assembled in Consequence of the first Election, they shall be divided as equally as may be into three Classes. The Seats of the Senators of the first Class shall be vacated at the Expiration of the second Year, of the second Class at the Expiration of the fourth Year, and of the third Class at the Expiration of the sixth Year, so that one-third may be chosen every second Year; and if Vacancies happen by Resignation, or otherwise, during the Recess of the Legislature of any State, the Executive thereof may make temporary Appointments until the next Meeting of the Legislature, which shall then fill such Vacancies.

No Person shall be a Senator who shall not have attained to the Age of thirty Years, and been nine Years a Citizen of the United States, and who shall not, when elected, be an Inhabitant of that State for which he shall be chosen.

The Vice President of the United States shall be President of the Senate, but shall have no vote, unless they be equally divided.

The Senate shall chuse their other Officers, and also a President pro tempore, in the absence of the Vice President, or when he shall exercise the Office of President of the United States.

The Senate shall have the sole Power to try all Impeachments. When sitting for that purpose they shall be on Oath or Affirmation. When the President of the United States is tried, the Chief Justice shall preside: And no person shall be convicted without the Concurrence of two thirds of the Members present.

Judgment in Cases of Impeachment shall not extend further than to removal from Office, and disqualification to hold and enjoy any Office of honor, Trust, or Profit under the United States: but the Party convicted shall nevertheless be liable and subject to Indictment, Trial, Judgment, and Punishment, according to Law.

**Section 4.** The Times, Places and Manner of holding Elections for Senators and Representatives, shall be prescribed in each State by the Legislature thereof; but the Congress may at any time by Law make or alter such Regulations, except as to the Places of Chusing Senators.

The Congress shall assemble at least once in every Year, and such Meeting shall be on the first Monday in December, unless they shall by Law appoint a different Day.

**Section 5.** Each House shall be the Judge of the Elections, Returns and Qualifications of its own Members, and a Majority of each shall constitute a Quorum to do Business; but a smaller number may adjourn from day to day, and may be authorized to compel the Attendance of absent Members, in such Manner, and under such Penalties, as each House may provide.

Each House may determine the Rules of its Proceedings, punish its Members for disorderly Behaviour, and, with the Concurrence of two thirds, expel a Member.

---

[1] This version follows the original Constitution in capitalization and spelling. It is adapted from the text published by the United States Department of the Interior, Office of Education.

[2] Altered by the Sixteenth Amendment.

[3] Negated by the Fourteenth Amendment.

Each House shall keep a Journal of its Proceedings, and from time to time publish the same, excepting such Parts as may in their Judgment require Secrecy; and the Yeas and Nays of the Members of either House on any question shall, at the Desire of one fifth of those Present, be entered on the Journal.

Neither House, during the Session of Congress, shall, without the Consent of the other, adjourn for more than three days, nor to any other Place than that in which the two Houses shall be sitting.

**Section 6.** The Senators and Representatives shall receive a Compensation for their Services, to be ascertained by Law, and paid out of the Treasury of the United States. They shall in all Cases, except Treason, Felony, and Breach of the Peace, be privileged from Arrest during their Attendance at the Session of their respective Houses, and in going to and returning from the same; and for any Speech or Debate in either House, they shall not be questioned in any other Place.

No Senator or Representative shall, during the Time for which he was elected, be appointed to any civil Office under the Authority of the United States, which shall have been created, or the Emoluments whereof shall have been increased, during such time; and no Person holding any Office under the United States shall be a Member of either House during his continuance in Office.

**Section 7.** All Bills for raising Revenue shall originate in the House of Representatives; but the Senate may propose or concur with Amendments as on other bills.

Every Bill which shall have passed the House of Representatives and the Senate, shall, before it become a Law, be presented to the President of the United States; If he approve he shall sign it, but if not he shall return it, with his Objections, to that House in which it shall have originated, who shall enter the Objections at large on their Journal, and proceed to reconsider it. If after such Reconsideration two thirds of that House shall agree to pass the bill, it shall be sent, together with the objections, to the other House, by which it shall likewise be reconsidered, and if approved by two thirds of that House, it shall become a Law. But in all such Cases the Votes of both Houses shall be determined by Yeas and Nays, and the Names of the Persons voting for and against the Bill shall be entered on the Journal of each House respectively. If any Bill shall not be returned by the President within ten Days (Sundays excepted) after it shall have been presented to him, the Same shall be a Law, in like Manner as if he had signed it, unless the Congress by their Adjournment prevent its Return, in which Case it shall not be a Law.

Every Order, Resolution, or Vote to which the Concurrence of the Senate and House of Representatives may be necessary (except on a question of Adjournment) shall be presented to the President of the United States; and before the Same shall take Effect, shall be approved by him, or being disapproved by him, shall be repassed by two thirds of the Senate and House of Representatives, according to the Rules and Limitations prescribed in the Case of a Bill.

**Section 8.** The Congress shall have Power To lay and collect Taxes, Duties, Imposts and Excises, to pay the Debts and provide for the common Defence and general Welfare of the United States; but all Duties, Imposts and Excises shall be uniform throughout the United States;

To borrow money on the credit of the United States;

To regulate Commerce with foreign Nations, and among the several States, and with the Indian Tribes;

To establish an uniform rule of Naturalization, and uniform Laws on the subject of Bankruptcies throughout the United States;

To coin Money, regulate the Value thereof, and of foreign Coin, and fix the Standard of Weights and Measures;

To provide for the Punishment of counterfeiting the Securities and current Coin of the United States;

To establish Post Offices and post Roads;

To promote the Progress of Science and useful Arts, by securing for limited Times to Authors and Inventors the exclusive Right to their respective Writings and Discoveries;

To constitute Tribunals inferior to the Supreme Court;

To define and punish Piracies and Felonies committed on the high Seas, and Offenses against the Law of Nations;

To declare War, grant Letters of Marque and Reprisal, and make Rules concerning Captures on Land and Water;

To raise and support Armies, but no Appropriation of Money to that Use shall be for a longer Term than two Years;

To provide and maintain a Navy;

To make Rules for the Government and Regulation of the land and naval forces;

To provide for calling forth the Militia to execute the Laws of the Union, suppress Insurrections and repel Invasions;

To provide for organizing, arming, and disciplining the Militia, and for government such Part of them as may be employed in the Service of the United States, reserving to the States respectively, the Appointment of the Officers, and the Authority of training the Militia according to the discipline prescribed by Congress;

To exercise exclusive Legislation in all Cases whatsoever, over such District (not exceeding ten Miles square) as may, by Cession of particular States, and the acceptance of Congress, become the Seat of the Government of the United States, and to exercise like Authority over all Places purchased by the Consent of the Legislature of the State in which the Same shall be, for the Erection of Forts, Magazines, Arsenals, Dock-yards, and other needful Buildings;—And

To make all Laws which shall be necessary and proper for carrying into Execution the foregoing Powers, and all other Powers vested by this Constitution in the Government of the United States, or in any Department or Officer thereof.

**Section 9.** The Migration or Importation of such Persons as any of the States now existing shall think proper to admit, shall not be prohibited by the Congress prior to the Year one thousand eight hundred and eight, but a tax or duty may be imposed on such Importation, not exceeding ten dollars for each Person.

The privilege of the Writ of Habeas Corpus shall not be suspended, unless when in Cases of Rebellion or Invasion the public Safety may require it.

No bill of Attainder or ex post facto Law shall be passed.

No capitation, or other direct, Tax shall be laid unless in Proportion to the Census or Enumeration herein before directed to be taken.

No Tax or Duty shall be laid on Articles exported from any State.

No Preference shall be given by any Regulation of Commerce or Revenue to the Ports of one State over those of another: nor shall Vessels bound to, or from, one State, be obliged to enter, clear, or pay Duties in another.

No Money shall be drawn from the Treasury, but in Consequence of Appropriations made by Law; and a regular Statement and Account of the Receipts and Expenditures of all public Money shall be published from time to time.

No Title of Nobility shall be granted by the United States: And no Person holding any Office of Profit or Trust under them, shall, without the Consent of the Congress, accept of any present, Emolument, Office, or Title, of any kind whatever, from any King, Prince, or foreign State.

**Section 10.** No State shall enter into any Treaty, Alliance, or Confederation; grant Letters of Marque and Reprisal; coin Money; emit Bills of Credit; make any Thing but gold and silver Coin a Tender in Payment of Debts; pass any Bill of Attainder, ex post facto Law, or Law impairing the Obligation of Contracts, or grant any Title of Nobility.

No State shall, without the Consent of the Congress, lay any Imposts or Duties on Imports or Exports, except what may be absolutely necessary for executing its inspection Laws; and the net Produce of all Duties and Imposts, laid by any State on Imports or Exports, shall be for the use of the Treasury of the United States; and all such Laws shall be subject to the Revision and Control of the Congress.

No state shall, without the Consent of Congress, lay any duty of Tonnage, keep Troops, or Ships of War in time of Peace, enter into any Agreement or Compact with another State, or with a foreign Power, or engage in War, unless actually invaded, or in such imminent Danger as will not admit of delay.

## ARTICLE II

**Section 1.** The executive Power shall be vested in a President of the United States of America. He shall hold his Office during the Term of four years, and, together with the Vice President, chosen for the same Term, be elected, as follows:

Each State shall appoint, in such Manner as the Legislature thereof may direct, a Number of Electors, equal to the whole Number of Senators and Representatives to which the State may be entitled in the Congress: but no Senator or Representative, or Person holding an Office of Trust or Profit under the United States, shall be appointed an Elector.

[The Electors shall meet in their respective States, and vote by Ballot for two persons, of whom one at least shall not be an Inhabitant of the same State with themselves. And they shall make a List of all the Persons voted for, and of the Number of Votes for each; which List they shall sign and certify, and transmit sealed to the Seat of the Government of the United States, directed to the President of the Senate. The President of the Senate shall, in the Presence of the Senate and House of Representatives, open all the Certificates, and the Votes shall then be counted. The Person having the greatest Number of Votes shall be the President, if such Number be a Majority of the whole Number of Electors appointed; and if there be more than one who have such Majority, and have an equal Number of Votes, then the House of Representatives shall immediately chuse by Ballot one of them for President; and if no Person have a Majority, then from the five highest on the List the said House shall in like Manner chuse the President. But in chusing the President, the Votes shall be taken by States, the Representation from each State having one Vote; a quorum for this Purpose shall consist of a Member or Members from two-thirds of the States, and a Majority of all the States shall be necessary to a Choice. In every Case, after the Choice of the President, the Person having the greatest Number of Votes of the Electors shall be the Vice President. But if there should remain

two or more who have equal votes, the Senate shall chuse from them by Ballot the Vice President.][4]

The Congress may determine the Time of chusing the Electors, and the Day on which they shall give their Votes; which Day shall be the same throughout the United States.

No person except a natural-born Citizen, or a Citizen of the United States, at the time of the Adoption of this Constitution, shall be eligible to the Office of President; neither shall any Person be eligible to that Office who shall not have attained to the Age of thirty-five years, and been fourteen Years a Resident within the United States.

In Case of the Removal of the President from Office, or of his Death, Resignation, or Inability to discharge the Powers and Duties of the said Office, the same shall devolve on the Vice President, and the Congress may by Law provide for the Case of Removal, Death, Resignation, or Inability, both of the President and Vice President, declaring what Officer shall then act as President, and such Officer shall act accordingly, until the disability be removed, or a President shall be elected.

The President shall, at stated Times, receive for his Services a Compensation, which shall neither be increased nor diminished during the Period for which he shall have been elected, and he shall not receive within that Period any other Emolument from the United States, or any of them.

Before he enter on the execution of his Office, he shall take the following Oath or Affirmation:—"I do solemnly swear (or affirm) that I will faithfully execute the Office of President of the United States, and will, to the best of my Ability, preserve, protect, and defend the Constitution of the United States."

**Section 2.** The President shall be Commander in Chief of the Army and Navy of the United States, and of the Militia of the several States, when called into the actual Service of the United States; he may require the Opinion, in writing, of the principal Officer in each of the executive Departments, upon any subject relating to the Duties of their respective Offices, and he shall have Power to Grant Reprieves and Pardons for Offenses against the United States, except in Cases of Impeachment.

He shall have Power, by and with the Advice and Consent of the Senate, to make Treaties, provided two-thirds of the Senators present concur; and he shall nominate, and by and with the Advice and Consent of the Senate, shall appoint Ambassadors, other public Ministers and Consuls, Judges of the supreme Court, and all other Officers of the United States, whose Appointments are not herein otherwise provided for, and which shall be established by Law: but the Congress may by Law vest the Appointment of such inferior Officers, as they think proper, in the President alone, in the Courts of Law, or in the Heads of Departments.

The President shall have Power to fill up all Vacancies that may happen during the Recess of the Senate, by granting Commissions which shall expire at the End of their next Session.

**Section 3.** He shall from time to time give to the Congress Information of the State of the Union, and recommend to their Consideration such Measures as he shall judge necessary and expedient; he may, on extraordinary occasions, convene both Houses, or either of them, and in Case of Disagreement between them, with respect to the Time of Adjournment, he may adjourn them to such Time as he shall think proper; he shall receive Ambassadors and other public Ministers; he shall take care that

[4]Revised by the Twelfth Amendment.

the Laws be faithfully executed, and shall Commission all the Officers of the United States.

**Section 4.** The President, Vice President and all civil Officers of the United States, shall be removed from Office on Impeachment for, and Conviction of, Treason, Bribery, or other high Crimes and Misdemeanors.

## ARTICLE III

**Section 1.** The judicial Power of the United States, shall be vested in one supreme Court, and in such inferior Courts as the Congress may from time to time ordain and establish. The Judges, both of the supreme and inferior Courts, shall hold their Offices during good Behaviour, and shall, at stated Times, receive for their Services, a Compensation, which shall not be diminished during their Continuance in Office.

**Section 2.** The judicial Power shall extend to all Cases, in Law and Equity, arising under this Constitution, the Laws of the United States, and Treaties made, or which shall be made, under their Authority;—to all Cases affecting ambassadors, other public ministers and consuls;—to all cases of admiralty and maritime Jurisdiction;—to Controversies to which the United States shall be a Party;—to Controversies between two or more States;—between a State and Citizens of another State;[5]— between Citizens of different States—between Citizens of the same State claiming Lands under Grants of different States, and between a State, or the Citizens thereof, and foreign States, Citizens, or Subjects.

In all Cases affecting Ambassadors, other public Ministers and Consuls, and those in which a State shall be Party, the supreme Court shall have original Jurisdiction. In all the other Cases before mentioned, the supreme Court shall have appellate Jurisdiction, both as to Law and Fact, with such Exceptions, and under such Regulations as the Congress shall make.

The trial of all Crimes, except in Cases of Impeachment, shall be by Jury; and such Trial shall be held in the State where the said Crimes shall have been committed; but when not committed within any State, the Trial shall be at such Place or Places as the Congress may by Law have directed.

**Section 3.** Treason against the United States, shall consist only in levying War against them, or in adhering to their Enemies, giving them Aid and Comfort. No Person shall be convicted of Treason unless on the Testimony of two Witnesses to the same overt Act, or on Confession in open Court.

The Congress shall have power to declare the Punishment of Treason, but no Attainder of Treason shall work Corruption of Blood, or Forfeiture except during the Life of the Person attainted.

## ARTICLE IV

**Section 1.** Full Faith and Credit shall be given in each State to the public Acts, Records, and judicial Proceedings of every other State. And the Congress may by general Laws prescribe the Manner in which such Acts, Records and Proceedings shall be proved, and the Effect thereof.

**Section 2.** The Citizens of each State shall be entitled to all Privileges and Immunities of Citizens in the several States.

A Person charged in any State with Treason, Felony, or other Crime, who shall flee from Justice, and be found in another State, shall on demand of the executive Authority of the State from which he fled, be delivered up, to be removed to the State having Jurisdiction of the crime.

No Person held to Service or Labour in one State, under the Laws thereof, escaping into another, shall, in Consequence of any Law or Regulation therein, be discharged from such Service or Labour, but shall be delivered up on Claim of the Party to whom such Service or Labour may be due.

**Section 3.** New States may be admitted by the Congress into this Union; but no new State shall be formed or erected within the Jurisdiction of any other State; nor any State be formed by the Junction of two or more States, or parts of States, without the Consent of the Legislatures of the States concerned as well as of the Congress.

The Congress shall have Power to dispose of and make all needful Rules and Regulations respecting the Territory or other Property belonging to the United States; and nothing in this Constitution shall be so construed as to Prejudice any Claims of the United States, or of any particular State.

**Section 4.** The United States shall guarantee to every State in this Union a Republican Form of Government, and shall protect each of them against Invasion; and on Application of the Legislature, or of the Executive (when the Legislature cannot be convened) against domestic Violence.

## ARTICLE V

The Congress, whenever two-thirds of both Houses shall deem it necessary, shall propose Amendments to this Constitution, or, on the Application of the Legislatures of two-thirds of the several States, shall call a Convention for proposing Amendments, which, in either Case, shall be valid to all Intents and Purposes, as part of this Constitution, when ratified by the Legislatures of three-fourths of the several States, or by Conventions in three-fourths thereof, as the one or the other Mode of Ratification may be proposed by the Congress; Provided that no Amendment which may be made prior to the Year One thousand eight hundred and eight shall in any Manner affect the first and fourth Clauses in the Ninth Section of the first Article; and that no State, without its Consent, shall be deprived of its equal Suffrage in the Senate.

## ARTICLE VI

All Debts contracted and Engagements entered into, before the Adoption of this Constitution, shall be as valid against the United States under this Constitution, as under the Confederation.

This Constitution, and the Laws of the United States which shall be made in Pursuance thereof; and all Treaties made, or which shall be made, under the Authority of the United States, shall be the supreme Law of the Land; and the Judges in every State shall be bound thereby, any Thing in the Constitution or Laws of any State to the Contrary notwithstanding.

The Senators and Representatives before mentioned, and the Members of the several State Legislatures, and all executive and judicial Officers, both of the United States and of the several States, shall be bound by Oath or Affirmation to support this Constitution; but no religious Tests shall ever be required as a qualification to any Office or public Trust under the United States.

---

[5]Qualified by the Eleventh Amendment.

## ARTICLE VII

The Ratification of the Conventions of nine States shall be sufficient for the Establishment of this Constitution between the States so ratifying the same.

Done in Convention by the Unanimous Consent of the States present the Seventeenth Day of September in the Year of our Lord one thousand seven hundred and Eighty seven, and of the Independence of the United States of America the Twelfth. In Witness whereof We have hereunto subscribed our Names.[6]

### GEORGE WASHINGTON
### PRESIDENT AND DEPUTY FROM VIRGINIA

**NEW HAMPSHIRE**
John Langdon
Nicholas Gilman

**MASSACHUSETTS**
Nathaniel Gorham
Rufus King

**CONNECTICUT**
William Samuel Johnson
Roger Sherman

**NEW YORK**
Alexander Hamilton

**NEW JERSEY**
William Livingston
David Brearley
William Paterson
Jonathan Dayton

**PENNSYLVANIA**
Benjamin Franklin
Thomas Mifflin
Robert Morris
George Clymer
Thomas FitzSimons
Jared Ingersoll
James Wilson
Gouverneur Morris

**DELAWARE**
George Read
Gunning Bedford, Jr.
John Dickinson
Richard Bassett
Jacob Broom

**MARYLAND**
James McHenry
Daniel of St. Thomas Jenifer
Daniel Carroll

**VIRGINIA**
John Blair
James Madison, Jr.

**NORTH CAROLINA**
William Blount
Richard Dobbs Spaight
Hugh Williamson

**SOUTH CAROLINA**
John Rutledge
Charles Cotesworth Pinckney
Charles Pinckney
Pierce Butler

**GEORGIA**
William Few
Abraham Baldwin

---

*Articles in Addition to, and Amendment of, the Constitution of the United States of America, Proposed by Congress, and Ratified by the Legislatures of the Several States, Pursuant to the Fifth Article of the Original Constitution*[7]

## [AMENDMENT I]

Congress shall make no law respecting an establishment of religion, or prohibiting the free exercise thereof; or abridging the freedom of speech, or of the press; or the right of the people peaceably to assemble, and to petition the Government for a redress of grievances.

## [AMENDMENT II]

A well regulated Militia, being necessary to the security of a free State, the right of the people to keep and bear Arms shall not be infringed.

## [AMENDMENT III]

No Soldier shall, in time of peace, be quartered in any house, without the consent of the Owner, nor in time of war, but in a manner to be prescribed by law.

## [AMENDMENT IV]

The right of the people to be secure in their persons, houses, papers, and effects, against unreasonable searches and seizures, shall not be violated, and no Warrants shall issue, but upon probable cause, supported by Oath or affirmation, and particularly describing the place to be searched, and the persons or things to be seized.

## [AMENDMENT V]

No person shall be held to answer for a capital or otherwise infamous crime, unless on a presentment or indictment of a Grand Jury, except in cases arising in the land or naval forces, or in the Militia, when in actual service in time of War or public danger; nor shall any person be subject for the same offence to be twice put in jeopardy of life or limb; nor shall be compelled in any criminal case to be a witness against himself, nor be deprived of life, liberty, or property, without due process of law; nor shall private property be taken for public use, without just compensation.

## [AMENDMENT VI]

In all criminal prosecutions, the accused shall enjoy the right to a speedy and public trial, by an impartial jury of the State and district wherein the crime shall have been committed, which district shall have been previously ascertained by law, and to be informed of the nature and cause of the accusation; to be confronted with the witnesses against him; to have compulsory process for obtaining witnesses in his favour, and to have the Assistance of Counsel for his defence.

## [AMENDMENT VII]

In suits at common law, where the value in controversy shall exceed twenty dollars, the right of trial by jury shall be preserved, and no fact tried by a jury, shall be otherwise reexamined in any Court of the United States, than according to the rules of the common law.

---

[6]These are the full names of the signers, which in some cases are not the signatures on the document.

[7]This heading appears only in the joint resolution submitting the first ten amendments, known as the Bill of Rights.

## [AMENDMENT VIII]

Excessive bail shall not be required, nor excessive fines imposed, nor cruel and unusual punishments inflicted.

## [AMENDMENT IX]

The enumeration of the Constitution, of certain rights, shall not be construed to deny or disparage others retained by the people.

## [AMENDMENT X]

The powers not delegated to the United States by the Constitution, nor prohibited by it to the States, are reserved to the States respectively, or to the people.
[Amendments I–X, in force 1791.]

## [AMENDMENT XI][8]

The Judicial power of the United States shall not be construed to extend to any suit in law or equity, commenced or prosecuted against one of the United States by Citizens of another State, or by Citizens or Subjects of any Foreign State.

## [AMENDMENT XII][9]

The Electors shall meet in their respective States and vote by ballot for President and Vice-President, one of whom, at least, shall not be an inhabitant of the same State with themselves; they shall name in their ballots the person voted for as President, and in distinct ballots the person voted for as Vice-President, and they shall make distinct lists of all persons voted for as President, and of all persons voted for as Vice-President, and of the number of votes for each, which lists they shall sign and certify, and transmit sealed to the seat of the government of the United States, directed to the President of the Senate;—The President of the Senate shall, in the presence of the Senate and House of Representatives, open all the certificates and the votes shall then be counted;—The person having the greatest number of votes for President, shall be the President, if such number be a majority of the whole number of Electors appointed; and if no person have such majority, then from the persons having the highest numbers not exceeding three on the list of those voted for as President, the House of Representatives shall choose immediately, by ballot, the President. But in choosing the President, the votes shall be taken by states, the representation from each state having one vote; a quorum for this purpose shall consist of a member or members from two-thirds of the states, and a majority of all the states shall be necessary to a choice. And if the House of Representatives shall not choose a President whenever the right of choice shall devolve upon them, before the fourth day of March next following, then the Vice-President shall act as President, as in the case of the death or other constitutional disability of the President.—The person having the greatest number of votes as Vice-President, shall be the Vice-President, if such number be a majority of the whole number of Electors appointed, and if no person have a majority, then from the two highest numbers on the list, the Senate shall choose the Vice-President; a quorum for the purpose shall consist of two-thirds of the whole number of Senators, and a majority of the whole number shall be necessary to a choice. But no person

constitutionally ineligible to the office of President shall be eligible to that of Vice-President of the United States.

## [AMENDMENT XIII][10]

**Section 1.** Neither slavery nor involuntary servitude, except as a punishment for crime whereof the party shall have been duly convicted, shall exist within the United States, or any place subject to their jurisdiction.

**Section 2.** Congress shall have power to enforce this article by appropriate legislation.

## [AMENDMENT XIV][11]

**Section 1.** All persons born or naturalized in the United States, and subject to the jurisdiction thereof, are citizens of the United States and of the State wherein they reside. No State shall abridge the privileges or immunities of citizens of the United States; nor shall any State deprive any person of life, liberty, or property, without due process of law; nor deny to any person within its jurisdiction the equal protection of the laws.

**Section 2.** Representatives shall be apportioned among the several States according to their respective numbers, counting the whole number of persons in each State, excluding Indians not taxed. But when the right to vote at any election for the choice of electors for President and Vice-President of the United States, Representatives in Congress, the Executive and Judicial officers of a State, or the members of the Legislature thereof, is denied to any of the male inhabitants of such State, being twenty-one years of age, and citizens of the United States, or in any way abridged, except for participation in rebellion, or other crime, the basis of representation therein shall be reduced in the proportion which the number of such male citizens shall bear to the whole number of male citizens twenty-one years of age in such State.

**Section 3.** No person shall be a Senator or Representative in Congress, or elector of President and Vice-President, or hold any office, civil or military, under the United States, or under any State, who, having previously taken an oath, as a member of Congress, or as an officer of the United States, or as a member of any State legislature, or as an executive or judicial officer of any State, to support the Constitution of the United States, shall have engaged in insurrection or rebellion against the same, or given aid or comfort to the enemies thereof. But Congress may by a vote of two-thirds of each House, remove such disability.

**Section 4.** The validity of the public debt of the United States, authorized by law, including debts incurred for payment of pensions and bounties for services in suppressing insurrection or rebellion, shall not be questioned. But neither the United States nor any State shall assume or pay any debts or obligation incurred in aid of insurrection or rebellion against the United States, or any claim for the loss or emancipation of any slave; but all such debts, obligations, and claims shall be held illegal and void.

**Section 5.** The Congress shall have the power to enforce, by appropriate legislation, the provisions of this article.

[8]Adopted in 1798.
[9]Adopted in 1804.

[10]Adopted in 1865.
[11]Adopted in 1868.

## [AMENDMENT XV][12]

**Section 1.** The right of citizens of the United States to vote shall not be denied or abridged by the United States or by any State on account of race, color, or previous condition of servitude—

**Section 2.** The Congress shall have power to enforce this article by appropriate legislation.

## [AMENDMENT XVI][13]

The Congress shall have power to lay and collect taxes on incomes, from whatever source derived, without apportionment among the several States, and without regard to any census or enumeration.

## [AMENDMENT XVII][14]

The Senate of the United States shall be composed of two Senators from each State, elected by the people thereof, for six years; and each Senator shall have one vote. The electors in each State shall have the qualifications requisite for electors of the most numerous branch of the State legislatures.

When vacancies happen in the representation of any State in the Senate, the executive authority of such State shall issue writs of election to fill such vacancies: Provided, That the legislature of any State may empower the executive thereof to make temporary appointments until the people fill the vacancies by election as the legislature may direct.

This amendment shall not be so construed as to affect the election or term of any Senator chosen before it becomes valid as part of the Constitution.

## [AMENDMENT XVIII][15]

**Section 1.** After one year from the ratification of this article the manufacture, sale, or transportation of intoxicating liquors within, the importation thereof into, or the exportation thereof from the United States and all territory subject to the jurisdiction thereof for beverage purposes is hereby prohibited.

**Section 2.** The Congress and the several States shall have concurrent power to enforce this article by appropriate legislation.

**Section 3.** This article shall be inoperative unless it shall have been ratified as an amendment to the Constitution by the legislatures of the several States, as provided in the Constitution, within seven years from the date of the submission hereof to the States by the Congress.

## [AMENDMENT XIX][16]

The right of citizens of the United States to vote shall not be denied or abridged by the United States or by any State on account of sex.

Congress shall have power to enforce this article by appropriate legislation.

[12]Adopted in 1870.
[13]Adopted in 1913.
[14]Adopted in 1913.
[15]Adopted in 1918.
[16]Adopted in 1920.

## [AMENDMENT XX][17]

**Section 1.** The terms of the President and Vice-President shall end at noon on the 20th day of January, and the terms of Senators and Representatives at noon on the 3d day of January, of the years in which such terms would have ended if this article had not been ratified; and the terms of their successors shall then begin.

**Section 2.** The Congress shall assemble at least once in every year, and such meeting shall begin at noon on the 3d day of January, unless they shall by law appoint a different day.

**Section 3.** If, at the time fixed for the beginning of the term of the President, the President elect shall have died, the Vice-President elect shall become President. If a President shall not have been chosen before the time fixed for the beginning of his term or if the President elect shall have failed to qualify, then the Vice-President elect shall act as President until a President shall have qualified; and the Congress may by law provide for the case wherein neither a President elect nor a Vice-President elect shall have qualified, declaring who shall then act as President, or the manner in which one who is to act shall be selected, and such person shall act accordingly until a President or Vice-President shall have qualified.

**Section 4.** The Congress may by law provide for the case of the death of any of the persons from whom the House of Representatives may choose a President whenever the right of choice shall have devolved upon them, and for the case of the death of any of the persons from whom the Senate may choose a Vice-President whenever the right of choice shall have devolved upon them.

**Section 5.** Sections 1 and 2 shall take effect on the 15th day of October following the ratification of this article.

**Section 6.** This article shall be inoperative unless it shall have been ratified as an amendment to the Constitution by the legislatures of three-fourths of the several States within seven years from the date of its submission.

## [AMENDMENT XXI][18]

**Section 1.** The eighteenth article of amendment to the Constitution of the United States is hereby repealed.

**Section 2.** The transportation or importation into any State, Territory, or possession of the United States for delivery or use therein of intoxicating liquors, in violation of the laws thereof, is hereby prohibited.

**Section 3.** This article shall be inoperative unless it shall have been ratified as an amendment to the Constitution by conventions in the several States, as provided in the Constitution, within seven years from the date of the submission hereof to the States by the Congress.

## [AMENDMENT XXII][19]

No person shall be elected to the office of the President more than twice, and no person who has held the office of President, or acted as President, for more than two years of a term to which some other person was elected President shall be elected to the office of the President more than once.

[17]Adopted in 1933.
[18]Adopted in 1933.
[19]Adopted in 1951.

But this Article shall not apply to any person holding the office of President when this Article was proposed by the Congress, and shall not prevent any person who may be holding the office of President, or acting as President, during the term within which this Article becomes operative from holding the office of President or acting as President during the remainder of such term.

This article shall be inoperative unless it shall have been ratified as an amendment to the Constitution by the legislatures of three-fourths of the several states within seven years from the date of its submission to the states by the Congress.

## [AMENDMENT XXIII][20]

**Section 1.** The District constituting the seat of Government of the United States shall appoint in such manner as the Congress may direct:

A number of electors of President and Vice-President equal to the whole number of Senators and Representatives in Congress to which the District would be entitled if it were a State, but in no event more than the least populous State; they shall be in addition to those appointed by the States, but they shall be considered, for the purpose of the election of President and Vice-President, to be electors appointed by a State; and they shall meet in the District and perform such duties as provided by the twelfth article of amendment.

**Section 2.** The Congress shall have power to enforce this article by appropriate legislation.

## [AMENDMENT XXIV][21]

**Section 1.** The right of citizens of the United States to vote in any primary or other election for President or Vice-President, for electors for President or Vice-President, or for Senator or Representative in Congress, shall not be denied or abridged by the United States or any state by reason of failure to pay any poll tax or other tax.

**Section 2.** The Congress shall have the power to enforce this article by appropriate legislation.

## [AMENDMENT XXV][22]

**Section 1.** In case of the removal of the President from office or of his death or resignation, the Vice-President shall become President.

**Section 2.** Whenever there is a vacancy in the office of the Vice President, the President shall nominate a Vice President who shall take office upon confirmation by a majority vote of both Houses of Congress.

**Section 3.** Whenever the President transmits to the President Pro Tempore of the Senate and the Speaker of the House of Representatives his written declaration that he is unable to discharge the powers and duties of his office, and until he transmits to them a written declaration to the contrary, such powers and duties shall be discharged by the Vice-President as Acting President.

**Section 4.** Whenever the Vice-President and a majority of either the principal officers of the executive departments or of such other body as Congress may by law provide, transmit to the President Pro Tempore of the Senate and the Speaker of the House of Representatives their written declaration that the President is unable to discharge the powers and duties of his office, the Vice-President shall immediately assume the powers and duties of the office as Acting President.

Thereafter, when the President transmits to the President Pro Tempore of the Senate and the Speaker of the House of Representatives his written declaration that no inability exists, he shall resume the powers and duties of his office unless the Vice President and a majority of either the principal officers of the executive departments or of such other body as Congress may by law provide, transmit within four days to the President Pro Tempore of the Senate and the Speaker of the House of Representatives their written declaration that the President is unable to discharge the powers and duties of his office. Thereupon Congress shall decide the issue, assembling within forty-eight hours for that purpose if not in session. If the Congress, within twenty-one days after receipt of the latter written declaration, or, if Congress is not in session, within twenty-one days after Congress is required to assemble, determines by two-thirds vote of both Houses that the President is unable to discharge the powers and duties of his office, the Vice President shall continue to discharge the same as Acting President; otherwise, the President shall resume the powers and duties of his office.

## [AMENDMENT XXVI][23]

**Section 1.** The right of citizens of the United States, who are eighteen years of age or older, to vote shall not be denied or abridged by the United States or by any State on account of age.

**Section 2.** The Congress shall have power to enforce this article by appropriate legislation.

## [AMENDMENT XXVII][24]

No law, varying the compensation for the services of the Senators and Representatives, shall take effect, until an election of Representatives shall have intervened.

[20]Adopted in 1961.
[21]Adopted in 1964.
[22]Adopted in 1967.
[23]Adopted in 1971.
[24]Adopted in 1992.

# Presidential Elections

| YEAR | CANDIDATES | PARTIES | POPULAR VOTE | % OF POPULAR VOTE | ELECTORAL VOTE | % VOTER PARTICIPATION |
|------|-----------|---------|-------------|-------------------|----------------|----------------------|
| 1789 | **George Washington** | | | | 69 | |
| | John Adams | | | | 34 | |
| | Other candidates | | | | 35 | |
| 1792 | **George Washington** | | | | 132 | |
| | John Adams | | | | 77 | |
| | George Clinton | | | | 50 | |
| | Other candidates | | | | 5 | |
| 1796 | **John Adams** | Federalist | | | 71 | |
| | Thomas Jefferson | Dem.-Rep. | | | 68 | |
| | Thomas Pinckney | Federalist | | | 59 | |
| | Aaron Burr | Dem.-Rep. | | | 30 | |
| | Other candidates | | | | 48 | |
| 1800 | **Thomas Jefferson** | Dem.-Rep. | | | 73 | |
| | Aaron Burr | Dem.-Rep. | | | 73 | |
| | John Adams | Federalist | | | 65 | |
| | Charles C. Pinckney | Federalist | | | 64 | |
| | John Jay | Federalist | | | 1 | |
| 1804 | **Thomas Jefferson** | Dem.-Rep. | | | 162 | |
| | Charles C. Pinckney | Federalist | | | 14 | |
| 1808 | **James Madison** | Dem.-Rep. | | | 122 | |
| | Charles C. Pinckney | Federalist | | | 47 | |
| | George Clinton | Dem.-Rep. | | | 6 | |
| 1812 | **James Madison** | Dem.-Rep. | | | 128 | |
| | DeWitt Clinton | Federalist | | | 89 | |
| 1816 | **James Monroe** | Dem.-Rep. | | | 183 | |
| | Rufus King | Federalist | | | 34 | |
| 1820 | **James Monroe** | Dem.-Rep. | | | 231 | |
| | John Quincy Adams | Indep.-Rep. | | | 1 | |
| 1824 | **John Quincy Adams** | Dem.-Rep. | 113,122 | 31.0 | 84 | 26.9 |
| | Andrew Jackson | Dem.-Rep. | 151,271 | 43.0 | 99 | |
| | Henry Clay | Dem.-Rep. | 47,136 | 13.0 | 37 | |
| | William H. Crawford | Dem.-Rep. | 46,618 | 13.0 | 41 | |
| 1828 | **Andrew Jackson** | Democratic | 642,553 | 56.0 | 178 | 57.6 |
| | John Quincy Adams | National Republican | 500,897 | 44.0 | 83 | |
| 1832 | **Andrew Jackson** | Democratic | 701,780 | 54.5 | 219 | 55.4 |
| | Henry Clay | National Republican | 484,205 | 37.5 | 49 | |
| | William Wirt | Anti-Masonic | 101,051 | 8.0 | 7 | |
| | John Floyd | Democratic | | | 11 | |
| 1836 | **Martin Van Buren** | Democratic | 764,176 | 50.9 | 170 | 57.8 |
| | William H. Harrison | Whig | 550,816 | 49.1 | 73 | |
| | Hugh L. White | Whig | | | 26 | |
| | Daniel Webster | Whig | | | 14 | |
| | W. P. Mangum | Whig | | | 11 | |
| 1840 | **William H. Harrison** | Whig | 1,275,390 | 53.0 | 234 | 80.2 |
| | Martin Van Buren | Democratic | 1,128,854 | 47.0 | 60 | |

| YEAR | CANDIDATES | PARTIES | POPULAR VOTE | % OF POPULAR VOTE | ELECTORAL VOTE | % VOTER PARTICIPATION |
|------|-----------|---------|--------------|-------------------|----------------|----------------------|
| 1844 | **James K. Polk** | Democratic | 1,339,494 | 49.6 | 170 | 78.9 |
|      | Henry Clay | Whig | 1,300,004 | 48.1 | 105 | |
|      | James G. Birney | Liberty | 62,300 | 2.3 | | |
| 1848 | **Zachary Taylor** | Whig | 1,361,393 | 47.4 | 163 | 72.7 |
|      | Lewis Cass | Democratic | 1,223,460 | 42.5 | 127 | |
|      | Martin Van Buren | Free Soil | 291,263 | 10.1 | | |
| 1852 | **Franklin Pierce** | Democratic | 1,607,510 | 50.9 | 254 | 69.6 |
|      | Winfield Scott | Whig | 1,386,942 | 44.1 | 42 | |
|      | John P. Hale | Free Soil | 155,825 | 5.0 | | |
| 1856 | **James Buchanan** | Democratic | 1,836,072 | 45.3 | 174 | 78.9 |
|      | John C. Fremont | Republican | 1,342,345 | 33.1 | 114 | |
|      | Millard Fillmore | American | 871,731 | 21.6 | 8 | |
| 1860 | **Abraham Lincoln** | Republican | 1,865,908 | 39.8 | 180 | 81.2 |
|      | Stephen A. Douglas | Democratic | 1,375,157 | 29.5 | 12 | |
|      | John C. Breckinridge | Democratic | 848,019 | 18.1 | 72 | |
|      | John Bell | Constitutional Union | 590,631 | 12.6 | 39 | |
| 1864 | **Abraham Lincoln** | Republican | 2,218,388 | 55.0 | 212 | 73.8 |
|      | George B. McClellan | Democratic | 1,812,807 | 45.0 | 21 | |
| 1868 | **Ulysses S. Grant** | Republican | 3,013,650 | 52.7 | 214 | 78.1 |
|      | Horatio Seymour | Democratic | 2,708,744 | 47.3 | 80 | |
| 1872 | **Ulysses S. Grant** | Republican | 3,598,235 | 55.6 | 286 | 71.3 |
|      | Horace Greeley | Democratic | 2,834,761 | 43.9 | 66 | |
| 1876 | **Rutherford B. Hayes** | Republican | 4,034,311 | 48.0 | 185 | 81.8 |
|      | Samuel J. Tilden | Democratic | 4,288,546 | 51.0 | 184 | |
| 1880 | **James A. Garfield** | Republican | 4,446,158 | 48.5 | 214 | 79.4 |
|      | Winfield S. Hancock | Democratic | 4,444,260 | 48.1 | 155 | |
|      | James B. Weaver | Greenback-Labor | 308,578 | 3.4 | | |
| 1884 | **Grover Cleveland** | Democratic | 4,874,621 | 48.5 | 219 | 77.5 |
|      | James G. Blaine | Republican | 4,848,936 | 48.2 | 182 | |
|      | Benjamin F. Butler | Greenback-Labor | 175,370 | 1.8 | | |
|      | John P. St. John | Prohibition | 150,369 | 1.5 | | |
| 1888 | **Benjamin Harrison** | Republican | 5,443,892 | 47.9 | 233 | 79.3 |
|      | Grover Cleveland | Democratic | 5,534,488 | 48.6 | 168 | |
|      | Clinton B. Fisk | Prohibition | 249,506 | 2.2 | | |
|      | Anson J. Streeter | Union Labor | 146,935 | 1.3 | | |
| 1892 | **Grover Cleveland** | Democratic | 5,551,883 | 46.1 | 277 | 74.7 |
|      | Benjamin Harrison | Republican | 5,179,244 | 43.0 | 145 | |
|      | James B. Weaver | People's | 1,029,846 | 8.5 | 22 | |
|      | John Bidwell | Prohibition | 264,133 | 2.2 | | |
| 1896 | **William McKinley** | Republican | 7,108,480 | 52.0 | 271 | 79.3 |
|      | William J. Bryan | Democratic | 6,511,495 | 48.0 | 176 | |
| 1900 | **William McKinley** | Republican | 7,218,039 | 51.7 | 292 | 73.2 |
|      | William J. Bryan | Democratic; Populist | 6,358,345 | 45.5 | 155 | |
|      | John C. Wooley | Prohibition | 208,914 | 1.5 | | |
| 1904 | **Theodore Roosevelt** | Republican | 7,626,593 | 57.4 | 336 | 65.2 |
|      | Alton B. Parker | Democratic | 5,082,898 | 37.6 | 140 | |
|      | Eugene V. Debs | Socialist | 402,283 | 3.0 | | |
|      | Silas C. Swallow | Prohibition | 258,536 | 1.9 | | |

| YEAR | CANDIDATES | PARTIES | POPULAR VOTE | % OF POPULAR VOTE | ELECTORAL VOTE | % VOTER PARTICIPATION |
|------|-----------|---------|-------------|-------------------|----------------|----------------------|
| 1908 | **William H. Taft** | Republican | 7,676,258 | 51.6 | 321 | 65.4 |
|      | William J. Bryan | Democratic | 6,406,801 | 43.1 | 162 | |
|      | Eugene V. Debs | Socialist | 420,793 | 2.8 | | |
|      | Eugene W. Chafin | Prohibition | 253,840 | 1.7 | | |
| 1912 | **Woodrow Wilson** | Democratic | 6,293,152 | 42.0 | 435 | 58.8 |
|      | Theodore Roosevelt | Progressive | 4,119,207 | 28.0 | 88 | |
|      | William H. Taft | Republican | 3,484,980 | 24.0 | 8 | |
|      | Eugene V. Debs | Socialist | 900,672 | 6.0 | | |
|      | Eugene W. Chafin | Prohibition | 206,275 | 1.4 | | |
| 1916 | **Woodrow Wilson** | Democratic | 9,126,300 | 49.4 | 277 | 61.6 |
|      | Charles E.. Hughes | Republican | 8,546,789 | 46.2 | 254 | |
|      | A. L. Benson | Socialist | 585,113 | 3.2 | | |
|      | J. Frank Hanly | Prohibition | 220,506 | 1.2 | | |
| 1920 | **Warren G. Harding** | Republican | 16,153,115 | 60.4 | 404 | 49.2 |
|      | James M. Cox | Democratic | 9,133,092 | 34.2 | 127 | |
|      | Eugene V. Debs | Socialist | 919,799 | 3.4 | | |
|      | P. P. Christensen | Farmer-Labor | 265,411 | 1.0 | | |
| 1924 | **Calvin Coolidge** | Republican | 15,719,921 | 54.0 | 382 | 48.9 |
|      | John W. Davis | Democratic | 8,386,704 | 28.8 | 136 | |
|      | Robert M. La Follette | Progressive | 4,831,289 | 16.6 | 13 | |
| 1928 | **Herbert C. Hoover** | Republican | 21,437,277 | 58.2 | 444 | 56.9 |
|      | Alfred E. Smith | Democratic | 15,007,698 | 40.9 | 87 | |
| 1932 | **Franklin D. Roosevelt** | Democratic | 22,829,501 | 57.4 | 472 | 56.9 |
|      | Herbert C. Hoover | Republican | 15,760,684 | 39.7 | 59 | |
|      | Norman Thomas | Socialist | 881,951 | 2.2 | | |
| 1936 | **Franklin D. Roosevelt** | Democratic | 27,757,333 | 60.8 | 523 | 61.0 |
|      | Alfred M. Landon | Republican | 16,684,231 | 36.5 | 8 | |
|      | William Lemke | Union | 882,479 | 1.9 | | |
| 1940 | **Franklin D. Roosevelt** | Democratic | 27,313,041 | 54.8 | 449 | 62.5 |
|      | Wendell L. Wilkie | Republican | 22,348,480 | 44.8 | 82 | |
| 1944 | **Franklin D. Roosevelt** | Democratic | 25,612,610 | 53.5 | 432 | 55.9 |
|      | Thomas E. Dewey | Republican | 22,117,617 | 46.0 | 99 | |
| 1948 | **Harry S Truman** | Democratic | 24,179,345 | 50.0 | 303 | 53.0 |
|      | Thomas E. Dewey | Republican | 21,991,291 | 46.0 | 189 | |
|      | J. Strom Thurmond | States' Rights | 1,169,021 | 2.0 | 39 | |
|      | Henry A. Wallace | Progressive | 1,157,172 | 2.0 | | |
| 1952 | **Dwight D. Eisenhower** | Republican | 33,936,234 | 55.1 | 442 | 63.3 |
|      | Adlai E. Stevenson | Democratic | 27,314,992 | 44.4 | 89 | |
| 1956 | **Dwight D. Eisenhower** | Republican | 35,590,472 | 57.6 | 457 | 60.6 |
|      | Adlai E. Stevenson | Democratic | 26,022,752 | 42.1 | 73 | |
| 1960 | **John F. Kennedy** | Democratic | 34,226,731 | 49.7 | 303 | 62.8 |
|      | Richard M. Nixon | Republican | 34,108,157 | 49.6 | 219 | |
|      | Harry F. Byrd | Independent | 501,643 | | 15 | |
| 1964 | **Lyndon B. Johnson** | Democratic | 43,129,566 | 61.1 | 486 | 61.7 |
|      | Barry M. Goldwater | Republican | 27,178,188 | 38.5 | 52 | |
| 1968 | **Richard M. Nixon** | Republican | 31,785,480 | 44.0 | 301 | 60.6 |
|      | Hubert H. Humphrey | Democratic | 31,275,166 | 42.7 | 191 | |
|      | George C. Wallace | American Independent | 9,906,473 | 13.5 | 46 | |

| YEAR | CANDIDATES | PARTIES | POPULAR VOTE | % OF POPULAR VOTE | ELECTORAL VOTE | % VOTER PARTICIPATION |
|------|-----------|---------|-------------|-------------------|----------------|----------------------|
| 1972 | **Richard M. Nixon** | Republican | 47,169,911 | 60.7 | 520 | 55.2 |
|      | George S. McGovern | Democratic | 29,170,383 | 37.5 | 17 | |
|      | John G. Schmitz | American | 1,099,482 | 1.4 | | |
| 1976 | **Jimmy Carter** | Democratic | 40,830,763 | 50.1 | 297 | 53.5 |
|      | Gerald R. Ford | Republican | 39,147,793 | 48.0 | 240 | |
| 1980 | **Ronald Reagan** | Republican | 43,904,153 | 51.0 | 489 | 52.6 |
|      | Jimmy Carter | Democratic | 35,483,883 | 41.0 | 49 | |
|      | John B. Anderson | Independent | 5,719,437 | 7.0 | 0 | |
|      | Ed Clark | Libertarian | 920,859 | 1.0 | 0 | |
| 1984 | **Ronald Reagan** | Republican | 54,455,075 | 58.8 | 525 | 53.3 |
|      | Walter Mondale | Democratic | 37,577,185 | 40.5 | 13 | |
| 1988 | **George H. W. Bush** | Republican | 48,886,097 | 53.9 | 426 | 48.6 |
|      | Michael Dukakis | Democratic | 41,809,074 | 46.1 | 111 | |
| 1992 | **William J. Clinton** | Democratic | 44,908,254 | 43.0 | 370 | 55.9 |
|      | George H. W. Bush | Republican | 39,102,343 | 37.4 | 168 | |
|      | H. Ross Perot | Independent | 19,741,065 | 18.9 | 0 | |
| 1996 | **William J. Clinton** | Democratic | 45,590,703 | 49.3 | 379 | 49 |
|      | Robert Dole | Republican | 37,816,307 | 40.7 | 159 | |
|      | H. Ross Perot | Reform | 8,085,294 | 8.4 | 0 | |
| 2000 | **George W. Bush** | Republican | 50,456,062 | 47.9 | 271 | 51.2 |
|      | Al Gore | Democratic | 50,996,582 | 48.4 | 266 | |
|      | Ralph Nader | Green | 2,858,843 | 2.7 | 0 | |
| 2004 | **George W. Bush** | Republican | 62,048,610 | 50.7 | 286 | 60.7 |
|      | John F. Kerry | Democrat | 59,028,444 | 48.3 | 251 | |
|      | Ralph Nader | Independent | 465,650 | 0.4 | 0 | |
| 2008 | **Barack Obama** | Democratic | 65,070,487 | 53 | 365 | 63.0 |
|      | John McCain | Republican | 57,154,810 | 46 | 173 | |
| 2012 | **Barack Obama** | Democrat | 65,899,660 | 51.0 | 332 | 58.9 |
|      | Mitt Romney | Republican | 60,929,152 | 47.2 | 206 | |

# *Justices of the Supreme Court*

| | TERM OF SERVICE | YEARS OF SERVICE | LIFE SPAN |
|---|---|---|---|
| *John Jay* | 1789–1795 | 5 | 1745–1829 |
| John Rutledge | 1789–1791 | 1 | 1739–1800 |
| William Cushing | 1789–1810 | 20 | 1732–1810 |
| James Wilson | 1789–1798 | 8 | 1742–1798 |
| John Blair | 1789–1796 | 6 | 1732–1800 |
| Robert H. Harrison | 1789–1790 | — | 1745–1790 |
| James Iredell | 1790–1799 | 9 | 1751–1799 |
| Thomas Johnson | 1791–1793 | 1 | 1732–1819 |
| William Paterson | 1793–1806 | 13 | 1745–1806 |
| *John Rutledge** | 1795 | — | 1739–1800 |
| Samuel Chase | 1796–1811 | 15 | 1741–1811 |
| *Oliver Ellsworth* | 1796–1800 | 4 | 1745–1807 |
| Bushrod Washington | 1798–1829 | 31 | 1762–1829 |
| Alfred Moore | 1799–1804 | 4 | 1755–1810 |
| *John Marshall* | 1801–1835 | 34 | 1755–1835 |
| William Johnson | 1804–1834 | 30 | 1771–1834 |
| H. Brockholst Livingston | 1806–1823 | 16 | 1757–1823 |
| Thomas Todd | 1807–1826 | 18 | 1765–1826 |
| Joseph Story | 1811–1845 | 33 | 1779–1845 |
| Gabriel Duval | 1811–1835 | 24 | 1752–1844 |
| Smith Thompson | 1823–1843 | 20 | 1768–1843 |
| Robert Trimble | 1826–1828 | 2 | 1777–1828 |
| John McLean | 1829–1861 | 32 | 1785–1861 |
| Henry Baldwin | 1830–1844 | 14 | 1780–1844 |
| James M. Wayne | 1835–1867 | 32 | 1790–1867 |
| *Roger B. Taney* | 1836–1864 | 28 | 1777–1864 |

*Appointed and served one term, but not confirmed by the Senate.
**Note:** Chief justices are in italics.

| | TERM OF SERVICE | YEARS OF SERVICE | LIFE SPAN |
|---|---|---|---|
| Philip P. Barbour | 1836–1841 | 4 | 1783–1841 |
| John Catron | 1837–1865 | 28 | 1786–1865 |
| John McKinley | 1837–1852 | 15 | 1780–1852 |
| Peter V. Daniel | 1841–1860 | 19 | 1784–1860 |
| Samuel Nelson | 1845–1872 | 27 | 1792–1873 |
| Levi Woodbury | 1845–1851 | 5 | 1789–1851 |
| Robert C. Grier | 1846–1870 | 23 | 1794–1870 |
| Benjamin R. Curtis | 1851–1857 | 6 | 1809–1874 |
| John A. Campbell | 1853–1861 | 8 | 1811–1889 |
| Nathan Clifford | 1858–1881 | 23 | 1803–1881 |
| Noah H. Swayne | 1862–1881 | 18 | 1804–1884 |
| Samuel F. Miller | 1862–1890 | 28 | 1816–1890 |
| David Davis | 1862–1877 | 14 | 1815–1886 |
| Stephen J. Field | 1863–1897 | 34 | 1816–1899 |
| *Salmon P. Chase* | 1864–1873 | 8 | 1808–1873 |
| William Strong | 1870–1880 | 10 | 1808–1895 |
| Joseph P. Bradley | 1870–1892 | 22 | 1813–1892 |
| Ward Hunt | 1873–1882 | 9 | 1810–1886 |
| *Morrison R. Waite* | 1874–1888 | 14 | 1816–1888 |
| John M. Harlan | 1877–1911 | 34 | 1833–1911 |
| William B. Woods | 1880–1887 | 7 | 1824–1887 |
| Stanley Matthews | 1881–1889 | 7 | 1824–1889 |
| Horace Gray | 1882–1902 | 20 | 1828–1902 |
| Samuel Blatchford | 1882–1893 | 11 | 1820–1893 |
| Lucius Q. C. Lamar | 1888–1893 | 5 | 1825–1893 |
| *Melville W. Fuller* | 1888–1910 | 21 | 1833–1910 |
| David J. Brewer | 1890–1910 | 20 | 1837–1910 |
| Henry B. Brown | 1890–1906 | 16 | 1836–1913 |

| | TERM OF SERVICE | YEARS OF SERVICE | LIFE SPAN |
|---|---|---|---|
| George Shiras Jr. | 1892–1903 | 10 | 1832–1924 |
| Howell E. Jackson | 1893–1895 | 2 | 1832–1895 |
| Edward D. White | 1894–1910 | 16 | 1845–1921 |
| Rufus W. Peckham | 1895–1909 | 14 | 1838–1909 |
| Joseph McKenna | 1898–1925 | 26 | 1843–1926 |
| Oliver W. Holmes | 1902–1932 | 30 | 1841–1935 |
| William R. Day | 1903–1922 | 19 | 1849–1923 |
| William H. Moody | 1906–1910 | 3 | 1853–1917 |
| Horace H. Lurton | 1909–1914 | 4 | 1844–1914 |
| Charles E. Hughes | 1910–1916 | 5 | 1862–1948 |
| *Edward D. White* | 1910–1921 | 11 | 1845–1921 |
| Willis Van Devanter | 1911–1937 | 26 | 1859–1941 |
| Joseph R. Lamar | 1911–1916 | 5 | 1857–1916 |
| Mahlon Pitney | 1912–1922 | 10 | 1858–1924 |
| James C. McReynolds | 1914–1941 | 26 | 1862–1946 |
| Louis D. Brandeis | 1916–1939 | 22 | 1856–1941 |
| John H. Clarke | 1916–1922 | 6 | 1857–1945 |
| William H. Taft | 1921–1930 | 8 | 1857–1930 |
| George Sutherland | 1922–1938 | 15 | 1862–1942 |
| Pierce Butler | 1922–1939 | 16 | 1866–1939 |
| Edward T. Sanford | 1923–1930 | 7 | 1865–1930 |
| Harlan F. Stone | 1925–1941 | 16 | 1872–1946 |
| *Charles E. Hughes* | 1930–1941 | 11 | 1862–1948 |
| Owen J. Roberts | 1930–1945 | 15 | 1875–1955 |
| Benjamin N. Cardozo | 1932–1938 | 6 | 1870–1938 |
| Hugo L. Black | 1937–1971 | 34 | 1886–1971 |
| Stanley F. Reed | 1938–1957 | 19 | 1884–1980 |
| Felix Frankfurter | 1939–1962 | 23 | 1882–1965 |
| William O. Douglas | 1939–1975 | 36 | 1898–1980 |
| Frank Murphy | 1940–1949 | 9 | 1890–1949 |
| *Harlan F. Stone* | 1941–1946 | 5 | 1872–1946 |
| James F. Byrnes | 1941–1942 | 1 | 1882–1972 |

| | TERM OF SERVICE | YEARS OF SERVICE | LIFE SPAN |
|---|---|---|---|
| Robert H. Jackson | 1941–1954 | 13 | 1892–1954 |
| Wiley B. Rutledge | 1943–1949 | 6 | 1894–1949 |
| Harold H. Burton | 1945–1958 | 13 | 1888–1964 |
| *Fred M. Vinson* | 1946–1953 | 7 | 1890–1953 |
| Tom C. Clark | 1949–1967 | 18 | 1899–1977 |
| Sherman Minton | 1949–1956 | 7 | 1890–1965 |
| *Earl Warren* | 1953–1969 | 16 | 1891–1974 |
| John Marshall Harlan | 1955–1971 | 16 | 1899–1971 |
| William J. Brennan Jr. | 1956–1990 | 33 | 1906–1997 |
| Charles E. Whittaker | 1957–1962 | 5 | 1901–1973 |
| Potter Stewart | 1958–1981 | 23 | 1915–1985 |
| Bryon R. White | 1962–1993 | 31 | 1917–2002 |
| Arthur J. Goldberg | 1962–1965 | 3 | 1908–1990 |
| Abe Fortas | 1965–1969 | 4 | 1910–1982 |
| Thurgood Marshall | 1967–1991 | 24 | 1908–1993 |
| *Warren C. Burger* | 1969–1986 | 17 | 1907–1995 |
| Harry A. Blackmun | 1970–1994 | 24 | 1908–1999 |
| Lewis F. Powell Jr. | 1972–1987 | 15 | 1907–1998 |
| William H. Rehnquist | 1972–1986 | 14 | 1924–2005 |
| John P. Stevens III | 1975–2010 | 35 | 1920– |
| Sandra Day O'Connor | 1981–2006 | 24 | 1930– |
| *William H. Rehnquist* | 1986–2005 | 18 | 1924–2005 |
| Antonin Scalia | 1986– | — | 1936– |
| Anthony M. Kennedy | 1988– | — | 1936– |
| David H. Souter | 1990–2009 | 20 | 1939– |
| Clarence Thomas | 1991– | — | 1948– |
| Ruth Bader Ginsburg | 1993– | — | 1933– |
| Stephen Breyer | 1994– | — | 1938– |
| *John G. Roberts Jr.* | 2005– | — | 1955– |
| Samuel A. Alito Jr. | 2006– | — | 1950– |
| Sonia Sotomayor | 2009– | — | 1954– |
| Elena Kagan | 2010– | — | 1960– |

# A Social Profile of the American Republic

| YEAR | POPULATION | PERCENT INCREASE | POPULATION PER SQUARE MILE | POPULATION PERCENT URBAN/ RURAL | PERCENT MALE/ FEMALE | PERCENT WHITE/ NONWHITE | PERSONS PER HOUSEHOLD | MEDIAN AGE |
|------|------------|------------------|----------------------------|---------------------------------|----------------------|-------------------------|----------------------|------------|
| 1790 | 3,929,214 | | 4.5 | 5.1/94.9 | NA/NA | 80.7/19.3 | 5.79 | NA |
| 1800 | 5,308,483 | 35.1 | 6.1 | 6.1/93.9 | NA/NA | 81.1/18.9 | NA | NA |
| 1810 | 7,239,881 | 36.4 | 4.3 | 7.3/92.7 | NA/NA | 81.0/19.0 | NA | NA |
| 1820 | 9,638,453 | 33.1 | 5.5 | 7.2/92.8 | 50.8/49.2 | 81.6/18.4 | NA | 16.7 |
| 1830 | 12,866,020 | 33.5 | 7.4 | 8.8/91.2 | 50.8/49.2 | 81.9/18.1 | NA | 17.2 |
| 1840 | 17,069,453 | 32.7 | 9.8 | 10.8/89.2 | 50.9/49.1 | 83.2/16.8 | NA | 17.8 |
| 1850 | 23,191,876 | 35.9 | 7.9 | 15.3/84.7 | 51.0/49.0 | 84.3/15.7 | 5.55 | 18.9 |
| 1860 | 31,443,321 | 35.6 | 10.6 | 19.8/80.2 | 51.2/48.8 | 85.6/14.4 | 5.28 | 19.4 |
| 1870 | 39,818,449 | 26.6 | 13.4 | 25.7/74.3 | 50.6/49.4 | 86.2/13.8 | 5.09 | 20.2 |
| 1880 | 50,155,783 | 26.0 | 16.9 | 28.2/71.8 | 50.9/49.1 | 86.5/13.5 | 5.04 | 20.9 |
| 1890 | 62,947,714 | 25.5 | 21.2 | 35.1/64.9 | 51.2/48.8 | 87.5/12.5 | 4.93 | 22.0 |
| 1900 | 75,994,575 | 20.7 | 25.6 | 39.6/60.4 | 51.1/48.9 | 87.9/12.1 | 4.76 | 22.9 |
| 1910 | 91,972,266 | 21.0 | 31.0 | 45.6/54.4 | 51.5/48.5 | 88.9/11.1 | 4.54 | 24.1 |
| 1920 | 105,710,620 | 14.9 | 35.6 | 51.2/48.8 | 51.0/49.0 | 89.7/10.3 | 4.34 | 25.3 |
| 1930 | 122,775,046 | 16.1 | 41.2 | 56.1/43.9 | 50.6/49.4 | 89.8/10.2 | 4.11 | 26.4 |
| 1940 | 131,669,275 | 7.2 | 44.2 | 56.5/43.5 | 50.2/49.8 | 89.8/10.2 | 3.67 | 29.0 |
| 1950 | 150,697,361 | 14.5 | 50.7 | 64.0/36.0 | 49.7/50.3 | 89.5/10.5 | 3.37 | 30.2 |
| 1960 | 179,323,175 | 18.5 | 50.6 | 69.9/30.1 | 49.3/50.7 | 88.6/11.4 | 3.33 | 29.5 |
| 1970 | 203,302,031 | 13.4 | 57.4 | 73.5/26.5 | 48.7/51.3 | 87.6/12.4 | 3.14 | 28.0 |
| 1980 | 226,545,805 | 11.4 | 64.0 | 73.7/26.3 | 48.6/51.4 | 86.0/14.0 | 2.76 | 30.0 |
| 1990 | 248,709,873 | 9.8 | 70.3 | 75.2/24.8 | 48.7/51.3 | 80.3/19.7 | 2.63 | 32.9 |
| 2000 | 281,422,426 | 13.1 | 79.6 | 79.0/21.0 | 49.0/51.0 | 81.0/19.0 | 2.59 | 35.4 |
| 2010 | 308,745,538 | 9.7 | 87.4 | 80.7/19.3 | 49.2/50.8 | 77.1/22.9 | 2.58 | 37.2 |

NA = Not available.

| | | | VITAL STATISTICS (RATES PER THOUSAND) | | | |
|------|--------|------|--------|---------|------------|-----------|
| YEAR | BIRTHS | YEAR | BIRTHS | DEATHS* | MARRIAGES* | DIVORCES* |
| 1800 | 55.0 | 1900 | 32.3 | 17.2 | NA | NA |
| 1810 | 54.3 | 1910 | 30.1 | 14.7 | NA | NA |
| 1820 | 55.2 | 1920 | 27.7 | 13.0 | 12.0 | 1.6 |
| 1830 | 51.4 | 1930 | 21.3 | 11.3 | 9.2 | 1.6 |
| 1840 | 51.8 | 1940 | 19.4 | 10.8 | 12.1 | 2.0 |
| 1850 | 43.3 | 1950 | 24.1 | 9.6 | 11.1 | 2.6 |
| 1860 | 44.3 | 1960 | 23.7 | 9.5 | 8.5 | 2.2 |
| 1870 | 38.3 | 1970 | 18.4 | 9.5 | 10.6 | 3.5 |
| 1880 | 39.8 | 1980 | 15.9 | 8.8 | 10.6 | 5.2 |
| 1890 | 31.5 | 1990 | 16.7 | 8.6 | 9.8 | 4.6 |
| | | 2000 | 14.7 | 8.7 | 8.5 | 4.2 |
| | | 2010 | 13.8 | 8.0 | 6.8 | 3.6 |

NA = Not available.
*Data not available before 1900.

| YEAR | TOTAL POPULATION | LIFE EXPECTANCY (IN YEARS) | | | |
|---|---|---|---|---|---|
| | | WHITE FEMALES | NONWHITE FEMALES | WHITE MALES | NONWHITE MALES |
| 1900 | 47.3 | 48.7 | 33.5 | 46.6 | 32.5 |
| 1910 | 50.1 | 52.0 | 37.5 | 48.6 | 33.8 |
| 1920 | 54.1 | 55.6 | 45.2 | 54.4 | 45.5 |
| 1930 | 59.7 | 63.5 | 49.2 | 59.7 | 47.3 |
| 1940 | 62.9 | 66.6 | 54.9 | 62.1 | 51.5 |
| 1950 | 68.2 | 72.2 | 62.9 | 66.5 | 59.1 |
| 1960 | 69.7 | 74.1 | 66.3 | 67.4 | 61.1 |
| 1970 | 70.9 | 75.6 | 69.4 | 68.0 | 61.3 |
| 1980 | 73.7 | 78.1 | 73.6 | 70.7 | 65.3 |
| 1990 | 75.4 | 79.3 | 75.2 | 72.6 | 67.0 |
| 2000 | 76.9 | 80.0 | 75.0 | 74.8 | 68.3 |
| 2010 | 78.3 | 80.8 | 80.3 | 75.7 | 74.5 |

## THE CHANGING AGE STRUCTURE

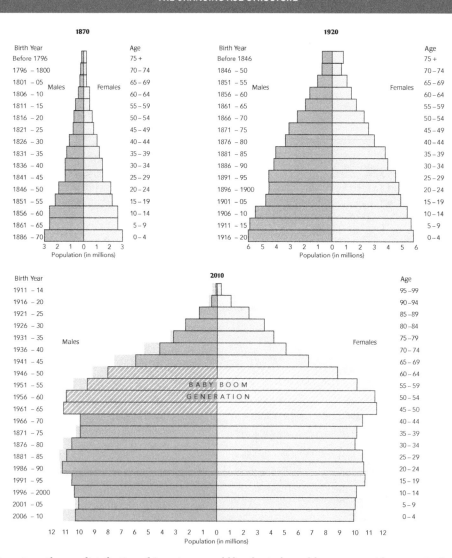

Before the twentieth century, the age distribution of Americans could be charted roughly as a pyramid, as seen in the figures for 1870 and 1920. High birthrates create a broad base at the bottom, while mortality rates winnow the population to a small tip of elderly. But by 2010, the pyramid had been transformed more nearly into a cylinder. Over the past two centuries fertility rates have undergone a steady decline, pulling in the base of the pyramid, while higher living standards have allowed Americans to live longer, broadening the top. Only the temporary bulge of the baby boom distorts the shape.

| | | REGIONAL ORIGIN OF IMMIGRANTS (PERCENT) EUROPE | | | | | |
|---|---|---|---|---|---|---|---|
| YEARS | TOTAL NUMBER OF IMMIGRANTS | TOTAL EUROPE | NORTH AND WEST | EAST AND CENTRAL | SOUTH AND OTHER | WESTERN HEMISPHERE | ASIA |
| 1821–1830 | 143,389 | 69.2 | 67.1 | — | 2.1 | 8.4 | — |
| 1831–1840 | 599,125 | 82.8 | 81.8 | — | 1.0 | 5.5 | — |
| 1841–1850 | 1,713,251 | 93.8 | 92.9 | 0.1 | 0.3 | 3.6 | — |
| 1851–1860 | 2,598,214 | 94.4 | 93.6 | 0.1 | 0.8 | 2.9 | 1.6 |
| 1861–1870 | 2,314,824 | 89.2 | 87.8 | 0.5 | 0.9 | 7.2 | 2.8 |
| 1871–1880 | 2,812,191 | 80.8 | 73.6 | 4.5 | 2.7 | 14.4 | 4.4 |
| 1881–1890 | 5,246,13 | 90.3 | 72.0 | 11.9 | 6.3 | 8.1 | 1.3 |
| 1891–1900 | 3,687,546 | 96.5 | 44.5 | 32.8 | 19.1 | 1.1 | 1.9 |
| 1901–1910 | 8,795,386 | 92.5 | 21.7 | 44.5 | 6.3 | 4.1 | 2.8 |
| 1911–1920 | 5,735,811 | 76.3 | 17.4 | 33.4 | 25.5 | 19.9 | 3.4 |
| 1921–1930 | 4,107,209 | 60.3 | 31.7 | 14.4 | 14.3 | 36.9 | 2.4 |
| 1931–1940 | 528,431 | 65.9 | 38.8 | 11.0 | 16.1 | 30.3 | 2.8 |
| 1941–1950 | 1,035,039 | 60.1 | 47.5 | 4.6 | 7.9 | 34.3 | 3.1 |
| 1951–1960 | 2,515,479 | 52.8 | 17.7 | 24.3 | 10.8 | 39.6 | 6.0 |
| 1961–1970 | 3,321,677 | 33.8 | 11.7 | 9.4 | 12.9 | 51.7 | 12.9 |
| 1971–1980 | 4,493,300 | 17.8 | 4.3 | 5.6 | 8.4 | 44.3 | 35.2 |
| 1981–1990 | 7,338,000 | 10.4 | 5.9 | 4.8 | 1.1 | 49.3 | 37.3 |
| 1991–2000 | 9,095,417 | 14.9 | 4.8 | 8.6 | 1.6 | 49.3 | 30.7 |

Dash indicates less than 0.1 percent.

| RECENT TRENDS IN IMMIGRATION (IN THOUSANDS) | | | | | PERCENT | | |
|---|---|---|---|---|---|---|---|
| | 1961–1970 | 1971–1980 | 1981–1990 | 1991–2000 | 1971–1980 | 1981–1990 | 1991–2000 |
| All countries | 3,321.7 | 4,493.3 | 7,338.1 | 9095.4 | 100.0 | 100.0 | 100.0 |
| Europe | 1,123.5 | 800.4 | 761.5 | 1359.7 | 17.8 | 10.4 | 14.9 |
| Austria | 20.6 | 9.5 | 18.3 | 15.5 | 0.2 | 0.3 | 0.2 |
| Belgium | 9.2 | 5.3 | 7.0 | 7.0 | 0.1 | 0.1 | 0.1 |
| Czechoslovakia | 3.3 | 6.0 | 7.2 | 9.8 | 0.1 | 0.1 | 0.1 |
| Denmark | 9.2 | 4.4 | 5.3 | 6.0 | 0.1 | 0.1 | 0.1 |
| France | 45.2 | 25.1 | 22.4 | 35.8 | 0.6 | 1.3 | 0.4 |
| Germany | 190.8 | 74.4 | 91.6 | 92.6 | 1.7 | 2.2 | 1.0 |
| Greece | 86.0 | 92.4 | 38.3 | 26.7 | 2.1 | 0.4 | 0.3 |
| Hungary | 5.4 | 6.6 | 6.5 | 9.3 | 0.1 | 0.1 | 0.1 |
| Ireland | 33.0 | 11.5 | 31.9 | 56.9 | 0.3 | 0.9 | 0.6 |
| Italy | 214.1 | 129.4 | 67.2 | 62.7 | 2.9 | 0.2 | 0.7 |
| Netherlands | 30.6 | 10.5 | 12.2 | 13.3 | 0.2 | 0.1 | 0.1 |
| Norway | 15.5 | 3.9 | 4.2 | 5.1 | 0.1 | 1.1 | 0.5 |
| Poland | 53.5 | 37.2 | 83.3 | 163.7 | 0.8 | 0.5 | 1.8 |
| Portugal | 76.1 | 101.7 | 40.4 | 22.9 | 2.3 | 0.3 | 0.3 |
| Spain | 44.7 | 39.1 | 20.4 | 17.1 | 0.9 | 0.2 | 0.2 |
| Sweden | 17.1 | 6.5 | 11.0 | 12.7 | 0.1 | 0.1 | 0.1 |
| Switzerland | 18.5 | 8.2 | 8.8 | 11.8 | 0.2 | 0.1 | 0.1 |
| United Kingdom | 213.8 | 137.4 | 159.2 | 151.8 | 3.1 | 2.2 | 1.7 |
| USSR | 2.5 | 39.0 | 57.7 | 462.8 | 0.9 | 0.3 | 5.1 |
| Yugoslavia | 20.4 | 30.5 | 18.8 | 66.5 | 0.7 | 0.5 | 0.7 |
| Other Europe | 9.1 | 18.9 | 8.2 | 57.7 | 0.2 | 0.0 | 0.6 |

| RECENT TRENDS IN IMMIGRATION (IN THOUSANDS) | | | | | PERCENT | | |
| --- | --- | --- | --- | --- | --- | --- | --- |
| | 1961–1970 | 1971–1980 | 1981–1990 | 1991–2000 | 1971–1980 | 1981–1990 | 1991–2000 |
| Asia | 427.6 | 1588.2 | 2738.1 | 2795.6 | 35.2 | 37.3 | 30.7 |
| China | 34.8 | 124.3 | 298.9 | 419.1 | 2.8 | 4.1 | 4.6 |
| Hong Kong | 75.0 | 113.5 | 98.2 | 109.8 | 2.5 | 1.3 | 1.2 |
| India | 27.2 | 164.1 | 250.7 | 363.1 | 3.7 | 3.4 | 4.0 |
| Iran | 10.3 | 45.1 | 116.0 | 69.0 | 1.0 | 1.6 | 0.8 |
| Israel | 29.6 | 37.7 | 44.2 | 39.4 | 0.8 | 0.6 | 0.4 |
| Japan | 40.0 | 49.8 | 47.0 | 67.9 | 1.1 | 0.6 | 0.7 |
| Korea | 34.5 | 267.6 | 333.8 | 164.2 | 6.0 | 4.5 | 1.8 |
| Philippines | 98.4 | 355.0 | 548.7 | 503.9 | 7.9 | 7.5 | 5.5 |
| Turkey | 10.1 | 13.4 | 23.4 | 38.2 | 0.3 | 0.3 | 0.4 |
| Vietnam | 4.3 | 172.8 | 281.0 | 286.1 | 3.8 | 3.8 | 3.1 |
| Other Asia | 36.5 | 176.1 | 631.4 | 735.4 | 3.8 | 8.6 | 8.0 |
| America | 1716.4 | 1982.5 | 3615.6 | 4486.8 | 44.3 | 49.3 | 49.3 |
| Argentina | 49.7 | 29.9 | 27.3 | 26.6 | 0.7 | 0.4 | 0.3 |
| Canada | 413.3 | 169.9 | 158.0 | 192.0 | 3.8 | 2.2 | 2.1 |
| Colombia | 72.0 | 77.3 | 122.9 | 128.5 | 1.7 | 1.7 | 1.4 |
| Cuba | 208.5 | 264.9 | 144.6 | 169.3 | 5.9 | 2.0 | 1.9 |
| Dominican Rep. | 93.3 | 148.1 | 252.0 | 335.3 | 3.3 | 3.4 | 3.7 |
| Ecuador | 36.8 | 50.1 | 56.2 | 76.5 | 1.1 | 0.8 | 0.8 |
| El Salvador | 15.0 | 34.4 | 213.5 | 215.7 | 0.8 | 2.9 | 2.4 |
| Haiti | 34.5 | 56.3 | 138.4 | 179.6 | 1.3 | 1.9 | 2.0 |
| Jamaica | 74.9 | 137.6 | 208.1 | 169.2 | 3.1 | 2.8 | 1.9 |
| Mexico | 453.9 | 640.3 | 1655.7 | 2249.4 | 14.3 | 22.6 | 24.7 |
| Other America | 264.4 | 373.8 | 639.3 | 744.3 | 8.3 | 8.7 | 8.2 |
| Africa | 29.0 | 80.8 | 176.8 | 355.0 | 1.8 | 2.4 | 3.9 |
| Oceania | 25.1 | 41.2 | 45.2 | 55.8 | 0.9 | 0.6 | 0.6 |

Figures may not add to total due to rounding.

| AMERICAN WORKERS AND FARMERS | | | | | | | |
| --- | --- | --- | --- | --- | --- | --- | --- |
| YEAR | TOTAL NUMBER OF WORKERS (THOUSANDS) | PERCENT OF WORKERS MALE/ FEMALE | PERCENT OF FEMALE WORKERS MARRIED | PERCENT OF WORKERS IN FEMALE POPULATION | PERCENT OF WORKERS IN LABOR UNIONS | FARM POPULATION (THOUSANDS) | FARM POPULATION AS PERCENT OF TOTAL POPULATION |
| 1870 | 12,506 | 85/15 | NA | NA | NA | NA | NA |
| 1880 | 17,392 | 85/15 | NA | NA | NA | 21,973 | 43.8 |
| 1890 | 23,318 | 83/17 | 13.9 | 18.9 | NA | 24,771 | 42.3 |
| 1900 | 29,073 | 82/18 | 15.4 | 20.6 | 3 | 29,875 | 41.9 |
| 1910 | 38,167 | 79/21 | 24.7 | 25.4 | 6 | 32,077 | 34.9 |
| 1920 | 41,614 | 79/21 | 23.0 | 23.7 | 12 | 31,974 | 30.1 |
| 1930 | 48,830 | 78/22 | 28.9 | 24.8 | 7 | 30,529 | 24.9 |
| 1940 | 53,011 | 76/24 | 36.4 | 27.4 | 27 | 30,547 | 23.2 |
| 1950 | 59,643 | 72/28 | 52.1 | 31.4 | 25 | 23,048 | 15.3 |
| 1960 | 69,877 | 68/32 | 59.9 | 37.7 | 26 | 15,635 | 8.7 |
| 1970 | 82,049 | 63/37 | 63.4 | 43.4 | 25 | 9712 | 4.8 |
| 1980 | 108,544 | 58/42 | 59.7 | 51.5 | 23 | 6051 | 2.7 |
| 1990 | 117,914 | 55/45 | 58.4 | 44.3 | 16 | 3871 | 1.6 |
| 2000 | 135,208 | 54/46 | 61.3 | 45.7 | 15 | 3305 | 1.1 |

| | GROSS NATIONAL PRODUCT (GNP) (IN BILLIONS)* | FOREIGN TRADE (IN MILLIONS) | | | FEDERAL BUDGET (IN BILLIONS) | FEDERAL SURPLUS/DEFICIT (IN BILLIONS) | FEDERAL DEBT (IN BILLIONS) |
|---|---|---|---|---|---|---|---|
| YEAR | | EXPORTS | IMPORTS | BALANCE OF TRADE | | | |
| 1790 | NA | $20 | $23 | $–3 | $0.004 | $+0.00015 | $0.076 |
| 1800 | NA | 71 | 91 | –20 | 0.011 | +0.0006 | 0.083 |
| 1810 | NA | 67 | 85 | –18 | 0.008 | +0.0012 | 0.053 |
| 1820 | NA | 70 | 74 | –4 | 0.018 | –0.0004 | 0.091 |
| 1830 | NA | 74 | 71 | +3 | 0.015 | +0.100 | 0.049 |
| 1840 | NA | 132 | 107 | +25 | 0.024 | –0.005 | 0.004 |
| 1850 | NA | 152 | 178 | –26 | 0.040 | +0.004 | 0.064 |
| 1860 | NA | 400 | 362 | –38 | 0.063 | –0.01 | 0.065 |
| 1870 | $7.4 | 451 | 462 | –11 | 0.310 | +0.10 | 2.4 |
| 1880 | 11.2 | 853 | 761 | +92 | 0.268 | +0.07 | 2.1 |
| 1890 | 13.1 | 910 | 823 | +87 | 0.318 | +0.09 | 1.2 |
| 1900 | 18.7 | 1499 | 930 | +569 | 0.521 | +0.05 | 1.2 |
| 1910 | 35.3 | 1919 | 1646 | +273 | 0.694 | –0.02 | 1.1 |
| 1920 | 91.5 | 8664 | 5784 | +2880 | 6.357 | +0.3 | 24.3 |
| 1930 | 90.7 | 4013 | 3500 | +513 | 3.320 | +0.7 | 16.3 |
| 1940 | 100.0 | 4030 | 7433 | –3403 | 9.6 | –2.7 | 43.0 |
| 1950 | 286.5 | 10,816 | 9125 | +1691 | 43.1 | –2.2 | 257.4 |
| 1960 | 506.5 | 19,600 | 15,046 | +4556 | 92.2 | +0.3 | 286.3 |
| 1970 | 992.7 | 42,700 | 40,189 | +2511 | 195.6 | –2.8 | 371.0 |
| 1980 | 2631.7 | 220,783 | 244,871 | +24,088 | 590.9 | –73.8 | 907.7 |
| 1990 | 5803.2 | 394,030 | 495,042 | –101,012 | 1253.1 | –220.5 | 3206.6 |
| 2000 | 9872.9 | 1,102,900 | 1,466,900 | –364,000 | 1788.8 | +236.4 | 5629.0 |

THE ECONOMY AND FEDERAL SPENDING

*For 1990 and after, gross domestic product (GDP) is given.

# Glossary

## A

**actual representation**   view that the people can be represented only by a person whom they have actually elected to office; this understanding of representation was the consensus among colonials during the imperial crisis and the basis of their objection to the British claim that Americans were virtually represented in Parliament.

**affirmative action**   practice of actively seeking to increase the number of racial and ethnic minorities, women, persons in a protected age category, persons with disabilities, and disabled veterans in a workplace or school. Such measures sometimes include the setting of quotas or percentages in hiring.

**amnesty**   general pardon granted by a government, usually for political crimes. Proposals of amnesty were made, with varying degrees of exception for high Confederate officials, by Presidents Lincoln and Johnson as well as by Congress in 1872. President Ford offered conditional amnesty in 1974 to draft evaders at the conclusion of the Vietnam War.

**anti-Semitism**   hatred, prejudice, oppression, or discrimination against Jews or Judaism. *Semite* originally referred to the descendants of Shem, which included both Jews and Muslims in the Middle East. More recently the term has come to refer primarily to Jews.

**appeasement**   policy of making concessions to an aggressor nation, as long as its demands appear reasonable, in order to avoid war. Hitler's full conquest of Czechoslovakia, violating his promises given at the Munich Conference in 1938, gave the term its negative connotation.

**armistice**   mutually agreed-on truce or temporary halt in the fighting of a war so that the combatants may discuss peace.

**artisan**   skilled craftworker, such as a blacksmith, a cooper, a miller, or a tailor. Master artisans constituted a large segment of the middle classes in American cities and towns from the beginnings of colonial settlement through the 1820s; they owned their own shops and employed a number of younger journeyman artisans, who owned only their tools, and trained even younger and less skilled apprentices in a craft.

**assimilate**   to absorb a culturally distinct group into the dominant culture. The debate over the process of assimilation, of immigrants "becoming American," has been a persistent fault line in American politics. The debate revolves around what qualities are American and the degree to which a dominant culture should define them. The debate is extremely difficult in a society in which immigration plays a crucial role—in a "nation of nations," as Walt Whitman described the United States.

**autonomy**   condition of being independent or, in the case of a political structure, the right to self-government.

## B

**balanced constitution**   view that England's constitution gave every part of English society some voice in the workings of its government. While the Crown represented the monarchy and the House of Lords the aristocracy, the House of Commons represented the ordinary people of England.

**barter economy**   networks of trade based on the mutual exchange of goods and services with little or no use of coin or currency.

**behaviorism**   school of psychology that measures human behavior, believes it can be shaped, and discounts emotion as subjective. Behaviorism was founded by psychologist John Watson and was first presented in his *Psychology as the Behaviorist Views It* (1913).

**benign neglect**   policy also known as "salutary neglect," pursued by the British empire in governing its American colonies until the end of the Seven Years' War.

**biocentric**   life-centered; also a theory of moral responsibility stating that all forms of life have an inherent right to exist and that humanity is not the center of existence.

**biogenetic engineering**   process of changing the DNA of a plant or an animal to produce desirable characteristics. Examples of desirable characteristics include fast growth and unusually large size. The health and environmental safety of genetically modified food products is a subject of debate in the scientific and lay communities.

**black codes**   series of laws passed by southern states in 1865 and 1866, modeled on the slave codes in effect before the Civil War. The codes did grant African Americans some rights not enjoyed by slaves, but their primary purpose was to keep African Americans as propertyless agricultural laborers.

**bloody shirt**   political campaign tactic of "waving the bloody shirt," used by Republicans against Democrats; it invoked the tremendous loss of life and casualties from the Civil War as a reason to vote for Republicans as the party of the Union and not to trust Democrats, who had often opposed the war. The tactic continued to work, with diminishing success, throughout Reconstruction.

**bonds**   certificates of debt issued by a government or corporation promising to repay the buyers of the bonds their original investment, plus interest, by a specified date of maturity. Bonds have been traditionally used by governments as a way to raise money during wartime or for large-scale projects.

**boom-bust economy**   periods of expansion and recession or depression that an economy goes through. Also referred to as *business cycle*. Major downturns in the cycle have occurred in the United States beginning in 1819, 1837, 1857, 1873, 1893, 1907, and 1929, the start of the Great Depression.

**bootlegging**   illegal transport or sale of goods, in this case alcoholic beverages during the 1920s. The term derived from the practice of hiding a container of alcohol in the upper part of a boot.

**boycott**   tactic used by protesters, workers, and consumers to pressure business organizations through a mass refusal to purchase their products or otherwise do business with them.

**brinkmanship**   policy of pushing a critical situation to the edge of catastrophe by using the implicit threat of nuclear war in order to persuade an opponent to back down. The strategy was developed by Secretary of State John Foster Dulles under President Dwight Eisenhower.

**bureaucratic state**   government run by administrative bureaus or divisions and staffed by nonelected officials.

**business cycle**   *see* **boom-bust economy.**

# C

**carpetbagger**   white Republicans, originally from the North, who came to live in the South after the Civil War. They received their nickname from hostile southerners who claimed that the newcomers arrived carrying all that they owned stuffed into a carpetbag and eager to get rich by plundering the South.

**cartel**   organization of private businesses that join to control production, distribution, and prices.

**caste system**   system of social stratification separating individuals by various distinctions, among them hereditary, rank, profession, wealth, and race. Slavery as a caste system not only separated whites from blacks but also assigned value to people according to shadings of color.

**cede**   to give up possession of, usually by treaty.

**celibate**   abstaining from sexual intercourse; also, unmarried. Celibacy is the abstention from intercourse, a state often motivated by religious teachings.

**charter**   document issued by a sovereign ruler, legislature, or other authority creating a public or private corporation. England's rulers issued charters setting forth the authority of corporations or joint stock companies to colonize sections of the Americas; state legislatures have issued charters to corporations; and the British (including American colonials) traced basic rights of representation to the Magna Carta (Great Charter) granted by King John in 1215 CE.

**checks and balances**   mechanism by which each branch of government—executive, legislative, and judicial—keeps the others within the bounds of their constitutional authority; James Madison emphasized this feature of the federal constitution to assure the Anti-Federalists.

**Columbian exchange**   transition of people, plants, insects, and microbes between the two hemispheres, initiated when Columbus reached the Americas in 1492.

**commercial economy**   economy in which individuals are involved in a network of markets and commercial transactions. Such economies are often urban, where goods and services are exchanged for money and credit; agricultural areas are also commercial when crops and livestock are sold in markets rather than consumed by those who grew or raised them. Commercial economies are less egalitarian, because wealth can be concentrated in the hands of fewer individuals. *See also* **semisubsistence economy.**

**committees of correspondence**   strategy devised by Samuel Adams in 1772 to rally popular support among American colonials against British imperial policies. The committees of correspondence drew up statements of American rights and grievances, distributed those documents within and among the colonies, and solicited responses from towns and counties. This committee structure formed a new communications network, one that fostered intercolonial agreement on resistance to British measures and spread the resistance from seaports into rural areas.

**community action programs**   programs designed to identify and organize local leaders to take steps to alleviate poverty and crime in their neighborhoods. Sociologist Saul Alinsky from Chicago organized the Industrial Areas Foundation to support community action programs in the 1960s.

**conformity**   degree to which people adjust their behavior, values, and ideas to fit into a group or society.

**conglomerate**   corporation whose various branches or subsidiaries are either directly or indirectly spread among a variety of industries, usually unrelated to one another. The purpose of a conglomerate is generally to increase shareholder value and ensure against market cycles by spreading its risk, rather than to improve market share or production efficiency by concentrating on excelling within a single industry.

**Congregationalists**   members of a Protestant denomination that originated in sixteenth-century Britain as part of the Puritan movement. While some early Congregationalists, known as Separatists,

concluded that the Church of England was beyond reformation, most strove to reform English religion and society while remaining within the Church of England. Early modern Congregationalists embraced Calvinist theological beliefs and held that each individual congregation should conduct its own religious affairs, answering to no higher authority. The Separatists founded Plymouth, the first northern colony, and the Non-Separating Congregationalists predominated elsewhere in seventeenth-century New England.

**conscription**   act of compulsory enrollment for military service, as opposed to a voluntary enlistment.

**consensus**   point of view generally shared by a group, institution, or even a culture. Scholars have analyzed and debated the institutions that contribute to the construction of a consensus viewpoint, ranging from schools and churches to the media in their various forms.

**constitution**   framework of government establishing the contract between rulers and ruled. American revolutionaries insisted on written constitutions to protect individual rights and liberties; by contrast, Britons understood the term *constitution* to mean the existing arrangement of government—not an actual document but a collection of parliamentary laws, customs, and precedents.

**consumer goods**   products such as food and clothing that fill the needs and wants of individuals. *Producer* or *capital goods,* in contrast, are the factory equipment and other machines used to manufacture or transport other goods or services.

**Continental Army**   main rebel military force, created by the Second Continental Congress in July 1775 and commanded by George Washington. After the 1776 campaign, most enlistments came from the poorest and most desperate in American society, and it was they who shouldered the burden of the fighting. During the harsh winter at Valley Forge in 1778/1779, the army acquired greater discipline and expertise and thereafter scored important military victories in the mid-Atlantic and the South.

**contraband**   goods seized by a government during wartime when the goods were being used by an enemy nation or being shipped to an enemy nation by a neutral nation. The term was also applied during the Civil War to escaped slaves who fled behind Union lines.

**Copperhead**   derogatory term used by Republicans to label northern Democrats who opposed the war policies of the Lincoln administration and advocated a negotiated peace.

**CORE** Congress of Racial Equality, an organization founded in Chicago in 1942. The group's inspiration was Krishnalal Shridharani's book *War without Violence,* which outlined Mohandas K. Gandhi's nonviolent philosophy for action. CORE believed that African Americans could use nonviolent civil disobedience to challenge racial segregation.

**corporation** business entity that has been granted a charter granting it legal rights, privileges, and liabilities distinct from the individual members that are a part of it. A corporation therefore may survive the death of the individuals who created and run it.

**Counter-Reformation** reform movement within the Roman Catholic Church in response to the Protestant Reformation, seeking to reform and reinvigorate the Church. Religious orders played a large role in the Counter-Reformation, particularly the Jesuit order, known formally as the Society of Jesus, and founded in 1534 by Ignatius of Loyola.

**covert operations** military or political actions carried out in secret to allow the responsible government or party to deny its role. Governments have often relied on such operations when overt military force is impractical or dangerous or when public negotiations are likely to fail.

# D

**de facto segregation** spatial and social separation of populations brought about by social behavior rather than by laws or legal mechanisms. Segregation (especially in schools) has often existed without being sanctioned by law. When the practice is accomplished through explicit legal means, it is known as *de jure segregation.*

**debt peonage** paying off a debt through labor when the debtor lacks sufficient cash or other assets.

**Deep South** South Carolina, Georgia, Florida, Alabama, Mississippi, Louisiana, and Texas.

**demographic** factors relating to the characteristics of populations. Demography is the study of populations, looking at such aspects as size, growth, density, and age distribution.

**depreciated** decreased in value owing to market conditions. Depreciation in the value of banknotes can occur when too much paper money is put into circulation or when users doubt the ability of the government to back up the paper currency with reserves of gold or silver.

**détente** relaxation of strained relations between nations, especially among the United States, the Soviet Union, and China in the 1970s and late 1980s. In seeking détente, once-hostile parties begin to emphasize their common interests and reduce their points of conflict.

**deterrence** prevention of an action by fear of the consequences; during the cold war, the theory that war could be avoided because each side knew that the other possessed large numbers of nuclear weapons. Thus any nuclear exchange threatened the survival of both sides.

**disenfranchise** to deny a citizen's right to vote.

**disenfranchisement** denial of a citizen's right to vote.

**doctrine of preemption** war undertaken in anticipation of imminent attack or invasion by another nation or in hopes of gaining a strategic advantage when war seems unavoidable. In that sense the Japanese government viewed its attack on Pearl Harbor as preemptive.

**domesticity** devotion to home life, and a woman's place at the center of that life. The ideal of domesticity became popular during the nineteenth century as industrialization was increasingly separating work and home as individual spheres.

**dove** see **hawks and doves.**

**dry farming** farming system to conserve water in semiarid regions receiving less than 15 to 20 inches of rain a year. Methods include leaving some fields fallow or unplanted to reduce water use, keeping soil broken to absorb water, and growing drought-resistant crops.

**due process** constitutional concept, embodied in the Fifth and Fourteenth Amendments, that no person shall be deprived of life, liberty, or property without legal safeguards such as being present at a hearing, having an opportunity to be heard in court, having the opportunity to confront hostile witnesses, and being able to present evidence.

# E

**ecosystem** a community and/or region studied as a system of functioning relationships between organisms and their environments.

**ecumenism** movement encouraging unity among religions, especially among Christian denominations and between Christians and Jews. Ecumenical movements promote cooperation and better understanding among different religious denominations.

**egalitarian** exhibiting or asserting a belief in the equality of humans in a social, political, or economic context.

**elect** in theology, those of the faithful chosen, or "elected," by God for eternal salvation.

**elites** class of people given special social, economic, or intellectual status within society. The singular noun *elite* can also be used as a plural, as in *the colonial elite.*

**embargo** government act prohibiting trade with a foreign country or countries, usually to exert economic pressure.

**enfranchise** see **suffrage** and **disenfranchisement.**

**Enlightenment** intellectual movement that flourished in Europe from the mid-1600s through the eighteenth century and stressed the power of human reason to promote social progress by discovering the laws that governed both nature and society. In the American colonies, the Enlightenment's influence encouraged scientists such as Benjamin Franklin to experiment and discover useful scientific knowledge, and it also persuaded a growing minority to accept more liberal religious views, known as "rational Christianity."

**escalation** process of steady intensification, rather than a sudden or marked increase, applied to the increasing American military presence in Vietnam. The term derives from an escalator, which gradually lifts its cargo to a higher level. Nuclear theorist Herman Kahn used the term geopolitically in his *On Escalation: Metaphors and Scenarios* (1968).

**evangelical** term that derives from a Greek word meaning the bringing of good news—in this case, the Gospel. Protestant evangelicals stressed the need for individual conversion and rebirth stemming from an awareness of sinful guilt and Christ's act of atoning, through his death, for their sins.

**excise tax** internal tax placed on the production or sale of a commodity, usually a luxury item or nonessential.

**executive order** declaration issued by the president or by a governor possessing the force of law. Executive orders are usually based on existing statutory authority and require no action by Congress or the state legislature to take effect.

**expatriate** one who leaves the country of one's birth or citizenship to live in another, usually out of a sense of alienation. The term is often applied to the group of writers and artists living in self-imposed exile in Paris during the 1920s and sometimes referred to as the "Lost Generation." That term was coined by the writer Gertrude Lawrence, describing the rootless generation of American expatriates who found life in the United States culturally sterile and promises of postwar freedom and democracy empty.

# F

**federalism** governing principle established by the Constitution in which the national government and the states divide power. A stronger commitment to federalism as the basis of a national republic replaced the system established by the Articles of Confederation, which granted virtually sovereign power to individual states.

**fission** splitting of a nucleus of an atom into at least two other nuclei, accompanied by the release of a relatively large amount of energy. The splitting of the nucleus of the uranium isotope U-235 or its artificial cousin, plutonium, powered the atomic bomb.

**Free Soil Party** antislavery party formed in 1848 by northern Democrats disillusioned with southern Democratic support for slavery. The party tried to widen its appeal by focusing less on outright abolition than on opposing the spread of slavery into the territories (the need to protect "free soil" and "free labor"). The party never gained strength, however; the Republican Party in the 1850s attracted the greater number of antislavery voters.

**freedmen** former slaves; the term came into use during the Civil War, as greater numbers of slaves fled or were freed under the terms of the Emancipation Proclamation, and continued to be widely used during Reconstruction. More recently historians have also used the gender-neutral term, *freedpeople*.

# G

**graduated income tax** tax based on a percentage of an individual's income, the percentage increasing as total income increases. Under such a system, wealthy individuals are taxed at a higher rate than are poorer individuals.

**Great Awakening** term used by some historians to describe periods of intense religious piety and commitment among Americans that fueled the expansion of Protestant churches. The First Great Awakening extended from the 1730s to the American Revolution; the Second Great Awakening includes the period from about 1790 to the 1840s; the Third Great Awakening took place during the late nineteenth and early twentieth centuries; the Fourth Great Awakening spans the latter half of the twentieth century.

# H

**habeas corpus** Latin phrase meaning, "you have the body." For centuries, the term referred in English law to the right of individuals to be brought before a court and informed of the crime alleged against them. The right of habeus corpus is meant to ensure that the government cannot arbitrarily arrest and imprison a citizen without giving grounds for doing so.

**hawks and doves** nicknames for the two opposing positions in American policy during the war in Vietnam. Hawks supported the escalation of the war and a "peace with honor." Doves, the peace faction, argued that the United States had intervened in a civil war and should withdraw its troops.

**hedge fund** an investment fund requiring high minimum contributions and thus used by a limited range of more affluent investors. Hedge funds are very lightly regulated by the government, often secretive, and undertake a range of high-risk investment and trading strategies.

**Hessians** German soldiers who fought with the British Army during the American Revolution. Some Hessians taken as prisoners of war later served in the Continental Army and settled in the United States after the Revolution.

**horizontal combination** strategy of business growth (sometimes referred to as "horizontal integration") that attempts to stifle competition by combining more than one firm involved in the same level of production, transportation, or distribution into a single firm.

**http://** abbreviation for HyperText Transfer Protocol, the set of Internet rules governing the transfer of data between a server and a computer as well as for exchanging files (text, graphic images, sound, video, and other multimedia files) on the World Wide Web.

# I

**impeachment** under the U.S. Constitution, the process by which members of the House of Representatives bring charges against a high government official for "Treason, Bribery, or other high Crimes and Misdemeanors." Once an individual is impeached, he or she must stand trial before the Senate, where a two-thirds majority vote is required for conviction. Conviction results in removal from office.

**imperialism** acquisition of control over the government and the economy of another nation, usually by conquest. The United States became an imperialistic world power in the late nineteenth century by gaining control over the Hawaiian Islands and, after the Spanish American War (1898), Guam, the Philippines, Cuba, and Puerto Rico.

**indemnity** compensation for loss or damage.

**indentures** contract signed between two parties, binding one to serve the other for a specified period of time. The term originated because two copies of the agreement were made, both indented in the same way at its edges, so that each party was provided an identical record of the agreement.

**inflation** increase in the overall price of goods and services over an extended period of time; or a similar decrease over time of the purchasing power of money. The latter situation can be caused by an increase of the amount of currency and credit available in an economy. In such cases, when the perceived value of paper money declines (as often happens in wars, when the government tries to raise revenues by printing money), sellers raise the prices of their goods to compensate.

**injunction** court order requiring individuals or groups to participate in or refrain from a certain action.

**interstate commerce** trade in goods that crosses state lines. Regulation of interstate commerce is reserved in the Constitution for the federal government and has become the constitutional basis for much of federal regulation of business.

**Iroquois League** Indian confederacy, also known as the Five Nations, that exerted enormous influence throughout the region. In 1712, a sixth tribe, the Tuscaroras, joined the confederation.

**isolationism** belief that the United States should avoid foreign entanglements, alliances, and involvement in foreign wars. The tradition had its roots in President George Washington's farewell address, which warned in 1796, "It is our true policy to steer clear of permanent alliances with any portion of the foreign world...."

**Issei**   *see* **Nisei.**

**itinerant**   traveling preacher attached to no settled congregation. Itinerants played an important role in the first Great Awakening, taking their inspiration from George Whitefield, who preached up and down the Atlantic seaboard. In the early nineteenth century, many Protestant denominations—especially the Methodists and the Baptists—made strategic use of itinerants to evangelize settlers on the frontier.

# J

**jihad**   Arabic term meaning "striving or struggling in the way of God." Although broadly the term can indicate a spiritual effort on the part of a Muslim believer to come closer to Allah, the expression is also used to denote a Muslim holy war against unbelievers.

**joint stock company**   business in which capital is held in transferable shares of stock by joint owners. The joint stock company was an innovation that allowed investors to share and spread the risks of overseas investment. Instead of only a few individuals owning a ship and its cargo—which might sink and bring ruin to its investors—joint stock allowed for smaller sums to be invested in a variety of different ventures.

**journeyman**   person who has served an apprenticeship in a trade or craft and who is a qualified worker employed by another person.

**judicial review**   doctrine set out by Chief Justice John Marshall in *Marbury v. Madison.* The decision established that the judicial branch of the federal government possesses the power to determine whether the laws of Congress or the actions of the executive branch violate the Constitution.

# L

**laissez faire**   a French term ("allow [people] to do [as they choose]") referring to an economic doctrine that advocates holding government interference in the economy to an absolute minimum and ideally having none at all.

**landed states and landless states**   some of the 13 colonies that became the United States had originally been granted land whose western boundaries were vague or overlapped the land granted to other colonies. During the Confederation period, the so-called landless states had boundaries that were firmly drawn on all sides, such as Maryland, New Jersey, and Massachusetts. The so-called landed states possessed grants whose western boundaries were not fixed. (See the map on page 186).

**libertarian**   advocate of a minimalist approach to governing, in which the freedom of private individuals to do as they please ranks paramount. A libertarian philosophy contrasts with the outlook of modern liberals, in which government plays a more active role in meeting the needs of citizens or in managing social and economic life for the common good.

**lien**   legal claim against property used to obtain a loan, which must be paid when the property is sold. Developing first in the South after the Civil War, the crop-lien system allowed merchants to claim a portion (or all) of current or future crops as payment for loans to farmers for seed, tools, and fertilizer. Merchants often insisted that indebted farmers raise a single cash crop, frequently cotton. That requirement helped to ensnare farmers in a cycle of debt as the price of such crops fell.

**loyalists**   supporters of the king and Parliament and known to the rebels as "tories." At the outset of the American Revolution, loyalists made up about one-fifth of the white population, but their ranks diminished steadily after about 1777, as the British army alienated many civilians in every region that they occupied.

**loyalty oath**   oath of fidelity to the state or to an organization. Plans for Reconstruction insisted that southerners returning to the Union take a loyalty oath of some sort, whether that they would be loyal henceforth to the United States or a more strict "ironclad oath" that they never had aided the Confederacy. At other times of stress—as during the Revolutionary era or during the cold war of the 1950s, loyalty oaths and loyalty investigations have been used by groups or governments to enforce obedience to the state or to a revolutionary movement.

# M

**managed economy**   economy directed by the government with power over prices, allocation of resources, and marketing of goods.

**Manifest Destiny**   belief, as Democratic editor John L. O'Sullivan put it, that it had become the United States' "manifest destiny to overspread the continent allotted by Providence for the free development of our yearly multiplying millions." The roots of the doctrine were both religious and political. Protestant religious thinkers had long seen American settlement as setting a pious and virtuous example to the rest of the world. The political ideology of the Revolution encouraged the notion that the benefits of democracy would spread along with the political expansion of the nation. Yet Manifest Destiny was also racist in its assumption of the inferiority of other peoples and cultures; and it encompassed a purely economic desire to expand the nation's commerce and power.

**"Maroon" communities**   collective attempts at escape typically undertaken by groups of newly arrived African slaves in the American South. Such slaves fled inland, often to the frontiers of colonial settlement, where they attempted to reconstruct the African villages from which they had been taken captive. Because of their size, such communities proved to be short-lived; they were quickly discovered by white slave patrols or by Indian tribes such as the Cherokees, who profited from returning runaways. "Maroon communities" in the Caribbean proved far more enduring and provided the bases for successful slave rebellions during the eighteenth and early nineteenth centuries.

**mass media**   forms of communication designed to reach a vast audience, generally a nation state or larger, without personal contact between the senders and receivers. Examples would include newspapers, movies, magazines, radio, television, and—today—some sites on the Internet.

**mercantilism**   European economic doctrine calling for strict regulation of the economy in order to ensure a balance of exports over imports and increase the amount of gold and silver in a nation's treasury.

**merchants of death**   term popularized in the 1930s to describe American bankers and arms makers whose support for the Allied cause, some historians charged, drew the United States into World War I.

**Mesoamerica**   the area stretching from present-day central Mexico southward through Honduras and Nicaragua, in which pre-Columbian civilizations developed.

**Methodist**   denomination that originated as a reform movement within the Church of England during the mid-eighteenth century, much as the Puritans originated as a reform movement within the English church during the mid-sixteenth century. The distinctive features of early Methodism on both sides of the Atlantic included a strict devotional regimen, an ascetic moral discipline, and an emphasis on evangelical conversion. By the Civil War, Methodists had become the largest Protestant denomination in the United States among both whites and African Americans.

**military-industrial complex** combination of the U.S. armed forces, arms manufacturers, and associated political and commercial interests, which grew rapidly during the cold war era. It is another term for the mutually supportive relationship of military contractors, the Pentagon, and sympathetic members of Congress, an alliance also known as the "Iron Triangle."

**militia** local defense band of civilians comprising men between the ages of 16 and 65 whose military training consisted only of occasional gatherings known as musters. Militias were organized in towns and counties throughout the American colonies from the beginnings of settlement, but they played a crucial role in the war for independence by supporting the Continental Army whenever the fighting moved into their neighborhoods.

**millennialism** belief in the thousand-year reign of Christ predicted in the Bible's final book, the Revelation to John. The belief that dedicated Christians could help bring about this reign of holiness by converting the world to Christianity proved to be a powerful impulse to reform.

**miscegenation** marriage, cohabitation, or sexual relations between persons of different races. Since race is a socially constructed identifier rather than one with any scientific or genetic basis, *miscegenation* as a term is used only in its historical context.

**monoculture** growth of a single crop to the virtual exclusion of all others, either on a farm or more generally within a region.

**mutiny** refusal of rank-and-file soldiers to follow the commands of their superior officers. Mutinies plagued the Continental Army between 1779 and 1781 as resentments mounted among soldiers over spoiled food, inadequate clothing, and back pay.

**mutually assured destruction (MAD)** national defense strategy in which a nuclear attack by one side would inevitably trigger an equal response leading to the destruction of both the attacker and the defender. Deterrence theory suggested that when both sides possessed the capability to inflict nuclear annihilation, even after being hit by a first strike, neither side would dare use such weapons.

# N

**national debt** cumulative total of all previous annual *federal deficits* or budget shortfalls incurred each year and owed by the federal government.

**nativism** outlook championing the supremacy of "native" cultural traits and political rights over those of immigrants from different backgrounds. Nativism flourished during the high immigration of the late 1840s and 1850s, evidenced by the rise of the American ("Know-Nothing") party. In the late nineteenth and early twentieth centuries, nativists pressed for the restriction of immigration and won their biggest victories when Congress enacted the National Origins Acts of 1921 and 1924. As immigrant numbers rose again in the late twentieth and early twenty-first centuries, the nativist debate again emerged.

**naturalization** act of granting full citizenship to someone born outside the country.

**navalism** theories of warfare and trade that rely on a nation's navy as a principal instrument of policy.

**neo-isolationist** term applied to those who after World War II believed the United States should avoid foreign entanglements. Neo-isolationists especially condemned the United Nations and its supporters, whom they contemptuously referred to as "one-worlders."

**"new" immigrants** called "new" because they differed substantially from earlier arrivals who had come mostly from northern and western Europe; these newcomers came to the United States between 1880 and 1920 from eastern and southern Europe. Unlike most earlier immigrants (with the exception of the Irish), these immigrants were non-Protestants: Catholics, Jews, and Russian Orthodox Christians.

**Nisei** American-born citizens of Japanese ancestry, contrasted with *Issei*, native-born Japanese who had moved to the United States. At the outbreak of World War II, Nisei referred specifically to Japanese Americans who lived on the West Coast (but not in Hawaii or the East Coast), who were interned during the war because of prejudice and the widespread fear that they sympathized with Japan.

**nomad** a member of a group of people who have no fixed home and who move about, usually seasonally, in pursuit of food, water, and other resources.

**normal schools** schools that trained teachers, usually for two years and mostly for teaching in the elementary grades.

**Northwest Territory** present-day states of Ohio, Indiana, Illinois, Michigan, and Wisconsin. The incorporation of this territory into the United States through the Northwest Ordinance of 1785 marked the major achievement of the national government under the Articles of Confederation.

# O

**Opposition** diverse group of political thinkers and writers in Great Britain, also known as the Country Party and the Commonwealthmen, who elaborated the tradition of classical republicanism from the late seventeenth century through the eighteenth century. They warned that the executive branch of government (the king and his ministers) was conspiring to corrupt and coopt the legislative branch of government (the House of Commons), thereby endangering popular liberties, and they called for political reforms to make Britain's government more representative of and more accountable to the people. Dismissed in England as a disaffected radical minority, the Opposition exerted a decisive influence on the political thinking of an increasing number of American colonials in the decades leading up to the Revolution.

**outsourcing** the contracting of goods or services from outside a company or organization in order to maintain flexibility in the size of the organization's workforce. Increasingly, outsourcing has used suppliers outside the United States in low-wage countries such as Mexico, India, and China.

# P

**pandemic** outbreak of disease that spreads across national boundaries or across the world.

**partisan warfare** armed clashes among political rivals, typically involving guerrilla fighting and the violent intimidation of civilians by militias. Partisan warfare between loyalists and rebels tore apart communities everywhere in the United States during the war for independence, but the fighting was especially fierce and protracted in the South. The success of rebel insurgencies there ultimately convinced many southern whites to support the cause of independence.

**patent**   legal document issued by the government giving the holder exclusive rights to use, make, and sell a process, product, or device for a specified period of time. The first patents in America were issued by colonial governments as early as 1641. Congress enacted the first patent law in 1790.

**paternalism**   attitude or policy of treating individuals or groups in a fatherly manner, by providing for their needs without granting them rights or responsibilities. The relation involves both a dominant and a subordinate party. Sometimes the dominance comes from gender, as in a male patriarchy, whereby females are given subordinate roles. But paternalism can also be expressed in relations between colonial and subject peoples, masters and slaves, or culturally different groups.

***pays d'en haut***   in the seventeenth century, the lands referred to by the French as the "upper country," the land upriver from Montreal as French fur traders passed into the Great Lakes beyond the southern shores of Lake Ontario. The trading lands stretched all the way to the Mississippi River.

**peculiar institution**   euphemism for slavery, perhaps revealing in its use. The institution was "peculiar" to the South in that it had been abolished in the North (and other parts of the world, increasingly). *Peculiar* also suggests the contradiction with the ideals of the Declaration of Independence, that "all men are created equal."

**per capita income**   average yearly income per person in a particular population; it provides one statistical measure of the relative wealth of a region.

**pluralism**   idea that identity cannot be reduced to a single shared essence. Under such a philosophy, distinct ethnic, cultural, and religious groups are tolerated and affirmed within a society. The philosophy contrasts with the belief, in American politics, that citizens should assimilate into a more uniform cultural identity of shared values. Contrasting metaphors portray an assimilationist United States as a melting pot versus a pluralist mixing bowl.

**plurality**   in elections, a candidate who receives a plurality wins more votes than any other candidate but less than half of all votes cast. Receiving more than half of the votes cast is called a *majority*.

**pocket veto**   means of vetoing a bill without formally doing so. Normally, if a president does not veto or sign a bill within 10 days of receiving it, the bill automatically becomes law. If it is received, however, within 10 days of Congress's adjournment, the president can simply "pocket" the bill unsigned, until Congress adjourns, and it does not go into effect.

**political culture**   patterns, habits, institutions, and traits associated with a political system. The political culture of the Jacksonian era, for example, was marked by a number of innovations: political nominating conventions, torchlight parades, campaign songs, badges, and other souvenirs.

**political machine**   hierarchical political organization developed in the nineteenth century that controlled the activities of a political party and was usually headed by a political boss.

**popular sovereignty**   doctrine that a territory could decide by vote whether or not to permit slavery within its boundaries. The doctrine was devised by Senator Stephen Douglas of Illinois as a way to placate southerners who wanted slavery permitted within Kansas Territory, forbidden under the Missouri Compromise. Meant as a compromise measure, the doctrine only inflamed the situation, as both sides worked to win a vote over slavery.

**Populism**   political outlook that supports the rights and powers of the common people in opposition to the interests of the privileged elite. The Populist Party evolved out of the economic distress of the 1890s among farmers and focused its anger against the era's large industrial corporations, railroad monopolies, and banks. But populism as an outlook and philosophy persisted long after the party had dissolved.

**pragmatism**   philosophical movement, led by philosophers Charles S. Peirce and William James, that stressed the visible, real-world results of ideas. Pragmatism was embraced by many progressives who wanted to promote the possibilities of change by abandoning the old notion that events were predetermined and inevitable.

**predestination**   basis of Calvinist theology and a belief that holds that God has ordained the outcome of all human history before the beginning of time, including the eternal fate of every human being. Believers in this doctrine found comfort and meaning from its assurance that God was directing the fate of nations, individuals, and all of creation toward his divine purposes.

**Presbyterians**   members of a Protestant denomination that originated in sixteenth-century Britain as part of the Puritan movement. Like their fellow Puritan reformers, the Congregationalists, the Presbyterians embraced Calvinist theology beliefs; but unlike the Congregationalists, Presbyterians favored a more hierarchical form of church governance, a system in which individual congregations were guided by presbyteries and synods comprising both laymen and ministers.

**presidio**   military garrison; as Spanish colonizers moved north from central Mexico in the sixteenth and seventeenth centuries, they constructed presidios to consolidate claims over new territory. Presidios often encouraged the growth of nearby towns and ranches and were probably more important as sites of diplomacy with Indians than as centers of military power. Poor funding and political instability led to the decline of the presidios after Mexican independence in 1821.

**privatize**   transferral of an economic enterprise or public utility from the control of the government into private ownership. The Bush plan for Social Security reform sought to place retirement contributions into investment accounts managed privately, rather than into a fund managed by the Social Security Administration.

**producer goods**   goods, such as heavy machinery, used to manufacture other goods, often consumer goods.

**psychedelic**   characterized by or generating shifts in perception and altered states of awareness, often hallucinatory, and usually brought on by drugs such as LSD, mescaline, or psilocybin. Advocates of the psychedelic state spoke of euphoria, mystic visions, and philosophic insights produced. Critical observers pointed to the potential of inducing not only hallucinations but also sometimes psychoses.

**public works**   government-financed construction projects, such as highways and bridges, for use by the public.

**Puritans**   members of a reform movement within the Church of England that originated in the sixteenth century and that ultimately formed the Congregationalist and Presbyterian churches. Calvinist in their theology, the Puritans strove to reform English religion, society, and politics by restricting church membership to the pious and godly, by according the laity greater power in church governance, and by enlisting the state to enforce a strict moral code that prohibited drunkenness, gambling, swearing, and attending the theater.

# Q

**Quakers**   Protestant sect, also known as the Society of Friends, founded in mid-seventeenth century England. The Quakers believed that the Holy Spirit dwelt within each human being and that religious conviction was the source of their egalitarian social practices, which included allowing women to speak in churches and to preach in public gatherings. Quakers settled the mid-Atlantic colonies in large numbers and founded the colony of Pennsylvania.

# R

**racialism**   *see* **racism.**

**racism**   form of discrimination based on the belief that one race is superior to another. Racism may be expressed individually and consciously, through explicit thoughts, feelings, or acts; it can be codified into a theory that claims scientific backing for its tenets. It can also be expressed socially and unconsciously, through institutions that promote inequality between races. In the early twentieth century, when racism became much more pronounced, the term *racialism* was also coined.

**reconquista**   military reconquest of the Iberian Peninsula from Islamic Moors of Africa by European Christian rulers. The campaign lasted on and off from 718 to 1492 CE.

**Redeemers**   southerners who came to power in southern state governments from 1875 to 1877, claiming to have "redeemed" the South from Reconstruction. The Redeemers looked to undo many of the changes wrought by the Civil War. Their goals included minimizing the role of African Americans in government and reducing their economic independence and strengthening the "New South" through industrial development.

**red-light district**   area in cities reserved for prostitutes. The term, first employed in the United States, resulted from the use of

red lights to show that prostitutes were open for business.

**repatriation**   act of returning people to their nation of origin. The term often refers to the act of returning soldiers or refugees to their birth country.

**republican motherhood**   redefinition of the role of women promoted by many American reformers in the 1780s and 1790s, who believed that the success of republican government depended on educated and independent-minded mothers who would raise children to become informed and self-reliant citizens. The ideal of republican motherhood fostered improvements in educational opportunities for women and accorded them an important role in civic life, but it also reinforced the notion that women should confine the sphere of their activities to home and family.

**republicanism**   belief that representative government safeguards popular liberties more reliably than does either monarchy or oligarchy and that all citizens must practice vigilance and self-denying virtue to prevent their rulers from succumbing to the temptations of power and becoming tyrants. This "classical republicanism" profoundly influenced the political views of many Americans from the middle of the eighteenth century to the middle of the nineteenth century.

**Romanticism**   intellectual and artistic movement that arose in the early nineteenth century out of a rejection of the Enlightenment values of reason and balance. Romanticism emphasized the individual's expression of emotion and intuition.

# S

**sagebrush rebels**   group of western cattlemen, loggers, miners, developers, and others who argued that federal ownership of huge tracts of land and natural resources violated the principle of states' rights. This group demanded that government transfer control to individual states, in respect of their right to make decisions about the management of both the land and the natural resources.

**scalawag**   white southerners who supported the Republican Party. The derisive nickname was given by their opponents. Perhaps a quarter of all white southerners voted Republican at some time during Reconstruction.

**scientific management**   system of factory production that stresses efficiency.

The system was pioneered by American engineer Frederick Winslow Taylor. In *The Principles of Scientific Management* (1911), his most famous work, he emphasized time-and-motion studies to enhance productivity. The book became the bible of efficiency experts and Taylor the "Father of Scientific Management."

**sedition**   words or actions that incite revolt against the law or duly constituted government.

**segregation**   system, imposed through law and custom, of separating people by race; first enacted into law in Tennessee (1875) with a statute separating blacks from whites on trains, one of the most prevalent public spaces for racial mingling.

**self-determination**   principle in international law that people have a right to determine their own form of government free from outside control. The principle contrasts with colonialism and imperialism, under which people are subject to foreign rulers.

**semisubsistence economy**   economy in which individuals and families produce most of what they need to live on. Such economies are overwhelmingly rural and also egalitarian, in that wealth is distributed fairly broadly. During the colonial period and early republic, much of the American economy was semisubsistence. *See also* **commercial economy.**

**separate but equal**   rationale for a policy of segregation granting equal facilities and services to African American and whites in schools, hospitals, transportation and lodging facilities, and other public places. The Supreme Court upheld such laws in *Plessy v. Ferguson* (1896). In practice such facilities were separate but seldom equal.

**separation of church and state**   principle that religious institutions and their representatives should exercise no civil or judicial powers and that civil governments should give no official sanction, privileges, or financial support to any religious denomination or organization.

**separation of powers**   principle that each branch of government—the legislature (Congress), the executive (the President), and the judiciary (the Supreme Court)—should wield distinct powers independent from interference or infringement by other branches of government. During the debates of the Constitutional Convention in 1797, James Madison successfully argued that this separation of powers was essential to a balanced republican government.

**settlement house**   social reform effort that used neighborhood centers in which settlement house workers lived and worked among the poor, often in slum neighborhoods. The first settlement house, Toynbee Hall in London, was founded in 1884. The first settlement house in the United States (The Neighborhood Guild, later University Settlement House) came in 1886 in New York City and was founded by Stanton Coit.

**Shi'ite and Sunni**   two major branches of Islam, a division not unlike the Protestant-Catholic split in Christianity. After the death of the Prophet Muhammad, followers disagreed over who should be his successor. Most believers accepted the tradition of having their leader chosen by community consensus (the Sunni branch), but a minority supported the claim of Ali, the Prophet's cousin. Over the years theological differences have separated Shi'ite and Sunni Muslims as well. Today the Shi'ites are dominant largely in Iran and southeastern Iraq.

**silent majority**   phrase coined by President Richard Nixon in a 1969 speech, referring to the large number of Americans who supported his policies but did not express their views publicly.

**sit-in**   form of direct action in which protesters nonviolently occupy and refuse to leave an area. Mahatma Gandhi employed the tactic during the Indian independence movement, and autoworkers used it in Flint, Michigan, in the late 1930s. Student movements around the world widely adopted the tactic in the 1960s.

**social mobility**   movement of individuals from one social class to another. In general, the stronger the barriers of class, race, gender or caste, the less social mobility exhibited by a society.

**socialism**   philosophy of social and economic organization in which the means of producing and distributing goods is owned collectively or by government.

**sociological jurisprudence**   legal theory that emphasizes the importance not merely of precedent but of contemporary social context in interpreting the law.

**specie**   coined money of gold or silver. Also referred to as hard money or hard currency. In contrast, banknotes or notes are paper money or paper currency.

**sphere of influence**   geographic region beyond its border over which a nation exerts political or economic control.

**spoils system**   practice of rewarding loyal party members with jobs in government. Known more formally as "patronage," the practice drew its name from the old saying "To the victor belong the spoils," in this instance, meaning the rewards of election victories.

**steerage**   least expensive accommodation on a passenger ship, located below decks and often used by immigrants for passage to the United States in the late nineteenth and early twentieth centuries.

**stock exchange**   market at which shares of ownership in corporations are bought and sold. The creation of what were markets for investment capital made it easier to raise the large sums of money needed for large industrial projects.

**stratified**   layered; in this case, according to class or social station. A highly stratified society has a greater variety of social levels, from the richest or most socially esteemed to the poorest or least socially approved. A society can be stratified according to wealth, race, religion, or a number of other social markers.

**subsistence farming**   see **semisubsistence economy.**

**subversive**   one who seeks the destruction or overthrow of a legally constituted government; also used as an adjective ( for example, *subversive conduct*) to refer more generally to behavior undermining the established social order.

**suffrage**   right to vote; also referred to as the franchise. To *disenfranchise* is to take away the right to vote.

**Sun Belt**   areas of the southern and western parts of the United States that experienced significant economic and population growth since World War II. That growth has been a contrast to the relative decline of the *Rust Belt*, the older industrial area from New England to the mid-Atlantic region across the upper Middle West.

**Sunni**   see **Shi'ite and Sunni.**

**supply-side economics**   theory that emphasizes tax cuts and business incentives to encourage economic growth rather than deficit spending to promote demand. Businesses and individuals, the theory assumes, will use their tax savings to create new businesses and expand old businesses, which in turn will increase productivity, employment, and general well-being.

# T

**tariff**   duty on trade, the purpose of which is primarily to regulate the flow of commerce rather than to raise a revenue. The Molasses Act of 1733, for example, imposed a hefty customs duty on molasses imported from non-British Caribbean islands to encourage American distillers to purchase molasses exclusively from the British West Indies.

**task system**   way of organizing slave labor in the South Carolina low country during the eighteenth century. Masters and overseers of rice and indigo plantations assigned individual slaves a daily task, and after its completion, slaves could spend the rest of the day engaged in pursuits of their own choosing. Gang labor, the system practiced in the Chesapeake, afforded slaves less opportunity for freedom within slavery.

**taxes**   duty on trade (known as external taxation) or a duty on items circulating within a nation or a colony (known as internal taxation) intended primarily to raise a revenue rather than to regulate the flow of commerce. The Sugar Act of 1764 was an external tax, whereas the Stamp Act of 1765 was an internal tax.

**Tejano**   Texan of Hispanic descent. In the early stages of the rebellion against Santa Anna, more than a few Tejanos supported the Texan drive for independence. But as Americans continued to arrive in Texas in large numbers, many viewed Tejanos with suspicion, and they were marginalized in Texan society.

**temperance movement**   reform movement, begun in the 1820s, to temper or restrain the sale and use of alcohol. It achieved its greatest success when the Eighteenth Amendment took effect in 1920, outlawing the manufacture, sale, transportation, and importation of alcohol. The amendment was repealed in 1933.

**tenement**   building, often in disrepair and usually five or six stories in height, in which cheap apartments were rented to tenants. Such dilapidated housing sprang up in cities across the United States in the late nineteenth and early twentieth centuries to lodge the growing numbers of immigrants, African Americans, and other poor populations moving to urban centers.

**theocracy**   system of government dominated by the clergy.

**totalitarian government**   system in which the state controls all aspects of economic, political, and even social life, usually through some form of dictatorship. Nazi Germany under Adolf Hitler and the Soviet Union under Joseph Stalin are examples of totalitarian regimes.

**trade association**   organization of individuals and firms in a given industry that provides statistical, lobbying, and other services to members.

**trust**   business arrangement in which owners of shares in a business turn over their shares "in trust" to a board with power to control those businesses for the benefit of the trust. Following the example set by John D. Rockefeller and Standard Oil, trusts blossomed in the late nineteenth century as a means of consolidating power over production, marketing, and pricing, often crowding out other competitors.

# U

**union**   organization of workers designed to improve their economic status and working conditions. Such organizations come in two varieties: the horizontal union, in which all members share a common skill or craft, and the vertical union, composed of workers from all across the same industry.

**Upper South**   the border states (Delaware, Maryland, Kentucky, and Missouri) and Virginia, North Carolina, Tennessee, and Arkansas.

# V

**vertical integration**   strategy of business growth that attempts to reduce costs by gaining control of the successive stages of a business operation, incorporating into a single firm several firms involved in all aspects of the manufacture of a product—from exploiting raw materials to manufacturing and distribution.

**Victorianism**   constellation of middle-class values attributed to the proper virtues of Britain's Queen Victoria. Victorianism responded to the instabilities of an industrial age in which factory work dominated the lives of struggling workers and middle-class clerks as well as down-at-the-heels landed gentry. The culture's emphasis on "refinement" and "manners" established a social hierarchy offering some sense of stability.

**virgin soil epidemic**   epidemic in which the populations at risk have had no previous contact with the diseases that strike them and are therefore immunologically almost defenseless.

**virtual representation**   view that representation is not linked to election but rather to common interests; for example, during the imperial crisis the British argued that Americans were virtually represented in Parliament, even though colonials elected none of its members, because each member of Parliament stood for the interests of the whole empire. *See also* **actual representation.**

# W

**"watered" stock**   stock issued in excess of the assets of a company. The term derived from the practice of some ranchers who made their cattle drink large amounts of water before weighing them for sale.

**welfare capitalism**   business practice of providing welfare—in the form of pension and profit-sharing programs, subsidized housing, personnel management, paid vacations, and other services and benefits—for workers. The practice was pioneered by Henry Ford under the philosophy that businesses in a capitalist economy should act for the common good of their workers. The philosophy, if not the businesswide practice, became popular in the 1920s as a way of reducing high rates of turnover among employees and integrating technological change into the workplace.

**Wisconsin idea**   series of progressive reforms at the state level promoted by Robert La Follette during his governorship of Wisconsin (1901–1906). They included primary elections, corporate property taxes, regulation of railroads and public utilities, and supervision of public resources in the public interest. A nonpartisan civil service group, recruited mostly from faculty at the University of Wisconsin, provided a cadre of expert bureaucrats to run the new programs.

# Y

**yellow journalism**   brand of newspaper reporting that stresses excitement and shock over evenhandedness and dull fact. The term "yellow journalism" derived from the color of the ink used to print the first comic strip, which appeared in William Randolph Hearst's *New York Journal* in 1895. Hearst's newspaper specialized in yellow journalism and is often credited with igniting public passions for war with Spain in 1898.

# Credits

## Text Credits

### CHAPTER 1

**Page 17,** Dueling Document 1
Quotation from Sherburne F. Cook and Woodrow Borah, *Essays in Population History: Mexico and the Caribbean,* 3 vols. Copyright 1971 by University of California Press—Books. Reproduced with permission of University of California Press—Books via Copyright Clearance Center.

**Page 17,** Dueling Document 2
Quotation from Massimo Livi-Bacci, "Return to Hispaniola: Reassessing a Demographic Catastrophe," in *Hispanic American Historical Review,* Volume 83, no. 1, pp. 3–51. Copyright, 2003, Duke University Press. All rights reserved. Republished by permission of the copyright holder, Duke University Press. www.dukeupress.edu.

### CHAPTER 4

**Page 93,** Dueling Documents 1 & 2
Quotation from The Salem Witchcraft Papers, Verbatim Transcriptions of the Court Records in three volumes. Edited by Paul Boyer and Stephen Nissenbaum, Da Capo Press, 1977. Salem Witch Trials Documentary Archive, http://etext.virginia.edu/salem/witchcraft.

### CHAPTER 24

**Page 662,** Dueling Document 1
Quotation from Marcus Garvey, "Go Back to Africa," speech at Madison Square Garden, March 16, 1924. Reprinted in Amy Garvey, *Philosophy and Opinions of Marcus Garvey: African for the Africans* (NH: Ayer Company Publishers 2e, 1967), pp. 118–123. Reprinted with permission of Ayer Company Publishers.

**Page 662,** Dueling Document 2
"We must oppose all segregation" from W. E. B. Du BOIS, "On Being Ashamed of Oneself: An Essay on Race Pride," The McGraw-Hill Companies wish to thank the Crisis Publishing Co., Inc., the publisher of the magazine of the National Association for the Advancement of Colored People, for the use of this material first published in the May 1933 issue of Crisis Magazine.

### CHAPTER 25

**Page 690,** Dueling Document 2
"Lorena Hickok to Harry Hopkins, January 1, 1935" in Richard Lowitt and Maurine Beasley, eds., *One Third of a Nation: Lorena Hickok reports on the Great Depression* (University of Illinois Press: Urbana, IL, 1981).

### CHAPTER 28

**Page 777**
Figure: Average Annual Regional Migration, 1947–1960 from Frank Levy, "Major U.S. Migration Flows in the late 1940s and 1950s." In *Dollars and Dreams: The Changing American Income Distribution,* Figure 6.1. © 1998 Russell Sage Foundation, 112 East 64th Street, New York, NY 10065. Reprinted with permission.

**Page 784**
Reprinted courtesy of Pepsi-Cola Company.

### CHAPTER 29

**Page 820,** Dueling Document 1
Quotation from Statement of Purpose of the SNCC (Student Non-Violent Coordinating Committee). Reprinted by permission of the SNCC Legacy Project, Inc.

**Page 820,** Dueling Document 2
Quotation from the Sharon Statement, 1960, Young Americans For Freedom. www.yaf.com, Young Americans For Freedom, 2300 M Street, NW, # 800, Washington, D.C. 20037.

**Page 821,** Dueling Document 3
Quotation from Port Huron Statement of the SDS, Michigan, 1962. Students for a Democratic Society, 1962, public document.

### CHAPTER 30

**Page 845,** Dueling Document 1
Gloria Steinem, What Would It Be Like if Women Win? From Alexander Bloom and Wini Breines, eds., *"Takin' It to the Streets": A Sixties Reader* (New York: Oxford University Press, 1995), pp. 475–477. Reprinted by permission of the author.

**Page 845,** Dueling Document 2
Phyllis Schlafly, "What 'Women's Lib' Really Means." From the Phyllis Schlafly Report 5, no. 7 (February 1972). Reprinted by permission of the author.

### CHAPTER 31

**Page 866,** Dueling Document 1
Quotation from *Listen America!* by Jerry Falwell, copyright © 1980 by Jerry Falwell. Used by permission of Doubleday, a division of Random House, Inc. Any third party use of this material, outside of this publication, is prohibited. Interested parties must apply directly to Random House, Inc. for permission.

**Page 867,** Dueling Document 2
Norman Lear, excerpt from "Liberty and Its Responsibilities," in *Broadcast Journalism 1979–1981: The Eighth Alfred I. DuPont Columbia University Survey,* Marvin Barnett, ed., (NY: Everest House, 1982). www.normanlear.com/backstory_writings.html. Used by permission.

**Page 875**
Figure: Poverty in America, 1970–1993 from Frank Levy, "Official Poverty Rates for Children, the Elderly, and the General Population." In *Dollars and Dreams: The Changing American Income Distribution* Figure 7.1. © 1998 Russell Sage Foundation, 112 East 64th Street, New York, NY 10065. Reprinted with permission.

### CHAPTER 32

**Page 926,** Dueling Document 2
Reprinted by permission of the publisher from *The Discovery of Global Warming: Revised and Expanded Edition* by Spencer R. Weart, pp. 201–204, Cambridge, MA: Harvard University Press, Copyright © 2003, 2008 by Spencer R. Weart.

## Photo Credits

Image Researcher: Deborah Bull; Assistant Researcher: Jullie Chung

### FRONT MATTER

p. iii (top): The McGraw-Hill Companies; (bottom): Library of Congress (LC-DIG-pga02419); p. iv: Library of Congress; p. xxiv: The Granger Collection, New York; xxvi: National Archives; p. xxvii: Private Collection/The Bridgeman Art Library International; Backgrounds (Laid paper): National Gallery of Art, Washington.

### CHAPTER 1

Opener: © Richard A. Cooke/Corbis; p. 4: © Heritage Images/Corbis; p. 5: Adalberto Rios Szalay/Sexto Sol/Getty Images/Getty Images; p. 6: Princeton University Art Museum. Museum purchase, Fowler McCormick, Class of 1921, Fund, in honor of Gillett G. Griffin on his seventieth birthday. Photo: Bruce M. White, © Trustees of Princeton University/Art Resource, NY; p. 7 (top) © Werner Formans/HIP/Image Works; (bottom) © George H. H. Huey/Corbis; p. 8: Courtesy of Cahokia Mounds State Historic Site, Collinsville, Illinois. Painting by William R. Iseminger; p. 9: Ancestor Figure, Kwakwaka'wakw, A50009d. Courtesy UBC Museum of Anthropology, Vancouver, Canada. Photo: Bill McLennan;

of the New-York Historical Society, USA/ The Bridgeman Art Library; p. 183: Miriam & Ira D. Wallach Division of Arts, Prints and Photographs. New York Public Library. Astor, Lenox and Tilden Foundations; p. 184: National Archives (596742); p. 185: unidentified artist, circa 1805. *The Plan of Civilization*. Oil on canvas, 35 7/8 × 49 7/8 inches. Greenville County Museum of Art, Greenville, SC, Gift of The Museum Association, Inc. with funds donated by Corporate Partners: Ernst and Young; Fluor Daniel; Director's Circle Members; Mr. and Mrs. Alester G. Furman, III; Mr. and Mrs. Dexter Hagy; Thomas P. Harntess; Mr. and Mrs. E. Erwin Maddrey, II; Mary M. Pearce; Mr. and Mrs. John D. Pellett, Jr.; Mr. W. Thomas Smith; Mr. and Mrs. Edward H. Stall; Eleanor and Irvine Welling; Museum Antiques Show, 1989, 1990, 1991, Elliott, Davis & Company, CPA's sponsor: Collectors Group 1990, 1991; p. 187: © Bettmann/Corbis; p. 189: © Wilberforce House, Hull City Museums and Art Galleries, UK/The Bridgeman Art Library; p. 190: The Library Company of Philadelphia (W26); p. 191: *The Skater (Portrait of William Grant)*, 1782, by Gilbert Stuart, American, 1755–1828. Oil on canvas, 245.5 × 147.4 cm (96 1/4 × 58 in.) Andrew W. Mellon Collection, © 2007 Board of Trustees, National Gallery of Art, Washington. 1950.18.1; p. 192: Courtesy, Winterthur Museum, Painting, *Rebecca Prichard Mills (Mrs. William Mills) and her daughter Eliza Shrewsbury*, by James Earl, 1794–1796, Charleston, SC, Bequest of Henry Francis du Pont, 1960.554; p. 193: Courtesy Winterthur Museum (1954.0093.001); p. 194 (left): Tate Gallery, London/Art Resource, NY; (right): The Library Company of Philadelphia; p. 195: © Reproduced by permission of The Society of the Cincinnati, Washington, D.C. (M1938.482); p. 196: © Francis G. Mayer/ Corbis; p. 197: Private Collection/Peter Newark American Pictures/The Bridgeman Art Library; p. 203 (top): Brand × Pictures/Punch-Stock; p. 204: Herrnhut, Archiv der Brüder-Unität; p. 205: Virginia Baptist Historical Society at the University of Richmond; p. 206: The Print and Picture Collection, The Free Library of Philadelphia. Will Brown, Photographer; p. 207: The Historic New Orleans Collection, accession no. 1960.46.

## CHAPTER 9

Opener: © Collection of the New-York Historical Society, USA/The Bridgeman Art Library; p. 210: The Granger Collection, New York; p. 214: copyright © The Metropolitan Museum of Art/Art Resource, NY; p. 216 (left): Independence National Historical Park; (right): *Alexander Hamilton*, c. 1972, (detail) by John Trumbull. Oil on canvas, 30 1/4 × 24 1/8 in. Gift of Avalon Foundation, © 2000 Board of Trustees, National Gallery of Art, Washington, DC; p. 217: Private Collection/Archives Charmet/The Bridgeman Art Library; p. 218: Gilbert Stuart (American painter, 1755–1828), *John Adams*, c. 1800/1815, oil on canvas, overall: 73.7 × 61 cm (29 × 24 in.) framed:

97.5 × 84.5 × 10.8 cm (38 3/8 × 33 1/4 × 4 1/4 in.) Gift of Mrs. Robert Homans, National Gallery of Art, Washington, DC; p. 220: Hulton Archive/Getty Images; p. 221: Courtesy, Winterthur Museum, Painting, *The Quilting Frolic*, by John Lewis Krimmel, 1813, Philadelphia, PA, Museum Purchase, 1953.178.2; p. 222: Miniature Panorama Scene (detail): "Scenes from a Seminary for Young Ladies," c. 1810–20. Saint Louis Art Museum, Museum Purchase and funds given by the Decorative Arts Society (89: 1976); p. 227, 228: The Granger Collection, New York; p. 233: Library of Congress (ppm-sca10755); p. 234 (left): Special Collections and College Archives, Skillman Library, Lafayette College; (right): Collection of The New-York Historical Society (1937.714); p. 239 (left): Library of Congress (LC-USZ62-70508); (right): From the Collection of the Henry Ford; p. 241: Monticello, The Thomas Jefferson Memorial Foundation, Inc.; p. 242: Jefferson, Thomas. Farm Book, 1774–1824; p. 145. Original manuscript from the Coolidge Collection of Thomas Jefferson manuscripts, Courtesy of the Massachusetts Historical Society; p. 243 (top): Howard University/Moorland-Spingarn Research Center; (bottom): Abby Aldrich Rockefeller Folk Art Museum, Colonial Williamsburg Foundation, Williamsburg, VA (#T94-121).

## CHAPTER 10

Opener: © Collection of the New-York Historical Society, USA/The Bridgeman Art Library; p. 246: Library of Congress; p. 247: © Bettmann/ Corbis; p. 250 (top): Library of Congress (LC-USZ62-103288); (bottom): The Lilly Library, Indiana University, Bloomington, Indiana; p. 252: *Princess*, by Adrien Persac. Louisiana State University Museum of Art, Baton Rouge. Gift of Mrs. Mamie Persac Lusk; p. 255: Charles Felix, Blauvelt, *A German Immigrant Inquiring His Way*, 1855, Oil on canvas, 36 1/8 × 29 in. (91.8 × 73.7 cm), North Carolina Museum of Art, Purchased with funds from the State of North Caroline, 52.9.2; p. 256: American Textile History Museum, Lowell MA; p. 258: Photo by Jonathan Parker/Lowell National Historic Park/National Park Service; p. 259: Gift of the American Art Council and Mr. and Mrs. J. Douglas Pardee/Digital Image © Museum Associates/LACMA; p. 260: New York Public Library/Art Resource, NY; p. 262: Library of Congress; p. 263 (left): Private Collection: (right): Biggs Museum of American Art; p. 265: *Interior of Fort Laramie*, Alfred Jacob Miller. © Walters Art Museum, Baltimore USA/ The Bridgeman Art Library; p. 266: Library of Congress (LC-USZ62-89594).

## CHAPTER 11

Opener: SuperStock; p. 272: Courtesy of the Cornell University Library, "Making of America" Digital Collection; p. 274: © Museum of the City of New York, USA/The Bridgeman Art Library; p. 277 *Politics in an Oyster House*, Richard Caton Woodville. The Walters Art Museum (37.1994); p. 278 (top):

*County Election* by George Caleb Bingham, 1851–52. Saint Louis Art Museum, Gift of Bank of America (bottom): The New-York Historical Society, 1858.11; p. 279: The Granger Collection, New York; p. 280: National Museum of the American Indian, Smithsonian Institution (P00452); p. 282: Joslyn Art Museum, Omaha, Nebraska (1991.19.2); p. 285: (top): Library of Congress Manuscript Division (MMC-2503); (bottom left): Library of Congress (LC-USZC4-4438); (bottom right): Courtesy of the J. Paul Getty Museum, Los Angeles, 84.XT.441.3; p. 287: "Webster's Reply to Hayne" Courtesy of The Boston Art Commission, 2004; p. 289: The Library Company of Philadelphia; p. 290: Museum of the City of New York, The J. Clarence Davies Collection/Art Resource, NY; p. 292: Gift of Stephen C. Clark. Fenimore Art Museum, Cooperstown, NY. Photograph by Richard Walker. (N0402.1955) p. 295: Library of Congress (3b35969).

## CHAPTER 12

Opener: Library of Congress; p. 298: Harriet Beecher Stowe Center, Hartford, CT; p. 299: Library of Congress (LC-USZC4-2671); p. 300 (top): Allen Memorial Art Museum, Oberlin College, Ohio; Gift of Lewis Tappan to Oberlin College, 1858; (bottom): The Granger Collection, New York; p. 301: Photograph by Richard Pieper. Courtesy of New York Parks, Recreation and Historic Preservation; p. 303: The McGraw-Hill Companies; p. 304: Stock Montage, Inc.; p. 305: From the Collections of Old Sturbridge Village, Sturbridge, MA (26.23.95); p. 306: Image copyright © The Metropolitan Museum of Art/Art Resource, NY; p. 307: A6 folio American Tract Society, Boston, MA n.d.s.n. Engraving, 53 × 46.5 cm © American Antiquarian Society; p. 308: Connecticut Historical Society, Hartford, Connecticut (920 B4135be vol. 2); p. 309: Library of Congress (LC-USZC2-9797); p. 310 (top): Courtesy Concord Free Public Library; (bottom): Library of Congress; p. 311: Apic/Getty Images; p. 312: Miriam and Ira D. Wallach Division of Art, Prints and Photographs, The New York Public Library. Astor, Lenox and Tilden Foundations; p. 313: © Lowell Georgia/Corbis; p. 314 (top left): Courtesy of the Trustees of the Boston Public Library/Rare Books. (Ms. B. 10.37); (top right): Library of Congress; (bottom): Photograph courtesy of the Pocumtuck Valley Memorial Association, Memorial Hall Museum, Deerfield, Massachusetts. L05.077 p. 315: Madison County Historical Society, Oneida, NY; p. 316: Coline Jenkins/Elizabeth Cady Stanton Trust; p. 318: Library of Congress (3a12793); p. 321 (left): AGE Fotostock; (right): Library of Congress (cph 3a44497).

## CHAPTER 13

Opener: 322: The J. Paul Getty Museum, Los Angeles; p. 324: National Archives of Canada, Documentary Art and Photography Division (C128473); p. 326 (top): University of Arkansas Department of Entomology. (IMG9368)/Scott Akin; (bottom): Museum of the City of New

canvas, 63 × 45 1/8 inc. (160.02 × 114.62 cm), Milwaukee Art Museum, Layton Art Collection, Purchase L1964.7. Photo credit P. Richard Ellis; p. 547: Hulton Archive/Getty Images; p. 548: Winslow Homer, *Blackboard,* 1877. © 2000 Board of Trustees, National Gallery of Art, Washington, Gift (Partial and Promised) of Jo Ann and Julian Gans, Jr., in honor of the 50th Anniversary of the National Gallery of Art (1990.60.1/DR); p. 549: Harpers New Monthly Magazine, May 1893, pg 837; p. 550: Shinn, Everett, *Sixth Avenue Shoppers,* n.d. Pastel and watercolor on board, 21 × 26 1/2″. Santa Barbara Museum of Art, Gift of Mrs. Sterling Morton for the Preston Morton Collection; p. 552: Image courtesy of Circus World Museum, Baraboo, Wisconsin with permission from Ringling Bros. and Barnum & Bailey® THE GREATEST SHOW ON EARTH®; p. 557 (left): Welgos/Hulton Archive/Getty Images; (center and right): Library of Congress.

## CHAPTER 21
Opener: © Bettmann/Corbis; p. 560: Library of Congress (3g03270); p. 562: © Courtesy Colorado Historical Society, All rights reserved; p. 563: Library of Congress; p. 564: Courtesy of the California History Room, California State Library, Sacramento, California (GL# 4216); p. 565: Courtesy of Cornell University Library, Ithaca, NY; p. 566: Library of Congress; p. 569: Charles Dana Gibson; p. 571: Collection of David J. and Janice L. Frent; p. 572: Library of Congress; p. 576 (top): Library of Congress; (bottom): Philip P. Choy, Professor of Asian American Studies at San Francisco State University (Plate 50); p. 577: Hawaii State Archives; p. 579 (right): © David J. & Janice L. Frent Collection/Corbis; (left): Chicago History Museum (ICHi-08428); p. 580: © Museum of the City of New York, USA/The Bridgeman Art Library; p. 581: Huntsville Public Library, Huntsville, AL; p. 584 (right): National Archives; p. 587: Library of Congress; p. 588: Courtesy Frederic Remington Art Museum, Ogdensburg, New York; p. 590 (top); Theodore Roosevelt Collection, Harvard College Library; (bottom): New York Public Library/Art Resource, NY;p. 591: New York Public Library/ Art Resource, NY.

## CHAPTER 22
Opener: Public Art for Public Schools/NYC School Construction Authority/Image © Stan Ries Photography; p. 594: Brown Brothers; p. 597: © Bettmann/Corbis; p. 598, 599: Library of Congress; p. 600 (top): Library of Congress (LC-DIG-ggbain-02461); (bottom): Illinois State Library; p. 602: *Gondolas in Venice Canal,* Venice, California, Photograph by Pacific Novelty Co. California Historical Society, San Francisco, [FN-29415]; p. 603 (top): Library of Congress; (bottom): Hulton Archive/Getty Images; p. 604: Without Sanctuary: Lynching Photography in America, plates 25 and 26 © 2000–2005 Collection of James Allen and John Littlefield/National Center for Civil and Human Rights; p. 605: (detail) National

Portrait Gallery, Smithsonian Institutions, Washington, DC/Art Resource, NY; p. 606: Culver Pictures, Inc.; p. 608 (left): Brown Brothers; (right): Library of Congress; p. 609: Library of Congress; p. 610: From the Collections of the Henry Ford (00.4.5767); p. 611: Courtesy of The Bancroft Library, University of California, Berkeley (1971.031:1902.03.118); p.613: Library of Congress (LC-H25-6497-MM); p. 614: Library of Congress; 616: Library of Congress (LC-DIG-ppmsca-06024); p. 619 (left): Illinois State Library; (right): Library of Congress.

## CHAPTER 23
Opener: Imperial War Museum, London, UK/ The Bridgeman Art Library; p. 624: Library of Congress (LC-DIG-jpd-02531); p. 626: Brown Brothers; p. 627: Image copyright © The Metropolitan Museum of Art/Art Resource, NY; p. 629: National Archives; p. 631: © Hulton-Deutsch Collection/Corbis; p. 632: Courtesy New Mexico State Records Center & Archives, Santa Fe, NM. Read Collection, Private Papers, Folder 54a, Series II, Ellis & Jenkins, 1892–1920, Box #9, Serial Number 8425, WWI, Felix Sanchez Photo Number 7224; p. 633: Rubenstein Rare Book, Manuscript, and Special Collections Library, Duke University (n967); p. 634: Library of Congress (3c00307); p.635: © Bettmann/Corbis; p.639: WPA Photo Collection, National Archives; p. 640: Cartoon by D.C. Boonzaier in "Die Burger," October 16, 1918; p. 643: Library of Congress; p. 644 (top): Culver Pictures, Inc.; (bottom): Library of Congress; p. 647: Library of Congress.

## CHAPTER 24
Opener: The Granger Collection, New York; p. 650: © Bettmann/Corbis; p. 652: (detail) From the Collection of the Henry Ford (THF 25002); p. 653: Nebraska State Historical Society (RG2183-1933-0411-1); p. 654: Dover Publications; p. 655: Hartman Center for Sales, Advertising & Marketing History, Duke University (BH1567); p. 656: Image copyright © The Metropolitan Museum of Art, NY/Art Resource, NY; p. 657: © Bettmann/Corbis; p. 658: Library of Congress; p. 659: Leif Neandross, The Roxy Theater. Courtesy of the Rambusch Company Archives, NY; p. 660: Library of Congress; p. 661: Archibald John Motley, Jr., *Blues,* 1929. Photograph © 1993 The Art Institute of Chicago. All Rights Reserved. Collection of Mara Motley, M.D. and Valerie Gerrard Browne. Image courtesy of the Chicago History Museum; p. 663, 664: Library of Congress; p. 666: John Steuart Curry, 1897–1946, *Baptism in Kansas,* (1928). Oil on canvas, 40 1/4 × 50 1/4 in. (102.2 × 127.6 cm). Whitney Museum of American Art, New York; gift of Gertrude Vanderbilt Whitney, 31.159. Digital Image, © Whitney Museum of American Art, NY. © Estate of John Steuart Curry; p. 667 (top): Courtesy of Christine Lesiak/NET Television; (bottom): Research Division of the Oklahoma Historical Society (OHS#16936); p. 668: Library

of Congress (3c30973u); p. 669: © Corbis; p. 673, 677: Library of Congress.

## CHAPTER 25
Opener: Library of Congress; p. 680: Library of Congress; p. 681: University of Washington Libraries, Special Collections (SEA0552); p. 682: Radio designed by Harold van Doren and J. G. Rideout. Made by Air-King Products CO., Brooklyn, 1930–33. The Brooklyn Museum of Art, purchased with funds donated by The Walter Foundation, [85.9] Photograph, Scott Hyde; p. 683: Hulton Archive/Getty Images; p. 684, 685: Library of Congress; p. 686: Louis Ribak, *Home Relief Station,* 1935–36. Collection of Whitney Museum of American Art, NY. Purchase, 36.148. Digital image, © Whitney Museum of American Art, NY; p. 687: *Riot at Union Square,* 1947 [date depicted: March 6, 1930]. Peter Hopkins, oil on canvas. Museum of the City of New York, Gift of the Artist, 66.82; p. 689: New York Daily News Archive/Getty Images; p. 694, 695: The Granger Collection, New York; p. 696: Library of Congress; p. 697: USDA Photograph Archives; p. 698 (top): Library of Congress; (bottom): SuperStock; p. 699: Courtesy of The Bancroft Library, University of California, Berkeley; p. 700: Amy Jones; p. 701 (left): State Archives of Michigan, #05060; (right): Walter P. Reuther Library, Wayne State University; p. 702: National Archives; p. 703: Library of Congress; p. 709: (top left): Wei/iStockphoto, RF; (center left): Oleg Kulakov/iStockphoto, RF; (top center): © Ingram Publishing/Fotosearch, RF; (bottom left): © IT Stock/PunchStock, RF; (bottom center): Anton Zhukov/iStockphoto, RF; (bottom right): Keith Webber, Jr./iStockphoto, RF.

## CHAPTER 26
Opener: Private Collection/Peter Newark Military Pictures/The Bridgeman Art Library; p. 712: National Archives; p. 713: © 1942 Edward B. Marks Music Company. Copyright renewed. All rights reserved. Photograph courtesy Franklin Delano Roosevelt Library, Hyde Park, New York; p. 715: © Corbis; p. 716: Central Press/Getty Images; p. 717: © Corbis; p. 722 (top): Library of Congress; (bottom): National Archives; p. 723: Tillamook Air Museum/Image courtesy of James West Davidson; p. 724: National Archives; p. 726, 727: Library of Congress; p. 729: Photo by Bill Manbo. © Takao B. Manbo; p. 732: © Bettmann/ Corbis; p. 734: D-Day Normandy. *The Rhino Ferry* by Orville Fisher. © Canadian War Museum, Beaverbrook Collection of War Art, 19710261-6230; p. 736: © Bettmann/Corbis; p. 738: National Archives; p. 739: Standish Backus Jr., Hiroshima, 1945. Courtesy of the Navy Art Collection, Naval Historical Center, Washington, DC; p. 741: Library of Congress (ppmsca 18531); p. 742 (top): National Archives; p. 743: National Archives (208-N-43440 [box 208 MO-105B]); p. 744 (top): © Brian Brake/Photo Researchers, Inc.; (bottom): National Archives.

## CHAPTER 27

Opener: © Bettmann/Corbis; p. 748: © Corbis; p. 749: The Truman Presidential Museum & Library; p. 750: AP Images; p. 751: Hulton Archive/Getty Images; p. 754: stills from "Duck and Cover," Federal Civil Defense Administration; p. 755: Ben Shahn, *For Full Employment After the War Register to Vote,* 1944. The Museum of Modern Art, New York. Gift of the CIO Political Action Committee. Photo © 2014, The Museum of Modern Art, NY/Art Resource, NY. Art © Estate of Ben Shahn/License by VAGA, New York; p. 757: © Corbis; p. 758: Rare Books and Manuscripts, Benson Latin American Collection, University of Texas, Austin; p. 760: Center for Legislative Archives, US Senate Collection, National Archives (A-072_10-19-1948); p. 762: © Baldwin H. Ward & Kathryn C. Ward/Corbis; p. 763 (top): © Warner Bros./Photofest; (bottom): Eve Arnold/Magnum Photos, Inc.; p. 766: Interim Archive/Archive Photo/Getty Images; p. 767: Library of Congress (2a10935); p. 768 (top): The CONELRAD Collection, www. conelrad.com; (bottom): Private Collection; p. 771 (top): Library of Congress (3c17876); (bottom): Eve Arnold/Magnum Photos, Inc.

## CHAPTER 28

Opener: Tom Kelly Archive/Archive Photo/Getty Images; p. 774: © Transtock/Corbis; p. 776: © R. Krubner/ClassicStock//Corbis; p. 778: Printed by permission of the Norman Rockwell Family Agency. Copyright © 1959 the Norman Rockwell Family Entities. Courtesy Curtis Publishing; p. 779: © Corbis; p. 780 (top): Elliott Erwitt/Magnum Photos, Inc.; (bottom): © PoodlesRock/Corbis; p. 782: Los Angeles Public Library; p. 783: © Corbis; p. 785 (top): © Warner Bros./Photofest; (bottom): © Bettmann/Corbis; p. 788 (bottom): © Bettmann/Corbis; p. 791: Time & Life Pictures/Getty Images; p. 792 (left): Photofest; (center): © Corbis; (right): Photofest; p. 796: AFP/Getty Images; p. 799 (left): © Corbis; (right): Image Courtesy of the Advertising Archives.

## CHAPTER 29

Opener: © Steve Schapiro/Corbis; p. 802: Drawing by Ruby. From *Children of Crisis: A Study of Courage and Fear, Volume I,* by Robert Coles. © 1964–67. By permission of Little, Brown and Company (Inc.); p. 804: Library of Congress (ppmsca 01271); p. 805 (top): Spencer Research Library, University of Kansas Libraries; (bottom): Dr. Hector P.

Garcia Papers, Special Collections & Archives, Texas A&M University-Corpus Christi Bell Library; p. 807: John Bryson/Time & Life Pictures/Getty Images; p. 808: © Bettmann/Corbis; p. 809: Charles Moore/Black Star/Stock Photos; p. 810: AP Images; p. 811: Michael Alexander/Black Star/Stock Photos; p. 812: Ed Whitfield/AP Images; p. 813: Library of Congress (LC-DIG-ppsca-08102); p. 814: George Tames/New York Times, 1957/Redux; p. 816: © Bettmann/Corbis; p. 817: AP Images; p. 819: McCain Library and Archives, University of Southern Mississippi; p. 821: © Jeff Morgan 16/Alamy; p. 822: © Bettmann/Corbis; p. 824: AP Images; p. 827 (left): Comstock Images/Getty Images; (right): McGraw-Hill Companies.

## CHAPTER 30

Opener: © Tim Page/Corbis; p. 830: © John Filo/Valley News Dispatch/Getty Images; p. 831 (left): AFP/Getty Images; (right): © Bettman/Corbis; p. 833: © Tim Page/Corbis; p. 834: AP Images; p. 836: © Bettmann/Corbis; p. 837: Julian Wasser/Time & Life Pictures/Getty Images; p. 839: © Bettmann/Corbis p. 841: "Farm Workers' Altar" 1967, by Emanuel Martinez. Acrylic on wood. 37 1/2 × 53 × 35 1/2 in. Gift of the International Bank of Commerce in honor of Antonio R. Sanchez, Sr. Smithsonian American Art Museum (1992–95)/Art Resource, NY; p. 842: Arthur Schatz/Time & Life Pictures/Getty Images; p. 843: © Corbis; p. 844 (top): Courtesy of MS. Magazine; p. 844 (bottom): Courtesy of the James West Davidson; p. 847: © Bettmann/Corbis; p. 848: Hulton Archive/Getty Images; p. 850: NASA (AS11-40-5873); p. 852: AP Images; p. 855 (top): Library of Congress (ppmsca 11992); (bottom): National Archives; p. 856: Sandra Baker/Alamy; p. 857: Library of Congress (LC-USZ62-53278); p. 858: David Bookstaver/AP Images; p. 859 (top): James P Blair/National Geographic Images; (bottom): Sandra Baker/Alamy, RF.

## CHAPTER 31

Opener: © Wally McNamee/Corbis; p. 862: AP Images; p. 864: © Bettmann/Corbis; p. 865 (top): Dennis Cook/AP Images; (bottom): Michael Ochs Archives/Getty Images; p. 867: New York Daily News; p. 870: © Bettmann/Corbis; p. 872: Wally McNamee/Woodfin Camp & Associates; p. 874: Yvonne Hemsy/Getty Images; p. 876: © Gerald French/Corbis; p. 879: Lana Harris/AP Images; p. 881 (top):

National Archives (NLNP-WHPO-MOF-0388[13A]); (bottom): © 2014 Artists Rights Society (ARS), New York/VG Bild-Kunst, Bonn; p. 883: Leonard Freed/Magnum Photos Inc.; p. 884: Dirck Halstead/Time & Life Pictures/Getty Images; p. 885: © Brad Markel/Corbis; p. 889 (top): National Archives; (bottom): Dirck Halstead/Time & Life Pictures/Getty Images.

## CHAPTER 32

Opener: © Jenny E. Ross/Corbis; p. 892: Alicia Patterson Foundation/Image © Robert Suro; p. 894: (Detail) Hmong story cloth by Dia Cha and Chue & Nhia Cha. All Rights Reserved, Image Archives, Denver Museum of Nature & Science; p. 895: Buzz Orr; p. 897: Tom Haley/SIPA Press; p. 898: Ron Edmunds/AP Images; p. 899: Illustration by Anita Kunz for the New Yorker Magazine. Anita Kunz Limited. Reproduced by permission of the artist; p. 900: Robert Nickelsburg/Liaison/Getty Images; p. 902: Image Source/Getty Images, RF; p. 903: Library of Congress; p. 904: Stephen G. Eick/Advizor Solutions; p. 905: © Mark M. Lawrence/Corbis; p. 907: Raccardo Savi/The Image Bank/Getty Images; p. 908 (left): © Peter Turnley/Corbis; (center): Brian Hendler/AP Images; (right): © Ralf-Finn Hestoft/Corbis/SABA; p. 910: © Reuters NewMedia Inc./Corbis; p. 911: David J. Phillip/AP Images; p. 912: Doug Mills/The New York Times, November 5, 2008; p. 914: Pete Souza/The White House/Getty images; p. 916: © Andrew Lichtenstein/Corbis; p. 919 (left): Lourens Smak/Alamy; (right): AP Images.

## ADDITIONAL CREDITS

Globe icon: Cartesia/Getty Images
Sun icon: Photodisc/Getty Images
*Daily Lives* (field): Design Pics/Michael Interisano/Getty Images
*Dueling Documents* (swords): Civil War Archive/Getty Images
*Conclusion* (map): Royalty-Free/Corbis
*Historian's Toolbox* (weathered wood): Darrin Kilmek/Getty Images

*After the Fact* images:
Magnifying glass: Richard Hutchings
Blank parchment paper: Christine Balderas/Getty Images
Roll of parchment, background: Oleksiy Maksymenko/Alamy
Antique books: Ingram Publishing/SuperStock
Row of books: Tetra Images/Getty Images

# Index

Note: Page numbers in *italics* indicate illustrations and their captions; numbers followed by *m* indicate maps; page numbers followed by *n* indicate material in footnotes; page numbers followed by *t* indicate material in tables.

New York City Draft Riots. *See* New York City
   opening moves in, 396*m*, 405–410, 409*m*,
      411*m*, 414
   soldiers. *See* Soldiers
   Union home front, 416–419
Civil Works Administration (CWA), 691, 709
Clark, George Rogers, 169, 225–226, 237
Clark, Maurice, 511
Clark, Mollie, 304
Clark, William, 225–226, 227
Clarke, Charity, 164
Clarke, Dr. Edward, 549
Class divisions. *See* Social class
Clay, Gen. Lucius, 752–753
Clay, Henry, 247, 277, 284, *369*, 370
   election of 1824 and, 273, 274, 275, 275*m*
   election of 1832 and, 288
   election of 1844 and, 357, 357*m*
   as leader of Whigs, 291, 295
Clayton Antitrust Act of 1914, 615–616
Clayton-Bulwer Treaty, 577
Clean Air Act of 1970, 848
Clean Air Act of 1990, 883
Clean Water Act of 1970, 848, 898
Cleaver, Eldridge, 811
Clemenceau, Georges, 636, 638
Clemens, Samuel (Mark Twain), 536, 581
Clergy, 89, 303, 341
   African American preachers, 205–206, 450, 461
   circuit-riding preachers, 123, 489
*Clermont* (steamboat), 250
Cleveland, Grover, 526, 540, 564, *564*, 567, 568, 581
   mounting tensions over Cuba, 578–579
   opens World's Columbian Exposition, 560,
      *560*, 567
Cleveland, Ohio, 255, 537, 557*t*, 606, 846, *847*
Clifford, Clark, 836
Climate change. *See* Global warming
Climate Change Conference of 2009, 915
Climatology, 475, 516–517
Clinton, Hillary Rodham, 896, 898, 899, 911, *914*
Clinton, Sir Henry, 168, 169, 171, 173, 175
Clinton, William Jefferson ("Bill"), 884, 887, 896,
   899–900
   election of 1992 and, 886, 886*m*, 896
   as president, 896, 897, 917
      economic recovery, 897–898
      health care reform, 898, *898*
      women's issues, 898, *899*
      Yugoslavian turmoil, 896–897, *897*
*The Closing Circle* (Commoner), 847
"Cloudscrapers," 536
Clovis (N.M.) discoveries, 22–23, *23*
Clovis tools, *23*, 24
Coal, 726, 870
Coaling stations in Pacific, 578, 581, 583*m*, 589
Coal mining, 525, 726
Coast Guard, 908–909
Cochise, 493
Cockfighting, 469
Cody, William F. ("Buffalo Bill"), 490–491, *491*, *492*
Coercive Acts, 149, 150, 151, 154, 155
Coeur d'Alene miners' strike, 483, 525
Coffeehouses, English, *125*
Coffles, *64*
Cohan, George M., 553, 632, *632*
Cohn, Roy, *763*, 768
Coigne, Jean Baptiste de, 169
Coit Tower, *698*
Coke (fuel), 468
Cola war, 784
Colder, Cadwallader, 146

Cold Harbor, Battle of, 425*m*, 426
Cold War, *746–747*, 747–769, *770*, 794*m*
   aftermath of. *See* Conservative era
   containment policies, 750, 786–791, 793
   domestic events, 761–764, 771
   foreign events, 764–769, 771
   global perspective of, 769, 797
   postwar prosperity and. *See* Economy
   rise of, 749–755, 752*m*
   in suburban era, 791–796, 797
Coles, Robert, *802*
Collective security system, 767
College students
   freedom riders, *808*, 808–809, 813*m*, 819
   protests by, 830, *830*, 834, 837
   radicalization of, 818–819, *819*
Colleton, Sir John, 70
Collier, John, 700
*Collier's* magazine, *516*
*Collier's Weekly*, 609
Collins, Michael, 850
Collyer, Robert, 532
*Colonias* (Mexican communities), 635
Colonizationism, 284, 285, 313–314
Colorado, 9, 361, 492, 567, 606–607
*The Colored Citizen* (newspaper), 464
Colored Farmers' National Alliance and
      Cooperative Union, 566
Colored Orphan Asylum, 435
Coltrane, John, 786
Columbian exchange, 37
Columbus, Christopher, 3, 5, 17, 28, 32–33, 34*m*,
   *36*, 55
Comanche Indians, *106*, 106–107, 128, 129*m*, 282,
   359, 362, 493
Comic books, 683, *683*
Cominform, 752
Commerce, 212*m*, 212–213, 382, *382*
   agriculture. *See* Agriculture
   cotton trade. *See* Cotton
   E-commerce, 901
   eighteenth-century seaports, 116–118, *118*
   regulation of, 57, 59, 197, 564
   tobacco trade, 59–60, *60*, 467, *467*
Commercial economy, 211–213, 212*m*
Commission for Relief in Belgium, 634
Commission on the Status of Women, 844
Committee for Industrial Organization (CIO), 701
Committee on Civil Rights, 756, 758
Committee on Public Information (CPI), 636
Committees of correspondence, 147
Committees of inspection, 144, 151
Commodity Credit Corporation, 693
Commoner, Barry, 847
*Common Sense* (Paine), 152, *152*, 159, 160
Commonwealth of Independent States, 880
Communications, *250*, 250–251, 902, *902*
   global networks, 526
   information systems, 507, *507*
   Internet, 901, 905
   telegraph, 250, 505, *506*
   telephone, 505, *506*, 507, *507*
Communism, 644, *687*, 761
   American fear of, 750, *750*
   anticommunism, 751, 761, *762*
   in China. *See* China
   in Europe, 751, 752
Communist Labor Party, 644
Communist Party, 644, 688, 713, 761, 762–763,
   *763*, 880
Community action programs, 814
Commutation fees, 418, 435–436

Companionate marriage, 657, 781
Complex marriage, 312
Compromise of 1850, *369*, 370–371, 371*m*, 372, 375
Compromise of 1877, 458
*Comptoir*, 81
Computed Axial Tomography (CAT scan), 875
Computers, 784, 875
Comstock, Anthony, 546
Comstock Law, 546
Comstock Lode, 483
Conant, James, 744, 745
Concentration camps, 728, *729*, 730–731, *738*
Concerned Women of America (CWA), 864
Concord, Battle of, 151–152, 158
Confederate States of America, 405, 407, 412, 416,
   428–429
   currency of, 415, *415*
   diet of soldiers, 420, *420*
   home front, 413–416, 427
   resources of, 405, *406*
   secession and, 394–395, 401
Confederation, 184, *184*, 195, 202
   Articles of Confederation, 184, 187, 197, 202
   disputes among states, 186–187
   fear of aristocracy, 194–195
   foreign interference, *185*, 185–186, 203
   Jay-Gardoqui Treaty and, 195–196, 202, 203
   Northwest Territory, 188*m*, 188–189
   postwar ambitions, 191–192
   postwar economy, 190–191
   Shays's Rebellion and, 196–197, 202, 203
   slavery and, *189*, 189–190, *190*
   state constitutions, *183*, 183–184
   western settlement, 185, 186*m*, 187, *187*, 202
   women and, 192–194
Conference Room Technique, *788*
Confiscation Act of 1861, 411, 433
Confiscation Act of 1862, 412
Conformity, 774, 778, *778*, 784–785, *785*
Conglomerates, 783–784
Congregational Church, 122, 123, 299
   disestablishment of, 195, 303
   Puritans, 84, 85, *308*
   Separatists, 86*m*, 86–87
Congress, 198, 254, 447, 603, 670
   Andrew Johnson's break with, 443
   caning of Charles Sumner, 388–389, *389*, 390
   comprehensive tax law, 416
   creation of Border Patrol, 664
   denies aid to Vietnam, 852–853
   Missouri Compromise, 235*m*, 235–236, 345,
      371*m*, 385
   partisan voting in, 218
   plan for Reconstruction, 445–447, 446*m*
   railroad land grants, 484–485, 486
   *See also* Law; *specific laws*
Congressional Medal of Honor, 608
Congressional Union, 600
Congress of Industrial Organizations (CIO),
   701–702
Congress of Racial Equality (CORE), 731, 756, 808,
   809, 811, 818, 834
Congress of Vienna, 267
Congress Party (India), 675
Connecticut, 89, 97, 98, 101
Connerly, Ward, 903
Connery, Sean, *792*
Connor, T. E. ("Bull"), 809
*Conquistadores*, 28
Conrad, Frank, 658
Conscience Whigs, 359, 369

# K

Kansas, 361
  dust bowl, 682–684
  exodusters, *462–463, 463–464, 464*
*Kansas Free State* (newspaper), 377, 378
Kansas-Nebraska Act of 1854, 385, 386*m*, 399, 401
Kansas Pacific Railroad, 490
Kansas Territory, 385, 386*m*, 391
  attack on Lawrence, *376–377, 377–378, 378*
  "Bleeding Kansas," 379, 388, 389
Kaskaskia, 169
Kasserine Pass, Battle of, 720, 721*m*
Keating-Owen Child Labor Act of 1916, 598, 598*n*, 616
Keegan, Dennis, 712
Kefauver, Sen. Estes, 781
Keith, Benjamin Franklin, 553
Keith, Minor, 576
Kelley, Florence, 598
Kelley, Oliver Hudson, 565
Kellogg, Frank, 671
Kellogg-Briand Pact of 1928, 671
Kelly, Abby, 316
Kemble, Fanny, 273, 337, 340
Kendall, Amos, 276, 277
Kennan, George, 750, 764
Kennedy, John F., *792,* 792–793, 916
  assassination of, 810
  election of 1960 and, 791–792, 792*m*
  as president, 793, 795, 796, 814
    civil rights issues and, 808, 809, 810
    Cuban missile crisis, 795–796, *796,* 797
    space program, 850, *850*
Kennedy, Robert F., 809, 814, 836, 841, 853
Kennedy, Sen. Ted, 906
Kenny, Sen. Richard R., 590
Kent State shootings, 830, *830,* 839
Kentucky, 185, 279
  as border slave state, 396*m*, 405, 406–407
  Grant's campaigns in, 408, 409*m*
Kentucky Resolutions, 219–220
Kerouac, Jack, 786
Kerr, Clark, 819
Kerry, Sen. John, 910
Kesey, Ken, 821
Key, Francis Scott, 234
Keynes, John Maynard, 704, 705, 769
Khomeini, Ruhollah (Ayatollah), 871, 873
Khrushchev, Nikita, *788,* 789, 790
  Berlin Wall, 795
  Cuban missile crisis, 795–796, *796,* 797, 839
Kickbacks, 449
"Killing the king" ritual, *183*
Kim Il Sung, 764, 765
Kindergartens, 548–549
King, Boston, 182
King, Rev. Martin Luther, Jr., 792, *808,* 811, 825, 834, 866
  assassination of, 813*m*, 836, 853
  "Letter from Birmingham Jail," 809
  march on Washington, *800–801,* 810, 823
  nonviolence strategy of, 806, 808
King, Rufus, 197, 235
King Caucus, 273
King Philip's War, 94, *94*
Kings Mountain, Battle of, 172, 172*m*
Kingston, New York, 264–265
Kingston Trio, 823
King William's War, 114, 128
Kinsey, Prof. Alfred, 781
Kinship groups, 473, 508

Kiowa Indians, 282, *282,* 362, *362,* 493
Kipling, Rudyard, 585
Kip's Bay, battle of, 165
Kirk, John, 387
Kissinger, Henry, 838, 839, 840, 849
  influence of, 866–867
  shuttle diplomacy, 869, 887
Kiss-Me Clubs, 654
Kitchener, Gen. Horatio, 574
*Kiva,* 7
Knights of Labor, 521–522
Know-Nothings, 386, 388
Knox, Philander, 609, 624
Korean Americans, 721, 893–894
Korean War, 764–765, 765*m*
  Chinese intervention, 765–766
  Eisenhower's assessment of, 767–768
  Truman vs. MacArthur on, 766, 767, *767*
Korematsu, Fred, 728
*Korematsu v. United States* (1944), 728
Kosovo, 897
Krupp, 560
Ku Klux Klan, 730
  during Reconstruction, 456, 457, *457*
  resurgence in 1920s, *667,* 667–668
Ku Klux Klan Act of 1871, 456
Kunz, Anita, *899*
Kuwait, 882, 882*m*
Kyoto Protocol of 1997, 907

# L

Labor contractors, 508, 893
Labor force, 117, 382, 384, 469
  demographic summary of, A-20
  during Great Depression, 682–684, 709
  international labor pool, 506–508, *508*
  late 19th and early 20th century, 517–520, 527
  manual laborers, 262–264, 434, 436–437
  multiracial, 483
  occupational distribution, *509*
  transformation of, 256–260
  unions. *See* Labor unions
Labor-Management Relations Act of 1947, 758, 759
Labor movement, 259–260
Labor systems, 520–526
  factory system, 246, 256, 380
  gang vs. task systems, 335, 451
  slavery as, 329, 398
Labor unions, 526–527, 692, *701,* 701–703, 849
  activism in, 523, *523,* 525
  blacks excluded from, 283
  company unions, 654
  job displacement and, 876–877
  of migrant farm workers, 684
  national unions, 521–523
  peacetime economy and, 758
  rise of factories and, 259–260
  in wartime, 634, 726, *726*
  yellow dog contracts and, 526, 654
  *See also specific unions*
Lackawanna & Northern Railroad, 466
*Laconia* (British liner), 626
*Ladies' Home Journal,* 675
Lafayette, Marquis de, 234, *234,* 628
LaFeber, Walter, 908
Laffer, Arthur, 874
La Flesche, Susan, 479
La Follette, Robert, 606, *606,* 609, 615
*La Follette's Magazine, 606*
LaHaye, Beverly, 864
LaHaye, Tim, 864, 865, 866

Lake Champlain, battle of, 234
Lake Erie, 847
Lake Erie, Battle of, 232*m*, 233
Lakota Sioux Indians, 476, 477*m*, 480, 493
Lalawethika ("The Prophet"), *227,* 229*m*, 229–230, 237
Lancaster, Penna., 138
Land
  gained in Mexican War, 361, 363
  Indian lands, 358–359, 368, 480
    ceded to U.S., 225, 232*m*
    demand for, 227, 278
    taken by colonists, 92–93, 94
  railroad land grants, 484–485, 486
  redistribution of, 446–447
  western land rush, *462–464, 463–464,* 487, *487*
Land Act of 1851, 368
Landed states, 187
Land Grant College Act of 1862, 416
Land-grant colleges, 464
Landis, Judge Kenesaw Mountain, 660
Land League, 482–483
Landless states, 187
Landon, Gov. Alfred ("Alf"), 696
Land speculation, 185, 187, 254, 287–288, 290–291
  Northwest Territory, 188, 188*m*
  San Francisco, 365, *365*
Lane, Ralph, 45
Lane Seminary, 313, 315
Lange, Dorothea, *703*
Language, 5, 541, 590
*La Raza Unida,* 842
L'Archevêque, Jean, *102–103,* 103–105, 114, 129*m*
La Salle, Robert Cavelier, Sieur de, 84, 104, 105, 106
Las Americas, 892, 894
Las Casas, Bartolomé de, 17, 34
*Las Gorras Blancas* (The White Caps), 480
Lasker, Albert, 655
Lathrop, Julia, 598
Latin America, 276, 365, 706, 789, 793
  American intervention in, 625, 625*m*
  Good Neighbor policy, *713,* 713–714
  Great Depression in, 673
  political reforms, 617
  poverty in, 815–816
Latinos, 635, 756, *758,* 776
  activism of, 840–842
  civil rights of, 804–806, *805*
  Jim Crow system and, 804–806, *805*
  migration chains, 891–892, *892*
  *pachucos,* 730–731
  in U.S. population, 893, *893*
  in Vietnam War, 833–834
Laundresses, 523, 525, 596
Law, 194, 253, 316, 480, 527, 598, 601, 607
  civil rights legislation, 443, 455, 470–471
  colonial, 67, 73, 110–111
  Jim Crow. *See* Jim Crow laws
  sociological jurisprudence, 595–596
  state laws, 317–318, 594
  *See also* Court(s); Supreme Court; *specific laws*
Lawrence, Kansas, *376–378,* 377–378
League for the Protection of the Family, 569
League of Nations, *641,* 641–642, *643,* 713, 714
League of United Latin American Citizens (LULAC), 684, 804, 840
League of Women Voters, 657, 714
Lear, Norman, 865, 866, 867
Leary, Timothy, 820, 821
Lease, Mary Elizabeth, 566
*Leaves of Grass* (Whitman), 310, *310*
Lebanon, 789, 868*m*, 877

Milholland, Inez, 599
Military-industrial sector, 755, 791
Militia(s), 113, 151–152, 162–163, 171–172, 173, 179
Miller, Alice Duer, *599*
Miller, Arthur, 92
Miller, Dorie, *722*
Miller, Flournoy, 659
Miller, John Chester, 241
Miller, Josiah, 377
Miller, William, 210
Mimeograph, 507
Mines Act of 1842 (Gr. Britain), 617
Ming Dynasty, 29
Mingo Indians, 130, 132, 138
Minié ball, 421
Mining, 483, 484, 485*m*
    coal mining, 483, 525, 687, 726
    copper mining, 351
    gold mining. *See* Gold mining
    silver mining, 37, *39*, 106, 483, 525
    strikes, 483, 525, 608, 688, 726
Minstrel shows, *285*, 286
*Miranda v. Arizona* (1966), 817, 827
Miscegenation, 332, 333, 338
Miss America pageant, 658, *658*
Missiles, 736, *746–747*, 840, 908
    Cuban missile crisis, 795–796, *796*, 797
    missile gap, 791, 792, 850
Missionaries, 302, 307, *307*, 541, 541*n*
    in California, 107, 110, 129*m*, *350*
    Protestant, 227, 298, 308
    Roman Catholic, 43, 55, 81, 308
    as shapers of Imperialism, 574, 575–576, *576*
Missionary diplomacy, 624–625
Missionary Ridge, Battle of, 430*m*
*Mission to Moscow* (film), 763
Mississippi, 39–40, 279, 442, 446, 571–572
    Black Belt of, 466, 671
    distribution of slavery in, 328, 328*m*
    Jackson State shootings, 830
Mississippian culture, 8, *8*, 10*m*, 12, 15, 39
Mississippi Freedom Summer, 810, 818, *819*, 844
Mississippi Plan, 457–458
Mississippi River, 84, 104, 252, *252*
    access to, 185–186, 225, 424, 430*m*
    Great flood of 1927, 670*m*, 670–671
Missouri, 396*m*, 405, 407
*Missouri* (battleship), 739
Missouri Compromise, 235*m*, 235–236, 345, 371*m*, 385
Missouri Indians, 348
Missouri Territory, 235
Mitchell, Albert, 638, 640
Mobil Oil, 784
*Moby-Dick* (Melville), 310–311
Moctezuma, 35, *35*, 38, 53
Model T Ford, 651
Modernism, 665, 677
Modoc War, 477*m*, 493
Mogollon culture, 7, 10*m*, 15, 21*t*
Mohawk Indians, 81, 82, 94, 169
Mohegan Indians, 93
Molly Maguires, 523, *523*
Mondale, Walter, 879
*Monitor* (ironclad), 407
Monmouth Courthouse, battle of, 169
Monopolies, 251, 253, 292
Monroe, James, 225, 234, 247, 273–274, 279
    Missouri Compromise, 235*m*, 235–236
    Transcontinental Treaty, 236, 353*m*, 375
Monroe Doctrine, 236, 585, 623, 717
Montagnais Indians, 80, 81

Montaigne, Michel de, 36
Montana, 492, 631
Montcalm, Louis Joseph, marquis de, 133, 135
Monterey, California, 107, 110, 350
Montgomery, Benjamin, 439–440, *440*, 459
Montgomery, Gen. Bernard, 720
Montgomery (Ala.) bus boycott, 806, 807
Montgomery (Ala.) *Mail*, 394
Monticello, 240, 241, *241*
Montreal, 84, 134*m*, 135
Montserrat, 68, 72*m*
Monuments
    Freedmen's Memorial Monument, 857, *857*
    to Lincoln, 698, 810, 857, *857*
    Vietnam Veterans Memorial, 856–859
Moody, Dwight Lyman, 540, 779
Moore, Gov. James, 71
*Moorehead v. Tipaldo* (1936), 704
Moral diplomacy, 624–626, 625*m*
Moral Majority, 865, *865*, 866
Moral reform, 297–298, *298*, 314, 321
Morgan, Brig. Gen. Daniel, 172, 172*m*, 173
Morgan, J. Pierpont, 513, 609, 613
Morgenthau, Hans, 767
Morgenthau, Henry, 704, 726
Mormons, 299, 312–313, *313*, 914
    promotion of women's suffrage, 600*m*
    settlement of Utah, *366–367*, 367–368, 375
*The Morning Post* (London), 623–624
Morocco, 230, 231*m*
Morris, Gouverneur, 197, 198
Morris, Robert, 197
Morse, Samuel F. B., 250, 505, 507
Morse code, 505
Morton, Gov. Oliver, 445
Morton, Levi P., *564*
Moss, Thomas, 572
Mossadeq, Mohammed, 788
Motion pictures, 657–659, *659*, 682, 720
    civil defense film, 754, *754*
    conservatism and, 865, *865*
    movie theaters, 657–658, 781
    *See also* Film industry; *specific films*
Motley, Archbald, Jr., *661*
Mott, Lucretia, 316
Mountain men, 265–266, *266*
MRI (Magnetic Resonance Imaging), 875
*Ms.* magazine, *844*, 845
Mubarak, Hosni, 913
Muckrakers, 596
Muhammad, Elijah (Elijah Poole), 685, 811
Muir, John, 610–611, *611*, 612
Muir, John (soldier), 829
Mulattoes, 56, 282
Mulberry Plantation, *73*
Muller, Curt, 596
*Muller v. Oregon* (1908), 596
Multiculturalism, *903*, 903–904
Multinational corporations, 784
Munich, Germany, 716, *716*, 749
Municipal governments, 538–541, 564–565, *815*
    boss rule, 538, 540, 605
    reformers and, 605–606
*Munn v. Illinois* (1877), 566
Murphy, Gov. Frank, 702
Murray, Judith Sargent, 194
Music, 552, 660, 703, 823, 895, 903
    jazz, 660, *661*, 786
    Mexican *corridos*, 485–486, 656
    patriotic sheet music, 623, *623*
    rock and roll, *785*, 785–786
Muskogean-speaking people, 16

Muslims, 685, 811, 871, 895–896, 909, 909*m*
Mussolini, Benito, 714, 715, 728, 732, 737
Mutiny, 169
*Mutualistas*, 685
Mutually assured destruction (MAD), 795
Myers, Jacob A., 539
Myspace, 902

# N

NAACP. *See* National Association for the Advancement of Colored People
Nader, Ralph, 846, *847*
NAFTA (North Atlantic Free Trade Agreement), 897–898
Nagasaki, 739
Naismith, James, 551
Nanboa, Don Pedro, 58
Napoleon I (Bonaparte), 230, 231, 232, 233, 236, 319
Napoléon III, Emperor of France, 424
Narragansett Indians, 93
Narváez, Pánfilo de, 34*m*, 39
Nasser, Gamal Abdel, 789
Nast, Thomas, *442*
Natchez Indians, 16, 18, 84, 113, 128
National Academy of Sciences, 870
National American Woman Suffrage Association, 599, 600
National Association for the Advancement of Colored People (NAACP), 605, 661, 699, 729, 756, 807, 808
    attacks on Jim Crow laws, 803–804, *804*
    Montgomery bus boycott and, 806
National Association of Colored Women, 572
National Association of Manufacturers, 577, 654
National Birth Control League, 656
National Climate Program Office, 874
National Consumers' League, 596, 598, 607
National debt, 190, 213, 224, 632, 877
National Defense Education Act of 1958, 791
National Energy Program, 870
National Environmental Policy Act of 1969, 847–848
National Geographic Society, 25
National Guard, 525, 630, 632, 702, *811*
    at Kent State, 830
    in Little Rock, Ark., 806, 807, *807*
National Industrial Recovery Act (NIRA), 691, 709
National Interstate and Defense Highway Act of 1956, 776, 783
Nationalism, 247, *627*, 645, 786–791
Nationalist Party (China), 713, 717, 761
National Labor Relations Act of 1935, 696, 701, 704, 709
National Labor Relations Board (NLRB), 696
National Labor Union (NLU), 521
National League of Professional Baseball Clubs, 551, 757
National Municipal League, 564–565
National Negro Business League, 573
National Organization for Women (NOW), 844, 864
National Origins Act of 1921, 664
National Origins Act of 1924, 664, 815
National parks, *258*, 610, 858
*The National Police Gazette*, 551
National Public Housing Act of 1937, 709
National Recovery Administration (NRA), 692–693, 696, 700, 704
National Republican party, 275, 277
National Rifle Association, 898–899
National Security Council (NSC), 764, *796*
National Socialist (Nazi) Party, 645, 688, 705, 714

Rural Electrification Administration (REA), 697–698, *698*, 709
Rush, Benjamin, 124, 194, 196
Russia, 631, 638, 641, 643–644, 645, 880
Russian Revolution, 630, 749
Russo-Japanese War of 1904–1906, *624*, 735–736
Ruth, George Herman ("Babe"), 660
Rutledge, John, 197

# S

Sacco, Nicola, 663, *664*
Sachem, 92
Sachs, Sadie, 598
Sadat, Anwar, 871, *872*
Safeguard operation (Ariz.), 905
Sagamore, 92
Sagebrush rebels, 874
Sahagún, Bernardino de, 38
Saint-Mihiel, battle of, 636, *638m*
Saladin, 32
Salem Village (Massachusetts), 87, 90
Salem witchcraft trials, 90, 92
Saloons, 552, 553, 561, 602
SALT I (Strategic Arms Limitation Treaty), 840
SALT II (Strategic Arms Limitation Treaty), 869, 871
Salt Lake City, *366–367*
Salvation Army, 540
Samoa, 587*t*
Sampson, Adm. William, 579
San Antonio, Texas, 106
Sanchez, Felix, *632*
Sanchez y Tapia, Lino, *106*
*A Sand Country Almanac* (Leopold), 756
Sand Creek Massacre, 476, *477m*, 493
San Diego, Calif., 107, 350
Sandinistas, *878m*, 878–879
Sandow, Eugen, 547, *547*
Sands, Dorothy, 883
San Felipe (Mexico), *368*
San Felipe de Austin, 351–352
San Francisco, 350, 366, 557*t*, 623, 823
    beginning and growth of, 365, *365*, 366
    earthquake and fire, 542
Sanger, Margaret, 598, 601, 656–657, *657*
San Ildefonso, treaty of, 136
San Jacinto, battle of, 352, *353m*
San José, census of, 108–109
San Juan Hill, battle of, 581, *581*, *588*, 588–589
Santa Anna, Gen. Antonio López de, 352, 359
Santa Fe Trail, 351, *353m*
Santee Sioux uprising, 475–476, *477m*, 493
*San Yi Man*, 893
Saratoga, battle of, *166m*, 167, 168, 177
Saturday Club of Boston, *310*
*Saturday Night Fever* (film), 865, *865*
Saturday Night Massacre, 852
Saudi Arabia, 882, *882m*, 907, 908
Sauk and Fox Indians, 230, 281
Savannah, Ga., 171, *172m*, *425m*, 429
Savings and loan (S&L) crisis, 886
Savio, Mario, 818–819
*The Sawdust Trail* (Bellows), *546*
*Sazanami* (Japanese ship), *624*
Scalawags, 448, 461
Scalia, Justice Antonin, 884, 914
Scandinavian immigrants, 383
*The Scarlet Letter* (Hawthorne), 310
Schaw, Janet, 115
*Schecter Poultry Corp. v. United States* (1935), 693
Schell, Jonathan, 877
Schenck, Charles, 637

*Schenck v. United States* (1920), 636
Schine, David, *763*, 768
Schism of 1840, 317
Schlafly, Phyllis, 845, 846
Schlesinger, Arthur, Sr., *657*
Schneiderman, Rose, 594, *594*
Schroeder, Gerhard, 907
Schweitzer, Albert, 915
Scientific management, 653–654
SCLC (Southern Christian Leadership Conference), 808
Scopes, John T., 666, 667
Scopes trial, 666–667, *667*
Scots-Irish immigrants, 96–97, 114, 117*m*
Scott, Dred, 390, *390*
Scott, Gen. Winfield, 359, 372, 405
Scottsboro boys, 685
Scruggs, Jan, 857
SDS (Students for a Democratic Society), 818, 820, 821
SEALS (Navy), 913
Seaports, *98*, 116–119, *118*, 121, 146, *146*, *176*
Sears, Richard W., 551
Sears, Roebuck "wishbooks," 489
Secession, 287, 370, 394–395, 401
    rejection of, 371–372
    slavery and, 396–397
Second Bank of United States, 247, 250, 287–291, 294
Second Confiscation Act of 1862, 446
Second Continental Congress, 159, 162, 177, 181, 184
    indifference to suffering of Army, 168, *168*
    lack of power of, 190–191
Second Great Awakening. *See* Great Awakening
Second Reform Act of 1867 (Gr. Britain), 275
Secret (Australian) ballot, 538, 539
Sectionalism, 189–190, 377–399, *400*, 401
    election of 1848 and, 369–370
    global perspective of, 397–398
    inflamed by theatrical presentations, 387, *387*
    political realignment of 1850s, 379, 385–390, 399, 401
    rising tensions, 360–361, 363
    social changes, 379–385
    triggers of war, 393–398, 401
    worsening crisis, 390–393
Secular utopian communities, 311
Securities and Exchange Commission, 691
Securities Exchange Act of 1934, 691, 709
Security Council (UN), 737, 909
Sedition, 636
Sedition Act of 1798, 219, 220
Sedition Act of 1918, 636
"Seeing the elephant," 356, *356*
Segregation, 283, 469, 623, 662, 810
    African American response to, 603, *603*, 605
    Jim Crow laws, 471, 493
    in New South, 470–471, *470–472*
    by religious beliefs, 778–780, *780*
    World War II and, 729–732
Selassie, Emperor Haile, 714
Selective Service Act of 1917, 631
Selective Service System, 833–834
Self-determination, 735
Seminole Indians, 211, 279, 280, 281
Semisubsistence economy, 211, *212m*, 332
Semple, "Nannie" McKenzie, *414*
Senate, *447*, 769
    Clinton impeachment trial, 899–900
    nullification debate in, 287, *287*
    Watergate hearings, 851–852, *852*

Seneca Falls Convention, 316, 599
Seneca Indians, 82, 169
Separate but equal doctrine, 471, *472*, 548, 804
Separation of church and state, 91
Separation of powers, 198
Separatists, 86*m*, 86–87, 91
Sephardim, 74
Septic systems, 776–777
Serbia, 896, 897
*Sergeant Pepper's Lonely Hearts Club Band* (Beatles), 823
Serpentine mounds, *2–3*, 4
Serra, Fray (Friar) Junípero, 107
Settan (Little Bear), 362, *362*
Settlement. *See* Frontier, settlement of
Settlement house movement, 540–541, 597, 598, 598*n*, 617
Seven Days' battles, 410, *411m*
*700 Club*, 863
Seventeenth Amendment, 393*n*, 607, 619, A-9
Seventh Cavalry, 476, 493
Seven Years' War, 133–138, 153
    British defeats in, 133
    British victories, 135–136
    change in policy and, 133–135
    maps of, *134m*, *137m*
    postwar effects of, 136, *137m*, 138
Sewage systems, 537
Seward, William H., 424, 427, 577
*Sex in Education* (Clarke), 549
Sexual behavior, 338, 546, 632, 781
    African American poetry, 663
    of counterculture, 820, 824
    double standard of, 304, 332
    homosexuality, 547
    new model of marriage, 656–657
*Sexual Behavior in the Human Female* (Kinsey), 781
*Sexual Behavior in the Human Male* (Kinsey), 781
Sexually transmitted diseases, 603, 632
Shadow churches, 207, *207*
Shafroth, John, 606–607
Shaftesbury, Earl of (Anthony Ashley Cooper), 70
Shakers, 311–312, *312*
Sharecropping, 451, 452, *452*, 458, 465–466, 565
Share Our Wealth plan, 694–695
Sharon, Gen. Ariel, 877
Sharon Statement (YAF), 820–821
Shaw, Pauline, 596
Shawnee Indians, 73, 84, 138, 169, 189, 226
    in Ohio Country, 130, 132
    "The Prophet," 227, 229*m*, 229–230, 237
Shays, Capt. Daniel, 197
Shays's Rebellion, 196–197, 202, 203
Sheen, Bishop Fulton J., 779
Shelley, Mary, *565*
Shenandoah Valley, *425m*, 428
Shepard, Alan, 850
Sheppard-Towner Federal Maternity and Infancy Act of 1921, 657
Sheridan, Gen. Philip, *425m*, 428
Sherman, Gen. William Tecumseh, 408, 425, *429*, *477m*, 493
    in Georgia, 423, 426, 427
    march to sea, 428–429, *430m*
Sherman, John, 589–590, *590*
Sherman, Roger, 159, 197
Sherman Antitrust Act of 1890, 513, 515–516, 564, 608
Sherman Silver Purchase Act of 1890, 563, 564, 569
Shi'ite Muslims, 871, 909, 909*m*, 910
Shiloh, Battle of, 408–409, *409m*, *423m*, 425
Shinn, Edward, *550*

Ships and shipbuilding, 31
    "Great White Fleet," 580, 623–624
    rebuilding of U.S. Navy, 574–575, 580, *580*
    steam-powered, 248*m*, *252*, 252–254, 534, 580, *580*
Shirer, William, 716
Shoe industry, 350
Sholes, C. Latham, 507
Shopping centers, 776
Shopping malls, 861–862, *862*
Shriver, Sargent, 814
Shuster, Joe, 683
Shuttle diplomacy, 869, 887
Siberia, 23–24, 25
"Sick" industries, 674
Siegel, Jerry, 683
Sierra Club, 610, *611*
Sievers, Viola, *727*
Silent majority, 837–838
Silent Sentinels, 599, 600
*Silent Spring* (Carson), 816, 846, 915
Silicon Valley, 876
Silver, 40*m*, 42
    discovered in West, 474, 475
    mining, 37, *39*, 106, 483, 525
Silver Bluff plantation, 329
Silverites, 569, 570
Silver standard (currency), 563, 569, 570
Simpson, A. B., 540
Sinclair, Upton, 609, 694, 695, 816
Singer, Isaac, 380
Singer Sewing Machine Company, 511, 577
Single-tax clubs, 514
Sioux Indians, 282, 355, 475, 476, 495
    Battle of Little Big Horn, 476, 477*m*, 493
    invasion of Great Plains, 347–348, *348*, 349*m*
    Lakota Sioux, 476, 477*m*, 480, 493
    Santee Sioux uprising, 475–476, 477*m*, 493
Siqueiros, David Alfaro, *698*
Sirhan, Sirhan, 836
Sirica, Judge John, 851
Sit-down strikes, 701, *701*, 703
Sit-ins, 731, 807
Sitting Bull, 476, 491, 493
Sixteenth Amendment, 613, 615, 619, A-9
*Sixth Avenue Shoppers* (Shinn), *550*
*The Skater* (Stuart), *191*
Skeleton Canyon, Battle of, 477*m*, 493
Skelton, Martha Wayles (Jefferson), 240, 243, *243*
Skidmore, Thomas, 311
Skinner, E. F., *500–501*
Skipworth, Lucy, 340
Skype, 902
Skyscrapers, *536*, 536–537
Slater, Samuel, 256
Slater Fund, 549
Slave(s), 159, 324, 328, 335, 340
    African vs. native born, 120–121
    maintenance of, 335–336, 337, *337*
    rebellions by, 68, 113, 122, 128, 222, 336
        running away, 336, *336*, 337
        White fears of, 174–175
    runaways, 177, 182, 324
        Dunmore's recruitment of, 173–175, *174*
        Maroon communities, *64*, *65*, 121
        as rebellion, 336, *336*, 337
Slave drivers, 330, 335, *335*, 340
Slaveholders, 224, *336*, 340
    class structure of South, 329–330, *330*
    encouragement of religion, 339
Slave Power, 361, 389, 390
Slave quarters, *331*

Slavery, 7, 9, *9*, 37, 62–68, *67*, 70, *189*
    abolition of, 74, 189, 352, 428
    of *conquistadores* in Texas, 39
    defense of, 341–343
    Denmark Vesey case, 286
    distribution of power in, 334–335
    in eighteenth-century seaports, 117
    in French Louisiana, 113–114
    Indians as slave owners, 280, *280*
    Missouri Compromise and, 235*m*, 235–236
    in Old South, 329, 334–341, 344
    as "peculiar institution," 190, 328, 334–335
    plantation monocultures and, 53
    secession and, 396–397
    sectionalism and, 189–190, 360–361, 363
    slave laws and codes, 67, 73, 282–283
    slave wars in Carolinas, 71
    systems of labor in, 120, 335, 451
    Western expansion and, 352, 359, 369–372, 375
Slave societies, 117, 119–122, *121*, 190, *190*
Slave trade, 31–33, 63, 327
    abolition of, 222, 235
    Atlantic slave trade, 63–68
    cost of slaves, *384*, 393
Slidell, John, 358
Sloan, Alfred, 656
Slums, 537–538
Smallpox epidemics, 13, 71, 115, 348, 349*m*
    during American Revolution, 170, 170*m*
    Indians and, 82, *82*, 281–282
    in Spanish colonies, 37, 56, 106
    trade routes and, 226
    western settlement and, 476
Smathers, Sen. George, 813
Smedes, Susan Dabney, 332
Smith, Adam, 57
Smith, Alfred E., 607, 671, 671*m*
Smith, Capt. John, 52, *53*, 87
Smith, Dewitt, 380
Smith, Jedediah, 265
Smith, Joseph, 312–313, *313*, 367
Smith, Rev. James, 4
Smith, Venture, 222
Smith-Connelly Act of 1943, 726
*Smith v. Allwright* (1944), 731
Smoot-Hawley Tariff, 686
Smuggling, 126
SNCC (Student Non-Violent Coordinating Committee), 808, 809, 811, 818, 820, 834
Snow Belt, 774
Social class, 272, 274, *274*, 541, 551
    class conflict, 259
    in colonial seaports, 118–119
    in England and America, 124
    juvenile delinquency and, 785
    middle class. *See* Middle class
    political parties and, 292–293
    suburban class distinctions, 778
    of Whites in Old South, 329–334, 398
Social control, 367–368, 546, 601–605, *603*, *605*
Social Darwinism, 514, 576
Social Gospel, 540
Socialism, 514–515, 585
Socialist Labor Party, 514
Socialist Party of America, 515, 614, 636, 637
Socialists, 311, 643
Social media, 902, *902*
Social mobility, 263, 264, 520, 893–894
Social reform, 596–601, 598*n*
Social Security, 695–696, *696*, 732, 849, 874
Social Security Act of 1935, 695–696, 704, 709
Social Security Board, 700

Social work, 597
Society, 116
    Chesapeake Bay colonies, 57, 59–61, 61*m*, 77, 120
    culture of suburbia, *778*, 778–782
    of early republic, 182, *191*, 191–195, 227, 228, *228*
    evangelicalism and, *303–307*, 303–308
    French Louisiana, *113*, 113–114
    market society, 245–267, *268*
    of Old South, 325*m*, 325–329, 328*m*
    pre-Civil War changes, 379–385, 381*m*
    of 1920s, 656–663
    social structure of Old South, 323–324, *324*
    Western expansion and, 363–368
Society of Cincinnati, 195, *195*
Society of Friends. *See* Quakers
Society of Jesus (Jesuits), 43, 55, 81
Sociological jurisprudence, 595–596
Sofaer, Anna, 14
Soil Conservation and Domestic Allotment Act of 1936, 694
Soil erosion, 326
Solar tax credits, 870
Soldiers
    African American, 234–235, 476
        American Revolution, *173*, 177
        Civil War, 413, *413*
        Spanish-American War, 580–581, *581*
        Vietnam War, 833–834
        World War I, 632
        World War II, 729–730
    Civil War, *402–403*, 419–422
        black soldiers, 413, *413*
        casualties, 404, 421–422, *422*, 423*m*
        diet of, 420, *420*
        hardships, 419, *420*, 421, 426–427
    in Vietnam War, 833–834, 839
    World War I, 631–632, *632*, 639, *639*
    World War II, 720, 758, 760
Solomon Islands, Battle of, 720, 735*m*
*Solos*, 664
Somme River, Battle of, 631
Somoza, Anastasio, 879
"Song of Myself" (Whitman), 310, *310*
*Song of Russia* (film), 763
Sons of Liberty, 142, 144
"Sooners," 487
Soto, Hernán de, 39–40, *40*
Soul music, 823
*Soul on Ice* (Cleaver), 811
*The Souls of Black Folk* (Du Bois), 605
The South, 214, 398, 561, 569, 803
    biracial worship in, 204–207, *204–207*
    colonial era, 51–75, 119–122
    market economy and, 247, 249, 251
    migration of blacks to North, 635–636, 665*m*
    pre-Civil War, *384*, 384–385, 393
    after Reconstruction. *See* New South
    during Reconstruction, 441–443, *442*
    resistant to women's suffrage, 600*m*
    temperance movement in, *303*, 303–304
    Tidewater region, 212*m*, 212–213, 330, 331
    upper South, 326–327, 340, 395, 396*m*
    *See also* Confederate States of America; The Old South
South Africa, 478, 825
South Carolina, 39–40, 68, 70–71, 72*m*, 442
    black majority of voters, 447, 448
    distribution of slavery in, 328, 328*m*
    nullification crisis, 286–287
    Sherman's march through, 425*m*, 429

Urbanization
air pollution and, 255
late 19th century
chronology of, *556*
city life, 541–547
global perspective of, 554
governments and reformers, 538–541
impact of, 557*t*, *557*
new urban age, 533–538
radical renovation of cities, 554
urban culture, 547–554
lower birthrates and, 775
in market society, 254–255, *255, 262*
*See also* Cities
Urban League, 699
Urban liberalism, 607
USA Patriot Act of 2001, 908
USS *Dolphin,* 625
USS *George Washington,* 640
USS *Memphis,* 659
USS *Merrimack,* 407
USS *Oregon,* 621–622, *622m*
USS *Philadelphia,* 230
USS *Shaw,* 712
Utah, 9, 361, 370, 371, 492, 600*m*
immigrants in, 541, 541*n*
Mormon settlement of, 363, *366–367,* 367–368
Ute Indians, 56, 359, 480
Utopian communities, 311–312

# V

Vallandigham, Rep. Clement, 418
Valley Forge, 168–169
Value politics, 846–849
Van Buren, Martin, 288, 295, 357, 369, 370
election of, 291, 343, 352
on political parties, 276, 360
as president, 281, *290,* 290–291, 294
Vance, Cyrus, 872
Vandenberg, Sen. Arthur, 761
Vanderbilt, Cornelius, 264, 506
Van Devanter, Justice Willis, 704
Vanzetti, Bartolomeo, 663, *664*
Vardaman, Gov. James K., 605
Vatican II, 819, 863
Vaudeville, 553, *553*
Venereal disease. *See* Sexually transmitted diseases
Vergennes, Charles Gravier de, 167, 168
Vermont, 185
Verrazano, Giovanni da, 34*m,* 41
Versailles, Palace of, 640–641
Versailles Peace Conference, *831*
Vertical integration, 511, 520–521, 529
Vesey, Denmark, 286, 336
Vespucci, Amerigo, 33
Veto power, 290, 441, 443, 601
Vick, Sarah Pierce, *332*
Vicksburg, capture of, 421, 424, 430*m*
Victoria, Queen of England, 304, 491, 544
Victorianism, 304, 544, 546, *546,* 602
Victory bonds, 632
Victory gardens, 634, *634,* 724
Vienna summit, 795
Vietcong, 787, 787*m,* 830, 831, *833*
Vietnam, 32, 717, 787
North Vietnam. *See* North Vietnam
South Vietnam, 787, 787*m,* 795, 853
Vietnam Era, 829–854, *854*
identity politics of, 840–846, 853–854
pragmatic conservatism, 849–853

value politics of, 846–849
Vietnam War. *See* Vietnam War
Vietnamese immigrants, 893
Vietnamization, 838
Vietnam Veterans Memorial, 856–859, *856–859*
Vietnam War, 825, *828–829,* 832*m,* 848, 849
invisible enemy in, 829–830, *830*
Nixon era of, 838–840
origins of, *831,* 831–833, 832*m*
significant events of, 855
social consequences of, 833–835
unraveling of, 835–838, 838*m*
Vietnam Veterans Memorial, 856–859, *856–859*
Villa, Pancho, 626, *626,* 630
Villasur, Don Pedro de, *102–103,* 104, *104,* 105
Vincennes, capture of, 169
*A Vindication of the Rights of Women* (Wollstonecraft), 192, 194
Vinland encampment, 19
Violence, 29, 221, 490, 824
against African Americans, 456, *667,* 668
assassination. *See* Assassination
civil rights movement, 806, 808, *809,* 809–810, 813*m,* 818
rape, 166, 171, 332, 338, 685, 897
religion and, 308, 313
*See also* Race riots; Riots and mob violence
Virginia, 132, 189, 407, 446, 807
colonial. *See* Chesapeake Bay colonies
distribution of slavery in, 328, 328*m*
House of Burgesses, 59, 141–142
*Virginia* (ironclad), 407
Virginia Company, 59, 60
Virginia Debate of 1832, 341, 345
Virginia Plan, 197–198
Virginia Resolutions, 219–220
Virginia Resolves, 142
Virgin soil epidemics, 37
Virtual communities, 902
Virtual representation, 142–143
*A Visit from the Old Mistress* (Homer), *441*
VISTA (Volunteers in Service to America), 814
Voice of America, 768
Voltaire (François-Marie Arouet), *167*
Volunteers in Service to America (VISTA), 814
V-1 buzz bombs, 736
Vonnegut, Kurt, *751*
Voting, 89, 125, 564, 672
disenfranchisement of black voters. *See* Disenfranchisement
"graveyard vote," 538
machine-age voting, 539, *539*
secret ballot, 538, 539
voter registration, *808,* 808–809, 810, 813*m,* 819
voter turnout, 276, 561, *561*
Voting Rights Act of 1965, 810, 811
V-2 rocket, 736

# W

WAAC (Women's Army Auxiliary Corps), 722
WAC (Women's Army Corps), 722
Wade, Sen. Benjamin, 441, 443
Wade-Davis bill, 441
Wages, 263, 520, 651, 781, 849, 886, 901
Ford's doctrine of high wages, 651–652
minimum wage laws, 793, 803
rise of, in 1950s, 783
stagnation of, 901–902
Wagner, Robert F., 607
Wagner Act of 1935, 696, 701, 704

Wagon trains. *See* Overland Trail
Wainwright Building, 537
Wald, Lillian, 605, 630
*Walden* (Thoreau), 309–310
Waldo, Daniel, 354
Walker, David, 284, 285
Walker, Dr. Thomas, 139*m*
Walker, James, 265
Walking cities, 535, 554
Walkley, Olive, 306
Walkley, Stephen, 306
Wallace, Gov. George, 815, 837, 838, 838*m*
Wallace, Henry C., 668, 732, 760
Wall Street, *507,* 615, 913
*The Wall Street Journal,* 670, 874
Walsh, Christy, 660
Wampanoag Indians, 87, 93
War(s), 71, 422, 793, 832
atrocities, 107, 165–166, 167, 171, 897
motives for, 93, 589
*See also* specific wars
War bonds, 416, 632, *635*
Ward, Aaron Montgomery, 551
War Department, 728, *729*
Ware, James E., 537
War Hawks, 231, 232
War Industries Board (WIB), 634
War Labor Board (WLB), 726
Warmouth, Gov. Henry, 449
War of 1812, 236, 247
British invasion, 233–235
decision for war, 231–232, 232*m*
naval and land battles, 233, *233*
War of League of Augsburg, 114, 128
War of Spanish Succession, 114, 128
*The War of the Worlds* (Wells), 682
War on Poverty, 814
War posters, *634,* 636
War Powers Resolution, 866
War Production Board (WPB), 724
Warren, Earl, 731, 825, 851
*Brown* decision, 804, 827
*Hernández* decision, 806, 827
reforms of, 817–818, *818*
Warren, Mary, 93
Warsaw Pact, 789
Washing Society, 525
Washington (state), 23, 492
Washington, Booker T., *572,* 572–573, 605, 608, 661
Washington, D.C., 224, 234, 636
Washington, George, 4, *130,* 131–132, *165,* 237
as commander-in-chief, 162, 163, *173,* 177, 234
Cornwallis' surrender, 176
inoculates troops against smallpox, 170
strategies of, 164–165, 175
at Constitutional Convention, 197, 198
as critic of slavery, 341
as Freemason, 275
as president, 213, *216,* 218, 220, 221
design for Washington, D.C. and, 224
Farewell Address, 218, 753
neutrality policy, 217–218, 221
Whiskey Rebellion, 209–210, *210*
as slaveholder, 342, *342*
surrender at Fort Necessity, 132, 133, 134*m*
Washington, Henry, 177
Washington, Jesse, 604, *604*
Washington, Lt. Col. William, *173*
Washington Mutual Bank, 912
*The Washington Post,* 873